TENNIS WEST

A History of the Western Australian Lawn Tennis Association from the 1890s to the 1990s

Published by Playright Publishing Pty Ltd.
P.O. Box 548, Caringbah. Sydney. Australia. 2229.

First published in 1995

National Library of Australia
Cataloguing-in-publication data

Phillips, Harry C.J.
Tennis West: a history of the Western Australian Lawn Tennis Association from the 1890s to the 1990s.

Bibliography
Includes Index

ISBN O 646 24768 9

1. Western Australian Lawn Tennis Association - History. 2. Tennis clubs - Western Australia - History. 3. Tennis - Western Australia - History. I. Western Australian Lawn Tennis Association. II. Title.

796.342060941

Designer: Mark Hand/Hand Graphic Design Pty Ltd
Editor: James Murray

TENNIS WEST

A History of the Western Australian Lawn Tennis Association from the 1890s to the 1990s

HARRY C. J. PHILLIPS

Playright Publishing Pty Ltd

CONTENTS

LIST OF ILLUSTRATIONS

ACKNOWLEDGMENTS

As the project to write the Tennis West history was commenced as far back as 1984 when I was lecturing in a unit titled 'Government Systems and Recreation' I have many people to thank for their contribution over the last decade. My family have helped me to endure the strains which began to surface after the initial research interest had faded. Jan, my wife, has read the drafts and helped inspire me to finish the task. Our daughters Michelle and Marina have also given me unflagging support and encouragement. Matthew Kiely, our son-in-law, assisted the cause with his willingness to proof the final draft.

Several of my tennis friends have read various chapters and made many constructive suggestions. Bill Edgar, Cec Gardiner, Dene Rundle, Andrea Mitchell, Pam Brand and Geraldine Watson (and Mrs Sayers) all assisted in this regard. Many others kindly sent me newspaper clippings, provided photographs or made suggestions. Arthur Marshall gave me access to many of his newspaper articles. Most of these communications have been recorded in the bibliographic section. I recognise how this assistance, together with many interviews, enabled me to broaden my understanding of tennis. Many fellow members of the Reabold Tennis club have also expanded my tennis horizons and cemented my commitment to the great game. Patron Dr Elizabeth Constable, and many committee members, particularly Robert Wallman and Alan Tognolini, displayed keen support. Greg McKay, a keen and capable Reabold player, gave initial sponsorship support on behalf of Sanax Medical and First Aid Supplies. Encouragement from younger generation members such as Damien Hampson has also been appreciated.

A former colleague Cam Rielly undertook the major initial editing task. His expertise greatly improved the quality of the work although I have to assume responsibility for the shortcomings. Glen Bennett, another life long friend, read the early chapters and offered encouragement when I began to tire. Two researchers, Tracy Hart and Yvonne Ball also assisted. Yvonne, one of the leading players in the State, gave additional editorial advice. Julie Martin at the Battye Library of Western Australia generously assisted in the collection of the photographs and other aspects of research. Richard Tredget (Camera and Photo Specialists), together with Photo Hendriks and Bob Prodonovich, helped in the production of some photographs. The courtesy of *The West Australian* newspaper was also appreciated as was Kevin Bradley's preparedness to permit photographs to be taken at Royal King's Park. Leading veteran player Bob Gordon willingly supplied a range of valuable photographs.

At Edith Cowan University we now have a sporting history unit to which departmental colleagues Professor Geoffrey Bolton, Dr Jan Ryan, Associate Professor Ed Jaggard and myself contribute. The endorsement of the University, which assisted with two grants, was appreciated. Indeed, the support of many colleagues at Edith Cowan has been important. Head of Department Dino Gava has long shared my interest in all sport and fellow political scientist Dr Quentin Beresford has also been most supportive. Christine Harvey, too, has helped considerably by typing so many of my sporting works.

My colleagues at the Legislative Assembly have been central to the exercise. One of my special tennis titles (along with Clive Wilderspin at Reabold and Jenny Massey at Fremantle) was victory in the Parliament's doubles tournament with Lorraine Allen. Others at the Parliament with a keen interest in tennis include

Legislative Assembly Clerk Peter McHugh and Deputy Clerk Doug Carpenter, Tamara Fischer, Michael Baker, Peter Metropolis, Andrew Young, Di Dinnie, Gerda Slany, Amanda Millson and Jan Graham. David Black shares with me a thirst for political history and sporting history. He understands the demands involved and has constantly given me encouragement to complete the task. Finally, at the Annexe the admirable help from Pat Roach, herself a keen and capable tennis player, has been of wonderful assistance.

As the Director of Playright Publishing, Gary Lester, has been a true professional throughout the exercise invariably endeavouring to produce a quality product. Geoff Pollard, President of Tennis Australia, had alerted Tennis West about Gary Lester's expertise. The support rendered by Geoff Pollard was timely and very helpful to the launch of the publication phase.

At Tennis West I have been appreciative of the cooperation I have received over many years. Harry Spilsbury was President when the project was commenced. Barry Sanders, also a former president, was involved in the early discussions. Incumbent President Alan Hicks and Vice-President Andrea Mitchell gave the project their imprimatur. Alan and Mary Hicks spent many hours carefully reading the completed text. In fact in the end Alan's contribution was stupendous and far beyond the call of duty of any President. Throughout the project I benefited from John Whitton's interest in the Association's history and his preparedness to assist in any manner. Two Directors, Dene Rundle and Treasurer Michael Lee have monitored the progress of the work. Julie Philp rendered valuable help. Recently appointed General Manager Gordon Allen and marketing officer Sue Turner were supportive. I hope their assistance has resulted in the completion of a resource that will be of use to Tennis West and an interest to the tennis and sporting community.

Near the conclusion of the project the marketing of the book required further assistance from the tennis community. Clive Wilderspin, Rob Casey and Christine Dorey, great players themselves, were valuable members of the marketing sub-committee. The co-operation from Veterans Club President Rob Ockerby and Ross Gerrands (Tennis Coaches Association) should also be recorded. Moreover, Auntie Olive (Mrs Crawley) and Auntie Ruth (Mrs Phillips) took the opportunity to help again what had become a family cause. Brothers and sisters James, Bill, Margaret and Pat gave support, while cousin Glenys (with Kevin) have taken a keen interest.

Harry Phillips, 20 October 1995.

FOREWORD

Every club, association and organisation has a history. Not all have it faithfully recorded but those who have give their future members and followers a heritage beyond equal. Such is now the case with Tennis West.

To the author of this publication, Harry Phillips, this has been a labour of love extending as it has over the last decade and is a memorial to his exceptional abilities and persistence. He has combined a number of talents to produce this remarkable book. To his academic skills as a writer and historian he has added an extraordinary thoroughness in research, together with his profound knowledge of sport to mould by intensity of resolve a truly authentic account of the history of the Western Australian Lawn Tennis Association.

It is a fascinating volume in easy to read format and is much more than just a history but in reality an absorbing story which will satisfy even the most discerning reader.

From the early unsettled days of the Association, through the dizzy heights of Australian Tennis in the 50's and 60's to the present revival of interest in tennis, every step has been formally documented.

To the tennis enthusiast, it is compulsory reading and is supplemented by an extremely comprehensive list of appendixes which provide exhaustive detail on all aspects of the sport in Western Australia.

In unreservedly recommending this magnificent publication, I am mindful of the tremendous contribution made by Harry Phillips and the constant support provided by his family in bringing the history of our great game in Western Australia to fruition.

To the reader - enjoy the content of this wonderful book.

To Harry and your family - sincere thanks from all in tennis for this monumental gift to our heritage.

Alan Hicks,

President, Tennis West

23 January 1995.

Chapter One

THE BEGINNINGS OF THE GAME

When Captain Fremantle formally took possession of the western third of Australia for Britain on 2 May, 1829 there was no Adelaide, no Melbourne and no Brisbane. Neither had the modern game of 'lawn' tennis been invented. The term 'tennis', though, was part of the vocabulary of the early settlers. Some of the more educated would have known that Shakespeare had mentioned playing with tennis balls and racquets in Act I, Scene II of 'Henry V'. In 'All's Well That Ends Well' (Act I, Scene I), Shakespeare had reminded those in all walks of life of how 'the Court's a learning place'. A few of the same pioneers may have noticed in 1839 a *Perth Gazette* (19/1/1839, 12) advertisement for many wares including tennis balls. This was also suggestive that some form of tennis game was known to the people of Perth.

The Perth Town Hall Clock Scoring in tennis has been linked to quarters of the clock. The early rules for lawn tennis were formulated in England. Some have been modified for Western Australia

As a word, 'tennis' first appears in a recognisable form in a poem by John Gower, in 1399, in the phrase 'of the tennis to win or lose a chase...' Even earlier, in 1380, Geoffrey Chaucer had characters speaking of playing 'racquets' (Clerici, 1975, 27). One view associates the term 'tennis' with an Egyptian town on the Nile, called Tinnis (in Arabic) or Tanis (in Greek). The city was famous for its linen and the earliest balls were made of that material (Brasch, 1986, 355). However, it seems more likely that the French *tenez* meaning play gave birth to 'tennis'; in English the word was originally *tenetz* (Glanville, 1981, 8).

Games involving racquets and balls had long been in existence (Clerici, 1975, 10-12). One of these was racquets. It began to be played in a debtors' prison near Fleet Street, London, about the time that Captain Arthur Phillip landed at Sydney Cove on 26 January 1788. The racquets were crudely fashioned from wood and the balls were possibly made of leather. Racquets, which was similar to modern squash, became a popular way of easing the monotony of prison life (Davison-Lungley, 1979, 74).

Another important forerunner of tennis was known as 'real tennis' or 'royal tennis'. It had a noble ancestry, being a pastime of Henry VIII. The courts where the king played are still in existence at Hampton Court, near London. Henry had borrowed the main elements of the game from France, where it was popular with the monarchy as early as the fourteenth century. Despite regal patronage, royal tennis did not spread quickly. By 1875, the year of the game's inception in the antipodes port of Hobart, it was played actively elsewhere only in Britain and France. In 1882, a club, characterised by a wealthy membership, was also founded in Melbourne. Although the rules were complicated, the similarities of the two versions of tennis are sufficient to regard royal tennis as the parent of lawn tennis (Kinross Smith, 1987,190).

The invention of lawn mowers facilitated the preparation of grass courts

Tennis (or lawn tennis, to give it its popular name) was properly born in Victorian England. People wanted a game that was more active than croquet and yet could be played on croquet courts or the lawns of stately country homes. Its growth was hastened by a technological breakthrough; the development of the India-rubber ball. By 1872 solicitor Harry Gem was able to write about a game he had devised that was like royal tennis but could be played outdoors on grass with balls made from rubber (Davison-Lungley, 1979, 75). The invention of lawn mowers facilitated the preparation of grass courts.

Authoritative works on the history of tennis, however, have not attributed to Gem a label suggesting he was the 'father' of modern tennis. Instead considerable credit is given to Walter Clapton Wingfield, a former major in the Indian Army, for taking the development of the new game a stage further. Wingfield called his game 'spharistike', a Greek word meaning 'ball game'. He patented a set of rules and a box which contained two racquets, balls, a net, net posts, white tape for marking the courts and assorted skewers. At a cost of £5/5 sales boomed among the English middle and upper class (Davison-Lungley, 1975, 75). Wingfield's customers included the Prince of Wales, the Duke of Edinburgh, the Crown Princess of Prussia, and various other British and foreign notables (Haley, 1978).

Spharistike was played on an hour glass shaped court and had a net some 1.5 metres in height. The scoring system was similar to that used in racquets and would be familiar to a modern squash player. To avoid charges of plagiarism, which were frequently fired at the Major, he considered the idea of introducing deuce when the score was thirteen all (Clerici, 1975, 66). 'Still it was a beginning and many would say the beginning' (Davison-Lungley, 1979, 75).

The Marylebone Cricket Club (MCC) which had been the governing body for the rules of royal tennis, cricket and croquet, was then suggested as a suitable authority under which to standardise the rules of lawn tennis. Within a few years, it was decided to adopt a rectangular court 26 yards (22.76 metres) long by 9 yards (8.23 metres) wide; lower the net to 3 feet (0.91

metres) at the centre; decrease the distance of the service line from the net to 21 feet (6.40 metres); use the royal tennis method of scoring by 15s; and permit one fault by the server. It has been asserted that the second serve was originally favoured because it would enhance the prospect of women playing the game. Ironically, especially for men, this rule change weighed the game in favour of the server. The dimensions of the court have not been altered since to lessen this advantage.

The strange progression from 'love' to game through 15, 30, and 40 was from royal tennis, though 45 was diminished to 40. Glanville (1981, 9) observed that the French gambled on the game in multiples of 15, reflecting the coinage system of the time. However, the same researcher was more convinced that the fascination and utility of the number 60 was the basis of the manner of scoring which followed the quarters of the clock. Bransch (1986, 362) in his study of the beginnings of sports also spoke of how the Babylonians believed in the cosmic significance of the number 60 which led to the division of every hour into 60 minutes. Sub-divided into quarters, it made 15 a popular unit. Moreover, in terms of time the scoring system which evolved for lawn tennis had the 'advantage' that a contest could normally be completed during an afternoon or evening. Most matches could be concluded within two hours although there were variations depending on the number of sets and the closeness of the contest. If many 'deuces' were necessary several more quarters of the clock could elapse.

Deuce is an Anglicised version of the French word *à deux*, meaning two, implying that two successive points must be gained to win a game (Bransch, 1986, 355). Also most sources suggest that the term 'love' is derived from the French *l'oeuf* , the shape of which suggests a zero. Yet despite the obscure origins of scoring, the method has been regarded as appropriate for more than a century, except for the need to win a set, so that 6/5 had to be converted to 7/5 or another two game margin. Later, in the 1970s, the tie break procedure was introduced at eight (then six) games all in a set.

A significant milestone in the history of tennis was the decision in 1875 of the All England Croquet Club to set aside one of its lawns at Wimbledon for tennis. Tennis proved so popular that in the following year the club changed its title to the All England Croquet and Lawn Tennis Club. In 1877 the club decided to hold a tennis championship, open to 'amateurs only', for a silver Challenge Cup presented by *The Field* magazine. A few years earlier, a distinguished royal tennis player, J.M. Heathcote, had written to the editor of *The Field* detailing the advantages of a tennis ball he had designed. The adoption of this ball made of rubber, but significantly covered with white flannel, considerably increased the amount of control a player could achieve. It provided new scope for the exercise of skill by tournament players

The first Wimbledon championship, with a draw of 22 players, was scheduled to begin on Monday 9 July 1877 and continue until play had been completed. No matches were programmed for the Friday and Saturday of that week in order to avoid a clash with the Eton versus Harrow cricket match. This prominent event in the social calendar of Victorian England regularly drew some 10,000 spectators (Haley, 1978, 126). Of course no play was permitted on the Sabbath.

After some delays caused by rain, the first Wimbledon final took place on Thursday 19 July. The finalists were a 26 year old Wimbledon resident, Spencer Gore and a former Cambridge blue, William Marshall. Gore, a Harrovian racquets player, was known for a heavy-cut underhand service and a tendency to storm the net. Marshall was a renowned 'royal' or 'real' tennis player. Gore defeated Marshall on a wet and blustery day before two hundred spectators with a scoreline of 6/2, 6/5, 6/2. The players wore white flannel shirts with ties, long cream trousers (with schoolboy belt), and white caps. The racquets bore traces of their 'real' tennis ancestry and were rather square tipped, with plain wooden handles. The balls were lighter than those used today.

The club reported a meagre profit of £10 for the first championship. But it was the start of something which was to spread to other countries and to other parts of the British Empire. But while cable links to such far-flung outposts as Perth were nearing completion, Wimbledon was understandably not yet sufficiently significant to command attention in the newspapers of the colony. The limited press space allocated to sport reported contests of agricultural shows, including ploughing matches, horse racing meetings and regattas on the Swan River (*Inquirer*, 1/8/1877). Rifle shooting contests were also popular, with Fremantle versus Perth matches being organised (*Western Australian Times*, 3/8/1877, 3).

As Wimbledon play was beginning, Swan River residents were supposedly being educated by reading accounts of the proceedings of the Legislative Council, where the battle for the secret ballot was being won. Another battle fought in newspaper ink was to determine the direction of the railway between Perth and Fremantle. Was the route to be north of the river or south? The north and south of the river divide was later to influence the organisation of Western Australian tennis. Later, too, Wimbledon became front page news. However, in 1877 the *Western Australian Times* (forerunner of the *West Australian*) devoted its front page to advertisements. Even then the Swan Brewery was vigorously promoting its products. The time for 'beer and skittles' may have arrived but tennis was not yet a well known game to the colonists.

From uncertain beginnings tennis was to grow to become an important part of the Western Australian culture. The establishment of an association to advance the game was fraught with difficulties. However, once the association found its feet, the sport advanced, although events of national significance such as Federation, the two world wars, depression and boom, influenced progress. And affairs largely outside the jurisdiction of the Association, such as the great divide between amateurs and professionals, the focus on Wimbledon and other Grand Slam events, together with the Davis Cup and even the Federation Cup have also been important in shaping tennis within Western Australia.

The absence of well-researched Australian sports histories have been noted on many occasions. This is a paradox, given that for many Australians 'sport is life and the rest is shadow'. It is the one national institution that few criticise. To play, watch, read and talk about sport is to uphold the nation and build its character. It is deeply rooted in the consciousness of the people (Horne, 1966). Keith Dunstan (1973, 1) even claimed that, for Australians, 'sport is the ultimate super religion'. This is not a solely modern view as when tennis was beginning to grow Henry Lawson was already writing, that in our Australian land, 'sport is sacred'.

Tennis, despite its significance to the lives of thousands of 'Sandgropers', has not been the subject of a historical analysis. This work represents an attempt to fill part of this vacuum with a study of the Western Australian Lawn Tennis Association, often referred to by its acronym WALTA. However, it needs to be recognised that not all tennis comes within the ambit of the Association. The histories of the many tennis clubs, some of which are not affiliated with the WALTA, are not specifically covered. This means that many club champions, administrators, characters and contributors to the tennis scene have not been documented. Nor are some of the important 'associate bodies' of WALTA such as those formed by the umpires and veterans treated extensively in this history. The Catholic Tennis Association and the Southern Suburbs Tennis Association are other important organisations which have left a mark on Western Australian tennis. They remain fertile areas for further research.

The history of the Association, now often known by its trading name of Tennis West, is treated chronologically. Each chapter deals with the issues of greatest significance for a particular era. Like most sport histories, the results of the various championship contests are included (Whimpress, 1992, 2-15). This need for tabulation may explain why academic historians have tended to ignore sport and unacceptably omit an important part of our culture. Fortunately this barrier is now being broken down.

Chapter Two

TENNIS: THE PREMIER FAMILY GAME

DISCUSSING the beginnings of lawn tennis in Australia, Brasch (1986, 419) claims that 'every residence of consequence [had] its tennis court'. This proposition held true in Perth and Fremantle where the first recorded tennis activities can be traced to Government House and the properties of leading families. The latter often owned large blocks with sufficient space for a tennis court. By contrast, those who lived in the so-called '60 foot' cottages had insufficient space. So, as there were no public courts, the opportunity to play tennis was restricted to people with a substantial stake in the community.

T.B. Beuttler, Headmaster of High (later Hale) School 1882-1888 winner of the 1888 Government House Handicap Gentlemen's Singles

Government House Courts

Lawn tennis was brought to Australia in the late 1870s and early 1880s (Brasch, 1986, 419). For instance in 1878 the Melbourne Cricket Club's Lawn Tennis Association had laid an asphalt court at the Melbourne Cricket Ground. A year later 100 people were regularly using the court, prompting a decision to lay a second court, this time with a grass surface (Yallop, 1992, 11). In Perth, two courts were constructed at Government House. At first, tennis was restricted to social play. However, by 1888 it was decided to conduct handicap tournaments for men and women. As the events were 'by invitation only' the draw read like a 'Who's Who' of Western Australia. The women's event, which commenced in June and was completed in July, was won by Miss Amy Moore. She had been allocated a generous '30' handicap. For her performance, Miss Moore received a 'handsome' inkstand.

By late August 1888 the men's tournament was completed with Mr T.B. Beuttler the victor receiving praise 'for his excellent all round play' (*West Australian*, 28/8/1888, 3). Beuttler had narrowly survived a first round match against F.D. North who was on the same 'scratch' handicap. North was also a prominent cricketer while Mr Beuttler was better known as Headmaster of the prestigious High (later Hale) School. Thomas Breame Beuttler, B.A. of Queen's College, Cambridge had been educated at Rugby. Throughout his headmastership from 1882 to 1888 he had promoted outdoor competitive sport introducing 'colours' at the school to denote excellent performance (Burton, n.d., 44).

The suburban tennis scene at the Barker 'Chanonry' homestead.

As this was probably the first occasion on which a local tournament was fully documented in the *West Australian*, the details as published are reproduced here. It should be recalled, however, that the contest was on a handicap basis. This was very popular although the formula was different and involved 'bisques'. A bisque was a stroke which could be taken at any point in the match. It appeared that Hilda Wright judiciously applied her two bisques in the 1888 tournament, as this helped her reach the ladies' final.

In a second form of handicapping the higher ranked players were deemed to 'owe' some points to their opponents in all or specified games. For example, if a player was handicapped 'owe 30' it required the competitor to win two points (to reach owe 15 and then love) before commencing to score in a game. In a refinement of this a player might be handicapped '30, 2/6', indicating that they had to gain two points before scoring in the second and sixth game. Sometimes the handicapping formula gave lesser players the advantage of 15 or 30 per game or nominated games. As in such instances fewer points had to be won to win a game it meant that some sets could be quickly concluded. Sometimes, too, matches were played on a first to nine game basis and when sets were played to six games the principle of advantage (of a two game lead) was not applied.

In handicap matches delicacy and gentleness were the norm and the volley was not *de rigueur*, or etiquette, because it curtailed rallies. Accounts indicate the ladies typically wore hair gathered in a bunch, with a straw 'gem' hat. Their tennis attire consisted of white blouses and long skirts, some three inches (eight centimetres) from the ground. The 'gentlemen' usually wore long cream trousers, or knickerbockers, often with wide and colourfully striped elastic belts with a shirt and tie surmounted by a striped tennis blazer. A straw boater or skull-cap was often part of the tennis uniform (Kinross-Smith, 1994a, 138)

Ladies Singles	Gentlemen's Singles
Mrs A B Wright (15) beat Miss L Stone (30) 9 games to 2.	Mr W A Gale (scratch), beat E Burnside (15) 6 games to 2, 6 games to 1.
Miss Hilda Wright (15 and two bisques) beat Mrs Beuttler (1/2 30), 9 games to love.	T Delay (scratch), beat C Y Simpson (scratch) 4 games to 6, 6 games to 4 and 6 games to 5.
Mrs Harper (scratch) beat Miss B Leake (1/2 30), 9 games to 8.	D B Ord (scratch), beat J de C Harston (1/2 15), 6 games to 4, 0 to 6 and 6 games to 5.
Miss Leake (15) beat Miss Jones (less 1/2 15), 9 games to 4.	R Gee (scratch), beat Lee Steere (1/2 30), 6 games to 3, 6 games to 6, and 6 games to 1.
Miss A Moore (30) beat Miss Gee (15) 9 games to 4	J D Booker (1/2 30) beat L Broome (1/2 30), 6 games to 1, 3 games to 6 and 6 games to 3.
Miss Lefroy (less 15) beat Miss M Stone (30) 9 games to 2.	T B Beuttler (scratch), beat F R North (scratch) 6 games to 5, 5 games to 6 and 6 games to 4.
Miss W Hickling (1/2 30) beat Miss D Lefroy (scratch) 9 games to 7.	
2nd Round	**2nd Round**
Miss A Moore beat Miss E Lefroy 9 games to 7.	D B Ord beat J D Booker 5 games to 5, 6 games to 4 and 6 games to 3.
Miss Leake beat Miss Lefroy 9 games to 5.	W A Gale beat R Gee retired.
Mrs A B Wright beat Miss Hickling, 9 games to 1.	T B Beuttler beat T A Delay 6 games to 2 and 6 games to 5.
Mrs Harper beat Miss W Hickling 9 games to 5.	
Miss Hilda Wright a bye.	
3nd Round	**3nd Round**
Miss Leake beat Mrs A B Wright 9 games to 8.	T B Beuttler beat D B Ord 6 games to 4 and 6 games to 5.
Miss Hilda Wright beat Mrs Harper.	W A Gale a bye.
Miss A Moore a bye.	
Source: *West Australian* , 10/7/1888, 3.	Source: *West Australian* , 28/8/1888, 3.

In 1891, the results of another handicap tournament at Government House were published in the *West Australian* . On this occasion, Mrs Fraser defeated Miss Leake 6/5 to win the prize of a ladies' bracelet. In the men's division C.Y. Simpson had a long match before conquering D.B. Ord 3/6, 6/1, 6/4 (*West Australian*, 27/7/1891, 3). Ord's reward, apart from the prestige, was a tennis racquet. In this tournament, Lady Forrest, the wife of the Premier, Sir John Forrest, was an entrant. Although Lady Forrest had a generous handicap she lost in the first round (*West Australian*, 27/7/1891, 3). However, for more than a decade she was a leading patron of tennis and her attendance was regularly reported at tennis tournaments and functions (*West Australian* , 16/9/1893, 2).

It is not surprising then, that the Forrests had a court at their Hay Street bungalow, opposite where His Majesty's Theatre now stands. This was another of the 'leading family' courts. However, the Forrests may have been guilty of considering the well-being of the tennis fraternity above that of other residents of Perth. For instance, in 1896, the Forrest Government created a Waterworks Board with the colourful tennis enthusiast, Edward Keane, as the first chairman. Keane had a grass tennis court on his Peppermint Grove property and undoubtedly knew the cost of court maintenance. Keane, therefore, probably realised at least one of the reasons why Forrest was listed as a 'selfish user of water by the Board' (Stannage, 1979, 275-276). He probably also knew one reason why he was later forced to resign his post. Tennis had facilitated Keane's appointment, but it also may have contributed to his downfall.

Forrest had earlier sold five acres (two hectares) of prime land at Peppermint Grove to Mr E. Barker for £500. Barker had come to Perth from Scotland and was one of the founders of the W.A. Trustee Company and the secretary of the prestigious Weld Club. At first Barker was active in yachting circles but when he married Ethel Wood, one of the leading young tennis players in the colony, the Barker's soon built an asphalt court, later converted to grass. As the history of Western Australian tennis unfolds, the imprint of the Barker family will become more obvious. As tennis began to grow in popularity, nearly all the leading tennis players of that era played at the Barker 'Chanonry' property. Even today, a tennis court remains on the site. However, the property has changed hands numerous times with one owner, the late prominent businessman Robert Holmes a Court, forging closer links with racing than with tennis.

Keith Barker, one of the two Barker sons has recalled that practically every home in his area had a court (interview with Keith Barker, 18/4/1986). However, only a few were acknowledged centres of tennis activity. One such location was the magnificent home of Mr McNeil in Peppermint Grove. McNeil (or 'Mac') was an entrepreneur and major owner of real estate. Another 'Mecca' for tennis was the Burt's 'Strawberry Hill' residence in Adelaide Terrace. Although Sir Archibald Burt had died in 1871, the influential family had continued to develop the property to include one of the best tennis courts in the colony.

North of the city, a focal point was a property located at Aberdeen Street, the home court of Ethel Wood and her sister Salina. Both became fine players. As mentioned above, Ethel Wood married Mr E. Barker, the owner of 'Chanonry'. Ethel was to later win the 1909 Open Ladies Singles championship of Western Australia. Significantly, photographs of gatherings at Aberdeen Street and other tennis centres indicate that many women were playing. Their large hats suited the climate but the long dresses, worn with corsets, must have restricted their mobility and been oppressive on warm days.

Another resident of the 'Northbridge' area was a printer named Orchard. Newspaper reports indicate that he made courts available for minor handicap tournaments. On one occasion in 1894, the *West Australian* (21/12/1894,2) reported:

> *There was probably a larger gathering of spectators than we have seen at any previous tennis match in this colony. The interest taken in the tennis matches, which, by Mr Orchard's kind favour have been held at Palmerston Street during the six weeks, has been throughout very gratifying to lovers of the game....*

Students of the game would also be interested to read some of the comments about the final match between A.W. Hoskings (later the 1897 colonial champion), and C.Y. Simpson (who had won the 1891 Government House handicap tournament). With Hoskings the victor 6/5, 6/2, 6/2 it was reported (*West Australian*, 21/12/1894, 2) how:

> *Both men played excellent tennis at times and first rallies were of frequent occurrence. Simpson's quickness about the court stood him in good stead. Whilst he several times got the better of his opponent at the net it is fair to say he had the worst of the luck in that most difficult department of tennis - the umpiring. Hoskings won by his facility in volleying.... He is an easy and collected player....*

Various reports suggested that tennis was beginning to capture the interest of the wider public (*West Australian* 4/10/1894, 13/12/1894, 15/12/1894 and 19/12/1894). The settings were still the private courts but references to umpiring and stroke play were indicative of many keen contests. This could be regarded as a sign that tennis was beginning to be more widely accepted as a 'sport' rather than a game, with the added attraction that it could be played by women. Undoubtedly one of the attractions of lawn tennis was its suitability for women. Major Walter Wingfield, credited with initiating developments in lawn tennis, had advertised the game 'could be played in the open air, in any weather by people of any age and both sexes' (Haley, 1978, 134). This propaganda had been supported by the appearance of comments by a leading British educator Herbert Spencer (himself a sportsman), who had begun a crusade in which he argued the unconventional view that sporting activities, incorporating both competition and play, should be made an intrinsic part of the educational and cultural life of [both] men and women.

Anthony Trollope, who in 1868 had published an anthology of sporting essays entitled *British Sports and Pastimes*, claimed that tennis was a game suitable for women. However, this was short of an endorsement for women's full participation in sport. The distinction Trollope made between tennis as a game and cricket as a sport might appear obscure now, but in those days games were often thought to be diversions like tip-cat, strat-ball and croquet. The latter, which had organisational links with tennis, was the novelty of the period. Games that offered no physical challenge were considered suitable for children or women (Haley, 1978, 125).

In 1871 Trollope was to travel to the Australia including a visit 'to the little known territory of Western Australia' (Trollope, 1953, 299) and was astounded with the amount of sport played in the colonies. In his judgement it 'almost' represented 'a national necessity' to play sport. He said he could not explain why the taste for sport had transported itself to Australia and not to the United States of America (Dowe, 1966, 168). The 'sports' Trollope mentioned were cricket, athletics, rowing, hunting, flat racing, and steeplechasing (Jacques and Pavia, 1976, 24). Tennis had yet to win recognition as a sport. But in Western Australia tennis had begun to be played as a 'handicap' game by women and men in the late 1880s and early 1890s. Government House and the private courts of leading citizens became the metropolitan locations for the game. However, to achieve a championship and competitive basis for status as a sport, it was necessary to establish an organisation of some kind. This did not occur until actual clubs began to emerge.

Chapter Three

METROPOLITAN CLUBS BEGIN

THE proliferation of family courts, mainly in select suburbs, probably delayed the establishment of the metropolitan tennis clubs that had begun to take place in the eastern colonies. In essence, though, the various homesteads operated informally as clubs. No constitutions existed but informal rules fostered 'handicap' competitions and restricted membership. Soon, however, gold 'the yellow fever of the nineties' was to produce massive demographic, economic and political changes in the 'Cinderella' colony. There were important consequences for tennis. Firstly, immigrants came largely from the eastern colonies, especially Victoria. The Victorian influence was to be particularly important for Australian Rules football. But tennis too, had become well established in Victoria. One newspaper even reported 'tennis enthusiasts are arriving by every steamer' (*Morning Herald*, 31/3/1896, 2). Secondly, the beginnings of industrialisation and the expansion of commercial and professional groups provided new sources of capital, property and organisational skills for different sports, particularly tennis, which appealed to this 'class'. Thirdly, the growth of suburbs around Perth and Fremantle established a basis for regional competition. Again this was probably more obvious in the case of Australian football and cricket, but it also had an impact on the organisation of tennis (Bennett, 1985, 106).

The first Perth and Fremantle tennis clubs

The first metropolitan tennis clubs that can be documented were in Perth and Fremantle. In December 1894, at the end of a newspaper account of a handicap tournament, the *West Australian* (21/12/1894, 23) noted:

> *Many will hail with pleasure.... the possibility of a tennis club, with a central ground and three courts, being established in time for the end of the cricket season. Such a club has been a long felt want in Perth. Those who are familiar with similar clubs in the eastern colonies and in the old country, know what an important factor they are in our social life, and how keen is the friendly rivalry incited amongst both sexes by this very fascinating game.*

Progress was soon documented in the sporting section of the *West Australian* (8/4/1895). Below a heading 'Lawn Tennis', which appeared in the same column as the scoreboard of a Fremantle versus Perth cricket match, it was reported:

> *A circular has been issued by several gentlemen inviting tennis players to form a private tennis club in Perth. The want of such a club, it is stated, has long been felt, the main deterrent having been the difficulty of obtaining a central and suitable block of land. A first rate site, however, has been obtained*

[where] it is proposed to lay down three tennis courts and lawns [and] to build a tea house and dressing rooms.

The article, written in a similar tone to that in December 1894, went on to describe how the co-operation of leading Perth residents had been necessary:

to form, such as exists in England and in the other colonies, not only to provide healthful and desirable exercise for both ladies and gentlemen but also to furnish that which is absolutely lacking in Perth - a place of general resort where members can readily meet their families.

Evidence suggests, however, that many difficulties were still to be experienced. A year later, a number of options for raising funds to purchase land for courts and a pavilion were still being circulated (*Morning Herald*, 23/5/1896, 2) and a request was published for 'influential gentlemen in the city who are very anxious to have a good club formed in a central position' to attend a deputation to the mayor (*Morning Herald*, 16/5/1896,2). Some of the promoters held influential positions. For instance E.A. Stone, was puisne judge of the Supreme Court and member of a prominent local family; A.C. Willis, was the colonial manager of the Union Bank of Australia; and A.K. Money an executive for the Australian Mutual Providence Insurance Company (Stoddart 1981, 660). They were assisted by Messrs Roberts, Young, Hindhaugh and Kelsey who reputedly understood how to ascertain the best terms on which land could be obtained (*Morning Herald*, 23/5/1896, 2).

Encouraged by the support of S.H. Parker QC, MLC, 'that grand supporter of sport' (*Morning Herald*, 23/5/1896, 2) the promoters held a series of well publicised meetings at Jacoby's Hotel before it was decided to build courts adjacent to the Perth Bowling Club on the Esplanade (*Morning Herald*, 21/7/1897, 2 and 22/7/1897, 2). In August 1898 it was announced that the membership of the club (60) was fully subscribed, and that the courts, which had been very well laid by Peter Dawson of Sydney were ready for use (*West Australian* 29/8/1898, 6). The cost of £150 for two courts was raised by the issue of 30 debentures at £5 each at the rate of seven per cent, to be repaid from subscriptions from players (*West Australian*, 11/7/1898, 6).

Members of the Bowling Club showed their confidence in the success of the tennis 'club' by taking up 20 debentures. It was decided that they would only have the right to use tennis courts after they had paid an entrance fee of 10 shillings and 6 pence and an annual subscription of one pound and one shilling. The finances of the tennis club were to be kept separate from those

Tennis on the Perth Esplanade

of the bowling club, although there was to be a joint committee of management (*West Australian* 11/7/1898, 6).

The Perth Club, however, did not survive (*Morning Herald* 4/5/1901, 2). It was taken over by members of a separate club known as WANDA, which was thought to stand for the Western Australian Never Say Die Association (interview with R. Noble 23/3/1992). Reports indicate that the WANDA club celebrated its opening on 26 August, 1898 in the presence of Chief Justice Sir Alexander Onslow and Lady Onslow, and leading surgeon Dr Saw and Mrs Saw (*Morning Herald* , 4/9/1899 and 26/8/1899). Both Onslow and Saw soon became leading proponents of the establishment of a tennis association. Once the WANDA club took over the courts its membership attracted people who became influential in tennis circles although it will later be demonstrated that it also included members who were reluctant to support the formation of a tennis association.

Given the rivalry in that era between Perth and Fremantle, it was not surprising that early in 1895 there had been a call for Fremantle people to also begin proceedings to establish a tennis club. Again at the foot of a column of cricket details, a caption 'Tennis Club at Fremantle' indicated that (*West Australian* 23/2/1895, 36):

> *A meeting of tennis players and others interested in the game was held at the Federal Hotel, Fremantle, on Thursday evening, when preliminary arrangements were made for the formation and conduct of a tennis club in Fremantle. It has been decided to limit the membership of the club to 30.*

Brian Stoddart, a leading sports historian, recognised that limiting the club to 30 might have been conditioned by available facilities, but he also claimed it was a 'sign of social restrictiveness'. 'Tennis', said Stoddart (1981, 660) 'was an important social activity for the emergent commercial-financial community and its service associates'. Among the members of the foundation steering committee of the Fremantle Club were H.F. Brandon (Fremantle Manager of the Bank of Australasia); W.R. Hodge (chief accountant for the *West Australian* Bank in Fremantle); R.M. Walker (principal of one of Perth's most important accounting firms); and James (Jas) Bassett (a Fremantle broker and agent).

It appears that, like Perth, the Fremantle steering committee also experienced several delays. The tennis writer in the *Morning Herald*(29/7/1896, 2) commented :

> *Those who once showed the keenest interest in the game are now conspicuous by their absence ... It is expected that during the next three months a good deal of much needed life will be infused into the game, and that trophies will be offered for competition. Here is a chance for some enterprising firm of business men to 'immortalise' themselves.*

Earlier, the same newspaper, which had begun to regularly publish a tennis column, had claimed that some tennis enthusiasts were urging the establishment of a second club at the port. It was argued (*Morning Herald*, 7/4/1896, 2) that:

> *If only two clubs could be formed in Perth and two in Fremantle an association could be immediately established on the same basis as those in other colonies. There is nothing like association tennis for improving one's play, for it forces a man to practise, and to play his very best in the matches, instead of 'fooling' away an afternoon on the courts.*

Support for the formation of an association did not immediately gain momentum. However, in late October 1896, the inaugural meeting of the Fremantle club elected its committee. The 'prime mover' of the club's formation was Jas Bassett who became secretary. The entrance fee was set at 10 shillings and 6 pence for men and 5 shillings for women, and the annual subscription fee at one pound one shilling and 10 shillings and 6 pence respectively (*Morning Herald*, 29/10/1896, 2).

The Fremantle committee decided to ask the Fremantle Municipal Council to keep its original promise to lay two asphalt courts. The club was prepared, when funds permitted, to provide three grass courts (*Morning Herald*, 29/10/1896, 2). F.W. Burwell, who had taken a keen interest in bowling and tennis at the port, had drawn up plans for the site set aside by the Council in Fremantle Park. The plans incorporated five tennis courts, a bowling green, and a grandstand (*Morning Herald*, 29/10/1896, 2).

Progress was slow, but by early 1897 the Council had completed the surfacing of two asphalt courts. At the annual general meeting after the 1897 season, it was reported that the land upon which the courts were constructed was not held under lease. Nevertheless, there was confidence that the Council had no intention of disturbing or removing the tennis courts. By that time, the club had accumulated a debt of £40. Worried by the strain, Bassett, who had been largely responsible for managing the club, decided to retire and Alf Kidson, a local identity and Member of the Legislative Council, assumed the presidency (*West Australian* 23/3/1898, 7) and was able to guide the club back into the black. The improved financial position was largely due to the well patronised Easter tournament which the Fremantle Park Tennis Club had begun to conduct. Somewhat pretentiously, this was called the 'Western Australian Colonial Championship' (*West Australian*, 14/12/1898, 6).

In 1900, a change of name was approved and the Fremantle Park Tennis Club became the Fremantle Tennis Club. In that year the famous engineer, Charles Yelverton O'Connor, became associated with the club. He was 'a man of fine physique with a taste for walking, swimming and riding [and had] become patron of several active sports in Fremantle' (Tauman, 1978, 240). The years near the turn of the century proved nearly as eventful for the tennis club as they did for O'Connor. The club's position was complicated by its ambivalent attitude towards the formation of a tennis association, which, as other clubs began to emerge, became a major issue. However, many of the new clubs experienced similar difficulties to the first Perth and Fremantle clubs.

New clubs

Establishing new metropolitan clubs had certainly proved to be difficult. In early 1896, the regular tennis columnist in the *Morning Herald* (24/3/1896, 2), writing under the pseudonym 'The Master', explained:

> *Lawn tennis is in a very backward state in this colony, not on account of the want of players - and good ones - but because of their inability to obtain grounds on which to put down courts. There are plenty of tennis enthusiasts to form a few clubs in Perth alone, and if only these could be started, and a couple of courts put down for each of them, an association would soon be formed, and the game boom.*

'The Master' frequently appealed to 'capitalists or representatives of capitalists' to lay down courts and lease them to a club at a fair interest rate (see *Morning Herald*, 25/2/1896, 2). However, there did not exist a reasonable prospect for this type of investment. So it was necessary to approach local government bodies for land and funds. These authorities, faced with requests for help from many more popular sports, were understandably reluctant to fund tennis, a relative newcomer.

It was necessary for the Perth and Fremantle clubs to forge links with bowling clubs to justify their quest for land. Tennis shared with bowling an appeal to both women and men. Tennis, like bowling, tended to be played at a leisurely pace. Both 'games' appealed to the same 'class of citizens but not necessarily the same age cohorts' (see Inglis, 1912, 234). This early partnership of tennis and bowling enthusiasts to secure land was to be repeated in many metropolitan localities and country districts throughout the State.

Another common link was a partnership between tennis clubs and churches. This link went beyond the realisation that one of the great champions of the era Dorothy Chambers (née Douglas) who won seven Wimbledon singles titles between 1903 and 1914 was the daughter of a vicar. Church authorities had the capacity to grant land for courts. Fostering 'a family game' on land adjacent to the church had a ready appeal for the clergy. One of the first outcomes of this partnership was the formation of the West Perth Tennis Club in 1898. Within 12 months, the club was to be become involved in the first tennis association in Western Australia.

A meeting of people interested in forming this club was held at the Presbyterian Church in Havelock Street, West Perth, in October 1898 (*West Australian*, 13/10/1898, 6). Within two months, the club's formal opening was reported in the press, with the President, the Reverend A. Moore, congratulating the committee 'upon the quickness with which they had accomplished their work' (*West Australian*, 26/1/1899, 6). Land at the rear of the church was rented at a 'peppercorn' rate. The membership list was quickly filled. And, with an outlay of a little over £100, a court was built, allowing the club to celebrate its start free of debt (*West Australian*, 26/1/1899, 6).

On opening day an exhibition match was played between A.H. Greene, the reigning colonial singles champion, and D.B. Ord, another prominent player (*Morning Herald*, 21/2/1899, 2). The warm conditions reminded the 60 guests that the elevated location of the courts gave the 'advantage of catching the afternoon breezes' (*West Australian*, 26/1/1899, 6). As funds were forthcoming, it was intended, under the direction of architect, A. Oswald Wilson, to add a second court and make a number of improvements, including planting of shrubs and flowers (*West Australian*, 26/1/1899, 6).

Whether concern for the environment could be traced to the composition of the club committee is a moot point. Three women, Mrs Rain, Miss Tassie and Miss Young, were members of the inaugural committee (*West Australian*, 26/1/1899, 6), but the earlier Perth and Fremantle Clubs had not included women committee members. However, at Fremantle Charles O'Connor's wife was frequently commended for her organisational skills and in Perth, Lady Forrest was even more regularly praised. Social functions, such as balls, dances and afternoon teas were very important aspects of the tennis scene.

It was a period of keen debate in the colony about the legal rights of women. In 1892, the Forrest government had passed legislation which permitted married women to own personal and real property in their own right. Seven years later, after protracted public debate, women were granted the vote. These initiatives helped to focus attention on the role of women in leisure pursuits including tennis (*Morning Herald*, 7/2/1896, 2). As the *West Australian* (21/7/1900, 7) indicated, under a heading 'Notes by Racquet':

> *In these days ladies endeavour to keep pace with men in all things. They appear now to be bestowing themselves in tennis, in as much as a match was played last week between teams representative of Perth and Fremantle, with the result that the latter proved too formidable and won somewhat easily. The*

Perth team consisted of Mrs Tomlin, Mrs Kelsall, and Misses M Lee-Steere and Staples, while for Fremantle the players were Mrs Rockliffe, Miss Price and the Misses Penny. A large number of people witnessed the match, and much interest was manifested in the play. I hope to hear of more contests, as playing in matches will improve the standard and make the ladies events at the annual tournament even more interesting than they have been in the past.

The West Perth Club, however, did not remain in existence beyond the turn of the century with its members presumably joining the nearby Mount Club (see *West Australian*, 16/1/1900). The Mount Club, which was to become Kings Park and, ultimately, Royal Kings Park in 1947, was to date its beginning from 1898. Within a year the membership stood at 41- including men, women, and juniors (*West Australian*, 14/2/1921, 8). Significantly, though, women soon withdrew their membership as a result of a decision to lay grass courts, which proved expensive to water. In 1904, it was decided that as men's fees were set at a higher rate than for women, play on the grass courts on Saturdays should be reserved for the former. This occasioned a 'walkout' by the women. Not until 1926, when more grass courts became available, were women permitted associate membership (*Western Mail*, 28/2/1935, 2).

Despite its later prominence in Western Australian tennis, the foundation of the Mount Club is not well documented. Nor was the formation of the Swan Club at Guildford reported in the Perth press. In the case of the Mount Club, it was probably deemed judicious not to publicise how some prominent residents of West Perth (including later administrators A.G. Rains and A.P. Mills) had succeeded in their application to the Kings Park Board for a grant of land in the Park for tennis. In 1898, Sir Winthrop Hackett MLC introduced to Premier Forrest a deputation seeking 'the conditional use of so much of Kings Park as was necessary for the construction of two tennis courts and the erection of an exceedingly modest dressing shed' (*West Australian*, 14/2/1921, 8). In the following year, the two asphalt courts were declared open for play, with Sir John Forrest serving the first ball to Lady Forrest.

Some years later the author of 'Notes on the Club's History' explained that Kings Park members 'gratefully remember[ed]' how the Chairman of the Kings Park Board, the late Lord Forrest (then Sir John Forrest) and the late Sir J W Hackett. (then Dr J W Hackett) were primarily responsible for the approval of the application (*Kings Park Tennis Club Souvenir: Report and History*, 1898 to 1924, n.d.). Yet hindsight suggests that, from the perspective of the future tennis association, the expression of generosity towards Forrest and Hackett should be re-evaluated. Forrest had recommended in January 1890 to Governor Broome, a 999 year lease to the Western Australian Cricket Association (WACA) for their playing field east of the city (Crowley, 1971, 244). Later, the WACA advantageously gained a freehold title. Forrest's action proved a great boon to cricket, but, despite Lady Forrest's support for tennis the only tangible evidence of where her interests lay was a 'tenants at will' arrangement for the Mount/Kings Park Club. Not only could the private club lose its prime location but there was no allocation of land for a future tennis association.

The WACA was formed in 1885, so the formation of an association in the developmental phase of cricket provided long run benefits. Perhaps one justification for the granting of the lease was the willingness of the WACA to have two asphalt tennis courts and a cycle track built by 1892 as part of the complex. It was a reminder that the absence of a tennis association in this first decade of self government meant that crucial opportunities were lost. The availability of 'homestead' courts in central Perth even led a tennis enthusiast to reason that as the courts at the WACA 'are so far away, and there is such difficulty getting to them, that it is practically useless to join the club there' (*Morning Herald*, 24/3/1896, 2).

A tennis division of the WACA was formed in 1892, although it was not until 1896 that women were admitted on the basis of not being able to play on Wednesdays or Saturdays (*Morning Herald*, 13/8/1896, 2). However, from the men's perspective, the links between tennis and cricket were very strong. One theory expressed in 1896 was that 'cricketers as a rule, are expert wielders of the racquet, and many of the players of the older game are the best tennis exponents in the colony' (*Morning Herald*, 7/4/1896, 2). This theory was soon to be tested by the performance of cricketers in the 'unofficial' colonial championship first conducted at the WACA courts in the spring of 1896. Since 1892, cricketers had performed well in handicap tournaments at the WACA and the 'friendly' Perth versus Fremantle contests (*West Australian*, 16/9/1893, 18/9/1893 and *Morning Herald* , 17/2/1893). For cricketers, though, tennis was an off-season game.

Developments in tennis also took place in many country centres but they were not always reported in the metropolitan press. However, the Katanning correspondent of the *West Australian* (22/8/1892) did file the following report in August 1892:

Lady Forrest, wife of Premier John Forrest, was a leading patron of tennis in Western Australia. (Courtesy Battye Library 681369P)

> *Within the past week a club has been formed here, and a spot has been cleared at the northern end of the town. Patrons of this healthful sport may be seen wielding the racquet on five afternoons.*

Tennis spread to the goldfields. By 1896, it was judged that 'tennis at the fields had apparently as many adherents as in the city' (*Morning Herald*, 28/4/1896, 2). In the same year there were reports of tournaments being conducted by the Geraldton club (*Morning Herald*, 12/2/1896, and 30/5/1896). Indeed, as far back as the late 1880s gravel courts were prepared at the northern end of Avon Park in York (*Westennis*, June 1978, 7).

The formation of small tennis clubs in country towns predated many metropolitan clubs. Historians have even theorised that tennis was frequently the first 'sport' to be established in country towns. In pioneering days people were too busy bringing their farms into production to attend team practices and matches. As Greble (1979, 64) has claimed 'individual sports had greater support than team sports in the earliest years'. In many country districts, gravel or clay courts and matched with scattered populations, actually assisted tennis to become popular. Only two people were needed for a match. The necessary equipment was simple, farmers could supply rolls of wire netting and a few bush posts, and farm machinery could level the courts. Although the dispersed clubs could not be harnessed to form an association, it seems that tennis clubs may well have been able to establish themselves more readily in their own right. In the metropolitan area, however, the early clubs generally had partnered bowls, cricket or church organisations. Nevertheless, when it came to deciding the leading players of the colony, the tournaments were held in 'the big smoke'.

Chapter Four

COLONIAL TOURNAMENTS

WITHOUT an association there was uncertainty about the status of the various tournaments. In tabulating the inaugural championships in each of the Australian colonies Bruce Matthews (1985, 4) designated 1895 as the first year for Western Australia as does *The Tennis Australia Handbook* (1993, 320). In fact, the 1895 tournament was the fourth in a series of annual handicap tournaments controlled by the tennis section of the WACA. The first Men's Western Australian Open Championship was not conducted until 1896. Twelve months later, the first Ladies' Western Australian Open was held. However, in 1898 there were insufficient entries for a women's championship, although the men's event went ahead after some doubts had been raised about its viability.

1895 The Handicap Tournament

Reports indicate the courts were specially 'tarred and dusted' for the 1895 event at the WACA (*Western Mail*, 18/10/1895, 2). In a close women's final, Miss Bell defeated Miss Macklin 6/3, 7/5 (*West Australian*, 10/10/1895, 3). In the men's final Frank Marrie defeated J.B.Spence 6/1, 6/4, with both players on the same handicap. The *Western Mail* (8/11/1895) indicated that:

> *Marrie played a first rate game throughout the tournament having had to meet all the toughest opponents. He won the final fairly easily from Spence, who was on the same mark viz. minus half fifteen. The tournament, owing to bad weather and other hindrances, has taken some six weeks to bring to a conclusion.*

Frank Marrie, won the 1895 Colonial Handicap Tournament but never won the WA Open Championship (Courtesy The West Australian)

Despite what the official records suggest Marrie never won the Western Australian Open Championship. He was transferred by his employer, a leading bank, to Boulder and this restricted his competitive tennis in Perth. Occasionally he travelled for championship play and even participated in some inter-club pennant fixtures. When he came back to Perth in 1903 he was reportedly delighted with the progress of tennis and the development of turf courts in the metropolitan area (*Morning Herald*, 11/7/1903, 7). By this time, too, a permanent Tennis Association had been established after the setbacks in the intervening years which Marrie had not witnessed at first hand. Significantly, Marrie was not able to play in the 1896 Open Championship where his 'accurate play' and 'wonderful judgement' would have provided him with a chance to win the inaugural Open (*Morning Herald* , 11/7/1903, 7). The *Western Mail* (10/9/1897, 23) reporter had indicated 'there [was] no player in Perth to beat him on the backline, his forehand and backhand strokes being always swift and low and a very good length'.

1896 The Inaugural Men's Open Championship

In late September 1896, 'The Marker' in the *Morning Herald* (29/9/1896, 2) expressed concern 'that the increased interest in golf and baseball had greatly affected tennis'. A month later the same columnist (*Morning Herald*, 31/10/1896, 2) in a more enthusiastic tone heralded the organisation of a tournament. It was added 'a great number of inter-colonial and English players in the colony, besides the local contingent, should result in a large entry'. To help give the event status the tournament committee of Messrs Kelly, S.J. Howe and R.H. Kelsey announced the establishment of a Challenge Cup prize fund. It was proposed that if the Challenge Cup (the same trophy title as for the Wimbledon men's singles) be won three times by the same player it was to become his property. Each competitor upon entering for an event and paying the entrance fee to the secretary was given the right to practice at the cricket association courts until the commencement of the tournament. This payment also entitled a player the right of free entrance as a spectator. One widely publicised rule stated that 'if a competitor fails to be present at the time indicated he will have to forfeit to his adversary' (*Morning Herald* 31/10/1896, 2).

Detailed commentaries of each day's play appeared in the newspapers. Also published was a complete entry guide, grading allocations for the handicap events and the daily match draw. For the championship, new tennis nets were erected by the WACA committee and quality balls, a major problem at that time, were secured from Melbourne (*Morning Herald* 31/3/1896, 2). Of course, the committee was powerless to lessen the strength of the prevailing spring breezes. As Perth has been ranked as one of the windiest cities in the world, it was an omen for the future that the wind caused problems in the first Open. (*Morning Herald*, 16/11/1896, 2).

Given this was the inaugural Western Australian Men's Singles Championship some of the detail published at the time is repeated here. The extracts provide both an indication of the style of play and the flavour of tennis writing in this era. As was the community custom, the Christian or given names of competitors were rarely mentioned by the journalists. A section of the report for the men's championship (*Morning Herald*, 23/11/1896, 2) read:

> *The next event was the final of the championship singles between Boddington and Greayer. Mr Pearce, who has been remarkably kind in that direction, consented to umpire. The first two sets of the match were good, but somehow slow on account of the fear of the players to bring off a smash or a strong winning stroke. Bursts of brilliancy came from Boddington at times, and certainly some of his strokes along the side lines were magnificent. He seems to put no force into them, but they travel at far too rapid a pace to enable his opponent to get anywhere near them. Greayer would be a 50 per cent better player if he could smash; for he got scores of balls eminently suited for the stroke, and all he could do with them was to pot them gently back. He, however, made some brilliant returns, getting balls back over the net which one would deem to be almost impossible to return. Boddington is to be heartily*

congratulated on winning the championship, for he played remarkably well in each of the three matches he contested.

The importance given to doubles contests would surprise many modern tennis fans. The description of the doubles went as follows (*Morning Herald*, 25/11/1896, 2):

A great deal of interest was attached to the lawn tennis tournament yesterday, as the finals for the championship doubles were fixed to be played. Kelsey and Currie who had previously defeated Greayer and Newsom, had to meet Boddington and Hoskings, and it was anticipated that the match would be a close and exciting one. The day was not a very pleasant one for the game, as a strong wind was blowing off the river, which made it extremely difficult to place with accuracy. Boddington won the toss, and chose the court, Currie thus having the service with the wind. The first game was the record one of the tournament, for the score was taken back to deuce no fewer than ten times. Eventually, after a hard fight, the game was won by Boddington and Hoskings. The same pair carried off the next, chiefly by judicious lobbing, and it began to be thought that the steadiness of the winners play was going to carry them on to victory. Kelsey and his partner then, however, came with a rush, and, playing a strong forcing volley game, won the next six games in succession and set, 6-2. Three of the games were won without their opponents scoring a point. The winners of the first set kept going, and were three games to one in the second set. They then lost both games with the wind and three all was called. The next two games fell to them, and although Boddington and Hoskings recovered to the extent of one game, Kelsey and Currie were not to be denied, and secured the following game and set. At the beginning of the third set it was thought that Boddington and Hoskings were even at that late period of the match going to make a bold bid for victory, for they won the first three games in succession. This was all they got, however, for their opponents made a spurt, and won the six requisite games in succession. This gave the victory to Kelsey and Currie, 6-2, 6-4, 6-3, and secured for them the title of 'champion double' of the colony. The score was hardly a fair criterion of the play, for many of the games were 'deuce' ones, and long rallies were frequent. The winners had a distinct advantage through knowing one another's play, and the losers missed several strokes through not knowing which player had to take certain strokes. The consequence was that, on one or two occasions, neither player tried for the stroke. Kelsey and Currie scored most of their strokes through combined net play, which was especially successful in consequence of the strong wind that was blowing. Boddington made some very pretty underhand drives, but his partner was rather weak in his returns. He placed well at times, but there was not enough power in his strokes.

Much of the remaining interest focused on the numerous handicap events. Although careful consideration had been given to the appointment of the handicappers, their judgements were invariably criticised. This was illustrated in the report of the major women's event (*Morning Herald*, 23/11/1896, 2):

The final of the ladies' singles did not provide a very exciting contest, for the handicappers had misjudged Miss Stewart's abilities as a tennis player and practically gave her the event. She beat Miss M. Lee-Steere 6-0, 6-4.

While handicappers invariably had a difficult task another facet of tournament tennis, namely seeding the competitors in each draw, was not always common practice. Some of the literature of the era was critical of seeding as it provided a favoured draw for leading players. The introduction of seeding to provide a more interesting competitive environment to each tournament had a chequered introduction. In this respect the guidance of the All England Tennis Club was not firm. Seeding on merit was not introduced until the 1927 Wimbledon championship. Earlier, in 1924, each nation was allowed to nominate up to four players in the singles (and two pairs in doubles) who were then drawn in different quarters. Partial or 'blind seeding' had been practised, particularly in the United States, before this formal rule change (Bransch, 1986, 361). As many of the events had very few entrants 'blind' seeding often meant keeping at least the two leading contenders on different sides of the draw.

1897- the Inaugural Ladies Open Championship

The 1897 'WACA' championship marked the first time that a women's championship in Western Australia had been organised although such championships had been held in some eastern colonies since 1884. The Wimbledon Ladies Championship was also dated from 1884 when Maud Watson (Great Britain) defeated her sister Lillian 6/8, 6/3, 6/3 in the final. However, the inaugural Western Australian women's championship did not attract much publicity and despite an extension of the deadline for entries, only six players were in the draw (which was presumably not seeded). The tournament draw eventually read as follows:

	Miss Stewart		
		Miss Stewart 6/1. 6/2.	
Miss Sadlier Miss Price	Miss Sadlier 6/3,6/1.		
			Miss Calder 6/3, 6/0.
Mrs Rockcliffe Miss Finnerty	Mrs Rockcliffe 6/1, 6/4.		
		Miss Calder 6/4, 6/1.	
	Miss Calder		

In the final, Miss Calder had no difficulty in defeating Miss Stewart. Moreover, the men's final was also one sided with A.W. Hoskings having a resounding 6/1, 6/0, 6/3 victory over prominent player D.B. Orr (*Morning Herald*, 30/9/1897, 2). Hoskings had obviously had his game sharpened in the semi-final when he had struggled to defeat A.H. Greene 6/3,5/7, 6/3, 6/3 (*Morning Herald*, 21/9/1897, 2).

The novelty of the Ladies' Championship did not attract additional publicity, although a good crowd attended finals day. This had been moved to a Wednesday because of the poor weather during the tournament. The Governor, Sir Gerard Smith, had offered the use of the Government House courts, one of the foundation tennis venues in Western Australia, to finish the championship. However, the prizes were not presented by the Governor. This role was performed by Lady Forrest at a windup dance arranged by the WACA committee under the direction of the tournament secretary. The function was attended by some 50 couples, with prominent women players including Mesdames Willis and E.S. Barker and Misses M. Lee-Steere, Brown, Woods, Calder and Marmion being given credit for the success of the occasion (*Morning Herald* 21/10/1897, 2).

The men's doubles championship was won by the well known brother combination of C.L. Oldham and G.V. Oldham. The Oldham's second set score over H.R. Orr and C.J.K. Wilkinson of 18/16 was described as a 'record one, not only for the colony, but also probably for Australia and England as well' (*Morning Herald*, 27/9/1897, 2). Given that tennis was just emerging from the family homestead phase, it is not surprising that brothers could combine to win the colonial championship. At Wimbledon the pattern of brothers combining to win the doubles had been well established. Herbert and Wilfred Baddeley had won four titles, the famed William and Ernest Henshaw had secured five titles, while in 1897 Reggie and Laurie Doherty were to win the first of their eight crowns in men's doubles.

The Championship had been preceded by an open championship at the Fremantle Park Tennis Club during the winter. A local identity, Mr Hindaugh, provided all the prizes for the tournament (*Morning Herald* 5/7/1897, 2). The significance of this championship should not be overlooked, because one of the obstacles to the formation of a tennis association in Western Australia was to be the absence of an agreement as to whether the colonial championship should be held in Perth or Fremantle. A local Fremantle player, E.W. Rosman, who had only taken up tennis upon his arrival from South Australia two years earlier, defeated A.H. Greene with a score of 6/2, 3/6, 6/4 (*Western Mail*, 10/9/1897, 23). Perhaps the three-set contest, as opposed to five, indicated there could be no serious claim that this tournament be regarded as the colonial championship.

The doubles championship was also a best of three sets contest. Victory went to Frank Marrie and J.H. Newsom. The latter, another tennis enthusiast employed at the Western Australian Bank, was a stylish volleyer who had won the 1894 championship of the Carlton Tennis Club in Victoria. It led the *Western Mail* (10/9/1897, 23) reporter to state that Newsom had 'been playing for a considerable time, but principally in country districts, where there is not much scope for improvement'. Newsom had been another of the many tennis players from Victoria who had sought prosperity in rural Western Australia before settling in metropolitan Perth.

The 1898 Tournaments

Significantly, the advertisement for the 1898 WACA Colonial Championship, which did not include a women's championship, invited players to lodge their entries at either a Perth or a Fremantle office. This advertisement appeared in the amusements column on the front page of the *West Australian* on 9 September, 1898.

Details of the tournament should provide some comfort for the modern competition player. Firstly, the entrance fee for an event was as high as 15 shillings. Conversion to today's dollars would support the argument that tennis at the time was almost solely an 'upper-class' game. Secondly, only the opening day of the tournament (24 September) was specified, making it difficult for participants to plan their schedules. Thirdly, as the men's singles were to be decided on the best of five set matches, the tournament was likely to be drawn out over several weeks.

Unfortunately, the spring of 1898 was one of the wettest on record. The tournament dragged on for weeks, with the final not being played until late October. Despite many complaints, the tournament directors still chose to restrict play to the two asphalt courts at the WACA. The earlier offer by the Governor to use the Government House courts was overlooked. The Committee also had their scheduling upset by many long matches. For instance, A.W. Hoskings, the 'crack' Fremantle player, defeated E.W. Rosman in a semi-final 6/3, 6/0, 1/6, 6/8, 6/1. It was claimed that 'better tennis than this [had] rarely been seen in the colony (*West Australian*, 26/9/1898, 6). However, in another marathon match Hoskings was beaten in the final by a courageous A.H. Greene 1/6, 2/6, 7/5, 6/4, 6/1.

The tournament scene of 1898 again revealed the growing status of the Fremantle event which had been moved to the Easter break. Newspapers claimed that the men's final between Roland Kelsey and G.V. Oldham was for the Championship of Western Australia (*West Australian* 7/4/98, 6). Kelsey had to withdraw on medical advice, so Oldham won by default and received a silver cigar case as a reminder of his success.

Ultimately, though, only an association could sanction tournaments and determine their status. Some tournament procedures, such as principles for seeding players and handicapping formulas, also had to be established. They could be expected to come within the ambit of an association which could also develop links with a national and an international body or federation.

J. H. Newsom, one of the leading players from Victoria. (Courtesy The West Australian)

Chapter Five

THE FIRST LAWN TENNIS ASSOCIATION

THE advantages of forming a tennis association to develop Western Australian tennis had been canvassed in Perth from 1896 onwards. Reports of colonial tournaments during the next four years occasionally carried references to informal meetings between tennis enthusiasts with the object of forming a tennis association (*West Australian* 25/4/1898, 6 and 10/8/1898, 6). Associations had already been founded in most of the eastern colonies. Queensland had established their association in 1888, the following year it was South Australia, then New South Wales in 1890 and Victoria in 1892. However, Western Australia had not followed suit.

Advocates of a tennis association considered such a body could help organise tournaments and clarify their status. It could establish rules for a much needed inter-club pennant competition. In addition, attention could be given to purchasing land for courts for a tennis centre in Perth and planning intercolonial tennis contests. These events had established some standing in the eastern colonies with keen rivalry between Melbourne and Sydney already obvious (Yallop, 1992, 11).

Yet, when it was predicted that tennis would 'take off' in the West, the game at Wimbledon had temporarily flagged. Spencer Gore, who had won the first Wimbledon, had speculated that 'lawn tennis would not go on'. In 1890 Gore wrote 'it is its want of variety that will prevent lawn tennis in its present form from taking rank among our great games' (Synder, 1993, n.p.). As the Wimbledon titles began to be dominated by a few families, the 1895 championship even recorded a loss of £35. Croquet players who had lost their status with the swift growth of tennis were invited to return to the club. However, this proved to be a temporary setback when before long the Wimbledon colours of deep green and purple (which became official in 1909) again set the tone of the tennis world.

The first association

An important meeting where progress was recorded towards the formation of a tennis association in Western Australia took place at the Hotel Esplanade (Perth) on 24 February, 1899. A.W. Hoskings, the leading Fremantle player and active official at tournaments, presided over a large attendance (*Morning Herald* 25/2/1899, 2). Club members from Fremantle, Perth, West Perth, and the WACA were present. The chairman explained that the Guildford club had indicated that it favoured of the formation of an association, although none of its members were present.

The report of the meeting (*Morning Herald* 25/2/1899, 2) indicated that:

> *It was unanimously resolved on the motion of Mr Kelsey, seconded by Mr Helsham that an association be formed.*

Draft rules were decided upon and were forwarded to the various clubs for consideration. It was hoped the clubs could arrive at a decision to be put forward at a general meeting to be held within three weeks. The general feeling of the participants was that the association would 'do a great deal of good for the game', as pennant matches could be organised during the winter and championship tournaments organised (*Morning Herald* 25/2/1899, 2). Eventually the meeting was adjourned to 17 March, Roland Kelsey being appointed as acting secretary.

It was soon apparent that the unanimous resolution to form a new association may have been premature. At the next meeting (again at the Hotel Esplanade) the attendance was small and there was evidence of disappointment. Ernest Allnut, a Fremantle merchant took the chair. Another Fremantle representative, H. Watson-Williams, participated, together with the prominent players E.W. Rosman, Frank Marrie, R.H. Thomas, F. Stewart (from Guildford) and Roland Kelsey. After long debate they resolved that the rules should again be submitted to the clubs and possibly agreed upon at a meeting scheduled for 10 April, 1899. This would give other clubs time to consider sending delegates. Moreover, some of the outstanding matters could be discussed when the spotlight moved to Fremantle for the annual Easter tournament (*Morning Herald* 18/3/1899,2).

When the delegates returned to the Hotel Esplanade after Easter there was, however, no delegate from Fremantle. Only Perth, West Perth, Guildford and the WACA sent representatives. Apparently agreement could not be secured to alternate the colonial championships between Perth and Fremantle. The acting secretary, Roland Kelsey, appealed to more clubs to join the Association, as it was clear that the absence of Fremantle would weaken the new body's initial standing (*Morning Herald* 6/4/1899, 2). Nevertheless, a set of association rules was agreed upon. It was also decided to conduct an inter-club pennant competition.

The initial meeting of the 'first' council of the first Lawn Tennis Association of Western Australia took place at the Hotel Esplanade on 25 April, 1899. Some preliminary business was undertaken. Thereafter a committee was appointed to draw up rules for the conduct of pennant matches (*Morning Herald* 26/4/1899, 2). The meeting was then adjourned to 4 May, on which occasion the following office bearers were elected:

Patron	Sir Alexander Onslow
President	S.H. Parker QC
Vice Presidents	Mr S. Burt QC Mr A. C. Willis Dr K. Kelsall
Chairman	R.A. Kelsey
Secretary and Treasurer	Mr M.N. Buzzacott

Understandably, the fledgling tennis association sought the stamp of high office with its initial appointments. The patron Sir Alexander Onslow, who had links with the WANDA Club, had been Chief Justice of the colony since 1882. Mr S.H. Parker had been a leading advocate of constitutional change and a colourful local jockey. Early in his career Parker, 'the people's Harry', had been a great public favourite and known as a 'friend of sport'. At one stage, when responsible government was granted in 1890, it was thought Parker had a strong claim to be the colony's first premier. However, John Forrest, his school 'mate' from Bishop Hale's School emerged as the logical choice. Nevertheless when Parker assumed the presidency of the tennis association he had become an extremely respectable judge with unimpeachable claims of belonging to the colony's landed elite (de Garis, 1981 b, 335, 338)

One of the new tennis association's vice-presidents, Septimus Burt, was actually a member of John Forrest's first cabinet. He was also one of Forrest's school friends and his partner in a pastoral venture, though for a time they had been estranged in their career paths (de Garis, 1981b,338). As previously mentioned, the Burt's 'Strawberry Hill' residence was one of the tennis centres of Perth.

S.H. Parker, 'The people's Harry and 'friend of sport' was the [illegible] Association's first President (Courtesy Battye Library 1120P)

Thus, some of the key personnel of the first association were those 'with the highest indices', in the colony. Many had been educated at Bishop Hale's school where headmaster T.B. Beuttler, a tennis player, had promoted competitive sports. The other members of the inaugural committee had demonstrated their commitment to the game by involvement in the formation of the early clubs. Vice-President A.C. Willis has already been mentioned as a key figure in the Perth Club and Dr K. Kelsall was active in the Perth and WANDA clubs.

The combined position of secretary and treasurer was filled by another Perth (then WANDA) founder, M. N. Buzzacott. He was a hard worker for tennis (*Morning Herald* 6/5/1899, 11). The same could be said of Roland Kelsey, who was elected chairman. Kelsey, who also had links with cricket, was a Hansard reporter at the Parliament.

The first clubs admitted to the Association were Perth, West Perth, Guildford and the tennis section of the WACA. Although the number of clubs was small, the formation of the Association was welcomed by the press. The *West Australian* (9/5/1899, 6) stated:

> *Popular though tennis is it has laboured under great disadvantages in this colony and it must be a source of gratification to all tennis players to know that the formation of a W.A. Lawn Tennis Association is now an accomplished fact. The advantages of such an association must be patent to all. Chief among them are the promotion and control of all championship tournaments.*

The *Morning Herald* (6/5/1899, 11) expressed similar views, although reference was also made to the difficulties which had been encountered establishing the Association. It was contended that:

> *What may be termed the tennis history of Western Australia has just begun, as, up to now, there have not been sufficient clubs or interest in the game for an association to be formed. Several enthusiasts have, however, for some time*

> *been using their best endeavours to attain this desirable object, and their efforts have been crowned with success, and the game may now be expected to improve very greatly both in the number of its adherents and in the standard of play. It has not been an easy task to form this association, for there have been antagonistic influences at work, and a deal of trouble has had to be undergone in order to bring about the satisfactory state of affairs that now exists.*

The assessment of 'Volley' in the *Morning Herald* had not appeared on the second page which the newspaper reserved at that time for sporting details and commentary. Instead, 'Volley' was published in the section of the paper which included guidance about the best chessboard plays and information about drama. Quotes from Shakespeare, news and reviews from the theatre in London, New York and Sydney surrounded opinion concerning the formation of the first tennis association in Western Australia. Tennis, despite its links with the colony's 'power' elite, was going to find it hard to remove its image as a mere leisure pursuit. Obviously, a new inter-club pennant series which had been organised by Kelsey and Buzzacott to commence on 20 May, 1899, would be a step towards tennis being more widely regarded as a sport.

Inter-club association pennants begin

Hopes for a healthy future of the new Association, and development of tennis as a sport, were at first enhanced by the organisation of a pennant competition for the winter months of 1899. The wide use of the term pennant or pennants in tennis, and other sports such as cricket, stemmed from the emblem (or pennant) which was awarded to the victorious team at the conclusion of the series of fixtures. The desire to establish a pennant series was perhaps the most immediate reason for the formation of the association. Moreover, as many tennis enthusiasts regard pennants as the 'life blood' of the game at club level, the format of the early pennants will be examined.

The rules for the winter 1899 competition were devised by Kelsey and Buzzacott and were to be the first of several formulas for inter-club competitions. The fixtures were to be played on Saturday afternoons by 'four man' sides. Each of the five teams in the competition was to play each side twice in the season. This meant a total of eight rounds. Each fixture was to begin with two doubles pairings (A and B) competing in two non-advantage sets. Then the reverse doubles were played before each team member met the equivalent ranked player for one set of singles. Thus each player in each fixture participated in five sets, leaving a total of 12 sets (all first to six games) for decision.

The availability of courts posed a problem. Courts at the disposal of the Association were located at the WACA, the Esplanade, and Guildford. As West Perth had only one court, its team had to have all its matches scheduled away from home (*Morning Herald* 6/6/1899, 11). Perhaps in an effort to ensure that no hitches occurred, West Perth was allocated a bye for the 20 May, 1899 opening of the season, when, in perfect weather and no wind 'the first association lawn tennis matches ... [were] contested in the colony'.

The *West Australian* (24/5/1899, 8) commented:

> *Judging by the keen interest evidenced in the games played on Saturday last under the auspices of the newly formed Lawn Tennis Association, it is very evident that those players whose enthusiasm prompted the formation of the association has[sic] given tennis the impetus the body needed.*

On the Esplanade, the WACA 'A' team of K. Bolton, V. Keane, F. Marrie and C.T. Wilkinson played the Perth team of A.M.P. McQuilkin, H.F. Helsham, M.N. Buzzacott and T. Rain. An extract of this description of this encounter, which was played before a large crowd, reads as follows (*Morning Herald* 25/5/1899, 10):

> *The courts were in splendid order, and a very good tussle was witnessed, the A team only just managing to win by seven sets to five. The visiting team was superior to the home players in the doubles, but the latter won three of the four singles. Bolton and Keane showed the better form in the doubles, and won their four sets straight off. Both men were in very good form at the nets, and nonplussed their opponents by their accuracy in this respect. Keane's service was also very good. Marrie and Wilkinson did not play particularly well together, and the latter had evidently not yet struck form. This pair drew with each of their opposing doubles. All four of the Perth men have the making of very good players. The underhand drive is popular with most of them, but net play was generally deficient. In the singles Bolton secured a love set, but all the other sets were close and exciting. Helsham's was the most meritorious win, for he took a set from Marrie. The latter evidently underrated his opponent's ability, and slackened off so much that he was unable to pull himself together again. Helsham played a better single than double. Keane and Buzzacott had a grand fight, and the score of 6-5 showed that there was very little between the players. Both men served splendidly. McQuilkin beat Wilkinson by a couple of games.*

The scores were:

Bolton and Keane (A) beat McQuilkin and Helsham (Perth) 6/1, 6/1; and Buzzacott and Rain (Perth), 6/1, 6/3.
Marrie and Wilkinson (A) drew with Buzzacott and Rain (Perth), 6/5, 5/6; and McQuilkin and Helsham (Perth), 5/6, 6/0.
Bolton (A) beat Rain (Perth), 6/0;
Marrie (A) lost to Helsham (Perth), 5/6 ;
Keane (A) lost to Buzzacott (Perth), 5/6;
Wilkinson (A) lost to McQuilkin (Perth), 4/6.

Total - WACA 'A' team, 7 sets; Perth, 5 sets

At the nearby cricket association courts the WACA 'B' team of J.G. Greayer, Kelsey, A.H. Greene and J. Innes met the Swan team of L.O.H. Bruyeres, P. Ramsden, Dr J.M.Y. Stewart and Dr F. Stewart. The contest was not so close although the reports of the rubber were lengthy.

The scores were:

Greayer and Kelsey (B) beat Bruyeres and Ramsden (Swan), 6/3, 6/0; and Dr. J. M. Stewart and Dr. F. Stewart (Swan), 6/2, 6/2.
Greene and Innes (B) beat Dr. Stewart and Dr. Stewart (Swan), 6/2, 6/1; and Bruyeres and Ramsden (Perth), 6/5, 6/5.
Greayer (B) beat Bruyeres (Perth), 6/0;
Greene (B) lost to Ramsden (Perth), 5/6;
Kelsey (B) beat Dr. J. M. Stewart (Perth), 6/2;
Innes (B) beat Dr. F. Stewart (Perth), 6/5.

Total - WACA 'B' team, 11 sets; Swan, 1 set.

On the following Saturday morning the *West Australian* listed the teams for the second round of fixtures. Some pre-match comments and arrangements were regularly featured in this first season. As Perth were to play Guildford, the Perth team were to leave Perth central station at 1.15pm and alight at the Woodbridge Station. It was also the first day of competition for the West Perth club, represented by Curlewis, Clarke, Young and C.Y. Simpson. The last player, it will be recalled had been a prominent 'handicap' performer at Government House, Palmerston Street and the WACA for more than a decade.

As the season unfolded it was apparent the West Perth and Guildford teams did not have the strength to match the two WACA teams and to a lesser extent the Perth side. In late August, the premiership was determined in the final WACA 'A' versus WACA 'B' clash. As had been the case throughout the season, the rubber was described in detail maintaining the code of the era; the omission of the Christian, or given names, of the players (*Morning Herald* 21/8/1899):

WACA 'A' versus WACA 'B'

Upon this match depended the result of the premiership for the season, and the consequence was that great interest was manifested in the meeting of the two teams from the Cricket Association. The game was played on the Association Ground on Saturday afternoon in delightful weather conditions. Some really good tennis was expected; but neither team played up to its best form. All the players seemed to be too erratic, and nearly every double had bad spells every now and then. For instance, in the first doubles between Keane and Bolton against Greayer and Kelsey, the former pair played very poorly for the first set and for half of the second set; then they improved considerably, and their opponents went off color altogether. This round of matches resulted in a draw. The "A" first double scored two sets against the "B" second double, the first of which was a good one, and chiefly noticeable for a fine effort by Greene. Marrie and Wilkinson in their two double matches won two sets and lost two, and they showed good general form. In the singles the "A" team overmatched their opponents, and won three out of four. Coming to the individual play, Keane and Bolton, when once they had started to get into their proper form in the second set against Greaver and Kelsey, played admirably, their volleying being excellent. They kept a uniform length, and were very quick in getting to the net. Keane's service was not quite as consistent as usual, but both Bolton and he have a good length second service, which stands them in good stead. In the singles Bolton had a great fight with Greayer, and just managed to win by the odd game. He showed great activity on the court. Keane was too consistent for Kelsey, and did not have much trouble in winning. Marrie and Wilkinson, as a double, have improved considerably during the season. The former serves better, and has improved in his ground strokes, while the latter is much more consistent than ever before. He volleys with accuracy, and is a good net man, in addition to having a fast underhand shot from the base line. Marrie easily won his single, while Wilkinson, after a ding-dong struggle, just lost to Innes. Of the losers, Greayer played a magnificent game in the early part of the afternoon, but the erratic play of his partner some what demoralised him later on. He has played many better singles than in his set with Bolton. Kelsey was not in good form, and had to depend upon his partner to make all the winning strokes. Greene is fast improving in his play. Some of his strokes in the doubles were excellent, and he volleyed with great judgment and accuracy. He did not seem to take much trouble in his single with Marrie, for, at that time, the match was won and lost, and the result of his set would not affect the issue. Innes has come on splendidly during the season, and ½-30 better now than he was when the matches began. He won his single against Wilkinson after a good fight. By winning the match on Saturday the "A" team has secured the premiership, and the "B" is left to fill the second position.

The scores were:

Bolton and Keane (A) drew with Greayer and Kelsey (B), 4-6, 6-5,and beat Greene and Innes (B), 6-4, 6-0;
Marrie and Wilkinson (A) drew with Greene and Innes (B), 5-6, 6-5, and
Greayer and Kelsey (B), 6-3, 2-6;
Bolton (A) beat Greayer (B), 6-5;
Marrie (A) beat Greene (B) 6-1;
Keane (A) beat Kelsey (B), 6-4;
Wilkinson (A) lost to Innes (B), 5-6.

Total -WACA 'A' , 8 sets 64 games; WACA 'B', 4 sets 51 games.

The premiership table at the end of the season revealed the imbalance of the competition and the dominance of the WACA teams:

Tennis Association Premiership Table 1899

Clubs	Matches	Won	Lost	Total Points
WACA 'A'	8	8	0	16
WACA 'B'	8	6	2	12
Perth	8	4	4	8
West Perth	8	2	6	4
Swan	8	0	8	0

Reviews of the 1899 association pennants characterised the first season as an unqualified success (*Morning Herald*; 5/8/1899, and 9/9/1899,). Fortunately, fine weather had generally prevailed. This had helped to allay the concern of those who also played cricket in summer that pennant postponements would delay the staging of the colonial championships. In turn this could make it difficult for them to meet their early season cricket commitments (*Morning Herald*, 5/8/1899, 11). There were also reports of a number of friendly matches being organised outside the official pennant program (*West Australian* 25/5/1899, 17/6/1899, and 19/6/1899).These were mostly between the registered pennant players and other groups such as Palmerston House (*Morning Herald* 3/7/1899, 2). Further evidence of the growth of tennis was the conduct of several handicap tournaments (both singles and doubles) and the arrangement of junior tennis matches.

One 'junior' match between teams selected from the tennis association and the West Perth Tennis Club, took place on the latter's court late in July 1899. In that era 'junior' did not necessarily imply that a person was 18 and under (which was the common handicap tournament age mark) but also included the idea of a reserve or second team. However, as the encounter was reported in detail, it augured well for the future of the pennant competition and the viability of the association (*Morning Herald* 31/7/1899, 2).

The second pennant season-1900

Perhaps the biggest boost to the prospects for the future of the Association was the decision in May 1900 of the strong Fremantle club to join the Association and participate in the pennant competition scheduled for the winter months (*West Australian* 26/5/1900, 6). Before the end of the month, a team of six WACA players went to Fremantle to 'try conclusions' in a friendly match. The visitors were 'hospitably entertained' but lost a close match by five games (*West Australian* 30/5/1900, 7). It was apparent, however, that the WACA were not going to be as formidable as they had been in the first season. Leading player Frank Marrie was again living at Boulder (*West Australian* 11/6/1900, 7). It had been learnt with regret that another good player Private Greene, of the Second West Australian Contingent, had been taken prisoner by the Boers (*West Australian* 2/6/1900, 7). It was further rumoured that Roland Kelsey, the Association's 'founding father', would not be able to play pennants (*West Australian* 11/6/1900,7). Obviously though, his services as an administrator and competent doubles player were too formidable because before the season was over he was playing pennants for the Fremantle 'A' team.

When the fixtures were published, the WACA and Fremantle clubs were both to have 'A' and 'B' teams, but as the competition still had an uneven number of teams, a series of byes was necessary. The season was to run from 26 May to 15 September 1900, with two Saturdays being left 'vacant' for any matches postponed due to inclement weather (*West Australian* 28/5/1900, 7). Unfortunately, on the first day of competition, the Swan Club (with the same group of players as the previous Guildford Club) had to forfeit to Fremantle 'A' as their courts were unplayable (*West Australian* 28/5/1900, 7). The Swan Club took no further part in the competition; apparently its withdrawal was accommodated, but it suggested that the competition was not as solidly structured as had appeared.

As the season progressed it became apparent that the 'premiers' would be either Fremantle 'A' or WACA 'A'. However, when the teams met for the second time on 19 August 1900 the Port side had a resounding victory. The scores and final premiership table (*West Australian* 21/8/1900, 7) were:

Tennis Association Premiership Table 1900

(The *Morning Herald* 17/9/1900, 2)

Clubs	Matches	Won	Lost	Total Points
Fremantle 'A'	10	10	0	20
WACA 'A'	10	8	2	16
Perth	10	5	5	10
Fremantle 'B'	10	4	6	8
WACA 'B'	10	2	8	4
West Perth	10	1	9	2

Kelsey and Rosman (F) beat Bolton and Keane (A) 6/3 and 6/2: and Collier and Wilkinson (A) 6/1 and 6/4.
Price and Magee (F) beat Collier and Wilkinson (A) 6/2, 6/5; and drew with Bolton and Keane (A) 1/6 and 6/1.

Magee (F) beat Bolton (A) 6-2.
Kelsey (F) beat Keane (A) 6-4.
Rosman (F) beat Collier (A) 6-4.
Price (F) beat Wilkinson (A) 6-0.

Total: Fremantle 'A' 11 sets, 67 games defeated WACA 'A' 1 set, 33 games.

The first lawn tennis Association fades

At the annual general meeting of the Association held at the Hotel Esplanade on 17 April, 1901 secretary J. Cox Innes' report was generally optimistic, the winter pennants of 1900 being described as manifesting 'great interest'. The annual WACA 'Colonial' championship was reported to have concluded within a three week time span although it was contended that if the event had been conducted on grass courts, the 103 entries would have been exceeded. Innes complained that the purchase of a Challenge Cup for the men's singles championship had been delayed too long so a sum of £8/8/- was collected in the room during the evening. It was claimed that the Association's finances were sound, but one area of concern was the cost of balls. As a means of reducing this expense, it was recommended that a sufficient number of balls be imported for the next 'State' championship (*Morning Herald* 4/5/1901, 9). It was also decided that the Association's colours would be black and white (*Morning Herald* 3/5/1901, 2). But in the short term, its future was to be black: for a brief period, the Association was soon to fade from existence.

Meanwhile, arrangements had been made for the WANDA club to lease the Esplanade courts and accommodate any Perth members. It saved the venue for tennis but it raised the question as to whether the merger would mean that the WANDA club would be a member of the Association. It was soon decided, however, that WANDA would not submit a team for the Association pennants. The WANDA label was significant. As previously asserted the letters reportedly stood for the 'Western Australian Never Say Die Association'. Many people in the south-western corner of the continent harboured reservations about joining the proposed Australian federation. Western Australia it was feared would lose its identity and control over its own destiny. Likewise, WANDA, by joining the Lawn Tennis Association of Western Australia would lose its autonomy. Even at the WACA and Fremantle Clubs there was evidence that some members were unhappy with the courts being used throughout the winter by pennant players (*Morning Herald* 14/5/1901, 2). It was a problem that was to bedevil clubs in the Association for decades. However, the final blow to the prospect of organising a winter pennant competition for 1901 came when it was announced 'that the West Perth club have been unable to make satisfactory arrangements for the leasing of the ground on which their court is built, and therefore the club is forced to disband (*Morning Herald* 11/5/1901, 2).

At the 13 May, 1901 meeting of the Lawn Tennis Association (at the Hotel Esplanade), it was decided not to conduct the winter pennant series. This was a great disappointment to those who had worked so hard for the establishment of the Association (*Morning Herald*, 14/5/1901, 2). Nevertheless there were expressions of confidence about the future of tennis. As 'Racket' commented in the *Morning Herald* (14/5/1901, 2):

> *The fact that there will be no pennant matches this season does not, I am glad to say, mean that the game of lawn tennis has in any way retrogressed in popular taste, for it is doubtful whether it ever had more devotees than at the present time. During the past year or two many new private courts have been built and the result is that scores of players take place in the game every Saturday. Private tournaments are being held in various suburbs. What will be done during the season is that club matches will be arranged and tournaments held.*

Friendly matches between the WACA and Fremantle were soon arranged (see *Morning Herald*, 4/6/1901, 2 and 9/7/1901, 2). The WACA also played against Palmerston House (*Morning Herald* 27/5/1901, 31), the Mount Club (*Morning Herald* 1/7/1901, 2) and Midland Junction (*Morning Herald* 9/7/1901, 2). Moreover the WANDA club soon became active in inter-club matches conducting ties against the Mount Club (*Morning Herald* 23/9/1901, 2), Fremantle (*Morning Herald* 9/9/1901, 2), York (*Morning Herald* 27/8/1901, 2) and the prestigious Weld club (*Morning Herald* 28/10/1901, 2). A handicap doubles tournament was organised at the WACA (*Morning Herald* 18/5/1901, 2) and another handicap tournament was held in the Fremantle suburb of Richmond (*Morning Herald* 31/7/1901, 2). Earlier, the Association had arranged to play matches against Coolgardie, Kalgoorlie and a combined Goldfields team (*Morning Herald* 3/5/1901, 2).

The first 'State' Championship

The tennis scene appeared active in the winter of 1901. However, proof that the Association had survived the crisis arising from abandoning the pennant series was probably still needed. One test was going to be the organisation of the first State Championship to be held since Western Australia had become a State in the new Commonwealth. It was scheduled to start at the WACA ground on Thursday 10 October, and conclude on Saturday 12 October, 1901. The three day program was an innovation made possible because an arrangement with the WACA trustees for the use of six grass courts.

The decision to play the tournament on grass immediately created keen interest. It was contended (*Morning Herald* 14/9/1901, 9) that;

> *Some people are rather chary about going on the grass after having practised on the asphalt, but they have no need to fear in that direction for they will find immediately that they will play better on the turf than they did on the hard courts. One peculiarity is that whereas a man who has been playing on grass finds it is impossible to play on asphalt, a man who has practised on asphalt finds no difficulty with the turf.*

A lull in the arrival of entries fuelled debate about the decision to use a grass surface and having two working days in the three-day program. Entries could be lodged at Perth (Mr Innes), Fremantle (Mr Higginson), Coolgardie (Mr Cochrane) or Kalgoorlie (Mr Ingle). It was expected that a large contingent from the Goldfields region would participate in the tournament. Finally, though, an entry of 151 was recorded, slightly better than in 1900.

It was usual to publish the names of entrants, their handicaps and the draw in the various newspapers (Morning Herald 5/10/1901, 7 and 7/10/1901, 2). The entrance fee for men was 10 shillings each for the twelve entrants and five shillings each for the eight entrants in the women's singles. The biggest field, at five shillings per player, was 43 in the men's handicap singles. At half this cost 14 entered the women's handicap singles.

Despite some bad weather, the tournament kept to schedule. The courts had been prepared on 'a fairly even surface' (*Morning Herald* 14/9/1901, 9) and the organisational performance of the committee, particularly that of secretary James Cox Innes, was commended. One report on the surface (*Morning Herald* 14/10/1901, 2) stated:

> *It was the first properly conducted tournament on grass that has been held in WA and there is not a single competitor who did not admit that playing on turf was infinitely preferable to the asphalt.... The standard of play in WA has been raised considerably by the tournament.*

The Ladies Championship was won by Mrs Matilda Walsh, from the Goldfields. She was well known 'on the coast' and was widely regarded as the best woman player of her day. Of special interest was her final score against Miss Staples (6/3, 6/2, 6/1). Each match in the women's singles and doubles championship was the best of five advantage sets. This was historic as it proved to be the only occasion when five set matches were played in the Open women's events. In the doubles final Walsh teamed with her regular doubles partner Mrs Ethel Barker to eventually win over Staples and Miss Price in a prolonged struggle, the final score being 6/8, 5/7, 6/3, 6/3, 6/3 (*Morning Herald* 15/10/1901, 2). Fortunately for Walsh, the handicap singles was conducted on a best of three sets (without advantage) basis. In this event, Walsh was able to easily defeat Miss Skinner 6/1, 6/2 to round off an outstanding tournament for the champion.

The men's championship was won by J.D. Cramond. This player had splendid credentials. In 1890 he had won the Victorian men's singles title and in 1899 had added the Western Australian (Perth) crown to his record. To win the first State title was a major achievement, as during the previous season he had been fighting in South Africa with the Second Contingent. In April 1901, just six months before the championship, 'Racket', the tennis columnist had commented (*Morning Herald* 27/4/1901, 11):

> *In the street the other day a man whom I could not recognise came up to me and mentioned my name, and asked how tennis was getting on. I had not the faintest idea who he was until he said, "Why, don't you remember Cramond?" Of course I remembered him, as a genial companion, a thorough sportsman, and one of the hardest nuts to crack on a tennis court that a man would like to meet ... When he went away to fight the battles of the country in South Africa a couple of years ago he was a very thick set and almost a stout man with a moustache. Now he is thin and almost boyish looking with no hair on his face.*

In the men's final Cramond had to fight hard against Association committeeman J.G. Greayer to win the first set 8/6. At 6/1, 6/1, the two remaining sets were more convincing. In the semi-final Greayer had shown good form with a 6/2, 6/3, 6/0 win against Keane (Ken) Bolton. However, Bolton was to win the doubles when he teamed with Keane to defeat Greayer and J. Magee 6/2, 6/4, 1/6, 0/6, 6/2. Cramond, for his part, was back in the winner's circle when he partnered Miss E. Marmion to defeat J. Carter and Miss M. Messer 6/4, 6/2 in the popular mixed handicap doubles.

Cramond probably considered his mixed doubles prize was a pleasant bonus to finish the tournament. However, the Boer War veteran soon had another fight on his hands. The dispute had had its origins in the previous 1900 season when it was decided to hold a play-off between the winner of the

Fremantle Easter Tournament and the Perth WACA Tournament to determine the colonial champion. On that occasion the Perth winner J.C. Johnston played Greayer who had secured the Fremantle title (*West Australian* 19/5/1900, 7). In the 1900 contest, Johnston (Perth) had defeated Greayer (Fremantle) in a long match 3/6, 6/3, 6/3, 3/6, 7/5 to claim the last colonial crown (*Westennis* August 1987, 10).

But in 1901 there was dissension about the need to have a play-off. Magee had won the Fremantle Easter title. However, he had not competed in the Perth tournament singles but had kept himself sharp by entering the doubles championship. This plan had apparently been based on the expectation that he was to challenge the winner at the WACA. This was not Cramond's expectation. In late October, when the Association met to review the tournament, Cramond tabled the following correspondence (*Morning Herald* 31/10/1901, 2):

> *I would be glad if you would place before the committee of the WA Lawn Tennis Association my refusal to play off with Mr Magee for the position of champion of the State. When I entered into the competition just played, I was not aware of the conditions which I now understand exist. Had I been aware of them, I certainly would have objected at an earlier stage. As the particulars, I understand, were not advertised previous to this meeting taking place, I consider that I am quite justified in acting as I am doing. Whatever decision your committee arrive at in this particular instance, I trust they will endeavour to avoid a similar case arising in future. In conclusion, I may add that I am not actuated by any personal feeling in the matter.*

Mrs Matilda Walsh from the Goldfields, widely regarded as the best woman player of her day. (Courtesy The West Australian)

Cramond's claim did not sway the meeting. It was moved and seconded 'that the championship of the State of WA for 1901 be awarded to Mr Magee, Mr Cramond the winner of the Perth Championship having refused to play him'. Before the motion was carried an amendment by Roland Kelsey 'that any verbal compromise which may have existed in the past in connection with the championship of WA shall cease to exist' was accepted (*Morning Herald* 31/10/1901,2).

During the meeting, it was resolved that a suggestion be made to the Fremantle Club to hold the 'Asphalt Championship of Western Australia' on its courts during Easter. It was unlikely that the Club would be agreeable but secretary J. Cox Innes gave notice that at the next meeting of the Association he would move 'that the championship of Perth be synonymous with the championship of the State' (*Morning Herald* 31/10/1901, 2).

The dispute over the status of the Perth WACA tournament was an obvious sign that the Association was not highly influential in the tennis scene. Two major reasons for its formation had been the conduct an of inter-club pennant competition and the need to clarify the status of tournaments. During 1901 the Association appeared to have failed on both counts. A further sign that the Association had lost its way was its apparent failure to call a further meeting to debate the motion. With the passage of time it was apparently decided to recognise Cramond as the winner of the first State Men's Singles Championship. Contemporary records kept by the Association and Tennis Australia support this interpretation. In 1901, the Association had not been dissolved but it had obviously become powerless.

Chapter Six

THE SECOND LAWN TENNIS ASSOCIATION

AS the winter of 1902 approached several attempts were made to entice a sufficient number of clubs to field teams for an association pennant series. The failure of these attempts may well have been a major reason for the Association becoming defunct (*Morning Herald*, 26/8/1902, 2). However, in late August a circular was sent to clubs in the metropolitan area asking them to send delegates to a meeting for the purpose of 'reforming' the Association (*West Australian*, 26/8/1902, 6).

Reforming and resuscitating

At this meeting in early October 1902, with Roland Kelsey, one of the driving forces of Western Australian tennis in the chair, it was moved by J. Cox Innes and seconded by a Mr Neville 'that the Lawn Tennis Association of WA be resuscitated' (WALTA *Minutes*, 1/10/1902). The motion was duly carried by the council of delegates in attendance from the WACA, WANDA and Claremont clubs. The Constitution and rules of the Association, which had been promulgated in 1899, were examined. Several amendments were carried out but essentially the same framework was adopted.

The amendments to the constitution mainly related to the organisation of pennant fixtures. A new clause was inserted which stated 'it shall be optional to engage in pennant matches'. This had been a contentious matter in the founding constitution, so it was hoped the amendment would encourage clubs not wishing to enter pennant teams to affiliate. It was also decided to give the council of delegates authority to arrange pennant matches for women. So far these had not been conducted, although there had been some friendly inter-club contests.

The officials elected were Patron: Mr Justice S. H. Parker; President: Dr A.J.H. Saw; Vice- Presidents: Sir George Shenton, George Parker, and W.H. (later Sir Walter) James, MLA; and secretary and treasurer: J. Cox Innes. Parker had been President of the Association when it was first established in 1899. In 1892 Sir George Shenton (who was not a member of the 1899 Association Committee) had stepped down from Sir John Forrest's first cabinet to become President of the Legislative Council. This had permitted him more time to devote to his many public activities and as one prominent historian (de Garis 1979, 66) has said 'late in the nineteenth century no board or committee was complete without him'. The other nominee for a Vice-President post was Walter James. As President of the prestigious Weld Club and a prominent 'conservative' politician, he was briefly the Premier. James certainly had the credentials for an executive post in the Tennis Association. Importantly, though, James had played and maintained links with the Australian football community, the 'working class' sport (Hunt, 1979, 112). At the turn of the century, tennis shared the winter season with football so James preferred to remain with the football scene and declined to accept the office of Vice-President (WALTA *Minutes*, 1/10/1902).

The absence of James' imprimatur was a disappointment for those striving to re-establish an Association. It was also a reminder that sharing winter months with the increasingly popular Australian football code could stifle the growth of tennis. In terms of other sports it was significant that George Parker, a prominent political figure and Weld Club member, had also been elected as a Vice-president for the Tennis Association. He had been a Trustee of the WACA and had been instrumental in securing for the WACA a long lease for its East Perth ground (Stoddart, 1981, 659). Given the influence of the WACA in tennis circles, it was not surprising that one of its officials held at least a symbolic post in the Tennis Association.

One extremely important new face was that of the President Athelstan John Henton Saw. As a brilliant scholar at Perth High (Hale) School during Mr Thomas Beuttler's headmastership, he won a scholarship to study at Trinity College, Cambridge. Later he became a leading physician in Perth also serving as a senior surgeon in the Australian forces in Egypt during the Great War. Saw shared with Winthrop Hackett and Walter James a commitment to establish sport in the new self-governing community, as well a desire to establish the University of Western Australia. After membership of the University Senate, he became the Chancellor (1922-1929). Earlier, at a by-election in 1915 Dr Saw was elected to the Legislative Council, briefly acting in 1916 and 1917 as a Minister without Portfolio. As he was active in seeking better accommodation for senior citizens (Stannage, 1979, 257) there is today a Saw Street which runs from the Home of Peace in Subiaco through Kings Park near the tennis courts.

Dr Althestan John Henton Saw OBE (1868-1929), inaugural WALTA President, unshakeably committed to the goal of a Tennis Association

It was apparent that Dr Saw was needed to utilise his influence and political skills to ensure a future for the Tennis Association. Despite a temporary setback when the 1902 Association later fell into abeyance, he remained unshakeably committed to its goals, again assuming this post which he held until 1910. To assist him in 1902 he had a solicitor Mr A.S. Hardwick as Chairman of the council of delegates and the hard-working J. Cox Innes as Treasurer and Secretary.

To facilitate re-establishing the Association, Dr Saw's committee had an immediate goal on which to focus. At the first meeting it had been resolved to conduct the 1902 State Open Championship at the WACA on Thursday, 16 October, Friday, 17 October and Saturday, 18 October. Before the 'resuscitation' of the Association, fears had been expressed that the tournament on the grass courts at the WACA would not take place (*Morning Herald*, 30/8/1902, 5). Plans were quickly made for an extended program of events, including a mixed doubles championship and a veterans' handicap singles. It was also resolved to divide the popular men's handicap into divisions. In the expectation of keen interest in the tournament, it was decided to issue season tickets at two shillings and sixpence per spectator (WALTA *Minutes*, 25/8/1902). Advertising would be placed on city trams (WALTA *Minutes*, 1/10/1902) and a band would play on each of the three tournament days. Lunch and afternoon tea would be served at the ground (*Morning Herald*, 16/10/1902, 2).

Negotiations with the WACA trustees for the use of six grass courts were successful. There was even speculation that the entries for the tournament would greatly exceed that of the previous year which had been the first 'Open' played on a grass surface. As the *Morning Herald* (30/8/1902, 2) reporter had observed in relation to the 1901 entry:

> *There was a great prejudice to fight against, for it was the first time that the tournament had been played on grass in the state, and the first occasion in which the events were begun early in the morning and continued throughout the day.*

Over the year, the number of entrants from the newly formed Claremont Club jumped from two to an expected 30 or 40. This was thought to reflect acceptance of the new arrangements (*Morning Herald*, 30/8/1902, 5). The Association had also received several applications from people in the country for advance programs. In particular, several players from Narrogin wanted to take part in the handicap events (*Morning Herald*, 13/9/1902, 7).

Much to the satisfaction of J. Cox Innes, the tournament chairman, many of the players who had fought out the major championship in the past, including Cramond, Bolton, Keane, Greayer, Kelsey, Parker, Kitchen, Carter, Stuart and Coventry, were in the draw. Among the leading new competitors were Saxon and Hill. The former was a Melbourne player of note, while Hill had made a name for himself in South Australia. Unfortunately, though, the women's field was to be weakened by the absence of Matilda Walsh and Miss Staples. Walsh was ill and unable to defend her title, while Staples had become Mrs Greene and had moved to Victoria with her husband (*Morning Herald*, 30/8/1902, 5).

Mr Justice Parker donated a cheque for £2/2/- as a prize for the Ladies' Championship (WALTA *Minutes*, 1/10/1902). J. Cox Innes secured the agreement of Alcock and Company to donate a handsome trophy and prize for the men's championships. However, perhaps the best news for Innes was notification that the Fremantle and Mount Clubs intended to join the Association (*Morning Herald*, 13/9/1902, 7). This meant the Association consisted of the WACA, Fremantle, Claremont, Mount and WANDA clubs. This embraced a membership of several hundred players. Understandably, it was contended that 'with such a force controlling the game and the tournament, the success of both is assured, (*Morning Herald*, 13/9/1902, 7).

It was soon obvious, however, that it was again premature to make judgements about the future strength of the Association. Within a week there was a report of a stormy meeting of WANDA members (*Morning Herald*, 20/9/1902, 24). There were expressions of annoyance concerning the action of the WANDA secretary, J. Neville, attending the meeting and endorsing a motion to 'reform and resuscitate' the Tennis Association. WANDA, it will be recalled, had not joined the 1899 Association. This mood was again to prevail in 1902. Nevertheless in his comment on the actions of the WANDA club, 'Racket' the *Morning Herald*'s tennis columnist said (20/9/1902,24):

> *It was necessary that the WANDA club should come in so that the Association might be reformed, and thanks to this Secretary, Neville, who takes a keen practical interest in the game, the Association was reformed and it was possible for full arrangements to be made for the tournament. Now it is to a certain extent immaterial whether the club is included or not, as all the other clubs have thrown their lot in with the Association.*

Entries for the tournament totalled 154, which was slightly more than in 1901, but below the initial forecasts. However, it was still considered highly satisfactory (*Morning Herald*, 3/10/1902, 2). The women's championship attracted only six entrants. The decision to reduce the women's championship to the best of three advantage sets (from five advantage sets in 1901) had not increased the draw. However, the field for the men's singles was one of the largest on record. This compelled the organisers to publish the conditions of play in the newsletter to ensure that when His Excellency Sir Edward Stone, the Administrator, attended the WACA ground on the Saturday afternoon, the finals would be in progress.

Conditions of Play

(Morning Herald,15/10/1902)

Appended are the conditions of play:

(1) The council shall have the entire management of the tournament.

(2) The entrance fees of all competitors must be paid to the honorary secretary of the Lawn Tennis Association before 6 o'clock on Wednesday, October 8, when the entries close. The draw will take place on the evening of Wednesday, October 8. Competitors' attention is particularly drawn to this condition.

(3) Play will commence punctually at 9 o'clock each day, at which hour, whatever may be the weather, all competitors must be on the ground prepared to play.

(4) No competitors will be allowed to wear boots or shoes with heels, spikes, or nails, except those known as 'steel point'.

(5) Any player not playing his match at the time specified by the council will be disqualified.

(6) Players must play their matches without any delay. No longer interval than three minutes between each set shall be allowed each player without the consent of his opponent, and in no case shall a longer interval than five minutes be allowed. If a player neglects to continue the game when requested by the umpire, he shall be wilfully wasting time between the strokes in the game, after one caution the umpire shall thereupon disqualify him, and award the match to his opponent.

(7) The council reserve the right to disqualify any competitor whose conduct during the tournament, in their opinion, shall be deserving of censure.

(8) The tournament will be conducted in accordance with the rules and regulations laid down by the All England Lawn Tennis Club for the carrying out of tournaments, save as altered by the program and these conditions.

The schedule of matches was maintained. The women's championship was easily won by Miss Black over Miss Rockliffe 6/1, 6/2. Black had her toughest match in the first round, when she dropped a set to the Fremantle player, Kitchen. Nevertheless, it was immediate success for Black, as she had arrived only a few days earlier from Victoria. In that State, Black had been the doubles partner of the legendary Miss P. Howitt, who had won three New South Wales Open titles and five Victorian Open Championships.

The victor in the men's championship was L. Saxon, who was also a former prominent Victorian player. In the final, Saxon defeated J.D. Cramond, the 'eventual' holder of the 1901 title. The match was a hard-fought five set marathon, with a score card of 3/6, 1/6, 6/3, 7/5, 6/1 in favour of Saxon. In the men's doubles final Saxon teamed with T. Kitchen, to win another five set match over Ernie Parker and J. Magee, 6/4, 3/6, 1/6, 7/5, 6/2.

Although Saxon had had an outstanding championship, winning titles in the men's singles and doubles as well as the mixed doubles (with Kitchen over Bolton and Mrs Barker 6/1, 6/8, 6/1), the tournament heralded the emergence of Ernie Parker as a future champion. Over the next decade, Ernie Parker established himself as one of Western Australia's finest sportsmen. His cricketing prowess took him close to gaining a test cap after he had become the first Western Australian to score a century in an interstate match. After winning several State Open Championships, he was the first Western Australian to win the prestigious Australian Open (then known as the Australasian Open) in 1913. As noted in the 1902 tournament, Parker was a finalist in the men's doubles. In the singles he defeated leading players, Greayer and Magee before losing in four sets in the semi-final to Saxon, the eventual winner, 4/6, 4/6, 6/1, 5/7.

'Racket' recalled how he had predicted that Ernie Parker, born in 1883 and then 19 years of age after being educated at Perth High (Hale) School and St Peter's College in Adelaide, was likely to be a future champion (*Morning Herald*, 20/10/1902, 3). It was also said that:

> *The tournament was far and away ahead of anything that had been held in the State previously; the weather was fine; the arrangements more complete, the attendance larger, the entries more numerous and the standard of player higher. The Hon. Secretary, Mr J. Cox Innes worked untiringly and he was well assisted by his Committee.*

The floundering

The success of the tournament should have enhanced the stability of the Lawn Tennis Association. However, this was not the case, as 'Racket' pointed out (*Morning Herald*, 20/10/1902, 3):

> *It is to be regretted that the opposition shown by all the clubs to the efforts of those gentlemen to improve the standard of the game should have caused them to announce, as they did at the conclusion of the tournament on Saturday, that their association with the management of the game in the State would cease entirely with the setting up of the affairs of the tournament.*

On 22 October, 1902, the Secretary presented a Statement of Receipts and Expenditures in connection with the tournament which showed a credit balance of £50/10/- The *minutes* of the meeting indicate that Mr Kelsey moved and Mr Bolton seconded 'that the balance be disposed of in purchasing prizes' (WALTA *Minutes*, 22/10/1902). There is no evidence that the second Lawn Tennis Association in Western Australia ever met again. Within a few months, though, there was yet another attempt to establish an Association. Perhaps it would be 'third time lucky'.

Chapter Seven

THE THIRD LAWN TENNIS ASSOCIATION

THE process of establishing a lawn tennis association in Western Australia was developing into a saga. The main objectives of the first Association had been to organise an inter-club pennant competition, clarify the status of major tournaments, develop a tennis centre and organise inter-colonial tennis contests. During the winters of 1899 and 1900 inter-club pennants had been conducted but the competition had been disbanded. After initial success with the designation of tournaments, the dispute over the 1901 men's championship of Western Australia had been a fiasco. The resuscitation of the Association in 1902 to conduct the annual tournament for that year had proven to be short-lived. With no tennis Association the future was gloomy for the sport in the West.

Those who had been frustrated in their attempts to form an association obviously realised that a different strategy had to be used. This led to informal negotiations to use grass courts at the Zoological Gardens Oval during the winter for pennant matches. If clubs electing to have pennant teams did not have to provide courts and so prevent social play on Saturday afternoons, the prospects of a viable association would be enhanced. Moreover, a move away from the WACA would help to establish the identity of the Tennis Association, which had remained a poor cousin to the Cricket Association.

The 1903 Tennis Association

After arrangements had been made with the Zoological Gardens Board for the use of the six grass courts, a meeting of members of clubs in Perth, Fremantle and the suburbs was held at the Hotel Esplanade on 3 April, 1903. The purpose of the meeting was to 'form an Association to control tennis on the coast' (*Morning Herald*, 4/4/1903, 2). When this suggestion was 'enthusiastically received', it was decided to contact all clubs on 'the coast' and ask them to affiliate with the Association, upon the payment of a certain sum to be fixed later. This levy would entitle each club to send two delegates to meetings of the committee and to form a controlling body. To cater for those combinations of players who might decide to form a club for the purpose of pennant matches without having courts of their own, it was decided to accept the inclusion of Cottesloe, East Perth and the Stock Exchange (*Morning Herald*, 4/4/1903, 2).

Once again it was Roland Kelsey who assumed the responsibility, as acting secretary, to attend to the correspondence and organise a meeting to formally structure the Association. A major problem was that of deciding whether teams that did not possess courts should still have delegates on the committee. This was overcome by ruling that, with the exception of the foundation clubs, a team without grounds (or a membership of 12) could not join the Association as a club. Nevertheless there appeared to be a climate conducive to the establishment of an Association. Most of the old rules had been considered and agreement upon the changes appeared to prevail. The 'antagonistic influences' that had characterised the 1899 and 1902 Association were not so obvious. Undoubtedly, one major source of encouragement was access to the courts at the Zoological Gardens Oval. It was even claimed 'that Western Australia led the way in tennis in the Commonwealth for in other states pennant matches had to be played on asphalt' (*Morning Herald*, 25/4/1903, 2).

The 'third time lucky' formal establishment meeting of the Lawn Tennis Association of Western Australia took place on Friday evening 17 April, 1903 at the Hotel Esplanade and involved Dr Deravin and W. Kitchen (Fremantle), J. Carter and E. Parker (East Perth), R. H. Kelsey (Stock Exchange), Messrs Crooks and Clyde (Claremont), A. Nairn (Cottesloe) and Messrs A.F. Abbott and A.V. Neville (WANDA). As WANDA had not authorised the presence of Abbott and Neville, and mindful of that club's previous reluctance to support an Association, Abbott and Neville were allowed to remain 'on sufferance' in order to provide suggestions with regard to the rules (*WALTA Minutes*, 17/4/1903).

In the chair was Dr Deravin, a prominent Fremantle doctor and renowned doubles specialist. A motion was moved and seconded 'that an Association be formed to be called the Lawn Tennis Association of Western Australia' (*WALTA Minutes*, 17/4/1903). The mover was W. Kitchen, an active committee man and fine player from Fremantle. Given that Fremantle did not initially join the 1899 Association (thus weakening the organisation from its beginning) it was significant that the club was solidly behind the 1903 initiative. The seconder was Ernie Parker from East Perth. He helped give the stamp of approval to the Association from a leading group of players.

The delegates representing the foundation clubs then adopted a Constitution. As the Constitution was relatively brief and provided a statement on the objectives of the Association and its basic structure, it is printed here:

CONSTITUTION

1. *The Association shall be called "The Lawn Tennis Association of WA".*
2. *The objectives of the Association shall be -*
   (a) *The general control of lawn tennis in Western Australia.*
   (b) *The arrangement of inter-state, pennant, trophy, and inter-club tennis, and all things that relate thereto.*
   (c) *The settlement of disputes between associated clubs.*
   (d) *The representation of the state at any conference of delegates convened for the purpose of discussing and considering any matter relating to lawn tennis.*
   (e) *The delegation of the management of any championship or inter-state meeting to any club or other body.*
3. *The Association shall consist of the amateur members of all associated clubs and affiliated teams.*
4. *The test of a bona fide club, except insofar as the foundation clubs are concerned, shall be -*
   (a) *Possession of a ground.*
   (b) *A membership of at least twelve members.*

(c) *A constitution to the satisfaction of the committee hereinafter defined.*

5. *Any aggregation of players may be enrolled as an affiliated team for the purposes of pennant matches; but they shall not have representation upon the committee.*

6. *Foundation clubs not having courts of their own shall retire from the Association upon withdrawing from pennant matches.*

7. *The officers of the Association shall consist of a patron, a president, not less than three vice-presidents, a treasurer and a secretary. They shall be elected by the committee at its first meeting in every year, and shall not enter upon their office until the termination of such meeting.*

8. *The management of the Association shall primarily be vested in a committee consisting of two delegates appointed by each club.*

9. *The committee shall at all times have full power to frame by-laws and elect sub-committees for the carrying out of the objectives of the Association.*

10. *It shall be optional for clubs joining the Association to engage in pennant matches.*

By the time the office bearers were elected at another meeting at the Hotel Esplanade on 6 May, 1903, the Mount Club (later Royal Kings Park) and significantly WANDA had joined the Association. The Midland Junction club had also made firm enquiries concerning membership (*WALTA Minutes*, 17/4/1903). As in 1902 and 1899, the Association's patron was a leading judicial figure namely Justice (later Chief Justice) S.H. Parker. Dr Saw, as previously indicated, also retained the Presidency. Roland Kelsey, in whose hand some of the initial records have been written, assumed the chairmanship, while the honorary secretary and treasurer was J. Carter. The latter, from the East Perth club, was noted for his attractive tennis (*Morning Herald*, 3/10/1903). In a sign reflecting the expected survival of this Association, an honorary auditor, Keane Bolton from Fremantle, was appointed.

Office Bearers-1903 Association

Patron	Mr Justice S.H. Parker
President	Dr A.J.S. Saw
Vice-presidents	Sir George Shenton
	Dr W. Hackett
	Dr Birmingham
	Dr Trotman
	Mr S.S. Stubbs
Chairman	Mr R.H. Kelsey
Honorary Secretary	Mr J. Carter
Auditor	Mr K. Bolton

Of special interest was the election of the vice-presidents. Sir George Shenton had agreed to retain the post from 1902. Two medical practitioners, Birmingham and Trotman, together with Mr S. Stubbs, were also elected as was Winthrop (later Sir Winthrop) Hackett. In 1898, Hackett had been the founding President of a tennis club in the South Perth area (*Westennis*, March 1988, 10-11). However, this club had not been an active participant in any of the three attempts to establish the Association. As the editor of the *West Australian* since 1887, Hackett wrote influentially on a range of topics. He strongly supported responsible government but he had doubts about the Commonwealth Constitution Bill which was the framework for federation in Australia (Battye, 1979, 95). Hackett may have had similar doubts about the

Tennis Association, in which clubs (like states) would lose their identity and viability. However, in 1903 Hackett was prepared to give his imprimatur to the Association.

It should not be assumed that Hackett was a token Vice-President. As President of the Zoological Gardens Board (established in 1897), he played a role in securing the agreement between the Director of the Board, Ernest Le Souef, and the Association for use of the turf courts on the Zoological Oval. This helped the Association to become a permanent body. It was certainly a contribution to tennis but, with hindsight, it must be wondered if Hackett's close friendship with Premier John Forrest (Battye, 1979, 94) could not have yielded a permanent, strategically-located tennis centre, a favour of similar proportions to that which the WACA had received. Nevertheless thoughts of an even better deal were far from Hackett's mind when he spoke at the opening of the courts for the 1903 winter pennant season. As he said (quoted in the *West Australian*, 8/6/1903, 6):

> *Better late than never. On behalf of the Committee who have these Gardens under their control I have not only to welcome you but to express very great pleasure at your having seen fit to accept these courts as the Association courts of Western Australia. It has ever been one of the principal objects of the founders of these Gardens to devote a part of them to the promotion of manly and athletic sports thus making a divergence from all other Zoological Gardens the world over. We are delighted to find that the idea has commended itself to the Association. That Association fills what has been a want in this State, and I am grateful to think we have been enabled to contribute a little help towards putting it on a footing unexampled in Australia whereby all the associated clubs can go through their matches at the time and on the one ground. I trust that you will be satisfied with that ground. What success it promises will be attributed to my friend, Mr Le Souef, and I am given to understand it has obtained the approval of so excellent a judge as your active chairman, Mr R. H. Kelsey, who you will allow me to say is one of the most valuable acquisitions that we have had to the manly sporting community of Western Australia. I have pleasure in declaring this ground open for the pennant matches of the present season.*

The occasion was also given prominence in the 'Social Notes' of the *West Australian*. The celebration of the opening of the courts was attended by 'a large number of well known people' and was described as 'one of the pleasantest events which have marked our social calendar for some time past' (*West Australian* 4/6/1903, 6). However, while it was certainly a social occasion Hackett, and Saw, probably understood the value of ritual in cementing bonds and creating the goodwill necessary for an Association to endure. There had been no comparable occasion to mark the beginning of the Association's activities in 1899, although newspaper editorials had brought the Association to public notice.

Surprisingly, Hackett did not publish an editorial extolling the creation of the new Association although sporting topics were obviously editorial material. Indeed, just a few days after the Association was founded an editorial was devoted to the subject of cricket (*West Australian*, 23/4/1903, 5). After claiming that 'there is much justification for regarding cricket as the national Australian game' it was suggested that better turf wickets and interstate competition were necessary to lift the standard of local cricket. Within another week an editorial praised the decision to send two crack riflemen to the imperial gathering at the Bisley Range, Surrey, where the Queen's Prize Competition was held (*West Australian*, 6/5/1903).

One explanation for the absence of a 'sport' editorial may lie in the previously expressed thesis that tennis was still regarded as a 'game', even a 'women's game'. It is noteworthy that Hackett, in his speech at the Zoo Oval, twice attempted to promote tennis as a 'manly' pursuit. Of course promoting tennis as a sport did not necessarily mean that women would not be equal partners. Hackett, for his part, was a strong advocate for opportunities for women and had campaigned for the women's vote. Ironically, on the day that pennant matches were first played under the auspices of the 1903 Association an editorial in the *West Australian* (6/6/1903, 6) opened with the observation that

Sir Winthrop Hackett (centre of photo), facilitated the Association's use of courts on the Zoological Oval in South Perth. Photo taken on the front lawn at the South Perth Club in 1905 (Courtesy Battye Library 5824P)

'every year, almost every month there is something new to announce in connection with the progress of women in the social and political arena'.

As a man of letters, and subsequently first Chancellor of the University of Western Australia (1911), Hackett, the presumed author of the editorial, was critical of Oxford and Cambridge denying women 'Bachelor' degrees. Women who satisfied the course requirements were only awarded 'certificates of proficiency'. Hackett was proud that this practice had not developed in the Australian universities. However, as the pennant season (for men) opened it was not possible to mention any administrative post being allocated to women in the Lawn Tennis Association. Nevertheless within a few weeks there was an example of significant progress for women. A. Neville, a WANDA delegate, mentioned 'the desirability of pennant matches for ladies to take place at the Zoo grounds on Wednesdays' (*WALTA Minutes*, 18/7/1903) and was authorised to communicate with member clubs. It marked the first step to establish a mid-week ladies' competition. Some shrewd minds may have reasoned that one way to ensure a viable Association was to mobilise the ladies' mid-week contingent. Meanwhile it was the men's pennants which were to be first organised.

Pennants (Men)

The Constitution provides a detailed set of rules and 'by-laws' for the conduct of pennants. A set of by-laws was also incorporated into the Constitution. Significantly, all matches were to be played 'under the laws of the game as accepted by the All England Lawn Tennis Association'. As in England, there was an endeavour in the colonies to preserve the amateur code of the game. The tennis associations in New South Wales and Victoria had in 1895 classified an amateur as a player who had 'never' violated any of the following conditions (see Yallop, 1992, 15-16):

(i) He has not knowingly competed with or against a professional lawn tennis player for a prize.

(ii) He has never entered a lawn tennis competition open to professionals, nor played lawn tennis for a stake, public or admission money or entrance fees, nor received money in lieu, or as a prize.

(iii) He has not instructed, taught or assisted in the pursuit of lawn tennis as a means of livelihood, nor for gain or emolument.

(iv) His membership in any lawn tennis club was not brought about, or does not continue, because of any mutual understanding expressed or implied whereby his continuing a member of any such club would be of any primary benefit to himself or his club.

(v) The pennant committee shall be the tribunal to decide whether a player is a professional or an amateur as defined by the above.

A Disputes Committee, with considerable powers, was to be established. To prevent frivolous appeals, a substantial fee (of 10 shillings and 6 pence) was to be lodged with the Secretary of the Association within three days of a dispute. If the decision was in favour of the club referring the dispute, the fee was to be refundable. Clubs were permitted to enter any number of teams for pennant matches. Competitors who had played twice for one club in one season could only play for another club with the special permission of the committee. This committee had the power to disqualify players for misbehaviour. In addition, the committee could award premiership points for any matches for which a protest had been lodged to either of the competing teams, or order the match to be replayed or to extend the playing time for any match. A set of fixtures was then published.

Winter Pennant Fixtures 1903

May 30 – Wanda* v Mount, East Perth v Stock Exchange Club, Fremantle* v Claremont, Cottesloe bye.

June 6 – Wanda v East Perth, Cottesloe v Stock Exchange Club, Fremantle v Mount, Claremont bye.

June 13 – Wanda v Stock Exchange Club, Mount v Claremont, Cottesloe v East Perth, Fremantle bye.

June 20 – Wanda v Fremantle, Mount v Cottesloe, Claremont v East Perth, Stock Exchange Club bye.

June 27 – Wanda v Claremont, Mount v Stock Exchange Club, Fremantle v Cottesloe, East Perth bye.

July 4 – Wanda v Cottesloe, East Perth v Fremantle, Stock Exchange Club v Claremont, Mount bye.

July 11 – Mount v East Perth, Stock Exchange Club v Fremantle, Claremont v Cottesloe, Wanda bye.

July 18 – Vacant.

July 25 – Mount v Wanda, Stock Exchange Club v East Perth, Claremont v Fremantle, Cottesloe bye.

August 1 – East Perth v Wanda, Stock Exchange Club v Cottesloe, Mount v Fremantle, Claremont bye.

August 8 – Stock Exchange Club v Wanda, Claremont v Mount, East Perth v Cottesloe, Fremantle bye.

August 15 – Fremantle v Wanda, Cottesloe v Mount, East Perth v Claremont, Stock Exchange Club bye.

August 22 – Claremont v Wanda Stock Exchange Club v Mount, Cottesloe v Fremantle, East Perth bye.

August 29 – Cottesloe v Wanda, Fremantle v East Perth, Claremont v Stock Exchange Club, Mount bye.

September 5 – East Perth v Mount, Fremantle v Stock Exchange Club, Cottesloe v Claremont, Wanda bye.

*In each case the balls for the matches will be provided by the first named club.

The pennant by-laws were modelled on those which had been used during the 1899 and 1900 seasons. Yet even tried and tested rules rarely cover all the contingencies. While the season was generally free of disputes, there was controversy over a fixture between WANDA and Claremont on 27 June, 1903. After matches had been stopped due to an exceptionally heavy shower of rain, the WANDA team left the courts believing that no further play was possible. Later the weather cleared and the two other matches (Fremantle versus Cottesloe and Stock Exchange versus Mount) were completed. It was initially reported that WANDA would have to forfeit the points as the Claremont players were ready to compete when the rain ceased (*Morning Herald*, 29/6/1903, 2). However, WANDA successfully protested, by indicating that pennant by-law 13 stated in part 'in the event of an adjournment before 4.30 pm, the match to be declared a draw' (*WALTA Minutes*, 18/7/1903).

In August there was an adjustment to the fixtures when it was resolved to permit teams to postpone matches scheduled to play on the same day as the interstate lacrosse match between Western Australia and South Australia. In those days lacrosse was a winter game which appeared to attract more community interest than tennis. Within a year the Lacrosse Association demonstrated its growing stature by conducting an interstate carnival, probably the first such national event held in Perth. However, the postponement of some pennant matches indicated that, despite some friction between the tennis and cricket authorities, there could be co-operation between sections of the broader sporting community in Perth. When the 1904 interstate lacrosse carnival was played at Fremantle Oval the Football Association relinquished the use of the oval (on 29 August) so that everything could be in readiness for the occasion (*Morning Herald*, 4/7/1904, 2). It was noteworthy that late in 1903 there had been attempts to gain the Tennis Association's support for affiliation with the newly-founded Western Australian Amateur Sports Club (*WALTA Minutes*, 5/11/1903).

The interstate lacrosse fixture did prompt Tennis Association delegates to begin negotiations for a visit by an interstate tennis team to Perth in March 1904. Three selectors, leading players (E. Parker, K. Bolton and H. Hill) were appointed to select Association teams for interstate and intrastate matches (*WALTA Minutes*, 5/11/1903). Later there was discussion about the Mars Buckley Cup which was an interstate tennis competition played in the eastern states (*WALTA Minutes*, 20/8/1906). In the short term, though, the pennant fixtures and proposed championship were the priority matters. In fact, the publicity afforded to the pennant fixtures was considerable. Tennis and other 'sports' had benefited from the keen rivalry which had developed between the *West Australian* and the *Morning Herald*. 'Racket' in the *Morning Herald*, 3/10/1903, 4) presented a review of the men's winter pennants which were judged:

> *... to have been the best yet experienced in Western Australia, for although there have been two previous seasons of pennant matches neither has been anything like so satisfactory or complete as the one just conducted. This year we have had real lawn tennis and not a hybrid edition of the game played on asphalt ...*

Much of the success of the season was attributed to the system of central courts, by which the three Association matches were played simultaneously at the Zoo Gardens on Saturday afternoons. However, boasts that the Association had set an example to the whole of Australia and how 'visitors were very much struck by the businesslike air pervading it and the great strides the game was evidently making in the State' (*Morning Herald*, 20/7/1903, 3) were tempered by criticisms about the delays and problems caused by unusually bad weather. As 'Racket' recorded (*Morning Herald*, 3/10/1903, 4):

> *Many tennis players blame the Association authorities because they do not have the matches in summer; but they speak without this book, for the courts are not available in the summer, the ground being needed for cricket. If those who are complaining at what the tennis authorities do will find equally good courts upon which the tennis matches could be played in the summer well and good; but if not they should cease their complaints.*

Unfortunately, incessant rain also marred the pennant final, which had been expected to attract a large gate. The quest for the premiership was keenly fought between Fremantle and East Perth. As both sides were locked on 22 premiership points (only one loss each) at the end of the qualifying rounds, a play-off was required. Fremantle eventually won by a mere six games with sets being even. The scores (*Morning Herald*, 28/9/1903, 2) were:

Doubles

O'Connor and Jordan (F) drew with Carter and Parker (EP) 6/3, 4/6 and beat Greayer and Coyne (EP) 6/4, 6/3.

Rosman and Taylor (F) lost to Carter and Parker 5/6, 4/6(EP) and beat Greayer and Coyne (EP) 6/2, 6/3.

Sub totals: Fremantle 5 sets 43 games; East Perth 3 sets 33 games.

Singles

Jordan (F) lost to Parker (EP) 2/6

Taylor (F) lost to Greayer (EF) 4/6

Rosman (F) beat Carter (EP) 6/3

O'Connor (F) lost to Coyne (EP) 5/6

Sub total Fremantle 1 set 17 games - East Perth 3 sets and 21 games.

Grand Totals

Fremantle 6 sets 60 games - East Perth 6 sets 54 games

This meant that the final premiership table read as follows (*Morning Herald*, 3/10/1903, 4).

Club	Pl	W	Sets	Game	L	Sets	Games	Pts
Fremantle	13	12	108	806	1	48	551	24
East Perth	13	11	100	754	2	56	624	22
Cottesloe	12	7	81	653	5	63	586	14
Stock Exchange	12	7	78	624	5	66	586	14
Wanda	12	3	60	567	8	76	616	7
Claremont	12	2	49	468	9	87	652	5
Mount	12	-	39	481	12	112	745	-

The qualitative and quantitative analysis of each team's performance, including doubles, is too detailed to reproduce. However, to illustrate the detail, only the shortest entry, that for the Stock Exchange (a club name providing an insight into the basis of local tennis), is reprinted here (*Morning Herald*, 3 /10/1903, 4):

Stock Exchange

The chief reason for the comparative success of this club during the season was that they rarely changed their team and the consequence was that the players got to know one another's style thoroughly, and very rarely did they interfere with each other. Hill and Kelsey had a very successful season as a pair. They played together in 10 matches out of the 12 and won 37 sets and 234 games to their opponents 3 sets 85 games. Thus, their adversaries averaged just over 2 games a set against them, while they averaged 5 games and 17/20 per set. They only separated once, and that was against a weak team, but they found it far better to keep together. The club were beaten five times during the season – twice by Fremantle by games, sets being equal, twice by East Perth, once 7–5, and the other times 8–4, and once by Cottesloe on games, sets being equal. They therefore had plenty of exciting finishes. Kelsey played in every match during the season, and Hill missed only one. Spence also only missed one match during the season. He was partnered most of the season by Hardwick, and although as a pair they were not very successful, they had many good battles, and put up some excellent fights against superior doubles. Hill was the most successful player in singles and doubles, and he is now getting back into something like the form he was in when he won the doubles championships of South Australia two years in succession. Appended are the performances of the players:

Doubles

Players	Won		Lost	
	Sets	Games	Sets	Games
Hill and Kelsey	37	234	3	85
Hill and Spence	3	19	1	17
Kelsey and Hardwick	5	41	3	30
Hardwick and Buzacott	2	15	2	20
Spence and Rosenstamm	4	43	8	63
Spence and Hardwick	8	86	20	149

Single

Hill	7	55	4	34
Kelsey	6	50	6	53
Rosenstamm	1	11	2	16
Spence	3	38	8	58
Hardwick	2	28	6	51
Buzacott	0	3	1	6

Women's Pennants

The coverage given to the men's winter pennants overshadowed a significant development in the Tennis Association's program: the conduct of women's pennants in the new Association's first season. The question was first raised at an Association meeting on 1 July 1903 (*WALTA Minutes* 1/7/1903) and delegates generally favoured the proposition as it was rumoured that five clubs Fremantle, Mount, WANDA, Cottesloe and Claremont, were prepared to compete (*Morning Herald*, 4/7/1903, 2). However, the Association appeared to be reluctant to take decisive action; this view was expressed in the *Morning Herald* (4/7/1903, 2):

> *... the ladies would have to make all the arrangements with regard to the formation of the association themselves, and then submit their proposals to the association for ratification. It rests with the ladies how to set to work in order to get a couple of rounds of matches in before the season closes. As far as the financial position is concerned, the committee of the association do not anticipate any difficulty in making arrangements with the Zoological Garden authorities.*

The advocates of women's pennants wasted no time. At the initiative of Mrs Ethel Barker, a leading player and future state champion, a meeting was held on 9 July at the WANDA Club courts. It was decided to play on the association courts on Wednesday afternoons. The secretary for the matches was to be Miss Mabel Steere, with Carter, the Association Secretary arranging the fixtures. Within four days a schedule appeared in the *West Australian* (13/7/1903, 6):

Following is the draw for the ladies pennant matches, to take place on the Zoological Gardens grounds, commencing on Wednesday next. Players are requested to be on the ground ready to play at half past 2 pm at the latest, in view of the shortness of the afternoons. The first named club is in each instance, considered the "home" team, and has to provide the balls, the obtaining of which is in the hands of Miss M. Messer, to whom clubs are requested to forward the necessary subscriptions forthwith:

July 15 – Wanda v Cottesloe, Mount v Fremantle, Claremont a bye.
July 22 – Wanda v Mount, Cottesloe v Claremont, Fremantle bye.
July 29 – Wanda v Fremantle, Mount v Claremont, Cottesloe bye.
August 5 – Wanda v Claremont, Cottesloe v Fremantle, Mount bye.
August 12 – Cottesloe v Mount, Fremantle v Claremont, Wanda bye.
August 19 – Cottesloe v Wanda, Fremantle v Mount, Claremont bye.
August 26 – Mount v Wanda, Claremont v Cottesloe, Fremantle bye.
September 2 – Fremantle v Wanda, Claremont v Mount, Cottesloe bye.
September 9 – Claremont v Wanda, Fremantle v Cottesloe, Mount bye
September 16 – Mount v Cottesloe, Claremont v Fremantle, Wanda bye.

'Racket' in the rival *Morning Herald* (11/7/1903, 7) commented:

... it is a very good thing that arrangements have been made for these matches, as the standard of play of the ladies in this state is very much below what it is in the other states. Constant play in matches, however, will tend to improve the standard in a very short time. The ladies are very keen on the matter, and there is no doubt that the matches will prove very attractive and interesting.

It was not to be the last time that women's pennants were described as 'attractive and interesting' nor was it the last occasion on which the standard of women's tennis in Western Australia was criticised. Unfortunately, the first round of fixtures on 15 July was washed out, so the historic first ladies pennant match under the auspices of the Association took place on Saturday, 18 July, when a fixture between WANDA and Cottesloe was played at the Association ground. Contrary to expectations the WANDA women won, mainly because of convincing performances in the singles:

Doubles

Misses Messer and Lee Steere (W) lost to Mrs Barker and Mrs Rockliffe (C), 5/6, 1/6 and beat Miss Woods and Mrs Mann (C) 6/1, 6/2.

Mrs Kelsall and Miss D Moore (W) drew with Mrs Barker and Mrs Rockliffe (C), 3/6, 6/5, and beat Miss Woods and Mrs Mann (C) 6/5, 6/1.

Sub total: Wanda 5 sets 39 games, Cottesloe 3 sets 32 games.

Singles

Miss Messer (W) beat Mrs Barker (C) 6/3

Miss Moore (W) beat Mrs Mann (C) 6/2

Miss Lee-Steere (W) beat Mrs Rockliffe (C) 6/5

Miss Kelsall (W) beat Miss Woods (C) 6/3

Sub total: Wanda 4 sets 24 games, Cottesloe 13 games.

Grant Total: Wanda 9 sets 63 games Cottesloe 3 sets 45 games

WANDA, at the bottom of the men's table, went on to win the women's inaugural series. Although results were periodically published (see *West Australian*, 19/9/1903, 15), there was no listing of premiership tables nor any of the analysis that characterised the men's season. Nevertheless, despite the Association's lukewarm attitude, the women had ensured that they would be part of the pennant scene from the beginning of the third Association's history. Also women indicated they wanted to be full partners in the tournament scene.

The 1903 State Open Tournament

While the winter pennant matches were being conducted, the delegates to the Association were engaged in a potentially damaging row over the venue for the 1903 State championship. Given, success of tournaments at the WACA, some delegates considered this should again be the location. Others contended that the arrangements which had been made with the Zoological Board should be cultivated and continued. At the 1 July meeting, after a long debate, it was resolved to hold the tournament on the Zoo courts (*Morning Herald* 2/7/1903, 2). The Zoo authorities had undertaken to top-dress and prepare suitable courts, with the Association to receive half of the gate receipts from the championship. In mid-August a special meeting considered criticism about the location of the tournament. Strong objection was taken to the previous motion which decided that the tournament should be held at the Zoo, on the basis that the courts would not be in satisfactory condition and that the location was inconvenient. A motion was submitted to rescind the previous decision, but lost on the casting vote of the Chairman (*WALTA Minutes*, 14/8/1903 and *Morning Herald* 22/8/1903, 6).

Another related matter was the commencement date for the tournament. At first, 22 October was suggested, but this was only week before the planned opening of the grade cricket season. Unfortunately, these matters were being discussed with little more than a month left in which to make the necessary arrangements. This provoked an angry response in some quarters. As one writer to the sporting editor of the *West Australian* (26/9/1903) commented:

> *In the first place, it would be impossible to arrange and bring to a successful issue a tournament of the dimensions of the annual Perth tournament in so short a time. Secondly, why should the Tennis Association consider the few cricketers who interested themselves in tennis during the winter months? I am sure Bolton, Parker and Coyne (the only three) are all such true sportsmen that they would willingly give up one Saturday or two if necessary to further the interests of tennis. Again, was not one of the great arguments brought forward by Mr Kelsey, in reference to holding the tournament at the zoo that we were not bound in time, and could wait until we would be assured of settled weather, and, by waiting, give the courts a chance to be as near perfection as Mr Le Souef could make them. Anybody who has viewed the courts at the zoo since they were lately top–dressed would see that they cannot be ready in a month's time to stand three days' hard wear and tear. At the meeting on Wednesday, I hear that only seven delegates attended out of fourteen – Fremantle and Mount being unrepresented ...*

Finally it was decided to start the three day State Championship on Thursday 19 November, 1903. But the strain was beginning to show on the association officials. Roland Kelsey resigned as chairman but helped to forestall further dislocation by agreeing to remain a delegate and tournament committee member. Carter, the secretary of the Association, intimated that his official duties prevented him from taking over the secretaryship of the tournament. So it was decided to ask Mr H. Willis, from Cottesloe and formerly secretary of the prestigious South Yarra Club in Melbourne, to take over. After Mr Willis declined the offer the task eventually fell to Mr H.E. Hill who soon became secretary for both the tournament and the Association. As a player of note from the 'East' and having offices in central St George's Terrace, Hill was considered an appropriate choice. It was claimed that it would have been 'impossible to have found a better man to take up the position of secretary' (*Morning Herald*, 10/10/1903, 4). The President, Dr Saw, indicated that as he was leaving for England on 19 November he would miss the championship, but promised to give first prize for the women's singles handicap (*Morning Herald*, 2/11/1903, 2).

In view of all the difficulties, the field of 111 entrants received for the State Open was considered an 'excellent' outcome (*Morning Herald*, 14/11/1903, 5; see also *Morning Herald*, 12/11/1903, 2, for entries list). Parker and Bolton, of cricketing fame, were in the draw but a major concern was the lack of entries (except for four woman handicap players) from the Fremantle Club. Indeed, Fremantle, the club with the largest metropolitan membership, arranged a club tournament while the Association conducted its championship. This demonstrated that the Association had still not fully consolidated its position in the tennis world. However, the Open championship confirmed predictions that Ernie Parker was a player with a great future. At nineteen Parker, who had learnt much of his tennis at High (later Hale) School and then St Peter's College in Adelaide, won the final over J.G. Greayer in four sets, 3/6, 6/1, 6/3, 6/2. For Greayer it was the fourth occasion he had been runner-up for the 'W.A. Open'. However, he did enjoy success in the men's doubles in partnership with K. Bolton, turning the tables on Parker and his partner J. Carter with a marathon 6/4, 1/6, 6/4, 4/6, 6/3 victory (*Morning Herald*, 23/11/1903, 2).

In the women's singles Mrs Matilda Walsh, the champion in 1901 (and runner-up in 1900), easily defeated Miss Black (the 1902 title holder) 6/2, 6/3. There had been no suggestion that the women's singles be the best of five sets as had been the case for the first 'State' championship in 1901. Organisers would have been keen to avoid a repetition of what had taken place in the 1902 Wimbledon Championship. The women's challenge round final between Charlotte Sherry and Muriel Robb had created a unique Wimbledon record. When, on finals day, rain halted the battle at one set all (6/4, 11/13) it was decided to restart the match on the next day from the beginning. Miss Robb won the second instalment 7/5, 6/1 so that altogether they had completed 53 games. Ironically this had been the length of the 1901 inaugural 'State' doubles final which Matilda Walsh and Ethel Barker had won at the WACA ground courts. For the 1902 State Open Matilda Walsh had led a powerful goldfields contingent to the 'coast'. In fact given the Fremantle boycott much of the success of the tournament was attributed to the entries from country towns.

Many of the major country centres were thought to be anxious to field teams against Association teams. However, there did not appear to be any prospects of affiliation. This was a matter for the future but the original plan had only been to establish an association on 'the coast'. If the Association could secure its metropolitan status it would be able to play a major role in the development of tennis in Western Australia. Its short term objectives for 1903, a successful pennant season and the conduct of the State Open, had been achieved; but its long-term future was still not firmly assured.

Chapter Eight

THE 'NEW' LTAWA JOINS THE 'NEW' ALTA

ON New Year's Day 1901, Australia celebrated its foundation as an 'indissoluble Federal Commonwealth'. Some writers have argued that sport helped to bond the colonies together to provide a basis for federation (Mandle, 1973, 46). The 'surging devotion' (Cumes, 1979) for sport, traced back to the colonial era, has been linked to the absence of 'high culture' because of the immaturity of a young country, the Australian distrust of the intellectual, the instant gratification of sport, and the search for identity and recognition (Stoddart 1986, 4). When the founding fathers were formulating the Constitution, sport was presumed to be above politics. It was not considered that sport, leisure and recreation should be included in the list of Commonwealth powers. There was no need for a jurist to define sport 'as a human activity requiring physical exertion and/or physical skill which by nature and organisation is competitive (Bloomfield, 1978, xii). Sport, and recreation, being essentially non-utilitarian, elective and private, were not considered appropriate areas for government involvement. The organisation and financing of sport was regarded as the responsibility of the local community. It meant volunteer labour, club fundraising, and possibly co-operation with local authorities for the use of facilities (Stewart, 1985, 49).

Inadvertently, though, governments did assist in the promotion of sport. Legislation for shorter working hours gave workers freedom for Saturday afternoons, releasing them for half a day from a life divided between the obligations for employment and the rules of the Sabbath. For the majority, Saturday afternoon provided an opportunity to watch or play sport. Later, when sport was recognised as the major secular religion, Sundays was also freed for sport. As a result, it has been suggested that a broad spectrum of Australian society could catch the 'Saturday afternoon fever'. Supposedly this provided an advantage over nations where only a privileged elite had sufficient leisure to indulge in competitive sport (Jenkinson, 1985, 21).

These hypotheses concerning sport in Australia have been applied more often to cricket than to tennis or other leading sports. Tennis, too, drew much of its support from the 'privileged' in society (Kinross-Smith 1985, 25) or these labelled as 'well to do' (Yallop, 1992) who had sufficient leisure to often play the game in business hours on working days. At Federation, tennis was trying to confirm its status as a sport. There was neither a firmly established Western Australian tennis association nor a national tennis body. Significantly, though, once the political federation was constituted, a tennis federation (which included New Zealand, an early participant in the political federation discussions), was readily established. Moreover, immediately the Australian public began to seriously follow international Davis Cup competition, the national 'devotion for sport' was harnessed to stimulate the growth of tennis throughout the country.

The Australasian Lawn Tennis Association (ALTA)

At one of the first meetings of the third tennis association of Western Australia, Roland Kelsey indicated that the editor of the *Australasian Tennis Magazine* had written to him about the desirability of creating a tennis federation in Australia (*WALTA Minutes*, 1/7/1903). So before the Lawn Tennis Association of Western Australia ('LTAWA' later the Western Australian Lawn Tennis Association, or 'WALTA') had consolidated its own position, its delegates were likely to decide whether to join the mooted federation. The Australasian Lawn Tennis Association ('ALTA') was formed in Sydney in September 1904, the outcome of a resolution passed by the New South Wales Lawn Tennis Association. It was decided to invite representatives from each of the states and New Zealand to discuss the formation of a national association, so that these two countries could become one nation under the laws governing the competition for international team contests, such as the Davis Cup. This body was to control interstate matches and to establish and conduct Australasian tennis championships.

The driving force behind the formation of the ALTA was undoubtedly Tom Hicks, then honorary secretary of the New South Wales Association. The first President was Mr W.H. Forrest who was succeeded in 1908 by Mr P.B. Colquhoun. In addition to Hicks and Forrest, delegates at the first meeting were from New Zealand and all States except Western Australia (Inglis, 1912, 167). The absence of a delegate from Western Australia was a problem which would concern officials in the West for decades. Facing even more formidable distance problems, New Zealand later decided that it preferred to be regarded as a separate tennis nation and withdrew its affiliation in 1922. The ALTA continued to function as the Australasian body until 1926, when the title was changed to the Lawn Tennis Association of Australia ('LTAA'). In the same year, the national headquarters, with the approval of Western Australia, moved from Sydney to Melbourne. Even in the early years the national lawn tennis association was widely known as the LTAA and this acronym was used until the new marketing name 'Tennis Australia' was adopted in 1986.

The absence of a Western Australian representative at the first meeting did not appear to reflect a reluctance to join the federation. The new LTAWA (WALTA) confirmed its decision to join the ALTA (LTAA) at a meeting at the Palace Hotel on 14 October, 1904 (*WALTA Minutes*, 14/10/1904). At the same meeting it was resolved that Messrs Hill, Parker, Deravin and Kelsey constitute a sub-committee to prepare a report upon the proposed constitution and rules of the council of the new LTAA (*Morning Herald*, 17/10/1904, 2). These men were all influential figures in the State tennis scene suggesting that the national body should be given careful consideration. Although the decision to join the LTAA was reported in the *West Australian*, it was perhaps surprising the editor, Winthrop Hackett, did not publish a leading article on the subject. Hackett's interest in federation and his administrative role in tennis have already been mentioned. One explanation may have been the prevalence of the view that the LTAA would not have much of an immediate impact on tennis in Western Australia. There is no record in the Association minutes of the sub-committee reporting back to the Association. The next reference in the minutes to LTAA affairs was the appointment of H.P. Willis of Sydney, as a delegate for Western Australia on the Council of the ALTA. As a former Cottesloe club player, Willis could be expected to have a 'feel' for the interests of the West (*WALTA Minutes*, 5/9/1905).

Later, the Western Australian Association requested various leading players, who visited the West for the Open Championship, to act as WALTA delegates to LTAA. At the time there were no Western Australians who travelled the 'circuit' to the various capital city venues which rotated the Men's Australasian Open Championship after the inaugural event held in Melbourne in 1905. This was also the first year that Australasia had entered the newly established Davis Cup competition.

Norman Brookes, 'The Wizard'

The Davis Cup and the International Scene

As mentioned, following the formation of the LTAA Australasia entered a team for the Davis Cup competition. The large silver punch bowl was presented by Dwight F. Davis, an American diplomat and tennis player, for international competition. The Davis Cup concept had an impact upon tennis throughout Australia that was probably not envisaged when the LTAA was first formed. In 1905 Norman Brookes, the gritty left hander, and Anthony Wilding, the classic stylist from New Zealand, played in the singles. Brookes and Alf Dunlop, both Victorians, took the court in the doubles. Australia defeated Austria five rubbers to love, but was then beaten by the United States of America with equal ease. The famous Doherty brothers Reg (known as 'Big Do') and Laurie (known as 'Little Do'), together with Sydney Smith from England then beat the Americans William Larned, Beals Wright and Halcombe Ward. In 1906 the irresistible English trio were again victors over the United States of America. The latter had outplayed the Australasian team of Wilding and Les Poidevin from New South Wales. Poidevin, a doctor by profession, was described by tennis historian Metzler (1979, 25) as 'an amazing man' who had shared with Western Australia's Ernie Parker the distinction of playing first class cricket whilst still being in the top bracket of Australian tennis players.

It is the next year, 1907, that will always be remembered in the annals of Australasian Lawn Tennis. Norman Brookes in his second trip to Wimbledon became the first overseas player to win the coveted gentlemen's crown with his trade mark, the flat-topped Renshaw racquet. In 1899 William Renshaw had won the men's singles for a record seventh time establishing in tennis lore the famous 'Renshaw smash'. This shot was not a feature of Brookes' game as he was artful with the use of spin and cut. In 1913 Brookes, widely known as 'The Wizard' was to win another Wimbledon men's singles championship but it was in 1907 in combination with the gifted Anthony Wilding that he gained the Australian public's admiration when he won a hard earned Davis Cup qualifying round victory over the United States of America. Thereafter, the Dohertys and Smith being unavailable, the representatives from the antipodes took advantage of the situation to narrowly win the Cup 3-2 from England's Arthur W. Gore and H. Roper Barrett. Interestingly members of the Western Australian tennis fraternity had an early chance to view the Cup. When the *Moldavin* berthed at Fremantle in the first week of November, 1907 local officials and players had the opportunity to converse with Brookes who had the Cup at hand (*Morning Herald*, 9/11/1907, 2).

Australasia's capture of the Davis Cup meant that the focus of the tennis world was upon Melbourne in November 1908 for the defence of the trophy. Newspapers throughout the nation, gave the contest wide coverage. As the event took place a week after the Melbourne Cup, devoted sports fans from all over Australia stayed on for the big tennis. The daily attendance averaged 5,000 - a very high admission price of seven shillings and sixpence being cheerfully paid (Inglis, 1912, 161). It was a classic – perhaps the most exciting Davis Cup battle ever staged. One racegoer said of the doubles contest on the Saturday, 'It was as if the Melbourne Cup was run neck and neck for half an hour' (cited in Dunstan, 1973, 147). The issue was in doubt until the very last stroke of the last rubber when Wilding defeated the American Fred Alexander in four sets. The outcome was that Brookes and Wilding became the toast of the nation (*Morning Herald*, 30/11/1908, 6 and 1/12/1908, 6).

The challenge round in Melbourne led Gordon Inglis, in his authoritative *Sport and Pastime in Australia* (1992, 159), to make the following observations about lawn tennis in Australia:

> *We always had plenty of genuine [tennis] enthusiasts but public recognition of the game's merits came as a result of the cup .... It was the introduction of the international element that draw the outsider. Previously lawn tennis had been hopelessly misunderstood. The scoffer always associated it with afternoon tea; he jibed at its scoring terms and was pleased to burlesque 15 love as a term of endearment when recorded in mixed doubles. The ignorant labelled it 'a ladies game' and beneath their notice. When they saw a quartette like Wright, Alexander, Brookes and Wilding fighting out five set matches for two hours under a blazing sun, it was apparent that not only science, but also physique was essential to the making of a champion. The Davis Cup of 1908 removed all misconceptions, and an understanding is all that is necessary to secure appreciation the pastime has taken its proper place.*

The Western Australian public was now treated to regular tennis columns in the newspapers and they were kept fully informed of the international scene. Davis Cup performances, major tournaments, interstate matches, comments about great players and reviews of the rules were regularly covered. The reference to rules may surprise some readers. However, as tennis, was still a very young pastime/game/sport, the rules required refinement. For instance, one rule which was regularly debated was the let cord during a rally. Western Australians read about the findings of an American committee that included William Larned and Beals Wright. The Committee reasoned that it would be unwise to make any changes to the existing provision which permitted let chords, because (*Morning Herald*, 11/7/1903, 7):

(i) There will be no change in the law in England during the coming season, and it would be a mistake, at a time when the two countries are trying to make the laws the same, to make a radical change.

(ii) It would add largely to the amount of umpiring required in a match, and the question of getting competent umpires is already a very serious one.

(iii) In many cases where a player at the net has been clearly passed it would be unfair to require the stroke to be played again because it touched the net. It would also take away much interest from the play to require a stroke that had been fairly won to be played again.

(iv) Many chance noises would be mistaken for the noise which the ball makes when it touches the net.

(v) It would tend to discourage players from getting as close to the net as possible, which seems at least unwise.

(vi) It would also add to the advantage that a player has when at the net by forcing the player in the back of the court to play higher for fear of touching the net.

The Davis Cup Competition gave public recognition to the merits of tennis

Although the Association was able to keep abreast of the rapid developments in tennis, a major difficulty arose when it came to enticing players who had made their name on the international scene to come to Perth. At the Annual General Meeting in April 1904, a sub-committee of Kelsey, Ernie Parker and H. Willis was instructed to attempt to arrange a visit to Western Australia by the famed Doherty brothers. It was understood the brothers had given preliminary indication to the Melbourne Cricket Club that they would visit Australia (*WALTA Minutes*, 14/4/1904). Since 1897 they had so dominated the Wimbledon scene that the period has been labelled the 'Doherty Era' (Clerici, 1975, 82). Reg, the older and taller brother, won the title in 1897, 1898, 1899 and 1900, and his brother in 1902 and 1903, 1904, 1905 and 1906). Poor health is reputed to have cost Reg the title in 1901, when he lost his crown to Arthur Wentworth Gore (Medlycott, 1977, 17).

The Association's overtures for a visit by the Dohertys failed because the brothers declined to make the long sea voyage to Australia. It was one of the many proposed visits by leading British players and teams that came to nothing. Wimbledon's prominence, in terms of its championships, players and laws was recognised in Australia, so the failure to attract English champions was a source of frustration. However, even attempts by the Association to entice to Perth for the Western Australian Open heroes such as Brookes and

Wilding were not successful. The best the West could realise was the publication of interviews in the press when these household names stopped over at Fremantle on their way to the United Kingdom. On one such occasion, Brookes was quoted as saying (*Morning Herald*, 12/5/1905, 2):

> *There is no doubt that the game of lawn tennis is going ahead rapidly in Australia on a whole not only as far as the popularity is concerned but also as regards the standard of play. There are more tournaments available for players who can get away to take part in them, and the annual interstate matches do a great deal of good. It is a very good thing that arrangements have been made whereby Australia can take part in the great international matches ...*

Given an inability to lure international players to the West, the Association carried on negotiations to bring an interstate team in Perth. However, in 1906 when the interstate matches (which occasionally included New Zealand) were formalised into a competition known as the Mars Buckley Cup, the Western Australian Association had reluctantly to remain outside the series (*WALTA Minutes*, 23/7/1906). Travel to and from Perth by steamer meant a round trip of several weeks. The time factor constituted as great a problem as the cost. Nevertheless, in the first decade of the century, some Australians apart from Brookes, took part in the interstate and international 'circuit'. This small group of players 'with means' included H.A. (Harry) Parker, Alf Dunlop, Stanley Doust, Rodney Heath, Horace (Horrie) Rice and Leslie Gaden. A number of women also played in the various eastern states tournaments, including Miss Shaw (later Mrs P.B. Colquhoun), Miss P. Howitt, Miss Gyton, Miss Addison, Miss Stewart, Miss Dransfield and Miss Payten (Inglis, 1912, 172-173). In 1906, a team of top New South Wales players (S.N. Doust, S, Jones, R.M. Kidson and Dr Bowker) came to Western Australia for the Open. Doust and Harry Parker, also from New South Wales, later competed in several Western Australian Opens.

Perhaps the best indication that Western Australia was beginning to appear on the national, if not the international, map was the decision by the LTAA to grant the WALTA the 1909 Australasian Open Championship. Officials of the Association interpreted this action by the LTAA as a vote of confidence in their management of the new 'sport'. After the difficulties that had preceded the formation of the 1903 Association, there was a need to consolidate and move towards the conduct of hallmark events.

Chapter Nine

GROWING MATURITY

THE addition of the international element, particularly in the form of the Davis Cup and to a lesser extent, Wimbledon, helped produce a surge of interest in Australian lawn tennis. Many more clubs joined the Association, the tournament scene improved, the pennant competition expanded and some interstate tennis was played in Perth. Two Australasian Opens, in 1909 and 1913, were mounted, together with an international match between Western Australia and the British Isles just as the storm clouds of war loomed. Less successful were the attempts to firmly establish tennis as a summer game and the creation of a viable tennis centre.

One symbolic act that marked the period of consolidation was the appointment of the Governor, Sir Frederick Bedford, as Patron (*WALTA Minutes*, 28/4/1904). It was the beginning of a tradition which has been retained by the Association. Sir Frederick and Lady Bedford showed a keen interest in its affairs and, like many of their successors, they patronised the game to the widespread satisfaction of the tennis community. The courts at Government House, to which the beginnings of competitive tennis in metropolitan Perth have been traced, continued to be used for social tennis and some charity events.

Governor Sir Frederick Bedford, patron of the Tennis Association in 1904. This link began a tradition. (Courtesy Battye Library 613P)

Open Championships (1904-1908)

Between 1904 and 1908, the most successful competitors in the State Open Championships were Ernie Parker and Matilda Walsh. In 1904 the Governor presented Parker with the Alcock Cup, one of many cups donated by the sporting goods firm Alcock and Co. ('The Alcock Trophies', *Western Mail*, 6/10/1906, 37). 'Racket' of the *Morning Herald*, (31/10/04, 5) observed:

> *As far as play during the tournament was concerned E F Parker, the champion, considerably outshone everyone. He never played better tennis than he did on Saturday, and the form he showed then would bear most favourable comparison with that seen at tournaments in the eastern States.*

There had been considerable discussion at Association meetings (almost rivalling the debate about the relative merits of Ayres and Slazenger balls) as to whether the championship should be the best of three advantage or five advantage sets. Eventually it was decided in favour of the latter for men and the former for women (*WALTA Minutes*, 6/8/1904). In 1904, Parker took some heat out of the question by defeating Keane Bolton in straight sets 6/4, 7/5, 6/4 with Ayres balls (*WALTA Minutes*, 28/5/1904).

There is no evidence of any dispute about the 1904 championship being played on the grass at the Zoo ground. A new pavilion had been erected and additional change rooms were made available by courtesy of the South Perth Tennis Club. Special ferry arrangements were made for the players and spectators (*Morning Herald*, 26/10/1904, 11). One innovation was the introduction of a Plate event for the losers of the first two rounds of the Open

(*WALTA Minutes*, 1/8/1904). The winners of the men's and women's championships were each to receive £3/3/-. The suffragette literature aimed at raising the awareness of opportunities for women was apparently having some indirect impact on tennis in the form of equal prize money allocation. The most thrilling match for the 500 spectators, who made good use of the new pavilion, was the women's final between Matilda Walsh and Miss Hone. After winning a set each, Hone, a prominent South Australian player, finally triumphed 7/5 in the third. So Walsh was denied a hat-trick of State Opens, although she had confirmed her standing as the leading woman player in the state. Undoubtedly the members of the Goldfields team would have preferred her to represent them in a match against the Association just before the tournament. The latter had won easily, 15 rubbers 31 sets, 199 games to 3 sets, 96 games (*Morning Herald*, 26/10/1904, 2).

Just as Walsh's hold on the Western Australian championship was temporarily broken by a 'tothersider', the same fate was to befall Parker in 1905. In a gripping final, he lost to the New South Wales 'circuit' player Stanley Doust 7/5 in the fifth. Played in front of an audience which included the Chief Justice of the High Court, Sir Samuel Griffith, Sir Edmund Barton, the first Prime Minister of Australia, and several members of the State Parliament (*Western Mail*, 28/10/1905, 38), the match was said to furnish the best display of lawn tennis yet seen on a Perth ground.

It was also considered that Doust had made 'himself a favourite with his sportsmanlike conduct'. So the Tennis Association was well pleased that it had encouraged him to play by waiving his entry fee (*WALTA Minutes*, 12/10/1905). It was still able to make a profit of £15 for the tournament. Importantly, though, the results at the Open did demonstrate that Parker could be classed as a leading player in the Commonwealth. Doust had twice won the Queensland Championship and was later to represent Australia in the Davis Cup. Some months earlier Parker had also played well against Horrie Rice in an exhibition match at the Zoo. This encounter had been hastily arranged by Roland Kelsey when Rice's passenger ship called at Fremantle. Rice, a short, nuggety, left-hander, was known for his competitive spirit and stamina. He had won many State titles and was later selected in the Davis Cup team. In 1907, Rice won the Australasian Open in Brisbane. This victory gave him the distinction of being the first left-hander to win the title. He is also thought to be the only Open champion to have played in knickerbockers (Johnson 1985, 33). In Western Australia, both Rice and Doust impressed association officials sufficiently for the two men to be asked to act for a term as delegates for Western Australia at LTAA meetings (*WALTA Minutes*, 9/11/1906).

The Ladies 1905 Championship was dominated by Matilda Walsh. In the singles final she easily defeated Mrs Kitchen (whose husband was a leading player and official), 6/3, 6/0. In the doubles, Mrs Walsh teamed with her regular partner Mrs Ethel Barker to win their third Open doubles crown. They were a formidable combination at major championships. However, mindful of the future of women's tennis, the Association decided to introduce a girls 17 and under singles event for the 1905 championship. Unfortunately, the entry fee of three shillings and six pence helped keep the draw small (*WALTA Minutes*, 29/9/1905).

In 1906, both Walsh and Parker were eclipsed by players from New South Wales in circumstances that created a furore. The Tennis Association, mainly through the efforts of Kelsey, had finally succeeded in arranging an interstate match between New South Wales and Western Australia, to take place a few days before the W.A. Open. The latter had been scheduled for October 24, 25, 26 and 27, 1906. However, as the New South Wales team of S.N. Doust, R.M. Kidson, S. Jones and Dr Bowker, was only going to provide competition for leading men, steps were taken to invite two top women players to Perth for the championship. Association clubs donated 'half a crown' each towards the expenses of Miss Payten and Miss Jones to sail to Fremantle with the New South Wales contingent.

Payten was regarded as the best woman player in Australia and some argued that she looked a better player than the current Wimbledon and United States Open winner of her day (Morning Herald, 17/10/1906, 10). 'Forty All' the *Western Mail* tennis correspondent commented (3/11/1906, 38):

> *Broadly speaking, Miss Payten is all that has been said of her, and in some respects she is more. For instance we were not told of her accuracy or, it was not insisted upon ... On the other hand from accounts that came to us it seemed that Miss Payten never served a ball that she did not follow to the net. As a matter of fact, Miss Payten occasionally follows in; more often she prudently waits on the baseline for the return.*

Jones was said to be not so capable a player as her friend [Payten] but nevertheless 'gets weight into her strokes' (*Western Mail*, 31/11/1906, 38). Her skill was sufficient to allow her to win easily against Walsh 6/4, 6/0, while Payten won the other semi-final, losing only one game. In a sensational development Payten informed the Association officials that she was unwell and could not play in the final. Jones then decided owing to her personal friendship for the admittedly superior player she would counter default, to enable Payten to win the Championship. Given the efforts of the Association to bring Payten and Jones to Perth, the defaults prompted an angry reaction, particularly when the duo went ahead and won the Ladies Doubles (*Morning Herald*, 30/10/1906, 3). The sick Payten also teamed with Doust to defeat Western Australia's favourite son and daughter Parker and Walsh, 6/0, 6/4 in the mixed doubles. It was not surprising that the state parliamentarians found it necessary to debate the merits of secession (*Morning Herald*, 'Editorial', 22/10/1906, 2).

The 1906 championship attracted a record entry. This had been greatly enhanced by the endeavours of Kelsey who was described as 'the moving spirit' of the carnival (*Western Mail*, 3/11/1906, 38) He had visited all the clubs by car between Claremont and South Perth. This increased the entries by some one hundred (*Morning Herald*, 15/10/1906, 4). Handicap events continued to attract many entrants and some players were even regarded as handicap specialists.

The conduct of the Association's first interstate match, followed by the participation of some of the nation's best players in the State Open was a sign of its growing status. Perhaps the resounding win by the New South Wales team was a portent of the future for Western Australia in interstate tennis. Those who had the honour of being the first selected to represent the State were E.F. Parker, J.C. Cramond, K. Bolton and T.H. Coyne. When Coyne was injured on the first day of competition, Kelsey was nominated as a substitute, duly taking his place in the team. The final score was New South Wales 11 rubbers, 27 sets, 194 games to Western Australia 1 rubber, 5 sets and 112 games. The distinction of being the first Western Australian to achieve a victory in a clash with an eastern state went to Cramond, who defeated the highly competent Jones in a marathon match 7/9, 8/6, 9/7 (*Morning Herald*, 22/10/1906, 2).

Mrs Constance Blackmore, Claremont doubles legend

Much to the disappointment of the Association's officials, it was not able one year later to entice any leading national players to the 1907 Open. As a newspaper commentator observed (*Western Mail*, 26/10/1907, 38):

> *This year we had confidently expected Brookes and Wilding and Parker and Doust; and we got ourselves ... We had last year tasted of a new sweet, and to go back to the old order of things and hold a tournament among ourselves was akin to a garden party without guests.*

Nevertheless, the 1907 Open did feature two great finals, with Parker and Walsh retaining their status as the respective men's and women's champions. Parker defeated Dr Griffiths in a five set marathon 6/1, 3/6, 7/5, 4/6, 6/2. Mrs Walsh won against Miss Ruse after losing the first set 4/6, 6/3, 6/3. Parker completed a clean sweep when he won the men's doubles with Cramond and the mixed doubles with Walsh. In the women's doubles there was a mild surprise when Blackmore and Ruse defeated the highly fancied Walsh and Barker (*Western Mail*, 23/10/1907, 38). The Blackmore and Ruse combination were to prove their prowess with five wins in the State Open doubles. The secret of their success was aggressive volleying at the net. Constance Blackmore, whose husband Alf was a great worker for tennis, remarkably appeared in nine consecutive Open doubles finals from 1905 until the outbreak of the First World War. As was to be expected Mrs Blackmore held a monopoly over the championship titles at her home club of Claremont.

In 1908 Parker and Walsh again received the Open singles trophies. However, the Open had some interstate flavour. The Barnard brothers from Victoria played Parker and Kelsey as a lead-up to the championship. The Victorians, with 4 rubbers 12 sets 94 games beat Western Australia 1 rubber, 7 sets and 81 games. In this contest E. T. Barnard defeated Parker 6/4, 3/6, 6/4, 6/3 (*Western Mail*, 24/10/1908, 37). But in the Open, Parker was able to turn the tables with a 3/6, 6/3, 6/3, 6/2 win (*Western Mail*, 31/10/1908, 45).

Parker was in England during 1908 and missed much of the winter pennant season (*Western Mail*, 28/3/1908, 3). While he was overseas, he performed well in both cricket and tennis. Although he had decided not to compete at Wimbledon, the Association was keen to gain national recognition for its favourite son (*Western Mail*, 28/3/1908, 37). However, the attempt to nominate him for the 1908 London Olympic Games did not bear fruit as no tennis player was included in the 1908 Australian Olympic team (*WALTA Minutes*, 23/3/1908).

Pennants

Another important aspect of the Association's consolidation period was the management of interclub pennants. Throughout these years the pennant scene was given wide publicity. Fixtures were listed, important matches described and premiership tables presented. End-of-season resumes of player and team performances were published, but many issues had to be addressed: the number of teams and divisional structure; the credentials of clubs to participate in the competition; the feasibility of summer pennants; the location of the association courts for the fixtures and even the brand of balls to be used.

In 1904, the Association had decided to set the number of men's pennant teams at 14. There were to be first and second divisions with one team having a bye each week. Fremantle, the Mount Club and South Perth had teams in each division. New clubs entering teams included Applecross, West Perth and the Weld Club. Missing from the 1903 league were Cottesloe and the Stock Exchange. Cottesloe had ceased to be an affiliated club in the men's division (*WALTA Minutes*, 28/4/1904) and remained one of only three sides in the women's division.

As the tables indicate (*Western Mail*, 17/9/1904, 38) East Perth were 1904 premiers in the first grade and Fremantle No.2 in the second grade. South Perth won the women's series.

FIRST GRADE 1904					
CLUB	P	W	L	D	Points
East Perth	12	12	0	0	24
Fremantle	12	9	3	0	18
South Perth	12	8	4	0	14
Perth	12	7	5	0	14
WANDA	12	4	8	0	8
Mount	12	2	10	0	4
Weld	12	0	12	0	0

SECOND GRADE 1904					
CLUB	P	W	L	D	Points
Fremantle	12	10	2	0	20
Claremont	12	7	3	2	16
Applecross	12	7	4	1	15
South Perth	12	6	6	0	12
WANDA	12	3	9	0	7
West Perth	12	1	11	0	2
Mount	12	1	11	0	2

LADIES					
CLUB	P	W	L	D	Points
South Perth	14	12	2	0	24
WANDA	14	10	4	0	20
Cottesloe	14	7	7	0	14

At the beginning of the 1905 pennant season there was debate on whether a group of leading players, calling themselves East Perth, should be able to participate as it was not a bona fide club. This continued to be a thorny issue for the Association. The matter was given greater importance because Subiaco, a newly affiliated club, had its application to field a pennant team denied. To 'add salt to the wound' East Perth did not drop a premiership point for the complete season. Perhaps the only surprise was the loss of three sets suffered by Ernie Parker in singles competition (*Morning Herald*, 30/9/1905, 3).

Over the next three seasons the number of teams and divisions expanded with the cost of nomination also increasing. For the 1906 winter season the scale of nomination charges for pennants were (*WALTA Minutes*, 16/3/1906):

First Grade: £6 Second Grade: £4 Third Grade: £3 Ladies Grade: £2

East Perth Team, 1904 Standing: T.H. Coyne and J.D. Crammond Sitting: J. Carter and E. F. Parker (Courtesy The West Australian)

Ladies Grade	P	W	L	Points
WANDA No.1	10	10	0	20
Claremont	10	7	3	14
South Perth No.1	10	7	3	14
WANDA No.2	10	4	6	8
South Perth No.2	10	1	9	2
Subiaco	10	1	9	2

WANDA NO.1	Won		Lost	
Doubles	Sets	Games	Sets	Games
Misses Steere & Low	32	208	4	107
Misses Messer & More	17	136	12	120
Singles				
Miss Elwyn	2	12	0	3
Miss Low	8	48	2	25
Miss Steere	8	48	2	25
Miss Moore	4	29	4	34
Miss Messer	3	27	4	32
Miss Low	8	48	19	25

East Perth again won the first grade men's pennants in 1906. The WANDA No.1 side easily gained the Ladies' Grade pennant. One win for women's tennis was the decision of the *Morning Herald* to add to their end of season resume of men's pennants a similar analysis of the Ladies Grade. So readers were provided with the following premiership details and statistics for the WANDA No.1 (and other) teams (*Morning Herald*, 22/9/1906, 5, and 15/9/1906, 5).

South Perth became a force in pennants and Subiaco grew in prominence. The powerful Fremantle team continued its uneasy relationship with the Association by failing to field a pennant team in 1906. However, in the same year East Fremantle joined the Association (*WALTA Minutes*, 3/9/1906). It nominated pennant teams for 1907 and soon found its members at the centre of a controversy. The East Fremantle secretary was obliged to write to the Association complaining that the Kings Park 'C' team refused to play their 'C' team in a scheduled fixture because of the alleged misbehaviour of the East Fremantle team on the previous occasion the teams had met (*WALTA Minutes*, 23/9/1907). Such disputes are usually difficult to resolve but the Association's response indicated that etiquette was regarded as important in lawn tennis (*WALTA Minutes*, 23/9/1907).

There was an attempt to introduce three-set contests in pennant matches but it was finally decided to add another singles set to the format. But the teams were required to simultaneously exchange team lists (*Western Mail*, 12/3/1906, 37). Nearly every season there was debate about whether the Association should endorse Slazenger balls or Ayres balls (*WALTA Minutes*, 6/5/1907 and 20/5/1907). After a bitter dispute the Ayres ball was adopted in 1907 but the following season a change to Slazenger balls was agreed upon (*WALTA Minutes*, 31/3/1908). The sporting goods companies clearly regarded 'endorsement' by the Association as beneficial to their market share.

At the end of the 1906 pennant season an Ayres Cup competition was inaugurated (*WALTA Minutes*, 24/4/1906). This was to be a knock-out tournament limited to resident Western Australian pennant players. In concept it was to be the forerunner of the Champion of Champions tournament introduced more than half a century later. However, the Ayres Cup was soon discarded when the Association dropped its endorsement of the Ayres ball. In the Ayres Cup competition Parker again proved himself as the outstanding player. For two consecutive seasons Parker's opponent in the final was Dr Griffiths, a prominent Kings Park player. Known for his authoritative lectures on tennis (*WALTA Minutes*, 6/7/1906 and 20/8/1906) he was capable of taking sets from Parker. In the Ayres Cup final of 1907 Griffiths won the first set from Parker but he could not maintain his form to defeat the champion (*Morning Herald*, 21/10/1907, 3). A few weeks earlier it had taken Parker five sets to defeat Griffiths in the 1907 State Open final. It also appears that Dr Griffiths was an extremely reasonable person as twice he was prepared to shift the Ayres Cup final to a mid-week date to enable Ernie Parker to meet cricket commitments.

The question of whether the pennant competition and tournament focus should be shifted to the summer continued to bedevil the Association. Mainly due to the efforts of Mr Alf Blackmore, a summer pennant competition was organised to commence in January 1907. There was an 'A' and 'B' grade for men and a Ladies' grade. It is clear some difficulties were encountered in the opening round as Kings Park is recorded as defeating St Albans by forfeit, while Subiaco scored points by the same method in the Ladies' Grade (*Western Mail*, 12/1/1907, 38). Later there were reports of some teams failing to pay fees (*WALTA Minutes*, 20/5/1907). The Association congratulated Alf Blackmore for his zeal but there is no record of summer pennants being reintroduced in 1908 (*WALTA Minutes*, 22/4/1907).

A Tennis Centre

The feasibility of summer pennants was also bound to another ongoing question for the Association, that of a tennis centre. Its agreement with the Zoological Board was frequently debated. The unavailability of the oval during the cricket season, the dubious quality of the playing surface, the South Perth location and the cost of hire were the main bones of contention. The arrangement was even criticised in Parliament. John Scaddan, a future Labor Premier, attacked the hidden labour and capital subsidy being afforded to tennis through the Zoological Gardens Board chaired by Winthrop Hackett. Scaddan contended that if the trustees of the WACA had sought such a grant for cricket they would not be heard (Hansard, Legislative Assembly, 7/11/1907, 6). Scaddan overlooked the fact that cricket had gained a central ground at a peppercorn rental. It was a deal that the Tennis Association had not been able to achieve. Scaddan, it seemed, believed that tennis was a game reserved for the 'well to do', who did not need even indirect public funding assistance. As a rising Labor politician he would have read newspaper articles describing how pennant matches at the Zoo were (*Western Mail*, 30/9/1905, 37):

> *watched by Lady Northcote and Lady Bedford, to say nothing of an unusually large number of persons who in any reputable society journal would be described by the one generic term of nice.*

Even before Scaddan became Premier in 1911, it was clear the Association could not expect direct or even indirect assistance from the government for a tennis centre. In September 1905, the Association had established a sub-committee to assess whether a centrally located ground could be obtained where pennants could be played throughout the summer (*WALTA Minutes*, 29/9/1905). Several delegates claimed to have spoken to the Agricultural Society about the use of the Claremont Showgrounds (*Morning Herald*, 30/9/1905, 3 and *Western Mail*, 30/9/1905, 37.) The summer pennant series of January 1907 was played at the Showgrounds, but the solution to the court problem remained elusive. Early in 1908, the Association received another sub-committee report on the Zoo, the showgrounds and the WACA Ground. Delegates were supplied with the following brief (*Western Mail*, 28/3/1908, 37):

> Grounds Considered: The "Zoo", Agricultural Show Grounds, and the W.A. Cricket Ground.
>
> The "Zoo" ground is available for a season between April and November 30 at a rental of £75 for 24 courts. Players and spectators to be charged 6d. admission on entering the "Zoo".
>
> Royal Agricultural Show Ground is available for a tennis season at practically any time of the year at a rental of £110 for 24 courts. No admission fee would be charged players or spectators.
>
> The W.A. Cricket Ground is not, in the opinion of the sub-committee, suitable, owing to its being used for other sports, and there being so many members' tickets in circulation.
>
> An effort was made to obtain from the "Zoo" and Show Ground authorities alternative quotations with and without admission money, but required to make up the difference in rental.
>
> Sufficient dressing-room accommodation will be provided by either ground.
>
> Members of your sub-committee inspected both grounds.

> The "Zoo" courts were found to be in excellent condition, and first-class matches could be played in very short time. The Show Grounds are not in as good condition at present, but your sub-committee are assured by the Society that first-class courts could be provided by, say, the end of July, and this assurance the members of your committee feel confident can be carried out.

The Association held a meeting for the purpose of giving players an opportunity to express their opinions on the report. East Fremantle, which was making its presence felt in the Association, was lukewarm toward any of the options. The club preferred the adoption of a home and away pennant system (*Western Mail*, 25/4/1908, 38). Again the decision narrowly favoured conducting Association pennants and major tournaments at the Zoo. It was obvious, though, that a consensus had not been achieved. New proposals, particularly consideration of a new location at Mueller Park in Subiaco, were on the agenda in 1909. And 1909 was to be an important year for the Association, as it was granted the right to conduct the Australasian Open in Perth.

The Association's annual general meeting in mid-1908 marked the end of a very important consolidation phase. Kelsey resigned as secretary. The post was assumed by S.V. Eaton, whose office in Gledden Building at the corner of Hay and William Street, Perth became the official office of the Association (*WALTA Minutes*, 29/6/1908). A few months earlier Roland Kelsey, described as 'the knight errant of lawn tennis' (*Western Mail*, 5/5/1906, 37), had his services recognised by the granting of life membership (*WALTA Minutes*, 24/4/1908). Fittingly, he was the first person to receive this award from the Association which had earlier examined the criteria for the honour (*WALTA Minutes*, 31/3/1908). Technically, the Association itself was formally the Lawn Tennis Association of Western Australia (LTAWA). Not until 1912 was the name Western Australian Lawn Tennis Association (WALTA) adopted (*WALTA Minutes*, 29/12/1912 and 10/1/1913). However, as the acronym

Roland Kelsey, The WALTA 'founding father' who in 1908 was the first person to be granted WALTA life membership. (Kelsey is pictured above standing on the left with E.G. Glyde (centre) and L.L Murray (right). Sitting: M. Lee Steere (left) and Mrs Fraser (right). Courtesy The West Australian)

WALTA had sometimes been used in the early days, it was obviously decided to clarify the situation.

Kelsey was credited for much of the remarkable development and the growing popularity of local tennis (*Western Mail*, 6/5/1905, 38). At the social function at the conclusion of the interstate match against New South Wales in October 1906, Dr Ernest Black, Vice President of the Association, presented Kelsey with a purse of sovereigns and had been reported as saying (*Western Mail*, 3/11/1906, 38):

> *Mr Kelsey's services to tennis in this State can never be overpaid. He created the game, and far above all he has nourished it to the present day.*

Kelsey was a fine player in his own right, sharing with A. Currie the first Western Australian Open doubles title in 1896 and invariably performing creditably in pennant fixtures. As mentioned previously, he represented Western Australia in its first interstate match, then played against Victoria in 1908 and was selected in 1913 to play for Western Australia against the British Isles. However, his role in the formation of the Association, his administrative activities in pennants, together with his work at annual tournaments and interstate tennis arrangements were his major achievements. As early as 1896 he had urged the establishment of an association to coordinate these tennis activities. This is not to suggest that Kelsey did not receive criticism in some quarters. He was an advocate of winter (rather than summer) pennants and was closely associated with the Association's controversial agreements with the Zoological Board. Even after stepping down from the Executive, he remained a key figure in the growth of tennis in the West, particularly when it came to assisting the Association in organising hallmark events, such as the Australasian Open and international visits.

Roland Kelsey's signature, Kelsey was a Hansard reporter at the Parliament of Western Australia.

The 1909 Australasian Open

Formal acceptance of the LTAA's offer to conduct the 1909 Australasian Open Championship was approved at the Association's annual general meeting held at the Palace Hotel on 9 June, 1909 (*WALTA Minutes*, 9/6/1909). The offer was further proof that the Association had consolidated its organisation. However, the short notice given for the arrangement of the Open, which was scheduled for late October, was an indication of how small-scale the event was in those years compared to the Grand Slam status of the modern Australian Open. In fact the first Open held in Western Australia was only afforded four lines in Bruce Matthews' (1985, 8) chronicle of Australian championships. Fortunately other research has helped to overcome this dearth of detail (Johnson 1985, 29-32 and Phillips, 1989).

The timing of the allocation of the Open to Western Australia was significant. The LTAA was experiencing difficulties with its structure. New Zealand was negotiating for different terms and for a few months even withdrew from the LTAA (Inglis, 1912, 168). The Western Australian Association approved additional representation for New Zealand to help ensure its membership of the federation, but it also sought the transfer of the head office from Sydney to Melbourne (*WALTA Minutes*, 6/6/1909 and 30/8/1909). The LTAA had permitted the 1906 Open to be held in Christchurch, New Zealand and the 1907 championship in Brisbane. The designation of Perth in 1909 was one method of ensuring that another distant member of the federation did not harbour secessionist tendencies.

One extremely difficult decision was where to play the championship. Negotiations with the Subiaco Council for the lease of courts at Mueller Park had reached an advanced stage. The rental would be comparatively low but there was concern about the quality of the grass surface. The other major venue was the Zoo (*WALTA Minutes*, 30/8/1909). Eventually the designated sub-committee opted for the prospect of a better surface (but higher rental) at the Zoo grounds in South Perth.

Although the Australasian Championship consisted of only two events, the best of five advantage sets for the men's singles and doubles championship, a 15-event tournament was planned (*WALTA Minutes*, 30/8/1909). The minor events, particularly the popular handicaps, were important for the financial success of the tournament, the entrance fee structure again confirming the game's reputation as an 'upper-class' pursuit.

The tournament committee (B.L Murray-Chairman, S.V. Eaton and J. Walter Marris) announced that most of the minor events, if scheduled on working days, would be played in late afternoons. Moreover, there would be no difficulty in scheduling times for the convenience of players. As the six-day tournament (commencing on 16 October and ending on 25 October) included two Saturdays and the final on a Monday public holiday, it was advertised that those engaged in business 'will have plenty of opportunity of seeing or playing in this meeting' (*West Australian*, 9/10/1909, 4).

Although the organisers were disappointed that they could not entice Norman Brookes to compete they were delighted to learn that Anthony Wilding would travel from New Zealand. This ensured the championship would have a major drawcard. Wilding was described at the time as probably in physique the best equipped player in the history of the 'lawn' (Innes, 1912, 161). He was a professional when tennis was supposed to be strictly an amateur code. An interview granted to the *West Australian* just one day after completing a long and arduous steamship voyage revealed the extent of Wilding's commitment. On his trip to Fremantle he had played against Brookes during a short stopover in Melbourne. While in Adelaide he had practised with leading South Australian players. On ship he had trained with a punching ball and by skipping. During the interview he explained (*West Australian*, 12/10/1909, 7):

Zoological Gardens Tennis Courts [illegible] Australasian Open Venue (Courtesy Battye Library 21125P)

> *I neither drink nor smoke, but I do not believe in too rigid a diet while training, for in tennis above all games one has to be careful not to overdo the work on the track as in a long and severe match a man needs some weight and stamina behind him to help him through.*

Modern experts in sports medicine may not accept all of Wilding's theories, but he left nothing to chance to be at the top of his form. Upon Wilding's arrival, when he was met by tournament officials he was initially booked into Perth's Palace Hotel (*West Australian* 12/10/1909,7), but he soon moved headquarters to the Windsor Hotel in South Perth, as this was more conveniently located for practice and training. Reports indicated that he practised hard and conscientiously (*Daily News*, 16/10/1909, 12 and *West Australian*, 12/10/1909, 7). He was very particular about court surfaces and facilities and the quality of racquets, balls and other equipment.

The substantial number of entries and record crowds confirmed the increasing popularity of tennis (*Daily News*, 21/10/1909, 8). The attendance of many dignitaries, such as the Governor and other leading politicians, helped give the event even more prestige. Nevertheless, the tournament committee had many other sports to compete with for publicity. On the first Saturday of the championship, wide newspaper coverage was given to what was thought to be the first marathon running contest in Western Australia (*Western Mail*, 16/10/1909, 26). The East Fremantle Football Club was undertaking a successful end of season tour of the eastern states. The grade cricket scores were presented in detail. College athletics, cycling and rowing were thoroughly reported. Even rifle shooting and billiards were given space. During the tennis championship, the Subiaco and North Perth Bowling Club opened their seasons. Of course, the allocation given to horse racing was considerable.

Tennis did make the sporting columns although most of the articles featured Anthony Wilding. Ironically, there was little to report about Wilding's on-court performance in the singles championship. The man destined to win four Wimbledons (from 1910) was too classy. His serve had too much twist and he hit his groundstrokes very hard (*Sunday Times*, 17/10/1909, 1). Wilding had resounding wins in the quarter and semi finals. Local champion Parker provided 'Sandgropers' with some hope when he reached the final. Amid reports that he was not well (*Western Mail*, 23/10/1909, 37) Parker played with determination but could not win a set and was beaten 6/1, 7/5, 6/2. There was some surprise when Parker and another leading local doubles specialist, J.V. Keane, defeated Wilding and his partner Tom Crookes, a local sports goods proprietor, in the doubles 1/6, 6/1, 6/1, 9/7. Wilding, though, was back in the winner's circle when he teamed with Miss D. Moore to defeat Parker and Miss Clement 6/1, 6/4 in the mixed doubles final (*West Australian*, 27/10/1909, 9).

The most gripping matches of the tournament took place in the women's championship which did not feature any entries from the other states. Fortunately, the weather was cool, as the women continued to be dressed in long frocks. Victory went to Mrs E. Barker over Miss Low 6/4, 4/6, 6/1. Mrs Barker, as Ethel Woods, had been one of the leading juniors in the colony, with a reputation for a splendid forehand drive (interview with K. Barker, 18/4/1986). She had married E.H. Barker, who owned 'Chanonry', the pioneer homestead tennis venue. After the birth of her two sons, Eric and Keith (who became leading players), Ethel Barker had been prominent in tournaments for more than a decade. Partnered by Matilda Walsh, she won three state doubles titles, but, until 1909 an open singles title had eluded her. As the newspaper report indicated (*West Australian*, 27/10/1909, 9).

Mrs Barker after playing in the ladies championship for many years won the event on Monday and she deserved to. She has never played better than during this tournament, the chief difference being the development of a really strong backhand shot. She hit very hard in the match with Miss Low and yet did not suffer as she had done so often in the past with inaccuracy.

Success in the Open singles was to come Miss Low's way in 1910 while Mrs Barker was to win her second Open in 1911 with a 6/2, 6/3 victory over Miss McDougall. The major 1909 tournament was a financial success although amateurism placed limits on the prize money and value of trophies. For his victory, Wilding received £6/6/- and the runner-up, Parker, £2/2/- In the women's singles, the respective value of the prizes for the finalists was £2/2/- and £1/1/- If tennis was regarded in some circles as a women's game, it was rarely suggested in this era that prize money and trophies for men and women should be equal. In fact, trophies, which became an early means for sponsorship in amateur sport, were limited to the men's events for this tournament. Anthony Wilding was presented with the Challenge Cup (held at the time by Fred Alexander from the United States of America). This cup was donated by the sporting goods firm Slazenger and Sons. Another sporting goods firm, Alcock and Company donated a trophy (valued at £15/15/-) for the title Champion of Western Australia. A rival company, Messrs F.H. Ayres, donated the trophy for the men's doubles championship.

Quests for Hallmark Events

The resounding success of the tournament gave association officials confidence about their capacity to conduct hallmark events. There was even a suggestion that the Association support a bid to conduct the 1912 Olympic Games in Perth (*WALTA Minutes*, 22/5/1912). News in 1912 that the LTAA was also considering alternative venues for the Davis Cup Challenge Round prompted Association delegates to forward the following unanimously endorsed resolution to the LTAA headquarters (*WALTA Minutes*, 22/5/1912):

Whereas (1) The Challenge round of the Davis Cup Competition was played in Melbourne in 1908, (2) No such challenge round has yet been played in WA, (3) We have in Perth more grass courts of better condition than are to be found in Melbourne, (4) The climate of Perth would permit the Challenge round being played in perfect comfort on dry courts at any date in October, November or December, (5) Being some 1500 miles nearer to their base Perth is much more convenient to the promised English and French team than is Melbourne, (6) The condition of the Davis Cup Fund in Australia is or should be such that the difference if any in the anticipated gate-money as between Melbourne and Perth is unworthy of consideration as against the manifest desirability of an even distribution among the State Associations of the successive Challenge Rounds.

The bid was not successful, but arrangements were made for the British Isles team, en route to England, to play a Western Australian team. Officials spared no effort to make the occasion memorable. A training squad of Parker, Gibbs, Kelsey, Hedeman, Leschen and Parsons was nominated. Yet just as the team disembarked some British press reports were published in the local newspapers indicating that one unnamed British player had been amazed at the rough and haphazard manner of doing things in Australia. The same player then had the temerity to state: 'I am bound to say the Americans impressed me more with their businesslike and practical arrangements' (*Western Mail*, 7/2/1913, 26).

Whether the same player had the same thoughts about the organisation of the international match at the Mueller Park Association Courts in early February 1913 is not known. The local press certainly praised the arrangements (*Western Mail*, 14/2/1913, 41). However, although the British Isles team had lost the Challenge Round and showed indifferent form in some encounters against other States, it resoundingly defeated Western Australia (*Western Mail*, 14/2/1913, 41).

Day 1
Dixon d Kelsey (WA) 6-2, 6-0
Lowe d Gibbs (WA) 6-0, 6-4
Dixon and Parke d Parker and Gibbs (WA) 3-6, 6-3, 4-6, 6-3, 6-1
Beamish and Lowe d Kelsey and Hedeman (WA) 6-1, 7-5, 6-2
Beamish d Parker (WA) 6-4, 6-2
Parke d Hedeman (WA) 6-4, 6-3

Day 2
Parke d Parker (WA) 8-6, 6-3
Beamish d Hedeman (WA) 6-1, 6-2
Beamish and Lowe d Parker and Gibbs (WA) 3-6, 6-3, 4-6, 8-6, 13-11
Dixon and Parke d Kelsey and Hedeman (WA) 3-6, 7-5, 6-1, 6-4
British Isles 10 rubbers 24 sets 173 games defeated
Western Australia 5 sets 106 games

The Western Australian representatives
E. F. Parker, I.R. Gibbs, R.H. Kelsey (Captain), A.H. Hedeman
(Courtesy The West Australian)

The 1913 Australasian Open

It was widely agreed that the visit by the British team had helped to promote Western Australian tennis (*Western Mail*, 21/2/1913, 41). In 1913 the LTAA again designated Perth as the venue for the Australasian Tennis championship. This tournament was to be preceded by an interstate match against South Australia. Again, the Association spared no effort to ensure that the championship ran smoothly. In contrast to 1909, there was no dispute about the venue. 'Short Lob' of the *Western Mail* (7/11/1913, 41) reported:

> *The Mueller Park courts should present a scene of activity that should totally eclipse the best of the old days, at the Zoological Gardens. It is understood that extra accommodation is to be provided for spectators. The courts are in good order.*

A special committee, with T. Hantke, as the tournament secretary, was appointed to support the hardworking Mr Jefferson, the honorary secretary. The referee was S.J. McGibbon from the Kings Park Club who was becoming an activist in Association affairs. McGibbon, with Kelsey, Kingsmill, Armstrong, Murray and Gwynne volunteered to make the necessary entertainment arrangements. In addition a number of women had made arrangements for afternoon teas, which were to be served in marquees. A season ticket covering admission to the ground (and a reserved seat in the stand) could be purchased at Nicholsons, the box office agents for five shillings (*Western Mail*, 7/11/1913, 1).

Were the spectators to enjoy a victory for the hometown hero Ernie Parker? Although Stanley Doust had overcome his irritation with the policy of not providing ball boys and won the State Open in 1910, Parker had won again in 1911 and 1912. The victory in 1912 was particularly meritorious as the draw included Horrie Rice and the 'prince of volleyers' A.B. Jones, who were members of the New South Wales team which resoundingly defeated Western Australia in a lead-up to the championship (Metzler, 1979, 12 and *Western Mail*, 8/11/1912, 41)). In 1909 the prestigious Australasian Open had eluded Parker when he was defeated by Wilding. So 1913 (as he was soon to turn 30), was Parker's best chance for the crown. But he would have to overcome a major challenge from the persistent Harry Parker from New South Wales who had won several State titles (including W.A. in 1906) and he was runner-up in the 1907 Australasian Open. Stout opposition could also be expected from the members of the South Australian team who had visited Perth for the national titles.

Western Australia won the interstate clash by seven rubbers to five (*Western Mail*, 14/11/1913, 41). In the Open the 'seedings' held, so the Parkers met each other in the final. Reports of the match indicate that the standard was high. The front page of the *Sunday Times* 10/11/1913, 1) said:

> *The tennis shown on both sides was superb and time and time again the spectators were wound up to the highest stages of excitement by the wonderful rallies and seemingly impossible returns by both players. Ernie Parker lost the first set but won the other three magnificently. His success was greeted by a storm of applause.*

Ernie Parker had been able to grasp the opportunity to become the first Western Australian to win the national Open. He had teamed with Tom Crookes to win the doubles title in 1909. In 1913 he was again successful in the doubles when, in partnership with Alf Hedeman, he received the winner's trophy over Harry Parker and Roy Taylor (South Australia) 3/6, 6/4, 6/4, 6/4. It was obviously a great thrill for the young Hedeman to win a national title. He was to play through the years of the Great War and reach the final of the next (and last) Australasian Open conducted in Perth in late 1921. For Parker, though, it marked the culmination of his wonderful sporting career.

Like so many of his contemporaries, he was to go to war and was killed in May 1918 in France. As it transpired, the two winners of the pre-war Australasian Open singles held in Perth - Anthony Wilding and Ernie Parker - both died during active service.

As had been the case in 1909, the Women's Championship carried only the status of the W.A. Open Championship. The title went to Mrs Mather, who defeated Miss Kent 7/5, 6/2. This was Mather's first Open win, but it was not to be her last: she became the dominant player in the early 1920s. Unfortunately, Kent, who was regarded as a fine player, never gained the Western Australian singles title although she won the Open doubles (with Miss Low) in 1910. Kent had beaten Mather in the early rounds in 1912 but the title went to Miss Ruse. As mentioned in this pre-war period, Miss Ruse, in partnership with Mrs Blackmore, won a remarkable five Open doubles titles. Ruse was able to achieve more honours in singles but Blackmore had no peer in doubles.

The Australasian Open was a great success, but there were new difficulties. Was too much attention being given to hallmark events? Before the Open much energy had been given to obtaining a satisfactory lease for the Association headquarters. Furthermore, the Constitution was in the process of being revamped (*Western Mail*, 7/8/1914, 41). The question of whether to conduct summer or winter pennants remained unresolved. It led one columnist to suggest that pennants had been relegated to the 'dust heap' (*Western Mail*, 3/1/1913, 41). As these problems were being addressed the nation was plunged into World War I, the Great War. For seniors, tennis was no longer a sport, a game or a leisure pursuit; it was virtually only played to raise funds for the war.

Chapter Ten

MUELLER PARK AND THE GREAT WAR 1914-1918

WITHIN the space of a few years, the Lawn Tennis Association had conducted two Australasian Open Championships. Several interstate matches had been arranged and some of Australia's best players had visited Perth. A team from the British Isles, after a decade of negotiation, had also visited. The Association was invariably praised for the organisation of these events. Tennis, particularly in many country districts, was thriving. However, much of the tennis activity was outside the jurisdiction of the Association and was not being translated into financial benefits.

A tennis centre

Many believed that the key to the Association's financial and administrative future was settlement of the venue question as the tenure at the Zoo was uncertain. One prominent delegate, Mr Stow, commented (*WALTA Minutes*, 31/3/1909):

> *after the treatment meted out to us last year by the Zoo authorities, however, it would be almost impossible to deal with them further. They had broken faith in every way and we should never give them another chance to do so.*

Officials approached the Subiaco Municipal Council to negotiate an extended lease on part of Mueller Park, in Subiaco. Its central location was well served by public transport. Importantly, too, some members of the Subiaco Council were receptive to approaches by sporting associations. Mayor White, who lived opposite Mueller Park dreamt that the area would become 'the greatest rendezvous of sport in Australasia, (Spillman, 1985, 187). In White's first mayoral report to the Council in 1909, he made clear his passion for the project and listed an astonishing number of facilities already available (Spillman, 1985, 189):

> *Your Council of the past showed its wisdom by agitating for and obtaining from the Government the magnificat reserve - Mueller Park - and no greater evidence of its popularity could be forthcoming than the number of playing areas applied for and Sports Associations that have taken advantage of this centrally situated ground. The council has constructed 14 tennis courts, and the area now comprises a maximum size recreation oval, 16 Association tennis courts, 4 croquet courts for the Western Australian Croquet Association, four bowling rinks, four tennis courts for the local club, and if one may be allowed to be prophetic, one can picture, in a very few years hence, all the pennant tennis matches, croquet matches, cricket, football, and bowling being contested on this park, which will certainly be one, if not the greatest rendezvous of sport in Australasia.*

In a prospectus the Association sought a 15-year lease, carrying a priority right of renewal for a future term, and granting the right to charge for admission to the ground when tennis was being played. Based on estimates by the Subiaco Council engineer for court construction, fencing, and reticulation, it was decided that the Association would pay a contribution of £250. The Subiaco Council was prepared to undertake the maintenance of the courts for the sum of £150 per year (*WALTA Minutes*, 18/1/1909). To raise the necessary funds, the Association registered under the Associations' Incorporation Act. This enabled it to authorise the issue of 250 debentures of one pound each repayable in five years and bearing interest at 5 per cent per annum. A limited number of life membership tickets at £10/10/- each was to be made available. Subscribers of three or more debentures and life membership holders, were to be given some concessions, including free access to the grounds. It was forecast that the annual subscriptions, gate money and other receipts, would be more than sufficient to meet annual expenditure, including maintenance and the interest on debentures (*WALTA Minutes*, 18/1/1909).

The terms negotiated between the Council and several Association sub-committees formed to review the Mueller Park proposition were less favourable than had been mooted in the prospectus. Indeed, although the final agreement of the lease may have been reported in the newspapers (which were sometimes used as a substitute for official records), it was not documented in the Association's minutes. Unfortunately, the Association, despite attempts to redress the situation (*WALTA Minutes*, 6/10/1910), was burdened with a greater share of maintenance costs that could be reasonably afforded (*WALTA Minutes*, 20/4/1910 and 21/2/1911).

The Subiaco Council's plans to make Mueller Park 'the great rendezvous of sport in Australia' were shelved during the War. Later, the Council briefly pursued a policy of developing the area for women's and children's sport (Spillman, 1985, 310). By that time it was was known as Kitchener Park. In 1916, the Subiaco Council, motivated by 'hatred of the Hun' decided to remove from the municipal map any street or place names which the Great War had made seem offensive (Spillman, 1985, 209). So Mueller Park, named after the German-born botanist Frederick von Mueller, had its name changed to honour Horatio Lord Kitchener, a British Army hero. The action overlooked the fact that von Mueller was a knighted British citizen who had spent many years in Western Australia.

Wartime tennis

Association tennis at Mueller (then Kitchener) Park was very restricted during the War, particularly as the crisis deepened. In September 1915, after a keen debate, it was decided not to close the courts (*WALTA Minutes*, 20/9/1915). However, their condition deteriorated as the Association found it difficult to meet the cost of maintenance. A deputation to the Subiaco Council failed to negotiate a substantial fee reduction. Early in 1917, it was found necessary to restrict the use of the courts by students of the nearby Perth Modern School. Use of the courts by the students was only to be granted if arrears in hire payments were met (*WALTA Minutes*, 16/2/1917). In October 1917 the grounds committee was authorised to hire the Subiaco Council horse-drawn cutter to remove the thick, high grass outside the actual court area (*WALTA Minutes*, 8/10/1917). The condition of the courts was poor but play was possible. By far the most usual matches at the Park were mixed doubles medal tournaments which were conducted regularly to raise funds for the war effort (*WALTA Minutes*, 16/2/1917).

The Association's wartime policy position was that clubs should not hold tournaments for profit. In the spring of 1914, there was a dilemma over whether to conduct the State Open tournament. At one stage it was decided that, due to the 'disturbing influences of the war', (*Western Mail*, 2/10/1914, 37) it would be cancelled. However, when the LTAA chose to go ahead with the 1914 Australasian Open, it must have swayed the local delegates; it was resolved to conduct the State Open in conjunction with the Subiaco club's annual tournament (*WALTA Minutes*, 15/10/1914).

The 1914 State Open was the last major tournament until 1919. Understandably there were no interstate entries, although earlier in the year Norman Brookes had played an exhibition match in Perth. An interstate match had also been played against South Australia in April. On this occasion, Ernie Parker had alarmed officials when he sent a telegram indicating he would not be available. As Parker had given no explanation for his decision, the chairman sent a reply telegram stating (*WALTA Minutes*, 13/3/1914):

> *My Council confidently relies on your carrying out honourable arrangements we have entered into with South Australian Association for interstate match - wish you luck!*

By late November the leading question about Ernie Parker was whether he could defend his Open title against the promising Alf Hedeman. It was reported that both had practised regularly on the WANDA Esplanade courts (*Western Mail*, 13/11/1914, 37). Parker, though, decided he was 'not sufficiently fit' to play singles and restricted his entry to partnering Hedeman in the doubles championship. This immediately made the latter a strong favourite for the singles title. But in one of the great upsets of the Open, Hedeman lost in the semi-final to E. Stokes, a prominent Goldfields player. The *West Australian* (28/11/1914, 13) reported how:

> *... Stokes striking that form which from time to time lifts him out of the rank and file, succeeded in defeating Hedeman - by many regarded as the assured winner of the event - with a sustained display of hard, clean hitting, and smart footwork.*

Hedeman was to win the men's doubles with Parker but Stokes did not go on to achieve victory in the men's singles. Instead, Arnold Leschen won the title. In the previous year there had been some criticism about his omission from the Western Australian team for the interstate fixture before the 1913 Australasian Championship. Leschen, as well as Stokes, was selected in the practice squad to play against the British Isles, but was again overlooked as an official team member. After the opening round of the 1914 Open, one reporter observed how (*Western Mail*, 27/11/1914, 37) 'in respect of Leschen ... it may be said that he possesses more than just a chance [to win the Open]'. Leschen was to prove the accuracy of this claim by defeating Stokes in the final 6/3, 5/7, 6/3, 7/9, 9/7. Fortunately for the organisers, Mrs Mather was able to win the Women's Open in straight sets 6/3, 6/3. Mather was beginning to place her imprint on the women's scene in a manner similar to that of Matilda Walsh a few years earlier. Despite a report of serious illness (*West Australian*, 5/12/1914, 10) Mather continued her dominance of the Open after the war, but Leschen left Western Australia, joined the services, later married and remained in England (*Western Mail*, 3/12/1919, 9).

The end of the tournament and the cessation of major championships for the remainder of the War was accompanied by one rare piece of good news. For several years, the Association had sought to stage a Davis Cup tie. Attempts

Secretary H.C. Jefferson, 'Won a better deal for the WALTA'

were also made to improve its share of Davis Cup profits. The secretary, Mr Jefferson, had continually lobbied the LTAA for a better deal for Western Australia. So the welcome news for New Year's Day in 1915 (*Western Mail*, 1/1/1915, 37) read:

> *In spite of the depressing effects of the war, the drought and the various other disabilities under which we are labouring at the present the members of the Lawn Tennis Association are in a state of exceeding jubilation. The reason is not hard to seek. It lies in the fact that during the last few days the Honorary Secretary (Mr Jefferson) has received from the Australian Executive the sum of £300 as the State share of the proceeds of the last two Davis Cup series.*

Under the Presidency of politician Mr (later Sir) Walter Kingsmill, the Association Council met regularly in 1915 and 1916. In September 1915 there was discussion about whether the Association should go into recess (*WALTA Minutes*, 10/9/1915). Some officials, such as Roland Kelsey, mindful of the difficulty of securing the permanent establishment of the Association, successfully argued for the continuation of the Council. Eventually, though, the demands of the War meant that meetings became irregular. The theme was reflected in a motion passed in March 1916, whereby 'Council offers its congratulations to R.H. Kelsey on his determination to serve his King and Country and wishes him God Speed and a safe return' (*WALTA Minutes*, 10/3/1916). Earlier the Council had considered an appropriate memorial to Anthony Wilding, who had been killed on active service in Belgium (*WALTA Minutes*, 10/9/1915). Near the end of the War, the Association's members were saddened to hear that Ernie Parker had been killed in France.

Many must have wondered if the Association would be revived when hostilities ended. No formal Council meeting took place after October 8, 1917. However, it should be realised that, even prior to the war, the Association was experiencing severe financial difficulties. Some administrative flaws were also apparent, with disputes arising over how the Constitution should be revamped. The pennant competition, often regarded as 'the life blood of the Association' (*WALTA Minutes* 31/3/1909), fell into disarray in the 1912 season. With pennants still being conducted in winter, the schedule of matches could not be completed due to the poor weather before the State Championship. After leaving the situation in abeyance for several months, the Association finally declared the teams on top of the respective premiership lists as the pennant winners (*WALTA Minutes*, 10/1/1913).

As mentioned previously, the Association had no jurisdiction over many small metropolitan clubs. Nor were any of the country tennis clubs within its ambit. The Association was organising hallmark events but it had no substantial revenue base. Given the drain on finances incurred by the courts at Mueller Park, it was necessary in late 1913 to debate whether the Association should remain in existence. Some considered it to be in dire financial straits as the debt stood at about £150 (*WALTA Minutes*, 20/8/1913). Finally, Roland Kelsey successfully moved a motion which read, 'That in the opinion of this meeting the WA Lawn Tennis Association should be carried on ....' (*WALTA Minutes*, 10/9/1913). Six weeks earlier, the Association had shown a measure of confidence in the future when it adopted as its official colours black and gold (*WALTA Minutes*, 14/7/1913). This was accompanied by a decision to raise the affiliation fee, hold an annual dance and conduct a monthly tennis day (*WALTA Minutes*, 10/9/1913).

While it was important to decide on symbols, it was necessary to solve the more fundamental problem of finance. Secretary Jefferson's resolve to increase the share of the LTAA's hallmark events has already been mentioned (*WALTA Minutes*, 10/5/1913). However, the person who was probably most responsible for attempting the necessary reforms was S.J. McGibbon, the Kings Park delegate. At one stage, he stated that his continuing as Association Chairman '.... would depend upon the support the clubs and individual members were prepared to give the Council in their efforts to place the Association in a sound financial position' (*WALTA Minutes*, 4/6/1913). McGibbon firmly believed that the Constitution of the Association needed to be amended to facilitate the affiliation, of clubs, particularly those in country areas. After McGibbon had initiated a survey to reveal the number of clubs which were not affiliated he succeeded in his quest to secure the required constitutional amendment (*WALTA Minutes*, 24/4/1915 and *Western Mail*, 7/5/1914, 41 and 25/9/1914, 37).

As country clubs were to be allowed to affiliate at a reduced fee, it was not surprising that preliminary plans were soon made for a Country Week tennis carnival in Perth (*WALTA Minutes*, 8/7/1915). However, as the carnival was scheduled for October 1915 the adverse war situation required its cancellation. Nevertheless, McGibbon's constitutional change was later to have a profound impact on the future, as it meant the Association was in a pivotal position, with responsibilities for tennis development throughout the state. Until then the Association was solely a metropolitan organisation. McGibbon also canvassed the view that individual members should voluntarily pay a levy. It was a forerunner of the levy which each club was later required to pay on behalf of individual subscribers. Another revenue measure linked to McGibbon was a proposal that each club organise a dance or ball and allocate a percentage of the profits to the Association. McGibbon was certainly an innovator. He was to suffer ill-health during the War (*Western Mail*, 25/9/1914, 37) but maintained strong links with the Association. He was later President from 1925 to 1938 and was honoured with life membership in 1926 (*WALTA Minutes*, 21/5/1926).

Thus the financial plight, which McGibbon worked so hard to alleviate, led to some potentially important changes in its structure and direction. In this context, one development which later gained a central place was the fostering of junior tennis. With the curtailment of senior competition play a vacuum was left for the juniors. At a meeting in June 1914, the Association Council appointed a sub-committee composed of Secretary Jefferson, and prominent delegates Mr W. Cooper and Samuel Glyde to draft rules for a schools competition (*WALTA Minutes*, 4/6/1914). The competition was open to all bona fide clubs and schools, although the players had to be under 19 years of age. The winning team was to receive a trophy known as the Slazenger Junior Championship Cup. It was also specified that each of the four members of the winning team was to be given a tennis racquet. Initially the rules were framed for boys but it was decided to conduct a parallel Slazenger Cup competition for girls. The latter competition was, however, to be administered by the Girls' Secondary School Sports Association on club courts.

Despite several newspaper references and Council requests entries for the Slazenger Cup competition, which required an entry fee of one pound for the knock-out format, were very disappointing. Eventually the inaugural final was played at Mueller Park in conjunction with the State Open. Details of the final scores between Claremont and Perth Modern School were published in the press (*Western Mail*, 4/12/1914, 27):

Anthony Wilding (top) and Ernie Parker, two champions killed in action overseas. (Courtesy The West Australian)

Keith Barker and his mother Ethel Barker, two members of a prominent tennis family. (Courtesy The West Australian)

Claremont (C) versus Modern School (MS)

Singles: E. Barker (C) beat Stirling (MS) 6-3
Gawler (C) beat Berthold (MS) 6-3
K. Barker (C) beat Rhys (MS) 6-2
Trounce (C) lost to Henzell (MS) 4-6

Doubles: Barker and Barker (C) lost to Berthold and Stirling (MS) 6-1, 3-6, 2-6.
Gawler and Trounce (C) beat Rhys and Henzell (MS) 6-3 4-6, 6-2.

Totals: Claremont 6 sets 49 games beat Modern School 4 sets 38 games.

The Barkers in the Claremont team were sons of the former State Champion, Mrs Ethel Barker. Although they lost the Slazenger Cup doubles tie they went on, in 1922, to win the State Open Doubles titles. At 'Chanonry', the boys known as Tom and Keith, had plenty of opportunities to develop their talents. Tom and Keith Barker were the last 'set' of brothers to win the State Open Doubles. However, they were not the first pair to claim this honour for a family. The Oldhams were victorious in 1897, the Barnards (from Victoria) in 1908 and the Krugers (W. and C.), in 1920.

When the Barker brothers won the 1922 senior doubles title they gained prestige, but their prize was a nominal few pounds. For the Slazenger Cup triumph they, and their team-mates Gawler and Trounce, had expected a tennis racquet. But at the Cup presentation, photographed for the *Western Mail* (4/12/1914, 27), Walter Kingsmill, the President, had the Slazenger Cup at hand but no racquets. Later, the Association, in consultation with the sponsors, decided that it was not financially feasible to honour the condition of donating racquets to the winning team members. The decision was reached after the Headmaster of Perth Modern School wrote a letter of complaint to the Council. Perth Modern School had won the girls section of the competition so the Headmaster was justifiably annoyed that the original competition condition had not been honoured.

The girls' final was not played until a few days before Christmas at the Y.M.C.A. courts in Wellington Square. It was claimed the 'lines were very faint while the court surface quickly destroyed the players confidence' (*West Australian*, 26/12/1914, 10). The girls from Ormiston College, who reached the final in the seven-team competition, were particularly disadvantaged because they were accustomed to playing on gravel courts. As the results indicate, Ormiston College was to prove no match for Perth Modern School:

Perth Modern School (PMS) versus Ormiston College (OC)

Singles: Miss Hanrahan (PMS) beat Miss Tripp (OC) 6-3
Miss Cowan (PMS) beat Miss Whitfield (OC) 6-1
Miss Steadman (PMS) beat Miss Harry (OC) 6-1
Miss Long (PMS) lost to Miss Beresford (OC) 4-6

Doubles: Misses Hanrahan and Cowan (PMS) beat Misses Tripp and Whitfield (OC) 6-4
Misses Steadman and Long (PMS) beat Misses Harry and Beresford (OC) 6-1

Totals: Perth Modern School 5 sets 34 games beat Ormiston College 1 set 16 games.

One problem in the conduct of the Slazenger Cup competition had been the different management of the girls' and boys' sections. The Association had controlled the boys' competition since its inception, whereas the girls competition had been under the auspices of the Girls' Secondary Schools' Sports Association. In 1916, the girls (like the boys since 1914) played on the Association courts. In the following year, the Association assumed full responsibility for both competitions and resolved that both finals should be reserved for the annual State Open Championships (*West Australian*, 19/11/1919, 11). Of course, the Open Championships had been cancelled during the War but the Slazenger Cup had become firmly established.

Chapter Eleven

THE LINWOOD 'DRIVE' 1919-1922

THE armistice which formally declared the end of the 'war to end all wars' was signed at the eleventh hour on 11 November, 1918. However, the Council of the Lawn Tennis Association did not convene until the autumn of 1919. This meant there had been an 18 month lapse since a quorum had been recorded. Most business had been carried out by Chairman McGibbon and Secretary Jefferson (*WALTA Minutes*, 24/6/1919). A small group of enthusiasts had been responsible for running the Slazenger Cup competitions and a number of mixed doubles medal tournaments. The latter had usually been conducted on public holidays, such as Eight Hours (Labour) Day and Foundation Day. The profits from these occasions were donated to the Patriotic Fund. Clearly, though, with the War over the steps taken to achieve recovery and development would be important.

Remembrance and recovery

One of the first items of business for the Council was the tabling of correspondence from George Parker, a prominent citizen and cricket administrator, whose son Ernie had been tragically killed in France serving as a bombardier. Ernie Parker bequeathed to the Association the Alcock Cup he had secured when he was the victor in the 1912 State Open Tennis Championship (*WALTA Minutes*, 3/4/1919). The terms and conditions of the trophy were to be the same as previously promulgated whereby it was necessary to win three State Men's Open Singles Championships before the Alcock Cup could be retained by an individual. Soon the Association moved to establish a memorial to Parker to recognise his great feats as a tennis player. However, it was notable that the *West Australian*'s (25/5/1918, 43) obituary concentrated on Parker's cricket achievements. The few sentences devoted to Parker's tennis record stated:

> *Ernest's great powers did not stop with cricket, for he was the champion tennis player of the State, and his game was always most delightful to watch. Quick, wristy, and always looking for a 'winner' he made play most charming. He won many championships here, and in exhibition games against Brookes, Wilding, Jones, H. A. Parker, and others, showed some wonderfully good tennis.*

Decades later, in 1992, when Ernie Parker was belatedly inducted into the Western Australian Hall of Champions, a more balanced resume appeared in *Sportview*, the periodical of the Western Australian Sports Federation (October 1992, 8). It should be recognised, however, that in the troubled times in which Parker died, the team dimension of cricket had community appeal but his obituary gave the impression that tennis did not attract the public interest in the same way as cricket. Nevertheless all sporting bodies faced challenges in rehabilitating their organisations after the Great War. Tennis had lost the services of many players and administrators. Some who had taken up the game again, in both the city and country, were members of clubs not affiliated with the Association. Some of the affiliated clubs, such as WANDA, East Fremantle and University, had fallen into debt or were in arrears with their contribution fees. The Association was not insolvent but it could not sustain operating at a loss. The courts at Kitchener (formerly Mueller) Park had proven to be a 'millstone'. Tennis equipment was difficult to obtain. In particular, tennis balls, even when purchased in bulk, were often costly and of poor quality.

George Linwood's drive was a key factor in the Association's recovery after the Great War

George Linwood

After the War, the first annual general meeting to elect the new administration was called on the eve of Anzac Day, 1919. Ironically, there was minimal change in the Executive. The practice of appointing the Governor as patron was retained. Parliamentarian Walter Kingsmill remained President while McGibbon and Jefferson stayed on as Chairman and Secretary respectively. (*WALTA Minutes*, 24/4/1919). Within six months there were important changes in personnel. A Gallipoli veteran, Mr William Corr, began more than 40 years of service when he took over as Treasurer from Reg Long. Then, when Jefferson was transferred in his employment to Victoria, later becoming a WALTA delegate to the LTAA, the secretaryship fell to George Linwood. Arriving in Perth from Tasmania in 1910, Linwood joined both Kings Park and WANDA clubs. He had assisted in administrative affairs and was known as a capable tournament and pennant player with a 'solid' drive. In contrast to W.R. Corr's long service, Linwood served only four years as secretary before he accepted an employment promotion from the New Zealand Insurance Company to its India branch. Within a few months of his departure, in April 1923, news was received of his accidental death in Calcutta (*West Australian*, 22/10/1923, 37). Immediately the Association took steps to perpetuate his name as he had a dynamic and lasting impact on its affairs (*WALTA Minutes*, 19/10/1923 and 15/2/1924). The trophy for the winner of the State Open Singles Championship was to be known as the Linwood Memorial Cup.

Linwood was a keen advocate of interstate tennis. He strove to ensure that major tournaments were well organised and publicised. Importantly, too, he attempted, in concert with McGibbon, to seek more affiliates in urban and rural areas. A country week carnival was inaugurated just after Linwood left office. In the same year (1923), the first schools tournament was also conducted. When speaking earlier at a farewell function arranged in his honour, Linwood after thanking enthusiasts such as Corr, Hedeman, Eaton and Allen for their help, reminded delegates to 'keep the interest in the game broad based and the Association cannot fail' (*WALTA Minutes*, 11/5/1923).

While not denying the influence of Kingsmill and McGibbon, it is appropriate to view the recovery and development phase as broadly spanning Linwood's term as Secretary. As Kingsmill said (*WALTA Minutes* 11/5/1923) 'The parting of Mr Linwood was one of the greatest losses the Association has sustained.' He further elaborated:

> *In the course of a few years Mr Linwood had removed the affairs of the Association from Queer-Street to Easy-Street, had systematised the Association's work, effected important improvements at the Kitchener Park grounds, secured the active interest of country clubs, promoted interstate visits, and in many other ways proved to be highly imaginative ...*

One of Linwood's first initiatives was to seek the transfer of the State Championship to the Christmas vacation period. An argument in favour for this shift was that it would facilitate the participation of country players and even interstate champions. There had been widespread criticism of the decision to conduct the 1919 State Championships in early November on the grass courts at Kitchener Park. Amid discussion of a theory that the seasons had perceptibly altered since the last Open in 1914, it was argued in the *West Australian* (26/11/1919, 9):

> *For the past two months virtually every club in the metropolitan area has been closed down for top dressing; and behold, this dismal period is abruptly terminated by the putting on of the State Championship tournament, the premier meeting of the lawn tennis calendar. Could anything be more incongruous?*

Later, the same newspaper argued that the Association should relinquish its control of the State Championship and award it to a club that was prepared to conduct the event at Easter (*West Australian*, 5/1/1921, 8). Despite misgivings about the date of the fixture, one of the major controversies Linwood and his Council members had to handle was that of whether entries would be accepted from players who were members of unaffiliated clubs. Unfortunately, little space was required to list the affiliated clubs (and their secretaries) and the short list underscored the reason for the debate (*WALTA Minutes*, April 1920):

- Bunbury (E. S. Hart)
- Claremont (V. B. Mursell)
- East Fremantle (W. Jennings)
- Kalgoorlie (W. Brearley)
- Kings Park (K. A. McDougall)
- Katanning (W. A. Richmond)
- Loton Park (R. W. Richardson)
- Narrogin (W. J. Mills)
- South Perth (J. H. Lord)
- St Johns (C. A. Hudson)
- Subiaco (J. S. Kerbey)
- WANDA (L. Copley)

The 1919 Open

After an exhaustive Council debate just before the 1919 Open, it was decided not to accept entries from members of unaffiliated clubs. In a major concession, this rule was not to prevail for championship events (*WALTA Minutes*, 10/11/1919). It appears, though, there were expressions of dissatisfaction with the decision, because when the Kings Park Club was granted permission to designate its Easter tournament as the Metropolitan Championship, it was resolved to suspend the rule which prohibited the participation of unaffiliated club members (*WALTA Minutes*, 5/3/1920). Delegates, however, did not wish to cloud the tournament with controversy. Instead, there was a desire to satisfy the demands for a more extended program. Among the new events were the War Service Singles Handicap, the WALTA Plate and the Boys Junior Singles Championship.

The War Service Singles was restricted to members of the allied forces who had seen active service on any front, while the Plate was a consolation for players defeated in the first or second round of the State singles championship. The junior boys singles was open to boys up to 19 years of age. In addition, the twin championship finals for teams of girls and boys, hitherto known as the Slazenger Cup, came together into a tournament for the first time.

With such a range of events, eight playing days were designated for the tournament. It was recognised there would be complaints by some players who were called upon to play at inconvenient hours on 'work days'. While it was said 'that those without consideration for others may be relied upon to furnish the loudest complaints' such tournament schedules were regularly adopted in England (*West Australian*, 19/11/1919, 9). Such arrangements, of course, helped preclude the 'working class' and thwart endeavours to broaden the base of tennis, When finals day was reached, it was expected that Mrs Mather, who had won the State Open in 1913 and 1914, would again secure the women's title. This expectation was realised, Mrs Mather easily defeating Miss Mountain 6/4, 6/2.

In the men's event there was less certainty. By popular acceptance, Alf Hedeman had been unofficially labelled as the State Champion since the untimely death of Ernie Parker (*West Australian*, 3/12/1919, 9). However, the Association's State title had eluded him. It will be recalled that when Ernie Parker withdrew from the State Open in 1914, Hedeman was regarded as the 'assured winner of the event'. He did, however, suffer a shock defeat in the semi-final. It would have been expected that Hedeman would then have gone to the European front, but a military doctor perversely rejected him for military service on the score that his physical fitness was doubtful. So Hedeman consoled himself by improving his already formidable (but unusual) game. Hedeman was known for his ambidexterity; he changed racquet hands for some shots. The extent of his improvement was going to be critical for his chances of victory. A youngster from the Claremont club, Rice Gemmell, who had seen military service in France, was making an impression in local club tournaments.

Both Hedeman and Gemmell fulfilled expectations and reached the final. It was reported that the 'onlookers to the last man wanted Hedeman to win' (*West Australian*, 3/12/1919, 9). They were not disappointed as Hedeman won 6/2, 5/7, 6/3, 6/2. In brilliantly capturing the second set, Gemmell indicated what the new E.F. Parker Memorial Open winner would have to expect when defending his title in 1920. It was not lost upon Hedeman, who on shaking hands across the net, generously remarked 'I think I've got it just in time' (*West Australian*, 1/12/1919, 8). For the time being, Gemmell had to be content with winning the War Service Singles Handicap over E. (Tom) Barker. But Gemmell's best days were ahead of him.

Gemmell and Mather

By 1920, with the State Open transferred to Christmas, Gemmell had emerged as the leading men's singles player in the state. Hedeman again did well to reach the final against Gemmell. It was Hedeman's strategy to rely on 'his machine like control', whereas for Gemmell the tactics were 'service, volley and smash' (*West Australian* 4/1/1921, 4). Hedeman stationed on the baseline was able to win the first and third set, but Gemmell's attacking style allowed him to gradually seize the initiative and take the match in the fifth set.

In the Women's Open Championship, it was again the attacking style of Mrs Mather that prevailed over Miss McDougall 7/5, 6/1. Mather and Miss Brook also won the Ladies Doubles and only an injury to Ivan Gibbs denied the lady champion a sequence of impressive mixed doubles titles. As a newspaper columnist (*West Australian*, 4/1/1921, 4) observed 'for years Mrs Mather has occupied a class alone'. In the 1919 Open, she had the extraordinary distinction of defeating her niece, Miss Mountain, in the final. The latter was no 'slouch' as she played with distinction for Victoria and with Esna Boyd won the first Australasian Women's Doubles title in 1922. But as Mather had also won in 1913 and 1914, it is to be wondered how many consecutive Open titles she could have secured had the War not intervened. As a consequence of her dominance, reports of tournaments generally restricted references to Mather to confirmation she had captured another title.

Mather's big test was to come in the State Open of 1921, when some leading women players from South Australia travelled to Perth for an interstate fixture and the championships. This was one of the most important to be played in Western Australia, as the men's singles and doubles were designated as the Australasian Open titles. Given the drive of Linwood and supported by a keen band of officials such as William Corr, Hedeman, S.V. Eaton, L. Copley and Tom Hantke, the Association had applied for the prestigious Open in March 1921 (*WALTA Minutes*, 18/3/1921). It then made provision, at a cost of some £300, for a temporary stand at Kitchener Park (*Western Mail*, 22/12/1921, 20). Given these expenditures it was hoped that leading men players such as Gerald Paterson (the 1919 Wimbledon champion), Pat O'Hara Wood and James Anderson could be enticed to Perth. However, sheer cost and time, the Davis Cup and other major championship commitments always made such visits difficult to negotiate.

With no 'stars from the east' in the Men's Australasian Open, it was expected that Gemmell would be the victor. He had displayed good form when he defeated Hedeman in straight sets a few weeks earlier in the Suburban Championship Final (*Sunday Times*, 4/12/1921, 2). In the Open, Gemmell again proved his superiority over Hedeman, with a straight set 7/5, 6/1, 6/4 victory. When Association President Walter Kingsmill presented the champion with what had been designated as the Wilding Memorial Medal, he remarked 'if the leading players from the Eastern States persist in declining to come West, the Association will have to send Gemmell to them' (*West Australian* 8/1/1922, 6). Kingsmill did not appreciate that the Australian Open would never again be held in Perth. Nor did he realise that his remarks would be recorded in the annals of Australian tennis history. For when Bruce Matthews (1985, 10) wrote a history of the Australian tennis championships, he published Kingsmill's claim, but reminded readers that Gemmell never made an impact on the eastern seaboard.

The judgement about Gemmell's standing in national terms was made in hindsight. Nevertheless, the championship did confirm that Mrs Mather, from the South Perth club, was a player with exceptional qualities. She had shown good form in the lead-up events. In the Suburban Championship, Mather had defeated Miss Stuart (*Sunday Times*, 4/12/1921, 2).

At the South Perth tournament a fortnight later, Mather beat an old rival, Miss Brook 6/0, 7/5. Then in the match against South Australia, two long sets were necessary to defeat the visitor, Mrs Rowe. This latter match had created unusual interest as many believed Mather would lose her Open crown. At last a final in which Mather had participated was described in detail in the newspapers. Part of one commentary (*West Australian*, 3/1/19222, 6) read:

> *To the great relief of Mr G A. Linwood and his co-workers, the biggest and most successful tournament ever held in Western Australia was brought to a*

Stylish Rice Gemmell, winner of the 1921 Australasian Open conducted at Kitchener Park in Subiaco

close last evening. Appropriately enough, the last stroke played left Mrs Mather lady singles champion of the State, despite the efforts of Mrs Rowe, the South Australian lady champion, to dethrone her. Under the rules of the game Mrs Mather was more deserving of victory than was Mrs Rowe - about two strokes more - notwithstanding that within the course of the match the victor won 17 games, whereas the loser scored 18. In the interstate match, on Christmas Eve, the local champion defeated the visitor 8-6, 1-6, 8-6. Truly it was a battle between highly skilled and most courageously determined opponents. Viewing the match as a whole, there was nothing to choose between them. Physical and nervous strain resulted in brief alternating patches of mistakes, and only during such patches was one able to get the score away from the other. Thus in the second set [by] subconsciously sparing herself - the local champion made many errors, and the visitor quickly ran away with the set. In the opening games of the third set it was Mrs Rowe's turn to lapse and lose control, which she did till the score was 5-1 against her. Mrs Mather tried hard for the seventh game, but Mrs Rowe, recovering, took four on the end, and so evened at five all. Mrs Mather made it 6-5, Mrs Rowe evened, Mrs Mather made it 7-6, and had the score at 40 love when a net cord shot from Mrs Rowe suggested the possibility of at least two more games having still to be fought. However, the local champion with an accurate placement made the next point the concluding one. It was a pretty match prettily fought, and a crumpled gumleaf on the court might have served to turn the issue. During the forenoon both ladies had contested the final of the mixed doubles championship, and in the early afternoon Mrs Rowe had played her part in winning, through three sets, the ladies' doubles championship. The frequency and volume of applause from the gallery served to confirm the opinion of competent judges that it was the most memorable ladies' match ever played in Perth.

In 1922 and 1923 Mather maintained her stronghold on the Association's Open (*West Australian*, 2/1/1924, 6). It was not until Mather moved to live in Victoria that the number one women's ranking in Western Australia could be disputed. Meanwhile, in the men's division, Gemmell continued his domination of the tournament scene. Only in 1922, after Gemmell had married and was temporarily away playing tournaments in the Eastern States, did the Open crown fall to another player. Even then, in 1922 Gemmell's spirit was apparently at Kitchener Park, as he made a special effort to telegraph secretary Linwood to convey best wishes for a successful tournament (*West Australian*, 23/12/1922, 8). On this occasion the Bunbury left-hander R.W. Phillips defeated C.L. Treloar in the men's final. Both players were labelled as 'retrievers' (interview with Keith Barker, 13/4/1986) but for the dogged Treloar it was to be the first of four runner-up trophies in the Open (*Daily News*, 2/1/1923, 2).

Mrs Violet Mather, for many years a 'class alone' in Western Australia (Courtesy The West Australian)

Another of Linwood's promotions was interstate tennis. It was not possible to accept an invitation by the NSWLTA to send a representative team for an interstate series in Sydney in May 1919 (*WALTA Minutes*, 3/4/1919). But the following year a team from New South Wales visited Perth. On their arrival, Kingsmill referred to 'the gentleness of the game' and expressed the hope that the leaders of lawn tennis in the State would show them as much of this part of the continent as possible (*Daily News*, 27/3/1920, 4). Perhaps the goodwill was too comforting as the Western Australian team of Gemmell, Gibbs, Hantke and Eaton scored a one set win over their more fancied rivals Rice, Goodman, Cross and Louden (*West Australian*, 29/3/1920, 3 and 31/3/1920, 5). The Council responded by formally conveying congratulations. There had been some disappointment with the size of the gallery, but the £26 profit was encouraging (*WALTA Minutes*, 8/4/1920). However, there were no illusions that Western Australia had become a power in interstate tennis nor were there suggestions that gates for such events would provide substantial revenues.

Before 1914, teams from the other States had often played in Perth, but in February 1921, for the first time, a representative Western Australian team went to Adelaide for interstate matches against South Australia, to be followed by individual participation in the South Australian Open championship. The women's team comprised Mesdames Mather, Brook, Stuart and Miss McDougall and the men's team Messrs Gemmell (as manager), Braham, Cleland and Gibbs. A small group of enthusiasts, led by George Linwood, gathered at the Perth Railway Station to wish the team bon voyage and good luck (*West Australian*, 12/2/1921, 8). But South Australia proved too strong. The best of the Western Australians, Mather, won both her singles and doubles. Gemmell and Ivan Gibbs performed well in the doubles, an event in which the young Cleland (the junior champion of the State) reportedly found himself out of his depth (*West Australian*, 21/2/1921, 8). Back home a few weeks later a Western Australian team of Gemmell, Treloar, Eaton, W. Kruger, Gibbs and Linwood was able to record a narrow victory against South Australia before the Easter Tournament (*WALTA Annual Report*, 29/4/1921).

In March 1923, as part of a policy of fostering higher standards of play, a fund was established for the purpose of sending leading players to the eastern States (*WALTA Minutes*, 9/3/1923). In the same month, Western Australia participated in a national tennis carnival in Adelaide. This historic event was given special standing by the participation of some of the nation's leading players including Gerald Paterson, the reigning Wimbledon champion. The Western Australian side consisted of C. Clydesdale, K. McDougall, R.W. Phillips and V. Trounce. The women's contingent was Miss McDougall, Mrs Mills, Miss Whitfield and Mrs Wood. While all were capable players, none were well known names. Only Phillips had won a State title, although, in fairness, McDougall was the runner-up in four State Opens (1911, 1912, 1920 and 1923). Her career had been overshadowed by the legendary Mather who (like Gemmell) had not been available for the Adelaide event. During the carnival, McDougall was the most competitive of the Western Australian women, but only Phillips was able to win a number of rubbers in the men's section.

For Western Australian tennis fans an opportunity to view top tennis had taken place in February 1920, when A.R.F. (Colonel) Kingscote played exhibition tennis in Perth. At the time Kingscote was regarded as the number one British player (Clerici, 1975, 206). He never won Wimbledon but succeeded in reaching what was called the final. In that match Kingscote had been unlucky to strike Gerald Paterson, the powerful Australian. Subsequently Paterson easily defeated Norman Brookes in the challenge round to win the Wimbledon title. That victory explains why the Association was continually negotiating for a visit to Perth by Paterson. Nevertheless Kingscote did have some drawing power, as his exhibition games enabled a modest profit to be achieved (*WALTA Minutes*, 5/3/1920). Generally, though, interstate visits and exhibitions were financial risks. It thus came as no surprise that the Association decided to approach the LTAA to ascertain if finance could be provided to enable leading players to visit Perth for major events such as the State Open at Christmas (*WALTA Minutes*, 15/8/1921). Many similar requests were later to be made to the LTAA.

Development

The Association Council was also doing its best to foster school tennis. Two delegates (C. Smith from South Perth and L. Copley from WANDA) were responsible for formulating a school tennis scheme (*WALTA Minutes*, 1/11/1920). There is no record of a plan being tabled but some significant moves took place during Linwood's secretaryship. The Slazenger Cup rules were revamped. An annual schools tournament, to be played between the months of May and August, was commenced in 1923. Earlier, in 1921, it was decided to include a girls' singles championship on the program for the State Open. Margaret Officer was to be the inaugural winner with a 6/3, 6/4 win over Miss Plaistowe. Officer graduated to being a leading woman player for several seasons, her record including the 1925 State Open title. However, there was immediate controversy about what constituted a junior. As the University Club protested against under 18 being the age limit it was temporarily altered to 20 years. The Association then approached the LTAA to make the junior age categories uniform throughout Australia (*WALTA Minutes*, 11/11/1921). Given the federal structure of the LTAA, it was a problem that took decades to resolve.

Another move to assist junior development was a recommendation that junior pennants for girls and boys be introduced on an under 21 basis. At the Council's first meeting after the War it had been agreed to hold winter pennants for Men's 'A', 'B' and 'C' grades as well as a Ladies Grade (*WALTA Minutes*, 3/4/1919). The Men's 'A' grade was cancelled but the other sections were played through the winter months. As had been the case before 1914, debate about how the pennant competition should be structured and whether the fixtures should be summer, autumn or winter, continued without clear resolution. Early in 1921 R.W. Richardson, a prominent player and administrator from the Loton Park club, was appointed convenor of a committee to examine the whole question of pennants (*WALTA Minutes*, 22/1/1921).

In the meantime it was decided that 'A' grade pennants were to commence on the first Saturday in April and be played on the first and third Saturday of each month thereafter (*WALTA Minutes*, 22/1/1921). Interestingly, steps were taken to avoid the clash of pennant dates with interstate football matches (*WALTA Minutes*, 10/7/1921). By the time Linwood resigned, the top grade pennants for men and women were being played in January, February and March. Lower grade and junior pennants commenced later. Significantly, tennis had eventually established itself as a summer game. The Suburban Championship was played in late November, the State Open at Christmas, the 'A' (and 'B') grade pennants in the summer and autumn and the Metropolitan Championship at Kings Park during Easter. Some pennants were played in winter but it was becoming accepted as the football season.

Much of the focus of the Richardson Committee had been directed toward the composition of the Men's 'A' grade. The report, tabled on 8 September, 1922 argued that, subject to the clubs entering players of a satisfactory standard, 'A' grade status in the men's pennants should be afforded to Loton Park, South Perth, Kings Park, Claremont, Subiaco and WANDA. These teams had made up the top six in the previous season.

In April 1921, the Association had decided to play all pennant matches at the Kitchener Park courts. S.V. Eaton, a member of the WANDA club, and Chairman of the Grounds Committee, was repeatedly given credit at Council meetings for the improved condition of the courts. Linwood was also praised for his negotiations with the Subiaco City Council. In addition, C.P.T. Ewing was thanked for his services in the preparation of the lease of the Association Grounds from the Subiaco Municipality (*West Australian*, 12/3/1923, 8). There remained sharp differences with the Subiaco Council on several matters of policy. Numerous requests to permit play at the courts on Sundays were refused (*WALTA Minutes*, 8/9/1922). An application for billboard (or perimeter) advertising was rejected (*WALTA Minutes*, 29/9/1920). Furthermore there were frequent disagreements about the water charges that should be levied (*WALTA Minutes*, 13/1/1922).

The concept of having a centrally located set of courts had been on the agenda even before the birth of the WALTA. Yet even with Linwood's drive, charisma and administrative skill, the matter was no closer to resolution. Soon there would be moves to examine other alternatives. In the meantime, though, Kitchener Park was to be the venue for the first Country Week carnival. This fixture, initially seriously suggested during the War, was to take place a few weeks after Linwood's departure. Of course the decision to conduct the carnival was in line with Linwood's policy of 'keeping the interest of the game broad based'.

Chapter Twelve

THE CALL OF THE RACQUET: THE MID TWENTIES

DURING the 1920s and 1930s, the space allocated to sporting news in the major Western Australian newspapers rapidly expanded and tennis shared this growth. At the beginning of the period, one writer attempted to explain why tennis had achieved such widespread popularity. Under the headline 'The Call of the Racquet: A Universal Game' (*Daily News* 27/12/1922, 3), readers were told:

> *The student of human nature who decides to pay a visit to Kitchener Park, Subiaco, this week will find plenty to interest him or her. Practically every type in the community excepting old age and infancy is represented in the huge and heterogeneous entry for the State tennis tournament. One can pass from a court upon which two boys in knickerbockers are indulging in a species of glorified pingpong to the centre court, where four local champions are volleying with almost unerring precision, and en route see a ladies' doubles game being played with an absorption that is seldom met with in the men's matches, or a pair of veterans unsuccessfully endeavouring to prove that they are as good as they were 20 years ago.*

Emphasis was given to the fact that a 'nimble foot, a well trained body, an active brain, and a skilled hand' were essential to success in tennis. It was a 'great individual game', in which genuine good fellowship and sportsmanship were expected. Moreover it was argued 'scores of tennis courts can be made on the ground taken up by one oval'. In a reference to cricket and football it was suggested that it was 'much better to be a poor player, yet a trier, than a watcher of good players'.

There was a reminder that in the 'older' games such as cricket, women folk 'who claim equality in most things' are not given opportunities. In tennis, husband and wife, brother and sister could play together and secure the maximum enjoyment from the game. The fact that tennis 'is a game that our sisters can play' was regarded as a factor in its appeal. It was stressed, however, that this was not a recognition that tennis was a 'girls' game. Tennis also required strength, skill and stamina which were 'traits' the 'older' games had developed. They 'had helped to build up the strength and character of Britons'.

The obvious need to refute the 'sissy' tag, partly by linking tennis to the accepted wisdom about the benefits of cricket, indicated that such views still prevailed in the community. The point of view contained in the final paragraph of the article underscored one of the policy dilemmas faced by the Association: the expectation that broadening the base of tennis had to occur in concert with producing champions. It was contended (*Daily News*, 27/12/1922, 3):

> *Let us not forget that tennis is only a game, to be played as a body and brain refresher, after work is done. However, the game has now assumed such an international character that we who play it for recreation's sake must see to it that Australia's champions - the equal in all sports of any men in the world - are given an opportunity to compete on even terms with their opponents from other lands. Tennis can do much more than any other game towards promoting better feeling between the nations; also every one wishes to see Australia live up to the very high standard set by the late Anthony Wilding and the greatest player of all time, Norman Brookes, to whose indomitable spirit and genius for the game, Australia owes such a debt of gratitude. It is up to Paterson, Anderson, Wood and Co. to "go-get" that Davis Cup, and rejoice the hearts of Norman Brookes, and every other Aussie.*

Broadening the base

It was necessary for the Association to include the recreational players within its ambit. And to gain the support desirable of the Education Department authorities, the game's qualities of strength, skill, stamina and ethical behaviour had to be demonstrated. Yet, to satisfy the public thirst for national and international success, the Association also had to provide a 'professional' sporting structure. These were not necessarily incompatible goals, particularly if the thesis is accepted that a broadly based popular game is likely to produce some elite players. A means of reconciling these goals lay in the increase of affiliates in both metropolitan and country areas.

The Association decided to accept affiliation by other organisations which had sprung up in response to the increased popularity of tennis. It also prepared a document extolling the benefits of affiliation (*West Australian*, 23/7/1923, 9). Although WALTA was originally composed of clubs or teams of pennant players (such as East Perth), it was now made possible for other tennis organisations to gain 'associate status'. Individual clubs within the associate organisations did not have delegate representation at the Council level, but capitation fees were set at a lower rate. It was obviously deemed judicious to incorporate them under the WALTA umbrella to create a broader base. All this meant better prospects for the coordinated development of tennis throughout the State. Perhaps, too, more champions could be produced.

The immediate impact of this stance was the establishment of formal communication links between the WALTA and the Fremantle Tennis Association. An inability to effectively accommodate the interests of the Fremantle players had been a major source of weakness of WALTA and its predecessors. Ironically, the Fremantle (Park) Tennis Club, one of the first tennis clubs officially established in the metropolitan area had fallen on hard times. The tennis needs of the Fremantle community were being met by a struggling East Fremantle Club and a number of small (one or two courts) clubs, often with church links. The most significant of these small clubs was the St John Tennis Club, the members of which played on courts at the Rectory grounds in Cantonment Street, Fremantle. The Club had affiliated with WALTA after the

War, but had not taken part in the pennant competition. However, when it was rumoured that the Cantonment Street site was likely to be sold, the St John executive approached the Fremantle Council for permission to return to Fremantle Park and the construction of six grass courts (Lee, n.d.).

On 10 October, 1921 a meeting was held at the Cabin Tea Rooms in High Street, Fremantle. The Fremantle Tennis Club was reformed, H.D. Beard (the father of a later President of WALTA, Morrie Beard) being elected President. Significantly Charles Hudson, who had been the St John Club secretary for five years, became the Fremantle Club secretary. Although Hudson was once described as 'the leading spirit of Fremantle' (*Western Mail*, 21/2/1935, 21) he was also 'the voice of reason' in terms of Fremantle being a partner with the WALTA. Hudson was keen to break down the image of WALTA as a Perth ogre. The new Fremantle Club thus immediately joined WALTA and participated in the pennant competition.

In 1923, a Fremantle Tennis Association was formed to arrange a series of matches in the district. The President of this Association, which was registered as a WALTA affiliate, was none other than Charles Hudson. At the time it was estimated that the Fremantle Association had a total membership of 270 players (*West Australian*, 7/3/1923, 6). The pennants were to be played on the various club courts but it was Hudson's dream that the Fremantle Association would establish its own grounds. In the meantime 'as the main string of the Fremantle Club' (Lee, n.d.) Hudson worked hard to secure a base for tennis in the district by providing opportunities for children from nearby schools to play on the club courts.

Charles Hudson, 'The leading spirit of Fremantle'

Later, in 1928, Hudson paved the way for the admission of juniors to the club. He was also instrumental in establishing a tennis scholarship for pupils at the nearby Princess May and Fremantle Boys' Schools. The winners of the respective school tournaments had their membership fees waived for a season and the runners-up reduced by half (Lee, n.d.). In addition, juniors were encouraged to enter the Slazenger Cup competition. Understandably, Hudson was made a life member of the Fremantle Club and from the WALTA perspective he played an important role in ensuring that the strength of the Fremantle tennis community was harnessed.

A promising development to broaden the base of tennis was the introduction of night tennis. In 1929, there were reports of the growth in the popularity of tennis under these conditions (Adamson, 1992, 45). An Open Electric Tournament was staged and a 'City Houses Night Tennis Association' was formed. In the 1929/1930 season from early October to early March, a total 26 clubs participated in night pennants for Men's 'A' and 'B' grades and Mixed 'A' and 'B' grades. Most of the teams represented leading business firms in Perth such as Boans, Bairds, Foy and Gibson, Dalgety and Company, Harris, Scarf and Sandover and Caris Brothers. The Patron was W.J. Winterbottom from member club Winterbottom Motor Company.

An indication of the close links of the new Association with the WALTA was evident from the list of office bearers which included S.J. McGibbon as President and R.W. Richardson as Chairman of the Council. Although the new Association adopted colours (blue and gold) and ratified a host of rules and regulations, the 'City Houses Night Tennis Association' did not survive the exigencies of the depression period. Despite this unsuccessful venture, there are still members of the tennis fraternity who believe the potential for night tennis during Perth's summer months has never been realised.

Country Week

Another significant affiliation question related to country clubs and associations. The inaugural Country Week Tennis Carnival, first mooted during the Great War, was set to commence on 24 March, 1923. The honorary secretary for the event was Mr F.W. Goldsmith. He had assumed the task of promoting the carnival and determining the organisational details. However, despite his great enthusiasm for the concept and support from the WALTA Council, the carnival did not attract much initial interest. It was estimated there were about 90 country clubs in the State, yet only five (Albany, Carrolup, Darlington, Katanning and Northam) ultimately took part in the Carnival at Kitchener Park (*West Australian*, 21/3/1923, 9). As each team was composed of only two members, it meant that 13 players (including reserves) participated. It prompted 'Fif-all' at the *West Australian* (27/3/1923, 9) to comment facetiously 'that only the aristocrats of the country clubs competed, that those who have most to learn from inter-club play contented themselves at home'. It was certainly surprising that Bunbury (which had won wide praise for the conduct of the South-West Championship) and Kalgoorlie had not entered teams. This situation compared unfavourably with the tally of 200 players representing 20 clubs who had just taken part in the Country Week cricket carnival. It also contrasted markedly with the resounding success of country tennis carnivals in the eastern States (*West Australian*, 21/3/1923, 9).

Advertisement (Source, The City Houses Night Tennis Association, Official Handbook, 1929/1930, 14)

The Carnival received considerable newspaper coverage (*West Australian* 22/3/1923, 23/3/1923 and 24/3/1923). Each tie consisted of three rubbers, two singles and one doubles. Each rubber was played on the basis of three advantage sets. Under these rules, Katanning's team members, Messrs Koehne and Taylor, won the tournament. However, neither reached the final of the singles championship which followed the teams event. The tournament was played on a knock-out basis and produced several close matches. But the easy manner in which E.O. Strang (Northam) defeated E.M. Ladyman the State junior champion from Carrolup (6/0, 6/2) was unexpected (*West Australian*, 22/3/1923, 8). Later, though, Ladyman did not miss his chance to begin imprinting his name in the annals of Western Australian tennis history. Widely known as 'Chappie', he won the country week men's singles titles in 1925 and 1926.

In keeping with one of the recommendations of a WALTA Country Week subcommittee, a conference was conducted at the end of the tournament. The expected credit balance did not eventuate, as the budget (reproduced below) was based on 15 clubs competing. The outlay for trophies, which often appeared disproportionately high in that era, was reduced by the generous donation of a Challenge Cup for the men's singles championship. Fortunately a Mr Martin Stott donated the perpetual trophy valued at £10/10/-

Country Week Tournament, 1923
Financial Aspect
(Say 15 Clubs Competing)

Revenue:		
Capitation fees from 15 Club	£15.15. 0	
Tournament Entrance Fees (doubles)	£ 7.10. 0	
Tournament (singles-20)	£ 5. 0. 0	
Sale of second-hand balls	£ 6. 0. 0	£34. 5. 0
Expenditure:		
Tennis Balls, 8 1/2 doz @ 27/- per doz	£11.10. 0	
Trophies	£11. 9. 0	
Printing and sundries	£5. 0. 0	£27.19. 0
CREDIT BALANCE		£ 6. 6. 0

F.W. Goldsmith for Sub Committee CWT

There was an inconclusive debate about the best time for the carnival. Some country delegates, ever conscious of the seasons, were prepared to promise that if the time was right, their clubs might be prepared to participate and affiliate. Over the next few years, there was a growth in the number of country affiliates. One delegate, Mr G.W. Lowe, was actually awarded a silver pencil 'as a small token of the Association's appreciation' for his efforts in enrolling 'associate' members (*WALTA Minutes*, 20/6/1924). In fact, by 31 December, 1927 there were 44 affiliate country clubs and only 13 affiliated metropolitan clubs. There were also ten affiliated branches (*WALTA Minutes*, 31/5/1928). Yet, despite the zeal of Goldsmith and backing by the Association, there was no corresponding expansion of the carnival. In 1926, a women's team event was added to the program but it was cancelled as only one team entered. By 1927, it was possible to complain how 'Country Week took 10 years or more of effort to establish and there are but 12 men's teams competing' (*West Australian*, 10/3/1927, 29). A further matter of disappointment was the decision by Goldsmith to move to Melbourne (*WALTA Minutes*, 6/7/1928).

Enid Morse, Inaugural Winner of Ladies'Country Week Singles 1927

One bright note in 1927 was the entry of 10 women's teams. Victory in the inaugural women's competition went to Katanning, with a narrow win over Beverley (*Western Mail*, 17/3/1927, 28). This was also the first occasion that a Women's Country Week singles championship was held. The winner, in a hard fought 6/4, 6/8, 6/2 final, was Enid Morse (Avon) from Mrs Edwards (Northam). Morse was the reigning State Junior Girls' Champion. In the absence of a donor, there was no perpetual trophy for her to receive. In 1931, the Association remedied this situation by donating a perpetual trophy for the 'Ladies Country Singles Championship'. In the interim, Morse made an impression in metropolitan tennis. Perhaps her best performance was that of reaching the 1930 State Open singles final. But winning Ladies' Country Week has never proved to be a stepping stone to the State Open Crown. Even Phyllis Richardson, the Albany champion, who won an exalted reputation in the 'bush' by winning six Country Week singles titles between 1928 and 1936, was unable to win the State Open. Early in her career, she reached the 1926 final, but was beaten 6/3, 6/2 by Mrs McBeth. Interestingly, Richardson's first Country Week title was achieved after a marathon encounter with Morse. The score (6/3, 1/6, 10/8) indicated just how evenly these players were matched in the early years of women's Country Week.

Another avenue of promotion for Country Week, again dating from 1927, was the City versus Country fixture. After being postponed because of rain, this inaugual contest resulted in wins for the City teams. In the men's division, a strong city combination led by Rice Gemmell, supported by H. Stapleton, K. Barker and R. Forsyth defeated the country team of H. Koehne, V. Halbert, M. Halbert and M. Adams by 10 sets 79 games to 3 sets 56 games. Koehne (Katanning) had won the 1927 Challenge Cup but the Halberts representing Cunderdin, broke Katanning's four-year mortgage of the team events trophy. At the Association's initiative the perpetual trophy became known as the F.S. Goldsmith Cup (*WALTA Minutes*, 30/3/1928).

In the women's fixture, also played at Kitchener Park, the score in favour of the City was 9 sets 75 games to 3 sets 56 games (*Western Mail*, 17/3/1927, 28). The City team included Mrs McBeth, winner of the State Open in 1924, 1925 and 1926, together with Miss Peter Smith who was destined in 1929 to gain the same honour. Leading juniors J. Duncan and L. Adrich were included in the team members. The Country team led by Enid Morse, included E. Townsend (Beverley), Mrs K. Edwards (Katanning) and B. Spencer, a member of the strong Northam side.

The schoolchildren's championship and schools' tennis.

Goldsmith's legacy was not restricted to the creation of Country Week. As a club captain at Subiaco, he promoted junior tennis and, not surprisingly, he was keen to enhance the breadth of the Slazenger Cup competition by including teams from country clubs and schools. This proposal presented many problems, but Goldsmith was also partly instrumental in establishing the school tennis tournament. In Victoria, for instance, a school boys and girls tournament had been conducted since 1908. On the opening day of this first championship in June 1923 a tennis columnist (*West Australian* 12/6/1923, 6) remarked:

> *Credit is due to Messrs F.S. Goldsmith and O.J. Negus, representatives of the Association for the work they have put into the organising of the fixture, the ultimate success of which now lies with Messrs E.C. Clarke (High School), S. Bradshaw (Modern School), Miss M. Lowe (Presbyterian Ladies College), to whom had been entrusted the job of putting onto court after school hours the matches necessary to determine six winners, three boys and three girls among the total of 161 entries.*

In the open singles there were 38 girls and 19 boys; for the 16 and under, 50 girls and 22 boys, and for the 14 and under, 21 girls and 11 boys. The girls applications came from Church of England Girls School (25); Presbyterian Ladies College (22); Sacred Heart High School (Highgate) (22); Modern School (14); Methodist Ladies' College (10); Perth College (8); and Girls High School, Claremont (8). The biggest entry for the boys events came from High (Hale) School (39); followed by Modern School (11), Scotch College (1) and Christ Church (1) (*West Australian* , 12/6/1923, 9). The ratio of 109 girls to 52 boys greatly surprised officials and it was hoped that this would foster a timely rejuvenation of the female support for the Slazenger Cup competition.

The bad weather provided some administrative headaches. As a consequence, the tournament was not completed until the 9 August, 1923. Importantly, though, the Association considered the event 'an unqualified success' and thereafter the tournament was placed on the calendar for each subsequent season. The winners (*WALTA Annual Report*, 1923/1924) were:

Open Championship: Girls - J. Nairn - Methodist Ladies College
Open Championship: Boys - W. Halliday - Perth Modern School
Under 16 Championship: Girls - J. Duncan - Presbyterian Ladies College
Under 16 Championship: Boys - H. V. Halbert - Perth High School
Under 16 Championship: Girls - F. Moir - Perth Modern School
Under 14 Championship: Boys - J. M. Noble - Perth High School

While the tournament was being conducted, there was a protracted debate at Association headquarters concerning the right of schools to affiliate. The position had been complicated by the decision of George Linwood in 1922 to allow schools to participate in the winter tournament junior series. At the time, this action was outside the rules of the Association's Constitution. But as Linwood was a great innovator and a persuasive advocate, his desire to help the juniors and broaden the base of tennis had prevailed (*West Australian* 23/7/1923, 10). Linwood, in conference with secondary school headmasters, had proposed an affiliation formula with a reduced capitation fee (*West Australian*, 16/5/1923, 6). Some club officials queried this idea and expressed concern that their club juniors might resign and play pennants with affiliated school teams. So the new secretary, E.J.T. Warren, the Treasurer, W.R. Corr and Alf Hedeman, the former champion player and now Vice-Chairman of the Council, had headed an investigation into the question. Pending the outcome, schools were temporarily denied the opportunity to compete in a junior pennant series held in the winter months. This meant that the only teams which participated in the 1923 series were South Perth, Kings Park, Claremont and University.

The Council finally resolved 'that any secondary or private school situated in the metropolitan area may become affiliated with the Association on such terms as the Council may from time to time determine' (*West Australian* 23/7/1923, 9). The school's affiliation fee was set at £2.2 and the capitation fee was to be one shilling, with a £5.5 ceiling. In the long run, however, the issue proved to be a storm in a teacup. Very few schools availed themselves of the option. It was consistent with 'broadening the base' but even by 1930 there were only four schools (St Mary's West Perth, Perth Boys School, Perth Modern School and Sacred Heart High School) registered in this category. Schools did not undermine the viability of junior pennants. Moreover, schools as well as clubs, retained the right to participate in the Slazenger Cup. The Association's Schoolchildren's Tournament was left open to all bona fide students, regardless of club membership. Nevertheless, the Council did pass a resolution to exclude business college and technical college students from eligibility (*WALTA Minutes*, 3/4/1925).

Some schools were fortunate to have on their staffs enthusiastic advocates of tennis. One of the most notable of these was Miss Mollie Lowe at Presbyterian Ladies College (PLC.). Her dedication to the concept of the Schoolchildren's Championship was mentioned in the 1924 Annual Report (*WALTA Annual Report*, 1923/1924, 2). As a coach Lowe was instrumental in PLC recording a series of splendid successive Slazenger Cup victories between 1920 and 1924. Just a couple of months after her resignation to move interstate, a member of her 1921 team, Margaret Officer, won the Association's 1925 State Open. Fittingly, the Association Council paid tribute to Lowe's 'tireless' contribution. At the same farewell evening, the Association decided, for the first time, to provide the same range of events for girls as boys at the State Open championship (*Western Mail*, 29/10/1925, 23).

When Mollie Lowe left the State, it was obvious her record of success at PLC was going to be difficult to surpass. However, at Sacred Heart Highgate the call of the racquet was being answered by the unassuming Sister Clements. She encouraged her students to play serious tennis (interview with Molly McGrath, 29/5/1989) as the church's tangible support for the family game of tennis had to be converted to results. Sister Clements was perhaps fortunate to have her dedication administratively supported by the well known Mrs Gilchrist who was not so much a coach as a manager for the girls. With the blessing of Sister Clements, she organised the girls for regular practice, tournament play, and Slazenger Cup campaigns. Sacred Heart recorded a remarkable sequence of 13 successive Slazenger Cup victories from 1928 to 1940. In this period it was claimed that 90 per cent of all top women players attended the school. In the 1933 season, Sacred Heart even fielded a team in the Ladies' 'A' grade pennant competition. Pride of place went to Molly McGrath, who became a legend in the 1930s with the dominance of championship events in Western Australia. Myrtle Herbert (1934) and Jean Glover (1935) were others from Sister Clement's school who went on to win State Open championships. Herbert was to share a record seven women's doubles titles at the Open.

The 'Call of the Racquet' was answered by many unsung heroes in schools and clubs. Schemes for junior promotion were often under discussion: in February 1925, E.S. Clark submitted details of a scheme for the coaching of juniors which was based on that operative in South Australia. Clark, along with other prominent WALTA identities Gilchrist, Smith, Mursell and Brearley were appointed to assist in the evaluation (*WALTA Minutes* 27/2/1925). One rule change provided that, 'any person who is a beginner at Lawn Tennis and who wishes to obtain practice with a view to qualifying for entry to a club, may be elected by the Council, on application, as a Playing Association Member, with the right to use the Courts and Pavilion on conditions approved by the Council' (*WALTA Minutes*, 4/2/1927). No master plan emerged but in 1927 one source claimed, 'the Association does all within the power of any control body to bring the standard of ... play into line with that of the eastern states' (*Western Mail*, 3/3/1927, 27). At the same time there was special praise for the support provided for juniors at the Claremont Club. It was said that Vernon Mursell and Rice Gemmell played 'week in and week out' with the young players. Their efforts had contributed to the emergence of several promising players including Cec Lamb and the Camm brothers. Also at Kings Park the development of juniors was 'given pride of place in its general progressive policy'. Here the future champions were thought to be Ron Ford and Bill Halliday with good prospects expected for Tom Scaddan and Harry Stapledon.

Sacred Heart Slazenger Cup Winning Team, 1928 and 1929
Back: Molly McGrath (King), Mrs Gilchrist (Sport's Mistress), Rene Gray (Coach)
Front: May McCutcheon and Kath [illegible].

In 1924, an interstate competition for teams of up to four boys under 21 years of age was established, following the donation to the LTAA of a perpetual trophy by Richard (later Sir Richard) Linton of Melbourne. Held in conjunction with the Australian Championships, the tournament was first played under a knock-out system. Under the rules governing the competition, there was the distinct possibility of a team being defeated in the first round. In 1930, largely at the insistence of Western Australia (*WALTA Minutes*, 19/3/1929), the rules were altered to provide that in future each state should play every other state in a round robin. Thereafter, state representatives had to hope for a good performance in the Australian championship. It was thus left to the State Selection Committee to decide if it was productive to send a team to the Linton Cup and Australian Championships.

The Western Australian Association decided to send a team to the inaugural Linton Cup, held in Melbourne in mid-January 1924. The team members were E.M. Ladyman and W.M. Cleland. Both had dominated the boys junior championship events in the early 1920s. Cleland it will be remembered, was also a member of the first senior team that had played in Adelaide in 1921. Ladyman, too, was mentioned making his mark in Country Week. The boys were accompanied to Melbourne by seniors R. Phillips and C.L. Treloar. As indicated in the Association's records (*WALTA Annual Report*, 1923/24, 2), 'it was not expected that our representatives would reach the finals of any of the events, but we have every reason to be satisfied with their standard of play throughout'.

The financial strain caused by sending both junior and senior players away to the Linton Cup and Australian Championships was under regular review. To the Association's credit it sought the introduction of an equivalent national junior series for girls (*WALTA Minutes*, 14/2/1931). In some quarters, though, there gradually developed the view that too much was being done for juniors. One who argued this line was the popular Alf Hedeman. Since curtailing his championship play, Hedeman had held several executive positions at the Association and the Kings Park club, In 1924, he was honoured with Association life membership (*WALTA Minutes*, 20/6/1924). As Hedeman had also achieved a creditable record in surf life saving administration (Jaggard, 1984, 19-20, 89) his voice was respected. At one meeting he warned the Council 'much harm was being done by newspapers writing up juniors of all ages and he thought an alteration should be made in this connection' (*WALTA Minutes*, 15/1/1929). Later Hedeman made an assessment of the junior programs of the 1920s when he stated (*WALTA Minutes*, 11/12/1931):

> *there had been too much fostering of juniors in the last ten years and that the system in practice was one of the causes of the low standard ... juniors should be left more to their own resources and make good in their clubs first.*

Significantly, on the same occasion Vernon Mursell, a leading contributor to junior development and future president contended that after the Linton Cup juniors 'come back with swollen heads and their play went to pieces in almost every case'. At the annual general meeting in 1930, after claiming there were too many tournaments, the President S.J. McGibbon, moved a motion 'that once a junior had won a junior event he [or she] should not be permitted to play again as a junior' (*WALTA Minutes*, 30/5/1930).

The debate over junior promotion was clouded by a lack of consensus about what constituted a junior. In 1927, the Association had opted for 19 years as the maximum age. This was one year older than the British standard and two years above that accepted by the main tennis body in the United States. However, in 1929, the LTAA (after surveying its state affiliates) changed its rules so that 'under 21 years be recognised for all junior events throughout the Commonwealth' (*Sunday Times*, 23/6/1929, 44). In choosing to comply with the resolution the Association's Executive, which had come into existence with the alterations to the Constitution in 1928, found itself entangled in the political issues of the day. The *Sunday Times* newspaper, secessionist in its editorial policy, regarded the decision as an unacceptable instance of central control by the LTAA. The resolution had ignored how Jack Crawford had just returned from an overseas tour as a member of the Australian Davis Cup team and then entered for the Australian Junior Championship. Crawford it was claimed had, 'won it in a walk so discouraging every bona fide junior in the Commonwealth' (*Sunday Times*, 30/6/1929, 44).

King's Park

The stance of the *Sunday Times* was keenly debated (*WALTA Minutes*, 9/7/1929 and 12/7/1929). Apart from attacking the raising of the junior age limit, the newspaper had queried whether sufficient delegates had been present to make the decision binding. Even more serious was the assertion of discontent about the outcome of the elections to the new Executive. The *Sunday Times* columnist stated (23/6/1929, 44):

> *Nor was the Council any happier with its election of association officials. Of nine officials with seats on the executive eight are prominent members of the Kings Park Club ... It seems anomalous that with 90 constituent bodies represented on the council eight-ninths of the executive officers should be chosen from one club. Yet it is undeniable that perhaps seven-eighths of the Kings Park men elected fully justify their election, while three of them, namely the president of the association, the hon. treasurer, and the secretary, may be said to grace the positions they occupy. The difficulty in securing wider representation in the list of officers lies with the constitution of the council, from which the officers are drawn. That body is far too cumbersome and, worse still, too fluid,*

> *with the result that at almost every meeting there are to be found voting delegates who know nothing of what has gone before and who, probably lacking real interest in the affairs of the association, will not attend again.*

In September, 1927 (*WALTA Minutes*, 27/9/1929) the Association informed the LTAA that there were 4,644 members of affiliated clubs and associations in the State. It was conceded there were still many clubs outside its ambit but the decision of the growing Catholic Tennis Association to affiliate was most welcome (*WALTA Minutes*, 6/7/1927). In terms of clubs and membership the Association was now a far cry from being a 'King's Park fiefdom'. Moreover the Association had responded to the expansion of the tennis base by creating an Executive which was separate from the Council of delegates. The necessary amendments to the Constitution were formally endorsed in October 1928 (*WALTA Minutes*, 26/10/1928). This was expected to improve organisational efficiency. What was not expected was the claim of King's Park domination.

Many of the major tournaments and exhibition matches were being played on the scenic King's Park courts, but this does not fully explain why WALTA, even with its predominantly King's Park Executive, was being chastised as a creature of the King's Park establishment. One theory concerns the administrative style of McGibbon, the WALTA President who was also very prominent in the King's Park hierarchy. No one doubted McGibbon's commitment to tennis and his role in broadening the base of the Association. He had been awarded life membership but he tended to be overbearing in the performance of his duties. One leading player likened him to 'God'. With McGibbon flanked by an Executive team from the Kings Park club, the domination thesis can be comprehended, although not necessarily accepted.

Sir Walter Kingsmill, President 1911-12, 1914-1922 Life Member 1922

McGibbon had been President since 1924. Two King's Park members, E.C. Riddle (1923) and A.G. Rains (1924) had preceded him. Rains had briefly held the same office in 1913 but, despite reports to the contrary, had never been made a life member (see *WALTA Minutes*, 15/4/1936, 20/5/1936 and 10/6/1936). Neither Rains nor Riddle, while capable officials, (see comments in the *West Australian* 19/6/1923, 6) held the Presidency for sufficient time to have their performance accurately judged. One President (apart from McGibbon) who satisfied the 'longevity' condition was Walter Kingsmill. He was in the public eye as a parliamentarian and the minutes document the highs and lows of his political career (*WALTA Minutes*, 8/9/1919, 6/5/1922 and 12/2/1922). In fact Kingsmill stepped down from the Presidency after he lost his seat in the Legislative Council and gained election to the Senate. As the Commonwealth Parliament in those days sat in Melbourne, Kingsmill offered to further assist the Association by making representation to the LTAA which had moved its headquarters to Melbourne. A prominent historian, Geoffrey Bolton (1983, 601) claimed that 'contemporaries considered Kingsmill too gentlemanly and easy going for the cut and thrust of party politics, and his administrative style lacked drive'. It is clear, too, Kingsmill had a very different presidential style to McGibbon. Nor was he not so closely identified with King's Park. Like McGibbon, he was made a life member (*WALTA Minutes*, 8/6/1923).

During the 'Call of the Racquet' period, two other officials, E.J.T. Warren (20/11/1925) and S.S. Glyde (6/7/1928) were honoured with life membership. Warren was known as an energetic secretary. Significantly, in 1925 the Council had decided to pay the secretary £100 per year (*WALTA Minutes*, 3/5/1925). In the same year Basil Murray, a former leading administrator, died. He had won praise for exercising his commercial skills for the benefit

The S.S. Glyde Perpetual Challenge Cup (Men's Open Doubles)

The George Linwood Perpetual Challenge Cup (Men's Open Singles)

of the Association when it was experiencing severe financial difficulties (see *WALTA Minutes*, 15/5/1925 and *Western Mail* 30/4/1925, 23).

Samuel Stedman Glyde was a stalwart of the Claremont club, and like Murray, had been Chairman of the Council. Again, like Murray, he was also an innovative thinker, particularly where cost cutting was being considered. He once proposed that the preliminary rounds of the Australian Open be played in the various State capitals (*WALTA Minutes*, 5/7/1930). On another occasion he vehemently opposed an increase in travel subsidy for selected interstate representatives (*WALTA Minutes*, 13/2/1931). As manager of a shipping company, Glyde was not afraid of work but, in the name of efficiency, he thought the WALTA Council should go into recess during the winter months. Before he retired from the Executive in May 1941, he had served on a range of committees. By this time he had become concerned about the commercialism that had crept into tennis. He wanted it to remain an amateur game. As a reflection of Glyde's commitment to the spirit of tennis, he once sought to have the verse from Kipling's poem, which is engraved above the player's entrance at sacred Wimbledon, similarly placed at the Association Courts in Kitchener Park. His motion was lost (*WALTA Minutes*, 23/10/1925) but Kipling's poetry eventually stood for many years on the archway at the Kings Park Club. Players could read:

IF YOU CAN MEET WITH TRIUMPH AND DISASTER AND
TREAT THOSE TWO IMPOSTERS JUST THE SAME

Champions

Glyde was a team man with a special interest in doubles. Fittingly, the State Doubles Open Championship trophy is now known as the S. S. Glyde Memorial Perpetual Challenge Cup. As a regular tournament committee member, Glyde had seen all the champions. In this period Rice Gemmell, until he relinquished his amateur status to conduct coaching duties in May 1927, had continued to dominate the men's singles championship. His sequence of victories in the State Open had given him permanent possession of the E.F. Parker Memorial Cup. In its place the Association had decided in 1924 to designate the State Open Men's Championship trophy as the George A. Linwood memorial. A fund established for the purpose was generously subscribed. Later, a miniature of the trophy was sent to Linwood's mother, who lived in Tasmania (*WALTA Annual Report*, 1928-1929, 6).

In the women's events, the departure of Mrs Mather in 1923 had left a vacuum. Until the emergence of Molly McGrath later in the decade, one of the most notable performers was Mrs McBeth (née Wedin) from the Fremantle Club. One reason why McBeth did not have the same reputation as Mather was her tendency to lose unexpectedly pennant matches in the Ladies' 'A' grade competition. Nevertheless, McBeth had the distinction of playing in four consecutive finals between 1924 and 1927. The first victory, under her maiden name, was over State player, Miss Whitfield, in 1924. McBeth's other title came in 1926 with an easy win over the rising Albany star, Miss Richardson. Unfortunately photographs of these champions are difficult to procure. This is mentioned in the context of an Association resolution passed in 1926 which indicated the 'Executive were empowered to take such steps as they thought necessary to obtain photographs of past champions and erect an honour board at the pavilion' (*WALTA Minutes*, 23/10/1926).

By 1927 no photographic collection had been acquired nor honour board procured. The favourite for the title in that year had been the experienced

Loton Park Suburban Tournament

Mrs McBeth. However, the victor was the Goldfields veteran Marion Barker After McBeth had won the first set at 6/3 Barker, at 38 years of age, staged one of the great fightbacks in the history of the Open. She won a keenly fought second set 7/5 and then easily took command in the third to win the set to love. After moving to Coolgardie at the tender age of 12 years, Marion Barker became a formidable country player reaching the State's top ten in her twilight years (*Westennis*, February 1992, 40).

One Council resolution that was acted upon involved State rankings (*WALTA Minutes*, 5/12/1924). Performances in the State Open Championship were of crucial importance and the LTAA had requested all State bodies to undertake this exercise. The first rankings for Western Australia, which included men and women, were published in 1926 (*West Australian*, 7/1/1926, 7):

	Men		Women
1.	R.T.H. Gemmell (Claremont)	1.	Miss M. Officer (Wanda)
2.	C.L. Treloar (Wanda)	2.	Mrs McBeth (Fremantle)
3.	R.W. Phillips (King's Park)	3.	Miss P. Richardson (Albany)
4.	R. Ford (King's Park)	4.	Miss M Barker (Fremantle)
5.	C.L. Evans (King's Park)	5.	Miss Whitfield (Wanda)
6.	N. Brearley (King's Park)	6.	Miss McDougall (Wanda)
7.	E.W. Sturm (Wanda)	7.	Miss Fraser (Loton Park)
8.	C. Lamb (Claremont)	8.	Miss P. Murray (Wanda)
9.	F. Edmondson (King's Park)	9.	Miss E. Morse (Avon)
10.	H.D. Stapledon (King's Park)	10.	Miss J. Duncan (Wanda)

As mentioned the definitions of 'junior' posed difficulties for the ranking exercise at both the WALTA and the LTAA. In Western Australia junior girls had only just been provided with a range of tournament opportunities. Therefore ranking was not attempted. The junior boys list was headed by the formidable Ron Ford from the King's Park Club. Others in order were; 2-C. Lamb (Claremont); 3-W. Halliday (King's Park); 4-J. Pilgrim (Kings Park); 5-G. Parker (North Perth); 6-H. Jacoby (Subiaco); 7-T. Scaddan (Kings Park); 8-A. Lang (Subiaco); 9-D. Law (Kings Park); 10-A.L. Blue (Loton Park). These inaugural ranking lists had been made available to the press but they were not recorded in the minutes. It was not until 1933 that the practice of publishing them in the annual report was adopted (see Appendix 10).

One major event which exemplified the 'Call of the Racquet' was the visit of the French team to Perth in the late summer of 1928. Since the Great War, Western Australians had been reading about the mercurial Suzanne Lenglen and the 'Four Musketeers', Henri Cochet, Toto Brugnon, Renè Lacoste and Jean Borotra. Much to the chagrin of the Australian sporting public the French had begun to dominate the Davis Cup competition. Their record in Grand Slam singles events was also formidable. In 1926 and 1927 the 'Four Musketeers' won the French, Wimbledon and United States singles. In early 1928, Borotra won the Australian singles title.

So the French were 'on top of the world' when they came to Perth. Moreover, apart from their tennis ability, both individually and as a team they were charismatic and exuded charm. They were regarded as a great advertisement for tennis (Egan, 1984, 37). Perhaps some of the glamour of the occasion was dulled by the absence of Lacoste and Cochet. However, this was compensated for with the presence of Australia's Davis Cup players Gerald Paterson, Harry Hopman and Jack Crawford. Apart from the international fixture, a series of women's exhibition matches were also staged. The Australian women's team of Meryl O'Hara Wood, Louise Bickerton, Daphne Akhurst and Esna Boyd was on its way to South Africa and Europe. Boyd had been run-

Kitchener Park Association Courts Stand for the 1921 Australasian Open Championship (Courtesy The West Australian)

King's Park Australia versus France 1928

ner-up for the first five Australian Opens, before claiming the 1927 title. Akhurst had done much 'to enhance the status of women's tennis in the 1920s by the exuberant and athletic manner of her play' (Johnson, 1985, 78). Then ranked number three in the world, she won the Open title in 1925, 1926, 1928 and 1930, before dying tragically in 1933.

One newspaper, citing Norman Brookes, described the matches as 'perhaps the best tennis ever seen in Australia' (*Daily News*, 12/3/1928, 6). The men's international was a close contest, with France 5 rubbers, 13 sets, 116 games defeating Australia 4 rubbers, 11 sets and 110 games. Harry Hopman was outstanding but Gerald Patterson, who complained that he had had too much tennis and travelling of late, was below form (*Daily News*, 12/3/1928, 6). The women's matches were also keenly contested. The last match on the three-day program was designated as the final of the Melbourne Cricket Club Ladies Doubles (after its postponement in Melbourne from the previous weekend). It provided a fitting climax with Akhurst and Bickerton defeating Boyd and O'Hara Wood 6/2, 10/8.

The Association's management of the fixtures was warmly praised. Members of the LTAA Executive, distinguished by the presence of Norman Brookes, suggested that Western Australia should apply to hold the Australian Championship in Perth once every six years (*WALTA Minutes*, 17/5/1928). It was also mentioned that Western Australia should consider shifting the date of its Open to October. The alteration to the national schedule would enable many leading Australian (and perhaps international players) to compete.

These recommendations were based on the assumption that Kings Park would be the venue. The grass courts were of high quality and the central location was ideal for visiting players and spectators. So, while the French visit was a great success, and provided a valuable injection of funds, it had left the WALTA Executive with a terrible 'hangover'. The main cause of the latter was not the numerous civic receptions held to entertain the French players, the Australian Davis Cup team and Australian women's team, but the question of what to do with the Association Courts at Kitchener Park.

Chapter Thirteen

'THE GOLDEN AGE', COURTS, CONSTITUTIONS AND CHAMPIONS

GIANNI Clerici, in his classic study *The Ultimate Tennis Book* (1975) depicted the late 1920s, and the years before the Second World War, as 'The Golden Age of Tennis'. He wrote of the 'divine' Suzanne Lenglen, the immortal 'Big Bill' Tilden, the Four Musketeers, Fred Perry, Queen Helen Wills and Donald Budge. Wimbledon had grown in status, there was keen interest in the Davis Cup, and the major national championships, the Wimbledon, French, United States and Australian Open began to be known collectively as the 'Grand Slam'. The tradition of the Grand Slam had begun in 1933 when Australia's Jack Crawford was going for his fourth major title of the year, the United States national championships at Forrest Hills. A sport's columnist in the *New York Times* (cited in Blacker, 1993, 425) wrote: '... if Crawford wins, that would be something like scoring a grand slam on the courts ...' Unfortunately, Crawford faltered at Forrest Hills and the Grand Slam was forgotten until 1938 when the great American player, Donald Budge, became the first player to achieve the feat in a calendar year.

Jack Crawford was the greatest of Australia's players between the wars. In Davis Cup competition he played in a record 58 matches, winning 36 between 1928 and 1937. His fluent, easy style set the fashion for a whole generation. When Crawford played in Perth in 1932, the occasion created intense public interest. Tennis, though, in this era was given wide publicity in Western Australia. The newspapers printed detailed accounts of local tournaments and club championships which were also the major source of revenue. The WALTA was still keen to be part of the international action, but it had to resolve one of its great conundrums – what to do with Kitchener Park in Subiaco.

Courts

Early in Sinclair McGibbon's long term as President (1925 to 1938), the Executive conducted preliminary negotiations with the Perth Road Board for the allotment of land for courts. The tract was called 'The Mt Lawley Reserve'. At a conference with other sporting bodies it was suggested that the area allocated would permit 60 or 70 courts to be laid. The Association was required to spend £500 per year for the first 10 years, with a total of £10,000 being required over 50 years, the minimum term for which the lease would be granted (*WALTA Minutes*, 27/2/1925). Secretary Eric Warren was of the opinion that 10 or 12 courts would be self-supporting from hire fees. However, he did not make any commitment on the Association's behalf. He was lukewarm to the proposal as he considered that dialogue should be undertaken with the King's Park Board to ascertain what prospects there were for obtaining grounds in King's Park (*WALTA Minutes*, 19/3/1926).

Predicably, nothing came of the 'Mt Lawley Reserve' or Warren's preferred King's Park proposal. Not even during Kingsmill's term as President, although he was also a member of the King's Park Board at this time, did the dream of an Association tennis centre at the park become a reality. So the Association reverted to considering the feasibility of alterations at Kitchener Park (*WALTA Minutes*, 30/7/1926). An architect's advice was sought on improving the pavilion and entrance to the grounds. Unfortunately, the costs of improvements would have placed undue strain on finances. The Association was also frustrated by reports that the Kitchener Park groundsman was not carrying out the instructions of either the Grounds-sub committee Chairman (S.S. Glyde) or his deputy G.W. Lowe (*WALTA Minutes*, 1/4/1927). Another setback resulted from the Subiaco City Council's ratepayer referendum on the subject of sport on Sundays. It was a close vote, but the outcome continued to deny Sunday play at Kitchener Park (*WALTA Minutes*, 10/6/1927). With these adverse developments, coupled to an inability to play international and interstate matches at Kitchener Park, McGibbon decided to force the issue. At the annual general meeting on 31 May, 1928, he proposed to the incoming Council:

(i) That a request be made to the Subiaco Council to grant an extension of the present lease of the Association grounds at Subiaco for a further period of 30 years.

(ii) That an effort be made to raise £6000 by debentures carrying 8% interest per annum plus 4% renting fund redemption.

(iii) That seats in a new Pavilion Grandstand be sold at £10 each for a period of 30 years with the right of transfer.

Initially, the influential Glyde questioned whether the resolution was strictly in order, as no notice of motion had been given. However, as other delegates thought the matter should be given immediate attention, the resolution was debated (*WALTA Minutes*, 31/5/1928). After the next Council meeting, a circular was sent to all affiliated clubs and associations seeking their views on the McGibbon proposals. Clubs were also asked if they were prepared to pay a capitation fee (per membership) of £1/5/- to fund the venture. At the same meeting a sub-committee under chairmanship of Vernon Mursell was appointed to revise the rules of the Association (*WALTA Minutes*, 8/6/1928).

The Council found that an overwhelming majority of the clubs were opposed to the levy. They considered the expenditure on the Kitchener Park facilities to be unwarranted. This was the tenor of the report presented by Mursell's sub-committee to a specially convened meeting of the Council. As each of the recommendations was accompanied by supporting arguments, the report led to debate about a range of concerns (*WALTA Minutes*, 24/7/1928). The sub-committee had unanimously agreed that:

(i) The Association abandon the Kitchener Park courts and the equipment it presently controlled.

(ii) International and interstate matches, the Australian Championships and the State Championships be allocated to the most suitable clubs capable of controlling the event.

(iii) Interclub pennant matches be played on club courts with the 'official' pennants being restricted to Mens' and Ladies' A Grade.

(iv) For Country Week, Slazenger Cup, and Schools' Tournaments courts be hired for these events.

At a special meeting to discuss the recommendations, the scope of the pennant competition was expanded to include lower grades and juniors. In essence, though, the committee's conclusions were adopted. In accordance with the decision of Council the grounds of the Association were 'handed over' to the Subiaco Municipal Council on 20 September, 1928 (*WALTA Annual Report*, 1928/1929). An agreement with the Council was ratified, with Rice Gemmell, the former champion player, hiring the Kitchener Park facility for coaching purposes. This action relieved the Association of an estimated annual loss on ground maintenance of some £300 (*Report*, 18/7/1928). No reduction in affiliation fees was proposed, but the report was prefaced with the suggestion that the capitation fee of four shillings and sixpence per member payable by metropolitan clubs be abolished (*WALTA Annual Report*, 1928-1929). Officials had been concerned for several years about the small number of affiliated clubs in the metropolitan area. Clubs such as Hensman, West Subiaco, Maylands, East Perth, Bassendean, Cottesloe and some branch associations had made it clear they considered the cost of affiliation, when coupled with the capitation fee, to be too high (*WALTA Minutes*, 28/7/1928).

As a result of the abolition of the capitation fee, there was a spate of applications for affiliation by metropolitan clubs. By the time the 1930 annual report was tabled, metropolitan affiliates had risen from 13 to 25. In terms of the Association's future, one of the most significant additions was the Hensman Park Club (*WALTA Minutes*, 5/10/1928). The immediate impact was to increase representation in the metropolitan 'south of the river' zone rather than to significantly improve the affiliation fee revenue. As an examination of the accounts for the year ended 31 March, 1930 reveals, affiliation fees were less significant as a revenue source than tournament fees. However, the accounts indicate the comparatively small scale of the Association's operations although it was broadening its base. With the onset of the Depression, it was important to note that, despite the small excess of expenditure over revenue, the Association (without the Kitchener Park lease) was now financially viable.

THE WESTERN AUSTRALIAN LAWN TENNIS ASSOCIATION INCORPORATED
REVENUE & EXPENDITURE ACCOUNT FOR THE YEAR ENDED 31st March, 1930.

Dr.

	£		£
To Country Week	13.12.11	By Affiliation Fees	61. 9. 0
To Coaching Scheme	31. 2. 6	By Association Membership Fees	2.12. 0
To General Expenses	38.18. 8	By Tournament Fees	191. 3. 2
To Insurance	2.15. 0	By Pennant Competition	6. 3. 0
To Postages	21.14. 5	By Slazenger Cup Competition	5.17. 7
To Printing & Stationery	14.18. 2	By Schools Tournament	6. 8
To Salary: Secretary	200. 0. 0	By Great Southern Junior Competition	2.17.9
To Telephone Charges	8. 5. 0		
To Expenses: Eastern State Team	£44.11. 6.	By Davis Cup Exhibition Match	88. 8. 9
		By Interest	3. 8. 2
		By Balance: being excess of Expenditure over Revenue for year ended 31 March 1930	£13.16.1.
	£376. 2. 2.		£376.2.2.

THE WESTERN AUSTRALIAN LAWN TENNIS ASSOCIATION INCORPORATED
BALANCE SHEET AT 31st MARCH, 1930

	£		£
To Sundry Creditors	41.14 4	By Sundry Debtors	75.16.3
To Debentures	19. 0. 0	By Subiaco Municipal Council	400. 0. 0
		By Miniature Cups	20.11. 9
To Add Interest accrued	9.10. 0	By Fixed Deposit (Bank of Aust'asia)	200. 0. 0
To Interstate Visits Fund	96.11. 3	By Cash at Government Savings Bank 96/11/3	
To Revenue & Expenditure Account Balance at 31 March, 1929 260. 8. 5	803.16.11	Cash at Bank of Australasia	163.17.2
Less Excess of Expenditure over Revenue for the year ended 31 March, 1930 £956.16. 5	13.16. 1		£790. 0.10

Audited and found correct
(Sgd.) C.H. KING) Chartered Accountants (Aust.)
W.F. BROADHURST) HON AUDITORS.

There was, however, still evidence of an undercurrent of unease concerning the Association's pivotal position in tennis. During the 'great debate of twenty eight' some clubs had spoken of the Association as a 'rival' organisation seeking to run revenue-raising tournaments rather than coordinating and developing tennis (*WALTA Minutes*, 28/7/1928). After some years of ferment Keith Barker, the well known King's Park member, told the 1932 annual general meeting (*WALTA Minutes*, 30/5/1932) 'the Association had too much power and should not be a controlling body'. After detailing the administrative changes he considered desirable, the meeting responded by establishing an influential committee to revise and simplify the Constitution and cut costs.

After a great deal of deliberation, the sub-committee presented a report and draft recommendations to the Executive, with a request that a special general meeting be called as early as possible to deal with the matter. This was duly held on 20 January, 1933. The recommendations were not adopted and a second sub-committee was appointed to act in concert with the Rules Revision Committee. The special general meeting also directed the sub-committee to draw up amendments on the basis that the Executive be subservient to the council of delegates and that the lowest possible affiliation fees be a major objective (*WALTA Annual Report*, 1932/33).

At a special general meeting held on 25 May, 1933, it was revealed that 11 of the 12 members of the Rules Revision Sub Committee (under the chairmanship of Vernon Mursell) had unanimously agreed to a new draft constitution. But a challenge came from Mr Herbert, the author of the minority report who favoured:

(i) the retention of the annual general meeting of Association members rather than the proposed annual meeting of delegates. The annual meeting provided the only opportunity for an expression of views of the 'ordinary' member on matters affecting his or her interests.

(ii) the abolition of voting powers for delegates representing country clubs. This loss of voting power would not destroy the interests of country clubs and associations as only a small proportion of such bodies have considered it desirable to be retained on the Council in the past.

(iii) the provision of a maximum affiliation fee for district associations.

Mr J.L. Walker, a future President of the Association and delegate from Mt Lawley, strongly defended the majority report. He was particularly critical of Herbert's stance on country club representation. Nevertheless, the latter's views received some support, particularly that considering the retention of the annual general meeting of members (rather than delegates). He considered insufficient attention had been given to reducing the cost of affiliation, with the result that there were hundreds of unaffiliated players in the metropolitan area alone (*WALTA Minutes*, 26/5/1933). Finally, though, it was the majority report, with some concessions to Herbert's maximum fee proposition, that received the necessary two-thirds majority and allowed the revised constitution to be accepted. It came into force on 1 April, 1934 and remained the framework for the Association's operations for many years.

Champions

With Western Australians in all walks of life experiencing hard economic times and voting in 1933 to secede from the Commonwealth, it was not surprising that costs and constitutional matters were central concerns at Association headquarters. However, despite the Depression, many champion players from the eastern states and overseas visited Perth. Local leading players, especially Ron Ford and Molly McGrath, also helped maintain public interest in tennis. The Association had found that the top tennis could still be marketed. Following the great success of the visit by the French team in 1928, negotiations took place for teams from both South Africa and the British Isles to tour Australia. However, a few weeks before the scheduled arrival of the South Africans in November 1929, a cable was received postponing the tour for financial reasons (*WALTA Annual Report*, 1928/1929, 3).

Ron Ford, champion in the 'golden age of tennis', the first Western Australian based player to represent Australia

Earlier in 1929 the tour by the British Isles team had come to fruition, but this was one international match that had not lived up to expectations. The English team of Dr J.C. Gregory, I.G. Collins, H.W. 'Bunny' Austin and an injured Mr Higgs contained no prominent names. This problem was exacerbated by the decision of the LTAA not to send any of the top bracket players to Perth. The Western Australian Association protested with vigour, but no Davis Cup players arrived and instead the LTAA decided to give local champion Ron Ford the opportunity to represent Australia. The other Australians were Dr Hone and Ernie Rowe.

The English team proved far too strong. A similar result followed when the English played a hastily arranged exhibition match against an Australian representative side which included Dr Hone and Western Australians Ron Ford, Harry Jacoby, Frank Edmondson and Cec Lamb. At the request of the LTAA, expenditure for the visit was kept at a minimum and not surprisingly only a small profit was made. In contrast to the French visit only a year earlier, there was no official entertainment except a welcoming party at the Palace Hotel. Fortunately, President McGibbon was able to persuade some Association members to organise a surf party and provide cars for the visitors (*WALTA Annual Report*, 1928/1929)

Ron Ford had thus gained the distinction of being the first Western Australian based competitor to play for Australia. At the time Ford was the top ranked player in the State. In fact, he held the Association's number one ranking between 1927 and 1934. Many regard his straight set win over Harry Hopman at Kooyong in 1927 as the highlight of his career. He was renowned for his speed around the court and great persistence. Proof of this attribute is shown statistically by his two State Open title wins. Both victories, in 1927 and 1930, were five-set encounters. In the first he defeated the unlucky Clarry Treloar 6/3, 4/6, 4/6, 7/5, 6/0. On the second occasion he defeated one of his most feared opponents, the erratic but sometimes brilliant, Max Carpenter 7/5, 4/6, 11/9, 4/6, 6/3. Ron Ford would probably have won more State Opens but, at the peak of his career, the LTAA was subsidising the visits of leading players to Perth. As a consequence, Bob Schlesinger won the

Open in 1928, Harry Hopman in 1931, Adrian Quist in 1932 and Reg Ewin in 1933. Nevertheless, on the local scene, Ford was highly formidable - although not unbeatable. In city, suburban and country tournaments he built up an impressive record, gaining over 100 titles. Nor should it be overlooked that in 1928, when Ford was at his best, there was no official State Open as the WALTA did not designate any tournament as the State Championship. Remarkably, Ron Ford also won the State Badminton Singles title on three occasions between 1931 and 1933.

Ford twice travelled overseas on 'official' tennis tours. In 1928, the Malay Tennis Association had requested the WALTA to send a team to enter the Malay Championship and tour the Malay states. A number of players were mentioned in the request but, for various reasons, they were unable to accept. Ultimately, at the expense of the Malay Association, Ford was engaged to play exhibition matches from June to August. His home was actually Parliament House as his father, Edward Ford, also a prominent sportsman, was the House Controller. This enabled Ron to practice regularly at the court in the parliament grounds and the nearby Subiaco and King's Park Clubs. Another of his favourite practice spots was a private court in Mount Lawley owned by the parliamentarian (and one-time premier) John Scaddan. Scaddan's son, Tom, one of Ford's friends, was a leading junior in the late 1920s.

Stan Mortimer, hard working WALTA Secretary

Ford's second 'official' overseas tour was more controversial. In response to an invitation from the All India Lawn Tennis Association, he was appointed Captain/Manager of a team to play in venues such as Colombo, Calcutta and Madras. Other members of the party were the leading players Harry Jacoby, W. F. 'Chum' Stephen and Gordon Davis. As the team was absent during the State Open in December 1933, there was criticism that the standard of this event had been lowered due to the Association's decision to sanction the India trip. Fortunately, there was some compensation when 'bad boy' Max Carpenter narrowly defeated Don Harris 6/0, 3/6, 6/2, 8/10, 6/2 in a great men's final. The women's final was also keenly fought, Molly McGrath beating Myrtle Herbert 8/6, 6/0.

During the State Open sharp criticism appeared in the press concerning the poor standard displayed by the Western Australians on the sub-continent. This drew an immediate response from hard working secretary Stan Mortimer at the WALTA headquaters. Mortimer declared (*West Australian*, 30/12/1933, 10):

> *I cannot believe that the cablegram in The West Australian this morning expresses the attitude of the All India Tennis Association in view of the fact that we were careful to ensure that the association was under no illusion as to the standard of play in this State ... it was emphasised that our men could not be classed with internationally famous players.*

Upon his return, Ford was quoted as admitting that due to the different surfaces and light his players were some 25 per cent below their form (*Ford File*). Yet officials of the All India Tennis Association sought to prolong the tour by two weeks and there were some good performances by each of the players (*Ford File*). In India, though, some of the criticism persisted. Madan Mohan, the Cambridge and Indian Davis Cup player, in reviewing the tour, said (*Ford File*):

> *All were impressed by the charming manner of the visitors and their sporting spirit on and off the court, but all were disappointed with their tennis. The project cost Indian tennis nearly four figures. The result is that the finances of the Indian Tennis Association, owing to this crazy scheme, are very low and*

> *money cannot be found to finance the visit of a really representative side to Europe. So all sorts of Toms, Dicks and Harrys [sic]of tennis are being given a chance to play for India.*

Financing visiting teams in an effort to raise the standard of local tennis and generate public interest is a strategy that WALTA policy makers have often employed. Sometimes there has been criticism but often praise. One of the more successful ventures which rivalled the encounter with the French team in 1928, was an international match between Australia and Japan, designated a 'test'. It was conducted during the Australia Day long weekend in 1932 when the sport-thirsty public saw their cricketer idol Donald Bradman score a marvellous double century in Adelaide in the cricket test. The special committee appointed to organise the tennis test spared no effort to make excellent arrangements at the King's Park venue. The Lord Mayor of Perth, Sir William Latham, welcomed the visitors and stressed that Japan had been a 'sincere friend and trusted ally of Australia ...' (*Daily News* , 29/1/1932, 1).

Officially, 5,273 spectators attended over the three days (*WALTA Minutes*, 10/3/1932). To the delight of officials a 'substantial' profit was recorded. Secretary Stephen Hart, nearing the completion of his term of office before later being made a made a life member of the Association, was commended and paid a gratuity of £31.10. Additional contributions were also made to the interstate visits fund (*WALTA Minutes*, 10/3/1932).

One factor which had contributed to the success of the occasion was the evenness of the teams. Japan had narrowly won the first test in Adelaide with its representatives Takeichi Harada, Jiro Satoh and Rvosuke Nugoi while Australia's team consisted of Jack Crawford, Harry Hopman and Alf Dunlop. In Perth, the Australians were to finally win a close, well publicised contest 7

Alf Dunlop, Jiro Satoh, Rvosuke Nugio and Jack Crawford leave the court during the 1932 test match between Japan and Australia played at the King's Park courts.

rubbers, 16 sets, 140 games to 5 rubbers, 10 sets and 113 games (*West Australian*, 3/2/1932, 10). Hopman had been hampered by an arm injury but Crawford was in splendid form. When asked to comment on Crawford's easy singles victories, Harada, the 33 year old Japanese captain, said (*West Australian*, 3/2/1932, 10):

> *Crawford was a tennis genius, capable on his day of beating any player in the world. Like most men of genius he was erratic, but when at the top of his form and in perfect physical condition he was unbeatable.*

Given the success of the Japan test match, the Association made an application on similar terms for another test against the United States of America in late December, 1932. After some discussion of the terms, the fixture was granted. A large committee was formed and arrangements entered into with the King's Park Club for use of its courts and appointments. However, with plans well advanced the test was cancelled as the demands of travel to Perth were regarded as being 'too strenuous' for the players. Later, a compensation payment of £150 from the LTAA helped to cushion the disappointment (*WALTA Minutes*, 12/5/1933 and 11/8/1933). Half of the amount received was reimbursed to King's Park for losses incurred in the preparation of its courts for the fixture.

The compensation might not have been forthcoming had Western Australia's delegates on the LTAA, H.A. Pitt and T.E. Robinson not made strong representation. Both gave long service in that capacity. Pitt had taken H.G. Jefferson's seat as a delegate in 1926. Jefferson, secretary at the WALTA before George Linwood, had moved to Melbourne and been an LTAA delegate for Western Australia between 1922 and 1926. Robinson had accepted the delegate role in 1930 after E.D. Gilchrist had resigned after four years in the position. Gilchrist had been a member at the King's Park Club. Robinson was a top player. Although pressing Western Australia's claims at the LTAA he represented Victoria against Western Australia in an interstate match held in April 1933. On that occasion, he lost to the brilliant Max Carpenter, 5/7, 0/6. In the doubles, partnered by leading junior Jack Purcell, he lost to Ron Ford and the emerging W. (Chum) Stephens 6/1, 3/6, 2/6 (*WALTA Annual Report*, 1932/1933).

One of the most exacting experiences for Robinson and Pitt, as WALTA delegates, surrounded the fifth test between Great Britain and Australia, scheduled to open at the King's Park courts on 15 February, 1934. The immortal Fred Perry, destined in a few months to win the first of his three Wimbledon single championships and said to be 'the first great European champion who did not come from a family of means', was in the British team (Clerici, 1974, 184) and the other members were F. D.H. Wilde, G.P. Hughes and H.G.N. Lee. Unfortunately there was an outcry when the Australian team of Hopman, Moon, Purcell and Ewin was announced although all except Gar Moon had been prominent in previous State Opens. Hopman had won the singles in 1931 and partnered King's Park's Keith Barker to clinch the doubles at the same tournament. Reg Ewin had lost to Adrian Quist in 1932 but had defeated Ron Ford in straight sets in the final a year later. Purcell had been favoured to win the title in 1933 but had been forced to withdraw from the tournament due to ill health (*West Australian*, 18/4/1933, 10). The problem from the perspective of the WALTA, hoping for a financial bonanza, was the absence of Jack Crawford (who lost the 1934 Australian Open final to Perry), Vivian McGrath, John Bromwich and Adrian Quist.

The Association's protests were forthright. As S.A. Mortimer, the incumbent Secretary, was quoted as saying (*Daily News*, 26/1/1934, 1);

> *If the wire of protest to the selectors asking for a reconsideration of their decision and for the inclusion of some Davis Cup players is not satisfactory, another emergency meeting will be called to further discuss this matter. There are so many aspects of the negotiations to be considered, any one of which may alter the local arrangements.*

Leading local players such as Molly McGrath and Peter Smith publicly expressed disappointment. Keith Haugh, the Subiaco Club champion, said: 'I was also dumbfounded when I saw the names of the selected team' (*Daily News*, 26/1/1934, 1). Mrs La Nauze, a South Perth stalwart whose son Jack, a leading junior, had brought credit to tennis by winning the Rhodes Scholarship in 1931, said 'from the point of view of one watching the game I don't think that I shall get my money's worth' (*Daily News*, 26/1/1934, 1). This sentiment was also expressed by members of the public. They wrote numerous letters to editors of the major newspapers using terms such as 'impertinence' and 'indecent'. One correspondent (*Daily News*, 26/1/1934, 5) stated:

> *I would suggest to local followers of the game that they boycott the match unless some alteration is made in the constitution of the Australian team. It is not only an insult to the Englishmen and the local association but also to the tennis public. We could field a team equally as good from this state.*

With delegates Robinson and Pitt at the centre of the negotiations, the team was eventually strengthened by the inclusion of Quist from the current Australian Davis Cup squad. This last minute change was a decisive factor in the success of the test, which might otherwise have been not only a financial failure but have seriously impaired the excellent record which the Association had established in conducting such matches. Eventually Great Britain won 7 rubbers, 20 sets, 170 games to Australia's 5 rubbers, 11 sets and 153 games (*West Australian*, 19/2/1934, 14). On the final day it was estimated that 2,500 spectators viewed the play, a new record attendance for a lawn tennis fixture held in Western Australia (*WALTA Annual Report*, 1933/1934).

Crowds again flocked to King's Park for an invitation international match in January 1935. Paying spectators totalled 7,877 (*WALTA Annual Report*, 1935/1936, 2). Well aware of the public relations disaster of 12 months before, the LTAA sent Bromwich, McGrath and Quist to play for Australia against a team of Davis Cup veterans: the Czech Roderick Menzel, Italian Georgio de Stefani, Spaniard E. 'Booby' Maier and South African V.G. Kirby. Although 'freak' Menzel was said to be the number seven in the world, he lost 7/5, 6/1 to junior John Bromwich (*Daily News*, 30/1,1935, 2). The Australian victory, by nine rubbers to two, was accompanied by press reports that the Europeans had experienced difficulties with the effects of atmosphere, court surfaces and balls. Menzel also complained about the decisions of the linesmen, the behaviour of the public and even the photographers (*Western Mail*, 7/2/1935, 25).

An international invitation tournament was arranged immediately after the match. As Menzel had suffered an injured arm, it provided an opportunity for one of Western Australia's best younger players, W.F. 'Chum' Stephens to play (*Daily News*, 7/2/1935, 8/2/1935, and 9/2/1935). The headline in the *Western Mail* (7/2/1935, 25), which announced Stephen's inclusion, was accompanied by a profile of that player as part of a regular series on ranked men and women. Although aged only 20, Stephens was the current number one player in Western Australia. A section of the resume indicated his rise to prominence:

> *After winning the under 16 and open (under 19) singles championships at the schools' tournament in 1930, and the open again in 1931, 'Chum' went on to defeat Max Carpenter for the State junior title held at the Leederville Club courts in 1932. This win was not expected, and was regarded at the time as a lapse on the part of Carpenter. However, the young Subiaco player began to make a name for himself the next year, his most meritorious performances being the winning of the Eastern Goldfields open singles title and the junior singles and doubles. These wins were followed by his first defeat of Ron Ford in the Northam Districts centenary championships, and this form was confirmed by his defeat of Ron, again in five sets in the final of the spring tournament held at South Perth that year. Stephen also retained his State junior title.*

Reference was also made to Stephens' selection for the earlier Indian tour and his ability to extend the leading Victorian Jack Purcell to five sets in the 1934 Easter tournament. Interestingly, comments were made about Stephens' technique in the following terms (*Western Mail*, 7/2/1935, 25):

> *Stephens' development has been gradual, but consistent. He has adopted the grips of the new school of Australian players, and has practically eliminated over-spin from his game. First taking care of keeping the ball in play, "Chum" has gradually increased the speed of his shots until he has reached his present standard of control of both speed and direction. With a good service, smash and volley, he has no decided weaknesses: at the same time there is lacking from his repertoire one outstanding natural shot that can be depended on for hitting out-right winners. It is the ability to make winners of a certain shot that has lifted a number of our players into international class. G Paterson, J O Anderson, V McGrath, and Bromwich all have some shot developed practically to perfection.*

'Chum' Stephens, 'No decided weaknesses'. (Courtesy The West Australian)

The keen spectator interest in the regular international fixtures did offer support to Gianni Clerici's thesis that this was the 'Golden Age of Modern Tennis'. But was this an apt description of Western Australian tennis, if women's tennis is included in the equation? Only one of the international tests or exhibition matches in Perth had been for women. At one stage it was hoped that the 1934 Wimbledon champion Dorothy Round and Nancy Lyle, her compatriot from Britain, would play in Perth on their way to the Australian Open in Melbourne (*Daily News*, 18/1/1935, 8). As it transpired, Round defeated Lyle in a tense Open final at Kooyong, but Perth was not included in their itinerary.

The evidence, though, appears to indicate that women's tennis was very much to the fore during this period. Much of the interest stemmed from a coterie of young players who had taken over from Mrs Mather and, to a lesser extent, Mrs McBeth. The latter remained on the scene and even reached the 1934 State Open final. The main attraction was Molly McGrath, but her great friend Peter Smith together with Jean Glover and Myrtle Herbert were also prominent. As previously mentioned, McGrath was educated at Sacred Heart Highgate, the stamping ground in those days of the State's leading women players. At the school premises, she practised for hours against a huge brick wall. While still at school, she won her first senior title, the 1928

Molly McGrath, in action, she was a household name in the golden age of tennis

Christmas Metropolitan Championship. Her semi-final defeat of Kalgoorlie's Marion Barker caused a sensation. Although Barker was the reigning State champion, she won only three games.

During 1929 Molly McGrath's form, as a 15-year-old, was exceptionally good. In this season a highlight performance was her victory in the 1929 Centennial Championship at the Mount Lawley club. She won the final in an epic contest against Peter Smith, her friend and regular doubles partner (*Sunday Times*, 10/11/1929, 2). Perhaps McGrath did not receive the recognition which was due on this occasion. Firstly, in the early planning stages it had been intended that the tournament would be designated as a major feature event. Eventually the WALTA tournament committee merely designated the regular Spring Championship as the Centennial Championship. Secondly, the championship was marred by an astonishing forfeit by the leading player Cec Lamb. Holding match point in the semi-final against Ron Ford, the young Lamb conceded the match. Ford then went on to defeat Harry Jacoby in straight sets in the final, a victory also overshadowed by the debate over Lamb's action. One columnist described it as 'a besmirching of the exalted tradition of tennis' (*Daily News*, 3/11/1929, 4). Jacoby, whose prospects of winning the men's title had been regarded as indirectly thwarted by Lamb's behaviour, gained some comfort in the well publicised mixed doubles. In this event, Jacoby partnered Peter Smith to defeat Ford and McGrath 6/2, 1/6, 6/4 (Sunday Times, 10/11/1929, 2).

The highlight of Peter Smith's tennis career was not the Centennial Championship but the State Open final in the same year (*Western Mail*, 7/3/1935, 23). After McGrath had been surprisingly beaten in an early round, Smith was able to take advantage of 'the break' and gain the title. Peter Smith, from Perth College, had been coached by her father (a newspaper tennis critic) whose philosophy was to develop the young player's technique before thrusting her into the tournament scene (*West Australian*, 6/2/1934, 3). This approach had paid dividends when Smith defeated Myrtle Herbert 6/3, 3/6, 6/4 in the 1929 Open. Herbert, who McGrath later admitted was a very dangerous player on her day (interview with Molly McGrath, 29/4/1989), did win the 1934 State Open. On this occasion Molly McGrath had not entered. By that time she had won four successive State Opens and was rarely beaten in other metropolitan and country tournaments. Her tennis was described 'as a sort of symphony of the game, serene and stately' partly because she 'tried not to be conscious of the gallery' (interview with McGrath, 29/4/1989).

Although she 'did not have it all her own way' Molly McGrath became a household name in Western Australia. She shared with Ron Ford the billing as the top tennis player in the state. Coincidentally, McGrath, like Ron Ford, was also a leading badminton player and shared with Ford the view that her doubles play was not, in relative terms, as good as her singles. Nevertheless (again like Ford) she was still successful in this aspect of the game. In partnership with Smith she had some major wins, although the Myrtle Herbert and Mary O'Mahoney combination were sometimes superior. In mixed doubles McGrath, partnered by Harry Jacoby, had a meritorious win over the eastern States stars Bob Schlesinger (Victoria) and Miss Wemyss (South Australia) in the 1929 State Open. Three years later McGrath teamed with Adrian Quist to gain another state title in this event.

Neither McGrath nor Ford later entered into administration at WALTA. Ford had been advised by the Wimbledon champion, Gerald Paterson, to keep clear of administration during his playing days. Later the demands of the proprietorship of a sporting goods firm precluded his nomination to the WALTA committee structure. In one episode McGrath and Ford adopted diametrically opposite stances on a decision by the WALTA selection panel. In 1931, McGrath was the only name forwarded by the selectors to the WALTA Council to compete in the Australian Championship. Sending only one player, and a woman at that, raised eyebrows. Nevertheless, given McGrath's splendid record at home, and two semi-final berths when competing away at the Australian Junior Championship, the criticism was muted. For the 1933 Australian Championships, the Association took a bold step sending McGrath, accompanied by Peter Smith, Jean Glover and Aisla Carcary, to Melbourne. No man was selected by the all-male selection committee. The Association was prepared to give practical effect to ensuring that women were to receive some of the 'specs' in the golden age of tennis. For Ford, though, it was a grave mistake not to send a junior boys team to compete in the Linton Cup competition and the Australian championships. So he hurriedly pencilled a letter to the sporting editor of the *Western Mail* (15/12/1932, 22), stating:

> *[I] can assure you that our juniors would hold their own with at least three of the other five states... How does the association expect the standard of tennis to improve if the juniors are not given a chance and have something to play for, instead of discouraging and disheartening them every year?*

On the same page, 'Volley' headed the tennis column 'Giving Our Boys a Chance' and argued for more resources for fostering junior talent in the boys section. According to McGrath the controversy soon subsided (interview with McGrath, 29/4/1989). Yet, when the WALTA Constitution was being revised a section [19/3] was inserted that specified that Council members had to be male. Despite the detailed reporting of tennis affairs, this was not highlighted in the press and not for more than a generation was this to be contentious.

Country Week champions Phyllis Richardson, and Eric Conway (Courtesy The West Australian)

Attire

Molly McGrath, however, was later the focus of another controversy. At the 1935 Spring tournament held at Loton Park, McGrath and Smith made a decision to wear shorts on the first Sunday of play. Actually the costumes looked like very short skirts, shorts camouflaged by a multitude of pleats (Molly McGrath File). 'Skimpy' shorts were the chosen medium of Helen Jacobs, the American (and Wimbledon) champion. Dorothy Round, who refused to play on Sundays, followed suit for a short term. The first major breakthrough had taken place in the 1920s when the strong willed French champion Suzanne Lenglen was determined to be attired to facilitate mobility to enhance her chance of winning. The press pounced when she wore calf-length frocks with sleeves above the elbows and hemlines with no petticoat. It was also well known that Queen Mary, a devotee of tennis, frowned upon Lenglen's new style.

Back at the tournament scene in Western Australia, McGrath and Smith quickly reverted to more traditional attire although wearing of stockings was progressively phased out. The debate continued in all the tennis journals but it was not a matter ruled upon by WALTA headquarters. Captains of the member clubs had the difficult task of policing standards of dress.

Arguments over the wearing of shorts was not restricted to women. As Yallop (1984, 67) observed 'it was also considered dubious for men to reveal their legs in shorts'. 'Bunny' Austin had worn shorts on centre court at Wimbledon in 1933. In the same year, Adrian Quist had worn shorts while travelling with the Davis Cup team and Hopman also accepted the new fashion. It was the latter who brought the matter to a head in Australian tennis while playing in the 1934 Australian Open. Five minutes before his match against Fred Perry, he was called to the match box and told he would not be allowed to play in shorts. Hopman, a sports writer for the *Melbourne Herald* replied, 'I am sorry to hear that: I will forfeit,' and reportedly went to the press office to file the story. Almost immediately, he was recalled to speak with officials and told he could take his place against Perry in shorts (Yallop, 1984, 67).

The gradual acceptance of clothing which permitted more freedom of movement was widely welcomed. This was particularly so in country areas which experienced high summer temperatures. In the early 1930s many of the leading metropolitan and Australian players played exhibition matches in the country. If their route to Perth was by train, Kalgoorlie was often the venue. Quist and Hopman played in Northam and Bromwich travelled to Collie. The Albany and Bunbury tournaments, usually held in January, were given a regular and prominent place on the WALTA tournament schedule. In 1932, the WALTA Executive sanctioned the tournament committee's future schedule of tournament commitments until the year 1939 (*WALTA Minutes*, 12/8/1932). It certainly read like a vote of confidence for the future of the Association.

Photographs published during the well publicised Country Week carnival indicated that the men invariably wore long cream trousers. When the *Western Mail* (21/3/1935, 24) printed a resume of Eric Conway, the Wyalkatchem star of the men's division in Country Week in the early 1930s he was duly attired in trousers. Between 1932 and 1935, Conway lost only one set in teams contests and the singles championships during the Country Week competition. As a measure of his stature as a player he had a meritorious victory over champion Ron Ford in a Town versus Country match. On the other hand Conway was not photographed with a hat or cap. This was in contrast to the women's legend of Country Week, Phyllis Richardson, who wore head-gear that would satisfy any modern day Cancer Foundation advocate of protection against the sun.

Umpires

Another development worthy of comment, was the announcement in 1929 that a Board of Umpires had been formed, with the politician John ('Happy Jack') Scaddan as Chairman and Mr L. Spencer as Secretary (*Sunday Times*, 28/7/1929, 24). This was an outgrowth of the Stewards Sub-Committee created by the Council in 1926 (*WALTA Minutes*, 4/6/1926). Significantly, the Stewards Committee had been commended in the 1928 Annual Report for its 'valuable work'. It was mentioned how it was composed of three leading Council members namely V.B. Mursell, C.T. Smith and G.W. Lowe (*WALTA Annual Report*, 1928). So while the Umpires Board was originally formed 'for the purpose of instructing, examining, and registering umpires' and welcomed 'to stamp out the evil of foot faulting' it never gained adequate autonomy from the Stewards Committee (*WALTA Annual Report*, 1928/1929). Significantly, too, President McGibbon chaired a sub-committee of Council which reported opposition to the concept of an Umpires Association as a body separate from the WALTA (*WALTA Minutes*, 11/1/1929).

One positive outcome of the short-lived Umpires' Board was the preparation of a Handbook compiled in co-operation with V.B. Mursell, the secretary of the Stewards Committee, and Stephen Hart, the dedicated secretary of the Association. At a price of one shilling, the Handbook contained considerable detail about the Association, the rules of the game, explanations as to foot faulting, the management of tournaments and the duties of umpires and linesmen (*WALTA Annual Report*, 1930). It was praised in the press as a very useful reference, particularly for pennants and tournaments. Earlier in the same year, there had been complaints about the standard of umpiring, coupled with an observation that it was difficult to recruit people for the task (*WALTA Annual Report*, 1928/1929). It was hoped that two or three suitable men could be chosen from each club to train themselves to act as umpires (*WALTA Annual Report*, 1929/1930).

The future was going to be faced without an Umpires Association. Perhaps the high standards of etiquette and behaviour which appeared to characterise the era led officials to believe that the status quo should prevail. Of greater importance was the need for the Association to face the future without a leasehold agreement for courts. As visiting players and officials had invariably praised the King's Park courts and its appointments officials decided to attempt to secure an agreement which guaranteed the use of this location for hallmark events. The final settlement with King's Park, recorded in the 1934/1935 annual report was the right to use the courts for interstate and international events on three days per year for an annual payment of £25 (*WALTA Annual Report*, 1933/34). The following year, again by arrangement between the Association and King's Park, a pavilion was erected on the western side of the centre court arena to provide better accommodation for the patrons. As the LTAA was assisting its state bodies to upgrade facilities, a grant of £1,000 was forwarded to Western Australia for this purpose.

The Association contributed nearly £1,700 and King's Park just less than £350. So, when the Lieutenant-Governor Sir James Mitchell opened the facility on 31 January, 1935, he was able to say the cooperative venture had cost slightly over £3,040 (*WALTA Annual Report*, 1934/1935, 2). Given the shortage of funds in this 'golden age' it was a rare but splendid example of cooperative federalism at work.

Chapter Fourteen

McGIBBON TO MURSELL (1938-1948)

Sinclair McGibbon, 'a get things done' President (1924-1938) became a life member in 1926

Vernon Mursell , a 'consensus' President (1938-1948) was honoured with life membership in 1949

THE transition of the presidency from Sinclair McGibbon to Vernon Mursell took place in September 1938. Two months later, a bronze tablet was affixed to what had been named the S.G. McGibbon Stand at King's Park to formally recognise the businessman's long service. He was a 'get things done' president who had already been bestowed life membership in 1926. Remarkably, McGibbon had earlier in the 1909/1910 season been President of Kings Park. When he stepped down from the WALTA Presidency, he again resumed the presidency at King's Park. His outstanding contribution to King's Park was also remembered when the gates to the western and eastern entrances of the club were erected and named the S.J. McGibbon Gates. In 1940, McGibbon donated the column for a sun dial located in the grounds of the King's Park Club from materials previously secured from the Houses of Parliament at Westminster in London. This dedication, only three years before his death, was a reminder of McGibbon's close ties with politics: he was active in conservative circles.

Vernon Mursell also had a long connection with WALTA, commencing as a delegate from the Claremont Club. At Claremont, he was a life member, an honour he also achieved in 1949 at the Association level (*WALTA Minutes*, 27/5/1949). Under the old Constitution, Mursell had served as Chairman of the Council and for many years was Chairman of the Selection Committee. By special request, Mursell agreed to remain as a member of this Committee despite the fact that he had assumed the presidency. His son, also named Vernon, was emerging as a potential champion with fine performances in the 1940 junior schoolboy singles and doubles championship. Mursell senior was himself a very capable player. He had captained the Claremont club's 'A' grade pennant team for several seasons and in the 1923 State Open doubles final had partnered clubmate Rice Gemmell to win the title.

Classic Events

A few months before the change in leadership, the third test match between Australia and Germany was staged. Australia had won the first two tests so it was important for the WALTA organising committee to stage a contest which would still draw large crowds. It had been rumoured that John Bromwich was reluctant to travel to Perth (*WALTA Minutes*, 10/1/38) and eventually advice was received that he had agreed to play in Perth subject to his parents' consent. This was tantamount to an indication that he was not coming. WALTA officials, still harbouring disappointment of the cancellation of a visit to Perth by an American team in January 1938 made strong representations through H.A. Pitt, to the LTAA. The outcome was considered satisfactory, as the Australian selectors chose Vivian McGrath and Adrian Quist.

With war clouds gathering over Europe again, there was keen interest in the German team of Baron Gottfried von Cramm and Henner Henkel. The tall, blonde von Cramm had reached three successive Wimbledon finals. In 1935 and 1936 his conqueror had been Fred Perry, but the match he lost to his great friend Donald Budge at Wimbledon in 1937 recalled one of the most dramatic events in tennis history. The Baron's aristocratic heritage and liberal education had quickly brought him into open disagreement with Hitler, but when he was preparing with Captain Ted Tinling for a crucial Davis Cup rubber against Budge he was allegedly called off court to take an urgent message. A few minutes later, von Cramm rejoined Budge and Tinling, informing them quickly, 'It was Hitler. He wanted to wish me good luck' (Clerici, 1975, 199).

Much to Hitler's displeasure, von Cramm, who had led 4/1 in the fifth set found the pressure too much. He said to Budge 'that was the greatest match in my life. I am glad I lost it to a man like you' (Clerici, 1975, 200). Unfortunately, it was the beginning of the end for von Cramm's tennis. He did not perform well in the Australian championship in January 1938 and was below his best when he arrived in Perth after the long train journey. While the *West Australian* newspaper reported Hitler's purges in Germany, von Cramm lost to McGrath on the first Friday and then to Quist the next day. Only a win in the doubles with Henkel salvaged some of his pride.

After returning from Australia, von Cramm was accused of 'sexual irregularities', specifically having a homosexual relationship. Homosexuality was not then, nor is it now, alien to the tennis community or to international society. Whether the charges against von Cramm were fabricated or politically motivated is not clear but he was tried and imprisoned (Clerici, 1975, 200). He survived the war but lost his life in a car accident in Egypt in 1976. Henkel was killed in the German retreat from the Soviet Union in 1943.

On the positive side, the test match broke all attendance records for international matches in Perth. In a close tie Australia won 3 rubbers 9 sets 90 games to 3 rubbers 8 sets 79 games. A net profit of £340 was regarded as a very satisfactory return particularly as the Association was carrying a £400 overdraft with the English, Scottish and Australian Bank. The financial situation improved after McGibbon made a successful compensation bid at the LTAA annual meeting for the exclusion of Perth from the visit of an American men's and women's team.

The State Opens

In the late 1920s and 1930s, Western Australians had been able to watch some of the world's best players in action. The LTAA's policy was to compensate those States which did not conduct Australian championships with annual visits by two ranked players. However, these players did not always come to Western Australia for the State Open. Although this championship had been held at Easter between 1930 and 1934, it had reverted to the Christmas period from 1935 onwards. So the ranked players often played in the prestigious Easter Tournament conducted by the King's Park club and left the native Western Australians to compete on a virtual 'State closed' basis. Before Colin Long (Victoria) defeated Max Bonner and Joy Wood (Victoria) won against Mary Prindiville in the 1940 State Open, a succession of local players had won the Association's premier singles titles.

Mary Prindiville won two State Opens under her maiden name of O'Mahoney. Three times she was ranked as number one player in Western Australia and was often listed in the top ten. This fine record in singles should

Mary O'Mahoney, (Prindiville) developed her tennis in the Catholic Tennis Assocation. (Courtesy The West Australian)

Myrtle Herbert, a fine record in doubles

not obscure her reputation as a splendid doubles player. One newspaper report in 1935 called her 'certainly the best woman volleyer in the State'. It added 'this player has the ability, rare amongst women, of playing the chop volley' (*Western Mail*, 21/3/1935, 24). With her Loton Park team-mate Myrtle Herbert as her most regular partner, O'Mahoney was the most formidable women's doubles player of her era. She continued to play competitively after World War II, by which time she had won six State Open doubles titles. Her husband Bernie Prindiville, also a Loton Park player, became a leading cricket administrator. So Mary's attention shifted to cricket especially when their sons, Terry and Kevin, developed into state players. Fortunately, their daughter Joan, with her husband Dan Carney of Royal King's Park, kept the family's strong tennis tradition going.

A major factor in O'Mahoney's development as a player was the range of opportunities provided by the Catholic Tennis Association (CTA), which clearly followed the dictum that tennis was a 'family game'. The strength of tennis in the Catholic schools challenges the thesis articulated by prominent tennis historian Graeme Kinross-Smith (1994a, 144) that the game in the Australian States was 'probably primarily a Protestant pursuit, surrounded by the business ethic and the concomitants of the Masonic lodge'. O'Mahoney did not play competitively as a junior nor did she have the benefit of individual coaching. Nevertheless she was introduced to tennis at school and there were regular CTA interstate carnivals, Perth being the venue in 1932. However, despite her record (which included taking a set off the formidable Nancye Wynne) O'Mahoney did not represent WALTA in an interstate match. She was too young to be included in the controversial 1933 'women only' team.

In retrospect, though, Mary O'Mahoney should not have been overlooked on so many occasions. She was victim of a view, particularly after Molly McGrath and Jean Glover had stepped aside, that women's tennis in Western Australia was weak. The *Daily News* (2/11/1937, 4) even carried a headline 'Women's tennis has flopped'. The author of this claim, Mrs Paterson, formerly a leading player, had been interviewed on her way through Fremantle with her husband, Gerald Paterson. In fact, the basis of her claim was a reflection about the international scene concerning the absence of the great Helen Wills Moody and Helen Jacobs from the United States Open championships. What counted was that Vernon Mursell and his co-selectors subscribed to this opinion on the local scene, which was again expressed at the end of the 1938 State Open. Although O'Mahoney had won the women's singles, doubles and mixed doubles titles, the *Western Mail* columnist (6/1/1938, 7) wrote:

> *Women's events in the tournament were generally a disappointment. There were meagre entries and little competition. Indeed what little competition there was almost completely nullified by the unfortunate forfeits of Miss Trewhella and Miss Carcary .... It has served to emphasise the poor standard of women's tennis.*

In men's tennis there were several players who were capable of winning major titles in the seasons leading to the cessation of championship play during World War II. 'Chum' Stephen and Gordon Davis virtually alternated the number one seeding spot which Ron Ford had previously held for so long. Other prominent players were Harry Jacoby, Max Bonner, Bill Halliday, Norm Wasley and Max McDermott. All of them, except Halliday, won a major singles or doubles Open title. From 1936, the WALTA selectors saw fit to send players of this calibre to the Australian championships and the Linton Cup competition.

However, there was considerable controversy after the players returned from the 1936 Australian championships. The WALTA Executive 'decided in the interests of the juniors who participated the report be not published in the press it being considered that too much laudation might prove harmful' (*WALTA Minutes*, 12/2/1936 and 14/2/1936). Nevertheless, the Executive recommended an exhibition match be held between the Linton Cup juniors and the top senior players. The author of the report, manager Bob Reitze, was supportive of this idea but strongly disputed the Executive's decision not to publish the report. Angry words were exchanged, particularly between Stan Mortimer and Reitze. Initially, it was thought that an apology by Reitze to Mortimer might resolve the disagreement (*WALTA Minutes* 22/1/1937), but finally Reitze tendered his resignation as manager of the 1937 interstate team and 'Chum' Stephen was given the combined role of captain-manager. Reitze had also disagreed with the Selection Committee (especially Mortimer) about the doubles pairing of 'Chum' Stephen and Norman Wasley (*WALTA Minutes*, 25/11/1936, 4/1/1937, 15/1/1937). Reitze, obviously at odds with the Executive, returned the Shield Match Committee Minute Book to the Association (*WALTA Minutes*, 22/1/1937).

Another controversy erupted in late 1939 when the Selection Committee, under the chairmanship of President Vernon Mursell, decided not to select a Linton Cup team. Mursell publicly claimed the team would not be strong enough (*West Australian*, 28/2/1938, 7). His Committee had already overlooked a Council request to give serious consideration to nominating a girls team for the Wilson Cup (*WALTA Minutes*, 9/6/1938 and 9/12/1938). For the Linton Cup the leading contenders were Wally Main and Geoff Hammond, the Association's schoolboy champion. Later, Wally Main was added to the senior team of Max Bonner and Max McDermott. Main later added 'fuel to the fire' when he reached the final of the 1940 Junior Boys Singles at the Australian Championships. How Western Australia would have fared in the Linton Cup (or Wilson Cup) will never be known. Unfortunately, the next Linton and Wilson Cup competitions were abandoned until 1946. Unluckily, as well, Main had to withdraw from the 1940 State Open because of injury (*Western Mail*, 21/3/1940, 46). Hammond, too, lost his golden opportunity to be a state team member.

'Chum' Stephen was one leading player who did not compete in Linton Cup tennis for Western Australia. But he was a regular senior representative for the State. As noted earlier, in February 1935 he was a 'last minute' replacement in an international fixture involving European and Australian players (*Western Mail*, 7/2/1935, 25). Stephen won his first State Open in straight sets over Ron Ford in 1935. His second Open title came in 1937 after a creditable four-set performance against Arthur Huxley, a young left-hander from New South Wales. On another occasion Stephen took the leading Victorian Jack Purcell to five sets. He was regarded as a very steady player who invariably struck good form early in the season and this enabled him to win five successive Spring Championships between 1935 and 1939.

One prize which eluded 'Chum' Stephen was the honour of winning the State Doubles title with his brother Ron. The Stephens', from Subiaco, narrowly failed to emulate the Oldham's (1897), Barnard's (1908), Kruger's (1920) and Barker's (1922) in the 1938 final at the nearby Onslow Park Club. They were beaten in a thrilling contest by Max Bonner and Max McDermott, 4/6, 6/4, 6/3, 5/7, 6/4. Unfortunately, 'Chum' also lost the singles final to Gordon Davis in five sets. Young Ron, however, impressively won the junior boys' singles final (*Western Mail*, 6/1/1938, 17).

Gordon Davis, a King's Park player with a splendid physique, fulfilled some of his early promise with a 1938 Open victory. He had toured India and Ceylon with the Western Australian team in 1934. Fifteen months later, the columnist at the *Western Mail* (28/3/1935, 23) felt compelled to comment:

> *Davis has the strokes and latent ability of a champion yet he does not reach the heights ... His results are not convincing and yet it is very difficult to realise that this young man has not got it in him to leave his mark on tennis in this State ... Gordon will not win singles matches until he decreases his margin of error and learns when to use his forcing shots.*

One sign that Davis was improving his game was his reaching the final of the 1936 State Open. Unfortunately, he lost in straight sets to Harry Jacoby. It was Jacoby's most prestigious title in a tennis life that spanned more than 50 years. Interestingly, Harry did not start playing tennis until the comparatively late age of 17 years. He learnt the basics on hard courts at Mundaring. In his first tournament, he made a creditable showing against Rice Gemmell and gained selection in the 1927 Linton Cup team. In this tournament, he performed well, taking sets from Don Turnbull and Jack Crawford. Another fine interstate performance was his defeat of leading Victorian, T.K. Fitchett, at Kings Park in 1933.

Harry Jacoby with John Bromwich

At home Jacoby was the big name at the WANDA club. He won six successive singles and doubles championships and captained four consecutive 'A' grade pennant premiership teams. After moving to King's Park, he continued his record of pennant success (*Western Mail*, 14/3/1935, 23). Jacoby's name then became synonymous with King's Park, both as a player and administrator. Many other WANDA members joined King's Park, portrayed in the thirties as 'the Mecca of Tennis' (*Western Mail*, 28/2/1935, 23). The restricted number of courts at the Perth Esplanade meant that once pennants ceased to be played at Kitchener Park, it was not viable for WANDA to have a mens and womens 'A' grade teams. It had never been possible to conduct a major championship at the WANDA courts. Indeed during the 1930s there was constant debate about whether the State Open should be held at locations other than King's Park. The question of whether the Open should be conducted at Christmas or Easter also exercised the minds of officials. From 1935 onwards Christmas was designated, with the venues in successive years being Subiaco, Leederville, Mt Lawley, Onslow Park and Loton Park. In 1940, though, it was back to King's Park at Easter. The matter had come under critical discussion again after the 1938 Open was held at the small Onslow Park Club. No leading players from the eastern states had competed. As the *Western Mail* (6/1/1938, 16) correspondent stated:

> *The officials of the Onslow Park Club handled the organisation of the tournament quite ably. The courts, however, were hardly up to championship standard and spectator accommodation was poor and inadequate. More attention should be paid to the comfort of spectators in State Championships and it would be better for Western Australian tennis if the most important tournaments were confined to clubs with the most suitable facilities.*

The commitment to hold the 1939 State Open at Loton Park, which had been made in 1932, was nevertheless honoured. The club's contingent of leading women players, reflected in its dominance of 'A' Grade pennants, had kept Loton Park in the news. Myrtle Herbert, from Loton Park, was to reach the final and, although spectators witnessed the first women's Open three-set final for several years, Herbert lost to Miss Trewhella from Fremantle. As the newspaper report (*West Australian*, 3/1/1939, 5) described the match:

Driving strongly and going for the sidelines with commendable courage, Miss Trewhella gained a well merited victory in the final of the women's singles championship against Miss M Herbert. Miss Trewhella took the first set at 6/1 in easy fashion, lost the second at 5/7 after a hard fight and then gained the ascendancy again to win the third comfortably at 6/2. Miss Trewhella's game lacked the variety of that of her opponent as she refused to go into the net when forced there. Miss Herbert on the other hand, came into the net whenever possible, but her volleying was by no means as certain as it should have been and she often lost the advantage which her tactics had gained her.

The Loton Park State Open marked the fulfilment of promise previously displayed by Norman Wasley. He was in the Linton Cup team in 1936 and 1937 and was a senior representative for the next two years. As was printed in the journal *Lawn Tennis in Australia* (15/1/1939, 24);

Wasley has at last found some solidity in his play. Previously he hurled his 15 stone into his shots indiscriminately. The two coaching periods under O'Hara Wood helped to round off his game. Time alone was needed to mature his new found strokes.

Norm Wasley, the only Association President to have won the State Open

In the preliminary rounds Wasley recorded fine victories over Gordon Davis, the defending champion and Max Bonner, the Spring tournament champion. His opponent in the final was 'Chum' Stephen, who had used 'his reliable groundstrokes and variation of pace to upset Halliday and McDermott' (*Lawn Tennis in Australia*, 15/1/1939, 24). In an epic 6/1, 10/8, 3/6, 3/6, 6/4 match, Wasley used his height (193 centimetres) and stamina to win. It appeared he had the potential to remain at the top. However, much to the chagrin of officials, he announced his retirement from competitive tennis (*WALTA Minutes*, 8/10/1939 and 11/11/1939). The WALTA secretary sent a letter of regret, but Wasley's later contributions to state tennis were not as a player but as an administrator in the WALTA and the Mount Lawley Club. He was President of the Association between 1962 and in 1971 was awarded life membership (*WALTA Minutes*, 14/10/71). He remains the only Association President to have won the State Open singles.

Coaching

Wasley's progress as a player was partly attributed to the coaching he received from Pat O'Hara Wood, the former Davis Cup player. By 1936, the LTAA had finalised arrangements for the institution of 'coaching and physical culture' classes for promising players in each state and allocated funds for the purpose. The state selectors therefore nominated their 1936 Linton Cup players Max Bonner, Jack Vincent and Norman Wasley for the program (*WALTA Annual Report*, 1936/1937, 4). In the following year Wasley visited Sydney for a month's physical training and coaching under O'Hara Wood. This was followed by a further two weeks of coaching in Melbourne immediately prior to the 1938 Australian Championships. To the satisfaction of Association officials, a confidential report said that Wasley made good progress during the sessions (*WALTA Minutes*, 16/2/1938).

While the WALTA Executive endorsed the LTAA's junior coaching initiative, there was some doubt about the effectiveness of the plan. The journal *Lawn Tennis in Australia* (15/5/1937, 7) recognised that one shortcoming 'is that all attention is being paid to male players. Women are not receiving anything like the same encouragement ...' The same journal (15/12/1937, 12) also published the views of Gar Moon, the 1930 Australian Open Champion, who wrote:

Clarry Treloar, champion player who became a leading professional coach (Courtesy The West Australian)

Coaching! In practically every paper one picks up there is talk of the coaching of juniors, either by the Australian Association or by some other body. There appears to be a coaching complex. 'Juniors must be coached' is the cry... Drastic changes to a player's style are hopeless. All that a player needs is balance and the knowledge of where a ball should be hit and why it should be hit there ... What coaching has Crawford, McGrath, Quist, Bromwich, Miss Wynne, Miss Westacott, Miss Egan or Miss Coyne ever had that has done them any good?

Similar views were sometimes expressed by delegates to the WALTA Council. Occasionally there was concern that too many juniors were overtrained (*WALTA Minutes*, 17/3/1936), but the commitment to do something apparently constructive prevailed (*Western Mail*, 7/3/1935, 11). In late 1934 (*WALTA Minutes*, 19/10/1935), a coaching scheme had been inaugurated under the control of a committee consisting of enthusiasts Vernon Mursell, Bob Reitze, William Corr and Bill Halliday. Twenty-five boys, all under 16 years and nominated by schools sports masters, received instructions from Clarry Treloar, the coach engaged by the Committee (*Western Mail*, 11/4/1935, 25). After the seven week course, which the boys attended twice per week, a Fremantle versus Perth junior match was conducted (*Western Mail*, 28/3/1935, 24).

The Coaching Committee periodically modified the format of this program as its composition changed (*WALTA Minutes*, 26/6/1941). However, in 1942 Mursell announced that 'due to evacuations from the metropolitan area in the period concerned the effort was reluctantly abandoned' (*WALTA Annual Report*, 1941/1942). Earlier President Mursell had eulogised Jack Cox, the Mount Lawley club player, for his contribution to junior development. Cox had become a prominent member of the Coaching Committee (*WALTA Minutes*, 9/4/1937).

Such coaching schemes, conducted at either the WALTA or LTAA level, were aimed at improving the standard of the top bracket of players, perhaps with the ultimate goal of Davis Cup or Wimbledon success. However, other forms of coaching were also introduced. Clarry Treloar, one of the most prominent coaches, in cooperation with the *Western Mail* published photographs of stroke production by the State's leading players (see *Western Mail*, 19/1/1939, 26/1/1939, 2/2/1939, 23/2/1939). The newspaper staff had visited some of the leading metropolitan clubs and photographed members in action. Captions conveying advice on techniques accompanied the pictures. A similar service was sometimes prepared for participants in the Country Week carnival. Treloar had also embarked on coaching at schools such as Fremantle Boys School, Princess May School and Perth Central School (*Western Mail*, 4/4/1935, 25).

The most effective practitioner of mass coaching, sometimes performed to music, was the legendary Herbert Edwards. His coaching practices left an indelible mark on Western Australian (and Australian) tennis. Even before the WALTA had confirmed its existence, Edwards had begun his career as a junior professional at Wimbledon in 1901. After the Great War he coached in South Africa and in 1921 was appointed 'professional' coach to the New South Wales Association, the first official appointment of this nature in Australia. In Western Australia, the Herbert Edwards School of Tennis was established at Kitchener Park in Subiaco. Rice Gemmell had previously coached there but in 1936 reapplied for amateur status (*WALTA Minutes*, 4/5/1936). In addition Edwards also left an impression as coach for Wesley College where future leading players Clive Wilderspin, Arthur Marshall and

Bruce Robinson were among his pupils. Even after his retirement, Edwards' fatherly guidance was still evident. His sons, Stan and Vic were prominent in tennis. Stan coached Betty Stove, the 1977 Wimbledon finalist, while Vic was closely associated with facets of the careers of Evonne Goolagong (Cawley), Jan Lehane, Fred Stolle, Bob Hewitt, John Newcombe, Kim Warwick, and Syd Ball (*Daily News*, 21/11/1984, 16)

Edwards (1945, 2) believed that lawn tennis was 'a science and only those who are prepared to build their game with careful study can expect to advance soundly'. He had made this assertion in his textbook titled *Lawn Tennis: Foundation Strokes and Rules*. At all times he enthusiastically conveyed his understandings of the fundamentals of tennis. He did not always see 'eye to eye' with officialdom at the WALTA, particularly when some of his pupils were allocated to sessions conducted by the rival coach Clarry Treloar (*WALTA Minutes*, 11/3/1941). There were also many disputes about the status of junior tournaments conducted by Edwards at Kitchener Park (see *WALTA Minutes*, 16/9/1941). Nevertheless the Association did not deny his important contribution to the sport. This was reflected in the foreword to his book, written by Vernon Mursell in his capacity as President of WALTA. As Mursell (in Edwards 1945, vii) wrote:

Herbert A Edwards, the architect of mass coaching who believed tennis was a science

> *During the last six years of war, with so many of our players with the Forces, Mr Edwards's unflagging energy in the interest of Tennis has been invaluable, and his genius not only for imparting his knowledge to young players, but in organising and controlling Junior Tournaments, without pecuniary advantage to himself, has been of great assistance to the game and to the Western Australian Lawn Tennis Association.*

Umpires

The text written by Herbert Edwards contained details of all key aspects of singles and doubles play. Significantly, he also included chapters on rules of the game; duties of the referee, umpires, and linesmen; and sections on court and gallery etiquette. These were important to Edwards' role as a lecturer and examiner for the Western Australian Lawn Tennis Umpires Association and President of the Australian Lawn Tennis Umpires Association. The umpires' body in Western Australia largely owed its formation to Edwards. An umpires sub-committee had been formed in 1929 but it had faded out of existence. Nine years later, Edwards tabled a proposal for an umpires association at an Executive meeting (*WALTA Minutes*, 12/1/1938 and 14/1/1938). Discussion continued for some months, as there was again uncertainty about the status that should be granted to such an organisation. Eventually the WALTA Council gave recognition to the Western Australian Lawn Tennis Umpires Association as an official association with the right to issue certificates of competency. The WALTA Council was represented on the Board of Management of the Umpires Association by two delegates (*WALTA Annual Report*, 1938/39).

The Umpires Association was soon servicing clubs conducting important tournaments. Sometimes, though, at State Championships time the number of umpires required strained the resources of the new organisation (*WALTA Minutes*, 17/4/1939). It was not long before members were embroiled in controversy over the interpretation of the foot fault rule (*WALTA Minutes*, 7/12/1938, 12/1/1939 and 11/3/1941) In 1929, the International Lawn Tennis Federation had modified the rule, but there was no clear understanding of its interpretation. Quinton Stow applied his legal training to a keen study of the rule. As a player at the King's Park Club, he had the opportunity to test the practicalities of his suggestions. In essence, the rule at the time meant that the server could take a step with the front foot, provided the back foot was not lifted until the ball had been struck, and provided further that the step did not take the player onto the line or into the court (Edwards, 1945, 90). If the rule was not policed, the server could gain an advantage by moving towards the net before the ball was struck. Not surprisingly, accusations of foot faulting were accompanied by the use of terms such as 'cribbing' and 'cheating'. In the 1941 pennant season it was even decided to establish a roving group of foot fault umpires to stem this practice in competition matches (*WALTA Minutes*, 11/3/1941).

Shield tennis

The pennant competition after 1932 became officially known as the 'Shield Match Competition' and gradually began to cater for more teams (*WALTA Minutes*, 10/6/1932), reaching a peak of 91 in the 1939/40 season before the exigencies of the war began to have an effect. The season usually commenced in December, with the winners being determined before Easter. There were generally three grades (A, B, C) in the men's competition and two grades (A and B) in the women's competition. A junior boys' series was always conducted and usually a junior girls' competition was organised. The matches were played on Saturdays although in 1935 consideration was given to Sunday play (*WALTA Minutes*, 11/9/1935). A small sub-committee of the WALTA Council (with a high turnover of chairmen) handled the administrative load and the innumerable disputes over the rules of the competition and the grading of teams. The rejection of Claremont's application for an 'A' grade men's team in the 1939/40 season was one example of a dispute which reached Council (*WALTA Minutes*, 8/11/1939). To overcome this annual problem, it was suggested that all metropolitan clubs be graded 'A', 'B' or 'C'. Thus any 'B' or 'C' clubs improving themselves were given the right to apply to the Grading Committee for promotion (*WALTA Minutes*, 21/3/1939).

In the years prior to the outbreak of the Second World War, the Loton Park club dominated the womens' 'A' grade in a manner reminiscent of WANDA after the Great War. In 1935 Loton Park was undefeated throughout the season (*West Australian*, 14/1/1935, 19). This feat was repeated in 1938 (*West Australian*, 24/1/1938, 7) and 1940 (*West Australian*, 12/2/1940, 10). However, in 1939, without Mary O'Mahoney, the Loton Park team of Myrtle Herbert, Mrs Mavis Cooke, Mrs 'Vi' Easton and Miss Bone had to survive a play-off against Claremont (*West Australian*, 18/2/1939, 10) before winning the premiership. The latter club had been premiers in 1933 when former State Open champion Mrs McBeth and ranked player Mrs Kiesey were in the team (*West Australian*, 27/2/1933, 5). It was said that Kiesey's 'outstanding attribute was her will to win' (*Western Mail*, 11/4/1935, 25).

The WANDA club had a strong men's team in the late 1920s and early 1930s. A sequence of 'pennants' from 1928 to 1933 was only broken by Subiaco in 1934. The top players at WANDA were Jacoby, Carpenter, Gawler, Barker and Reynolds. Subiaco had an outstanding season in 1934 when the team was unbeaten. This club had a number of consistent players such as Hough, Thornander, Garside and Hawley (*West Australian*, 5/2/1934, 6). Thereafter, King's Park were formidable with a series of premierships in 1935, 1936, 1938 and 1940. This record could be attributed to the number of ranked players representing the club such as Ford, Jacoby, Davis, Halliday and Kinnane.

One matter that was continually before both Executive and Council was that of clearances and transfers. This was a subject of special interest to Ken Miller from the Leederville Club. He was later to become WALTA President (1953–1962) as well as President of the Western Australian National Football League (WANFL). The latter links made Miller well versed in clearances. Resolution of the matter was deferred on several occasions as it was not thought necessary to impose a clearance system which could become unnecessarily restrictive and controversial (*WALTA Minutes*, 9/1/1940, 12/1/1940, 8/3/1940, 6/8/1940, 5/11/1940, 10/2/1941). Tennis, and particularly shield tennis, was very much an amateur business, even though club championships, especially those in the more prominent clubs, were keenly contested and widely reported.

One side effect of the growing debate over the increasing professionalism in tennis was the inability of professional coaches such as Clarry Treloar and Rice Gemmell to play in the club shield competitions. Even in this era, the merits of professionalism were being raised in some quarters of the tennis world. Professionalism broadly meant playing or coaching for monetary gain. Many of the major disputes about professionalism were fought in the national and international board rooms. Tennis writers and newspaper columnists kept the issue alive. Some concerns were expressed at the WALTA Council (*WALTA Minutes*, 10/6/1938) and there was discussion about the use of trade names for trophies. Dunklings, a prominent firm of jewellers, requested the Council to endorse their decision to donate a number of spoons for competition between country clubs. The WALTA Executive, through its secretary Stan Mortimer, indicated that the use of trade names was contrary to policy (*WALTA Minutes*, 11/9/1935) and the LTAA had advised WALTA officials that it disapproved of employees of sporting manufacturers acting as coaches during their ordinary hours of employment (*WALTA Minutes*, 9/6/1939). It also requested assurances from Max Bonner that his name be disassociated from the sale of racquets (*WALTA Minutes*, 7/11/1939).

On one occasion, Executive member Quinton Stow, sought the opinion of the Council 'upon the position of a player who engaged in press work as a sideline for reward' (*WALTA Minutes*, 7/7/1937). This recalled a notable episode involving the great American Bill Tilden. The United States Lawn Tennis Association told Tilden, who had won the Wimbledon championships in 1920 and 1921, that he could not write for newspapers. Tilden resigned from the Davis Cup team and there was a public outcry, with threats of a breakaway association being formed. Tilden was wooed back but the issue was not resolved (Yallop, 1984, 64). Later Tilden, who in 1931 had a service measured at 263 km/hr (163.6 m.p.h.) (McFarlan, ed, 1990, 305) turned professional. Ironically, soon after Stow had raised the question of tennis players writing for newspapers, the WALTA Executive began negotiating with Tilden to play in Perth. However, the terms - 60 per cent of the gate after deduction of taxes, with a minimum of £1,000 - were too risky for an Association with an overdraft (*WALTA Minutes*, 6/4/1938).

It was understandable that the big names in tennis were attracted to writing about the sport. International, national, association and club tennis continued to be widely reported. In Perth, the Daily Newspapers, the *West Australian* and *Daily News* reported tennis in detail, while the weeklies, the *Sunday Times* and *Western Mail*, had regular columnists. The latter provided an extensive photographic coverage of players and clubs. Details of club tournament draws and scores were published regularly. At a WALTA Council meeting in 1936, the leading player and educationist Bill Halliday made it clear that the Council's concern about the lack of success of the Linton Cup team could not be attributed to the lack of publicity 'or public praise' (*WALTA Minutes*, 14/2/1936). To him, the major problem was the lack of opportunity for competitive tennis. Later, experts spoke of the need for winter practice (*WALTA Minutes*, 14/4/1939) and even the value of forming a club of ranked players (*WALTA Minutes*, 11/8/1939).

Illustrative of the keen competition between newspapers for tennis stories was the action of the editor of the *West Australian* in the winter of 1936. He wrote to the WALTA Executive and expressed disappointment that rival newspapers were receiving local tennis information before his newspaper (*WALTA Minutes*, 12/6/1936). In this quest for tennis news, the *Western Mail* negotiated an agreement with WALTA to designate this paper as its official voice. Before the WALTA Executive endorsed this agreement, it consulted with the Western Australian Golf Association (WAGA) to determine whether it was satisfied with the *Western Mail* as its official organ. As the WAGA confirmed its support for the *Western Mail*, in early 1938, this became the paper printing WALTA news (*WALTA Minutes*, 8/12/1937, 10/12/1937 and 12/1/1938). After two successful seasons, war demands began to reduce the space for sport. Fortunately for the WALTA, the Council was able to accept an offer by Mr L. Eichhorn, an activist in tennis circles, to act as a publicity officer (*WALTA Minutes*, 9/7/1940). Eichhorn soon had to contend with a decision by the Australian Broadcasting Commission (ABC) to discontinue broadcasting tennis results. However, after approaches from the Association, tennis was back on the air in 1941 (*WALTA Minutes*, 13/12/1940, 7/1/1940 and 8/4/1941).

Country affairs

The Association's desire for the ABC to publicise tennis was very important to its rural support, particularly during Country Week. The number and quality of the teams competing was a good barometer of the economic performance of the state. Support had fallen away during the Depression but a surge of interest was evident in the late Thirties. William Corr, a long serving member of the Executive, reported that the standard of play in 1938 'was perhaps the highest since the inception' of Country Week (*WALTA Minutes*, 14/3/1938). This was the only occasion that Kalgoorlie legend Herb Blacker won the singles title. Blacker held a State ranking partly due to the reputation he gained for outstanding performances against national champions, such as

Herb Blacker, (left) is pictured here in 1930 at Kalgoorlie with Harry Hopman, Eddie Johns and Bob Schlesinger (Victoria)

Hopman and Bromwich, who sometimes played goldfields' representatives during scheduled stop-overs at Kalgoorlie, which broke the long train journey to Perth.

Country Week was conducted in 1939, 1940 and even 1941 before being suspended until 1947. In the last few pre-war carnivals, Vern (Arthur) Hall emerged in the men's section to take over the mantle from Wyalkatchem's Eric Conway. Hall never gained a state ranking (as Conway had done), but he was unfortunate that the war coincided with his best tennis years. His first Country Week singles victory in 1939 was described as a 'surprise'. It was expected that Herb Blacker (Eastern Goldfields), the reigning champion, would defeat his less experienced opponent. However, Hall won 6/2, 6/4 and began to create an enviable record in the event (*West Australian*, 4/3/1939, 15). Perhaps Hall's most notable achievement in open company was his victory in the State Hardcourt Singles Championship (named the J. Norman Perpetual Cup), when it was conducted at Katanning in January 1948 (*WALTA Annual Report*, 1947/1948). After the war, he also won the first three Country Week singles titles. In 1949, the last time he won the singles title, he also teamed with Harry Spilsbury (who was later to hold senior office at the WALTA) to win of the men's 'A' grade team championship for Pingelly-Narrogin.

Vern Hall, a fine Country Week record (Courtesy The West Australian)

In the women's section of Country Week several different players won the singles after Phyllis Richardson won her last title in 1936: Miss Collins (1937), Miss Counsel (1938), Miss Gould (1939), Mrs Lings (1940) and Miss Graham (1941). In 1940 it was necessary to cancel the women's handicap singles, which had been included two years before to cater for the increased numbers of entries. Statistics indicate that individual and team entries for both women and men peaked in 1938.

One keen advocate of developing both women's and men's country tennis was Mervyn Copley, a delegate at the WALTA Council. In early 1939 he gave a notice of a motion which read in part 'that an endeavour be made to assist the Country Association and clubs to raise their standard of play' (*WALTA Minutes*, 10/2/1939). Copley's series of proposals included visits of country towns by ranked players, assistance to leading country players to compete in the State Open, special provisions for juniors to aid their prospects of interstate selection and more inter-association and inter-club matches (*WALTA Minutes*, 13/1/1939).

Earlier, Herbert Edwards had proposed that leading players visit country towns (*WALTA Minutes*, 11/8/1937). Some thought that Edwards' mass coaching should be available in country centres. At the WALTA, a sub-committee composed of J.L. Walker, S.A. Mortimer and W.A. Corr had been established to investigate proposals to zone the state into tennis districts (*WALTA Minutes*, 8/10/1936). Coincidentally, this matter was placed on the agenda at the Country Week Conference in March 1939 at the same time that Copley's proposals were debated. The deliberations were lengthy as was the WALTA Council's examination of the recommendations (*WALTA Minutes* 10/3/1939). But the timing was unfortunate with war imminent. The lack of progress was too frustrating for Copley and in late 1940 he resigned from the Council (*WALTA Minutes*, 10/10/1940).

Wartime Activities

In July 1940 the WALTA Council tabled LTAA recommendations for tennis activities during wartime. The WALTA was to make available its organisation for the promotion of physical education (*WALTA Minutes*, 12/7/1940) and

State championships were to be discontinued but exhibition matches were to be permitted for the raising of patriotic funds. Suggestions that the barriers against amateurs competing with professionals be relaxed for fundraising purposes were rejected, because the 'benefits likely to be derived ... would not be commensurate with the risk involved (*WALTA Minutes*, 11/9/1941 and 14/11/1941).

The Association complied with these guidelines and the State Championship was placed in abeyance. The City of Perth Championship, scheduled for Christmas 1941 and originally rostered to Peppermint Grove, was conducted by the Nedlands Club. A small loss was incurred despite the WALTA Executive's policy of waiving the tournament fee (*WALTA Minutes*, 14/2/1941 and *WALTA Annual Report*, 1941/1942). Nevertheless, the Association was able to supply nets and balls (which were in short supply) and facilitate the building of tennis courts at the Northam Army Camp, where many Western Australians were stationed for military training (*WALTA Minutes*, 8/4/1941). Some financial support was also given to the RAAF Flying School at Cunderdin (*WALTA Annual Report*, 1941/1942).

During the war the Association sponsored medal competitions, special tournaments and exhibition matches. One highlight was the visit of John Bromwich. He had achieved hero status in Australia by combining with Adrian Quist to win the Davis Cup in Philadelphia in 1939. Bromwich and Quist, the famed doubles combination, kept the tie alive after losing both of the opening singles matches. By winning the final two singles rubbers, Australia gained custody of the Cup during the war. History had repeated itself, for Australia held the Cup during the Great War. In June 1941, Bromwich played in Kalgoorlie, Northam, Perth and Fremantle and the proceeds, nearly £300, were donated to the patriotic funds (*WALTA Annual Report*, 1941/1942).

President Mursell, with the endorsement of Council, approved the creation of a Tennis War Patriotic Fund. This enabled the identity of the Association's contributions to be preserved as part of its support for Western Australian Sportsmen's Organising Council Fund. By 1942, some 80 clubs and associations had contributed to the fund (*Annual Report*, 1941/1942). Later, funds from the WALTA school tournaments were included. The enthusiastic Herbert Edwards was largely responsible for the organisation of the Schools and Junior Spring Championships. Not only was junior tennis given a stimulus but, in the process, funds were raised for patriotic bodies and the Red Cross (*WALTA Annual Report*, 1942/1943).

The War drastically curtailed the activities of the Association. At the annual general meeting in 1942, difficulties were reported in arranging committees to carry on its affairs. On the same evening, the Floreat Park delegate, Mr Clemon, complained that the 'Annual Report lacked enthusiasm and detail' (*WALTA, AGM Minutes* 1943). However, under the genial guidance of Mursell there was never any question of the Association dying out or going into receivership. Such problems had faced the Association during the Great War. There were some hard decisions; for instance Secretary G.H. Carlisle took a salary cut in 1942 (*WALTA Minutes* 11/9/1941). Importantly, though, the main components of the junior program, including the Slazenger Cup competition, were sustained. Wesley College took a firm grip of the boys' section in this competition and one of its members, Clive Wilderspin, had begun to dominate the junior scene. He was to emerge as one of Western Australia's greatest sports people.

Chapter Fifteen

WILDERSPIN FOR WIMBLEDON: THE POST WAR DECADE

ON Australia Day 1945, a special conference of club presidents and secretaries was held to consider the issues associated with returning to 'normalcy' (*WALTA Annual Report*, 1944/45). Not surprisingly, it was unanimously decided that the time was not opportune to recommence full scale-activities. Many players were still serving in the armed forces. At home, particularly in country areas, there was an acute shortage of tennis balls. Under rubber control regulations, clubs were restricted to 25 per cent of their 1941 purchases. So it was decided to review the situation after entries had been received for the 1945/1946 series of summer shield matches.

Returning to normal

Two months after the US Air Force bombed Hiroshima and Nagasaki in August 1945 and ended the war with Japan, the Association Executive appointed a sub-committee to survey metropolitan club members about future policies (*WALTA Annual Report*, 1945/1946). As many clubs and district associations had become defunct or had severely restricted their activities during the war, it was necessary to be extremely sensitive to the wants of the clubs to ensure their re-affiliation and continued support. In 1948 when Mursell stepped down from the Presidency due to ill health, still confident of the future of the WALTA, he was able to declare that the Association had regained its pre-war strength (*WALTA Minutes*, 20/5/1948). In terms of affiliated clubs and aggregate membership he was correct. Even the expectation of growth was fulfilled, although there was some levelling of numbers around 1950. At that time Australia had the highest ratio of courts to population in the world and a 1948 Gallup Poll had showed that tennis was by far the most frequently played of all outdoor sports (Fewster, 1984, 276). As there was no reason to believe these statistics did not apply to Western Australia, there was cause for optimism.

Clive Wilderspin, a household name in Western Australia

Wilderspin and other leading players

Throughout the war and its aftermath, the Association continued to direct a significant proportion of its limited resources to junior development. Junior pennants and junior tournaments had continued. Leading junior girls had an opportunity to play in a special ungraded (then graded) women's pennant competition. Yet hopes that these opportunities for juniors would heighten the standard of play were not realised in the short term. In December 1945, the Selection Committee reported to Council (*WALTA Minutes*, 12/12/1945):

> *The view was unanimously accepted that with the exception of C. Wilderspin the comparative standard of the remaining junior boys was doubtful and definitely below that of pre-war, but not withstanding disposition and for 'tactical' reasons the Association should send a team of boys to compete in the Linton Cup and Australian Championship this season.*

The Committee requested that Wilderspin, J. Fletcher, D.C. Hamilton and T. Genge practice at the Mount Lawley Club with senior players. Unfortunately, it was indicated at a later meeting that 'the form of T.M. Genge was not considered to be up to standard' so he was not included in the official Linton Cup team. Trevor Genge, who later became a ranked senior player and leading umpire was, however, given permission to travel with the team at his own expense (*WALTA Minutes*, 18/12/1945). This was a better deal than the junior girls received. When the Executive ratified the Linton Cup team, it unanimously resolved that 'the standard of play of junior girls did not warrant the nomination of a team' (*WALTA Minutes*, 13/12/1945).

1949 Linton Cup Victors
Back: John Blacklock, Norm Wasley (Manager), Clive Wilderspin
Front: Noel Pearse and Brian Tobin

The Western Australian boys finished fourth in the Linton Cup. Manager Geoff Hammond (whose duties included umpiring the Australian championship match in which former Sandgroper Max Bonner defeated the ageing Jack Crawford) was able to report upon the particularly promising play of Clive Wilderspin. It was the first occasion that the young Clive had an opportunity to display his talents in eastern states company, and within a year, although Wilderspin was still only 16, he had made significant progress. The influential Harry Hopman was reported to be very impressed with his strokes and match temperament (*articles, Wilderspin file*). So when the LTAA resumed control of its ranked players and promising juniors, Wilderspin, together with team-mate John Blacklock, was brought under this provision. The latter had also come under notice and, with Wilderspin, was included in a national training squad.

During the 1949 Linton Cup series, Wilderspin was outstanding. He won all his singles matches with the loss of only nine games and, with the support of Blacklock, Brian Tobin (later President of the LTAA for 12 years to 1989) and Noel Pearse, Wilderspin brought the Linton Cup to the State for the first time. The Association Executive proudly formed a sub-committee 'to consider the form of recognition to team members of the 1949 Linton Cup' (*WALTA Minutes*, 22/2/1949). In addition, they were to celebrate Clive Wilderspin winning the Australian junior singles title and, in partnership with Blacklock, the Australian junior doubles title.

Soon after the triumphs of 1949, Wilderspin was invited by the LTAA to participate in a two-month tour of South Africa. After carefully considering advice, particularly from his father and tennis administrator Eric Wilderspin, he decided to pursue a diploma of engineering course rather than accept the tennis opportunity. When Adrian Quist came to Hensman Park some months later to play in the Spring Tournament, he asserted that Wilderspin 'had made a very wise choice' by placing his engineering course ahead of tennis (*Wilderspin file*). In the context of the times the decision was applauded but as leading Reabold player, Bill Edgar, later reminded 'Quist was a wily master of psychology'. In preparation for the tournament, Wilderspin practiced hard with Max Bonner. One of Bonner's tips was 'when changing ends cross the net on the opposite side to Quist'. Bonner had remembered how he once led Quist in the quarter-final of the Australian Open by two sets to love. At the changeover, the ex-Davis Cup star said to Bonner 'if you keep playing like this you will be in the Australian Davis Cup team' (interview with Bill Edgar, 30/8/1989). Unnerved Bonner became tentative and lost the match to Quist in five sets and never represented Australia. Although Wilderspin steered clear of Quist at the net, he was easily defeated. He did, however, later represent Australia, although not as a Davis Cup player.

Arguing that Wilderspin should live in Perth 'or fall prey to the sporting goods manufacturers', Herbert Edwards, the coach, columnist and commentator, contended in a newspaper article (*Wilderspin file*, 29/1/1947) that Wilderspin should be awarded a scholarship to complete his education in Sydney or Melbourne. Edwards was of the view that 'Wildy was WA's Best Ever'. At the time Herb Blacker, the country champion, supported this claim in a radio interview when he said 'Clive Wilderspin is undoubtedly outstanding in this State at present. The only player I could compare with Clive ... would be Rice Gemmell. Ron Ford, Harry Jacoby, 'Chum' Stevens, Gordon Davis and others were all good players but I don't think they were as good as Clive Wilderspin'. Of course, Wilderspin never moved east, where Lew Hoad and Ken Rosewall, among others in his age bracket, progressed so rapidly. At home, though, he was rarely beaten in domestic tournaments or when playing shield matches for Hensman Park. Remarkably, he was the state's top ranked player from 1947 to 1963, with 1959 and 1960 being the only exceptions. He had a national ranking but never won an Australian senior title although in 1954 he partnered Neale Fraser to be runner-up in the Australian Open Doubles Championship to Rex Hartwig and Mervyn Rose.

For several seasons, the State Open eluded Wilderspin. In 1949, when Bill Sidwell (NSW) won the title, he was forced to withdraw with a foot injury (*West Australian*, 16/4/1949, 2). On several occasions, he was defeated by players of outstanding calibre. The LTAA's policy of sending ranked players to states which did not hold the Australian Open or Davis Cup ties ensured that it would be difficult to win this most prestigious event. A list of finalists for the first post-war decade makes impressive reading. Included among the winners were Dinny Pails (1946), Frank Sedgeman (1948 and 1950), Ken McGregor (1951), Ken Rosewall (1953) and Rex Hartwig (1952 and 1955). Wilderspin was runner-up in 1950 and 1952. The same fate befell Max Bonner. Before the war, he was a finalist against Colin Long. In 1946, he lost to the muscular Dinny Pails, who, in the same year was the number one seed for the Wimbledon championship. In 1947, Bonner was beaten in straight sets by Victorian Les Brodie.

In the semi-final of the 1952 State Open, Wilderspin recorded a brilliant, pulsating win over Lew Hoad. The spectators had witnessed a wonderful fightback, with Wilderspin winning, 2/6, 0/6, 6/4, 9/7, 8/6. Then in the subsequent final between Wilderspin and Hartwig, before a crowd said to be the biggest since the visit of the French stars in 1928, the Western Australian lost in five gruelling sets, 12/10, 6/3, 1/6, 2/6, 6/1. In the marathon first set Wilderspin had a set point at 8/7 but lost the game after serving three double faults. In the fifth set the demands of the previous day had began to tell. For his part, Hartwig, had played an easier semi-final although his opponent John Blacklock gave a good performance and extended the visitor to four sets.

Wilderspin was becoming a household name in Western Australia. As a result it was suggested that a 'Wilderspin for Wimbledon' fund be established to raise £800 to enable him to compete at the 1953 championship. Five years earlier, at Harry Hopman's instigation, a 'Sedgman for Wimbledon' fund had been supported by the WALTA Council (*WALTA Annual Report*, 1947/1948). For its part, the WALTA Executive began corresponding with the LTAA to ascertain the procedures for accreditation at Wimbledon (*WALTA Minutes*, 4/8/1952). It was recognised that the exercise had to be handled with care, as Wilderspin's amateur status could easily be impaired. This problem had arisen in the Sedgman case and at one stage there had even been debate about whether his wedding gifts contravened the amateur code.

The support for the Wilderspin fund from metropolitan and country clubs was so encouraging that air booking's were made for his departure on 12 April, 1953. However, the need for the fund evaporated when he became the first Western Australian tennis player to be chosen in an Australian overseas team. This helped to create interest in the 1953 State Open, for which a record total of more than 1,000 entries had been received (*West Australian*, 25/3/1953, 18). Ken 'Muscles' Rosewall and Don Candy were the two LTAA ranked players at King's Park for the championship and as Wilderspin had taken Rosewall to five sets in the New South Wales and Victorian championship there was an air of expectation. Reporting on semi-final day, 'Smash' of the *West Australian* (6/4/1953, 13) under the sub-heading 'Disappointing' reported:

> *The spectators expected a good performance by Wilderspin who will shortly leave for Europe with the Australian team, but he gave a disappointing display against Candy who slowed the pace and allowed his opponent to make the errors.*

As there had been some debate as to whether Wilderspin should have been chosen ahead of Rex Hartwig and Don Candy in the Australian team, this rare poor display gave the eastern states sports writers some basis for criticism (*Australian Tennis*, May 1953, 7,10). So the LTAA soon had to contend with a Victorian request to establish a 'Hartwig for Wimbledon' campaign. Wilderspin, though, was close to the top and still only 22 years of age. The tour, under the guidance of disciplinarian Harry Hopman (whom Wilderspin respected) was obviously going to be of immense value.

Playing on the clay courts of Europe offered a challenge to a Western Australian accustomed to grass surfaces. However, in doubles Wilderspin soon adjusted. Playing from the favoured right court to take advantage of his strong forehand, he partnered Mervyn Rose to reach the semi-final of the Italian Open. A few weeks later in Paris, the same pair defeated Vic Seixas and Gardner Mulloy in the semi-final of the French Open but lost the final to Hoad and Rosewall. After playing quite well on the grass at Queens Club, Wilderspin entered the Wimbledon stage. On Centre Court he played brilliantly, but lost a 64-game marathon second round doubles encounter. Suffering from a slightly strained tendon, Wilderspin managed to defeat the giant German Ernst Buchhal in straight sets, then lost to his 'bogeyman' (and Wimbledon doubles partner) Ian Ayre of Queensland (*Western Mail*, 23/7/1953, 13).

The President of the WALTA, Mr Justice Walker, who was a guest of the All England Club for the 1953 Wimbledon Championship, was publicly warm in his praise of Wilderspin as an Australian representative (*Wilderspin file*). While very competitive and extremely determined, Wilderspin also displayed outstanding qualities of sportsmanship. Walker was also mindful of these qualities when he articulated the view that Wilderspin would be able to greatly lift the standard of play in Western Australia and simultaneously maintain an excellent image for local tennis. Not surprisingly, in September of the same year Wilderspin was named to accompany Mervyn Rose on a goodwill tour to Japan (*WALTA Minutes*, 7/9/1953). He also toured Ceylon (Sri Lanka) and New Zealand. This was the beginning of regular travel for leading players. But only the world's top 10 could be regarded as circuit players and Wilderspin was not yet in that category.

In 1954, Wilderspin won the elusive Western Australian Open by defeating Ashley Cooper, the future Wimbledon champion, in a high-standard final. A year later, he was outplayed by Hartwig in a tournament so disrupted by bad weather that the Royal King's Park Club was able to successfully submit an insurance claim to compensate for lost revenue (*West Australian*, 11/4/1955, 12/4/1955, and 13/4/1955). In 1956 Wilderspin was again the victor. After brilliantly defeating Roy Emerson, another future Wimbledon winner, he met Rose in the final. It was a tight four-set match in which Rose disputed line calls and annoyed the large crowd with frequent outbursts (*West Australian*, 3/4/1956, 26). The following day, Wilderspin had another four-set doubles title win when he partnered Blacklock to defeat leading state representatives Alan Hicks and Bruce Robinson (*West Australian*, 4/4/1956, 18). A loss in the mixed doubles semi-final with women's champion Jill Langley (after winning the first set 6/0) cost him the triple crown.

The modest Wilderspin was always news in Western Australian tennis. He was a regular contender for Sportsman of the Year awards. In 1953, he went close to top billing but football legend Merv McIntosh was declared the winner. Yet it should not be forgotten that during this period a number of other players emerged with very good credentials. Blacklock has already been mentioned. Keith Holten and Dawson Hamilton were highly ranked. Hamilton, from the Goldfields, was also an outstanding cricketer and squash player (Terrell, 1993, 183). Two juniors from Wesley College, (Wilderspin's old school) Bruce Robinson and Arthur Marshall were prominent, rising respectively to four and five in senior ranking. They later became important figures in Western Australian tennis, Marshall in particular enjoying success at Wimbledon. Brian Ford, son of the former state number one, Ron Ford, shared with Marshall the distinction of taking a set from Hoad. Alan Hicks, a tall thin six footer (183 cm.) from Kalgoorlie, was a fine sportsman who had fortunately chosen tennis. Hicks, too, won a set from Hoad in a Linton Cup match at White City in 1951. In fact Hicks served for the match at 6/5 in the third set, but eventually lost 7/9. Other ranked players who could be listed include Claremont's Geoff Strang, the unorthodox Alick Bridge (originally from South Australia), Vern White from Royal King's Park, Sam Hodsdon and Ron Harris.

Seedings below number one were very important at that time, as the top seed always played number eight. Hicks cheerfully complained that he was 'locked in' at number eight, continuously playing Wilderspin in the quarter-finals (interview with Alan Hicks, 26/6/1989). When questioned about playing Hicks under the old seedings, Wilderspin chose instead to comment upon the slow pace of Hicks' left-handed serve. Wilderspin believed that Hicks could sometimes 'be all over you at the net' before the looping ball arrived. 'Wildy', known to some of his contemporaries as 'Mick', had a sense of humour and could tell a yarn. In one amusing incident, Wilderspin has recalled how a ball was temporarily lost in a championship match at Mandurah when Hicks managed to 'donkey lob' a serve in his pocket. 'Mick' did not realise what had happened and opponents Arthur Marshall and Bruce Robinson were nonplussed. Hicks, it is speculated, had got to the net ahead of his service so did not see what had occurred (interview with Clive Wilderspin, 20/12/1993).

The enthusiastic and immaculate Max Bonner in action

Most of the younger brigade of ranked players, sharing with Hicks a sense of awareness about the seedings, had been chosen in the Linton Cup team. Apart from interstate competition these representatives benefited from squad training. After 1949, Max Bonner, who had returned from Victoria as a professional coach, regularly conducted the training. It was not WALTA policy to designate an official State coach, but the immaculate, 'call me Uncle Max', Bonner was a positive influence. Bonner established himself as a venerated figure in many quarters of Western Australian tennis (*Westennis*, December 1991, 42-43). As mentioned, he had proven his skills against illustrious players such as Quist, Pails, Hopman, Sedgman and Bromwich (whom Bonner thought saw the ball so early he could check the flagpole for wind direction before he played his shot). Bonner's influence as a coach, particularly in schools was profound. For instance his record at Hale School was itself outstanding. In 1950 he was invited to coach some Hale boys on a trial basis at the Royal King's Park courts. The enthusiastic Bonner remained for some 35 years with the school naming its courts (in 1985) 'The Max Bonner Courts'. He insisted that at least every person on court could 'at least look like a tennis player'. At all times, his charges were exhorted to achieve bigger things as he would say, 'win that rally, champ, and you've won a free trip around the world'. As a coach he taught the finer points of the game but he was also about developing character and equipping youth for life itself. At Hale, at other schools, and at the WALTA, he was able to erase the simplistic belief that tennis was not a team game and that it encouraged too much individuality (Tregonning, 1993, 194).

Max Bonner 'became a legend in his own lifetime'. He had expanded the scope of his coaching duties when Herbert Edwards was beginning to scale down his coaching role, although his sons Stan and Vic kept the Kitchener Park enterprise going. Vic Edwards later moved to the eastern states and, as already mentioned, played an important role in the rise to stardom of Evonne Goolagong (Cawley). The subsequent publication of Cawley's biography has elaborated on his influence (*Goolagong Cawley and Jarratt*, 1993). Yet, while Bonner and Edwards were the big names in coaching, many of the leading players had not received concentrated professional coaching. Most, however, can recall receiving encouragement from a particular tennis enthusiast. Those in the latter category are too numerous to list but one, Roger Ryan, typifies the amateur coach. Ryan gave his time to provide students at St Brigids' Convent in West Leederville with a chance to learn the rudiments of the game. He would have been proud that his daughters Roma and Joan later became leading players for Subiaco. Conscious of his limitations, Ryan sent his best products to the 'finishing' school of Herbert Edwards for some further guidance, and even more importantly, for some publicity (interview with Margaret Robinson, 27/9/1989).

One prominent player who came through the ranks relying on voluntarism was Keith Holten. He had missed Linton Cup selection before Max Bonner trained the state squads. Holten was apparently of the view that he could have received more assistance from the Association. This matter was aired publicly when George Worthington, the New South Wales player, convincingly won the City of Perth singles titles during the 1948 festive season. Worthington, after defeating Keith Holten 6/0, 6/1, 6/1 in the final, 'referred to the poor showing of local players ... who lacked experience against top ranking players' (*Daily News*, 5/1/1949). Holten objected to being made the scapegoat for local players and said (*Daily News*, 5/1/1949) that:

> *(He) wanted to emphasise that his success had been entirely due to his own efforts and to the encouragement of the Nedlands club. He had seen the WALTA send players to the Eastern States for experience - players of his own age who had since dropped out of competition, but he had never in any way been helped.*

Long-serving secretary, G.H. Carlisle, conceded that Holten had improved after joining senior ranks, but the rapid development by some players always leaves the Association selectors vulnerable to similar charges. Carlisle, after expressing surprise at the claim, reiterated that 'encouragement was given to junior players according to their merits ...' (*Daily News* 7/1/1949). Holten turned professional and began coaching in 1950 but his case did help to lead to consideration of six (instead of four) juniors being sent to the Australian Championships and Linton Cup competitions (*WALTA Minutes*, 10/10/1949). What also prompted the decision to send more juniors was pressure from the WALTA on the LTAA to conduct a coach-in-residence scheme for juniors who displayed potential at the Australian championships (*WALTA Minutes*, 1/4/1948).

The LTAA implemented the coaching scheme at the beginning of the 1950s, several promising Western Australian junior boys and girls being selected. The first were the Eastern Goldfields duo of Alan Hicks and Les Grafton. Immediately after the 1950 Australian Championship, they received special coaching and physical education 'drill' under the supervision of former Davis Cup player Pat O'Hara Wood. Arthur Marshall and Bruce Robinson were selected in both 1951 and 1952. Jill Langley was also twice (1952 and 1953) included in the program. Other top juniors who received the benefit of this coaching (later given by Harry Hopman) were Mary Blacklock and Margaret Heron in 1951 and Bruce Francis and Don Watts in 1953. Watts, also a competent squash player, later became a state selector before becoming a leading educationist. For those who argue that tennis provides considerable scope for 'match-making' it should be noted that Mary Blacklock later married Alan Hicks and Margaret Heron likewise married Bruce Robinson.

International and interstate matches

One strategy to strengthen tennis that was vigorously pursued in the first decade after the war was the scheduling of exhibition matches with international and interstate players. The WALTA delegates at the LTAA, still H.A. Pitt and T.E. Robinson, often helped the WALTA Executive to obtain satisfactory terms. The exhibition matches were regarded as valuable sources of additional revenue. As Australia and the United States were perennial finalists in the Davis Cup, there was keen public interest in seeing the leading Davis Cup players in Perth. Many of these competitors were also prominent in the various Grand Slam events.

At the end of the Davis Cup Challenge Round played in late 1946, the victorious Americans, Jack Kramer and Fred Schroeder, played a two-day exhibition in Perth against Adrian Quist and Les Brodie commencing on New Year's Day 1947. The matches were enthusiastically patronised by a public eager for top tennis. At the annual general meeting in March 1947, President Mursell reported that the audited accounts for the year disclosed a substantial surplus of over £425, due in the main, to the financial success of the exhibition matches (*WALTA Annual Report*, 1946/1947). Later, the Association narrowly missed a further chance to boost its funds when a series of exhibition matches between the 1947, Australian Davis Cup players, scheduled for 29 March, 1947 had to be cancelled. The players were on their way to Wimbledon, but a last-minute change in the shipping timetable led to the program being abandoned (*WALTA Annual Report*, 1946-1947).

In January 1948, another international match between the United States and Australia was played at the Royal King's Park courts. However, the revenue to the Association dropped from £705 to £103 (*WALTA Annual Reports*, 1946/1947 and 1947/1948). The Association was still in the black but the public support was not as enthusiastic. The participating teams were not as strong and the match failed to make headlines (*West Australian*, 10/1/1948, and *Sunday Times*, 11/1/1948, 7). The American team, which won by four rubbers to two rubbers, was Edward Moylan (ranked 8 in the US) and Jim Brink not ranked in the US) and the Australian representatives were Jack Dart (ranked 8 in Australia) and the bespectacled Colin Long (ranked 6 in Australia).

One emerging factor in the exhibition scene was the marketing of professional tours. This was not a new phenomenon in world tennis but it had not significantly affected Australian or Western Australian tennis before. In the 1930s, WALTA officials gave brief consideration to arranging a visit by the great Bill Tilden, who had turned professional. In October 1948, the Association was invited to conduct matches between a new troupe of professional players headed by Jack Kramer (the 1947 Wimbledon champion) (*WALTA Minutes*, 24/9/1948). A regular visitor to Western Australia, Dinny Pails, was also to participate. Finally the Association considered the financial commitments to be too unacceptable, so the offer was declined (*WALTA Annual Report*, 1948/1949).

During 1948, the Association was also presented with the option of Doris Hart, the American champion, playing in Perth. LTAA delegate H.A. Pitt considered that unless Doris Hart was accompanied by a ranked player such as Nancye Bolton (Wynne) the visit would not capture much interest (*WALTA Minutes*, 4/11/1948). Hart had twice been runner-up at Wimbledon, although she was later to win the title in 1951. Eventually Hart did play in Perth, in mid-January 1949. A fortnight later, she defeated Nancye Bolton in the women's Australian Open singles final. Hart made news when she contended that Australia's tennis stars needed more encouragement (*Daily News*, 13/1/1949, 6), but she endeared herself to the public with praise about the cleanliness of Perth. Other participants in the exhibition were Joyce Fitch (runner-up to Bolton in the 1946 Australian Open), together with Frank Sedgman and 'foot fault offender' George Worthington (*Daily News*, 12/1/1949, 11). Although the fixture was well received by the players, there was no financial profit to the Association. It confirmed the view expressed at a meeting in the spring of 1948, 'that the Association was concerned only in meeting the possible demand of the tennis public, the matter of financial benefit being a secondary consideration' (*WALTA Minutes*, 24/9/1948).

The promising performances of Wilderspin enabled a different marketing strategy to be employed when an international match was played at Royal

King's Park under LTAA auspices on 10 and 12 February, 1950. Wilderspin was included in the Australian team, along with Don Candy and Ken McGregor. The internationals were the European Jaroslav Drobny and Eddie Sturgess of South Africa. The series of closely contested matches was attended by large and appreciative audiences. The internationals won the tie, which provided a very satisfactory financial return (*WALTA Annual Report*, 1949/1950) In late December of the same year, the Association was fortunate to be able to stage another exhibition match between American representatives Art Larsen and Dick Savitt and Australian Davis Cup players McGregor and Rose. The honours were again carried by the visitors with public support resulting in financial benefit (*WALTA Annual Report*, 1949/1950).

Maureen 'Little Mo' Connolly, played in Perth in 1953.
Maureen Connolly (left) and Julie Sampson, (right) arrive at Perth Airport on 27 January, 1953. (Courtesy The West Australian)

In 1952 the Association altered its financial year ending from 31 March to 30 June, but the 15 month period to June 1952 was not accompanied by any overall revenue boost from international exhibition matches. Attempts at various times to secure visits from American and Swedish players did not come to fruition. Later, though, the LTAA did provide Western Australia with a compensation package. The wait was worth it, as the famous Maureen ('Little Mo') Connolly graced centre court at Royal King's Park in late January 1953. It was the first occasion on which a reigning Wimbledon champion had played in Perth. Connolly's great stature as a player tended to overshadow the fact that Julie Sampson (the United States junior champion), Nell Hopman, Helen Angwin, Rex Hartwig and Clive Wilderspin also participated. The immaculate and compact Connolly was actually a little jaded at the end of an arduous Australian tour and, on the first day, she lost a set to Angwin. Teaming with Wilderspin she then lost the mixed doubles to Sampson and Hartwig (*West Australian*, 31/1/1953, 10), but on the final day, she gave a dazzling display in the singles to make the occasion a memorable one for women's tennis. On this topic, Connolly said 'your women need a lot more overseas experience. International trips, say on Davis Cup lines, would help them a great deal to learn strategy. With that experience there is no reason why they cannot be right up to world class' (*West Australian*, 28/1/1953, 13). For her part, 'Little Mo' who was soon to win the Grand Slam, said she was 'keen to return'. Fate did not permit this to happen; but she gave many Western Australians a glimpse of her remarkable prowess.

Further proof that Western Australians would patronise quality tennis came in January 1954. In the 'hype-ridden Davis Cup atmosphere', Vic Seixas and Tony Trabert represented the United States in exhibition matches against Rose and Hartwig for Australia. The tie resulted in a win for the U.S. 4 rubbers and 11 sets to 2 rubbers and 7 sets. On the first day's play, Hartwig and Rose defeated Seixas and Trabert 9/7, 10/12, 6/1, 5/7, 6/2. Next day the result was reversed, with the Americans winning 7/5, 2/6, 6/1, 4/6, 12/10. 'Smash' of the (*West Australian*, (18/1/1954, 19) reported:

> *Many people had joined long queues in the hope of gaining admittance but as on the previous day hundreds were turned away ... It was obvious that in future WALTA will have to make greater provision for the public when world class players are brought here.*

Fortunately for WALTA officials, they had negotiated with the LTAA an 80:20 split of the net profit (*WALTA Annual Report*, 1953/1954). Less than a month later, the profit-sharing ratio proved of little consequence when Western Australia hosted the fifth tennis test match between South Africa and Australia. The 1979 Gleneagles Agreement restricting sporting contacts between Commonwealth countries and South Africa was far in the future but no official South African tennis team returned to Perth until January 1993 for the Hopman Cup. The visitors' team comprising A. Segal, O. Williams, I. Vermaak, Mrs H. Redick-Smith and Mrs J. Wipplinger had a resounding eight rubbers to nil victory over Australia represented by Brian Bowman, Bill Gilmour, Helen Angwin and Norma Ellis. None of the players was a top line international. Furthermore, the test series had already been determined, with South Africa winning the A.N.Z.A. Cup for competition between the two countries. Not surprisingly, the crowds were very disappointing (*West Australian*, 12/3/1954, 20). Publicity for the test included a novel story which had a happy ending when Eric Wilderspin, the WALTA official, was able to procure a boomerang for Mrs Wipplinger (*West Australian*, 12/3/1954, 20). Another headline, however, condemned the LTAA for its handling of the tour and failing to maintain the goodwill generated by Australia's tour of South Africa in 1952. A writer in the *Sporting Globe* (*Wilderspin file*) noted:

> *It beggars (sic) comprehension how we, the leading tennis nation in the world, could have been so downright rude to representatives of a sister dominion ... The South Africans in private have spoken their piece, as they were thoroughly entitled to do.*

At this time, with the State Open only a few weeks away at Easter, the Western Australian public was receiving more than its usual share of international tennis. Before the international matches between Australia and the United States, and then South Africa, the WALTA administration had hosted the first interzone final of the 1953 Davis Cup. Played in December 1953, at Royal King's Park, it was the first time the WALTA had conducted a Davis Cup fixture. For nearly 50 years the Association had been seeking a Cup tie. Officials would have preferred Australia to be a competing nation but, as it transpired, Belgium played India. The tie was won by Belgium which earned the right to play the United States in the second interzone final. Reports indicated that about 5,400 people attended an efficiently managed event (*WALTA Annual Report*, 1953/1954).

Suggestions that Western Australian fans might be able to expect regular Davis Cup fixtures came in mid-December 1956, when the WALTA was allocated the higher profile second interzone final between India and the United States. This was a gala occasion attended by the top executives of the LTAA and members of the international press. The State Governor, Sir Charles Gairdner, as patron of the Association, officiated at the draw and watched several of the keenly fought matches. The opening singles rubber was a tense five-set struggle with Herb Flam defeating Ramanathan Krishnan 7/5, 4/6, 10/8, 2/6, 6/4. Eventually the United States of America cruised to a 4-1 victory. The team, captained by the popular Bill Talbert, included Vic Seixas, Sammy Giammalva and Mike Green. Tony Trabert who had been a team regular, had turned professional and was no longer eligible to play. Even without Trabert, ticket sales totalled 7,715, with gross receipts amounting to £5,471 and expenses £1,722. The Association and Royal King's Park shared the ground rental of £937, leaving £2,812 available to the competing nations to cover travelling expenses to Perth and share in the profits (*WALTA Annual Report*, 1956/1957). It now seems 'small bickies' but the Davis Cup revenues in the 1950s provided considerable financial assistance to Australian tennis.

Earlier, in January 1955, just a fortnight after Australia had lost the Davis Cup to the United States and before the Australian Championship, Tony Trabert had played in Perth. Partnered by his regular 'second string' Seixas (who had won Wimbledon in 1953), Trabert played Australia in an international match. Top drawcards Hoad and Rosewall ensured wonderful tennis. Despite complaints from Rosewall that he had not wanted to come to Perth but had been forced to do so by the LTAA (*West Australian*, 14/1/1955, 18), the Australians gained some revenge with a narrow 4 rubbers to 2 rubbers win. Rosewall 'with his stroking and control almost faultless' (*West Australian*, 15/1/1955,15) thrilled the gallery of nearly 8,200 spectators over the two days with straight-set wins over Trabert and Seixas (*WALTA Annual Report*, 1954/1955).

An international tennis fixture again opened the calendar year of 1956 when Americans Herb Flam and Gill Shea played the Australian team of Ashley Cooper and Mal Anderson. Although the standard of tennis was high the attendance over the two days was only 4,276, about half the number who had gone through the turnstiles a year earlier (*WALTA Annual Report*, 1955/1956). Before their departure the Americans described Royal King's Park as 'ideal' for interzone Davis Cup tennis (*West Australian*, 9/1/1956, 16). During the decade since the war, the Association had been able to offer the public, at the King's Park venue, a wealth of international talent. In some WALTA circles, though, there was agitation for the rejuvenation of interstate tennis. It was recognised that interstate tennis structured on the lines of the Sheffield Shield cricket competition was not viable, although such an objective had been sought when the Mars Buckley Competition was inaugurated in 1906. Rather, it was the WALTA policy to reach agreement with the South Australian Tennis Association. These states were thought to be comparable in tennis strength and with a common border travel costs were reduced. President Vernon Mursell offered to donate £100 for a Challenge Cup (*WALTA Minutes*, 11/6/1954). The South Australian Association, perhaps harbouring some reservations about the long-term viability of the competition, did not accept the overture.

When Western Australia did play South Australia on 29 March, 1953 the *West Australian* columnist (30/3/1953, 14) incorrectly labelled it 'as the first official interstate match played in Perth'. It was, however, the first time that Western Australia scored a resounding 12 rubbers to nil victory. Wilderspin was said to be 'a class above the rest of the players' (*West Australian* 30/3/1953, 14). Obviously, though, his team-mates John Blacklock, Alick Bridge and Dawson Hamilton had all pulled their weight against a weak South Australian team, but if WALTA officials felt satisfied that they had reinstated senior interstate tennis they were soon to discover they had actually ignited one of the worst feuds in the Association's history. This was about the lack of opportunities in women's tennis exemplified by the omission of women from the interstate fixture.

Significantly, when Western Australia played South Australia in a return match in Adelaide a year later, Pat Holmes and June McLeod were included in the team with Wilderspin and Blacklock. In a close contest, Wilderspin just managed to defeat the improving Brian Bowman. Holmes performed convincingly, living up to the reputation for determination she had gained under her maiden name of Cunningham. Later, as Pat Stanley, these same traits became evident when she turned her hand to administration. Nevertheless on the final day, after a straight-set singles victory, Pat Holmes teamed with the tall McLeod to save five match points and eventually win the deciding doubles 3/6, 11/9, 6/4 (*West Australian*, 13/1/1954, 14). One of McLeod's best performances was to come a fortnight later, when she reached the semi-final of the Australian junior girls' singles championship.

Pat Cunningham/Ho mes/Stanley, a determined player anc administrator

During the next three seasons, the Western Australia versus South Australia fixture was conducted with the two women and two men team composition retained. Wilderspin was a member of each team. Twice his partner was Dawson Hamilton and in 1957 the selected colleague was Doug Napier. Of the women team members Jill Langley was also chosen on each occasion. Her colleagues were, respectively, Mrs Mary White, (the State Open title winner in 1953 and 1954), former Kalgoorlie player Margaret Stewart, and again June McLeod in 1957. Each contest resulted in a seven rubber to five rubber scoreline with Western Australia winning in 1955 and 1956 and South Australia in 1957 (*WALTA Annual Reports*, 1954/1955, 1955/1956; and 1956/1957).

Each series with South Australia was conducted either just prior to the Western Australian Open at Easter (at home) or before the South Australian and Australian Championship in January (away). Compared with international matches, the encounters did not attract much public interest and gate takings were negligible. Indeed for the first meeting in Perth, an approach to the government to allow admission to be charged on a Sunday was denied (*WALTA Minutes*, 27/3/1953). This meant the only source of revenue was to be donations from the crowd.

The Women's Tennis Progress Movement

There was certainly no expectation that the inclusion of women in the teams would add to spectator appeal. In fact, a South Australian delegate at the LTAA publicly claimed that 'women players as a drawcard were not worth two pennyworth of gin' (*Wilderspin file*). The LTAA, as well as the WALTA, was beginning to receive trenchant criticism for its handling of women's tennis. There was dissatisfaction with the low number of overseas tours which the LTAA provided for leading women players. Then, when a women's team was selected for international and Wimbledon experience, Adrian Quist was appointed manager. Reflecting the extent of disagreement, the appointment required a casting vote to be validated (*WALTA Minutes*, 10/3/1955).

At the national level, Nell Hopman, Nancye Bolton and Thelma Long were at the forefront of efforts to improve the women's lot in tennis. At the Australian Open in 1956, Mary Carter (later Reitano) and Daphney Seeney (later Fancutt) had refused an attempt by officials to move their semi-final match from the centre court to accommodate the men's semi-final. They went 'on strike' by locking themselves in the change rooms until officialdom was eventually forced to buckle and accede to the women's demands. What was needed as a catalyst was an Australian woman such as Maureen Connolly, but if women's tennis was not being developed, it was unlikely that a champion would emerge.

Success by Australian men at Wimbledon, a string of epic Davis Cup victories and a fine local hero in Wilderspin all militated against publicity being given to women's tennis in Western Australia. Due to rule 19(3) of the 1934 Constitution, no women could be a member of the WALTA Council or Executive. Even when it was decided to adopt Frank Grove's suggestion that the composition of all the committees of the Council be published in the Annual Report, women's names were conspicuous by their absence. A new outlook was necessary if the situation was to change. This is perhaps best illustrated when the Executive was asked to decide whether it was policy to permit men and women linespersons to officiate in the same match. The Executive resolved to advise the Umpires' Association that (*WALTA Minutes*, 5/4/1954):

> *The Association did not have a definite policy in regard to linesmen, but that generally it preferred male linesmen, and would consider female linesmen provided a sufficient number were available to take all the lines in any one match.*

It is difficult to reliably gauge how concerned the Executive really was about women's tennis. Ken Miller, who was President of the Association for nearly 10 years until 1962, had presided over the recording in the minutes of the reaction to the omission of women from the previously mentioned match against South Australia. In the face of mounting criticism 'members were requested to do everything possible to break down the spirit of animosity which appeared evident in this regard' (*WALTA Minutes*, 23/3/1953). Nevertheless, in the short term it was decided 'no useful purpose could be served in appointing a special advisory committee on women's tennis' (*WALTA Minutes*, 13/4/1953). Not surprisingly, this did not alleviate the concern as two years later the Executive received a letter from 'The Women's Tennis Progress Movement' requesting permission for a deputation of five to attend a Council meeting to present their views. The case was first presented to the Council by the Alexander Park delegate Mr H.F. Watts, whose two children, Don and Val (later Bandy) were leading players. Watts stated that he had the pleasure of being indirectly associated with the movement. It was based 'not on grudges or personal grievances but on a keen and earnest desire to assist in the administration of tennis in this state' (*WALTA Minutes*, 9/6/1955).

Among some members of the Association there was clear resistance, as a series of devices were used to obstruct the actions of the movement. Former President J.C. Walker 'queried if the movement was a representative body' (*WALTA Minutes*, 7/6/1955). Walker then used his legal expertise, which had included terms as Solicitor-General and Chief Parliamentary Draughtsman for Western Australia as well as being a Puisne Judge of the Supreme Court, to ascertain if the group had office bearers, a ratified constitution and a list of members (*WALTA Minutes*, 9/6/1955). Watts conceded that none of these conditions could be satisfied, but he was able to report that the Council would receive a deputation at its July 1955 meeting. By the time of the meeting, the identities of those who were to lead the deputation for the 'Women's Tennis Progress Movement' had become known. Importantly these three women - Val Bandy, Margot Arcus and Jill McLeod - were leading players and had won a host of state titles. Val Bandy, as Val Watts, had won the State Junior title as early as 1940, at a time when no Wilson Cup teams were being sent from Western Australia. She also gave early indication of her doubles prowess by sharing the Open Women's Doubles title. After the war Bandy continued to play at the top level for many seasons, although the State Open title eluded this keen competitor. In 1951, she was to be beaten by Joan Ryan in a three-set final and was runner-up in the doubles. Bandy had the rare distinction of playing in five consecutive Open doubles finals, with victories in 1950, 1952 and 1953. Margot Arcus (nee Grace) also remarkably appeared in six Open doubles finals claiming the trophy in 1949 and 1955. As Margot Grace, she had won the State Open in 1949 but she had never represented the state in junior or senior competition. On the other hand June McLeod, the third member of the deputation, had played for Western Australia in the Wilson Cup and at a senior level against South Australia.

To accompany Bandy, Arcus and McLeod were parents and Council delegates Messrs Watts and McLeod. The main purpose of the deputation 'was to stress that women play such an active part in the game that it is right they should have direct representation on the council' (*West Australian*, 14/7/1955,19).

Val Bandy (Watts), a top player, who with Margot Argus and Jill McLeod lead the deputation for the 'Women's Tennis Progress Movement'

They were armed with the knowledge that in most other Australian states, and particularly New South Wales, women had representation in the state bodies. It was their intention to urge that the WALTA Constitution be amended to provide for women delegates to be appointed. This was clearly going to be a formidable task as, when the matter had been first raised at Executive, Morrie Beard (a future Association President) had made it clear that there was a formal procedure for club delegates to follow when seeking constitutional amendments (*WALTA Minutes*, 7/6/1955).

The deputation, which had its case thoroughly prepared, was received quite cordially by the Council on 14 July, 1955. Bandy provided a brief description of the movement's history. 'As a consequence of the current unrest on the part of women due to their non participation in the running ...' of tennis in Western Australia the first meeting of the movement had been attended by some 50 people. When a petition was circulated at least 650 signatures had been received. It was stressed that the, 'only aim of the movement was a temporary one to achieve its objective in allowing women to be represented on the Council and that the Movement would then disband'. June McLeod's research indicated that the representation objective had been achieved in other states while Margot Arcus conveyed some of the thoughts of the leading national player Nancye Bolton on the matter. According to Bolton, the administration of tennis had discernibly improved since women were elected to the Victorian Council (*WALTA Minutes*, 14/7/1955).

Council members queried if any juniors had signed the petition. They also sought more detail about the constitutional arrangements the women were seeking to ensure their representation. Norman Wasley, a keen advocate of interstate tennis and junior coaching, expressed disappointment on behalf of the State Selection Committee about the absence of leading women players in recent tournaments. One delegate submitted that it may be necessary to establish a separate federation to accommodate the Movement's aim (*WALTA Minutes*, 14/7/1955). In other sports such as bowls and hockey separate men's and women's bodies were in existence. Only time would tell what policies, if any, the Council would pursue. However, as the hierarchy of the WALTA was resistant, the Women's Tennis Progress Movement failed to achieve its objective. Success was not to be forthcoming for a decade.

Other leading women players

The absence of a woman with a national ranking militated against resources being devoted to women's tennis. Joyce McDermott (who as Joyce Wood of Victoria) had won the 1940 Western Australian Open, did have impressive credentials. After marrying Linton Cup player Max McDermott, she had settled in the West and had a mortgage on titles in the immediate post-war seasons. This included singles, doubles (often with Mary Prindiville) and mixed doubles with her husband until severe back problems prematurely ended her career. Nevertheless, it was mainly the war and the isolation of Western Australia that prevented her from rising to greater heights.

Some of the other leading players have already been mentioned in the context of the Women's Tennis Progress Movement and senior interstate representation. Three women won two State Open singles titles each. Mrs Helen Collins from the Subiaco Club took the title in 1950 and 1957. She had a reputation for 'hitting everything back'. Another with a similar reputation was Mary White, who had come from Victoria and played at King's Park. Her 1953 win over Joan Ryan (later Davies) is believed to be the longest final in the history of the Open. The set scores of 7/5, 4/6, 9/7 means the record stands at 38 games. This epic final thwarted Ryan's bid for a 'hat-trick' of State Opens; the physical education teacher at Methodist Ladies College had previously won the Open in three-set encounters in 1951 and 1952.

In Wilson Cup competition, Mary Blacklock, competing in her third successive Wilson Cup competition, had a sensational year in 1952 when she defeated top ranking Australian juniors Jenny Staley (later Hoad) and Mary Carter. Mary Blacklock, and brother John, had been leading juniors at the powerful Hensman Park club. Other top junior girls at the club, apart from Pat Cunningham, were Una 'Muffie' Prater and Peta Corry. Prater (later Rogers) then became active in squash and continued to play competitive tennis. The first junior to be selected in four consecutive Wilson Cup teams (1949-1952) was Subiaco's Margaret Heron. She was also the first woman player in Western Australia to undertake a private tour to play in the major tennis centres of Europe. In 1958, she was also the first woman (as Margaret Robinson) to turn professional. Her fine technique and relaxed style were obviously key factors in enabling her to play quality tennis for a further 40 years and permit her to represent Australia in veterans' tennis. While a 'trail blazer' in her own way, one characteristic Robinson did share with several of her Wilson Cup colleagues was her willingness to stay in tennis. Joan Hanlin (later Van Noort), Verna Calnon (later Hutchison), Maureen Sayers (later Scott), Laura Einihovici (later Raiter), and Lillian Cartledge (later Lake) all fit this category.

By common agreement, though, the woman who showed the greatest potential was Jill Langley. She performed creditably in the Wilson Cup and senior interstate matches. At 15 she won the State hardcourt title. In 1955, Langley received a national junior ranking, becoming the first Western Australian woman to achieve this status. After losing two State Open finals (to Mary White in 1954 and the South Australian Mrs Thiele in 1955) she comfortably beat Jill McLeod 6/2, 6/1 in 1956. At one stage there were discussions about the possibility of Langley being chosen to represent Australia. In Perth, she had benefited from Max Bonner's tuition. She temporarily moved to the eastern states in an attempt to gain more competition and was runner-up, with Bill Knight of Great Britain, in the 1957 Australian Open mixed doubles final. There was no financial assistance for players and even while playing in the Open, Langley had to return to work during the hours she was not on court. Eventually, she played at Wimbledon; she had the capacity, given the opportunities to achieve at the international level. As one sportswriter wrote, 'she was well built and versatile, she volleys and smashes strongly and is a good tactician who favours the net game' (*Wilderspin file*). Like her good friend Margaret Robinson, she continued, as Jill Bignell, to be involved in Western Australian tennis.

Joan Ryan, (later Davies) winner State Open 1951, 1952

Mrs Helen Collins, winner State Open 1950, 1957 (Courtesy-The West Australian)

Mary Blacklock, (later Hicks) 'a sensational year in 1952'

Publicity

One of the features of Jill Langley's style was her emphasis on attack. This helped draw publicity for her performances (*West Australian*, 28/3/1956, 21). However, Association officials frequently expressed concern about the relatively poor coverage of local tennis. In March 1946, the WALTA had negotiated with newspapers attempting to have championship draws published without charge (*WALTA Minutes*, 5/3/1946). Less than a year later, secretary Carlisle also wrote to the *Daily News* seeking reinstatement of tennis notes in that newspaper (*WALTA Minutes*, 11/2/1947). This was a far cry from the late 1930s, when newspapers were prepared to publish draws from private clubs

Margaret Heron, (later Robinson) on right with Mary Blacklock on left 'Top player, coach and veteran'

Jill Langley, (later Bignell) winner State Open 1956 'The woman who showed the greatest potential'

and give extensive coverage to both men's and women's tennis.

One tennis matter which did create a sensation, even in the local newspapers and magazines, had an international origin. Trying to find something distinctive to wear at the 1949 Wimbledon and abide by the 'all-white' rules, Gussy Moran, from the United States, and clothes specialist Ted Tinling designed a short dress and placed a two centimetre width of lace trim around the knickers. Although Tinling had worked at Wimbledon as master of ceremonies for over 20 years, he resigned when he was informed that he let 'vulgarity into tennis' (Snyder, 1993, n.p.).

Despite the 'Gorgeous' Gussy's publicity, tennis attire was not a matter which troubled the WALTA Council of male delegates. In the immediate post-war years, men had universally reverted to wearing shorts in match-play. Yvon Petra was the last man to win the Wimbledon singles final wearing long trousers when, in 1946, he defeated Australian Geoff Brown in five sets. Brown's fate of runner-up status in the singles, doubles (with Dinny Pails) and mixed doubles, with Dorothy Bundy, was well documented in the press although not on the scale of John Bromwich's 1948 defeat in the Wimbledon final. Bromwich had two match points against American Bob Falkenberg before he succumbed to the pressure of the occasion.

Highlights of Wimbledon were invariably featured in the newspapers and on radio. What the WALTA sought was more coverage of local tennis. Ron Halcombe of the ABC considered the Association should appoint a liaison or publicity officer. ABC management refused to pay royalties for tennis broadcasts, contending that broadcasting should be on the same basis as newspaper reporting for which no rights were paid (*Daily News*, 12/1/1949, 6). The Executive lobbied Halcombe for more air time for tennis and then decided to appoint a publicity officer. At first Brian Kinnane from King's Park, who held a state ranking in the 1930s (and 1946) was recommended, but he declined (*WALTA Minutes*, 12/9/1947 and 14/11/1947). Eventually lawyer Geoff Hammond was persuaded to accept the position. Subsequently a sub-committee under the chairmanship of Executive member Frank Grove recommended the establishment of a permanent Council Publicity Committee (*WALTA Minutes*, 6/8/1951).

Juniors

Officials obviously regarded favourable publicity as important to the development of tennis. Similarly, the junior coaching system and the fostering of tennis in schools was important. R.S. Whittington in *An Illustrated History of Australian Tennis* (1975, 69-70) claimed that one of the major reasons for Australia's post-war tennis supremacy was its nation-wide coaching system. Other reasons given were the opportunity for tough competition in the Linton and Wilson Cups, the support given by some sports goods manufacturers (notably Dunlop and Slazenger), and the influence of Harry Hopman. The WALTA had been a full partner in the establishment of a national coaching scheme. Subsidies were also provided to clubs to encourage junior coaching. Moreover, Western Australia had supported the Linton and Wilson Cup competitions, despite the cost. The WALTA was incorporated in the national plan but the champions from Western Australian were few in number.

The WALTA expanded its school competition with the introduction of the Herbert Edwards Cup for girls under 15 years of age. At first there were objections to the donor's name being used, as it was thought to be providing a commercial advantage to Edwards as a coach (*WALTA Minutes*, 2/2/1947).

When the competition was first conducted in 1944, it was won by Presbyterian Ladies College. Two of the team members Una Prater (later 'Muffie' Rogers) and June Lynn (later June Craig, a Minister in the Government of Sir Charles Court) played Wilson Cup for the State. The school had normally also performed well in the Slazenger Cup. After 1950, this competition was expanded to a second division, the trophy being known as the Mursell Shield.

Immediately after the war, officials made several attempts to have tennis designated a major sport in schools. Discussions were held with the Education Department and principals in the private schools. The outcomes were never entirely satisfactory to the Association. At one time the viability of the Slazenger Cup for boys was threatened by the absence of the major private schools partly because Wesley College had gained an apparent perpetual mortgage over the trophy. It won in every year from 1941 to 1950 (except 1948 and 1949). In that period, Wesley could boast of a string of top players including Clive Wilderspin, Dawson Hamilton, John Blacklock, Trevor Genge, Arthur Marshall and Bruce Robinson.

One unusual administrative responsibility for Association officials was that of deciding whether its junior tournaments should be conducted during poliomyelitis epidemics which periodically swept the state. Just before the Association's Schoolchildren's Tournament in September 1953, it was necessary to abandon the tournament, despite the fact that entries had closed and the draw been made. The entries were a record despite the severity of the epidemic (*WALTA Annual Report*, 1953/1954). At the Schools' Tournament the following year (1954), 256 boys and 276 girls submitted 790 entries over 24 events. Singles championships for girls and boys began at under 11 and were contested for all age groups, including 18 and under (*WALTA Annual Report*, 1954/1955). Ten years earlier, in 1945, there had been championships for each age group, although the entries totalled only 341 (*WALTA Annual Report*, 1944/1945). After the war, however, there were more tournament opportunities for young players aged from 14 and above. Apart from the Schools Championships, the State Championship (at Easter), the City of Perth Championship (at Christmas) and the Spring Tournament all had events for these juniors.

The Catholic Tennis Association and the Fremantle District Association also organised well-patronised junior tournaments. From 1950 the latter regularly conducted a junior championship in late January (*WALTA Minutes*, 7/12/1950). In 1951, there were some expressions of concern about an overlap of tournament dates between the WALTA School Tournament and a similar event organised by the Catholic Tennis Association. However, a motion moved by Morrie Beard, and seconded by Eric Wilderspin, that the WALTA fixture take precedence lapsed (*WALTA Minutes*, 14/12/1951). There was a growing recognition of the contribution of affiliated associations to tennis and a reluctance to provoke unnecessary conflict. One important development in this regard was the growth of the Southern Suburbs Association. Its history has been documented elsewhere (Cunningham, 1978) but it was an important element in meeting the 'anyone for tennis' demand.

The Schoolchildren's Tournament had to be played on hired courts; the State Open and international fixtures at King's Park while other major tournaments were rostered among metropolitan clubs. The State Hardcourt Championship was assigned to a country club, with the first post-war event ending in triumph for Kalgoorlie's hometown champion Herb Blacker. A legend on the Goldfields, Blacker defeated Ron Stephen in the final (*Kalgoorlie*

Miner, 4/6/1946 and *Sunday Times*, 9/6/1946, 10). Given the different locations of the major tournaments, a suggestion by Clarrie Mallett that an annual tennis calendar be printed containing these details was later accepted (*WALTA Minutes*, 12/2/1954). Occasionally clubs could not meet their roster commitments. For example, in 1948 the Subiaco Club accepted a request that it conduct the Spring Tournament in lieu of Claremont. In this case, no levy was charged on Subiaco (*WALTA Minutes*, 9/11/1948).

Tennis centre

It was considered that many of the difficulties associated with rostering tournaments and adjusting levies would be alleviated if the WALTA had its own tennis centre. As the existing agreement with Royal King's Park was due to lapse in 1955, Vernon Mursell was at the forefront of moves for a WALTA centre. While still President, he persuaded the Executive to establish a committee of five, with the power of co-option, to seek the Association's own courts and headquarters, and ascertain the likely costs (*WALTA Minutes*, 1/7/1948). Other members of the Committee were the incoming President, J.L. Walker; H.B. Angus; Frank Grove and Ken Miller. Unfortunately the committee's work soon fell into temporary abeyance because of the ill-health of Mursell.

Nevertheless the Committee's first report was presented in late 1949. It indicated that representations had been made to the King's Park Board but there was no prospect of land being made available in King's Park. The Subiaco Council had confidentially mentioned some possibilities. Perhaps the best prospect was President Walker's indication that the Governors of Hale School were contemplating selling 100 acres (40 hectares) of land at Scarborough. Walker, an old Halean, thought it might be advisable to obtain an option on this property. As an indication of some seriousness, it was recommended that £500 be transferred to a Headquarters Reserve Account (*WALTA Minutes*, 13/12/1949).

Eventually, Mursell's ill health forced his resignation from the Headquarters sub-committee (*WALTA Minutes*, 10/8/1950). Earlier he had expressed dissatisfaction at money being spent on grandstand facilities at King's Park which the Association did not own (*WALTA Minutes*, 14/7/1951). More disappointment was shown when it became apparent that the Hale School Governors had decided not to sell part of the Scarborough tract. However, Frank Collopy, who gave the Association valuable service, asked if consideration had been given to the availability of vacant land near Herdsman Lake (*WALTA Minutes*, 10/8/1950). Perhaps the closest the Association came to consideration of a new tennis centre was when sketch plans were drawn up for an application to the Perth Road Board for an allotment of an area of land in Inglewood (*WALTA Annual Report*, 1952/1953).

Finally, much to Mursell's chagrin, the attraction of the existing King's Park private club courts proved too strong. Negotiations between the Association and the Royal King's Park Tennis Club were finalised towards the end of 1953 and its headquarters were officially declared at Royal King's Park. The two organisations entered into a partnership under which half of the profit of every partnership fixture was to be directed to an improvement fund. The balance was to be allocated in a ratio of 60 per cent to the WALTA and 40 per cent to Royal King's Park. This ratio was also to apply to any compensation received from the LTAA for the cancellation of hallmark events in Perth. And the basis for distribution of the net gate taking's of the annual State Championship was to be 60 per cent to the club and 40 per cent to the Association (*WALTA Annual Report*, 1953/1954).

Shield tennis

The decision not to build a tennis centre meant that major shield matches at venues such as the Zoo or Kitchener Park, which had once been the case, would not prevail. Clubs which had played pennants on this basis (e.g. WANDA) would not be part of the shield program. WANDA, despite its proud history, had gone out of existence after World War II and had donated its residual funds to the Association. This enabled the Association to provide handsome perpetual trophies for some of its junior championships (*WALTA Annual Report*, 1947/1948). Nevertheless, on the basis of clubs providing home courts, the shield competition gradually expanded. In most seasons, the competitions began in mid-November and were completed before the State Championships at Easter. Some 'B' and Junior grades commenced later and did not complete the season until the beginning of winter.

Shield Teams

1945-1946	Teams	1955-1956	Teams
Men's 'A' Grade	8	Men's 'A' Grade	10
Men's 'B' Grade (2 sections)	13	Men's 'A' Reserve	5
Men's 'C' Grade (2 sections)	13	Men's 'B' Grade	17
Junior Boys (2 sections)	12	Men's 'C' Grade (3 sections)	27
Ladies 'A' Grade	7	Junior Boys (2 sections)	15
Ladies 'B' Grade	8	Ladies 'A' Grade	7
Ladies 'C' Grade	6	Ladies 'B' Grade	10
Junior Girls	7	Ladies 'C' Grade	13
		Junior Girls (2 sections)	13
	74		117

The grade structure, except for the addition of Men's 'A' Reserve, did not change during the 10-year period. 'A' grade teams of four played four singles and two doubles to the best of three sets. However, the sets were not advantage sets. After 1947, a final-four system was introduced. In the first seven seasons after the resumption of the shield competition five clubs won the 'A' men's division. In the women's competition, the Subiaco Club won four successive victories from 1949/50 to 1952/53. Its members included a number of Ryans, not all of whom were related. Match cards could include Rona Ryan, Joy Ryan and Joan Ryan. Others in the formidable team were Margaret Heron, Margot Arcus (Grace) and Gwyn White.

Subiaco: A force in Women's Pennants in the early Fifties Joy Ryan, Joan Ryan, Gwyn White (seated), Rona Ryan and Margaret Grace

In the mid-1950s Royal King's Park had the distinction of winning both the men's and women's A grade in successive seasons. Who could deny that King's Park was the 'Mecca of Western Australian Tennis'? Replicas of the shields reveal the names of many at the forefront of Western Australian tennis:

	Men		Women
	A. R. Bridge (Capt)		Mrs L. Bandy (Capt)
	A. R. Hicks		Mrs V. White
1953-54	V. J. White	1953-54	Mrs P. Holmes
	J. C. Bahen		Miss J. Langley
	H. D. Jacoby		Miss P. Corry
			Miss J. Earle
			Miss L. Blackburn

	Men		Women
	A. R. Bridge (Capt)		Mrs V. J.White
1954-55	D. C. Hamilton	1954-1955	Miss J. Langley
	A. R. Hicks		Mrs L. Bandy (Capt)
	V. J. White		Miss J. Earle
	H. D. Jacoby		Miss L. Blackburn
			Miss A. Bolton

One unusual pennant dispute between the Association and Royal King's Park arose from the latter's policy of using taped rather than chalked lines. It was a reminder of how Major Wingfield had included taped lines in his original Spharistike package when he was promoting a new game as the forerunner of tennis. In February 1947, the Council resolved to request King's Park that

Royal King's Park 'A' Grade Premier Team 1952/1953 Standing: John Bahen, Harry Spilsbury, Lloyd Chrystal. Sitting: Alick Bridge and Alan Hicks

all courts used for shield matches be chalked not taped (*WALTA Minutes*, 11/2/1947). Eric Wilderspin, a shield committee member, was particularly concerned about the possibility of the tapes causing injury to players. Hugh Guthrie, a King's Park delegate (and later President of the Club) questioned some of the evidence that Eric Wilderspin had presented (*WALTA Minutes*, 30/5/1947). The dispute subsided, the club using tapes for social play and marked lines for shield matches and tournaments. King's Park remained the venue at which all tennis players, metropolitan and country, junior, senior or veteran sought to play, but being a private club it was not possible for all major Association fixtures to be held there.

Brian Ford, leading player, professional and businessman who took a set off Lew Hoad.

Country tennis and taxes

For many years after the war, Country Week carnivals were conducted at King's Park. After the 1947 Carnival, it was agreed to reimburse the men's and women's singles winners with return train fares to participate in the State Championships which were normally conducted within a fortnight of Country Week. For a time, assistance was also given to some promising Goldfields' juniors to play in the State Championships. Alan Hicks and Les Grafton were two of the leading juniors who benefited (*WALTA Minutes*, 7/8/1950). For the 1948 Carnival, provision was made for junior events, but the response (as had been the case for handicap events in 1940) was disappointing (*WALTA Annual Report*, 1947/1948). The junior section gradually grew, although a suggestion in 1949 that a men's and women's doubles championship competition be played in addition to mixed doubles was not adopted (*WALTA Minutes*, 10/2/1949). Nevertheless, the senior competition was keen, although at times there were protests about the lack of publicity (*WALTA Minutes*, 6/3/1951). Occasionally, too, the Association Council heard requests to do more for the coaching of country juniors. Bob Reitze, who had built a reputation for managing junior tennis teams, was one who took this view (*WALTA Minutes*, 14/11/1947). He advocated that the Association arrange exhibition matches in country towns by leading juniors such as Arthur Marshall, Bruce Robinson, Don Watts, Alan Hicks and Brian Ford (*WALTA Minutes*, 6/3/1951).

The 1952 Linton Cup Team Left to right: Don Watts, Bruce Robinson, Arthur Marshall and Bruce Francis

In 1951, there was a record entry of 263 players from 25 clubs. Sadly, in the same year, the death of F.S. Goldsmith occurred. He had been one of the driving forces in establishing Country Week and his name had been perpetuated by the donation of a cup for the men's team competition. The singles trophy was won on five occasions by Laurie Quan between 1950 and 1956. With support mainly from Ted Hamilton and the 'net storming' Les Grafton, the 'brick wall' Quan had led the Eastern Goldfields team to a sequence of Country Week titles. Although Quan was unable to win a major metropolitan singles championship, he held a State ranking for several seasons and in 1952 reached as high as number four (Terrell, 1993, 184-185).

In the women's section, the competition was not so clearly dominated by one team or player although Moora's Betty Fairclough won the singles in 1948, 1949 and 1950. She helped steer Moora to team wins in 1949 and 1950. Unlike Quan, she did not receive a State ranking or regularly participate in the State tournament scene. One experienced judge regarded Betty

Laurie Quan, Country Week Singles Winner 1950, 1951, 1952, 1953, 1955, 1956.

Fairclough as being 'in Jill Langley's class'. She played a strong serve and volley game (interview with John Whitton, 4/10/89). In the early Fifties, the country clubs and associations were given strong representation on the Association Executive by Hugh Guthrie. He later became a Member of Parliament and a Speaker of the Legislative Assembly. In October 1951, clubs outside a radius of 15 miles (24 kilometres) from the GPO were designated 'country' clubs and by 1955 the aggregate membership of such clubs exceeded that of city clubs. This was a significant change and explained newspaper headlines that read 'Tennis is Booming in the Country' (*Clive Wilderspin file*).

The growth of tennis in rural areas was a satisfactory development. Breaking down the perceived division between the urban and rural sectors of Australian society is always difficult whether for governments or sporting associations. Sometimes during the decade the Association became involved in political issues. In one instance, the Association's bank the (E S & A) had asked for support in a campaign to combat the Federal Labor government's bank nationalisation legislation. The tennis community has often been portrayed as 'upper class' and not supportive of Labor. Nevertheless, after a spirited debate, it required the casting vote of the Chairman (Mursell) to recommend to the Council that the Association join in the mass petition. Three days later, the Council 'unanimously resolved that the Association join the petition to His Excellency the Governor General and make such further expressions as might be advised by the E S & A Bank' (*WALTA Minutes*, 12/9/1947).

The Association's officers also joined a campaign to abolish the entertainment tax. It was absorbing a third of gate takings and a further percentage of profits (*Clive Wilderspin file*). On this matter the WALTA liaised closely with the LTAA. The tax was not abolished but a reduced scale of charges was welcomed (*WALTA Annual Report*, 1948/1949). Opposition to the sales tax on sporting goods was less successful. Again the LTAA presented the case to the government, claiming it was detrimental to the fostering and promoting of schemes for the improvement of health and the development of national fitness (*WALTA Annual Report*, 1951/1952).

As 1951 was the Jubilee Year of the Commonwealth, special trophies were made available by the State Sporting Committee from Commonwealth Government funds. While there were some rumblings about the true quality of the trophies (*WALTA Minutes*, 8/3/1951), the Association designated the State Hardcourt Championship and the State Open Championship as celebration events. The former championship was held at Pingelly in March 1951. Reigning state junior champion, and Wilson Cup player, Pat Cunningham won the women's trophy. In a major 'boilover', John Blacklock gained the men's trophy at the expense of Clive Wilderspin. Bruce Robinson and Mary Blacklock (later Hicks) were the respective junior trophy winners. Six weeks later, at the State Open the senior championship winners were presented with jubilee trophies. Davis Cup star Ken McGregor defeated Mervyn Rose while Joan Ryan (later Davies) narrowly beat Val Bandy in the women's division.

Administration

During the Jubilee celebrations, the Association decided to recognise the services of some of its living life members. Gold life membership badges were struck to a suitable design. At a public dinner past president Vernon Mursell, former secretary and treasurer Stephen Hart, long serving treasurer William

Corr, and champion player and administrator Alf Hedeman each received a badge (*WALTA Minutes*, 12/10/1951). Just 12 months later Corr and Quinton Stow received presentations for long service (*WALTA Minutes*, 15/12/1952). Corr had received a similar award nearly 25 years earlier but it was Stow's first documented public recognition by the Association. 'Willie' Corr received life membership in 1935, while Stow gained this honour in 1953. From the King's Park Club, Stow had been a valued member of the Executive for many years. Two years later, Justice Walker, was also honoured with life membership. He had been a member of the Council since 1930 and on the Executive from 1933 to 1948, when he assumed the presidency, which he retained until September 1954.

The award of life membership had an interesting twist when it was proposed to honour H.A. Pitt for his 28-year term as Western Australia's delegate to the LTAA (*WALTA Minutes*, 28/6/1954 and 12/8/1954). In the interim, Pitt, had been appointed an honorary life member and Vice-President of the LTAA. Eventually he indicated an inability to accept life membership of WALTA 'should there be a clash of interests between the two associations', but added that 'on ceasing to hold office [Vice President] of the LTAA he would be willing to reconsider his decision' (*WALTA Minutes*, 9/12/1954).

Pitt died in August 1955, but a happier ending accompanied recognition of T.E. Robinson's long service (1930-1964) as a Western Australian delegate to the LTAA. In 1955, he was honoured by the Association at a dinner in Perth. Later, following a donation from Robinson, a scoreboard was built overlooking the centre court at King's Park. This structure became known as the T. E. Robinson Scoreboard. Finally, in 1955, Robinson became a life member of the WALTA (*WALTA Minutes* 29/91955). On this occasion, there appeared to be no concern about 'conflict of interests'.

In terms of its own governance, the WALTA Council amended aspects of its 'man's world' Constitution effective from 14 December 1951. Changes included a provision to elect trustees, the termination of the financial year (on June 30), provision for the conduct of ballots, and the creation of the office of Immediate Past President. Constitutional alterations were not automatic,

Alf Hedeman, champion player and leading administrator Life member 1924

Quinton Stow, long service to the WALTA Executive Life Member 1952

Justice James Walker, President 1948-1954 Life Member 1955

W.R. 'Willie' Corr, long serving Treasurer. and Life Member 1935
The Corr Cup has been dedicated to his memory

for an attempt to increase affiliation changes was defeated. President Walker, who in 1911 had been captain of the Ravensthorpe tennis club while in legal practice (*Phillips River Times*, 15/3/1911) before moving to Perth and joining the Mount Lawley club in 1924, had been involved in tennis club business long enough to recognise the great sensitivity to affiliation levies. However, it should be understood that club membership fees, a separate issue, were always set at the club level by their respective managements. As such club fees were rarely, if ever, a matter for the Association. Most clubs adopted the procedure of adding the WALTA affiliation fee to the club membership charge. By general consensus the level of these rates were modest in comparison to the cost of club membership in many other parts of the world.

In 1954, James Walker stepped down from the presidency. As a student of the Perth High School (later Hale) he had the distinction, in 1904, of being the first Western Australian to be selected for the Rhodes Scholarship. It is noteworthy that the trustees in selecting the scholarship winner were to have due regard to several criteria including (*West Australian*, 23/5/1904):

(i) literary and scholastic attainments;

(ii) fondness for and success in manly outdoor sports, such as cricket and the like.

Whether tennis satisfied the 'manly' outdoor sports criterion is not known. Presumably, though, Walker's pursuit of cricket, football and even boxing gave him the sporting credentials (correspondence with Len Walker, 16/12/1993). In a lifetime committed to sports administration, outside his legal career, Walker was later president of the North Perth Cricket club and a member of the Cricket Committee of the Western Australian Cricket Association. Moreover, he had close links with Australian rules football employing his judicial expertise as Chairman of the Protests and Disputes Board of the Western Australian National Football League (WANFL).

Walker's successor as President of the WALTA was Ken Miller He was also a person with a broad background in sporting administration particularly at the WANFL and school sports. Miller had joined the WALTA Council as early as 1936, in connection with the activities of the Junior Committee, and three years later had joined the State Selection Committee. Just before Walker's resignation, George Carlisle, the Association's secretary for 19 years, also resigned. In 1948 a sub-committee had been established to examine the secretary's remuneration. A salary increase was forthcoming as there was recognition of the greatly expanded duties of the position (*WALTA Minutes*, 9/2/1948). His successor Rod O'Shannassy was soon to experience further administrative responsibilities in this allegedly 'amateur' sport.

Chapter Sixteen

TOWARDS OPEN TENNIS 1957-1968

In September 1956, the LTAA supplied the Executive at the WALTA with its definition of an amateur tennis player. It was specified that any lawn tennis player was an amateur:

> *who does not receive, or has not received after attaining the age of sixteen years, directly or indirectly, pecuniary advantage by playing, teaching, demonstrating, or pursuit of the game.*

In addition it was stated that the 'game' definitely referred only to lawn tennis (*WALTA Minutes*, 29/9/1956). It was the version of the game which had been firmly endorsed by the WALTA hierarchy as the shadow of professionalism became more pronounced. In Western Australia, some leading players had been prematurely lost to the tournament scene when they became registered coaches. In addition, the administrative expertise of this sector was barred to the Association, but whether tennis in Western Australia was as adversely affected by professionalism as other parts of the world was a moot point. What exposed disagreements over WALTA policy towards open tennis was the practice of bringing troupes organised by Jack Kramer (and including famed players such as 'Pancho' Gonzales, 'Pancho' Segura and Frank Sedgman) to Perth and other Australian capital cities. As events transpired, the decade before open tennis proved to be extremely difficult for the amateur 'volunteers' who were administering tennis.

Policy on open tennis

In some quarters it was contended that Kramer enhanced tennis by bringing leading players to Perth. At times the WALTA received a welcome boost to its revenues when the 'Association courts' at King's Park were used as the venue for the matches (*WALTA Annual Report*, 1959/1960). However, Quinton Stow, from the Royal King's Park Club, told a specially convened Executive meeting in 1958 that 'the professionals were endeavouring to eliminate one state at a time' (*WALTA Minutes*, 21/10/1958). Perhaps there was substance in this allegation because in 1960 the WALTA gave support to the LTAA which briefly adopted a policy of barring the Kramer professionals from using the Association courts in each state (*WALTA Minutes*, 11/5/1959, and *WALTA Annual Report*, 1960/1961). In Perth this meant that the troupe played at venues such as Subiaco Oval and the Perry Lakes athletics stadium. Although the courts were hastily prepared, the matches had an electrifying atmosphere which gave tennis a real charge in Western Australia. Jack Kramer's main agent in Perth was Max Bonner and most of the entrepreneurial and organisational work was at his direction.

Norm Cunningham, President of the Umpires Association, a strong advocate of open tennis

One memorable occasion took place in late November 1959 at Subiaco Oval when Sedgman, McGregor, Pails, Segura, Gonzales and Bonner thrilled the crowds with scintillating play. In January 1964, Rosewall, Hoad, Laver and Sedgman played at Perry Lakes Stadium. A few months earlier the WALTA had sent a circular to all clubs and affiliated bodies requesting them not to support professional tournaments (*Cunningham file*). However, the success of the Perry Lakes venture led sections of the press to severely criticise the stance adopted by the WALTA towards open tennis (*Cunningham file*). Despite his links with 'semi-professional' Australian Rules football, President Ken Miller had firmly supported the amateur traditions of tennis, which began to be colloquially labelled as 'shamateurism'.

One of the most forthright advocates of open tennis in Western Australia was Norm Cunningham. He had the advantage of assessing the welfare of the game from a number of perspectives. For 10 years until 1965 he was President of the Western Australian Umpires Association. Later he held the national presidency of the umpires organisation. This was regarded as an honour, as the post was not rotated on a state by state basis. Cunningham was also an activist in the Southern Suburbs Tennis Association, his own club being known as Carrington. This Association, which had been founded as early as 1932, was a WALTA affiliate with a large membership in its own right. Moreover, Cunningham's daughter Pat had been one of the leading women competitors in the first post-war decade. Though Norm was not a champion player, he was a hard worker who certainly believed the only way for tennis to go was 'open'. For instance, in 1955 he urged that constitutional amendments be made to facilitate open tournaments. No action transpired apart from Cunningham's initiative being conveyed to the LTAA (*WALTA Minutes*, 13/10/1955 and 7/11/1955).

Cunningham rarely missed an opportunity at the WALTA Council to argue for open tennis. He did not subscribe to the widely held view that open tennis would undermine public interest in the Davis Cup (*WALTA Minutes*, 14/2/1959). At times, though, Cunningham annoyed members of the WALTA Executive, because he was able to encourage the Umpires Association to provide its members to the visiting professionals. This was possible because the Umpires Association was not constitutionally affiliated with WALTA. On one occasion, WALTA Treasurer Harry Spilsbury formally recorded an Executive expression of disappointment that the Umpires Association was not an affiliated body (*WALTA Minutes*, 6/3/1958). The matter held special significance for Spilsbury, not least because the Umpires Association during Cunningham's presidency regularly sought a subsidy from WALTA to assist its provision of umpires for 'amateur' tournaments (see *WALTA Annual Report*, 1966/1967 and *WALTA Minutes* 13/5/1965). Cunningham, though, won praise from the WALTA for encouraging young people to start umpiring. On one occasion, he even offered six top-grade racquets to novice umpires (*WALTA Annual Report*, 1966/1967).

Determining policy on open tennis questions became increasingly difficult. Consensus with the other states was not always easy to achieve. In hindsight, some of the decisions are difficult to comprehend. It meant that the expertise of many who had so much to contribute was not utilised. Professionals could not be 'officially' members of local clubs (*WALTA Minutes*, 10/2/1958) nor were they permitted to be members of club management committees (*WALTA Minutes*, 4/4/1968). On one occasion, an offer by a professional to instruct, without remuneration, undergraduate teachers in the rudiments of tennis was left in abeyance (*WALTA Minutes*, 9/1/1964). However, an application by coach Bruce Francis to permit professionals and amateurs to appear together in a social match was permitted providing there was no financial gain to the participants (*WALTA Minutes*, 11/1/1961). Earlier Spilsbury, had told the Council that in New South Wales two country clubs, which had permitted professionals to play on their courts, had had their affiliation cancelled (*WALTA Minutes*, 12/2/1958).

Alick Bridge, A leading player in the State

For many players, it was important they did not unnecessarily endanger their amateur status. Reports were quickly lodged at WALTA headquarters if instances of 'professionalism' were observed. This was the case with Bill Same from the Alexander Park Club when he was seen coaching juniors at two metropolitan high schools (*WALTA Minutes*, 9/3/1960). Within 30 days of the report, Same applied to the WALTA Executive to be registered as a professional (*WALTA Minutes*, 11/4/1960). On the other hand, Clive Wilderspin had earlier informed the Association of his apprehension that the appearance of his photograph on a cigarette packet, presumably without his authorisation, would threaten his amateur standing (*WALTA Minutes*, 10/5/1956). Other leading pennant players expressed concern about the grey area of assisting junior development by helping professional coaches. This matter was also discussed at the WALTA Executive level, but no resolution was reached (*WALTA Minutes*, 4/4/1966).

As the number of professional tennis coaches grew, questions were raised about an accreditation procedure. What relationship should WALTA establish with the professionals, who suffered various sanctions? This matter was given focus in June 1957 when correspondence was received from Mrs Helen Collins, Miss June McLeod and Messrs Ron Hunt, Jim Vallve and R.N. Bennett notifying the Association that they intended to act as professional coaches (*WALTA Minutes*, 13/6/1957). Clarrie Mallett, an active member of the Executive, immediately supported the application and expressed delight that Collins and McLeod could foster the development of women's tennis (*WALTA Minutes*, 13/6/1957). Nevertheless, Morrie Beard suggested that some standard should be demonstrated before approval was given. State player Alick Bridge, who was destined to be the WALTA number one ranked player in 1959, thought the Association should ensure that only 'reliable' coaches were allowed to teach the game (*WALTA Minutes*, 13/6/1957).

A motion was passed recommending a policy of accrediting coaches be adopted, subject to them being accepted by Council (*WALTA Minutes*, 13/6/1957). The applications were to be considered individually before approval was granted. In the course of the debate, President Ken Miller recognised that the Association did not have the power to refuse permission to the applicants to engage in professional duties. This was why Bridge thought it wise to consider what policies had been adopted in other states (*WALTA Minutes*, 13/6/1957). However, while information was being sought from other state associations in the LTAA correspondence was received from Stan Edwards, the acting secretary of a proposed Western Australian Lawn Tennis Professionals Association. He requested that the WALTA form a panel of three to examine professionals wanting to be registered as coaches. Replies from the other state associations indicated that professional bodies had either been established or that legal advice was being sought to assist their formation. The pattern was also to create accreditation panels with membership from both the respective state associations and professional bodies. The Executive, therefore, recommended that, 'WALTA agree in principle to the registration of professional coaches, the formation of the professionals association, and to admittance by examination' (*WALTA Minutes*, 10/10/1957). Yet a professional coaches association was not formed until 1971, when it was duly recognised by the WALTA. Even a WALTA resolution as late as 1969 continued to deny professional coaches a position on either the WALTA Council or Executive.

A steady stream of players joined the professional coaching ranks. Arthur Marshall transferred in 1958, followed a year later by Bruce and Margaret Robinson. Brian Ford became a professional in 1960, followed two years later by Eddie and Mary Edwards. In 1963 Rob Kilderry and Gordon Smith made the status transfer. Clive Wilderspin, who had restricted his tournament play, turned professional in 1964. Within a year Doug Napier, the first left-hander to have the state's top ranking, was also lost to amateur tennis. Later Brian Bermingham, Bill Jowett and Kerry Varney registered as professionals. All of these players were excluded from the tournament and pennant scene. The Robinsons and Brian Ford joined the squash racquets association where they were permitted to play pennants but were excluded from state selection. However, turning to squash was not acceptable to all. Some found being professional so restrictive that they sought reinstatement as amateurs. In this category were John Glidden, Bill Same and Ron Hunt. Such players had to stand down for a minimum of 12 months before their amateur status could be recognised (*WALTA Minutes*, 12/5/1966).

The professionals sometimes experienced distress as a result of their initiatives. In 1964, Brian Ford organised a junior tournament sponsored by Coca-Cola. One minor difficulty was the coincidence of the opening day of the junior tournament with the final day of the Metropolitan Hardcourt Championship. Although Ford undertook to avoid any clashes, he was displeased to be informed that the WALTA had decided not to sanction the Coca-Cola event. Indeed it was resolved that, 'Mr Ford be advised that the Association could not approve a tournament being staged by a private person or an unaffiliated organisation' (*WALTA Minutes*, 5/7/1965). In fact, the tournament went ahead with WALTA President Norm Wasley and Vice-President Eric Eastman undertaking negotiations with the Sales Manager of Coca-Cola for a tournament with a similar schedule to go ahead in 1966 (*WALTA Minutes*, 6/12/1965). Wasley was originally not sympathetic to open tennis but his commitment to junior development prevailed in this instance. Fortunately, from an 'illegal' beginning, the Coca-Cola tournament, often aggressively promoted by Arthur Marshall, was to become one of the most strongly patronised events on the junior calendar.

The Coca-Cola company also underwrote the preparation of a tennis coaching film (*WALTA Minutes*, 10/8/1967). Likewise, the Rothmans Foundation made available a coaching film. The cigarette company was also engaged in the publication of a tennis manual (*WALTA Minutes*, 6/12/1965). The Rothmans Foundation was to become a major sponsor of sport throughout Australia and financially supported junior coaching schemes throughout the state. Coaches of the calibre of Max Bonner, Bill Gilmour and Dinny Pails were hired to conduct the sessions (*WALTA Minutes*, 11/2/1965, 6/4/1967 and 5/9/1968). Leading coaches were also engaged for the beginning of Shell Petroleum's support for country junior coaching clinics. This scheme was to far outlast the Rothmans program. In the mid-Sixties, such sponsorship 'deals' were a tentative beginning to using sport as a major marketing tool. These developments were undermining the amateur traditions of tennis. Given Wasley's commitment to amateur tennis and the prevailing mood of

Hedley O'Neil (far right), O'Neil, a Leederville Club delegate who sought open tennis for each Grand Slam event. He is with WALTA legends John Bahen, Geoff Strang, Dawson Hamilton, and Keith Holten

the Executive, it was perhaps surprising that the WALTA was to claim credit for having initiated the final movement in Australia towards open tennis. The 1966/67 *WALTA Annual Report* included the following statement by Wasley:

> *Accompanied by Mr Beard [the Vice President] I attended the 1967 Annual Conference of the LTAA held in Melbourne on the 1 February 1967 when the question of Open Tennis was the major issue. Western Australia was responsible for bringing this matter into the limelight in December 1966 and subsequent events have brought world prominence to the subject.*

Not that the WALTA support for open tennis was without reservation. The original WALTA motion was for an open tennis trial at only one venue, namely Wimbledon. When Leederville delegate Hedley O'Neil attempted to amend the motion to include all Grand Slam events, he was unsuccessful (*WALTA Minutes*, 8/12/1966). The WALTA Executive was very nervous that its proposed open tennis trial at Wimbledon would be subject to 'the intrusion of many curly amendments coming in from other states'. So a committee comprising Norm Wasley, Quinton Stow, Morrie Beard and Eric Eastman was set up to 'investigate all avenues of possible amendments'. Final instructions to the delegates at the LTAA were, if necessary, to be communicated by telephone (*WALTA Minutes*, 9/3/1967).

Open tournaments

Internationally, the quest for open tennis overtook what was happening in Australia. The All England Lawn Tennis and Croquet Club had been planning to 'open' its imposing gates since 1962. In 1968 the Club decided to go ahead with an open event and was rewarded with one of its strongest fields. In Western Australia, the transition to open tennis was far from smooth. As President Wasley reported at the 1968/1969 annual general meeting (*WALTA Annual Report*, 1968/1969):

> *It has been a difficult year for the Lawn Tennis Association of Australia. Difficulties accompanying the introduction of open tennis to Australia were manifold. High sums of money were demanded by the professional groups and negotiations were protracted and trying. In addition LTAA finances were*

found to be in a most precarious position.

The WALTA as host of the first Open State Title in the Commonwealth, held between 1 January and 5 January 1969 paid $750 toward the cost of bringing professionals to Australia, the return air fares of the players who competed in Perth and financially assisted the leading registered amateurs competing (*West Australian*, 7/1/1969, 19).

Slazenger Australia gave support, while the major sponsor was T. E. Wardle Pty Ltd, a leading supermarket chain. This had helped offset the prize money allocation of $4,300. During the tournament a heat wave was estimated to have cost the Association some $5,000 in revenue. The $1,000 first prize for the men's championship went to American professional Marty Riessen. He gained a five-set victory over the firm favourite Ken Rosewall in the final. The women's final was won by Margaret Court who previously as Margaret Smith, had already established herself as one of the world's greatest players. In 1975, she married prominent businessman Barry Court (son of future premier Sir Charles Court) and became a resident of Perth. Margaret Court received $400 for her victory over Lesley Hunt, the promising Western Australian player. However, as Hunt was still an amateur, the $250 runner-up prize was shared between Court and beaten semi-finalists Ann Haydon-Jones and Francoise Durr (*West Australian*, 6/1/1969, 22). Perhaps the highlight of the tournament was Hunt's splendid semi-final victory over English professional Haydon-Jones. Her score of 6/4, 4/6, 8/6 followed a quarter-final win over the Victorian player Judy Tegart, who had narrowly (9/7, 7/5) lost the first open Wimbledon final to Billie-Jean King (*West Australian*, 4/1/1969, 31). Hunt looked destined for big things. At times, though, it is easy to overlook the advantage of playing at home: within six months Haydon-Jones captured the Wimbledon crown on her home soil.

One pleasing feature of the 1969 first 'open' WA Open was the increase in individual entrants from Western Australian players. A year earlier, Eric Eastman, as President of the Royal King's Park Tennis Club which was conducting the tournament, had expressed disappointment about the lack of support from local entrants. Nevertheless the last amateur Open was described 'as among the most successful held in Perth' (*West Australian*, 9/1/1968, 20). The appearance of dual Wimbledon champions in Billie-Jean King and Margaret Court proved a big drawcard. The crowd for the final was only 300 below the 3,920 seat capacity. Most of the spectators were probably disappointed when King confirmed her reputation, at that time, as the world's number one player by defeating adopted Western Australian, Court 6/2, 6/4 in the final. For King, the success helped to erase memories of an earlier visit to Perth. As one of a dozen international amateurs in Perth for the 1965 Open (*WALTA Annual Report* 1964/1965) Billie-Jean Moffitt, as she was then known, had been sensationally defeated by Jan Longson, the Cottesloe club player who was about to depart as captain with Lesley Hunt, Barbara Wall, Anne McKenzie and Sandra Stephen for the 1965 Wilson Cup tourney in Melbourne. Although Moffitt had won the first set 6/3 Longson then gave 'a great exhibition of controlled stroke play winning many points with powerful cross court forehand drives' (*West Australian*, 7/1/1965, 31). With the scorecard in the final two sets reading 6/2, 7/5 the (*West Australian* 1/1/65, 2) columnist described the victory, in the long match, as 'unequalled in WA women's tennis'.

Three years later, in 1968, it had taken Billie-Jean King only 45 minutes to defeat Margaret Court. This short duration was in marked contrast to the men's final. It took four and a half hours and 88 games for Bill Bowrey (NSW) to defeat Ray Ruffels (NSW) 6/8, 11/9, 6/2, 17/19, 6/4. It is not known whether the elapsed time created a record. Certainly, no final in the history of the WA Open has included so many games. The standard of the play by both players was high, particularly the return of service and ground shots. This was despite the match being played in high winds, the players having to leave the court four times because of rain (*West Australian*, 8/1/1968, 34).

Jan Longson(right), pictured with Lorna Jowett, defeated Billie-Jean Moffitt (King) in 1965. The victory was described as 'unequalled in WA women's tennis'.(Courtesy The West Australian)

In the decade leading to open tennis, the most prestigious Association championship had generally drawn good quality fields. The annual report regularly listed the visiting stars and their achievements. However, to attract these players it was necessary to often shift the dates for the fixture in accordance with LTAA guidelines. Although Christmas was the most common time, the 1963 Open had been held in early November. Sometimes the junior events were held on different occasions. Yet, despite the alteration of the dates and the presence of good players, there were often poor attendances. For instance, the crowds for the 1964 Open, held from 7 December to 15 December 1963, were down (*West Australian*, 17/12/1963, 24). It is difficult to assess the impact of the reported poor sportsmanship of 'bad boy' Bob Hewitt, the Wimbledon doubles champion (*West Australian*, 17/12/1963, 24). What is clear is that the experiment during the championship of playing exhibition tennis at night had only proved moderately successful (*WALTA Annual Report*, 1963/1964).

The regular attendance of ranked players at the Open meant that the WALTA honour boards were to be decorated with the names of Wimbledon and other grand slam title holders. In the women's division, apart from Court and King, these included Angela Mortimer (1958), Maria Bueno (1960), Christine Truman (1963), Lesley Turner (1964) and Francoise Durr (1967). The men's victors included Mal Anderson (1958), Andres Gimeno (1959), Neale Fraser (1960), Roy Emerson (1962 and 1965), Bob Hewitt (1963), Fred Stolle (1964), and Tony Roche (1967). The listings confirm that if the Western Australian public could not always watch the top professionals, they were able to witness play by the world's leading amateurs.

One consequence was the absence of Western Australians from the list of title holders. In 1959 both the women's and men's singles finals were fought between overseas champions. This was the first time this had occurred in 54 opens since the inception of the event. In the men's singles Andres Gimeno (Spain) had a straight set win Earl Buchholz from the United States. In the men's doubles there was another three-set win to Ulf Schmidt and Jan-Erik Lundquist (Sweden) over Gimeno and Luis Arilla. The women's singles final was a contest between 19-year-old René Schuurman and her South African compatriot Sandra Reynolds. After Schuurman won the singles, she teamed with Reynolds to defeat Victorian Eva Duldig and 15-year-old Western Australian junior Helen Paterson (*West Australian*, 12/1/1959, 20).

An exception to the sequence of visiting stars winning the WA Open came in 1961 when Dorothy Whitely, an 18-year-old from the Alexander Park Club, won the women's singles final with 'accurate placements' against Wilson Cup teammate Helen Plaisted (*West Australian*, 3/1/1961, 30). The championship was a most successful one for Whitely, as she won four titles and was runner-up in a fifth event. This was a rare occasion when a competitor was permitted to enter in so many championship events. Whitely's junior status enabled this situation to arise although it did cast light on the capacity of an individual to afford the fees for so many events. In Western Australian tennis, the cultural

Dorothy Whitely, (later Lee) State Open Winner 1961. A great tennis personality

element of egalitarianism was 'a powerful influence' which weighed upon the WALTA Executive and Council of delegates to avoid prohibitive fees for championship entry.

Thus 1961 was the third year in succession in which Dorothy Whitely had won the junior girls singles when she defeated Victorian Ann Jenkins in straight sets. With another Wilson Cup team member, Helen Plaisted, the all-conquering Whitely defeated Diane Gugeri and Helen Paterson 6/3, 7/5 in the junior girls' doubles. Partnering legend Clive Wilderspin in the senior mixed doubles final, Whitely won against 'Fiery' Fred Stolle (NSW) and Plaisted. Whitely's only reverse came in the women's doubles final, in which she and Joan Davies were beaten by Plaisted and Eva Duldig of Victoria.

Whitely's success demonstrated that she had benefited from the competition in the eastern states. This venture had not been without incident, as the WALTA Executive refused to allow her request to delay using her 1960 Wilson Cup travel ticket while she competed in the eastern states tournaments. An Alexander Park delegate, Keith Treadgold, protested unsuccessfully about the Executive's action at the WALTA Council (*WALTA Minutes*, 14/8/1960). Unfortunately, the funding arrangements for such ventures were largely ad hoc as playing on the eastern circuit was not frequently attempted on an unofficial basis. While Whitely was away, she played in the Queensland, New South Wales and Victorian championships and received 'advanced' tuition from coach Vic Edwards in NSW. Back in Perth, his brother Stan Edwards gave Whitely further coaching (*West Australian*, 3/1/1961, 30).

For three successive years (1959, 1960 and 1961), Whitely received a national junior ranking, number five in 1960 was her best standing. Despite touring overseas she was never quite able to secure a national senior ranking. Despite this, she remained in the game and as Dorothy Lee she continued for many seasons as a leading pennant player and personality for Alexander Park. Dorothy did not win another State Open, although some of her other singles successes included the Spring Tournament and State Hardcourt. In doubles, she appeared in the 1963 Open final with Pam Brand, but lost to Lesley Turner and Judy Tegart. The following year partnered by Robin Ebbern, she was again runner-up in the doubles to Margaret Smith (Court) and Helen Plaisted.

Helen Plaisted, was another who achieved a creditable record in the Open. In the 1961 final, she was narrowly beaten by Whitely 8/6, 6/2. Twice (1961 and 1965) Helen Plaisted claimed the Open doubles crown. In the 1961 Wilson Cup, Plaisted played outstanding tennis and in 1962 she gained the top senior State ranking; her best national ranking as a junior was eighth in 1961. She gained major titles in the City of Perth, State Hardcourt and Spring Championships and then attempted to improve her game by living in Melbourne for a year. In 1964, at only 21, she qualified for the women's singles at Wimbledon but she was beaten by Carol Caldwall of the United States in the first round. She then teamed with Brian Tobin (later President of the Tennis Australia and then the International Tennis Federation) to reach the quarter finals of the mixed doubles. While she was in England she played in the British Open Squash tournament and teamed with legendary Heather McKay in an Australian team to defeat Great Britain in an unofficial 'test'. At home Plaisted also had the distinction of being the State's number one squash player. Fortunately her squash commitments did not prevent Plaisted from achieving a high profile in tennis. Her 'head to head' confrontations with her arch rival Whitely always kept her in the news. Later, as Helen Muir, she became a prominent professional coach, sports-goods proprietor and successful national and international competitor in veterans' tennis.

Visiting players taking part in the State Open were often promising national juniors: this made the junior titles often extremely difficult to win. In 1957, Jan Shearer from South Australia defeated Kalgoorlie's Jan Blackburne for the junior girls singles. Blackburne, a dogged and determined player, was also runner-up in the same championship in 1958 and 1959. The victor in 1958 was Delys Blackburn from Mount Lawley, who gained the number one junior ranking in that year. Jan Blackburne's 1959 loss was to Whitely, who recorded a hat trick in this event. In 1962, the title went to the leading New South Wales junior Kay Dening with Helen Paterson from Cottesloe the losing finalist. Paterson, whose father Jim gave dedicated service to tennis in the area, was a most promising junior with a classic style. Earlier in the season she had impressed in the Wilson Cup competition with a series of competitive performances (*West Australian*, 30/12/1961, 20).

Helen Plaisted (later Muir), champion tennis and squash player with 1959 Wilson Cup team members From left to right: Helen Plaisted, Lyn Millard, Dorothy Whitely, Jan Blackburne

The dominance of interstate juniors was maintained in 1963 by Kay Dening when she defeated Pam Brand in the final. Thereafter, the record was much better for local players. Subiaco's Sandra Stephen, the daughter of 'Chum' Stephen, defeated Anne McKenzie 6/2, 0/6, 6/2 for the 1964 title. In 1965, Jan Longson narrowly beat rising star Lesley Hunt 11/9, 7/5. For the next four years, Hunt thwarted challengers from both east and west. Lynley Griffiths (Reabold) and Vicki Lancaster (East Fremantle) were the successive runners-up in 1966 and 1967. Anne Coleman (Fremantle) took a set from Hunt in 1968 but a year later lost in straight sets. After national success, Lesley Hunt was then selected (in 1968 under captain Harry Hopman) in an official Australian touring team, the first Western Australian woman from local ranks to achieve this honour. In 1971 and 1972, Hunt was also a member of the Australian Federation Cup team. Again she was the first 'local product' to gain this honour.

Hunt won a host of senior titles including the State Hardcourt, the City of Perth, and the Spring Championship. Another of her Western Australian titles was the Champion of Champions. This was established in 1964 as an event for affiliated club champions and major title holders. Whitely was the first women's winner and Lesley Hunt (Loton Park) won in 1966. In 1965, however, Lesley Hunt had to lower her colours in the final to Pam Brand from Alexander Park. In the same year Brand's performances in Europe allowed her to be one of the few Western Australian women to play at Wimbledon. Later, as Pam Hatt, she became a leading professional coach and administrator, and managed many junior teams to the eastern states. In veterans' competition she achieved considerable success, particularly in 1987 when she won the Australian (40 years and over) veterans womens singles and doubles and the mixed doubles. She also captained the Australian Young Cup veterans team in overseas competition.

Lesley Hunt, one of the State's great players. First local women from Western Australia to be chosen for Australia and first to play Federation Cup tennis

Another leading player of the 1960s was Gwenda Don; her elder sister Lorraine, who shared her determination, was also a prominent competitor. Gwenda's victories included the State Hardcourt (1961) and City of Perth (1962) Championships. She was a member of the 1962 and 1963 Wilson Cup teams, upholding her reputation as a fine doubles player. At the end of the 1963 Australian Championships, in company with Helen Paterson (and the Linton Cup boys Alan Wall and Fred Street), she was honoured with selection in the Shell National Coaching class. At the 1963 State Open she won the under 21 singles and in 1965, after Jan Longson had eclipsed Billie-

Pam Brand, (Hatt) leading player as a junior, senior and veteran. Prominent professional

Jean Moffitt (King), it was Don who eliminated 'Jan the giant killer' with a battling 6/4, 6/8, 6/4 victory. Don (later McIntosh) was the number one ranked player for the 1964 calendar year after having been the WALTA nominee for the 1963 Sportsman of the Year award.

On the men's side, a fine player of this era was Brian Bowman. He had made his name in South Australia having even played for that state against Western Australia. In 1954, he was chosen for test matches against South Africa. Thirteen years later Bowman had the distinction of touring New Zealand as manager of a mixed doubles team chosen to compete in the New Zealand Championship (*WALTA Annual Report*, 1966/1967). Since 1960 Bowman had been a Western Australian. His performances in the Open have been mentioned and he briefly challenged Wilderspin as the top player in the State. When the latter turned professional, Bowman had four successive years (1964 to 1967) as the top ranked men's player in the state. His 'purest' stroke making and ease of play left a profound impact (interview with Don Menzies, 4/7/1989). At the end of his playing days Brian Bowman also left his imprint as an administrator: he became a member of the WALTA Executive, with roles in junior development and State selection.

A young player who showed great promise when Brian Bowman was at the top was Tim Clayton, who was ranked as high as number two in the 1964 senior listings. Earlier in 1961 and 1962, after displaying considerable talent at Wesley College, Clayton was designated the State's top junior boy. This status was confirmed after he had brilliantly defeated John Newcombe, who, for three successive years (1961, 1962, and 1963) was the top-rated junior boy in Australia. However, although he was selected in the 1962 Australian Touring Team, farming commitments at Kulin then curtailed his quest to be a permanent top player.

Another emerging junior was Gary Penberthy, who shared with Tim Clayton a rural background. As a junior, he was ranked second in Australia for 1966 and the same year was chosen as captain of the Australian junior Davis Cup team that travelled to the United States. At an Orange Bowl event for juniors in Miami, he reached the semi-finals with future international stars in the field such as Jimmy Connors, Eddie Dibbs, Manuel Orantes, Bob Lutz and Stan Smith. Penberthy, a crafty left-handed artist, opted not to attempt the senior circuit. He remained on the scene as a leading senior, then veteran, and administrator (*Westennis*, March 1978, 4).

Brian Bowman, top ranked player who was a 'purest' stroke maker

The player who took over the mantle in 1968 as the State's number one men's competitor was Tony Hammond. He achieved the rare distinction, as Wilderspin had done, of being twice simultaneously ranked as the top senior and top junior in Western Australia. On three occasions (1967, 1968 and 1969), Hammond gained an Australian junior ranking. In this period he monopolised the junior singles at the State Open. In 1966 and 1967 he won against strong eastern States representatives and in the following two years his respective opponents in the final were fellow Linton Cup representatives Geoff Hodsdon (Reabold) and Gary Same (Alexander Park). Hammond later moved to Melbourne, where he was under the guidance of coach Keith Rogers. During his time as a circuit player he had wins against players of the calibre of veteran Frank Sedgman and Bill Bowrey, beating the latter when he was the reigning Australian Open champion. Just as Bowrey (the 1968 WA Open Champion) married a champion player, Lesley Turner (the WA Open winner in 1964), Hammond married Libby Worner, a Wilson Cup player for Western Australia. Libby also received a national ranking and played on the seniors Virginia Slims Circuit. Later their son, Tim, represented Western Australia at a very young age. In another direction, Tony and Libby Hammond were also deeply involved in the tennis scene as coaches and owners of a business selling tennis equipment and other sporting goods.

Tim Clayton, talented sportsman who represented Australia in an overseas team (Courtesy The West Australian)

Four generations of Hammonds have been associated with Western Australian tennis and the family could itself provide a comprehensive history of many Western Australian Open championships. The story began when Les Hammond started playing tennis before the Great War. Although wounded in action, he returned, not as an Open competitor, but as a competent club player. Both Les and his wife, Alice, worked tirelessly for tennis and were awarded life membership at the Nedlands Club. Mention has already been made of son Geoff, who missed the 1940 Linton Cup when no team was selected. Geoff went on to become a solicitor and married Betty Bahen, a stylish King's Park player, who had achieved a State ranking. Geoff Hammond has often provided legal opinions to the Association. He continued, however, to play inter-club pennants and tournaments. Success in the Open was not forthcoming, but on one occasion Geoff won the City of Fremantle men's championship. The Hammond links with the game were reinforced when Geoff's and Betty's daughters, Sharman and Deborah, matched their father's feat at Hale School by helping Loreto College win a Slazenger Cup.

Two colourful and often controversial characters who had preceded Tony Hammond as leading juniors and ranked seniors were Rob Kilderry and Wayne Millen. Twice, in 1958 and 1960, Kilderry beat Millen in two tight sets for the Open junior boys' singles. On three occasions (1958, 1959, 1960) Kilderry and Millen were chosen in the Linton Cup team. Perhaps Kilderry's best senior win was his 1961 State Hardcourt title victory. Millen came close to the top, winning the men's South-West Championship singles. Kilderry became a professional coach and was deeply involved the Western Australian tennis scene but the demands of academic life and later business restricted Millen to pennant competition.

Kilderry and Millen both shared a keen desire to improve the game. Millen sometimes put his suggestions in writing to the Executive while Kilderry challenged many of the sacred cows of local tennis. Performances at the Wilson and Linton Cup levels had to be improved, although these events should not necessarily dominate the junior program as tended to be the case. In the decade before open tennis there were no Linton Cup or Wilson Cup victories. After the 1964 carnivals, which included brother and sister, Alan and Barbara Wall in the respective cup teams, it was claimed that Western Australia could have finished better than fourth in the Linton Cup 'if the matches had been played on grass courts' (*WALTA Annual Report*, 1964/1965). There was even newspaper speculation that Western Australia would win the 1965 Linton Cup in Sydney (*Weekend News*, 18/1/1964, 33). In fact the best results came from the girls in the Wilson Cup. In 1965, Western Australia finished third. In 1966, with New Zealand in the competition, it was third place again, and in 1967 it was also third. In 1968 Western Australia moved to second position. A year later the situation was repeated by Lesley Hunt, supported by Vicki Lancaster, Anne Coleman and Christine Matison. In earlier carnivals Jan Longson, Barbara Wall and Lynley Griffiths had also performed well. This excellent series of results in the Wilson Cup was a far cry from the situation in 1957, when the selectors argued that 'our junior girls tennis was below the required standard', and had decided, amid controversy, not to select a Wilson Cup team (*WALTA Annual Report*, 1956/1957).

Tony Hammond, he was simultaneously ranked as the top junior and top senior in the State (Courtesy The West Australian)

The 1960 Linton and Wilson Cup teams are pictured right
Back: Frank Harris, Tim Clayton, Rob Kilderry and Wayne Millen
Front: Helen Paterson, Helen Plaisted, Sam Hodsdon (Manager), Diane Gugeri and Dorothy Whitely

The policy of sending four junior boys and four junior girls to the prestigious Linton and Wilson cup competitions and the Australian Championships, established in the 1950s, was maintained in the 1960s. Of course, there was often debate about the selection of the team, because the policy often appeared to be to select the top two players to be accompanied by two youngsters for experience. In 1963, to help avoid claims of favouritism towards certain clubs, the WALTA Council had passed a motion preventing more than one selector, apart from the chairperson, being on the panel from the same club (*WALTA Minutes*, 5/4/63).

Professional coach Arthur Marshall, who gave local tennis publicity in his newspaper column 'Cross Court' often aired the selection controversies. The teams were usually announced after the Spring Championships, usually one of the first tournaments of each season, so later results could embarrass the selectors. In November 1963, Marshall said 'later selection after more tournament results, or organised round robin tournaments through the winter seem obvious solutions' (*Weekend News*, 10/11/1963, 33). The observation was made in the light of proven performer Richard Coulthard's surprise omission from the 1963 Linton Cup team. Left-hander Coulthard subsequently recorded an impressive win over Fred Street, who had been selected in the Linton Cup team. One of Marshall's proposals to help avoid this kind of controversy was in itself controversial. Marshall maintained (*Weekend News*, 10/11/1963, 33):

> *Statistics show that only a fraction of the girls selected continue to compete in tournaments after they turn 21. This wasted expense could probably be put to better use by limiting the girls' team to two, thus enabling the best four boys to be included and still two young ones for experience.*

The success of the girls in the Wilson Cup, Lesley Hunt's championship performances, and the appointment of Helen Waters to the selection panel following the constitutional amendment allowing women delegates were factors militating against the acceptance of Marshall's proposal. However, there was more support for Marshall's view that something had to be done for players who had recently graduated from junior ranks. There was certainly a desire to have senior interstate matches. Despite constant negotiations, they proved difficult to stage. In December 1965, Western Australia played South Australia in Adelaide. The Western Australian team which had to lower its colours was Brian Bowman, Tim Clayton, Lesley Hunt and Gwenda Don. This had been the first interstate match since February 1957, except for an encounter later in 1957 when a Western Australian women's team of Helen Collins, Margaret Heron, Mary Edwards and Helen Waters played a combined universities side (*WALTA Minutes*, 13/6/1957).

To provide seniors with some opportunities and incentives to remain in the game, a number of leading ranked players were invited to accompany the junior teams. On occasions they acted as managers and chaperones. Brian Bowman, as the leading men's player, toured as a senior from 1964 to 1967. Dorothy Whitely was the women's senior in 1962, 1964 and 1965. In 1966, Gwenda Don was chosen and the following year Pam Brand was the women's senior representative. In a special endeavour to provide a lift to senior tennis, four senior players were sent away with the 1968 Wilson and Linton Cup teams. The Manager on this occasion was Barry Sanders, who held several positions on the Executive. This decision was made possible by the efforts of many volunteers from clubs and organisations who worked hard to build up the Eastern States Visitors Fund.

A special feature of the 1966 combined senior and junior tour was the inclusion of the Tasmanian Championship in the itinerary. The seniors selected were Richard Coulthard, Henry Ladyman, Dorothy Whitely and Sandra Stephen. Their performances were not exceptional but they provided an excellent example for the juniors. On the tour, Lesley Hunt won the Tasmanian junior girls singles title. She became the first Western Australian player on record to win an Australian Junior Girls' Singles title and then partnered the doubles expert Vicki Lancaster to win the national junior girls' doubles. At the end of the Australian Championships, Hunt, Lancaster and Tony Hammond were selected to participate in the national Shell coaching series (*WALTA Annual Report*, 1967/1968).

Feature events

Given the failure to win agreement for a national interstate tennis competition, some members of the Council argued that Western Australia should again stage an Australian Open. A Council meeting in October 1966 passed a motion supporting 'this state making application to the LTAA to have Western Australia included in the roster for the conduct of the Australian Championships when same expires in 1972' (*WALTA Minutes*, 13/10/1966). When the application was debated at the LTAA Conference in early 1967, it was narrowly defeated on the casting vote of the President (*WALTA Minutes*, 9/11/1967). Unease pervaded the Executive. At a meeting in October 1967, Vice-President Eric Eastman spoke strongly against submitting a further application for the Australian Open, claiming that no financial benefit would result, only 'prestige'. It would be necessary to find a sponsor prepared to guarantee at least $5,000. Such an event would also probably detract from the WA State Championship, because the existing advantage of two ranked players coming to Perth at LTAA expense would be lost (*WALTA Minutes*, 5/11/1967).

A few days later Eric Treasure, father of leading player Kerryl Treasure (later Chute) and leading umpire in his own right, moved that the Council rescind a previous motion to seek the Australian Open (*WALTA Minutes*, 9/11/1967). He repeated some of Eastman's arguments and raised the spectre of increased affiliation fees to meet expenses. Moreover, if there was a mass exodus of amateurs to professional ranks the Australian Championship would 'count for nothing'. In a lengthy debate others contended that the loss of two ranked players had been overemphasised. An increase in the popularity of tennis would result from the press coverage. The cost of sending the Wilson and Linton Cup teams (and seniors) held in conjunction with the Australian Championship would not have to be met once every seventh year when Perth had its turn. Some of these arguments were perused but as open tennis was soon to change the tennis agenda forever the Executive's reluctance eventually prevailed with a decision not to seek the Australian Open carnival.

One hallmark event, the Davis Cup second interzone final between Italy and the United States had been held in Perth in December 1960. The success of earlier Davis Cup zone finals was obviously a factor in the LTAA again considering that Royal King's Park was a suitable venue. A feature of the tie was the remarkable comeback by the Italian team. On the first day, the Italians, Orlando Sirola and Nicola Pietrangeli, were both respectively beaten by Earl Bucholz and Barry MacKay. The matches were close but the results left the impression that Italy was most unlikely to become the first European nation since 1937 to reach the Challenge Round. It was thought this adversely affected the gate and net profit. The overall attendance, which included the completion of matches on a fourth day, was a disappointing 6,112 persons. Eventually the Italian pair won the doubles against Buchholz and 'Chuck' McKinley, who was to be the 1963 Wimbledon champion. Then, surprisingly, the Italians won the reverse singles to win the tie.

The souvenir program included messages from David Brand, the Premier of Western Australia, and Norman Strange, President of the LTAA. Strange described the Davis Cup as 'the greatest all the year round international sporting event' and claimed that it made 'a very definite contribution to international understanding' (*Davis Cup Programme*, 1960, 1). Brand remarked that a 'Davis Cup Challenge Round and a cricket test match should be amongst the next important steps in our sporting progress'. He noted that Perth had already been selected as the host city for the 1962 Commonwealth and Empire Games. Later the WALTA, in concert with most sporting and community organisations, contributed to the fund raising for the Games and was associated with the King's Park tennis venue being made available for the conduct of the wrestling division of the Games (*WALTA Annual Report*, 1961/1962).

King's Park headquarters

The King's Park centre court area and stand were occasionally hired out to entertainers such as the Harlem Globetrotters, an Aboriginal theatre group and a Holiday on Ice show. However, although the amenities were improved to cater for a crowd of 4,000 the venue was not a major source of revenue. Nevertheless, an electronic scoreboard was installed to improve playing facilities. Unfortunately light reflection on the board at certain hours of the day reduced its efficiency. Unfortunately, too, ill-health prevented the board's donor from attending the ceremony to mark the official presentation of the 'T.E. Robinson Scoreboard' (*WALTA Annual Report*, 1963/1964). In 1964, Robinson had stepped down as Western Australia's delegate to the LTAA, a role he had filled since 1930. It was soon with deep regret that the Association, in January 1966, recorded his death.

In co-operation with the Royal King's Park Tennis Club, the Association contributed nearly £8,000 to the building of a new squash centre, bar facilities and amenities at King's Park. The additional facilities meant the Association was able to negotiate a rental agreement by which the undercroft of the McGibbon Stand was utilised for its main office and sub-committee meetings (*WALTA Annual Report*, 1964/1965). Thus, at the Association's annual general meeting on 23 September, 1965 President Wasley stated that, 'it is now felt that the facilities available are sufficient for the present needs in Perth and the Headquarters Area compares favourably with other venues available in Australia for international or major events' (*WALTA Annual Report*, 1964/1965). A year later, the President was able to report upon the improved office accommodation and the installation of two honour boards for the men's and women's State Singles Championship, the result of generous donations from Frank Wilkins and Morrie Beard. At that stage, Beard was Chairman of the Tennis Development Committee and the Finance Committee. Wilkins was a stalwart of local tennis but he did not hold executive office at the Association. A few years later, C.H. 'Chum' Champion, who did serve for several years on the Executive, donated another honour board for the listing of past presidents and life members (*WALTA Annual Report*, 1967/1968). The Presidents' board, which listed men, was accurate. But the tabulation of life members contained omissions (Kelsey and Kingsmill) and included Rains whose life membership cannot be verified in the records.

Women at the WALTA

By the mid-Sixties, the quest for a tennis centre, separate from the King's Park location, had been left in abeyance. An issue that could not be overlooked forever was the constitutional inability of women to be members of the WALTA Council and Executive. In 1955, there had been a concerted but unsuccessful attempt to delete the word 'males' from Rule 19(3) of the Constitution (*WALTA Minutes*, 29/9/1955) and resentment simmered for years. At the national level women players had also begun a series of 'battles' with the male-dominated power stucture organising Australian tournaments and overseas tours. In 1961, with interest in women's tennis revitalised by the emergence of top players like Margaret Smith (Court), the women staged a self-imposed lockout in the Kooyong dressing rooms during the Australian championships. They were seeking more centre court for women's matches. Earlier Margaret Smith had protested about the conditions provided for the women's teams on tour under the management of Nell Hopman. The latter, however, did play an important role in establishing the Federation Cup, an international competition for women conducted with a similar format to the Davis Cup (Kinross-Smith, 1994a, 148-149).

At a July 1964 meeting of the WALTA Council, Brian Morrell of the Mount Lawley Club, seconded by David Punch, a South Perth delegate, formally moved that Rule 19(3) be amended. Morrell reviewed the contribution of women to tennis and submitted that the time was opportune to admit them to the Council as delegates. Punch supported this line of reasoning, as did delegates from Alexander Park and Leederville. On the other hand, Lloyd Chrystal, one time Chairman of the WALTA Selection Panel and competent player, submitted that the Royal King's Park Tennis Club was opposed to the motion. The negative prevailed; the 23 votes in favour did not constitute a two-thirds majority of the 37 delegates present (*WALTA Minutes*, 24/9/1964).

Equal opportunity legislation was still 20 years away. However, during the period equal pay judgements were being introduced into public sector wage awards. Thus, when a special committee was charged, in mid-1965, with the responsibility of revamping the WALTA Constitution, there was an expectation that Rule 19(3) would be changed. When the final draft appeared, Rule 19(3) remained as it had been cast 30 years earlier. Immediate action by Morrell remedied the omission. Eventually 16 amendments were approved by the Council, including an increase in the permitted maximum affiliation fees, admission to affiliation of a new category of membership in associated bodies and, significantly the right of admission of women to act as delegates (*WALTA Annual Report*, 1965/1966).

One explanation for the initial reluctance to amend Rule 19(3) of the Constitution was the prevalence of the belief that the Women's Auxiliary, founded in 1961, was working in close harmony with the Association. Within 18 months its success supported the opinion that it was 'the most suitable arrangement' (*WALTA Minutes*, 9/5/1963). Women who sought to give administrative support to tennis could do so in the Auxiliary. In one listing of the functions of the organisation, it was indicated that the Auxiliary (*WALTA Annual Report*, 1965/1966):

- conducted the Linton and Wilson Cup raffle,
- provided lunches for participants in the Shell Coaching Week,
- catered for the Metropolitan Hardcourt Championship,
- catered for official Association functions,
- assisted with raising funds to send teams to participate in events in the Eastern States,
- organised and controlled the Ladies Mid-Week Pennants.

The acknowledged driving force behind the formation of the Auxiliary was Helen Waters, its founding President. Waters had already been made a life member for her services to the Mount Lawley Club. She had also made her name as a fine player, rising to number four State-ranked player in the 1957/1958 season. In the 1958 State Open, she partnered Wimbledon champion Angela Mortimer to win the doubles final over Jill Langley (Bignell) and Margaret Robinson. A win in the Metropolitan Hardcourt women's doubles championship with Pat Holmes was a further demonstration of her skills. Her status as a player, the Umpire of the Year Award in 1960, and more than a decade as secretary at Mount Lawley obviously provided her with the right credentials to overcome the barriers to women in tennis.

As to be expected, she was active in seeking the amendment to the Constitution to permit women to enter in the decision-making structure of the WALTA. Since September 1961, she had represented tennis as a proxy delegate in what was known as the 'Associate Sporting Committee'. In the following year she became the fully-accredited tennis representative on this Committee which was the forerunner of the Western Australian Sports Federation. In 1967, she became the first women to join the Executive

(*WALTA Minutes*, 21/9/1967) and later, the first woman on the State selection panel. Another role which she filled was a position on the Junior Development Committee, where she watched her son Peter develop to be an 'A' grade player with a State ranking. She also participated in the Interstate Visits Committee and the Country Affairs Committee. She maintained the presidency of the Women's Auxiliary until 1980 and in 1983 retired from the Executive. Fittingly, in the same year, she became the first woman to be given the honour of life membership of the Association (*WALTA Minutes*, 13/10/1983). Having earned the title of Mrs Tennis, she had foreshadowed the moves for equal opportunity which the Australian government was now placing on the statute books.

Helen Waters, accomplished player who was the first woman member of the WALTA Executive and first woman life member(Courtesy The West Australian)

One of the enduring legacies of the Waters leadership of the Auxiliary was the inauguration in the 1962/1963 season of a ladies mid-week pennant competition. The 11 teams were divided into two divisions. The division one victors were the powerful King's Park combination, while Applecross won the second division. A special feature of the competition, conducted on Wednesday morning, was its all doubles format. A team of four played three doubles matches, each of two sets. The format proved popular, as by the 1967/1968 season the competition had grown to six divisions, with 42 competing teams (*WALTA Annual Report*, 1967/1968.

Shield tennis

While the growth of the ladies mid-week competition was pleasing, there was some concern that the shield competition required review. The introduction of an under-16 division was an important innovation in the 1962-1963 season. Leederville delegate Hedley O'Neil, who was always prepared to offer solutions, even suggested the introduction of mixed doubles play. Mount Lawley's Brian Morrell had also mooted the introduction of mixed doubles (*WALTA Minutes*, 4/7/1960). In April 1968, a questionnaire was sent to all clubs seeking their suggestions for changes (*WALTA Annual Report*, 1967/1968). Meanwhile, steps had been taken for both the men's and women's annual 'A' grade shield competition winners to be recognised with memorial trophies. Slazenger's donated a perpetual shield in memory of David Blacklock, their late managing director, who had been a tennis enthusiast. In the 1966/1967 shield season, Royal King's Park became the first winner of the Blacklock Shield as the men's 'A' Grade premiers (*The Retailer*, January 1954, 56,72, 73).

The designation of a memorial shield for the men's 'A' grade prompted similar moves for the women's 'A' grade. An opportunity arose from sad circumstances when Laurie Toole, a great volunteer worker for the Association, died of a heart attack on 25 March 1967. Toole played his early tennis in the 1930s on the goldfields and later represented the Goldfields Association on the WALTA Council for many years. As a teacher he was devoted to the development of tennis in schools and was a member of the WALTA's Junior Development Committee for over 20 years. He also served on the Executive from 1953 to 1957 and for nearly a decade (up to 1963) was the Association's honorary publicity officer.

One of Toole's firmly held views was that the WALTA was too conservative in its policy of sending players to the eastern states (*WALTA Minutes*, 28/9/1961). A bachelor, Toole lived in Subiaco within view of the Subiaco Tennis Club and this club benefited so much from his zeal. He also maintained links with the Goldfields and encouraged its leading players to

Alexander Park, celebrate another Shield victory
Left to right: Dorothy Whitely, Leonie Dallimore, Loma Jowett, Pam Brand and Sally Cawley

Subiaco, including Margaret Stewart, June Irving and Rob and Rick Kilderry. As late as June 1966, he returned to Kalgoorlie to watch Brian Bowman and Lesley Hunt win the major singles titles at the State Hardcourt Championship. It was to be his last visit. A band of six anonymous donors presented a memorial shield in September 1967 to the President Norm Wasley and the inscription read 'In honour of a man who devoted a lifetime to the promotion of tennis' (*WALTA Annual Report*, 1967/1968). The trophy was for the women's 'A' grade and Alexander Park, led by Dorothy Whitely, were the first winners. Toole never knew that one of his own nieces, Mary Sawyer (later Collins), would later rise to the top of women's tennis in the West.

Alexander Park fielded a leading 'A' grade women's team in the Sixties. It had not won its first premiership until 1957 when Mrs Helen Collins captained the grand final side (against Royal King's Park), strongly supported by Maureen Sayers, Margaret Enderby and Beryl Wattelworth. The latter had experienced an undefeated season (*West Australian*, 18/2/1957, 26). This victory occurred before Dorothy Whitely emerged to lead Alexander Park with other top regulars Pam Brand (Hatt), Loma Jowett and Sally Cawley. In the 1966/1967 season Loton Park, with the formidable Lesley Hunt at number one, broke its sequence of four consecutive premierships.

At the beginning of the Sixties, it appeared that Cottesloe, rather than Alexander Park, would dominate the women's 'A' grade. In the 1959/1960 season it won the competition with a team of juniors with an average age of 16. It was claimed to be the first team of junior players to win an A grade pennant (*West Australian*, 16/2/1960, 18). As Pat Adamson (1992, 157) notes in her authoritative history of the Cottesloe club, the combination was led by Ann Edgar and included Helen Paterson (16), Diane Gugeri (15), Gwenda Don (15), Margaret Anderson (16) and Diane Blackwell (15). The reserve, Barbara Gandy, who played only one match, was the only senior listed. However, in the following 1960/1961 season Cottesloe was narrowly defeated in the grand final by Claremont (*West Australian*, 20/2/1961, 29). Over the next few seasons, Cottesloe remained strong with Helen Plaisted and Jan Longson as key players but another premiership proved elusive in that period.

It appears that the women's shield matches did not always receive good press coverage. In December 1965, Helen Waters, on behalf of the Women's Auxiliary, expressed concern at the lack of publicity given to the women's 'A' grade pennants; representatives claimed that only 25 of 198 lines of pre-pennant publicity were devoted to women's pennants (*WALTA Minutes*, 8/7/1965). A few months earlier there had been discussions about means of promoting more interest in the game in general. One proposal was to play the feature match of each round at King's Park. It was even suggested that the tie could be telecast (*WALTA Minutes*, 8/7/1965).

Pennants, however, continued without much change, although, there was a shift in ascendancy in men's tennis from the south of the river club Hensman Park to north of the river teams Royal King's Park and Claremont. From 1956 to 1962, Hensman Park had been virtually unbeatable. In fact, in the 1960 Grand Final, Hensman Park No. 1, with Clive Wilderspin, John Blacklock, Frank Harris and Don McMurtry, defeated Hensman Park No.2 represented by Doug Napier, Peter Greaves, Glen Diggins and Colin Bell. Obviously this did not stimulate much interest in the shield competition grand final, as the results (*West Australian* 15/2/1960, 20) were not even accompanied by an account of the fixture.

In 1963, Royal King's Park comfortably defeated Hensman Park in the grand final by 11 sets, 87 games to 5 sets, 57 games. Brian Bowman, as the King's Park captain, played a major part in his team's victory by defeating Doug Napier in the main singles match 6/5, 6/4, and then teaming with Lloyd Chrystal to 'halve' the important doubles match against Napier and Colin Bell with a score of 6/2, 4/6 (*West Australian*, 18/2/1963, 29). Bowman, also played a very important role in King's Park's 1964 shield victory. But to win premierships the number one player needed competent support and King's Park was fortunate to have other strong players such as Graham Bancroft, Lloyd Chrystal, Don Watts, Tim Clayton, Tony Hammond, Rod Cadwallader and Rudy D'Orsogna.

Doug Napier, in action a top shield and tournament player

Perhaps one of the unluckiest teams was the 1963 Claremont combination. Claremont was unbeaten in the qualifying rounds but lost a sudden-death play-off in the semi-finals which were played on a one versus four and two versus three basis. This prompted calls for the introduction of the Page final-four system which was used in league football, because it gave the top team two chances to reach the grand final. One supporter of the Page principle would undoubtedly have been Don Menzies, the leading Claremont player. Menzies had shown his class by defeating all the opposing number one players in the preliminary rounds. Wins over Les Grafton, Wayne Millen, Bowman and Napier and even a 'tie' with Wilderspin were included in his pennant triumphs (*Weekend News*, 16/2/1963, 33). However, when the grand final was played in 1963 there was no Claremont, and hence Menzies was not a participant.

Fortunately for Don Menzies, his Claremont team won the 1965 grand final. Yet even on this occasion the semi-final again nearly proved to be jinxed. After a convincing win over Fremantle, the latter team lodged a protest on the grounds that as Gary Penberthy had not played in the semi-final a week earlier, he could not participate in the replay which had become necessary (*West Australian*, 15/2/1965, 26). With the appeal dismissed, Claremont won the grand final against King's Park. The emerging Penberthy won his two sets against the proven Bowman and Menzies 'halved' his match against Chrystal. Other members of the victorious Claremont team were the highly-rated Geoff Strang and Trevor Genge. They had been supported throughout the season by Peter Dyson and Howard Hunt.

Juniors

The pennant competitions for the David Blacklock and Laurie Toole Memorial Shields were important for leading players in maintaining a competitive edge for local tournaments. One who was prematurely lost to this scene was the country player Hugh Thomson. In 1964, he had shown promise at Country Week when he teamed with fellow junior David Hatt (later an 'A' grade player and member of the boards of management of Australian Institute of Sport and the Western Australian Institute of Sport) to win the teams event for Toolibin, a clay court club located west of Narrogin. Thomson played in the annual Town versus Country match and took part in an exhibition game against Ted Hamilton, a legend in country areas (*WALTA Minutes*, 7/12/1964). Thomson missed Linton Cup selection, so he chose a new route for a promising Western Australian player by accepting a three-year tennis scholarship at the University of Mississippi. Apart from undertaking his studies, Thomson represented the university in tennis and played the American circuit. He remained one of the best credentialled of professional

Claremont: Shield Winners 1964/1965
Standing: Trevor Genge, Geoff Strang, Don Menzies (Captain)
Front: Peter Dyson, Gary Penberthy, Howard Hunt

club coaches. Since that time, a regular trickle of young players has gone to the United States to further their tennis.

As coach and columnist Arthur Marshall was apt to regularly remind his readers, many of those who followed Thomson to the United States did not return as 'tennis fixtures' to Western Australia. Rod Cadwallader, Jim McDonald, Howard Hunt, Max Nalder, Myron Pushyk and Phil Chamberlain were listed in this category (*Sunday Times*, 5/10/1986, 133). For most, though, it was an avenue to professional coaching rather than a step to the circuit, which was becoming highly structured and regularised, with high stakes for the top players.

New means of promoting junior tennis continually occupied the delegates to Council meetings, as there was always a formal report on aspects of junior development. In 1961, the Association endorsed a Hensman Park initiative to conduct a North of the River and a South of the River Tournament for juniors living on the respective sides of the Swan. Juniors resident beyond 25 miles (40 kilometres) of the GPO could play in either tournament (*WALTA Minutes*, 12/3/1964). Conducted during the May school vacation, the tournaments were generally very successful. In 1967, however, Hensman Park was obliged to conduct both the North and South division as no club had made application for the North of the River tournament. This had been preceded by a lower number of entrants in the School Children's Tournament (*WALTA Annual Report*, 1964/1965). It was evidence that, during the mid-Sixties, tennis was being threatened with decline. It did prompt the Association to concentrate more of its coaching on squads in addition to the Wilson and Linton Cup levels. For instance, in July 1963, squads below the Wilson Cup of 10 boys and 10 girls were selected to train on Sunday mornings under professionals Bruce Robinson and Arthur Marshall (*WALTA Minutes*, 11/7/1963). A primary schools competition was introduced in 1965. The trophies for these events for boys and girls (known as the Academy Plate) were donated by Marshall whose range of coaching strategies encompassed many schools, most of them in the Fremantle area (*WALTA Annual Report*, 1964/1965). The innovative Marshall had also pioneered the concept of resident tennis camps during school vacations. As such camps were well patronised many other professionals adopted this idea.

In 1963, the Public Schools Association named its interschool competition the Wilfred Corr Cup. Wilfred Corr, an accountancy teacher, had retired in 1960 from Hale School. He had been a life member at WALTA since 1935. After his return from the Great War he had been active in tennis administration, particularly in the junior area. 'Willie' Corr, who lived until he was 96 years of age, would have been pleased to observe that the Corr Cup competition was well structured and placed on a permanent footing by the private schools. This contrasted with the introduction of mid-week matches for Education Department high schools. As a result of recommendations from the Junior Development Committee, chaired by Bill Jowett, the State Schools Sports Association in March 1965 introduced mid-week matches among three-year high schools on lines similar to the competition previously instituted for senior high schools (*WALTA Annual Report*, 1964/1965). It was an encouraging step, but the competition soon lost direction and not all high schools participated.

Significantly, though, John Curtin Senior High School recorded two successive wins in the Slazenger Cup competition for boys. Apart from Modern School (an Education Department school with special entry requirements) private schools had previously dominated the Slazenger Cup. Of course, Curtin's cause had been aided by the presence in its 1964 team of champion Gary Penberthy. Keith Hince, another ranked junior and future leading professional coach was a member of both winning teams. Meanwhile Sacred Heart, Leederville, after three more Slazenger Cup victories had accumulated by 1964 a record 21 wins in the girls section. Loma Jowett, a leading junior from Alexander Park, who later gained a senior ranking, was a member of the three winning Slazenger Cup teams. Twice she was partnered by Anne McKenzie who soon rose to be number four in the State. Then in 1965 and 1966 Lesley Hunt led Our Lady's (later Mercedes) College to two Slazenger Cup wins. With Jill Coward, Judith Edmiston and Mary Sawyer, all of whom were winning their share of junior tournaments, the school's success was not surprising. In the Catholic school system, tennis was widely fostered as a family game. Tennis courts were constructed in the school grounds and coaching was provided. Perhaps the same could be said of Methodist Ladies College, which had four successive wins in the Slazenger Cup. Christine Randell was in three of these teams, whilst success came twice to Eve Shipley and Jill Cowan.

New Directions

Methodist Ladies College in Claremont was one of the several private schools in the 'establishment' suburbs where tennis was firmly based. The expanding metropolitan population of the late Fifties and Sixties meant new suburbs and schools where tennis needs had to be met. In June 1958, the Council requested Ralph Doig, one of its Executive members, and an officer in the Premier's Department to act as a liaison officer for the Association with the State Housing Commission and Town Planner (*WALTA Minutes*, 12/6/1958). The Executive also resolved to write to the Local Government Association to help ensure the adequate provision of tennis facilities (*WALTA Minutes*, 7/7/1958).

Negotiations with local government authorities were continually on the agenda. The 1959/1960 *WALTA Annual Report* even included a note of congratulation to the Perth City Council for the assistance given to the newly-founded Reabold Club in the Floreat area. In fact, Reabold's lease conditions appear to have been less generous than those for Higgins Park when it was established as a club a few years earlier, and clearly less advantageous than City Beach, which had a much longer history. The Perth City Council, like many other local government authorities, did not have a uniform policy on assistance to tennis. Therefore the advice provided by WALTA officials when a club was being established was invariably necessary.

There was a steady rise in the number of affiliated metropolitan tennis clubs from 29 in 1958 to 38 in 1968. Scarborough, Nollamara, Wembley Downs and Hamersley were establised in rapidly growing north-western suburbs corridor. On the other hand, in 1963, the Subiaco Tennis Club, which had a proud history of nearly 60 years was officially taken over by the Kitchener Park Bowling Club (*WALTA Minutes*, 11/7/1963) and aggregate individual membership figures (including both metropolitan and country clubs) fell from 12,330 to 10,843 during the decade. In economic terms, the State was in boom but in tennis there were indicators that the sport (and game) was losing its appeal.

The Association remained solvent, although Treasurer Harry Spilsbury often warned against too much reliance on sundry income (*WALTA Annual Report*,

Ken Miller, leading tennis and football administrator. Life member in 1963

1965/1966). Affiliation fees had been increased in money terms in the 1960/1961 season and fund raising took many forms. At one stage it was decided to conduct a walkathon. Later there was the so-called 'inaugural' tennis ball. Actually the same idea had been tried as a revenue raiser in 1928. The 1967 occasion proved more successful than its forerunner, but a year later, on 30 April, 1968, there was a disappointing attendance at the Embassy Ballroom. So it was back to the successful but relatively small-scale raffles and stalls, conducted by the Women's Auxiliary (*WALTA Annual Report*, 1967/1968).

Concern about the lack of interest in senior tennis was expressed in correspondence from Arthur Marshall (*WALTA Minutes*, 12/11/1957). In his judgement, senior players should be given the opportunity to obtain some benefits from the game. In essence, the only existing incentive was a State ranking. After some delay, the issue was debated by Council. It was agreed that the clubs and the Association had to give more thought to promoting tennis for young people aged between the ages of 19 and 21, by the incorporation of more intermediate-age events in tournaments. Other suggestions included more inter-club social functions and, perhaps, more district tennis (*WALTA Minutes*, 13/4/1961). It was recognised that more statistical information was needed about the extent of the apparent decline in tennis.

Counter-attractions, particularly surfing, were loosening the hold of tennis on the young. The administrators also had to contend with internal frictions generated by the decay of amateurism. In September 1967, Vice-President Morrie Beard made a spirited call for more help. He spoke with concern about the fall in voluntary efforts in shield matches and school tennis. There was only one nominee for the Executive when there should have been 10. There was also a need to increase affiliation fees, which had been eroded by inflation. The dejected Beard said that 'plenty are capable, but few are willing' (*WALTA Minutes*, 21/9/1967). Of course he was not addressing the outstanding exceptions, such as former President Ken Miller and former Executive member Frank Grove, appropriately honoured with life membership. The award to Grove in September 1961 (*WALTA Minutes*, 28/9/1961) was followed by that to Miller in August 1963 (*WALTA Minutes*, 8/8/1963).

One blow to the administration was the resignation in September 1966 of Rod O'Shannassy. He had learnt his tennis at Wesley College, become a State-ranked junior, played 'A' grade for Mount Lawley and been the WALTA secretary for 13 years (*Weekend News*, 3/11/1966, 25). A commitment to tennis was necessary because the salary allocated to the secretarial post was comparatively low. Given the Association's financial conservatism, requests for salary increases were not automatically met (*WALTA Minutes*, 8/10/1962). Nevertheless, in a review of the Association's progress during his term of office O'Shannassy was more positive in tone than some members of the Executive.

Developments O'Shannassy considered significant were Western Australia's inclusion in the Australian tennis circuit, the admission of women to the Council, the substantial increase in the number of tournaments and coaching for juniors, the establishment of headquarters at King's Park with office accommodation (from 1966) and the attempt to improve senior tennis by the promotion of interstate games with South Australia. It is noteworthy that the development which he listed as most significant was the division of the country areas into eight administrative zones (*Weekend News*, 3/11/1966, 25).

Country affairs

Frank Grove, life member in 1[illegible]

One of the controversial administrative initiatives undertaken by the Association, in the face of the apparent decline of tennis, was the zoning of the country regions. A sub-committee, consisting of Norm Wasley, 'Robin' Clayton and Eric Eastman was formed in 1957 to investigate country tennis issues (*WALTA Minutes*, 22/1/1957). A zoning plan, first mooted in the 1930s, was tentatively endorsed but attempts to bring the plan to fruition did not meet immediate success. In 1962, it was endorsed and the amendments to the Constitution necessary to accommodate the change were made (see *WALTA Annual Reports*, 1961/1962 and 1962/1963). Zones were required to conduct annual general meetings at which a Management Committee was to be elected. The zone managements were to be responsible for a range of general activities, including the coordination of a calendar of zone activities such as tournaments, pennants and junior development, incorporating the Shell coaching camps. They were also to coordinate entries for the annual Country Week Carnival. Moreover, the zones were to liaise with the WALTA office, and provide forums for the discussion of issues relating to tennis and provide direction to delegates for voting at Council meetings.

While the zones did provide a structure for lobbying on issues of concern to the WALTA or local and state government bodies, each annual conference of city and country representatives invariably debated its merits. At headquarters there were second thoughts, as affiliation numbers in the country areas dropped. In his address to the annual general meeting in 1966, President Norman Wasley said (*WALTA Annual Report*, 1965/1966):

> *The zoning plans continued with moderate success, the difficulty in administration being that common to most sporting bodies, namely, the ability to find persons with the time available to render service in an honorary capacity.*

The decline in 'voluntarism', usually thought associated with city life, had spread to country areas and did not augur well for rural tennis or, ultimately, the Association. Whether J. M. ('Robin') Clayton, who represented country tennis on the WALTA Executive from 1958 to 1964, or his replacement Brian Morrell, subscribed to this view is not known. Nevertheless, Country Week continued to be keenly contested. For a short period in the mid-Sixties it was a Country Fortnight as the annual carnival in late January or early February, was spread over two weeks. As late as 1958 'country' still encompassed Safety Bay/Rockingham, which in 1958 and 1959 won the women's team section. The metropolitan boundary was later extended. At the annual conference of delegates in 1966, it was also decided to enforce the regulation that only members of clubs affiliated with a zone could participate in the Carnival. The zones and their respective secretaries at this juncture were (*WALTA Annual Report*, 1965/1966):

Geraldton Districts	-	Mrs E. Hayward; Bluff Point
Moore Districts	-	Mr I. Hassan; Kondinin
Central Districts	-	Mr P. G. York; Tammin
Great Southern	-	Mr H. Ladyman; Katanning
Eastern Districts	-	Mr K. Brayshaw; Narembeen
South West Districts	-	Mr L. Marsh; Bunbury
Southern Districts	-	Mr N. A. Field; Albany
Eastern Goldfields	-	Mr J. Pippin; Kalgoorlie

Pat Jenzen, (left) at 40 years of age wins another Country Week title from Helen Graham

Most of the winners of the Country Week men's singles made their names in the 'Big Smoke'. Cliff Fitzpatrick, a mathematics and science teacher, who won in 1957 was later a ranked player and valuable shield member for the Royal King's Park Tennis Club. Left-hander Alan Hicks, with victories in 1957 and 1958, had already made his mark on the State scene. Stylist John Evans, who won the title in 1961, was another mathematics teacher at Eastern Goldfields Senior High School, who was later to win the prestigious 1968 Champion of Champions event. Henry Ladyman was twice successful, while Ken Harris won three singles medals. Both had represented Western Australia in the Linton Cup and both achieved senior rankings. Other winners were Maurie Baddely and Colin Bell. The former, who had a solid all-round game, never really tried his luck in Perth, but Bell was a top performer in the city.

The winners of the Women's Country Week singles were more inclined to achieve success in Perth than had been the case in the past. Jan Blackburne from Kalgoorlie, while still a junior dominating the schoolgirl championships, won three consecutive titles in 1958, 1959 and 1960. As Jan de Tastes she later made her presence felt, particularly in veterans' competition. Margaret Enderby (1957), Pam Brand (1961), Mrs Joy Jones (1964) and Mrs Helen Walker (1968) each won the singles title. Margaret Enderby held a junior ranking. As mentioned Pam Brand was to be a leading metropolitan competitor and influential force in Association business, particularly with respect to development of opportunities for women.

Mrs Judy Keenan and Miss Ros Hall, who won the Country Week singles title in 1962 and 1963 respectively, were sisters. Ros Hall was to later carve a niche for herself in this event. With incredibly relentless play, she won on eight occasions as Ros Giles. Another player with a sequence of wins was Mrs Pat Jenzen. She had a very steady game which paved the way for her to take the title in 1965, 1966 and 1967. Jenzen, who contributed to the organisation of many carnivals, was later very successful in the Veterans' club when she moved to Perth. However, the earlier metropolitan opportunities for this group of Country Week regulars were very limited, so they did not feature in the Association rankings.

Publicity

As in the past, there were occasional complaints about the lack of publicity given to Country Week carnivals (*WALTA Minutes*, 22/1/1957). One school of thought believed that many of the problems facing tennis could be overcome by better publicity. With the advent of television it was considered this medium would foster interest (*WALTA Annual Report*, 1958/1960). Ralph Doig, Chairman of the Publicity Sub-Committee, actually negotiated coverage of the Spring and City of Perth Championships during the 1960-1961 season. Generally, though, an expectation that the medium would create renewed interest in local tennis was not fulfilled. There was an attempt, however, to place the Association's publicity on a more professional footing by appointing a part-time publicity officer for a three-year term from 1 January 1964 at £500 ($1,000). The statement of duties read (WALTA correspondence 4/2/1964):

(i) Publication in the *Sunday Times* and The *West Australian* of Shield Match results.

(ii) Publication in the metropolitan press of Shield fixture and tables with appropriate 'write ups'.

(iii) Publication in appropriate newspapers of forthcoming tournament fixtures and later results of same.

(iv) Publication in country press of some tournaments, pennants and other fixtures and zone and country club affairs.

(v) Attend monthly Council meetings and arrange press reports of appropriate items.

(vi) Such other duties as specified from time to time by Association Executive.

Brian Morrell (right), 'Minister for Almost Everthing', who was granted life membership in 1967
Brian Morrell is pictured here with Doris and Geoff Strang

Doug Napier from Hensman Park believed the publicity officer should also play a role in seeking sponsors (*WALTA Minutes*, 12/3/1964). Dudley Croft, who was appointed to the position, soon expressed the view that there was a lack of coordination, for publicity purposes, among the various sub-committees. Croft found the task exacting and resigned in November 1964, having held the position for less than a year (*WALTA Minutes*, 12/11/1964). Brian Morrell, fast becoming the 'Minister for Almost Everything', assumed the position until Norman Barrett took over. He was followed in November 1967 by Albert Porges (*WALTA Annual Report*, 1967/1968).

Despite these changes in the publicity officer position a number of new ideas were implemented. For a while the Association received considerable air time on a commercial radio station (*WALTA Minutes*, 11/8/1960). The practice of publishing annual tennis supplements in the *Sunday Times* commenced (see *Sunday Times*, 10/10/1963, 8/10/1964 and 17/10/1965). These advertised club membership vacancies and invariably attempted to highlight the family attractions of tennis. It was common to offer family membership discounts. Fees, though, by comparison with most other sports were invariably modest so tennis, for those willing, was available to most people.

By the middle years of Norm Wasley's presidency, from 1962 to 1971, he developed a reputation for conducting a convivial Christmas party for media people together with some of the leading professional coaches (*Weekend News*, 2/10/1964). As previously mentioned, Arthur Marshall wrote a weekly column 'Centre Court Chatter' for the *Weekend News* which focused on local pennants and tournaments, often providing human interest sidelines.

It was suggested that a *Who's Who of West Australian* Tennis (*WALTA Minutes*, 11/5/1964) be compiled and the preparation of a yearbook was also mooted. To aid publicity it was decided to initially lodge shield match cards at the *West Australian* office. For a time an effort was made to publish premiership tables in *Tom's Weekly*. This newspaper was distributed free to metropolitan households to advertise Tom's the Cheap Grocer's supermarket products (*WALTA Minutes*, 4/4/1968). Costs, however, were always a matter for concern and given the apparent decline in voluntarism, local publicity was difficult to obtain. The Association, however, did play a role in public relations by sending representatives to church services for sportspersons (*WALTA Minutes*, 5/4/1965) and to such occasions as Commonwealth Day at Government House (*WALTA Minutes*, 10/5/1965).

Whether open tennis would significantly alter the publicity given to tennis was difficult to forecast. Leading advocates of open tennis such as Norm Cunningham were extremely confident. Ironically, Norm Cunningham relinquished to Vic Anderson the Presidency of the Umpires Association just as open tennis was introduced. Even Norm Wasley, who had earlier expressed reservations about open tennis told the 1968 annual general meeting (*WALTA Annual Report*, 1967/1968):

> *I firmly believe with the advent of Open tennis, a great step forward has been taken and I confidently look forward to the re-establishment of tennis as a major spectator sport.*

In addition Wasley felt that 'the future of tennis as a major participant sport is assured while so many volunteers continue to give their time in services ...' Voluntarism, even if the President was 'talking-up' its importance was vital for the Association. Earlier in the President's Report, the granting of life membership to Brian Morrell was noted (*WALTA Minutes*, 9/11/1967). Morrell had been one of the great volunteers at a time when the divide between amateur and professional had made people like him harder than ever to find. Often, of course, voluntarism took the from of a commitment by a family. This, too, was the case of the Morrell family with Harcourt, Brian's younger brother, later being awarded life membership at the Mount Lawley Tennis club.

The great Margaret Court (Smith), captured a record eight WA Open titles and moved to Perth

Chapter Seventeen

WHERE IS IT HEADED? (1969-1976)

As tennis historian Richard Evans (1988, 4) has asserted, 'until 1968 tennis was a divided game. There were amateurs and there were professionals and heaven forbid that they should ever meet'. Evans made this observation from an international perspective but even in Western Australia the professionals were widely regarded as another breed. This meant that for several years following the introduction of open tennis, there was some resistance at the Association level to welcoming professionals as equal partners. It also meant that planning was needed to determine the directions open tennis should take. A further factor was that professional tennis was not a united body. By 1968 there was a men's troupe managed by World Championship Tennis (WCT) including Newcombe and Roche and known as the 'Handsome Eight'. A rival group of professionals, under George McCall's banner, including Laver, Rosewall and Gonzales, were known as the 'ancient eight'.

The Local Professionals

As early as February 1969 the standing of teaching professionals was discussed by the Executive after the Cottesloe club had sought rulings on a number of questions. Could professionals be accepted as 'normal' club members? Could they participate in pennants and tournaments and be eligible to compete in the Champion of Champions event? And, importantly, could professionals become office bearers of the Association or individual clubs? (*WALTA Minutes*, 9/2/1969).

At the ILTF (International Lawn Tennis Federation) meeting in Monaco on 10 July, 1968 it had been affirmed that 'only those who are accepted by their own national association as having no direct financial interest in the game may participate in its administration on a national or international level'. Open tennis, at first meant the right to play in selected tournaments. It was not an entitlement to hold an administrative position in the Association or at an affliated club.

The Executive and Council were presented with a list of teaching professionals who requested they be classified as eligible to compete in tournaments open to registered players (*WALTA Minutes*, 13/2/1969). The list was virtually a *Who's Who* of Western Australian tennis: Max Bonner, Alick Bridge, Gary Penberthy, Keith Holten, Rob Kilderry, Bruce Robinson, Margaret Robinson, Norm Collins, Helen Collins, Doug Stewart, M. Passmore, K. Varney, Arthur Marshall, Bill Jowett, Brian Ford, Maureen Smith, Clive Wilderspin and Colin Bell.

Letters were tabled from leading players Tony Hammond and Jill Coward (later Howard), indicating their decisions to remain amateurs. They were given permission, along with Alan Wall, to conduct private overseas tours (*WALTA Minutes*, 6/3/1969). When a perplexed delegate asked for more information about the standing of teaching professionals, President Norm Wasley confessed that the matter was still very much in the melting pot. It was in the hands of the LTAA, and in all probability at the next ILTF Conference the category of 'registered' players would disappear and all competitors would become players (*WALTA Minutes*, 13/2/1969).

At the WALTA a separate file was opened for matters relating to open tennis. Before long it was bulging, although many issues were gradually resolved. At the Annual Country Conference, held on 20 January, 1970, it was explained that, as registered players could not automatically participate in all country tournaments, the prospectus for country tournaments should now state, 'This tournament is open to Amateur and Registered Players'. It was also made clear that an amateur playing against a registered player did not in any way damage his or her amateur status.

In April 1972, Alan Hicks, as Chairman of the State Selection panel successfully moved at Council (*WALTA Minutes*, 13/4/1972) 'that teaching professionals be made eligible for selection in State teams, provided they comply with all the conditions laid down for amateurs'. In speaking to the motion he contended that over the past three years the tennis professionals 'had shown good faith ... were very keen and were putting plenty back into tennis, and had done a lot to bring on younger players'. The contribution of teaching professionals was also recognised by Barry Sanders, as Chairman of the Shield Match Committee.

While the avenues for professionals continued to be 'opened', an amendment to the Constitution in 1976 made it clear that 'no person teaching tennis in a professional capacity shall be eligible to be a member of a selection and ranking committee'. This provision remained in effect until 1990. Even then, the chair of the selection panel could not be a professional. Yet following the 1976 amendment, Quinton Stow, a member of the Executive and principal of a legal firm, indicated that he could see no legal reason why a professional could not be on the Council or a member of the Executive (*WALTA Minutes*, 7/10/1976).

Understandably, the professionals recognised the need to form their own association. In May 1971, the youthful and vital tennis professional, Rob Kilderry, advised the WALTA that another attempt was being made to form a professional association with the object of improving the quality of coaching and the standard of tennis in general. A request for the use of the Association rooms for an inaugural meeting was granted. Diplomatically, Kilderry also invited the attendance of WALTA nominees.

The response suggested some unease; it was considered inappropriate for the WALTA to be represented at the meeting as it 'should not align itself with the proposal, and should wait until such time as the body had been properly constituted and formed, and its Constitution had been fully accepted by the existing Australian Professional Association' (*WALTA Minutes*, 13/5/1971).

Reports indicate that 11 professionals attended the meeting on 11 May 1971. It was decided to hold a further meeting later in the month to determine whether an association would be created. As a result the WALTA was advised of the formation of the Tennis Professionals Association, provided with a copy of its Constitution and notified of the elected Committee, which included some of the best known names in Western Australian tennis (*WALTA Minutes*, 8/7/1971):

Patron	Ross Hutchinson, MLA
President	Bruce Robinson
Vice Presidents	Arthur Marshall and Clive Wilderspin
Hon. Secretary/Treasurer	Rob Kilderry
General Committee	Russell Seymour, Brian Ford, Doug Napier

Bruce Robinson, ranked player and leading professional coach who was the inaugural President of the Tennis Professionals Association

By early October, the WALTA was informed that the Tennis Professionals Association of Western Australia had been admitted to full membership of the Australian professional body (*WALTA Minutes*, 7/10/1971). Although this removed an impediment to recognition by the WALTA, discussions about the links between the two bodies were protracted. In June 1973 two members of the WALTA Executive attended a general meeting of the Tennis Professionals Association and further negotiations led to associate status being granted. All appeared well when professionals Bruce Robinson and Russell Seymour were welcomed to the WALTA Council in early November 1973 (*WALTA Minutes*, 8/11/73), but despite the apparent goodwill there were continual reminders of past frictions. When professional Pam Hatt, who had become a delegate to Council as early as 1969 (*WALTA Minutes*, 9/10/1969), sought a copy of the Council Minutes, she was refused on vague 'constitutional grounds' (*WALTA Minutes*, 14/3/1974). Earlier an initiative by professional Brian Ford to conduct a 'private' Coca Cola Tournament' at Hensman Park that overlapped with the State Hardcourt Championships at Corrigin attracted a rebuke from Council. It was resolved (*WALTA Minutes*, 2/9/1971):

> *To write to the newly formed Professionals Association drawing attention to these facts, maintaining that such action was not conducive to good relations, and that this Association does not approve the dates selected.*

Fortunately this affair did not become a major issue, as the Hensman Park Club replied regretting the oversight and indicating that Ford had given an assurance of full cooperation in the future (*WALTA Minutes*, 3/9/1971). On a more constructive note, in the spring of 1971 the Tennis Professionals Association, in association with the National Fitness Council, organised a series of 12 weekly lectures by Gundars Tilmanis at the University of Western Australia. Tilmanis, a highly-competent player in his own right, was a keen student of the game with qualifications in physical education. Soon, as part of their own accreditation program, the Tennis Professionals Association made passing an Umpires Association test a prerequisite to the granting of full accreditation (*WALTA Annual Report*, 1974/1975). It was an indication that the professionals wanted their coaching role based on a more methodical, even scientific-basis.

In the course of the negotiations about associate status the Tennis Professionals Association in August 1973 placed before the WALTA Executive a 14-point charter of desirable innovations (*WALTA Minutes*, 2/8/1973). The suggestions included better tennis etiquette, court behaviour, dress, attention to foot faulting, knowledge of the rules (including the need for an umpire to blow a whistle for each tie-break) and incentives for juniors to join clubs. There was also a generous offer to play practice matches with State squad members.

One proposal, about which the WALTA sought more detail from the professionals, was the ranking of junior players in all age groups. However, after consultation with the State selectors and the Junior Development Committee (*WALTA Minutes*, 8/8/1974), the WALTA decided to reject the idea. Although junior rankings had been adopted by some of the other State associations, local tennis did not immediately follow suit in this direction.

At the senior level, leading players were finding that the transition to open tennis made it difficult to resolve the conflicting demands of the new circuit and the expectations of the LTAA and State associations. In one instance, Western Australia's Lesley Hunt (along with Judy Dalton and Kerry Melville) became embroiled in a dispute with the LTAA over participation in New Zealand tournaments which were to be conducted at the same time as Australian state events. It was suggested the state associations should authorise the LTAA to put a proposal to the three women to play the 1971/72 Australian circuit, rather than overseas, and offer them the travel, accommodation and prize money arrangements afforded to the Davis Cup players (*WALTA Minutes*, 9/12/1971). For a short time Hunt, Melville and Dalton were deemed by the LTAA to be 'ladies not in good standing' (*WALTA Minutes*, 10/2/1972) and their subsequent reinstatement was described by WALTA Vice-President Eric Eastman 'as a money motivated complete backdown by the LTAA' (*WALTA Minutes*, 10/2/1972). According to him '$15,000 from the Bonnie Bell Milk Comp[any] considerably influenced the [LTAA] decision'.

'Tennis; where is it headed?'

In this atmosphere, the administrators of Western Australian tennis decided to seize the initiative and confront the LTAA with a position paper entitled 'Australian Tennis - Where is it Headed?' The submission, which the *WALTA Minutes* (5/12/1972) indicate was written by Executive Member Harry Spilsbury, indicated that, in recent years 'expediency had governed many decisions'. It was contended (*LTAA File* 2, March 1973):

> *As early as April 1964, this Association (WALTA) endorsed a resolution which recognised that open tennis had to come. In doing so, it had some realisation of the consequences, but in the long run, the domination of professional groups would be broken and to some degree a free-lance situation would develop. That is gradually happening. A natural consequence has been the intrusion of money in substantial amounts into the sport and while this Association accepts that financial demands which would have seemed exorbitant a decade ago now have to be faced, it also maintains that those demands should not be met through the sale or disposition of the Associations' birthright, namely control and management. We also look at the future with some concern because we see little sign of cohesion nationally by the states. The grass roots of tennis are in the states and unless they are individually strong, the LTAA, a loosely knit federation of states, cannot hope to be strong itself.*

It was argued that as the 'have not' states had surrendered the right to conduct the Australian Championship to Melbourne and Sydney, they should share a second major fixture (in addition to each State Championship), which was financially supported by the LTAA. The state associations should control these tournaments, even though a promoter might be paid a fee. In addition, a per capita player membership plan was suggested to raise revenue to be distributed to the State Associations. The submission further asserted that it was 'degrading' to have 'to offer a carrot' to Australians to play for their country in international competition. At the same time, there was a realisation that winning the Davis Cup was a financial bonanza upon which Australian tennis had, unfortunately, come to rely.

It was claimed that the paper was well received at the 1973 LTAA Annual Conference. However, it was one of the final items on the agenda and some of the delegates left before it was debated. Nevertheless, the President of the LTAA, Wayne Reid, took the trouble to provide written responses to its main suggestions (*WALTA Minutes*, 11/1/1973). From another quarter, though, the LTAA had to contend with new pressures from the Association of Tennis Professionals (ATP) which had been formed in 1972. In 1973, there was a boycott of the Wimbledon tournament by the players' union in the wake of the controversial suspension of Nikki Pilic for failing to play a Davis Cup match for his native Yugoslavia. Also in 1973, the Women's Tennis Association had been founded. This was followed by the creation of the Australian Women's Tennis Foundation (AWTA) in 1974. Later, in 1990, the AWTA became the Australian Federation Cup Foundation. The AWTA's formation had taken place three years after the creation of the Virginia Slims circuit for women. With Billie-Jean King in the vanguard the separate tour for women (except for Grand Slam tournaments) greatly increased the publicity, prize money and negotiating strength of women's tennis.

Perhaps concerned that the LTAA might not be sufficiently decisive about the Western Australian initiatives, Spilsbury also recommended a course of action at home in Perth. At Council in April 1973, after reminding delegates of the advent of huge prize money tournaments, he successfully moved the motion:

> *That the Executive appoint a Committee to give urgent consideration to the preparation of a Master Plan covering improvements of facilities in the Headquarters area, and to report back to Council by 30/9/1973.*

In September 1973, the committee chaired by Eric Eastman and including Spilsbury and David Punch, had failed to report. Perhaps Hedley O'Neil, the circumspect Leederville delegate, should have been a member as he had suggested to Council in February 1972 that a master plan of the headquarters should be formulated (*WALTA Minutes*, 14/2/1972). Some priorities were determined, but no master plan was to eventuate. Glen Anderson, a future Reabold President and life member, was one delegate who continued to ask whether the Association would ever get its own headquarters (*WALTA Minutes*, 8/11/1973).

The needs of tennis were also discussed with the newly-created Western Australian Department for Recreation (from July 1972), which had resulted from the merger of the Youth Council and National Fitness Council. It reflected the growing role of government in the planning and funding of recreation and sport. Federally, too, an increased role for the national government had been assessed by Professor John Bloomfield (1973) of the Department of Human Movement at the University of Western Australia, in a major report on recreation and sport for the Whitlam government.

In this atmosphere, Barry Sanders, as the Chairman of the WALTA Tennis Development Committee, submitted to the Department of Recreation early in 1973 that (*WALTA Minutes*, 8/3/1973):

(a) Tennis has a special place amongst sports as it is considered the ideal

Bruce Durston, appointed as the full-time development officer in 1976

activity through which the aims of a Recreation Ministry can be achieved;

(b) This game is administered by voluntary officials mainly for the benefit of amateur players;

(c) This Association seeks Government funds to finance a full time administrator, more coaching, capital and consumable equipment, North-West and country coaching tours on a regular basis, and State team trips to national events beyond this State.

(d) The Government must introduce tennis as a major activity into primary schools as a matter of urgency. Funds must be made available for the necessary equipment and training demonstrations.

(e) Community use of High School tennis courts should be encouraged;

(f) Government funds should be made available in new areas at the planning stage in consultation with this Association as to location and space requirements;

(g) Better public courts and pavilions are required and Government funding should be introduced to make this possible.

The government's response to this 'wish list' was lukewarm and tennis failed to win special status in the primary school curriculum. In fact, the Education Department pursued a policy of introducing students to a wide range of sports in the schools. Even cricket and football, along with tennis, had to surrender time to minor sports. However, wider community use of high school courts did eventuate in some areas.

One significant outcome in 1976 (*WALTA Minutes*, 5/8/1976), was the appointment of a full-time development officer. This was made possible by a 50 per cent subsidy from the Community Recreation Council (CRC). Bruce Durston was the successful applicant. He had a long connection with tennis in the Corrigin area where he had farming property. At various times he had been the captain and president of the Corrigin Tennis Club where he had also formed a junior club in the town. Another of Durston's roles had been President of Zone 5 (*Westennis*, December, 1976, 1). Soon after his appointment, he was involved in a number of projects, including an administrators' seminar in October 1976 and a productive trip to some new clubs in the North-West. He also commenced collating information on court requirements and construction and guidelines for the formation of new clubs.

The CRC grants were a welcome additional source of income for tennis. At the WALTA Council, affiliated clubs were urged to lodge their applications after obtaining the forms from their respective local government offices. Apart from funding for the field officer position, grants took the form of assistance for courts, umpires stands, seminars, fencing and even newly introduced ball machines (*WALTA Minutes*, 10/5/1975). The funds were sourced from the Department of Recreation and distributed on a competitive basis with other sports by the Associated Sporting Committee. In 1975/1976 tennis bodies received \$17,690 out of a total grant money of \$120,400. Tennis was thus receiving about 15 per cent of the allocations (*WALTA Minutes*, 20/1/1976).

The Associated Sporting Committee, the forerunner of the contemporary Western Australian Sports Federation, had dated from 1956 and Helen Waters represented tennis from then until 1980. The Committee administered the Sportsman of the Year Awards, which always drew entrants from tennis. Significantly, too, it administered grants for junior squad coaching, tennis camps for state players, travel for state teams, and association office equipment and assistance including typing, duplicating and printing.

Funding from governmental sources was becoming very significant and it was obvious that the Association needed more expertise if it was to attract grants and influence policy making. Much of this work had been carried out by the Tennis Development Committee under Barry Sanders. It was particularly active in planning for new clubs in the growth corridors of the metropolitan area. Another of its functions was to assist the establishment of the Tennis Foundation of WA (Inc.).

The Tennis Foundation

Following the creation of tennis foundations in the eastern States, steps were taken in Western Australia to follow suit. The possibiliy of attracting sponsorship by creationing a foundation outside the direct control of the Association needed investigation. After the draft constitution had been presented to Council, several delegates sought assurances that the Foundation would cooperate with the WALTA. The Foundation was to promote participation in the game at all age levels and foster the formation of new clubs and playing facilities, giving particular attention to encouraging tennis in schools (*WALTA Annual Report*, 1972/1973).

The Association retained the right to appoint the chairman and one member on the seven-person Management Committee; secretarial work was to be done at the Association office. The Association was to make a financial contribution for the first three years (WALTA, Minutes, 11/5/1972) of $750 per year to be funded from two sources: interest earned from profits gained from the highly successful Federation Cup tie in late December 1970 and by the savings from abolishing the publicity officer position, which would become redundant.

Ultimately, the WALTA contribution was limited to $100 per year, but a $5,000 sponsorship, considered as the minimum necessary to launch the Foundation, was secured from sponsors Slazenger Australia Ltd, (Morris Williams from that company being a key figure) and Dunlop Australia Ltd (Footwear and Garment Division). Additional sponsorships were then obtained from Rothmans Pall Mall (Australia) Ltd and Tom The Cheap Grocer. Andrew Millen was appointed Director. An experienced executive and member of the Royal King's Park club, Millen also had family connections with the sport - his son Wayne having been a leading player in the 1960s and daughter Joan (Kelly) also prominent in tennis circles.

Millen immediately visited the peak educational bodies as part of the drive to establish tennis in schools and tennis facilities throughout the state. Companies such as Hamersley Iron Pty. Ltd. were approached to assist professionals to conduct coaching clinics in Pilbara towns. Soon the Foundation claimed to have been largely responsible for the floodlighting of the South Fremantle, Melville, Morley, Balga, and Kewdale high schools with the aim of opening them to the public for night play (*WALTA Annual Report*, 1973/74).

Around this time, the LTAA with support from WALTA, attempted to establish a Patrons' Club to bolster its funding (*WALTA Minutes*, 5/3/70), but in the early 1970s, with soaring inflation and economic difficulties, sponsorship opportunities evaporated. These problems also afflicted the Foundation.

Major sponsors withdrew and Millen decided to relinquish his position as Chairman effective from 31 December 1974, but he agreed to continue until 30 June 1975 on a non-charge basis to wind up the Foundation (*WALTA Minutes*, 14/11/1974). Some of the assets, including racquets and stocks of *Tennis Hints* were donated to the Education Department. A surplus of $543 was used to purchase perpetual trophies for junior tournaments and to help defray costs of a forthcoming under 16 tour of the eastern States (*WALTA Minutes*, 5/6/1975).

The Foundation, a product of the early years of open tennis, did not appear to have the strong backing of the Association, of which the objectives appeared to be congruent. When substantial sponsorship could not be gained the Foundation was dismantled particularly as the Association's membership, through its affiliated clubs, was showing signs of significant increase.

WALTA membership and finances

One of the main objectives of the Foundation had been to encourage greater participation in tennis. Given the growth of professional tennis, it is pertinent to ask how Association membership fared in terms of participation in the first seven years of open tennis. Was it seven years of feast or seven years of famine?

Actually the membership numbers increased, although President Morrie Beard publicly expressed the view that the figures, particularly in the junior categories, were not accurately reflecting the growth of tennis. He told a (*Sunday Times* 6/10/1974, 64) reporter:

> *Never before have so many youngsters been taking more interest in the sport ... and this is both in the city and the country ... My association welcomes this, but we do find that with modern trends, the membership of clubs is not increasing accordingly.*

Not surprisingly, this led to requests for strategies to ensure that people who used public courts contributed to the development of tennis (*WALTA Minutes*, 10/4/1975). No solutions were devised to overcome this perceived conundrum. However, the first seven years of open tennis witnessed the Association's aggregate membership rise from 5341 to 6848 (see Appendix 11). The 14 per cent increase between 1974 and 1975 was the biggest jump since 1963 (*WALTA Annual Report*, 1974/1975) Yet, the number of affiliated clubs was static. Bassendean withdrew from the Association, as did another old club Daglish. In late 1973 the Catholic Tennis Association withdrew its associate status (*WALTA Minutes*, 27/9/1973). On the other hand, a notable new club to affiliate in 1974 was Corinthian Park. Such enthusiasm accompanied its establishment that it led some to humorously query whether WALTA should affiliate with Corinthian Park. Responding to the population growth south of the river, tennis stalwarts Alan and Mary Hicks played a leading role in its creation (*Corinthian Park Tennis Club: A Short History - The First Ten Years*, n.d.).

One measure adopted in 1974 to provide a link between the Association and clubs in the North-West of the State, including Carnarvon, was a decision to designate them 'associate bodies' for a symbolic eight dollar levy. This did not arrest a drop in country membership in 1974, when an increase in fees took effect. Generally, though, as mentioned the trend was upwards. Direct televison coverage of Wimbledon had begun in 1971, with John Newcombe winning an epic men's final and Evonne Goolagong defeating Margaret Court in the first all Australian final. This coverage had given impetus to local tennis. Some observers also referred to the growth of tennis in the United States of America and wondered whether placing the sport on the open market had facilitated its growth in that nation. There was speculation that tennis in Western Australia was growing outside the ambit of WALTA, as there was an escalation in the number of community courts established by local government authorities. But the local game was not being driven by 'private capital' as it was in the United States.

The financial reports suggest that the Association was being prudently managed during this era. In 1973, Spilsbury relinquished his position as Honorary Treasurer after 14 years and his successor was another accountant, R.A. (Bob) Casey, whose son Rob had established himself as one of the best players in the state. The financial year ended 30 June 1970 had showed a loss of $1,724 from general operations and Spilsbury had stated that 'once again it will be necessary to re-examine the future conduct of the Association' (*WALTA Annual Report*, 1969/1970). In the following financial year the staging of the Federation Cup resulted in a profit. This was a special bonus, as losses were frequently made on the Western Australian Open.

When R.A. Casey tabled the Association's financial report for the year ended 30 June 1976, he documented extraordinary percentage rises in expenditure from a modest 4 per cent in 1973 to 32 per cent in 1974, 36 per cent in 1975 and 26 per cent in 1976. Again, however, there was only a small operating deficiency before the distribution from the LTAA and other headquarters hire income, resulted in a final surplus of $2,470 (*WALTA Annual Report*, 1975/76). The Association had survived the years of high inflation, but on the revenue side there was still a heavy reliance on affiliation fees and fundraising activities coordinated by a Committee chaired at the time by Eric McManus. Funds raised by this Committee for the year ended 30 June 1976 totalled $11,039, made up of:

Miss WA Tennis	$ 3 ,693
Tournament Levies	$946
Women's Auxiliary	$1,292
Voluntary Donations Scheme	$238
Bingo	$4 ,870

A Miss WA Tennis contest was integral to fundraising. Inaugurated in 1969 as part of an Australia-wide promotion to identify a 'Miss Prestige Tennis', the competition raised over $21,000 in its first seven years and was a major source of revenue for interstate trips by players (*Westennis*, December 1976, 1). It was not always easy to attract an adequate number of contestants, which varied from a minimum of 11 to a maximum of 15, four clubs (Alexander Park, Hensman, Royal King's Park and South Perth) being the most consistent supporters. Another award, known as the Miss Charity Queen, went to the entrant who raised the most funds. Helen Waters, chaired the fundraising committee for five years and was tireless in her efforts to make the event a worthwhile and memorable experience. Attracting sponsors was a major task and success varied from year to year. Fashion parades, wine tasting evenings, walkathons, beachathons and quiz nights were the main fund raising activities.

Helen Waters also continued to play an important role with the Women's

Auxiliary, which contributed significantly to revenues. It organised the Linton and Wilson Cup raffles, the Ladies Gala Day and catering for tournaments and regularly assisted the Interstate Visitors Fund. Since its inception in 1961, the Auxiliary had remarkably the same main office-bearers; Helen Waters as President, Mrs Gwyn White as Secretary, and Mrs Mary Ward as Treasurer (*Westennis*, April 1978, 2). Tennis has always relied heavily on its unsung heroes.

A voluntary contribution scheme was established to encourage all players, to add an extra amount to their annual subscription cheques as a donation to the Interstate Visitors' Fund. However, revenue from this source was never substantial; tennis players, like most other Australians, preferred a small wager at a bingo night. Yet it all helped as the Association could not financially survive on its sometimes controversial levy, tournament fees or occasional hallmark events.

Hallmark events (including the Federation Cup and State Opens)

One of the most important international tennis events ever held in Perth was the ninth annual Federation Cup competition. It was played at Royal King's Park between 26 and 29 December, 1970. The Federation Cup, an international women's teams event conducted with a similar format to the Davis Cup, had, from its inauguration in 1963, been held at one location each year. The host was responsible for all expenses, including travel, accommodation and promotion. Early in 1970, when it appeared that Australia would be allocated a future Federation Cup tie, the Executive decided to place a bid with the LTAA to conduct the event (*WALTA Minutes*, 22/1/70).

With as many as a dozen national teams promising to participate, the news that Perth would be the venue was greeted with elation by local officials. Norm Wasley, as President, issued a press release which highlighted the friendliness of the people, the cleanliness of the city and the importance of 'the Sunshine State' because of its huge mining developments. Arrangements were made for visitors to tour the 'magnificent and rugged scenery' of Western Australia (*WALTA press release*, n.d.).

A sub-committee to conduct the tournament was chaired by Ken Miller, Vice-President Morrie Beard headed the sponsorship and publicity committee. Harry Spilsbury was to monitor the financial side. Brian Bignell and Don Hopkins, who were respectively President and Vice-President of Royal King's

The 1971 Federation Cup Committee Les Angel, Harry Spilsbury, Don Hopkins, Ken Miller, Morrie Beard and Brian Bignell (Courtesy The West Australian)

Park, represented the venue club. Secretary of the WALTA, Les Angel, had his correspondence workload greatly increased by acting as the sub-committee secretary for the conduct of the Cup. Fortunately it was an event for which volunteers were relatively easy to find. There was no need to suggest to Council, as was the case for a later State Open, that each affiliated club should nominate five per cent of its membership to be placed on a helpers' roster (*WALTA Minutes*, 26/9/1974).

A strong drive was made for sponsorship assistance. Federal Minister Vic Garland, the federal member for Curtin in the heart of tennis territory, was approached to ascertain if the Commonwealth Government would assist (*WALTA Minutes*, 3/9/1970). While support did not eventuate, the State Government of Sir David Brand made a donation. Approaches to major private companies were also successful and the Executive (*WALTA Minutes*, 19/8/1970) was informed in August 1970 of the following major sponsors:

Qantas	$5,000
BP	3,500
Western Australian Government	2,000
Alcoa	2,000
Western Mining	700
Swan Brewery	500

Berger Paints donated $200 worth of their product to help smarten the appearance of the McGibbon Stand located on the western side of the centre court (*WALTA Minutes*, 3/12/1970). Painting was scheduled to be completed on Christmas Eve as part of the 'last-minute' rush to have everything ready.

At the same time, referee Vic Anderson was making an urgent call for umpires (*WALTA Minutes*, 17/8/1970). This assignment was one of the most important in his distinguished career. In his younger days he had been an 'A' grade player in New South Wales and Queensland. This gave him an awareness of the competitors' perspective which was always evident in his refereeing style. At Royal King's Park he had been President and had served on the Management Committee for 13 years. He was to be referee for more than a dozen Western Australian Opens and numerous major international fixtures and local tournaments. At Wimbledon he had twice officiated as a central umpire and linesman. Fittingly, Anderson also held the office of President of the Western Australian Umpires' Association and was later honoured with life membership of that body. A year before the Federation Cup series, he had been awarded an Australian Umpires' Association Honour Award (*Westennis*, April 1986, 7).

Although the work of referees and umpires rarely make headlines, the Federation Cup received excellent media coverage. The crowds, totalling more than 14,000, were the largest that had ever attended a tennis event in Western Australia. Having two resident Western Australians (Margaret Court as captain and Lesley Hunt) and the popular Evonne Goolagong in the Australian team, intensified interest in the fixture.

In the final, a brilliant performance by Goolagong and a courageous display by Court enabled Australia to win the Federation Cup for the fifth time. Goolagong showed maturity beyond her years to defeat Virginia Wade, 6/4 6/1. Court, trailing after the first set of her match against Britain's captain, Ann Haydon-Jones, overcame the effects of cramp to win the second singles

Winning Federation Cup team Lesley Hunt, Margaret Court and Evonne Goolagong

6/8, 6/3, 6/2. Hunt with very good service made a promising debut in the competition when she combined with Court to defeat the British pair, Wade and Winnie Shaw, in straight sets 6/4, 6/4.

Wasley commended the 'colossal effort' of the organising committee in staging 'a long remembered event and one which we can feel justly proud' (*WALTA Annual Report* 1970/1971). Royal King's Park was also recognised for its joint role in the preparations. Of special significance was the profit of about $20,000. Tennis in the West had received a great boost in the early days of its search for identity, as the ramifications of open tennis became more apparent. It was unlikely, though, that Western Australia could expect to be allocated hallmark events on a regular basis to lift is profile and profits. Nevertheless, the Executive, without real expectation of success, immediately applied to conduct the next Federation Cup (*WALTA Minutes*, 22/1/1970). There was, however, still the annual Western Australian Open and there was the prospect of an Asian circuit event.

On the evenings of the 7 and 8 January, 1970, following the Federation Cup and the Western Australian Open, a round robin professional tournament was conducted. The gross receipts were to be divided in the ratio of 65 per cent for World Championship Tennis and 35 per cent for the Association. Top-flight players John Newcombe, Tom Okker, Nikki Pilic, Tony Roche, and Roger Taylor drew very good crowds. Roche won the event and the Association received a favourable dividend (*WALTA Minutes*, 22/1/1970).

Another international event which provided excellent exposure was the West Coast Classic. The inaugural Classic, conducted in late October 1975 at the Perth Entertainment Centre, is believed to be the first major Western Australian indoor tennis tournament to have been conducted by the Association. Sponsorship by Nissan Datsun, Hitachi, Trans Australia Airlines and the Western Australian Government Tourist Bureau ensured the financial success of the tournament: a $7,000 profit resulted. The keenly-fought singles final was won by Harold Solomon from 'Sandy' Mayer. In the doubles the victors were Paul Ramirez and Brian Gottfried over Ross Case and Geoff Masters. A year later, with a similar group of sponsors, the Association received a $5,000 share of the profits from the second West Coast Classic. Ray Ruffels eventually won the singles from Phil Dent in a thrilling five-set match. Dick Stockton and Rosco Tanner won the doubles from El Shafei and Bob Carmichael.

The promise of visits by international players invariably enhanced the likelihood of successful sponsorship deals. This meant that negotiating for the Western Australian Open was often a delicate exercise. The Open had an interesting history in the first seven years of open tennis. In 1969, 1970 and 1971 it was conducted by Royal King's Park Tennis Club in cooperation with the WALTA. In the following year the same arrangement prevailed except that for the first time the Australian Junior titles were included in the program. In 1973 the WALTA conducted the Open and employed Tennis Camp of Australia to promote and financially underwrite the event. This arrangement, which was yet another indication of the uncertainty about the future of tennis, prevailed for three years and was initially met with resistance at Association headquarters. Much of the opposition appeared to stem from the fact that the Executive (and Council) first heard about Tennis Camp's mooted role from radio reports (*WALTA Minutes*, 28/9/1972). The subsequent granting of the requested date for the Western Australian Open, as part of a national circuit, helped to allay some of the concern. Clarification of profit sharing, guarantees and player expenses had a similar effect (*WALTA Minutes*, 5/4/1973).

In September 1973, John Brown from Tennis Camp of Australia, and his promotions manager, Brian Beers, visited Perth. Beers, who was later to be the first Executive Director of the Association, was to focus on sponsorship matters while John Brown spoke to Council highlighting the promotion of the forthcoming State Open. His address was well received. Said Brown, 'top players are now essential so that the tournament does not become sub-standard. Any sub-standard tournament does nothing for tennis either in this State or Australia generally. To nominate a $15,000 tournament was the first duty, top players follow and sponsorship must be found, and this is the problem at the present' (*WALTA Minutes*, 27/9/1973).

Securing sponsorship was partly dependent on the ability of tournament organisers to sign television rights. The minutes give an account of the frustrations involved. One concession to television, which gradually won the approval of the tennis establishment, was the adoption of the tie-break system. This was the first major change since 1877 to the scoring system. After several formulas were tried the 12-point system was adopted. When the game score in a set was 'six games all' the first player to win seven of the next twelve points won the set. If necessary, additional points were to be played until a two-point advantage was secured. The tie-break was introduced to tournament play in the 1970 United States Open, adopted for Wimbledon in 1971 and accepted for the 1972 Australian Open. Western Australian followed suit in the same year. However, it was not until 1 January, 1976 that all the tie-breaker rules were resolved. From then on it was accepted that the receiver of the first serve in the tie-break would serve the next game. At one stage the tie-break was regarded as 'neutral' from a service viewpoint (*WALTA Minutes*, 2/10/1975).

Another subtle yet significant change in the administration of the State Open arising from changing social values came as a consequence of a petition presented to the Executive in April 1973 with 76 signatures requesting the appointment of ball-girls to perform similar duties to those of ball-boys. Its response was to pass the petition to the State Open Tournament Committee when it was appointed for the 1974 championship (*WALTA Minutes*,

The athletic Kerry Harris (Sewell) in action

5/4/1973). The matter did not reappear in the minutes, but photographs of the 1974 Open show that ball-girls had arrived.

In 1974, Margaret Court's stranglehold on the Western Australian open was temporarily broken. Court had been a dominating force with five titles in the first seven years of 'open' Opens. Evonne Goolagong won in 1972 when Court was not in the draw. Goolagong also secured the title in 1974 but the final was against Kerry Harris of Victoria. The latter had upset Court in a splendid semi-final, 7/5, 6/4. However, Harris could not reproduce such fine form in the final against Goolagong. The effervescent Goolagong, after having been forced to battle in her semi-final against Lesley Hunt (7/5, 7/5) had expected a tough final. As it happened, there was another 7/5 first set scoreline, but then the mercurial Goolagong took control over Harris for a comparatively comfortable 6/1 second set victory.

To have defeated Court at Royal King's Park ensured for the 24 year-old Harris a place in the history of Western Australian tennis. A few years later, after marrying Geraldton region farmer Pat Sewell, she became a resident Western Australian. Records indicate that Harris (Sewell) was never given a WALTA ranking, but in 1972 and 1973 she rose to be number five on the Australian rankings. Between 1972 and 1974 she had the unique distinction of being in three consecutive Australian Open doubles finals. In 1972, in partnership with Helen Gourlay she won the crown. In the following two years, partnered by Kerry Melville, she was beaten respectively by Court and Virginia Wade and then by Goolagong and Peggy Michel.

Harris, with her fine serve and volley game, was a formidable doubles player. In singles, too, she was able to rise to be a world top 20 player who could boast of wins over many of the games greats. This list included Richey, Stove, Durr, Melville, Krantzcke, Hunt, Gourlay and Dalton. She was a finalist at the prestigious Virginia Slims tournament in Philadelphia and a semi-finalist at the Australian Open. If Harris had been given the tennis opportunities of contemporary youth, and played under the present (fairer) seedings system, which does not so clearly favour the top eight, it is not inconceivable that a Grand Slam singles victory could have been achieved.

Perhaps the same questions could be posed about Lesley Hunt. In 1969, at 17 years she lost 7/5, 6/1 to Court in her only appearance in a Western Australian Open final. In 1968 she was also the runner-up in the Wimbledon junior girls singles although she won the French and US Junior Championships. Thereafter, she established an imposing record capable of reaching the finals (and winning) major women's events such as the Italian, Swiss and Canadian Opens as well as the Virginia Slims tournament. She was invariably in the top six in Australia and in 1974 was voted by the international sportswriters as number seven in the world. Some of her wins were against Goolagong, Reid, Wade, Durr, Jones, Dalton, Richey, Casals and even a young Steffi Graf. In 1974 Lesley Hunt received the 'Match of the Tournament' award at Wimbledon for her epic narrow loss to Chris Evert, who went on to win the title. She is able to celebrate membership of the 'final eight club' for both the Wimbledon and US Open championships in which she competed on a dozen occasions. After suffering a serious back problem in 1979, Hunt turned to coaching leading circuit professional players and undertaking radio and television commentary as well as writing books on tennis. This was her role for nearly a decade when she returned to Western Australia to become active in the coaching scene and play State Grade pennants with considerable success. In 1993 she was inducted into the Western Australian Hall of Champions, a rare honour for tennis players.

The State Open in the years following the adoption of open tennis invariably attracted a host of top international and national players, so it can be understood how a player of Lesley Hunt's calibre did not win a major State Open title. This was also applicable to the men. Tony Hammond, Gary Penberthy and Rob Casey who were ranked at number one during these seasons in Western Australia, were not serious contenders for the State Open title as the fields were too strong. Thus, the list of Open winners for men from 1969 included Marty Reissen (USA); Alan Stone (1970); Alex Metreveli (USSR-1971 and 1972); Patrick Proisy (France-1973); Colin Dibley (1974); Ross Case (1975); and Ray Ruffels (1976).

The succession of 'tothersiders' and internationals dominating the Open led to moves to introduce a State closed tournament. The idea had been around for decades. Eventually, on two weekends including the Labour Day holiday in March 1975, a State closed tournament was played, with a very large number of entries at the Bayswater club. Rob Casey won the men's singles and Christine Matison (Dorey) the women's singles. To complete a clean sweep, Matison took the women's doubles with Maureen Smith and then partnered Casey for the mixed doubles title. Veteran Arthur Marshall also had a good tournament when he shared the men's doubles with the highly-ranked fellow Fremantle player Ross Oliveri and the men's veterans' doubles with professional colleague Bruce Robinson.

The success of the first bona fide State Closed ensured its permanence on the tournament calendar. Labour Day weekend was maintained for the fixture, the City of Perth tournament being transferred to Christmas. When the second State Closed was held at Alexander Park, it was coupled with a reminder of one of the tragedies in Western Australian tennis. The men's singles championship, by resolution of the Council (*WALTA Minutes*, 4/12/1975), was to be known as the Andy Fanowrios Memorial Trophy.

In September 1975, a boating expedition involving leading tennis players ended tragically when Andy Fanowrios was drowned. In 1971, Fanowrios had been ranked as high as number two in the State. He had won two State Hardcourt titles and a Spring Championship. At Alexander Park he was establishing himself as a top coach. In addition he was also taking a leading role in training several state squads and Shell coaching clinics. On 19 October, 1975 the shocked tennis community organised a memorial fund for the Andy Fanowrios School of Tennis at the Alexander Park club. Spot prizes and a raffle led to the raising of over $1,600 (*WALTA Minutes*, 11/3/1976), and for a time several local coaches helped Mrs Ros Fanowrios to keep the tennis school going.

The coaching responsibilities at Alexander Park were taken over by Rob Casey who was the first recipient of the Andy Fanowrios State Closed Trophy. For the women's singles at the State Closed it was also decided to name a perpetual trophy. However, the name of a woman was not chosen. Instead, the work of Clarrie Mallett, who had served on committees for 27 years, was recognised (*WALTA Minutes*, 4/12/1975). The Clarrie Mallett trophy winner was Lyn Cooper, who was to remain as one of the top-flight performers in Western Australia for another 15 years. In those years, Cooper, like Mallett, made a significant administrative contribution to tennis. She managed several junior teams, was a member of the junior development committee and served on the State selection panel.

Lyn Cooper, a top flight player for over fifteen years (Courtesy The West Australian)

Michelle Pekovich (centre), showed promise but retired early Sue Taylor (later Mack), (above) remained near the top for two decades

The 1976 State Closed was a title that Cooper was to cherish as it was the last major singles crown she captured. Apart from an earlier 1973 Champion of Champions trophy, Cooper was often runner-up to Christine Matison (Dorey). Matison began to establish an imposing record, winning all the singles titles with the exception (at the time) of the State Open. Sue Taylor (Mack) from Higgins Park won a State Hardcourt, City of Perth and Champion of Champions trophy. Vicki Lancaster (South Perth) and Anne Coleman (Royal King's Park) were also title winners, but all found Matison their nemesis. Although Matison was not tall or powerful she always maintained balance and had an excellent backhand. 'Mentally', in the sense employed in tennis vocabulary, Matison had no peer.

In the mid-seventies, Michelle Pekovich, another Fremantle player, emerged as a genuine challenger to Matison's local dominance. At one stage she appeared to even have an international future. She was selected in an Australian team for a goodwill tour of China and had the experience of playing and travelling with such legends as Rosewall and Fraser. Later, Pekovich was included in an Australian under-21 team to tour Europe and compete at Wimbledon. However, after twice winning the State Closed and rising to number four ranking in the State, she chose not to continue the grind of challenging Matison (*Westennis*, April 1978, 7).

In the men's division Rob Casey's tournament record was comparable to that of Christine Matison in the women's section. Early in his tennis career Casey had shown every indication that he would become a fine player with an excellent temperament. In January 1972, when the Linton Cup competition was conducted in Perth, he was captain of the victorious team. As this gave Casey a rare niche in the history of Western Australian tennis, it will be discussed in the context of interstate competition.

A few months after the Linton Cup triumph, Casey was selected to represent Australia in a series of junior tournaments and international matches in Vancouver, Canada. A hurried send-off function was arranged in the association rooms before his departure in late July 1972 (*WALTA Minutes*, 10/8/1972). Casey and his colleague, Ernie Ewart from Victoria, acquitted themselves admirably and Casey was selected to join the Australian Davis Cup training squad.

At the Association, the Chairman of Selectors, Alan Hicks, spoke of 'the elation', which had resulted from Casey's selection (*WALTA Minutes*, 12/10/1972). As he was then studying at the University of Western Australia, it was necessary for Casey to miss the Spring tournament and make arrangements to take his examinations in Melbourne. He passed his examinations, but failed to gain selection in the Davis Cup team. Casey duly finished his Arts degree and became one of the State's greatest players including the distinction of being number one ranked player for six years. Later in veterans' competition he won national representation as a member of the 1991 Italia Cup team and in the same year was a semi-finalist in the International Tennis Federation over-35 singles and doubles competition. He also gained a reputation as a leading coach and served four years as the President of the Tennis Coaches Association of Western Australia. His credentials led to his appointment as a Manager and Coach of national youth teams including the victorious 1990 Youth Cup team for an Asian/Australian event in Hong Kong. He then played a part as an administrator in tennis including a term as a member of the Executive at Tennis West. In addition Casey wrote widely about tennis and given his communicative skills and knowledge of the game, was sought on the 'seminar circuit'.

Casey's great rival on the local tournament scene was Gary Penberthy. It will be recalled that Penberthy captained an Australian Junior Davis Cup team that went to the United States of America in 1966. Like Casey, however, Penberthy chose to establish his career in Western Australia rather than be a circuit player. As a cagey left-hander, he posed problems for all local players in tournaments and pennants, although for most of the time Casey was his master. This meant that Penberthy had a mortgage on the number two ranking and was the runner-up in many championships. Yet he was still able to capture the State Hardcourt, Spring and City of Perth titles and establish a fine record with five Champion of Champion trophies. His deft skills were also evident in doubles. With friend Peter Dyson (a prominent coach) he began to accumulate numerous doubles titles.

During this period, the name of Penberthy became established as one of the most revered in Western Australia tennis. He and his wife Laraine, a keen tennis fan, gave their time to the game in a positive, friendly manner. At one stage, while filling the role as Association coach, Penberthy donated his fee back to the WALTA. Gary Penberthy was invariably able to develop an excellent rapport with the various State squads and in 1978, when he was designated as the official Linton Cup coach, the team managed second place to a strong Queensland team.

Christine Matison (later Dorey), 'Mentally' she had no peer

Rob Casey, one of the State's greatest players and coaches

Juniors

A highlight of the junior program was the WA victory in the 1972 Linton Cup series. Dr R.G. Linton, son of the donor of the Cup, was on hand to make the presentation to the team captain, Rob Casey. Other members of the team were Phil Sofoulis, Ross Olivieri and Phil Chamberlain. With excellent press coverage and keen spectator interest, the team went through the competition, which included New Zealand, without recording a loss. Casey lost only one rubber and in that match he held match point. In the final encounter, he had some anxious moments when he lost the first set 8/10 to John Eastburn, a ranked junior from New South Wales. In a manner which was an omen of his senior career, Casey fought back to win the next two sets 6/3, 6/0. Sofoulis, after having set point against him, won in two sets against Richard Carey. It capped a fine series for Sofoulis, who had an outstanding carnival and remained undefeated throughout. Of course it should not be overlooked that when Casey had been defeated against Victoria it was Sofoulis who had kept Western Australia's cup hopes alive.

With the Linton and Wilson Cups being played in Perth for the first time, many months of preparation had been carried out by Barry Sanders as the chair of the organising committee. Coach Rob Kilderry, manager Geoff Strang, and physical education instructor Bruce Sinclair all played integral roles in the quest for the Cup. Kilderry, a keen student of the game, was credited with convincing Casey and Sofoulis of the need to consider all aspects of stroke play rather than being drawn into a big-hitting game (*West Australian*, 29/1/1972, 83).

Gary Penberthy, ageless champion player and contributor to tennis

To honour the success of the team, a function was held at the Royal King's Park pavilion in late April, 1972. Three members of the 1949 winning team Noel Pearse, Clive Wilderspin and manager Norm Wasley were present. John Blacklock and Brian Tobin were absent from the state. There was an air of expectation about the future, as both Casey and Sofoulis were young enough to defend the Linton Cup in New Zealand the following year. However, the team (including Oliveri and John Hunt) was able only to finish fifth. They

Phil Sofoulis, who with Rob Casey, was a star in the 1972 Linton Cup victory (Courtesy The West Australian)

were competitive, but without the rare advantage of playing at home on grass the so-called 'breaks' did not go with the boys. Nor did the breaks go with Barry Tognolini: he was unlucky to miss selection in the victorious 1972 Linton Cup team and in the following year he again narrowly missed being chosen. Fortunately Tognolini was not deterred as he then developed a reputation as one of the state's best doubles players. Support from more experienced brother, Jim Tognolini, a top player who knew the trials and tribulations of tennis, had obviously been rendered.

In New Zealand in 1973 bad luck also dogged the Wilson Cup team, as leading performer Sue Taylor (Mack) was very sick for most of the tour. The others chosen for the trip were Ann Layman, Pauline Saunders (Linney) and Mary Sawyer (Collins). They were all to develop into fine players, with Sawyer later challenging the dominance of Christine Dorey, but they could only manage sixth place on this occasion. Touring New Zealand was an extraordinary experience in the postwar era, a reminder of the time when Australia and New Zealand had an integrated administrative structure and played as 'Australasia' in the Davis Cup.

The inclusion of New Zealand appeared to reduce the chance of a victory in the Wilson Cup for remote Western Australia. In 1968, 1969 and 1970 Western Australia, with Lesley Hunt and Vicki Lancaster, had respectively twice finished second and third. Lesley Hunt and Vicki Lancaster were not in the 1970 side, but strength had been kept in the squad with the inclusion of Lyn Cooper and Elizabeth Worner, both of whom had achieved a national junior girls' ranking.

By 1976, Western Australia was again in serious contention for both the Wilson and Linton Cups. With a new wave of very promising juniors, both finished in second place. These teams were reduced from the traditional four to three members. The Wilson Cup team was composed of Joanne Hall, Michelle Pekovich and Ann Layman. At 14 years of age, Layman was one of the youngest players to be selected for a Wilson Cup team. She was a tall and athletic player with a fine service. Partnered respectively by Pekovich and Mary Sawyer (Collins), the promising Layman twice reached the final of the national junior doubles event. Later, in senior competition, Layman's aggressive game always posed a threat to the top seeds and it is surprising that she did not win more titles.

The Linton Cup team members were Lawrence Hall, John Hunt and Myron Pushyk. During this period, Hall from the Higgins Park Club, was making a name for himself, including being the Association's nominee for the Western Australian Sportsman of the Year. In April 1974, after being nominated to play in a 'round robin' in Melbourne with two other promising juniors, Chris Johnstone and Geraldine Sayers, the promising Hall was chosen as a member of the Australian junior team to play in an Avenire Tournament at Milan, Italy (*WALTA Minutes*, 18/4/1974). The tall, talented and sometimes volatile Hall reached the last 16, only to be beaten narrowly by the eventual winner of the tournament (*WALTA Minutes*, 11/7/1974). Later, Hall was included in a national touring party to Japan (*WALTA Minutes*, 10/7/1975).

Barry Tognolini, one of the State's best doubles players

Hall had been a member of an inaugural under-16 team which had toured the eastern States between 12 January and 30 January, 1974. After playing in Frankston and Beaumaris in Victoria, the party participated in the national championships in Canberra, where Hall gave a great display to win the Australian under-15 title. Overall, the championship performances from

Western Australian juniors were creditable, particularly as only two players had been seeded for the Canberra event.

Manager Ken Tobin, an 'A' grade player in his own right and an innovative tennis thinker, provided a detailed report of the tour. After thanking David Punch for his part in bringing the tour to fruition, Bob Benzie for his organisation and his wife Barbara for her role as chaperone, Tobin recommended to Council (*WALTA Minutes*, 14/2/1974) that:

- *Earlier team selection is recommended with matches against country zones and metropolitan teams.*
- *Western Australian to take the initiative and invite teams from all States to play in Western Australia.*
- *Sponsorship to be sought.*
- *Composition of the team could be four under sixteen boys and girls and two under fourteen boys and girls. The team was (WALTA Minutes, 8/11/1974):*

  Boys : Lawrence Hall, Chris Johnstone, Reg Luttrell, Tony Luttrell, Gary Rainbird, Peter Smith.

  Girls : Kathy Bovell, Janine Keenan, Judy Lange, Michelle Pekovich, Geraldine Sayers, Colleen Taylor.
- *Travel should be as a team, not by car.*
- *The team had made a great impression and were a credit to the State.*

Ken Tobin, it should be recognised, would not have submitted a glowing report if the team had not warranted such an evaluation. For instance, in early 1975 he managed the junior (Wilson and Linton) and senior State teams tour to Sydney, Melbourne and Hobart. After noting the excellent performances of Christine Matison, Lawrence Hall and Vicki Lancaster he was critical of the behaviour of some players. The Manager's report referred to the temperamental displays of State representatives including 'swearing loudly and smashing racquets'. Furthermore, as Tobin stated, 'it was puzzling in that they were enthusiastic prior to selection, they were enthusiastic after selection, but upon arrival in the Eastern States their attitude was negative (*WALTA Minutes*, 13/2/1975).

Ann Layman, athletic player

Joanne Hall, prominent in the mid-Seventies

Nevertheless, the Junior Development Committee, mindful of Tobin's approval of the earlier under-16 tour had decided to promote a similar venture in 1975. On this occasion, under the management of Bob Benzie who had striven so hard for such tours, the team played two tournaments in Victoria before proceeding to Manly for the Australian Junior Hardcourt titles. As had been the case in the previous year, the team members financed themselves, although they were assisted by the Manager arranging bingo evenings. The Association contributed $500 towards the manager's expenses (*WALTA Annual Report*, 1974/1975).

Reports again indicated that the tour was a profound success. The new faces were Linda Polley, Judy Wheatley, Andrew Paskos, Anthony Di Francesco, Terry Vinci, Roger Grant and Keith Begley (*WALTA Minutes*, 14/11/1974). The latter two were to become leading names in Western Australian tennis. They, with Chris Johnstone, were also members of the inaugural Reid Cup team for boys. The honour of being in the first Reid Cup team for girls went to Judy Lange, Elizabeth Sayers and Judy Wheatley. Sayers was only 12 years of age and the youngest competitor in the Cup series.

Keith Begley, became a well known name in WA tennis

The under-16 junior tour and its replacement, the Reid Cup, were part of the strategy to broaden the opportunities for comparatively isolated Western Australians to experience more interstate competition. For several years the Association had been advocating an under-16 competition on similar lines to the Linton and Wilson Cups (*WALTA Minutes*, 13/2/1975). When the LTAA endorsed the concept, and President Wayne Reid donated two perpetual trophies for the first series (including New Zealand) to be played at Brisbane in January 1976, the decision was greeted with satisfaction at WALTA headquarters. Less successful in the short term were the attempts to develop an interstate senior competition, possibly to be known as the Ken Rosewall Shield (*WALTA Minutes*, 10/1/1975).

Two other ventures that did not come to fruition were tours to Japan and Bulgaria. After lengthy negotiations, carried mainly by Benzie, a planned tour by two junior boys and two junior girls to Kagoshima, in Japan, was cancelled (*WALTA Minutes*, 6/3/1975). In August 1976, Myron Pushyk, Lyn Cooper and Michelle Pekovich were nominated for an 'amateur' team to visit Bulgaria (*WALTA Minutes*, 5/8/1976). Much to the disappointment of the players the plan fell through.

Within Australia, other opportunities were emerging for interstate competition. In January 1976, a coaching camp at Narrabeen (NSW), sponsored by computing company IBM, was attended by Geraldine Sayers, Andrew Paskos, Scott Nicholas and Kathy Bovell. The latter was charged with the responsibility of presenting a report on the tour to Council (*WALTA Minutes*, 24/2/1976). A month earlier, Elizabeth Sayers, Denise Cole, Andrew Paskos and Terry Vinci were nominated to compete in the National Berri Cup Junior Tennis Championships.

For boys as young as 12, a 'little Davis Cupper' competition was sponsored by Esso Australia. Shane Johnstone was the first Western Australian to be chosen for matches to be played at Hobart from January 7 to January 11, 1976. For women of between the age of 16 and 35 years, who had not previously toured overseas to play tennis, a new tournament sponsored by Cleo and Max Factor was unveiled. Each State Association conducted its own finals with a national final scheduled for January 1975. Joanne Hall, from Higgins Park, who had seen her brother Lawrence in the limelight, defeated her more fancied senior opponents Kerryl Chute and Maureen Smith to win the Western Australian title (*West Australian*, 15/12/1975, 54). At the time, Hall was second in the junior girls' rankings behind Michelle Pekovich. In 1974, 1975 and 1976, the powerful stroking Hall had been a member of the Wilson Cup team.

The Association was coming to grips with negotiating sponsorship deals to assist the junior program. Shell became involved in an annual program for country juniors. A successful approach was made to the Rothman's Sport Foundation for financial assistance to conduct coaching schools (*WALTA Minutes*, 18/4/1974). Of course it meant being sensitive to the requirements stance of the sponsor. At the Council meeting of May 1974, it was asked why an eastern States coach, Bill Gilmour, had been invited to run a training school for local coaches in lieu of local professionals. The answer, as minuted, states 'because Rothmans preferred it this way'. However, executives of the Rothman Foundation denied that they made this specification. They insisted that the minutes be corrected and the matter resolved by discussions between the professionals and Rothmans (*WALTA Minutes*, 11/7/1974).

During this period the Association continued to organise junior training squads with leading professional coaches. A well-organised training camp at Point Peron was temporarily part of the program. Each year an analysis was undertaken of the entries for the annual Schools' Tournament at Robertson Park during the August school vacation. It was often difficult to explain the oscillations in the entry numbers, which were generally around the 300 mark. Another major tournament for juniors, known as the State Underage Championships, which was first conducted by the Hensman Park club in January 1974 with 306 individual entrants, also complicated comparisons with previous years.

Some concern was expressed about how the Schools' competition, incorporating the historic Slazenger Cup, had declined in terms of the number of participating schools (*WALTA Annual Report*, 1975/1976). Although CBC Fremantle, with Barry Tognolini in the team, won in 1969 and St Louis, led by Rob Casey, was successful in 1970 it was Hale School that dominated the early 1970s. Dean Williams, who later rose to be the number two squash player in the world, displayed his racquet skills with three Slazenger Cup wins before being selected in the Linton Cup team. Kim Wallman, who was later prominent (with brother Robert) at the Reabold club, was also in three winning combinations. Before Hale, led by Chris Johnstone, won again in 1976 and 1977, Wesley College was able to capture the Cup in 1974 and 1975. Ian Berson, Clive Timms and Phil Searle were in both teams.

In the girls' division the Slazenger Cup was returned to Catholic schools in the early 1970s (Loreto 1971, St Joachim's 1972 and Mercedes 1973) before Presbyterian Ladies College, led by Judy Lange, won the competition in 1974 and 1975. Then, in 1976 and 1977, Melville Senior High School broke the hold of the private schools with successive Cup victories. In both years the same players Denise Cole, Glynis Mitchell, twins Jenny and Sue Mitchell and Margaret Casserly were listed as team members. Would this victory encourage more government schools to enter the Slazenger Cup, Mursell Shield, Herbert Edwards Cup and Academy Plate competitions?

The entries for the Slazenger Cup, and other trophy events, had dropped but school physical education programs were broadening their offerings to include many sports. This was also the case in the Catholic education system. In these schools tennis had traditionally been given an important focus and, when coupled with the opportunities provided by the Western Australian Catholic Lawn Tennis Association, an impetus had been given to the standard of women's tennis in the State. Gradually, though, there was a swing to participate in the expanded range of shield tennis and tournament opportunities provided by the WALTA.

Shield tennis

In the 1969/70 shield match season, which was highlighted by the entry of teaching professionals, 198 teams entered the competition. The men's and woman's 'A' grade had six team divisions. There were 64 other men's teams and 25 other women's teams. For women, the mid-week competition had six divisions, with a total of 41 teams. This meant that the number of senior men and senior women playing competitive tennis outside tournaments within the metropolitan area was comparable. In the junior section, there were 18 registered under 19 boys' teams, and the same number of under 16 teams. For the girls, on the other hand, the number of teams registered in the same age groups were only six and 15 respectively.

Seven years later, it was possible to point to the steady growth in the number of participants in the interclub shield competition: the number of pennant teams had risen to 278, of which 181 were in the men's section and 97 were in the women's section. A men's veterans' division had been introduced, as well as the women's over-35 competition. There were now 10 midweek ladies divisions with a total of 78 teams. This meant that the ratio of men to women playing pennants still remained fairly constant.

In keeping with the historical trend, there remained a higher number of junior boys' teams than girls' teams. In the under-19 age group, there were three boys' divisions and two girls' divisions, whereas in the under-16s there were five boys divisions compared with only two for the girls. One important innovation, from the 1972/1973 season, was the introduction of an under-14 division in junior pennants. At this level, there were an equal number of three divisions for both boys and girls. The competition in most age groups was strong. In that era the under-19 pennants had 'a high profile'. Many leading juniors played 'A' grade on Saturday afternoon followed by junior pennants on Sunday morning.

The role of Chairperson of the Shield Match Committee continued to be an exacting task. Barry Sanders filled this role until 1971, when Merv Hill took over for four seasons. He provided a set of guidelines for the Committee which was described as 'a very useful Association Archive' (*WALTA Annual Report*, 1974/1975). Dene Rundle, of the Hensman Park, club then began a stint of several seasons as the Chairman. In his first year he was responsible for reintroducing a winter pennant series. It was probably not appreciated that more than 70 years earlier the quest for the formation of a permanent tennis association had been driven in part by the demand for a winter pennant competition by fledging clubs in the metropolitan area. Forty-eight teams competed in what became a permanent part of the competitive scene. During this time the Shield Committee lost the services (due to the sudden death) of Bill Halliday, who had undertaken the unenviable task of recording the shield match results. In his youth, Halliday had been a leading player with a State ranking and as a prominent educationist, he had maintained his commitment to tennis with administrative assistance.

Another initiative which stemmed from Rundle's committee was the introduction of a transfer system. Similar 'clearance' plans had been high on the agenda during Ken Miller's presidency between 1953 and 1962. In 1972, the idea was again given a strong airing (*WALTA Minutes*, 14/6/1972). However, on this occasion the shield rules were unanimously amended to require any shield match competitor who wanted to transfer to another club to complete an Approved Transfer Application which ensured that the respective clubs agreed to the clearance. The transfer could be rejected on the grounds of the applicant being unfinancial or the transfer being detrimental to the shield match competition. The shield match committee adjudicated if there was a dispute about the criterion 'detrimental to the Shield Match competition' (*WALTA Minutes*, 8/4/1976).

Disputes, however, proved to be very rare. As the system regularised the transfer of players between clubs, there was no suggestion that it be abolished. However, other minor changes were made to the pennant system. When leading professional Bruce Robinson wrote in his regular *Sunday Times* (1/4/1973, 64) column that the 1973 womens 'A' grade final between Royal King's Park and Fremantle had been marred by the absence of umpires and singles sticks, steps were taken to ensure that losing teams provide umpires for future finals. Suggestions that inter-district rather than inter-club competitions be introduced were not adopted (*WALTA Minutes*, 5/4/1973). Nor was a satisfactory solution found to complaints about senior and junior shield matches being played in the December and January holiday periods (*WALTA Minutes*, 8/3/1973).

One matter often under review was the starting time for pennant matches. Hedley O'Neil, from Leederville, suggested to Council that 'A' grade matches begin at an earlier time (*WALTA Minutes*, 12/4/1973). On the related question of daylight saving, the Association advised the Chief Secretary's Department of the support for the concept. It did not recognise the political furore that daylight saving was to cause, particularly in rural areas. It, along with the tie-break, would allow clubs to complete pennant matches before the light had deteriorated as well as providing more late afternoon opportunities for pennant practice and social play (*WALTA Minutes*, 1/6/1972). The metropolitan Scarborough and Reabold clubs also supported daylight saving (*WALTA Minutes*, 13/7/1972).

For more than a decade from 1973, Fremantle dominated the women's competition. It took the lead from Royal King's Park, which won three womens' premierships between 1969 and 1972. In 1970, Claremont, with Christine Matison, Lyn Cooper, Libby Worner and Sue Coote denied King's Park the 'hat trick' when they overwhelmed Alexander Park by six rubbers to nil in the grand final. King's Park's strength had stemmed from players such as Helen Young (nee Patterson), Anne Watts (nee McKenzie), Jan Maddison, Gay Benzie and Jill Larritt. Even more formidable was the 1973 Fremantle final round team of Christine Matison (transferred from Claremont), Maureen Smith, Michelle Pekovich and Pauline Saunders (Linney). This marked the first of a sequence of four straight premierships. Other players who contributed to Fremantle's dominance included Judy Scarrott and Rosalind Fisher.

In men's 'A' grade between 1969 and 1976 premiership honours were shared by four clubs: Claremont, University, Bayswater and Royal King's Park. In 1970, Claremont achieved the rare double of a men's and women's senior shield title. Claremont's strength in the men's competition stemmed from Gary Penberthy, Peter Dyson, the experienced Geoff Strang and the promising Rob Casey. Other team members included Ken Tobin and David Hatt. In the 1970 grand final, a masterly pairing of Peter Dyson with Geoff Strang led to the first defeat of the season for the highly-fancied East Fremantle doubles combination of Kerry Varney and Arthur Marshall (*West Australian*, 20/4/1970, 28).

University, which before the advent of the Murdoch, Curtin, Notre Dame and Edith Cowan institutions, meant 'The University of Western Australia', celebrated its last years as the sole 'varsity' in the State with premierships in 1971 and 1972. On both occasions, University was regarded as the surprise winner entering the grand final after victory in the preliminary final. The 1971 winning grand final team against East Fremantle was made up of Peter Rigg, Phil Holten, Mal Hodsdon and Gundars Tilmanis. In the following year, Tilmanis and Holten were joined by Rob Kilderry and Neil Eddington when they defeated a strong Bayswater-Alexander Park team of Gary Penberthy, Andy Fanowrios, Gary Same and Glyn Shipley by a solitary game. The final result was University 3 rubbers, 7 sets and 64 games to their opponents 3 rubbers, 7 sets and 63 games. The tie came down to the final set in the doubles which Eddington and Holten won 6/2 against a despondent Same and Shipley.

By 1976, the scene which had been changed by player movements, saw Bayswater being dubbed 'one of the strongest teams ever to compete in the men's 'A' grade pennant tennis' (*West Australian*, 22/3/1976, 67). The team lived up to expectations when it recorded a most convincing win in the grand final, with a five rubbers to one score over Claremont. Bayswater's Penberthy, Keith Hince, Myron Pushyk and Ron Williams were too good for their respective opponents Casey, Dyson, Peter O'Dea and Ken Tobin. Only a narrow 7/6, 6/3 win by Casey over Penberthy avoided a 'white-wash'.

The country scene

One development strategy used in this period, was to send leading State players, who figured prominently in the shield competitions, to country centres. Each annual report invariably commented on the value of these visits. Thus, in September 1970, tennis in the north of the State was said to have received 'a great stimulus' when leading players Loma Jowett (Alexander Park), Christine Matison and Andy Fanowrios, with secretary Les Angel as manager, were flown by chartered aircraft (sponsored by the North Corp Committee of the National Fitness Council) to Pilbara and Kimberley centres. They played exhibition tennis, conducted coaching clinics, showed films and provided administrative assistance. As a measure of the success of this tour, a month later the Tom Price club, was prepared to organise a return visit by Alan Hicks and Peter Rigg accompanied by Loma Jowett and Christine Matison.

Of special interest was a trip to Nungarin on Sunday, 18 February, 1973 to celebrate the opening of four floodlit grass courts. Exhibition matches were played by Tony Hammond, Phil Holten, Christine Matison and Moira Whitely. The hospitality was described as 'fantastic' and nearly 40 juniors took part in the morning coaching activities (*WALTA Minutes*, 8/3/1973).

With such visits being so well received, Fred Dreyer, as Chairman of the Country Affairs Committee, later recommended to Council that each country zone be visited by an official and team of players once a year. The zones were to make arrangements for accommodation (*WALTA Minutes*, 10/6/1976). Fred Dreyer had taken over the responsibility for the Country Affairs Committee after Merv Hill had held the post for four years. Another approach to providing top tennis in the country took place in January 1972, when arrangements were made for the Australian Davis Cup team to break its journey for an exhibition match at Kalgoorlie. Later in the same month, three Soviet players in Perth for the Western Australian Open took part in the South-West Championships at Bunbury.

However, for the tennis players in rural areas Country Week remained the highlight. In 1970, team entries reached 128, equalling the 1962 record. The timing of the Carnival was regularly debated. In 1972, it was generally agreed that the lower number of entries could be attributed to the early (3 January to 7 January) dates. It was immediately decided that in the future Country Week would not be held before 15 January (*WALTA Minutes*, 4/1/1972). In 1972, though, several other factors had to be taken into account. Revised dates for the Australian Open necessitated an alteration to the Western Australian Championship dates, along with the need to keep the King's Park courts in good condition for the scheduled Linton and Wilson Cup competitions. Apart from the seasonal demands of the farming community, the dates of the very popular Country Week cricket carnival had to be included in the equation. Numbers jumped by 10 per cent in 1973, when a mid-January date was selected. In the following year, a 10 per cent drop was recorded and it appeared that the decision to move the venue to the Bayswater club, after some 20 consecutive seasons at Royal King's Park, was a factor.

At the annual Country Conference held in conjunction with the Carnival, there was praise for the organisation provided at Bayswater, particularly by Bob Benzie, who had served for some years on the Executive as the Country Affairs representative. Nevertheless, there was also a yearning to return to the 'Mecca', King's Park. At the 1976 Conference, a motion was forwarded requesting that every effort be made to return Country Week to its 'original home' on a rotating basis (*WALTA Minutes*, 20/1/1976).

Whether at King's Park or Bayswater the performances of Roslyn Giles from Katanning were outstanding. She dominated the women's singles championship with six titles in seven years, as well as helping Katanning to win the team competition. Giles had a fine, steady game, an excellent temperament and was known for her excellent tactical play. Unfortunately, she did not have the opportunity to play continuously in the major tournaments conducted by the Association, so, despite her prowess, she never received a State women's ranking.

Fred Dreyer, recommended country visits by leading players and WALTA officials

On the other hand, the outstanding Country Week player in the men's section was school teacher Colin Bell. He competed regularly in the major championships and was a leading pennant player for Hensman Park. Between 1973 and 1976, Bell won four straight Country Week men's singles titles. With assistance from John Pugh, Bill Sandilands and Ian Goodchild, he was also a member of the victorious Albany-Kendenup (or Albany) 'A' grade winning team on three occasions. Bell's name was to be engraved eight times on the perpetual Country Week singles trophy. No other player has neared this achievement in the men's singles. On one occasion in the State Open he narrowly lost to the future Wimbledon champion Arthur Ashe with a meritorious 6/3, 4/6, 10/8 scorecard. Later Bell demonstrated a keenness to improve coaching methods when he wrote a thesis entitled '*Tennis Coaching in Western Australia*' (Bell, 1976).

Bob Benzie (left), a hard worker for the WALTA Hon. Jim Brown M.L.C. (right) draws a Wesfarmers Country Week raffle

Junior tennis was regularly on the agenda of each annual Country Conference. An innovation in 1974 was the decision to invite the winners of the boys' and girls' under 16 and under 19 title winners at Country Week to play in the City of Perth Tournament, the Association assisting with accommodation and paying the entry fees. At the 1976 Conference, advice was received from Mrs M. Morrell that she wished to commemorate both her and her late husband's interest in Country Week by a donation to purchase perpetual trophies for the boys' and girls' under-19 competitions. A motion to this effect was carried with acclamation after it had been moved by 'great worker' Les Angel (*Westennis*, October 1991, 5), the Association Secretary who was known for his keen interest in rural affairs (*WALTA Minutes*, 20/1/1976).

The issue of publicity was yet again raised. In 1969, there was disappointment that the draw for Country Week was not being published in the newspapers (*WALTA Minutes*, 21/1/1969). Only occasionally was the championship covered in the metropolitan papers. Generally, the local town newspapers were the main source of information on performances of country players. For instance the *Geraldton Guardian* (24/1/1970) carried the headlines of 'Successes in Perth' when Ken Harris and Roger O'Farrell, for the fourth year in a row, secured the team title when they did not drop a set to Albany-Kendenup in the final. At that carnival, O'Farrell reversed the result of the previous two years by defeating Ken Harris 6/4, 6/3 in the singles event. Harris had held the singles trophy since 1967 when he had beaten Rudy D'Orsogna. However, it was not only Country Week play that was failing to reach the press. Publicity became a particularly important issue for the Association during the 1970s.

Publicity

In October 1970, David Brewtnal took over as publicity officer from Albert Porges. A year earlier, Dunlop/Slazengers and Spaldings, through their representatives in Western Australia -Williams and Wood Pty Ltd and Chrystal (W.A.) Pty Ltd - had renewed their agreement to continue financial support for a publicity officer. Brewtnal, like his predecessor, reported tournament results, pennant scores, and major association activities. But there were rumbles of discontent about the extent of the publicity which was being gained for tennis (*WALTA Minutes*, 2/4/1970 and 7/5/1970). When Brewtnal tendered his resignation in late 1972 to go on a working holiday, the sporting goods companies did not renew their support for a publicity officer. It was

Colin Bell (right), Country Week champion Colin Bell with Alan Gooch and umpire Charlie Brown

expected that the newly-formed Tennis Foundation would perform the publicity function, but this proved to be a forlorn hope so the Executive decided upon decisive action by obtaining Council's approval for a detailed set of recommendations (*WALTA Minutes*, 9/8/1973).

The Publicity Officer was to be renamed 'Field Officer'. The salary was set at $3,120 per annum, with additional expenses up to $750. The position was 'not seen as a 7½ hours a day, 9 to 5 job, but rather one involving those hours of the day or night considered appropriate to discharge ... duties' (*WALTA Minutes*, 9/8/1973). The 'duty statement' read:

Duty 1 - Tennis Promotion

(a) To work in close liaison with the Tennis Development Committee particularly in new club activity.

(b) To assist affiliated clubs in membership drives and at the direction of the Executive to canvass generally for new members.

(c) To pay particular attention to promotion of tennis in schools and foster the interest in tennis on the part of sportsmasters and sportsmistresses and graduating teachers.

(d) To attend all metropolitan clubs at least once per year either in committee or on playing day.

Duty 2 - Tennis Publicity

1) To arrange press publicity for the following -

   (a) Association and club items of interest.

   (b) Shield match commentaries and results.

   (c) Results and commentaries of all Association tournaments.

2) To attend as many tournaments and fixtures of affiliated clubs and associations in the country districts ... and to publicise the same and results thereof.

3) To carry such other duties of a publicity nature as the Executive may require ....

4) To attend such meetings of the Executive as required and all meetings of the Council of the Association plus such other meetings of sub-committees as the Executive may require.

The successful applicant was Gary Carvolth, the well-known local media personality. His appointment took effect from October 1, 1973. Within six weeks a 'get-together' was conducted to try to establish (or cement) good relations between the Association and the media. This function had already begun to become an annual affair but Carvolth was able to greatly expand the scope of media exposure.

Apart from his publicity role, Carvolth also pursued sponsorships and promoted the activities of the Association throughout the State. At one stage, this led to some concern about the size of the telephone account (*WALTA Minutes*, 2/5/1974). Fittingly, in March 1975, Carvolth was a guest speaker at a university seminar on 'Marketing of Sport'. Tennis, at least during this period, appeared to be at the forefront of sports marketing. A regular annual feature, a tennis lift-out in the *Sunday Times* newspaper at the beginning of the season in October, was retained (*Sunday Times*, 6/10/1974).

The Association also continued to send representatives to youth rallies and Church services for sports people. For the Youth Pageant held at the WACA ground in 1971 to celebrate the State's population reaching one million, leading young players Lyn Cooper and Tony Hammond were designated (*WALTA Minutes*, 11/2/1971). At the 1975 Commonwealth Youth Rally, Lawrence Hall and Michelle Pekovich attended (*WALTA Minutes*, 5/6/1975). It was, however, often the seniors who volunteered to attend the annual church service for the sporting community held at St Nicholas's Anglican Church in Floreat Park. In 1973, for instance, dedicated Executive members Sam Hodsdon and Eric McManis represented the Association (*WALTA Minutes*, 7/3/1992). McManis may have thought that visit earned him some goodwill a year later when he narrowly escaped more serious injury in a traffic accident near the wheat-belt town of Kellerberrin. He had been liaising with zone officials; public relations has always meant attending to the interests of country clubs.

Publicity also took advantage of the advent of screen printing technology with the sale of T-shirts with catchy phrases such as 'Tennis is a Love Game' or Humphrey Bogart's 'Anyone for Tennis'. What was needed as tennis headed into the open era, was a magazine that detailed the Association's activities. This was being contemplated and was close at hand.

Veterans

One initiative that had been discussed for some seasons was the formation of a Veterans' Club. Since the early 1960s many senior players had regularly grouped for matches as the Governor's team. Successive State Governors, in their capacity as Patrons, sponsored matches against schools and community organisations. Victorian John Young, the first President of the Veterans' Club of Australia, which had been founded in March 1970, urged local enthusiasts to form a State branch.

In 1972, politician, football star and coach extraordinaire Ross (later Sir Ross) Hutchison is reputed to have taken the initiative and sought a five dollar membership fee from each of a dozen seniors relaxing after playing at Royal King's Park. Informally, it was decided that former State Open champion Harry Jacoby would be President and prominent lawyer Geoff Hammond would act as the secretary-treasurer. Within a short space of time, Jacoby asked Hutchison to take the presidency. When the first annual meeting was conducted on 2 April, 1973 Hutchison was confirmed as the President, with Dr Don Paskos as the Vice-President. Dr Graham Hartill became the Secretary-Treasurer, with John Bahen, John Casson and Geoff Strang assuming committee positions. They had been elected from among 41 men who were the inaugural members. The 'Vets' had begun as a group of leading business and professional men. The 'Who's Who' list read as follows (*The First Decade*, n.d., 5):

> Harry Jacoby, Ross Hutchison, Geoffrey Hammond, Eric Daley, Graham Hartill, John Casson, Ron Hunt, Wallace Scarff, Eric Eastman, Morris Beard, John Bahen, William Gray, Lionel Sangster, Alick Bridge, Max McDermott, George Larkin, Geoffrey Strang, John Leonard, Alan Barblett, Keith Holten, Brian Bermingham, Clive Wilderspin, Lindsay Cox, Andy Millen, Lang Hancock, Valston Hancock, Russell Seymour, Howard Lange, Ivor Gordon, Bill Harrigan, Max Bonner, Harold Broadbent, Ross Graham, Bernie Bignell, Don Paskos, Imre Simkovic, Don Hutchison, Don Clayton, Ken Brooks, Ray Ellershaw and Alan Hicks.

The national Veterans' Constitution specified 45 years as the minimum age for entry to the 'Vets'. However, when the first tournament was conducted in September 1973 at the East Fremantle Club, the events were for male players aged over 40. There had been some controversy about the most appropriate entry age. Nevertheless, the scale of both the tournament and the club's membership listing began to rise. By 1976, there were 120 financial members. Matches were played against metropolitan clubs and two fixtures were organised against the state junior squad. Midweek matches were played against several schools. Significantly, too, the club donated funds to the Association to enable members of the Linton and Wilson Cup teams to compete in the Victorian, New South Wales and Australian junior championships. A small sum was also given to Mary Sawyer and Lawrence Hall to assist them with their overseas trips. These decisions indicated that the associate status adopted by the Veterans' Club as early as 1973 involved assisting junior tennis.

Ross Hutchinson, M.L.A. Veterans' President

Members began to visit eastern capitals for the Australian individual and team championships. In January 1976, the championships came to Perth. Past greats, such as Sedgman, Hartwig, Rose, Howe and Pails helped arouse interest. Local legend Clive Wilderspin had a memorable win over Sedgman but Hartwig was too strong for Wilderspin in the 45 years (and under) singles final. The latter event, together with the doubles, had attracted prize money for the first time in a national veterans' championship.

The profit recorded was $3,115. Major sponsors were the Oak Insurance Company and the Town and Country Building Society. The willingness of mining magnate, and keen tennis player, Lang Hancock to offer his private aircraft to bring a number of leading players form Melbourne was welcomed. The Veterans' Club comprised Western Australians with significant standing in society and so was well placed to facilitate the Association's entry to open tennis. Whether the Association itself would be able to win support from the benefactors congregating in the Veterans would be clearer in the future.

Life memberships

Between 1969 to 1976, three senior administrators, namely Norm Wasley, Eric Eastman and Morrie Beard were recognised with life membership. They had led the volunteer 'army' which assisted the small office at the WALTA to organise and facilitate the development of tennis on an increasingly sophisticated basis.

Wasley's life membership was endorsed by Council on 9 December, 1971 soon after he had resigned the Presidency. He had held that office for eight demanding years after being Vice-President for nine years. From 1949 he had been on the Executive as well as serving six years as President at Mount Lawley. Wasley possessed a special ability to relate to young players. He had served a long term on the junior development committee as well as 10 years on the State Selection Committee. From 1947 to 1951, he had managed the Linton Cup team, including the victorious 1949 combination. It will be recalled that Wasley was a member of the Linton Cup team in prewar years before he won the State Open singles title in 1939. Importantly, he was willing to listen to new ideas and was keen to ensure the Association kept pace with a changing environment.

On 9 October, 1975 the Council took the unusual step of simultaneously ratifying the life memberships for Morrie Beard and Eric Eastman. The latter had

Eric Eastman, OBE a dedicated sports administrator and life member

served on the Executive for over 20 years and as a delegate for a longer period of time. He was a Vice-President for over a decade and was President of Royal King's Park for a term in 1951/1952 and later from 1967 to 1969. However, when Eastman stood for the Presidency he was beaten by 28 votes to 19 at the annual general meeting on 25 September 1975 (*WALTA Minutes*, 25/9/1975). This result clearly hurt Eastman who indicated he did not desire to maintain a position on the Executive. He continued to contribute, however, with committee service including roles associated with finance, tournaments, The Rothmans Foundation, Shell coaching, country affairs and the LTAA.

Eastman was well known for his organisational role in many State Open Championships, where his membership at Royal King's Park was pivotal. Not only was he honoured with life membership in 1964, but when he died suddenly on 3 November, 1979 a plaque in appreciation of his 33 years of service was mounted at the entrance to the complex which housed the squash courts, offices, bar and dining room. For his services to sport' administration, Eastman also received the OBE. This award was gained on the basis of his service to hockey as well as tennis. This combination could be regarded as rare, but Eastman was renowned as a person of rare qualities who served both sports with dedication.

Morrie Beard had just completed four years as President of WALTA when he was honoured with life membership. He had joined the Claremont club in 1931 and by 1935 (when only 19) was a committeeman. A solid shield player, he left his main mark as an administrator. After war service, Beard eventually became President at Claremont and was subsequently elected a life member. One aspect of his work that won acclaim was his role in assisting with the organisation of major tournaments and international fixtures. As far back as 1953, he was prominent in mounting of the interzone final between Belgium and India. His contribution to the Federation Cup has already been mentioned. In 1975, Beard assumed the role of tournament director for the Hitachi West Coast Classic and, after stepping down from the Presidency, continued his association with the Classic.

Morrie Beard, Association President and life member

For many years, Beard was a Claremont delegate to the Council and in 1953 became a member of the WALTA Executive. Like other members of the Executive, he served on numerous sub-committees. When he did retire from the Presidency Beard drew attention to the tremendous changes that had taken place during his 25 years on the Executive. He said that 'though the game generally has amateur grass roots, tennis has moved in recent years from amateur to a definite professional outlook'. He thanked the professional association 'for the increasing part they now take in tennis administration ...' (*WALTA Minutes*, 25/9/1977).

The first seven years of open tennis had been neither feast nor famine for tennis. The Association had continued to grow and remained financially sound despite a difficult economic climate. It was apparent, however, that it would have to aggressively market its product if it was to hold or increase its share of the sponsorship dollars that were now such an important feature of professional sport.

Chapter Eighteen

WESTENNIS 1977-1984

As the WALTA moved towards what it recognised as its seventy-fifth anniversary, President Barry Sanders suggested that it should document its history (*WALTA Minutes*, 3/3/1977). One reminder of the place of tennis in the sporting culture was the publication in July 1974 of a standard seven cent postage stamp depicting a tennis player, in a non-Olympic sports series. Tennis had been played at the Olympic Games between 1896 and 1924. But the Olympic movement, like tennis, was losing its bid to retain its amateur code. In 1984, tennis became a demonstration Olympic sport, with reinstatement coming at the 1988 Olympics. News, too, that the Wimbledon tournament was to celebrate its centennial in 1977, with the opening of a tennis museum, had obviously helped prompt the tennis history initiative. In early 1978 the Executive chose Charlie Johnson, one of its members from the historic Fremantle club, to investigate the feasibility of such a project. Then Hensman Park's Gwyn Thomas, a new member of the Executive, was given the task of overseeing the proposed history in her role as the Chairwoman of the Publicity and Promotions Sub-Committee. It was soon apparent that other matters deserved a higher priority. The growth of the WALTA necessitated attention to its internal communications. One of the most significant developments was the introduction of *Westennis*, the Association's own news medium.

Westennis

The desirability of an Association newsletter or even a magazine had been frequently discussed. Sanders, aware that such an idea had been canvassed in the other States, was keen to have a regular publication distributed to all member clubs and even to newsagencies. *Tennis Magazine*, which has a national focus, had been published since early 1976, but its circulation in Western Australia was very low. Moreover, at the WALTA, other avenues of communication and publicity had to be considered as Gary Carvolth, the high-profile Field Officer, had resigned late in 1976.

In December 1976, the first issue of *Westennis*, subtitled 'Official Publication of the Western Australian Lawn Tennis Association (Inc.)' was published. Sanders indicated in a President's Message:

> *One of my ambitions on becoming your president was to see an Association newspaper launched and I now offer congratulations to David Punch and his Development Committee on achieving this objective. A major problem in modern society is proper communication and although clubs are fully represented on State Council, I often feel that too little information filters back to our 12000 members. I am hopeful that this publication will fill the gap and keep all tennis players informed of what is happening ....*

About 7,500 copies were distributed by hand to city clubs and by post to

The first issue of Westennis in December 1976

country area clubs. Alan East, a well-known sporting journalist, assisted editing the four-page publication, which had been partly funded by limited advertising. Harry Spilsbury provided an article on the forthcoming State Open and Sam Hodsdon, as Chairman of the State selection panel, listed the composition of the State teams. The Miss Tennis contest was highlighted and there was a feature article on Bruce Durston, the newly-appointed Tennis Development Officer. Other features included a call from Charlie Brown of the Umpires' Association for recruits. The keen rivalry in the shield match competition, including the introduction of a player of the year contest, was highlighted by Dene Rundle from the Shield Match Committee. Fred Dreyer, as Chairman of the Country Affairs Committee, mentioned the forthcoming (January 1977) Country Week carnival and described how country and city clubs had attended an inaugural Western Australian Tennis Administrators' seminar conducted in early October at the Yanchep holiday resort. Mary Sayers (Happ), of the Tennis Development Committee, also wrote about the seminar.

The publication filled a void as it enabled members of the tennis community, particularly those living in the country areas, to be informed of Association affairs rarely mentioned in the press. Within a year *Westennis* had expanded to eight pages and become a quarterly. However, attempts to improve advertising revenue were only moderately successful. As small losses were made on most issues, this led to regular debate as to whether *Westennis* should be retained. In the December 1978 issue, a questionnaire was published offering an incentive prize from Permanent Building Society, to encourage readers to respond about the value of the magazine.

No formal report was tabled at Council but eventually a decision was made to improve the quality of *Westennis* by making it more attractive to both readers and sponsors. The first issue in Volume 7 appeared in December 1982 with 32 pages of content on gloss paper. The front page, highlighted with a photograph of a youthful Pat Cash promoting the BP State Open, featured a yellow and gold band. These two colours were also used in some of the key advertisements promoting the sponsors WA Trustees, Kentucky Fried Chicken, and Tennis Courts (WA). Soon, in 1984, gold and green became official national colours but officially the WALTA retained its black and gold, as had been decided in 1913.

The future of *Westennis* seemed more secure. Streamlining of publishing techniques had led to better quality without radically increasing costs. In 1982 the State's economic performance temporarily faltered, but over the next few years sponsorship improved. A cover price was not set for *Westennis*, so it was necessary to fund the magazine from advertising revenue. More than 40 firms had responded to a call for *Westennis* advertising, handled by Russell Stanley, a member of a well-known tennis family. Content analysis of the 1982 issues of *Westennis* show that about 40 per cent of space was devoted to advertising. This does not alter the fact that there was a wealth of tennis news for Association members. One matter which was always given considerable space was the State Open. Any writer of a history of the Association would soon have become aware that it was a fixture with a longer history than the Association itself. Contemporary organisers of the event realised that every possible medium had to be utilised to publicise the Open. It was usually the only tournament that attracted players of national and international standing.

Mary Sawyer (Collins), a talented player who reached the State Open final in 1979. In the same year she was semi-finalist at the Australian Open.

State Opens and other majors

One of the results of securing high-profile players for the State Open was that Western Australians failed to win the historic event. Between 1977 and 1984 no Western Australian reached the men's singles final, although in the women's section the picture was different, particularly after 1984 when the women's event was downgraded.

In 1979, Mary Sawyer (Collins) was the women's singles runner-up when she lost to Jill Davis of Dallas, Texas. After an excellent tournament there was expectation that Sawyer would win the final. She was not one to make excuses, but it was known 'she had a sore throat and a stiff neck' when she went down in straight sets to the 18-year-old university physical education student (*West Australian*, 15/1/1979, 89). Collins had risen rapidly to prominence and represented a threat to Christine Dorey (Matison), the number one State woman in domestic competition. A highlight of Sawyer's career was her performance in reaching the semi-final of the 1979 Australian Open, which she lost to Sharon Walsh of the United States in a tough match 7/6, 6/4. A year earlier Matison had also reached the Australian Open semi-final, being beaten 7/5, 6/4 by Betsy Nagelsen in another close encounter.

Although Dorey was known for her 'never say die' qualities, a place in the 1981 final was denied her when Ann Minter, then one of Australia's leading juniors, staged a remarkable fightback in a semi-final. The unseeded Dorey was leading 7/6, 5/1 and 40-love when Minter decided to relax and hit out. The strategy was successful, as Minter (the number two seed) eventually won the final two sets, 7/5, 6/3 in a match that lasted for more than two hours on centre court at King's Park. Dorey had saved two set points in the first set, then Minter had denied her three match points in the second set. Later Minter claimed that the crowd had been so parochial in their support of Christine Dorey that it had inspired her to lift her game. She was quoted as saying that 'the crowd was so biased against me I decided I was not going to lose for them' (*West Australian*, 17/1/1981, 84). Ironically, the desire of the crowd to see a local in the final had probably worked against Dorey.

In the women's doubles, however, Dorey who had been Lesley Bowrey's winning partner in 1976, was the runner-up on several occasions. Twice she was partnered by circuit friend Pam Whytecross. In 1983 Elizabeth Sayers teamed with Dorey for another runner-up trophy against Whytecross and Lesley O'Neil (NSW), the 1978 Australian Open winner. In 1982, however, Sayers (Smylie) who was to win the Wimbledon title three years later, gained her only Western Australian Open Doubles title in partnership with Amanda Tobin.

In 1982, Sayers and Tobin had also fought out the singles final in unusual circumstances. Sayers (who had won the Queensland Open in 1980) became the first Western Australian-born player in 21 years to win the women's section, after staging a stirring comeback after light rain had interrupted play for 20 minutes. Sayers, who was trailing 5/2 at the break of play, went for a run in the picturesque King's Park and returned to the court a more adventurous player who produced scintillating winners from every corner of the court to

Elizabeth Sayers (Smylie), stirring fightback to win the 1982 WA Open

shatter Tobin, the number one seed and titleholder. Reeling off eight games straight, and 11 of the last 14 after the rain, Elizabeth Sayers won 7/5, 6/3 to receive a cheque for $1,500 from the Town and Country Permanent Building Society (*West Australian*, 18/1/1982, 89).

Although Amanda Tobin lost the singles final in 1982, her overall record in the Western Australian Open was meritorious. She won the title in 1978 and 1983 and, as Amanda Dingwell, in 1984. Tobin, who was nationally ranked, but below the top 10 international level, depicted the best of the women's draw. Wendy Turnbull had been the victor in 1977, by defeating the promising Czechoslovakian star Renata Tomanova. Turnbull did rise to four in the world but in 1977 she was only seven in the Australian rankings. Twelve months earlier Turnbull had made a deliberate decision to shake off the image of being purely a doubles player. So the Perth win, when coupled with wins in the Japanese and Austrian Opens, helped to enhance her reputation as a singles player (*West Australian*, 20/12/1976, 59).

The type of player able to win the men's section of the Open in these years was also nationally ranked but not a leading international. So the title winners were Ray Ruffels (1977), John Marks (1978), Mark Edmondson (1979), Colin Dibley (1980), John Fitzgerald (1981), Eddie Edwards (1982), Wally Masur (1983) and Brian Levine (1984). There were some highlights for resident Western Australians, but they were mainly confined to giving a fine performance against a leading player. For instance, in 1977 Rob Casey took a set off Bob Carmichael, the veteran Victorian. In the 1982 event, in which only five Western Australians were able to make the 64 draw, Casey reached the third round in good style before losing a close match to Brad Drewett, 4/6, 6/7. In the following year, Roger Grant and Brad Properjohn were competitive against respective seeded players Wayne Hampson and Syd Ball (*Western Australian*, 5/1/1983, 92).

Amanda Tobin (Dingwell), Four WA Open wins

In a review of the 1979 championship, State squad coach Rob Kilderry had injected a note of optimism with a claim that 'the gap between the eastern states and WA is being narrowed rapidly because of the more positive approach to tennis being adopted in this state'. Kilderry predicted that 'within five years ... this approach [particularly more scientific training methods] will see WA producing a big share of the national champions' (*Sunday Times*, 7/1/1979, 99).

In Kilderry's judgment, Casey and Gary Penberthy were capable 'of pushing the top Australian players'. Another reason for his optimism had been the performances in junior tournaments of Chris Johnstone and Lawrence Hall. The latter had achieved a victory over leading United States player Tim Wilkinson. By 1981, it appeared that Kilderry might have been right as both Johnstone and Hall had an outstanding day early in the championship. Hall, as an unseeded 21-year-old, upset the seventh seeded American Rick Fisher, 6/3, 6/4, while Johnstone (20) displayed good form in beating the highly-regarded Peter Doohan on the centre court 6/3, 6/3. Almost unnoticed on the same day was an observation in the *West Australian* (15/1/1981, 92) that Patrick Cash, who battled for three hours before losing to Colin Dibley, was 'regarded in some circles as the No 1 player in the world in the 16 and under age group'.

It must be said that most of the occasions on which Chris Johnstone hit the headlines for subsequent Western Australian Opens resulted from surprise early exits from the tournament. In 1982, he lost to Victorian junior Tony

Withers and a year later was fined $50 for hitting a ball into the northern-stand at Royal King's Park in the course of losing a close three-setter to John Benson, his doubles partner. Although there was the consolation of later winning the doubles title against Peter Doohan and Michael Fancutt with a third set-tie break, Johnstone was critical of both the umpiring and the manner in which the tournament was not being run in full compliance with Men's International Professional Tennis Council conditions (*West Australian*, 5/1/1983, 92). It soon became clear that the WALTA had only received a copy of some rule changes as late as 29 December, to be effective from 1 January 1983. Given that the controversy had arisen, Harry Spilsbury, who had become President in 1982, was forced to make these facts known. Ron Keenan, President of the Umpires Association, was reported as saying 'the players should be more understanding of the dilemma ... caused by the late arrival of the rules' (*West Australian*, 6/1/1983, 75).

Lawrence Hall, helped to temporarily lower the gap between the Eastern States and Western Australia

The prize money for the 1983 WA Open rose to $40,000. With national inflation running high in those years, it is not possible to accurately convey the real value of the prize money but in unadjusted terms it had risen from $17,000 in 1977. A major supporter was BP Australia, which had begun sponsorship of tennis in Western Australia for the Federation Cup in 1970 and had continued since then. By 1983, the Town and Country Building Society and Swan Television Channel (STW 9) had also been important contributing sponsors for five years. A related exercise had been the need for WALTA officials to negotiate television time for the event. The increase in prize money enabled the men's section of the Open to be allocated Association of Tennis Professionals (ATP) points. This had first taken place for the 1980 Open. Organisers had been seeking to achieve this status to enhance the prospect of attracting leading players.

Having been granted ATP status it was imperative that the Association fit the Open into the national tournament schedule and this resulted in an early January time slot. Actually this date had been adopted in 1978, as it enabled top junior events to be included in the schedule. Top juniors already on the international circuit were able to fight out the junior events and then 'shake up' the seniors. Yet, while ATP points lifted the quality of the draw and raised more spectator interest, the scale of international tennis was becoming so vast that the public was beginning to 'lose track' of the tennis calendar. The consequence was that Grand Slams, particularly Wimbledon, were deemed to be even more significant in the tennis tour. The corollary was that the WALTA often found it difficult to promote the Western Australian Open for it was just another of the numerous circuit tournaments.

One problem which sometimes arose, which was not unexpected by the locals, was the hot weather. This not only discomforted the visitors but also the juniors who participated in the annual junior coaching clinic, a feature of the Open and well attended by many budding players. However, in 1978 with the switch to January, the free two-hour coaching session run by Arthur Marshall and supported by visiting Australian players, had to cater for 700 children in heat-wave conditions. On quarter-final day senior players Bob Carmichael and Mal Anderson fought out a close singles encounter while the temperature rose to a record 44.7 C. The cost of victory for the 37-year-old Carmichael may have been too high, as he then lost a four-hour final to the 25-year old John Marks, 6/2, 6/7, 4/6, 6/4, followed by a remarkable 14/12 concluding set (*West Australian*, 16/1/1978, 72).

The West Coast Classic, the Women's Classic and Davis Cup ties

An important reason to lift the status of the WA Open arose from uncertainty about the future of the West Coast Classic. It was a matter of 'third time unlucky' when the event was conducted at the Perth Entertainment Centre in late October 1977. The Classic was part of an Asian tennis circuit, the tournaments being played in Brisbane, Sydney and Perth constituting the Australian leg. Despite the Herculean efforts of Morrie Beard, the Classic did not remain in the tennis calendar. Although it was the LTAA's responsibility to find a major sponsor, both the LTAA and WALTA worked on the problem without success after Hitachi desired not to continue as major backer. *Westennis* (October 1978, 1) reported that the 'Classic was a victim of player greed and the weakening of the Men's International Professional Council, who allowed a big prize-money event to be played in Japan at the same time; against all the principles of the Asian circuit'.

The 1977 Hitachi West Coast Classic had been won by Vitas Gerulaitis from Geoff Masters. Another star, Jimmy Connors, was also in the draw, but was forced to default in an earlier round because of injury. Allan Stone and 1977 singles winner Ray Ruffels secured the doubles title, with the WALTA sharing some $9,000 dollars profit from the venture.

Four years elapsed before an LTAA-WALTA partnership resulted in the staging in mid-November 1981 of the National Panasonic Women's Classic. In 1980, National Panasonic had been associated with the LTAA in sponsoring its first Women's Classic in Adelaide. The inaugural champion was Hana Mandlikova in the singles, with Betty Stove and Pam Shriver taking out the doubles. With the world's superstars due to appear in the Perth event, there was a reminder from Premier, Sir Charles Court, that the $125,000 prize money was the highest offered for a tennis tournament, and, outside horse racing, the second highest ever recorded for a sporting fixture in Western Australia. Sir Charles remarked that the event put 'women's tennis firmly in the spotlight in a city which has long been on the international men's circuit ... in fact [this is] the first international 'women only' individual championship staged in Western Australia' (*National Panasonic Women's Classic Programme*, 1981, 5).

But despite the rumoured desire of the players that the event again be conducted at Royal King's Park, the rich tournament was never again allocated to the West. It had been widely regarded as a success, even though local fans had been disappointed to witness the defeat of one of the star attractions, the 1980 Wimbledon champion, Evonne Goolagong, by American Jane Preyer, with a comparatively easy 6/3, 6/3 scoreline. The crowd did receive some joy on at least two counts. Firstly, Elizabeth Sayers (Smylie) won the junior 18 and under final from Ann Minter in a close 7/5, 6/2 match and secondly, the evergreen Christine Dorey, despite an absence from the circuit for nearly four years, played superbly to reach the third round after being given entry to the tournament with a 'wild card'. She then faced the daunting task of playing Andrea Jaeger, the 16-year-old number one seed who was ranked four in the world. Not surprisingly, Dorey lost 6/1, 6/2 although Jaeger did not go on to take the winner's cheque.

After losing the final to Pam Shriver with a score of 1/6, 6/7, Jaeger complained that being called 'superbrat' had contributed to her defeat. At a press conference Jaeger said: 'I don't see how you guys can expect me to play when you rip me apart in the paper.' Shriver, too, thought it was 'going too far' to compare Andrea Jaeger with 'superbrat' John McEnroe (*West Australian*, 23/11/ 1981, 88).

The loss of the National Panasonic Classic was partly compensated by the decision of the LTAA Council in June 1982 to award a Davis Cup tie to Perth. WALTA officials were only given three months in which to organise the event. Not only did it promise an all-too-rare opportunity to promote tennis through a major event of international stature, but it was the first time Perth had been the venue for a Davis Cup fixture with Australia as a participating nation. On five previous occasions Perth had hosted Davis Cup ties, but this encounter was to be a semi-final between Australia and its traditional rivals the United States.

President Barry Sanders was named as chairman of the organising committee, with a mandate to go into 'overdrive' to ensure a well-planned exercise. Harry Spilsbury took responsibility for the documentation and contracts, while Morrie Beard headed the Grounds Committee. As the Entertainment Centre was the venue, nearly a decade before the high-profile Perth Wildcats basketball team made it their home, it was necessary to construct scoreboards, court-side boxes, camera platforms, a masseurs' room, players' dressing rooms and sponsors signs.

There were some anxious moments before the French 'green set' courts for the Entertainment Centre were completed. In addition, two practice courts at Cherokee Village, some 20 kilometres north of the city, were also constructed under the supervision of Monsieur Tay, an expert from Paris, to ensure a perfect bounce. Later, after the tie had been decided, the Americans questioned the wisdom of Australia selecting this surface. Described as the 'great green set gamble' it is significant the surface fell out of favour for future Australian Davis Cup ties.

Responsibility for the 'courtesy' aspects of the tie was given to David Punch, who coordinated the accommodation, VIP rooms, transport, entertainment, amenities for sponsors, a cocktail party, an official function for the Davis Cup draw, and a Davis Cup dinner. Dot Connolly, liaised with the Entertainment Centre on ticket sales: season tickets to affiliated clubs and passes for organising committees, ballboys, linesmen, workers, box-holders, the media, sponsors and team members all had to be organised.

The marketing and publicity committee was chaired by Dene Rundle. All 36 courtside boxes were sold in record time, media releases were written and advertisements secured. It was reported that a significant media attendance was afforded to Davis Cup captain Neale Fraser's Australian team announcement. This resulted in 2,000 tickets being sold in a week. However, interest appeared to flag until the arrival of the players, which coincided with the end of the league football season. An attendance of nearly 16,000 over the three nights was achieved, although it was considered that a singles win on the first night to Australia would have pushed the number of spectators over 20,000, a figure that would have satisfied Dene Rundle. The latter's role also encompassed visiting the airport to chauffer John McEnroe, the volatile American. It was an experience that Rundle was not to forget, as McEnroe's 'rudeness' was apparently deplorable (interview with Dene Rundle, 23/3/1986). In reference to McEnroe's court behaviour a sports historian (Whimpress, 1992, 7) recently wrote, 'one of the unasked questions in world tennis is why umpires and linesmen have not taken defamation actions against John McEnroe when they have been publicly humiliated'.

Paul McNamee (top) and Peter McNamara (above), the Wimbledon doubles champions of 1980 and 1982, playing doubles for Australia in the Davis Cup at the Perth Entertainment Centre in 1982

Finance, with the gate ironically boosted by McEnroe's presence, was handled by Fred Dreyer, with Alan Hicks as match chairman controlling playing times, umpires, referees, linespersons, ballboys and ballgirls, uniforms and the 70 dozen tennis balls. With so much correspondence the secretarial role was filled by Leonie Bell, who had previously been a senior employee at the WALTA office.

The tie was described as a 'great success on every score,' except that the United States defeated Australia by 5 rubbers to nil. On the first night McEnroe (one of the few leading players still using a wooden racket) overcame an inspired Peter McNamara to win 6/4, 4/6, 6/2, 6/4, while 'double handed' Gene Mayer, in his Davis Cup debut, won in four sets 6/4, 3/6, 6/4, 6/2 against John Alexander. When McEnroe and Peter Fleming avenged their Wimbledon doubles loss to McNamara and Paul McNamee with another four-set win 6/2, 6/2, 3/6, 6/4, the tie had been decisively decided. In the return 'dead rubbers' McEnroe beat a plucky Alexander 6/4, 6/4 while Mayer had a straight set win 6/3, 6/3 over Mark Edmondson, who had replaced the injured McNamara.

The healthy financial return, coupled with the splendid organisation, enhanced the prospect of future Davis Cup ties being granted by the LTAA. However, as Sanders later warned in *Westennis* (December, 1982, 9) 'local tennis fans must remember, however, that even if our organisation is as good as any, a number of other cities could produce similar financial results and therefore maximum local support is essential if we are to have our share of top events'.

The uncertainties of sport were exemplified late in 1983 when Australia recorded a surprising, but meritorious Davis Cup victory against Sweden in Melbourne. Within two months, in late February, Australia's Melbourne heroes Pat Cash, John Fitzgerald, Paul McNamee and Mark Edmondson were in Perth to clash with Yugoslavia in the first round of the 1984 Davis Cup competition. This was the first Davis Cup match at Royal King's Park for seven years, although it had come only 16 months after the Australia versus the United States semi-final at the Entertainment Centre.

The Yugoslav team came in late February 1984 to the sweltering Perth summer, and grass courts from the cold and clay courts of central Europe. The odds were against the visitors, although they performed better than the five rubbers to nil outcome would suggest. On the first day, the crowd enjoyed seven hours of tense tennis played in oppressive conditions. McNamee eventually defeated Slobodan Zivjinovic 9/7, 4/6, 9/7, 10/8 while Fitzgerald also took four sets 2/6, 7/5, 6/1, 6/2 to win his singles rubber. The conditions on doubles day were exceptionally humid, but McNamee and Edmondson were easy winners 6/4, 6/1, 6/4, over Zivjinovic and Merko Ostaja.

The third day provided more pleasant weather conditions and despite the tie having been decided, another excellent crowd witnessed the play. There was some criticism of the Yugoslav captain for playing 'second string' members of the team in the 'dead rubbers'. This resulted in Fitzgerald easily defeating 16-year-old Bruno Oresar 6/3, 6/4, while McNamee had more difficulty in his 6/4, 10/8 win (in 2 hours 20 minutes) over Branko Horvat. Although the Davis Cup competition did not have the following it commanded in the halcyon days of Hoad and Rosewall in the 1950s a keen interest remained. And, the earlier, gripping victory against Sweden had helped to generate support. This was exemplified by the Cup's capacity to

Gordon Smith (left) receives a gift from Ken Harris (right) Both Smith and Harris worked hard for country tennis. Harris achieved a fine record as a player

draw spectators from outside the tennis community. Moreover, the business community maintained sponsorship: in this tie, the international sponsors NEC, Coca-Cola and Lacoste combined with local companies including Dunlop-Slazenger and Peters WA Ltd.

A special event which preceded the Yugoslav fixture was a visit to Geraldton, 450 kilometres north of Perth, by the Australian Davis Cup team for a series of exhibition matches. The Geraldton club provided first-class grass courts for the matches, which created keen local interest. Although the town was scoured for suitable seating it proved insufficient for some 700 spectators who attended. The reigning Davis Cup holders Cash, Edmondson, McNamee and Fitzgerald, together with captain Neale Fraser, were in keen demand. The Zone President, former Country Week champion Ken Harris, had realised this marketing advantage and played a key role in deciding to have the exhibition held on 18 February, 1984. Community spirit was mobilised and the costs underwritten. Local television station, with Arthur Marshall as commentator, provided nearly three hours of coverage. Lang Hancock flew both the Australian team and the WALTA President Spilsbury, to and from Geraldton in his private jet. This gesture considerably helped Geraldton's financing of the event. Given that the Sunseeker Hotel looked after the players and several sponsors also contributed, the venture was judged to be an outstanding success.

For the tie against Yugoslavia, the LTAA permitted arrangements for the coveted Davis Cup trophy to be on display in Perth. At a special function at the Royal Perth Yacht Club, history was made when the famed America's Cup was exhibited with the Davis Cup. It was a reminder of two of the most notable Australian sporting achievements for 1983. In yachting, the Western Australian business tycoon Alan Bond had triumphed, but in tennis, no Western Australian was a Davis Cup team member in 1983 and in fact no 'Sandgroper' had ever represented Australia in Davis Cup play. The program for the previous Australia-United States match had carried a two-page insert titled 'Why no WA Representatives?'

The resume, containing photographs of four of Western Australia's best male players Rice Gemmell, Clive Wilderspin, Gary Penberthy and Rob Casey stated in part:

> *Based on population, Western Australia has enjoyed more than it's [sic] share of sporting success in the heady atmosphere of national competition. Some of the major sports in which Western Australians have distinguished themselves are cricket, hockey, football, lacrosse, athletics, bowls, rifle shooting and swimming .... Why then has no Western Australian ever been able to gain selection in an Australian Davis Cup team?*

There were references to a range of interrelated factors, such as the lack of finance, restricted competition arising from isolation from the eastern States, and wide use of grass court surfaces. The 'tyranny of distance', which contributes to anti-centralist sentiments, can be employed in team sports to beat the best from the east but in tennis the isolation factor limits opportunities for competition. In the article it was also contended that some players tended to develop a feeling of 'self satisfaction' after winning local titles. Significantly, the period between 1977 and 1984 did witness several attempts to overcome the barrier of distance before the launching on 1 January, 1985 of the McDonald's Tennis Australia Junior Program.

Karen Vahala, represented Australia as a junior in September 1983 at the Sports Goofy (Walt Disney) competition in the United States of America

The junior scene

Associated with the Davis Cup was the 'Little Davis Cupper' concept. In conjunction with the United States versus Australia tie at the Entertainment Centre, seven 12-year-old boys from each State and the Australian Capital Territory had been selected to play tennis and absorb the atmosphere of the clash. Jason Lindeman, registered with the City Beach club, who had posted a number of outstanding performances in the 12 and under year group represented Western Australia. Two participants in that program notably Todd Woodbridge from New South Wales and Richard Fromberg from Tasmania, later gained Davis Cup selection. As Lindeman did not achieve that standing, it could be asserted it was another case of a young Western Australian player 'not making the grade'. In this instance, however, Lindeman soon moved to Victoria and hence should not be included on the Western Australian register. Other promising players named as Little Davis Cuppers included Scott Marshall, Jamie Hevron, Ian Berry, Evan Arnold, Damien Messer and Grant Frick. Although they did not become senior Davis Cuppers, they later played a role in the development of local tennis, particularly in the area of coaching. For instance Grant Frick combined with his brothers, Paul and Wayne, to establish the 'Frick Brothers Tennis School'.

The Little Davis Cupper scheme was part of the LTAA Junior Development Program which in early 1980 saw the introduction of the innovative 'Operation Springboard' sponsored by the S.C. Johnson company (labelled Johnson and Wax in the tennis literature). Initially this involved forming squads in each State comprising the top four boys and girls from the 12 and under group. A tournament was to be conducted to provide the basis for selection. It included an intensive training program for three hours weekly throughout most of the year. Two boys and two girls from each of these squads attended a national training camp in May 1980. Later in the same year a team was selected to compete in some major tournaments in the United States.

In Western Australia it was resolved that the Johnson and Wax squad should come under the overall responsibility of the Junior Development Committee, although it would be necessary for the State Selection Committee to monitor the performances of the players and the coach (*WALTA Minutes*, 2/4/1980). The latter post was filled by experienced professional Bruce Robinson. The girls chosen for the inaugural squad were Louise Finucane, Julia Ledder, Melinda Mead, and Rochelle Varney while the four boys were Tim Burrows, Jason Robinson, Carl Turich, and Mark Whitton. In May Julia Ledder, Mindy Mead, Jason Robinson and Carl Turich were nominated to attend a National Training Camp in Brisbane. However, no Western Australian was able to gain selection for the following tour of the United States of America.

The first Johnson and Wax squad member to be chosen to represent Australia for the world under-12 championship was Karen Vahala from the Alexander Park club. After defeating each number one girl from each State in her age group (with the exception of Bylinda Potter from New South Wales) she travelled in September 1983 to the Sport Goofy (Walt Disney) competition in the United States. Vahala appeared to be an outstanding prospect as her Australian selection had come at the conclusion of her second year in the Johnson and Wax squad. A bio-mechanics testing program, devised under the guidance of Dr Bruce Elliott at the Department of Human Movement at the University of Western Australia, was implemented to support this initiative. Funding had been granted by the Western Australian Institute of Sport (WAIS) which since its foundation in 1980, had sought to determine how it could produce a champion Western Australian tennis player. The Institute's Executive Director, well-known sporting identity Wally Foreman, had been a promising tennis player at the Reabold club in his junior days.

The Johnson and Wax program was scaled down before the sponsorship was finally withdrawn. One feature was the inclusion of top country juniors in the squads and it was regarded as being of sufficient quality to entice Rodney Lewis of Kalgoorlie to participate in 1981, while in 1982 Ashley Johns (Kalgoorlie) and Tracey Drake-Brockman (Lowden) participated. Only time would tell whether the Johnson and Wax aim of providing a 'springboard' for new stars had been fulfilled. In the meantime, a range of other programs were being given various forms of sponsorship. To the old-timers it appeared the juniors were receiving a wealth of assistance. However, the junior environment at the State, national and even international levels, was becoming more competitive. Problems, too, were emerging in the form of injuries, 'burnout', 'ugly parents' and unacceptable court etiquette.

One form of incentive, for both juniors and seniors, prevalent from the mid-Seventies was the various points competitions that led to awards in the form of trophies, money and 'trips' to participate in selected tournaments. In early 1976, the Commercial Bank of Australia (CBA) announced that they would provide $50,000 sponsorship for a series of National Under-Age Tournaments culminating with the playing of a National Under-age Championship in Melbourne in January 1977. In each age group for both boys and girls from under-13 to under-17, points were allocated according to the tournament category. Later, the under-18 age group was added, as an incentive to keep the older juniors in the game.

At the first CBA Junior Championship, Elizabeth Sayers displayed her promise with a magnificent 7/5, 6/4 victory over Jackie Pinto from Victoria in the under-14 age category. Sayers was then selected to tour the United States with the Australian Bonne Belle Cup team. This brought immediate recognition for Elizabeth in the form of the Radio 6IX Junior Sportsman monthly award (*WALTA Minutes* 10/3/1977). Subsequently, though, it was often unclear whether it was better for Sayers, and other leading juniors, to remain playing in their age group at home, often with weaker competition, in order to seek the national title.

In early 1977, CBA announced it would increase its bank's sponsorship for three years. The sponsorship formula was based on setting aside monies for the travel component and allocating each tournament a specific sum. In 1979, for instance, CBA gave $750 for the North and South of the River 'C' category tournaments: $1,100 for each 'B' category, which included the State Open Under Age, the State Closed and the Spring; and $1,200 for the 'A' category State Schoolgirls and Schoolboys Championship. It was a moot point as to whether the juniors carefully studied the point allocations although the winners (and sometimes the points) were regularly given space in *Westennis*. In the March 1978 issue, information was given to readers about the Western Australian representatives at the CBA age event at White City. The players were:

Boys		**Girls**	
Under/18	Chris Johnstone	Under/18	Denise Cole
Under/17	Terry Vinci	Under/17	Robyn Wood
Under/16	Brad Properjohn	Under/16	Julie Tolcon
Under/15	David Turner	Under/15	Elizabeth Sayers
Under/14	Michael Thorpe	Under/14	Louise Lavtas
Under/13	Jamie Hevron	Under/13	Alison Rushforth

Brad Properjohn (right), a junior CBA points winner who later won the Western Australian Open Championship

On this occasion, Sayers was inadvertently entered in the wrong age group but still reached the final of the under-16 feed-in event. In the boys' section David Turner reached the under-15 final. Generally, though, the Western Australians found the conditions difficult, as constant heavy rain in Sydney meant that the early rounds were transferred to the clay courts at Rockdale. Expertly managed by Mrs Mary Hicks, an ex-Wilson Cup player, the contingent was considered to have benefited from the opportunity to travel and compete against some of the best juniors in Australia.

Given that the CBA trips were available for four seasons, several juniors were fortunate to win their age groups on two or more occasions and gain considerable interstate experience. David Turner, already mentioned for his 1978 performance, also made the semi-final the following year and attended each national final in January at Beaumaris (1977), White City (1978), Milton (1979) and White City (1980). Michael Thorpe was another who played at each venue and then became a professional coach, a career also pursued by brother John Thorpe. Unfortunately, Michael Thorpe was tragically killed in a motor vehicle accident in May 1990. On the other hand, Turner was lost to the game when he opted not to continue at the senior level.

A recipient of three trips was Brad Properjohn. He remained in tennis, became a professional and played in Germany for several seasons. In 1988 he won the State Open singles title. As previously mentioned the State Open proved a nemesis for Chris Johnstone, but he had two CBA national final rounds in his junior days. Other junior boys with two tours were Jamie Hevron (a Little Davis Cupper in 1977) and Terry Vinci.

In the girls section, top performer Elizabeth Sayers played in the first three national events, winning the feed-in on her last occasion. Robyn Wood and Louise Lavtas also showed great promise, to gain the points to accompany Sayers on each occasion. From a tennis perspective it was disappointing that Wood and Lavtas chose not to continue at the competitive level in the sport. Joanne Greig was another who twice toured on the CBA points system. She had immense potential, but did not remain long enough in senior tennis to fulfil this promise. Sisters Sue Johnson (Clark) and Joanne Johnson (Wade) from Fremantle also won two trips, being together in 1980. Both represented the State in several junior teams and stayed in tennis. Some of Sue's best moments in the game were still to come while Joanne went on to train as a physical educationist and become a State selector.

When the CBA sponsorship concluded another incentive points competition was inaugurated for junior tennis. This competition embraced seven major junior tournaments during 1980 and 1981. Known a 'The Player of the Year', it was given 'substantial sponsorship' by Kentucky Fried Chicken. The sponsors financially assisted the tournaments, however for the players, trips were initially replaced with trophies (including some monetary prizes). Points were allocated according to the status of the tournament, with an award in each age group from the 12 and under to the 18 and under age groups. The overall top points winner in the boys and girls sections won the Player of the Year prize. A special incentive or improvement prize was also designated for one girl and one boy. In 1984, the Colonel, the trade name for Kentucky Fried Chicken, introduced a Grand Slam competition for the 11, 13 and 15 years age groups. A Grand Slam of major tournaments (State Open Age, North/South of the River and Schoolchildren's) was to be rewarded with a fully-paid trip to the eastern States for tournament experience.

Denise Cole, a junior CBA points winner who later (as Denise Stevlin) won the State Open Doubles Championship
She is pictured here with Judy Lange (Kozak) receiving the Slazenger Cup from WALTA official Barry Sanders

At each tournament venue, the Kentucky Points were posted at a vantage point. Again *Westennis* (December 1982, 21) printed current totals and occasional news of the award functions which were conducted with a generous spread of Kentucky Fried Chicken products. A highlight of the ceremony for the Colonel's 1982 Junior Player of the Year awards (named after the company's founder) was a message from Evonne Goolagong Cawley, who was able to congratulate the winners:

Girls 1982 Colonel's Player of the Year - Paula Parentich.
Boys 1982 Colonel's Player of the Year - Jason Robinson.
Girls 1982 Colonel's Most Improved Player - Jodie Bottrill
Boys 1982 Colonel's Most Improved Player - Lawrence Fiorentino.

Individual Age Group Winners-1982

Girls

18 and under-Jenny Byrne (80 points)
17 and under-Kerry Hurst (84 points)
16 and under-Kerry Hurst (108 points)
15 and under-Julia Ledder (100 points)
14 and under-Julia Ledder (140 points)
13 and under-Paula Parentich (180 points)
12 and under-Karen Vahala (172 points)

Boys

18 and under-Kurt Robinson (80 points)
17 and under-Ian Berry (108 points)
16 and under-Jamie Hevron (168 points)
15 and under-Damien Messer (164 points)
14 and under-Jason Robinson (172 points)
13 and under-Dean Danzi (136 points)
12 and under-Jason Lindeman (156 points)

Just as the Grand Slam in international tennis is elusive, it proved likewise in the Colonel's junior tournaments. In 1984, only Paula Parentich and Carl Turich won the Grand Slam. The following year Pablo Campillos, a member of the Sproule Stevens team in 1984, and later a 1986 Reid Cup team member, gained the Grand Slam against formidable opposition in a strong age group which included promising players Mark Lueba, Darren Patten and Damien Hampson. In 1985, the only other player to achieve a junior Grand Slam was Graeme Cox, who had begun to make considerable progress in his game. A few years later Cox won a tennis scholarship to the University of Utah, in Salt Lake City (*Westennis*, August 1991, 37)

Another junior initiative was sponsored by RAC Insurance Pty Ltd. It aimed to complement and expand the existing programs in two ways. Firstly, a country component incorporated a special coaching week in Perth during the January school holidays for 12 to 14-year-olds. The sponsorship provided funds to enable the country zones and the Pilbara to conduct a play-off competition for selection of players to take part in the squad.

The second component included the selection of the best available boy and girl in the 18, 16, 14, and 12 age groups to take part in the Australian junior circuits. Youngsters invited to the program included two from the Pilbara area. For instance, in 1982 those selected to take part were Ashley Johns and Karen Vahala (12s), Jason Robinson and Julia Ledder (14s), Jamie Hevron and Jenny Byrne (16s), and Scott Marshall and Elizabeth Sayers (18s). Each received air fares but the players had to meet other costs. What needs to be remembered is the continuity factor in the RAC sponsorship. It has proved to have a long lasting effect in improving the standard of tennis in Western Australia.

Another junior sponsorship characterised by its long life was the Shell Coaching Scheme. This did not have an interstate travel element, but was directed towards country players. During the season, a number of junior clinics in county towns formed the basis of the program culminating in a Shell junior coaching week in January. Given that Shell junior schemes had 'become a household name' in country areas, it was not surprising that, in 1981, Shell significantly increased its financial support to the Association. Yet how broadly based such schemes should be was a matter for some conjecture. Perceptive senior coach Rob Casey queried whether the resources were spread too widely to be of real benefit. On the other hand, the WALTA officials had cause for concern over reports that a very promising Aboriginal girl from North Merredin had not been identified for additional coaching (*WALTA Minutes* 5/3/1981). Tennis had been unable to attract significant numbers of Aboriginal children, so the question also remains whether the Shell, and other programs, catered adequately for them.

One scheme, of shorter duration, which provided opportunities for interstate junior competition, came under the umbrella of the National Panasonic 16 and under Pathfinders Program. Part of the assistance was provided to State associations to conduct three 16 and under tournaments, from which players could earn points to be used by the Australian selectors to select an overseas team funded by National Panasonic. Provision was also made for selected players to attend a national training camp under the guidance of leading Australian coaches. Jenny Byrne, who was showing considerable promise in local tennis, caught the national selectors' eye, to be invited to the 1982 camp in Canberra. Kurt Robinson, the son of the prominent professional coaches Bruce and Margaret Robinson, was also selected to attend and in the following year Byrne was again a member of the squad.

Given that Jenny Byrne was soon to emerge on the national scene the first reference to her in the tennis awards columns was very modest. In the 1978/1979 *WALTA Annual Report* it was noted that she had received of a $70 Hitachi scholarship in the under 13/14 age group. Although Hitachi withdrew its backing for the professional West Coast Classic, it directed its support to junior development and funded national training camps and State camps for selected players. At one stage there were expressions of concern from Hitachi representatives that its scholarship forms were not being widely distributed (*WALTA Minutes* 12/10/1978). Furthermore, at the WALTA Council a letter was tabled from the Mingenew club expressing concern at the lack of opportunity for country juniors to obtain such scholarships (*WALTA Minutes*, 5/4/1979).

The venue for the first national camp, in early 1978, was the Koala Park Tennis Resort on Phillip Island in Victoria. David Turner, Shane Johnstone, Robyn Lamb and Elizabeth Sayers were selected from Western Australia. In August, Turner and Lamb were again invited to attend. Then, in January 1979 Lamb was back at Phillip Island accompanied for her third camp by Scott Marshall and Michael Thorpe. A report on the latter camp by Scott

Marshall's father, Arthur, gave special credit to Lamb. With 16 boys and eight girls at the camp it was stated that, 'Robyn Lamb stood out as the leader in the girl's section and was by far the fittest girl - better than half the boys (*WALTA Minutes*, 5/4/1979). Clearly, Lamb had impressed the national selectors with her fitness and potential.

Previously, she had been given the opportunity of playing in the National Berri Cup Junior Championship in Adelaide. Dixie Marshall, Shane Johnstone and David Turner were also in the contingent. Turner recorded the best performance, reaching the singles semi-finals. In December 1978, Scott Marshall (Dixie's younger brother), Michael Thorpe, Judith Clarke and Jenny Howlett were nominated to represent the state in the second National Berri Championship. No Western Australian performance was outstanding.

Inclusion in the Berri Cup was determined from a round-robin of selected players. At times, there were examples of commitment far beyond normal expectations. For the 1979 round robin, the last to be conducted under the Berri sponsorship, it was recorded that an aspiring player Dianne McMahon had travelled 660 kilometres from Albany to compete. The players who won through were Peter Lebedevs, Ian Berry, Joanne Greig and Kerry Hurst, but at the first national level they too found it hard to make an impression. There are times in tennis, as in all sports, when players like McMahon need to be naive or unaware of the realistic prospects of success in order to prepare for future challenges. Joanne Greig, for instance, had immense potential, but she needed interstate experience to realise this promise.

Chris Johnstone, won selection in the 1979 Australian team (Courtesy The West Australian)

Other schemes were officially sanctioned, including a coaching camp at Narrabeen in New South Wales, sponsored by IBM, attended by Denise Cole, Erica Smith, Keith Begley and Roger Grant (*WALTA Annual Report*, 1976/1977). Grant was selected with Chris Johnstone in a special squad under the direction of the legendary Mal Anderson. This had been in recognition of the performances of Grant and Johnstone during the Australian 1977/1978 season. Johnstone was to gain the number two national ranking in the junior boys with Grant being listed at number nine. Both performed well in the Australian and New Zealand Junior Championships, Johnstone reaching the final in the Australian and then capturing the New Zealand title. His performances with Grant in the doubles were also worthy of commendation. Then a series of notable victories by Johnstone as he emerged from the junior ranks led to his selection in the official 1979 Australian team.

The LTAA successfully negotiated to have tennis included as a founding sport of the Australian Institute of Sport, located in Canberra. The Commonwealth Government had become increasingly involved in sports funding and policy after the previously cited report by Professor John Bloomfield (1973) had been prepared for the Whitlam government. The Australian Institute of Sport was launched by the Fraser government in 1980, with Bloomfield as the inaugural chairman. The first Western Australian to be chosen in the tennis program was Scott Marshall on what was designated as 'half scholarship'. Marshall had shown considerable promise winning the Victorian and South Australian 16-and under singles titles. Just how he, and others nominated for the Institute program, would develop under the coaching staff of Ray Ruffels, Helen Gourlay and Bob Carmichael was of keen interest to administrators. For the residents at the Institute school, classes operated in the mornings, with intensive practice, running and weight training in the afternoons. A tournament schedule, including overseas experience, was tailored for the squad.

Scott Marshall, participated in the AIS tennis program

The WALTA was also successful in its quest to include Western Australia in a secondary schools team competition, known as the Jack Pizzey Cup. This was inaugurated in 1963 by the then Minister for Education in Queensland, J.A.C. Pizzey. The competition was intended to include all States, but until 1978 the Cup was only conducted between New South Wales and Queensland. Thereafter, the competition was national in scope, with Western Australia first competing in Sydney in 1979.

In conjunction with the Pizzey Cup was a separate singles tournament for boys and girls. The inaugural championships, known as the Banfield Cup, were won by Peter Doohan (NSW) and Elizabeth Little (Victoria). From 1980, Colgate-Palmolive sponsored the singles, which then became known as the Colgate Cup. Many future leading players who had competed in either the Banfield Cup or Colgate Cup, without necessarily winning, had included Wendy Turnbull, Evonne Goolagong, John Alexander, Phil Dent, Mark Edmondson, Ross Case, Wally Masur, Liz Minter, Ann Minter and Laurie Warder.

A key concession which WALTA officials were able to extract was permission to include students from both private and government schools in the team. This simplified team selection, as it was left under the jurisdiction of the WALTA, which was also to meet the expenses incurred by the managers. The competition provided opportunities for interstate experience for the eight boys and eight girls in the full team. Each tie against other competing States and territories comprised six singles rubbers and three doubles rubbers. Points were allocated on the basis of singles and doubles victories, plus bonus allocations for winning either the boys or girls section.

Particularly before the growth of the Australian Institute of Sport and the conduct of several satellite tournaments (which tended to result in leading young players leaving school at an early age) the Pizzey and Colgate Cups attracted most of the top-calibre juniors in Australia. The Western Australian teams found it difficult to finish in the top three, particularly as some States included students from a sixth high school year, whereas the Western Australian norm was five years of secondary schooling. The first Pizzey Cup carnival attended by Western Australia in Sydney in August 1979 was managed by school teachers and former Champion of Champions winners Lyn Cooper and John Evans. The second team, managed by Rob Murton and Kerry Hickey, travelled to Canberra in April 1980. Neither side provided any outstanding performances, particularly in Canberra where the players were unaccustomed to the clay surface, but the managers judged the tournament structure to be beneficial as it provided a week of sustained and keen competition (*WALTA Minutes*, 10/7/80). This was a model which WALTA authorities were keen to endorse. Sending juniors to the east for the possibility of a first-round loss was a waste of resources. In the Colgate Cup, too, the old Wimbledon principle of avoiding first-round clashes with fellow nationals was followed, so a Western Australian could not draw a Western Australian in the first round.

Accompanying the report by Rob Murton and Kerry Hickey on the Canberra Pizzey Cup was a reference in the minutes to an Australian Schools' team to tour the United States 16 August to 15 September, 1980. It was indicated that Robyn Lamb, a member of the 1980 Pizzey Cup team, was listed as the second reserve to tour. But there was an addendum which said, 'at this stage it is unlikely that she will be asked to go on tour' (*WALTA Minutes*, 10/7/1980). As events transpired the talented Lamb was not in the final selected team.

A highlight of Western Australia's participation in the following Pizzey Cup carnival in Adelaide in December 1981, was the performance of Jenny Byrne, who won the Colgate Cup singles trophy in the girls section 6/2, 6/4 against Jo-Anne Brew from Victoria. Byrne was included in the All-Australian Schoolgirls Honour Team. At the end of each Pizzey Cup carnival, the team managers selected this team on the basis of performances during the competition. This was always a great incentive for the competitors, as inclusion in an Australian team, even if nominal, was an honour to cherish.

The conduct of the Pizzey Cup competition was rotated around the States and the Australian Capital Territory. In September 1983, it was Western Australia's turn to be the host. Unfortunately, the event was marred by adverse weather conditions for the first three days at the Sorrento club. As the club is only a few kilometres from the Indian Ocean, the interstate players, in particular, found it difficult to adjust to the wind. For another reason, too, the spring date was unsatisfactory as the students were preparing for tertiary entrance examinations. The outcome was a decision to transfer the event to a more suitable month, such as April or May. Thus, the next Pizzey Cup competition was held in Burnie, Tasmania during April 1984.

Even at home, under managers Peter Collier and Maureen Smith, Western Australia was only able to finish fifth after notching wins over the ACT and Tasmania. In the Colgate Cup, Jamie Hevron and Colin Napier did best by reaching the quarter-finals before they met each other, with the former going one further round. Generally, though, it was agreed that Western Australia had hosted the carnival in an efficient and friendly manner. Special credit was due to Norm Gratte as the Chairman of the organising committee. John Evans as referee, and match chairman Jack Eastcott were singled out for special praise, while Carmel Oud and Sue McMahon did a fine job of organising accommodation for 96 of the participants. Sue Mahon's daughter Alison was a team member, as was Joanne Johnson, daughter of the Chairman of the Publicity Committee, Charlie Johnson. The latter was keen to point out that Chris Limb from the Sorrento club had provided a vital link between the clubs and the Association.

By 1984, two more interstate competitions had been instituted in an attempt to strengthen the base of junior tennis in Australia. It will be recalled that, back in 1976, WALTA had been instrumental in the introduction of the Reid Cup. The Association also strongly supported the simultaneous introduction of the Sproule/Stevens competition for 14 and under boys and the Mary Hawton competition for girls in the same age category (*Westennis*, December 1982, 23). However, some reservations were expressed about the introduction of the Rod Laver and Margaret Court Cups for boys and girls in the 12 year age group. Particularly for young, primary-aged school children, the issues of 'burnout', injuries, bad behaviour and even 'ugly' parents were reasons for concern. Significantly, at this time *Westennis* (December 1983, 26) published the first of many articles providing 'Guidelines to Parents'. Parents, of course, had to meet many expenses. Some found the burden too much for their children to continue at this level of competition.

The inaugural 14 and under competition was conducted in Adelaide in January 1983. Both the boys and girls teams were thought to contain an emerging group of particularly promising players The Sproule/Stephens and Mary Hawton teams had four rather than the traditional three members. School teacher and student of the game, Geoff Mueller, managed the third-placed boys, David Culley, Anthony Cunningham, Dean Danzi and Carl

Kurt Robinson, continued the Robinson family tradition in tennis

Turich. The girls, Lisa Askey, Tracey Drake-Brockman, Julia Ledder and Paula Parentich, who finished fifth after losing several close encounters, were managed by Pam Hatt, an experienced professional.

Senior professionals Bruce and Margaret Robinson were also called upon to guide the12-and under boys and girls for the first Rod Laver and Margaret Court Cups in Sydney in January 1984. The boys Graeme Cox, Jason Evans and Alex Floyd, and girls Stephanie Martin, Jacqueline Quinn, and Natasha Vahala could only manage sixth place. Of course the rationale for eventually permitting participation in an interstate carnival for this age group was not necessarily based upon winning the trophies but providing opportunities for bona fide player development.

The focus on the Rod Laver and Margaret Court Cups had meant that Western Australia's fine performance in finishing third in the Linton Cup was easily overlooked. Managed by Rob Casey, the team members were Brad Williams, Kurt Robinson and Colin Napier. Each of the players went on to represent Western Australia in the senior Challenge Cup. Napier made the State hardcourt final at Esperance in 1984 but was beaten by Casey. Williams was in the news when he won the Tasmanian Open in 1985 after 'notching' up some very good wins on the satellite circuit against such players as Brett Custer and Peter Carter (*Westennis*, April 1985, 5). Unfortunately, Williams was lost to tennis when his talents were directed to other sports, so how good he could have been remains conjecture. On the other hand, Robinson remained a ranked player for many seasons, occasionally winning an important singles title and having his share of success in doubles. Furthermore, he remained in the family coaching business helping to keep the Robinson name, established by Margaret and Bruce, to the fore. Four other Robinson sons Mark, Paul, Chris and Ben were also prominent in tennis coaching.

Although the period from 1977 to 1984 saw an increase in the number of junior teams representing the state, there was only one occasion when Western Australia was able to win a carnival trophy. In January 1981, Elizabeth Sayers (captain), Robyn Lamb and Sue Johnson went through the Wilson Cup series undefeated to be outright winners. However, some matches were extremely close, but for the excellent fighting qualities of the team, it could have been another case of simply going close to winning the Cup, as in 1968, 1969 and 1980.

Against New South Wales, with one singles win each, the deciding doubles was crucial as Western Australia was down a set and 1/3 in the second before Sayers and Lamb managed to recover and win in three sets. Both Sayers and Lamb were splendid, aggressive doubles players. Manager Lyn Cooper was also an expert in this aspect of the game. So the team had confidence that if a tie came down to the doubles, Western Australia could win. Yet, in a very competitive competition, Sayers and Lamb surprisingly lost the doubles rubber against Queensland. At one stage, Sayers also trailed in her singles against Linda Cassell, but managed a close win in three sets. Lamb, playing her best tennis under pressure, won through in her rubber.

As the carnival neared completion, the tie between Western Australia and Victoria, the two undefeated teams, was played in atrocious conditions. Strong gusting winds, the odd rain squall and flying sand made play difficult for the players in such a vital contest. Sayers lost her only singles match in two years of Wilson Cup competition to Brenda Catton, after leading 5/3 in the third set. Momentarily it appeared that the Wilson Cup would not come west, but Lamb played a fine match to defeat Sharon Hodgkin, 6/4, 7/6. This was followed by a decisive Sayers and Lamb doubles win.

The weather had caused the match schedules to be severely disrupted so it was necessary for the teams to remain another day to achieve an outcome. Western Australia defeated South Australia with two singles wins to confirm the Cup win. This provided an opportunity for the third member of the team, Sue Johnson, to take part in the doubles. Johnson, who had performed well in the age competition events before the carnival, played a supportive role in the Wilson Cup victory.

Wilson Cup Winners 1981 Left to right: Susan Johnson, Rob Kilderry (Coach), Elizabeth Sayers and Robyn Lamb

Back in Perth, with time to reflect on the meritorious performance, a celebration function was held by WALTA. The contributions of Lyn Cooper as manager and Rob Kilderry as State coach were recognised as was the assistance given by Doug Napier, as manager of the accompanying Linton Cup team.

Although a celebration was fitting, it was timely to ask if the junior thrust was beginning to yield results or was the Wilson Cup victory an aberration? It was probably important to recognise that, despite the costs incurred, as a distant state Western Australia's participation in the various cups was proving beneficial. These competitions were accompanied by national championships which provided more chances for interstate play. The decision at this time by the LTAA to permit the rotation of the venues around the States for junior Cups and national championships was to assist the isolated Western Australia. In addition, the introduction of the feed-in concept, which the legend Clive Wilderspin had earlier persuaded State Council to introduce in junior tournaments (*WALTA Minutes*, 10/3/1977), had ensured additional matches for players who had early round loses.

Another factor contributing to success appeared to be the more specialised training being implemented in State squad and camp training. The latter had been regularly organised in various forms. For instance, in August 1979, 40 leading seniors and juniors attended a live-in camp at Guildford. Later, in 1983, junior squads were given a training session with Neale Fraser, the long-serving Davis Cup captain. Fraser, who later discovered he had family links with the goldfields region (*Kalgoorlie Miner*, 30/10/1993, 32), was reported to have stated (*Westennis*, October 1983, 3):

> *The WALTA appears to have the right development programmes and coaches with the ability to impart the knowledge. In general, the young players are not working hard enough - the ball is in their court.*

Following his visit to Perth, *Westennis* published an article 'Tennis Tips' by Neale Fraser. Surprisingly, he did not emphasise the need for hard work although local professional Maureen Smith later took up this theme as a guest columnist under the heading 'WA Kids Must Work Harder' (*Westennis*, 1984, 2, 29). The issue of *Westennis* in December 1983 included another 'Tennis Tips' column which was written by Ray Ruffels, who had also just concluded a visit to Perth to survey the junior scene in his capacity as national coach and head tennis coach at the Australian Institute of Sport. After meeting with the State selectors, administrators, State squad coaches, members of the Tennis Professionals Association, university and college academics and attending a player and parent forum, Ruffels said (*Westennis*, December 1983, 17) that:

> *WA had the coaches and the technical expertise to develop top players but it was essential for our youngsters to increase their access to tough competition.*

Bruce Elliott, highly competent player and State selector who made a scientific contribution to tennis

They should play in major Eastern States tournaments and Australian titles in their age groups to achieve greater confidence.

The visits to Perth by Fraser and Ruffels had been preceded by that of Alice Tym, an outstanding coach from the United States. Ranked as high as number 13 in the world in 1969, she had been voted as the 'US Coach of the Year' while serving as head coach at Yale University. The initiative for the visit could be credited to professional coach Pam Hatt, who had met Tym on trips to the United States in 1981 and 1982. Tym conducted a series of public lectures and coaching sessions provoking local juniors to think more constructively about their game (*Westennis*, March 1983, 3).

The preparation process for the state teams had been regularly altered, as new age groups were added to the WALTA interstate contingent. By 1984, three state squads, generally consisting of eight girls and eight boys, were selected to undergo training programs with the best available coaches. The squads were grouped in ages: 17 years and under (Rob Casey and Maureen Smith); 15 years and under (Peter Dyson and Christine Dorey); and 11 years and under (Bruce Robinson). To assist with the funding of these squads, the WALTA negotiated sponsorship with the Commonwealth Bank and Custom Credit Corporation.

Dr Bruce Elliott of the University of Western Australia, coordinated a physical training program for each squad, with specialist testing being conducted with the top 13 year-old players. Dr Elliott, a biomechanics expert and highly competent player in his own right, was by that time a State selector. In 1983, with Rob Kilderry, he published *The Art and Science of Tennis*. Later the Professional Coaches Association, noting the scientific contribution Elliott was making to their profession, recognised his work with special awards. Elliott also regularly published articles in *Westennis*. Sometimes his research colleagues were prominent tennis players such as Tony Marsh and Peter Overheu (*Westennis*, August 1990, 43). The latter, after many seasons as an 'A' grade player was to become a State selector.

The strong Carl Turich (left) is pictured with promising Johan Anderson

The Tennis Professionals' Association also began to provide interstate opportunities, gaining a Milo sponsorship from the Nestlé Company to fly to Melbourne the finalists in the boys' and girls' 16 and 14 year groups. In 1984, a 'Little Masters' tournament conducted by the professionals, resulted in Carl Turich, Jason Robinson, Paula Parentich and Natalie Crutchley (16s) and Pablo Campillos, Graeme Watson, Karen Bucens and Angela Jacka (14s) being able to test themselves against the best in the east. At that stage, the strongly built Turich looked a future champion. As early as 1981 the Australian selectors had indicated they were impressed with his prospects (*WALTA Minutes*, 10/6/1981). Later he was to win a scholarship to the Australian Institute of Sport. In 1987 Turich was selected (with Richard Fromberg in the team) for an Australian youth tour to Europe. Further tournament experience was gained in Canada and the United States. Although Turich won the Australian Junior Closed Doubles and played the satellites he eventually opted not to pursue a tennis career on the circuit (*Sunday Times*, 1/3/1987, 105).

Given that a semi-final win in the 'Little Masters' meant a ticket to the east, it not surprising that it was this rather than the final that was keenly fought. It was also an occasion on when the State selectors, responsible for the seedings, had their determinations brought under close scrutiny. State selectors always have an unenviable task whether their focus be seedings, annual ranking's, State team selection or even squad nomination. Apart from specific complaints to the Executive, there were some lengthy debates in Council about some of the selectors' decisions, or the rationales they employed (*WALTA Minutes*, 22/9/1977 and 13/10/1977). The selectors were made keenly aware that the junior scene was often contentious.

Three main reforms were introduced to allay criticisms. Firstly, to provide the selectors with more time to deliberate, it was decided to break tradition and no longer simultaneously announce the State teams at the trophy ceremony of the annual Spring tournament (*WALTA Minutes*, 9/10/1980). Secondly, it was decided to allocate each of the five selectors to specific age groups. This was thought to make the task more manageable, as attempts to cover each competition category in the mens and boys, womens and girls and mixed events was too formidable (*WALTA Minutes*, 4/3/1981). Thirdly, was to move towards the allocation of points on a basis similar to the international circuit ranking system. Of course the latter required accurate recording procedures and these were not always in place. In this respect confusion about age groupings exacerbated the problem, so the WALTA in 1980 adopted the International Tennis Federation eligibility date of 31 December for all age groupings (*WALTA Minutes*, 8/6/1980). The October 1984 issue of *Westennis* noted that the WALTA had installed a new microcomputer but its use appeared to be confined to pennant premiership tables, mailing lists and financial accounts rather than the tabulation of seedings points.

Geoff Strang, Claremont stalwart who was a State Selector for more than a decade

To reinforce the reforms it was decided to publish a 'Meet Your Selectors' article in the February 1983 issue of *Westennis*. Pen pictures of each committee member were included. By this time Geoff Strang had been a selector for many seasons, Clive Wilderspin since 1975, Doug Napier had already accumulated five years at the task, Kerryl Chute, Hensman Park legend and the only woman, had been on the committee two years, while Gary Penberthy had only joined in September of 1982. The tennis community, and especially the 'ugly parents', were certainly made aware that the seedings and selections were undertaken by a formidable group of knowledgeable tennis seniors. A later *Westennis* issue (April 1984, 30) explained how the selection process took place and what criteria were used.

One of the most demanding tasks for the selectors has always been seeding the Schoolchildren's Annual Tournament and over the years events (including younger age groups) have been added to the program. As the tournament is conducted by the Association, rather than being allocated to tendering clubs, the number of entries is regarded as a barometer of development. In fact while the Schoolchildren's Tournament continued to be important it could no longer be regarded as the premier under age junior titles event of the year as more tournaments had been added to the yearly shedule.

In 1977 there was an expression of disappointment that the number of entrants in the Schoolchildren's Tournament was down 371 to 253. This was attributed to the late distribution of entry forms; and by 1984 the number of entrants had risen to 490 although the ratio of boys to girls (333 to 157) caused some concern. It is not known if the disputed practice of limiting the number of events in which a competitor could enter was evaluated. In that year tournament tradition was broken with the transfer to the Trinity College synthetic surfaces in Manning, the Western Australian Institute of Technology (later Curtin University) and the Willetton Sports Club. The change had followed complaints and a players' petition in 1983 about the condition of the grass courts at the Perth City Council's Robertson Park and McCallum Park.

Kerryl Chute, Hensman Park legend who served as a State selector

Tradition, however, was retained with the Association continuing to conduct the Slazenger Cup competitions. Aquinas College was very successful with victories in 1978, 1979 and 1981. Brothers John and Michael Thorpe, later to become professional coaches, were in two winning combinations. The Robinson brothers Paul (1978) and Kurt (1981) helped the Aquinas cause, as did Mike Hendriks. Scott Marshall, in 1980, assisted Wesley to victory as his father Arthur had done thirty years earlier. For the earlier occasion Bruce Robinson, father of Paul and Kurt, was also in the Wesley team with Arthur Marshall.

In the girls' section, Catholic schools were again to the fore. Iona College won on three occasions (1978, 1979 and 1982), Newman College had successive wins (1980 and 1981) while Santa Maria College won in 1983. Several of the team members were prominent in the tournament scene. They included Elizabeth and Catherine Sayers (Iona); Joanne Greig, Robyn Lamb and Jenny Howlett (Newman); together with Paula Parentich and Joanne Johnson from Santa Maria College.

By 1984, the Slazenger Cup, Mursell Shield, Herbert Edwards Cup, and the Academy Plate had for four years been under the heading of the 'Rural and Industries Teams Competition'. The Bank (later BankWest) had broadened its support to tennis at both junior and senior levels, and after being a co-sponsor for several Western Australian Open events, from 1982 backed the Champion of Champions tournament. The latter was an impressive title but some of the leading players in the stronger clubs could not compete as entry was limited to major tournament winners and club champions.

Given the prevalence of sponsorship and the range of opportunities at the junior level, only rarely matched in senior circles, a view prevailed in tennis circles that once players reached the seniors they were regarded as 'has beens'. Attempts were made by administrators to try to counter this by initiatives such as a regular interstate senior competition. 'Player of the season' awards were also introduced, as had occurred in the junior age groups. The main object of these strategies was to keep leading seniors in tennis rather than producing a Western Australian champion.

The senior scene

As always, an interstate senior tennis competition remained high on the agenda. However, the road to tennis greatness lay through the circuit and with the Davis Cup and, to a lesser extent the Federation Cup and senior interstate tennis could not hope to capture public interest in the summer in the same way as Sheffield Shield cricket. Some members of the sporting fraternity advocated a national league football competition. There was similar speculation surrounding basketball and soccer. Eventually, in 1982, a Western Australian team, the Weststate Wildcats entered the National Basketball League (NBA).

Eventually, though, in tennis the lobbying from the West led to an interstate teams competition being held in January 1979, at Burnie, in Tasmania. All states were represented, with Rob Casey, Ian Bersan, Christine Matison (Dorey) and Lyn Cooper being chosen from Western Australia. After exciting narrow wins against Victoria and New South Wales, with captain/manager Casey defeating Bill Gilmour and Cooper winning against Jan Wilton, the team easily defeated the remaining states to win what became known as the Challenge Cup. The prize for the victors, sponsored by the New Zealand

The Sayers' clan as depicted in the WA Open Program, January 1978, 40

Lawn Tennis Association, was a tour of 'the land of the long white cloud'. However, Barry Tognolini and Tony Di Francesco replaced Casey and Bersen for the New Zealand national titles and matches against regional teams. In the nationals, Matison performed well to reach the semi-finals.

Perth was the venue for the second year of the competition. There were indications that it was winning acceptance when stronger teams were chosen than at Burnie: players such as Ray Ruffels, Wayne Hampson, John Fitzgerald, John Trickey and Peter Campbell were among the men who competed and, in the women's section, Kym Ruddell, Sue Saliba, Jenny Dymond and Karen Gulley were in the field. Defending champions Western Australia were represented by Casey, Gary Penberthy, Matison, and Mary Sawyer (Collins). Again Western Australia performed creditably, remaining undefeated until the final day. Then, in a cliff-hanging tie, it lost by one set to Victoria 3 rubbers 8 sets 76 games to 3 rubbers 7 sets and 88 games.

The tournament committee, chaired by Dene Rundle and including Barry Tognolini, Gwyn Thomas, Dot Connolly, and Leonie Bell, with Vic Anderson as the referee, was credited with having organised the fixture most efficiently. However, there were rumbles from some States about the wisdom of the competition and the number competing fell. In Hobart in 1982, Western Australia again took the Cup under the leadership of Penberthy supported by Reg Luttrell, Dorey and Elizabeth Sayers. In an interesting sequel, Reg Luttrell's brother Tony and Sayers' sister Geraldine later represented the state in the same competition. While tennis is often portrayed as a family game it is only rarely, even at the state level, that brothers and sisters reach top levels. Reg Luttrell's highest State ranking was four, while Tony reached number three. They often formed an outstanding doubles combination and later had an impact on the tennis scene. In the case of the Sayers sisters, Elizabeth reached number one and Geraldine was ranked at eight. Two other Sayers' sisters, Mary and Catherine, also played 'A' grade in these years. Remarkably, playing for University in the 1982 'A' grand final Elizabeth, Geraldine and Mary, with Joy Ducat (and Catherine as a reserve), went within one set of defeating Fremantle. In addition, brothers Mervyn and Anthony were very capable sportsmen, with Mervyn being chosen to play first class cricket.

To further encourage interest in senior tennis, a Shield Player of the Year competition was inaugurated in the 1977-1978 season. At first it was sponsored by the Nevarda clothing company which had strong links with Western Australian tennis. Director Brian Nevard was a keen player at both Reabold and King's Park. He held the Presidency at Reabold and was made a life member in recognition of his services. Nevard held a special interest in promoting team play in pennant matches. He had regularly sponsored a similar award at Reabold. At his suggestion, both the WALTA and Reabold competitions recognised participation in grades other than the 'A' or first.

Although the pennant player of the year competition concept may have stemmed from Nevard, as he was a frequent visitor to tennis headquarters, the credit for the scheme has been attributed to the Player Advisory Group which the Executive of the Association had fostered as part of its quest to improve senior tennis. Under the chairmanship of Alan Hicks, these players had begun to express their views on such matters as shield competitions, teams and tournaments and had sought a player of the year competition and the reintroduction of the Metropolitan Hardcourt Competition (*WALTA Annual Report*, 1975/1976).

At first, the players' group had no formal status, but in the 1977/1978 *WALTA Annual Report* the members were identified as Hicks (Chairman), Casey, Cooper, Matison, Napier, Penberthy, Maureen Smith, Barry Tognolini and Ken Tobin. The group continued until December 1984, after which President Harry Spilsbury paid tribute to its contribution to tennis making special reference to Rob and Pauline Casey, Jeff King, Penberthy and Tognolini (*Westennis*, December 1984, 4). Several members were prominent in the inaugural Nevarda Shield Player Award as well as a similar Player of the Year competition launched during the 1976/1977 season. In the latter competition, sponsored by Parameter Pty. Ltd., points were accumulated on the basis of all Western Australian tournaments, shield matches and senior interstate competition.

Player of the Year Competition 1976/1977

Men		Women	
1 Rob Casey	444	1 Mary Sawyer	304
2 Gary Penberthy	360	2 Christine Matison	276
3 Myron Pushyk	192	3 Sue Mack	212
4 Rod Cadwaller	164	4 Ros Fisher	174
5 Hugh Thomson	162	5 Kerryl Chute	152
6 Ross Oliveri	144	6 Lyn Cooper	140
7 Barry Tognolini	120	7 Michelle Pekovich	128
8 Doug Napier	106	8 Judy Lange	112
9 Chris Johnstone	104	9 Jill Larritt	108
10 Ian Bersan	102	10 Bernadette Heavey	96
		11 Jan Maddison	96

Nevarda Shield Player of the Year 1977/1978

Women

Maureen Smith	263.31	Glynis Mitchell	167.05
Judy Lange	258.14	Anne Watts	165.93
Cathy Ainscough	184.45	Robyn Wood	163.99
Michelle Pekovich	183.90	Jenny Smith	159.81
Lyn Cooper	177.39	Sue Mack	154.16
Jan Maddison	169.36	Elizabeth Sayers	153.52

Men

Rob Casey	233.31	Barry Tognolini	188.10
Tony Di Francesco	210.48	Roger Grant	181.39
Ian Bersan	206.55	Rob De Crespigny	181.29
Chris Johnstone	204.50	Phil Holten	177.03
Gary Penberthy	202.43	John Reynolds	151.40
Rob Murton	196.41	Alan Wall	141.28

The Player of the Year Award was continued but the Shield Player of the Year was discontinued after the 1982/1983 season. There were changes to the sponsorship arrangements with Mel O'Neil, who was to become a leading tennis administrator, privately backing the Shield Player Award for the 1980/1981 season. In the following season, STW Channel 9 began a long association with the Player of the Year Competition. Casey and Dorey held a virtual monopoly of the modest winner's cheque, with only Penberthy breaking though in the men's section and Lyn Cooper in the women's in 1978/1979 (in addition to Mary Sawyer in the inaugural year when Christine Matison (Dorey) was restricted in the number of events she played). However, the Shield Player of the Year was often won by lesser known competitors who were not always members of 'A' grade teams. In the men's competition Henry Michael (1979/1980), Keith Utley (1980/1981) and Jamie Hevron (1982/1982) were perhaps in this category while in the women's grades Jill Harrington (1978/1980), Melanie Kersten (1981/1982), and Jan McIntyre (1982/1983) were fine pennant performers who were not top-ranked players.

Shield competition

Although the Shield Player of the Year trophy was not monopolised by Casey and Dorey, they were both sufficiently prominent in the senior pennants to twice win the award during its five-year history. Dorey was the leading player in the dominant Fremantle 'A' grade team, which won six of the eight premiership finals played between 1977 and 1984. In fact, from 1973 to 1985, Fremantle won the Laurie Toole trophy on 13 occasions and in the 1980/1981 season were undefeated in the home and away season. The semi-final series was also negotiated but Higgins Park sprang a major upset victory in the grand final. Fremantle, as firm favourites, opened confidently, with Dorey defeating Mary Collins 7/6, 6/2. But Robyn Lamb, Glynis Mitchell and

Ann Layman representing Higgins Park proved too good for their opponents, the Higgins doubles combinations completing the rout for a five rubbers to one victory. Higgins had been strengthened in this department by the inclusion of strong-serving Layman, who had returned from university studies in the United States.

Fremantle had experienced an earlier grand final loss in 1977, when star players Christine Matison (Dorey) and Michelle Pekovich were unavailable due to tournament commitments in Victoria. This meant that Lyn Cooper (Nedlands) was able to record an easy 6/2, 6/2 win over Ros Fisher. When Bernadette Heavey surprised by winning a tight match 6/4, 7/6 against the competitive Maureen Smith, it was clear Fremantle was in difficulties. Judy Lange played strongly to beat Radhika Menon, then teamed with Judy Cole to win the doubles and clinch victory.

Yet it was not always a case of luck turning against Fremantle. In 1983, it finished the home and away series on top of the ladder but were beaten by Nedlands in the first 'grand final'. However, the rules for that season provided the top team with the right in such circumstances to a replay. Exercising this option, Fremantle won 3-7-74 to 3-7-68 in a dramatic finish when the fixture had to be completed at 10 a.m. on Sunday morning after six and half hours of play on Saturday had not resolved the tie. At that stage, the final doubles match between Fremantle's Christine Dorey and Maureen Smith and Nedland's Lyn Cooper and Judy Lange was poised at one set all. Eventually, the Fremantle duo won 6/1, 6/7, 6/2 to claim the Shield (*West Australian*, 28/2/1983, 71).

In 1984, the grand final was also closely fought between Fremantle and Nedlands. An afternoon of keen competition left Fremantle with a one-set advantage (3-8-74 to 3-7-67) with Dorey leading the way with victory over Cooper. The straight-set win was almost a replica performance of the previous year. A feature of the contest was the performance of Nedlands veteran Gwenda McIntosh (Don) who defeated Wilson Cup junior Joanne Johnson 7/5, 6/7, 6/4 and then combined with Ann Layman to win another three-set encounter 4/6, 6/2, 6/4 against sisters Sue and Joanne Johnson.

In the late Seventies, Fremantle was also a force in the men's 'A' grade competition, with successive Shield grand final victories played in 1977 and 1978. A highlight in 1978 was Fremantle's capacity to win both the men's and women's trophies. One factor in its success was thought to be the establishment of an Aces Club: a group of Fremantle identities which helped to raise finance for tennis promotion (*West Australian*, 20/2/1978, 56). This body was able to utilise the business acumen of club player Bob Gordon who later became a prominent sporting entrepreneur and successful veterans' tennis competitor. In 1978, the Aces were instrumental in flying leading juniors Chris Johnstone and Roger Grant back from Sydney for the grand final against Hensman Park. The two players were certainly needed, as Fremantle, in a thrilling finish, won by only two games: 3 rubbers, 7 sets, 66 games to 3-7-64 (*West Australian*, 20/2/1978, 56). It also meant that Fremantle's decision to recruit the state's number one player, Rob Casey, as club coach had paid dividends.

In the grand finals, though, Casey experienced mixed fortunes. In 1977, he was narrowly defeated by keen rival Gary Penberthy, when Fremantle met the strong Bayswater combination. However, singles wins by Chris Johnstone over Keith Hince and Owen Worley over Paul Holmes paved the way for

Fremantle to win on games; 3 rubbers, 7 sets, 71 games to 3-7-64. In 1978, Casey defeated Hensman's Keith Begley, in three sets, but in 1979, when Fremantle was again pitted against Bayswater, Penberthy was back to win in three sets on grand final day. On that occasion, Bayswater denied Fremantle a premiership 'hat trick' in another close encounter, 3-8-72 to 3-7-67. Roger Grant and John Gordon won their singles and combined in the doubles to give the port club three rubbers, but it was not enough for the title. Hince for Bayswater defeated Worley in straight sets and then combined with Penberthy to win the doubles against Casey and Worley.

Peter Dyson, prominent professional and sport's retailer

Between 1979 and 1982 the Blacklock Shield was won by Bayswater, Higgins, Maylands and Scarborough. Maylands won again in 1983, before Scarborough had wins in 1984 and 1985. Scarborough's 1985 premiership was surrounded by controversy, as the teams ran out of light with the result still in doubt. As the rules provided for a total replay of an unfinished grand final, Scarborough was able to reverse the situation of being down and facing defeat against Higgins on the Saturday, winning on the Sunday. This rule was later amended to prevent total replays. Another provision, drawing for opponents, which had the effect of altering the teams ranking of players (apart from the number one), was removed after a trial for only the 1984/1985 season. Yet, no matter what new rules were adopted, it seemed that Casey and Penberthy kept on appearing in grand finals for various clubs.

Scarborough's first 'A' grade premiership, decided on 13 February 1982, came after a grim struggle with Hensman Park, with the tension continuing until well after 7 p.m. on centre court at King's Park. Casey, who had not lost a pennant match for the whole season, had given Scarborough a good start with a straight set victory over Barry Tognolini. On the adjacent court, Penberthy 'scraped home' 7/6 in the third to give Scarborough a two-nil lead, before Hensman levelled when Phil Searle beat Rob Prowse and veteran Doug Napier proved too experienced for Geoff Voller. The doubles were split, which meant Scarborough had a set in hand to win its first flag (*West Australian*, 15/2/1982, 73).

Hensman Park were also runners-up in the 1980/1981 season when Maylands won its inaugural premiership. Maylands was well served by its number one player, Lawrence Hall, although his brother Tony was beaten in the one-sided grand final by Barry Tognolini. Other members of the victorious Maylands team were the prominent professional coaches Peter Dyson and Phil Holten (*West Australian*, 16/2/1981, 90). Later Dyson followed the direction of some other professionals with engagement in a retailing business known as Subiaco Sports.

Another club winning its first flag in this period was Higgins Park. Indeed, 1980 was a year for Higgins Park to savour, as it was undefeated, although the grand final card 3-7-66 to opponent Bayswater 3-6-62 was hardly decisive. As in league football, the winning margin is not significant, but losing premiership players after the grand final can mean that a second consecutive flag is beyond reach. This happened to Higgins after the 1979/1980 season, when the Hall brothers transferred to Maylands.

In the 1980 clash between Higgins Park and Bayswater, Lawrence Hall saved two opening set points in the tie-break over Penberthy, before winning in straight sets 7/6, 6/2. Tony Luttrell made it 2-0 for Higgins Park by outplaying Alan Shaw, before Bayswater kept its hopes alive with a 6/1, 6/4 win by David Turner against Gavin Bosworth. In a tense match, Bayswater's Keith

Hince edged out Tony Hall to level the singles at two wins for each team. Temporarily Bayswater then went ahead when Shaw and Turner defeated Bosworth and Tony Hall, then Lawrence Hall and Tony Luttrell scored a 6/1, 7/5 win over Penberthy and Hince, to give Higgins Park the flag.

The men's competition, in particular, was characterised by the frequent transfer of players from club to club. In 1977, a transfer system was introduced to regularise these movements. It did not operate in a restrictive manner, as had occurred in league football, and was considered a success. Of course, the financial rewards were modest compared with football and the incentives for players were limited to reduced fees and uniforms. Some clubs gave no concessions to their 'A' grade players.

One matter which the Council sought to resolve was the niggling question of the payment of ball fees in shield matches. It was decided not to permit home clubs to charge visiting team ball fees. This still left a grey area when matches were played on neutral courts, as in the end-of-season finals. For the home and away season, it did overcome a source of disagreement.

The ball fee principles and transfer regulations also operated in the lower grades, where the scale of the shield competition had grown steadily. For the 1976/1977 season the Chairman of the Shield Match Committee spoke of 'a new record of 181 men's and 97 women's teams entered the summer competition'. By 1984, with Peter Barrett in the chair, the committee indicated that 454 teams entered the summer competition but only 150 were in the women's divisions. An autumn night doubles competition was introduced, while the winter competition steadily expanded to over 200 teams (*WALTA Annual Report*, 1984/1985). The growth was welcome although it greatly complicated the recording at the WALTA office. Attempts at computerising the data promised a more productive return than was realised.

At one stage there was a concerted effort to produce a uniform set of by-laws under which pennants (ie. shield), including the thriving midweek ladies' competition, could operate (*WALTA Annual Report*, 1984/1985). However, this objective was not fully realised, although progress was made. For instance, the midweek ladies' competition had a separate committee, with its own members undertaking the recording. After nearly 20 years in office, Helen Waters and Mary Ward stepped down in June 1980 from their respective positions as President and Treasurer of the Women's Auxiliary, the umbrella body for the midweek competition. Three years later, Gwyn White retired after 23 years as secretary. Her son Ian continued the family service to tennis as an administrator (and competent player) at the Alexander Park Tennis Club. However, for her part Gwyn White continued to partake in pennants which she had done for nearly fifty years (*Westennis*, October 1983, 21). These women had presided over the formidable growth of the midweek shield match competition. By the 1984/1985 season, entries had risen to 162 teams from 40 clubs for the summer competition. There were also some 50 teams in a winter hardcourt competition which had also been initiated.

The ladies' midweek competition did much to provide women with competitive opportunities. Despite this the number of women entering tournaments was still lower than that of men. Nevertheless, with the doubles format proving so popular with midweek women it was not surprising that when plans were finalised to conduct a tennis attraction as part of Western Australia's 150th celebration in 1979, it was decided to conduct a 'doubles classic'.

Dubbed the 'tournament with a difference' it was conducted during the

Foundation Day long weekend in June at the University of Western Australia's Plexipave courts. Plexipave agreed to be the major sponsor with $500, with an additional $200 from Bunnings and radio promotion from 6PM. In the spirit of the celebrations, contestants were encouraged to dress in period costume; there was even a costume event as well as a mixed 'gotcha' handicap doubles. Of course, there were the customary men's and women's doubles championships.

Some of the leading organisers of the 'classic' were also among the leading players. Tournament director Gary Penberthy had just won the Spalding Player of the Year award, while champion Rob Casey was in charge of publicity. Secretary/Treasurer was Mary Sayers, a member of the prominent tennis family which advocated more doubles play to foster interest in the game. Holding the tournament as winter commenced was unusual and this helps to explain why no results were published in the *West Australian*. Its sports columns were filled with league football and racing coverage. Not since the early years of the century had the newspaper reported on local senior tennis tournaments in winter.

The doubles classic was to become a permanent feature of the senior tournament scene, with a mortgage on the Foundation Day long weekend. It was the only significant change during the 1977 to 1984 period in the tournament schedule after the players advisory body successfully reinstated the Metropolitan Hardcourt event in early September. There was concern when the Spring Tournament was not conducted in 1981, but it regained its October spot on the calendar when it became a hardcourt event. The State Hardcourt Championship was designated for the Queen's Birthday long weekend, which usually coincided with the last week in September and the grand final of Australian Rules Football in Melbourne. In one year, 1984, the desire of players to watch the grand final was easily accommodated when it rained throughout the day at an otherwise hospitable Esperance. This was the most distant venue from Perth for this championship, normally held in a country centre.

The City of Perth retained its Christmas spot, the City of Fremantle competition being conducted during the Australia Day long weekend in late January. The State Closed continued to be allocated to the Labour Day holiday in early March. A weekend near the Easter break was allocated to the Champion of Champions title. Many country tournaments coincided with these public holiday dates and the Roster Committee ruled that no metropolitan tournaments could be sanctioned during the Easter break. Geraldton and Kalgoorlie were able to stage some of the most lucrative tournaments on the calendar. Country Week continued to be conducted in the January period, although there was often discussion about the most suitable dates.

Country Week

The scale of Country Week continued to expand, with the men's sections increasing from six in 1977 to 13 (with an additional veterans' category) in 1984. In the same period, the number of women's grades went from three to seven, plus a veterans' division. The boys' and girls' junior championships were retained for the 18s, 16s and 14s age groupings.

The men's 'A' grade teams competition was dominated by Katanning in 1977, 1978, and 1979. It was well served by Peter Rigg, Henry Ladyman and Barry Jones. In the first two years Rigg also captured the singles title. Thereafter.

Ros Giles (Centre), Country Week legend Ros Giles is pictured above with Keith Wilson, the Sport and Recreation Minister and Katanning team member Joy Ducat (Fleay)

Geraldton teams claimed the Goldsmith trophy for five successive years. In 1980, after Geoff Jamieson and Max Correy (Geraldton) narrowly won the title from Ken Harris and Don Patten (Binnu-Geraldton), it was calculated that in the men's 'A' grade, the district fielded five teams or 40 percent of the 'A' grade competition (*Westennis*, March 1980, 4). The singles championship again became the domain of schoolteacher and metropolitan 'A' grader Colin Bell (three wins) and another schoolteacher and metropolitan 'A' grader Alan Gooch (two wins). Unlucky Henry Ladyman, like famed Argentinian Guillermos Villas, who was known as the 'eternal second' for much of his career, gained four runner-up trophies.

The women's 'A' grade team trophy was, however, spread around between seven different teams in the eight year period, only Katanning being twice successful. Katanning's players included Joy Jones, Vicki Ladyman and Ros Giles. In successive years (1978 and 1979) Ros Giles added two more Country Week titles to her impressive record raising questions again about her stature compared with her metropolitan peers. Not surprisingly, it was decided to extend the invitations to eligible country competitors to compete in the annual Champion of Champions event. Hard hitting Anne Watts (nee McKenzie), an experienced metropolitan pennant player, won Country Week in 1980 while Judy Lange, a leading member of the strong Nedlands 'A' grade team, was eligible to play due to residence in the country arising from a teaching appointment, dominated the women's singles championships in 1983 and 1984.

Gauged by the tone of the annual Country Week Conference, formally minuted in the WALTA records, much was being done to cater for tennis outside the metropolitan area. It was clear that the commitment of the country representative on the Executive was a factor that ensured strong representation of rural views. From 1977 until March 1984 this role was filled by Gordon Smith, widely praised for understanding the rural perspective. He was an 'A' grade player for Fremantle, where he was awarded life membership for his services to the club.

Sensitivity to the interests of country players was important in channelling the rural demand for sport into tennis and thereafter into affiliation. Recommendations to alleviate the problems of country sports were tabled in a 1983/1984 Legislative Council Select Committee report. However, despite attention to rural sport needs, membership statistics and affiliation revenues reveal only minimal growth over the period from 1977 to 1984.

Membership and finances

As the calculation of affiliation fees was based on the submission of membership statistics (on a per head basis) at 31 December each year, there was a temptation, akin to a taxpayer underestimating his or her income, to underestimate membership numbers. As tax avoidance became a national sport in the late Seventies and early Eighties it is not known how many clubs succumbed to the temptation to understate their membership and hence their 'tax' or dues to the WALTA. The official record indicates that country membership fell away in the early 1980s although numbers grew in the metropolitan area at a rate higher than the general population increase. There was a slow but steady growth in the number of affiliated metropolitan clubs, mostly in outer suburban areas such as Armadale, Memorial Park (Gosnells), Lesmurdie, Thornlie, Whitfords, Wanneroo, Sorrento, Kwinana and Safety Bay. Earlier the WALTA Executive had been successful in its quest to have tennis clubs included in the new metropolitan street directories. Closer to Perth, the Blue Gum Park Tennis Club, at Brentwood, almost immediately became a force in local tennis in 1978 with Maureen Smith as the club professional.

The Association's financial position remained sound. Fred Dreyer was the Treasurer for five years from 1976. After an interlude of one year, when educationist Peter Barrett held the position, experienced businessman Dene Rundle (in 1984) assumed this most demanding post. Remember, too, that accountant Harry Spilsbury became President of the WALTA in 1982, and had earlier rivalled William Corr's long term as treasurer. In a statement in *Westennis* (December 1983, 6) early in his Presidency, Spilsbury explained how the composition of the budget had changed:

> *Do you, the average club member, city or country, know that in 1982/1983...*
>
> - *members of the Executive and the General manager raised $106,000 through various sponsorships, almost twice as much as was received in affiliation fees?*
> - *The fund raising and Women's Auxiliary Committee contributed $17,900 from fund raising ventures?*
> - *We charged $20,900 as administrative fees to various tournaments and activities so those benefiting - the direct participants - in those activities had to contribute to our office operating costs?*
> - *[Expenditure] on activities solely for country players was $16,000 compared to $10,700 in country affiliation fees?*

Sponsorship was clearly becoming a very significant part of the revenue base. Each annual report documented the sponsorships from private and government sources. A Department of Youth, Sport and Recreation grant continued to subsidise the Tennis Development Officer position and the October 1983 Annual General Meeting was told by Spilsbury (*WALTA Annual Report*, 1982/1983) that:

> *A highlight of material long term significance for our Association is the introduction of the Sports/Culture Instant Lottery from which funds estimated at around $6 million annually will provide a tremendous fillip to sport in this State. I am sure that the many initial teething troubles currently being experienced with regard to SILDAC's policy guidelines and funding will be eliminated in the next twelve months and we can then realistically look forward to achieving considerable expansion of promotion and projects in both city and country.*

Another development, in 1981, which also became institutionalised, was the adoption of an LTAA levy. Conscious that such a proposal would experience a similar 'rocky road' to proposed increases in Association affiliation fees, President Sanders prepared this statement for *Westennis* (April 1981,1):

> *I think that most members will see the need to have 'bread and butter' income to cover administration costs and it is hoped a progressive attitude will be taken by all. We hope to circulate suitable explanatory material soon but in the meantime it could be assumed that the per head levy will not exceed one dollar per year and certainly your Executive is hoping for your whole-hearted support.*

Meanwhile the Association, through its fund raising committee continued with its Miss Tennis Quest. Promotion required considerable planning and energy but the funds raised for the Interstate Visits Fund were formidable. The early issues of *Westennis* were notable for the considerable space given to appeals for entrants from metropolitan and country clubs. There were tables of the amounts raised and photographs of the winners. Roger Burrows from Corinthian Park, well known for his smart attire, good humour and easy manner, often presided as master of ceremonies at the awards presentation. For instance, the front page of *Westennis* for March 1979, was headlined MISS TENNIS TITLE TO SALLY CHRYSTAL. A record net amount of $7938 was raised, made up as follows:

Beth Cunningham	Alexander Park	$212.23
Jenny Smith	Canning	444.60
Jean Anrobus	Claremont	322.73
Jillian Porter	Corinthian Park	864.60
Susanne Vidler	East Fremantle	1,040.56
Denise Cole	Fremantle	415.29
Nola Piper	Hensman Park	431.97
Denise Gunman	Higgins Park	439.60
Rae Armstrong	Leederville	526.44
Sally Worner	Loton Park	268.06
Judy Lange	Nedlands	663.29
Sally Chrystal	Reabold	400.00
Virginia Saunders	Scarborough	1410.66
Robyn Leschen	South Perth	211.87
Jenny Harman	Southern Suburbs	186.06
Total		$7,837.96

A fine photograph of Sally Chrystal was included on the front page. Chrystal was a very capable player who had won the women's championship and pennant player of the year at Reabold. She later married Mike Hendriks, a dual club singles champion at Reabold and President of the club. Sally's father Lloyd Chrystal was steeped in tennis lore having been President at Reabold and Royal King's Park as well as an Executive member at the WALTA. In addition between 1984 and 1992 he was Chairman of the WALTA/Royal King's Park Joint Standing Committee He was an 'A' grade player with a special capacity for splendid doubles performances.

The same issue of *Westennis* also included an expression of appreciation from Helen Waters, the long standing chairperson of the Interstate Visits Fund, and to Mrs Moira Thorpe for the many hours she had spent in making the annual Linton and Wilson Cup raffle so successful, yielding a net profit of about $1,700. Moira Thorpe was well known for the support she gave to furthering tennis with voluntary assistance to juniors. At one stage, she undertook the tedious task of recording the points for the CBA player awards. As her sons John and Michael invariably appeared, this eased the burden.

The Women's Auxiliary continued its numerous fund raising activities as part of the range of support roles to tennis. As already mentioned Helen Waters was to eventually step down as President to later in 1982 be the first women to be granted life membership of the Association. In 1983, Gwyn White also handed over her secretarial position; one of her favourite memories was her role, some 30 years earlier, to umpire the exhibition match between 'Little Mo' Connolly and Julie Sampson (*Westennis*, October 1983, 21).

The veterans

After the organisation of the very successful Australian Veterans' Carnival in January 1980, a separate Womens Veterans' Association was formed. Margaret Napier was the inaugural President with Maggie Venerys, Pat Stanley, Margaret Robinson, Estelle Smith, Doris Strang, Audrey Chrystal and Dot Connolly comprising the committee. Both the men's and women's associations maintained separate committees, although there was considerable cooperation, both on the court and socially before they amalgamated in 1984, with a strength of 370 members (215 men and 155 women). Records indicate that Elsie Crowe, Pat Stanley, Anne O'Connor, Maureen Graham and Moira Churack were present (at 6.00 p.m. on 20 September, 1984) to celebrate the new look club 'with a glass of champagne'. Meanwhile members received a copy of the publication entitled *The First Decade*. This brief history of the Club had been researched by Ross Hutchinson, Vern Beckett and Harold Broadbent. Don Clayton was credited with compiling the sources and prominent sporting journalist Alan East, edited and published the booklet (*Annual Report 1984/1985, Veterans Tennis Club of Western Australia*)

Drawing particularly upon the guidance of Reabold stalwart Don Clayton the Veterans refined their Constitution. Later a regular publication known as *Vetscene* was distributed to members who were charged very low membership fees. This magazine was the equivalent of *Westennis* which was compiled at headquarters. The combined men's and women's Veterans organisation was soon recognised as a positive force in Western Australian tennis although occasionally the organisation had to contend with 'converts' from other sports who sometimes lacked an education in the etiquette of tennis.

With so much expertise available, it was not surprising that the 1980 Championship had won so much praise. One reason could be that Clive Wilderspin was Chairman of the Carnival Committee. Apart from his great record as a player, there were few who could 'match' him in the organisation of championships on time and on budget. With 30 men's and 20 women's teams entered in the various age groups, Western Australia was successful in the men's over-40 and over-55 age groups, and the women in over-55 category. However, no Western Australian won a title in the individual events, some of which were played in searing heat made more manageable by the beauty of the setting of the Royal King's Park grass courts. Nevertheless, such conditions did not preclude 'senior' legends such as John Leonard, Harry Jacoby, Keith Holten and Ross Hutchinson enjoying their participation.

The veterans continued to conduct their own annual tournament, visit metropolitan clubs on Sunday mornings and play against selected schools in midweek matches. Each year there was an exodus of teams to play in the Australasian National Championships. Sometimes the victories received recognition but often they did not make the news. For instance, Moira Churack, well known in the veterans and club circles, wrote a short article for *Westennis* (April 1984, 5) about Western Australia winning the 'prestigious 55 years and over championship at the 1984 Brisbane Carnival. The members of the team were Nancy Plaisted (captain), Pat Jenzen, Elsie Crowe, Ethel Priestley and Gene Matthews as reserve.

Regular donations to fund State junior teams and, on some occasions, to help individual promising players in their overseas trips continued on the veterans' program. Other forms of assistance included coaching clinics for juniors in country areas and the organisation of 'generation gap' tournaments, with veterans competing in doubles with promising young players.

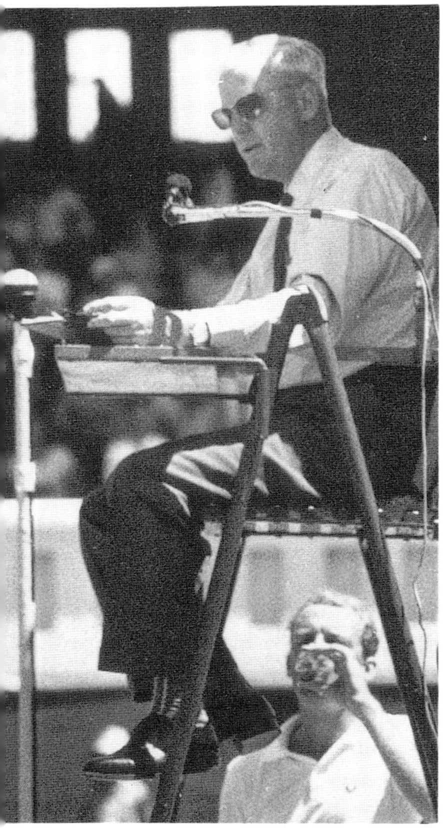

Vic Anderson, the umpire's stand

Umpires

The Veterans invariably conveyed to juniors the principles of tennis etiquette and of being a true sportsperson. The Umpires Association, too, stated that veterans tournaments 'were a delight to umpire, as the players were absolute 'Gentlemen' [sic] (*WALTA Annual Report*, 1984/1985). Whether this could be attributed to maturity or the fact they had learnt the etiquette of tennis before the McEnroe era, was debatable. The Veterans' Association did not make many calls on the Umpires Association, which struggled to gain sufficient recruits to umpire hallmark events such as the Davis Cup ties, West Coast Classics, as well as major senior and junior domestic tournaments. Seeking more women and younger umpires was particularly difficult.

Charlie Brown maintained his mortgage of the Norman E. Cunningham Umpire of the Year Shield with 11 successive awards. Not until after Brown's retirement in 1984 was Maggie Venerys able to break the monopoly. On the other hand, one award that was of necessity rotated was the Alf Shave Trophy for novice umpires. Significantly two women Elaine Skipworth and Margaret Napier, received this trophy: women's umpiring was just beginning.

An inaugural Referees and Umpires Seminar was held in Melbourne before the 1981/1982 season and attended by Vic Anderson, Charlie Brown and Ramon Connolly. In due course, Connolly became a qualified umpire with the Men's International Professional Tennis Council (MIPTC). In Western Australia, he was credited with revising the umpires' score sheet to incorporate scoring for the 12-point tie break. Later he became the President of the Umpires Association, quietly and efficiently going about his task and making (with his wife Dot, of the Leederville club) a substantial contribution to the development of tennis in Western Australia.

After the Davis Cup tie in February 1984, Norm Cunningham also retired from active umpiring. He was a foundation member of the Umpires Association, which had accorded him life membership. In 1977, he had received the British Empire Medal, for his services to sport. Although his contribution to the Umpires Association was noteworthy it should be remembered that he was a force in the organisation of the Southern Districts Tennis Association and forward thinker about being particularly strong in his advocacy of open tennis. His daughter, Pat had been a ranked player and remained as a keen supporter of the game. Significantly her younger son, Steven Stanley, upheld the family umpiring tradition by also becoming qualified with the MIPTC.

When Charlie Brown retired he was granted life membership of the Umpires Association. For eight years he was the Secretary/Treasurer of the Association in addition to his lecturing and examining roles. In 1981, he also had a term as the President of the Australian Lawn Tennis Umpires Association. His name was synonymous with the local tournament scene, where he maintained excellent rapport with the players. One of his credentials was his long experience as a player of shield tennis. He greatly enjoyed playing at his home club at (Mount Lawley), where he was also a life member (*Westennis*, December 1983, 5).

The dedication of umpires was rarely recognised, although one of the less obvious benefits of *Westennis* was its ability to provide news of the affairs of the Umpires Association. Another positive function of *Westennis* was its recognition of the roles of various administrators and most issues carried short articles about them.

John Whitton (left), WALTA General Manager with a keen interest in the history of tennis
Whitton is pictured above with country legend Rex Richter

Administration

The October 1978 issue of *Westennis* carried a headline 'Changes in the WALTA Office; Administration in Operation'. By this time the Association had progressed from having mainly part-time staff to employing three full-time personnel in addition to the tennis development officer, Bruce Durston. Many important functions were still being performed by volunteers. Moreover, nearly all affiliated clubs, with the exception of the Royal King's Park Tennis Club, operated with volunteer office bearers. Whether more 'paid' management would be necessary in the future was more regularly being debated. Even at the WALTA office the reliance on 'voluntarism' made it difficult to apply 'business efficiency' criteria to performance.

Gwyn Thomas (left), with other WALTA workers David Punch and Ramon Connolly.

In May 1978, John Whitton was appointed as the first general manager/secretary, an expanded role by comparison with that of predecessor, Hugh Cahill, who had been at the WALTA since 1976. Whitton was destined to have a much longer term with the Association. He joined the Alexander Park club in 1949 at the age of 14 after having his tennis fostered at Perth Boys High School by Laurie Toole. Later, Whitton was a member of various clubs, including Hensman Park, Royal King's Park and Belmont and for some years was also President of the Southern Suburbs Association. He was also associated with many country clubs as a result of being transferred by his employer, Elder Smith, to various towns such as Dowerin, Corrigin, Northam and Moora. His country service inculcated an abiding interest in rural affairs, and when he later took over the role of tennis development officer in 1990 he won plaudits for his commitment to country tennis. Another role undertaken by Whitton was the compilation of *Westennis*. He was able to shape gradual improvements to the magazine, which he always ensured included highlighting the history of tennis in Western Australia.

Successive issues of *Westennis* in 1979 and 1980 carried profiles of Gwyn Thomas and Dot Connolly. Both had been recently elected to the Executive. Until constitutional changes had enabled Helen Waters to become a member, it had been a male preserve. Thomas played her early tennis at Carnarvon and Katanning before moving to Hensman Park. Her committee experience at Hensman stood her in good stead in assuming a variety of roles, including being the inaugural chairwoman of the Publicity and Promotions Committee. Her work in the Women's Auxiliary, including a term as President, was also significant. For several seasons, Thomas had also undertaken the arducus task of recording Shield match results. Yet whether assisting with the organisation of the Federation Cup, publication of *Westennis*, the conduct of the Miss Tennis fund raising quest, the organisation of the Champion of Champion tournaments, she did it all with vitality and a sense of humour. Given Gwyn Thomas's participation in Association affairs in the 1980s *Westennis* printed a second profile of her credentials. The same issue included a profile of Executive member Peter Fleischer, who was maintaining the

Ramon Connolly and Dot Connolly, decades of help to tennis

Dene and June Rundle Hensman club members who gave outstanding service to tennis

tradition of a Royal King's Park member playing a central role in Association affairs (*Westennis*, February 1884, 20).

Before her election to the WALTA Executive in 1979, Dot Connolly had been involved in tennis for 35 years. She joined the Leederville club during the war years and became a committee member in 1954. In 1967, she was granted life membership at Leederville - a recognition she shared with her husband Ramon, whose role as an umpire has already been mentioned. At Leederville, the honour boards are dominated by the name Connolly, as Dot and Ramon had five children, Dot herself winning the women's singles at Leederville on 15 occasions between 1947 and 1979. For many years, Connolly held the Chair of the Tournament Roster Committee and of mid-week pennant supervisor for several seasons. There were very few tasks that Dot had not undertaken at WALTA, and Leederville. Later the scale of Dot Connolly's service was more formally recognised when she shared with Peter Barrett the honour of being awarded an inaugural 'Grand Slam Award' in appreciation of dedicated services in the development of tennis in WA' (*WALTA Minutes*, 15/12/1994).

Westennis (December, 1979, 6) carried a profile of 'Brian Bracewell - A Welcome Convert', who had been introduced to tennis by his wife, Lois, after being a keen cyclist. Soon after joining the Melville/Palmyra Club in 1967, he held a number of committee positions, including that of President. With strong support from his family, he established a very successful sub-junior program at Melville/Palmyra.

In 1972, Bracewell became a delegate to the Council and was then elected to the Shield Match Committee. From 1978, when he became a member of the Executive, he immediately assumed the position as Chairman of the Shield Match Committee. However, Bracewell never allowed himself to be completely 'bogged down' with detail. He was invariably innovative and some years later led the task force in a major review of the shield match competition. Like many converts, he sustained his commitment to the cause (in this case tennis) with enduring enthusiasm.

There is always some debate about the most demanding portfolio occupied by volunteers in the WALTA administration. Two roles are often mentioned: Treasurer and Chairperson of the Shield Match Committee. Dene Rundle filled both posts with distinction having 15 years on the Executive, beginning in 1975. As an accountant in public practice and manager of an importing firm, he was well qualified for the Treasurer's role. For the Shield Match Committee, he had the benefit of having played many years of pennants in seniors and veterans. While living in Katanning, Corrigin and Quairading, he won club championship titles as well as regularly holding the position as either President or Captain. At Hensman Park, his metropolitan club, he had three years as President and more than 20 years as a delegate on State Council. Even after stepping down from the Executive (before returning to the new Board of Directors in 1993), he continued to undertake several important select committee roles such as those concerned with constitutional review, corporate planning and organisational review. Much of this work was done with the significant assistance of wife June, whose father Herb Blacker, was a very prominent Goldfields' player. June Rundle held several committee posts at Hensman Park and in her own right gave outstanding service.

Another Hensman couple, Doug and Margaret Napier, filled many WALTA roles. Both had been President of the Hensman club, with life membership being simultaneously accorded to the partnership. At WALTA, Doug was a selector from 1978 and chair of the Committee from 1986 to 1990. In his junior days, Doug played Linton Cup, once achieving a win over Rod Laver. For Laver, it may have been a case of being unable to cope with a fellow left-hander. However, Napier was a fine player with many years of 'A' grade pennants (including several premierships) at Hensman and 13 club singles titles. In 1960 he was the top-ranked player in the State, ahead of the formidable Clive Wilderspin who was at number two.

Margaret and Doug Napier, Life Members at Hensman who also filled many roles at the WALTA.

In 1989 Doug Napier, an executive with New Zealand Insurance, was transferred to Darwin. Margaret's departure meant that the WALTA had to find a new match Chairperson for the Schoolchildren's State Championships; the umpires temporarily lost the services of one of their members; and Hensman lost its President. In the interim, sons Gary and Colin continued the Napier tradition. After three years, the return of the Napiers to Perth was accompanied by speculation that Doug was prepared to take on the best in his age group in the Veterans' competition. With schoolmate and friend Ken Harris, he had already won the Australian Veteran 40s doubles title (*Westennis*, August 1989, 13).

One of the most outstanding enduring contributions to the WALTA came from Barry Sanders, who held the Presidency from 1975 to 1982, before gaining life membership in the same year. He also received the prestigious May Campbell Award for service to sport. Earlier, in conjunction with his employment at the Western Australian Water Authority, he was awarded a Churchill Fellowship to study problems of water pollution and the control of water re-use. As a well educated person, with a Bachelor of Engineering degree, Sanders was an innovative thinker, always prepared to explore new opportunities for the development of tennis. Understanding the need for communication he fostered the introduction and improvement of the *Westennis* magazine. He had excellent debating skills and often spoke at length at functions for affiliated clubs.

Early interest in tennis for Sanders began at Hale School and the Dalkeith Tennis Club. In the 1940s and 1950s, Bill Sanders, his father, had been a delegate representing Dalkeith. With tennis administration in his blood, Barry had become President of the University Tennis Club. Perhaps history was made some years later when his daughter Jane attended State Council as a delegate for the same club. For his part, Sanders was a delegate to Council for several decades and in 1961 began 30 years of service on the Executive. His roles included Chair of the Shield Match Committee and the Tennis Development Committee, as well as that of State selector. He was a key figure in most international and national events held in Perth and a member of numerous WA Open committees. On several occasions he managed state junior teams, a commitment stemming from his strong belief in the need to foster youth. In 1974, he was chosen to manage an Australian tour of New Zealand. Although he was not a champion tennis player he developed excellent rapport with the players.

These travels led Sanders to understand that the WALTA required direct representation on the LTAA Council. Each year there were expressions of appreciation at the annual general meeting to people such as Jack Loughrey who were prepared to act as Western Australian delegates while living in Melbourne, the headquarters of the LTAA (*Westennis*, April 1990, 30). However, Sanders was able to ensure that a resident Western Australian delegate attended LTAA meetings. He also sought the venue rotation of interstate

events to help ensure that Western Australia occasionally enjoyed the benefits of a 'level playing field'. Indeed, the political imperatives of tennis administration were recognised by the perceptive Sanders, who also sought to ensure that the WALTA utilised the resources of government for the sport's future.

Barry Sanders became President at 42 and, when employment pressures led to his decision to step down eight years later (in 1982), he was prepared to remain on the Executive, continue his normal contribution to hallmark tennis events and pursue the elusive goal of seeking a tennis centre which required exhaustive delicate negotiations with each tier of government. This was a project high on the agenda of Harry Spilsbury, who succeeded Sanders.

State Government funding was a significant source of revenue and the federal Hawke government, elected in 1983, was indicating its preparedness to finance the building of sporting facilities. Bob Hawke, was a tennis fan, and during his student days in the West had been a member of the University Tennis Club. He was known to be concerned about reports that the Australian Open would lose its Grand Slam status if a suitable national tennis stadium was not built, but whether the WALTA was going to be a beneficiary was yet to be determined. What was clear was the significance of a new sponsorship package that the LTAA had negotiated with McDonald's, the international family restaurant chain.

Barry Sanders, President of the WALTA, and life member, who was on the Executive for more than 30 years

Aerial view of Royal King's Park Tennis Club, Perth, W.A.

Chapter Nineteen

McDONALD'S 1985-1994

New Year's Day 1985 was marked by Tennis Australia entering a sponsorship partnership with McDonald's, which was seeking to extend its market share in Australia. It was keen to demonstrate its national credentials by financially assisting Australian sports in international and domestic competition. Tennis, an international game which could be played by both males and females, young and old, and champions and social players, demonstrated ideal sponsorship potential. Moreover, as Glanville (1982,14) noted:

> *Tennis, for all the vast emphasis that has been placed in modern times on serve and volleying, and the consequent premium on tall, powerful players with long reach, has remained essentially democratic in a physical sense.*

Although at the social level there were signs that tennis was healthy, among the juniors there was a need to broaden the appeal of tennis to all socio-economic groups. Tennis had to modify its marketing strategies in the face of a new wave of sports that was capturing the loyalties of young Australians - little athletics, a T-ball rage, and the modified rules versions of a host of major and minor sports. Not all the developments in junior sport were desirable and this led the Western Australian Sports Council in 1987 to persuade the State's Minister for Sport, Graham Edwards, to commission an inquiry into junior sport to investigate coaching standards, ethics, resources, government support, research and media coverage (See Junior Sport Report, 1987). In tennis, the leading juniors received the sponsorships for clothing, footwear and the new, higher-powered rackets while most of the top seniors were paying their own way.

The WALTA, as it moved towards its centennial, had to revamp its organisation and even adopt a modern marketing name, Tennis West, just as the old LTAA in 1986 had become Tennis Australia. A survey was conducted through *Westennis* to determine what marketing title was preferred by the tennis community (*Westennis*, October 1988, 14) and the Promotions and Publicity Committee offered a small prize for a new logo competition. After considerable deliberation, Tennis West began marketing the Nineties with a new logo. Although the modern design, depicting a racket handle, was well received it was only used for a few years. Tennis Australia, recognising advantages emanating from national sponsorships and marketing strategies, persuaded the member State Associations to adopt logos with common features. In August 1993 the Tennis West Council resolved (*WALTA Minutes*, 12/8/1993):

> *The Tennis West logo be changed to a format similar to [that] being adopted*

Tennis West Logo 1990-1993

Tennis West Logo 1993

by other States, which is a copy of the Tennis Australia logo, but using state colours and the individual state association name beside the logo.

McDonald's junior development (and State coach).

McDonald's Junior Tennis Australia was first visible in Western Australia in early January 1985, when large banners were on view at the State Open Age tournament at the Belmont club. The scheme was initiated as part of a Tennis Australia junior development project of which McDonald's was contracted to make a substantial contribution. President Harry Spilsbury, as a delegate to the LTAA, was quoted as saying, 'I am sure the Australian program is the envy of many countries' (*WALTA Annual Report*, 1985/1986). In the first year (1985), excluding funds the various States had earmarked for junior schemes from their resources, the juniors' program was budgeted at almost a million dollars:

• LTAA (Tennis Australia) resources including Australian Government Funding	$560,000
• McDonald's Junior Tennis Australia (MJTA)	$350,000
	$910,000

To help coordinate the program and make the best use of these resources, a McDonald's National Board was established, responsible to the LTAA 'in the same way as any sub-committee' (*Westennis*, February 1985, 7). But the composition of the Board appeared to have a profile notably higher than that a normal sub-committee with John Newcombe (Chairman) and the former South Australian Tennis Association President and ranked player, Barry McMillan, as Executive Officer. Other members were Ashley Cooper, Ken Rosewall, Tony Ryan (Chairman of LTAA selectors), Ray Ruffels (LTAA national coach), Carol O'Sullivan (LTAA women's coordinator), and Geoff Pollard, the New South Wales Tennis Association President. The latter, in 1989, was to succeed Brian Tobin as President of Tennis Australia. Earlier Pollard had served on the Custom Credit Operation Tennis for junior development. In his junior days Pollard was runner-up to John Newcombe in the 1961 Australian Junior Championship and was chosen to represent Australia in Junior Davis Cup teams. Given that Pollard was a university lecturer in demography it was obvious he could apply such expertise to his position as the Deputy Chairman of the National McDonald's Board as well as his post at the helm of Tennis Australia (*Westennis*, October 1989, 39).

Pollard was soon to prove himself to be a very 'federal' President with a keen appreciation of the health of the respective State Associations. For the McDonald's program a governing board was established in each State, with the WALTA Vice-President Alan Hicks being appointed as the founding Chairman in Western Australia. The other foundation members were Eric McManis (Chairman, Junior Development), Doug Napier (Chairman of Selectors), Jeff King (President of the Tennis Professionals Association), Maureen Smith (Professional Coach) and Norm Sinclair (McDonald's). When appointed the State coach was to be a member, helping to ensure that the Committee would play an important role in the direction of Western Australian junior tennis.

Initiatives in the early days of the program included country camps at Bunbury, Geraldton, Katanning and Merredin; State squad visits to Albany and Bruce Rock managed respectively by Doug Napier and Alan Hicks; an inaugural city versus country junior teams match; sponsorship of outstanding juniors to participate in eastern states' tournaments; the introduction of the McDonald's Invitation Classic, based on a round robin tournament; and revamped State squads involving more intensive training.

Although the appointment of a state coach was not a direct result of the McDonald's sponsorship, the decision to implement the national junior plan in partnership with McDonald's gave impetus to the need for the introduction of the position. Earlier, in the October 1984 issue of *Westennis* Spilsbury had written in the President's Corner under the headline 'State Coach':

> *Our venture into the employment market brought us many replies from aspirants, both Australian and overseas ... [but] the selection panel decided not to make an appointment, but to try again in a few weeks. The employment of a state coach still remains our No 1 priority.*

John Fairchild, in 1986 became the inaugural full-time WALTA State Coach

At the time, there was some newspaper criticism that Chris Johnstone, winner of the Queensland Open, runner-up in the South Australian Open and a mixed doubles semi-finalist at Wimbledon for two years in a row, had his application overlooked (*Daily News*, 12/12/1985, 58). Johnstone, whose highest ATP ranking had been 70, was still only 25 years old and battling to succeed on the circuit. It was clear, however that the WALTA appointment committee did not wish to 'buy Western Australian'.

In March 1986, John Fairchild was selected as the full-time state coach. He had the credentials to fulfil his primary duty of coaching junior squads and, at 38 he was still sufficiently youthful to stand the physical rigours of this task. He had been a top player in South Australia before leaving in 1971 to coach in Europe. He began coaching at Lew Hoad's Tennis Camp in Spain and became a licensed national coach. After three years, Fairchild moved to Karlsruhe, then to Heidelberg in West Germany. At the latter venue, he had coached many leading juniors, including Boris Becker and teams including Steffi Graf and Mimi Jausovec. He had maintained his own high standard of play in the over 35 years tournament scene (*Westennis*, April 1986, 3; *West Australian*, 28/2/1987, 190).

Although Fairchild supported the view that McDonald's squads should extend the base of junior players, he clearly believed that there was a need to invest in elite juniors. This was demonstrated when three extremely promising juniors, Donna Blackwell, Narelle Kimpton and Stephanie Martin, were selected, with Fairchild as manager, to play a series of tournaments from mid-1988 in Europe. The strategy was generally applauded although a minority 'ginger group' contended a larger team should have been selected. The exclusion of boys was another bone of contention. The fact is that the trio was judged at that time to have best prospects for future success (*Westennis*, October 1988, 11).

In the European summer of 1990, the MJTA Board combined with the Association to organise another overseas tour for promising juniors to compete in West Germany, where the momentum for national unity was already gathering strength. The team manager was Jeff Schneider, who took over as State Coach early in 1990. The team was made up of Anthony Lewis, Donna Blackwell, Paul Kilderry, Erica Martin, Blake Brinklow and Tim Hammond. The tour was considered highly successful from both a tennis and educational viewpoint. Of special significance in Schneider's view (*Westennis*, October 1990, 4) was the fact that 'the clay courts create physically superior athletes with high ball skills and mental toughness, something our juniors need more of'.

Jeff Schneider, State Coach 1990-1993

Schneider, like his predecessor had gained considerable experience in West Germany, as head coach at the Olympia Neumunster Tennis Club. He had also successfully represented Schleswig-Holstein. Between 1979 and 1981 he had been an ATP grand circuit player after very promising performances in junior ranks. As a schoolboy he had represented Victoria in the Reid and Linton Cup, then had captured several senior titles in his home State. When appointed, Schneider was still only 30. He had been conducting his own coaching business in Melbourne before being attracted to the west to join the South Perth club as coach and State grade pennant player (*Westennis*, April 1990,7). When he tendered his resignation, because of family commitments in late 1993, it came as both a surprise and a disappointment. The December/February issue of *StrungOut*, which had replaced *Westennis* on a subscription basis during 1993, carried the news to the tennis community with a cover page heading 'Goodbye and Thank You'.

In contrast to the delays which preceded John Fairchild's appointment as the inaugural State Coach, Tennis West was quickly able to announce a replacement for Schneider. In early March 1994, President Alan Hicks formalised one of Tennis West's 'worst kept secrets' that Geoff Masters was the successful applicant for the State Coach position, to be known as Director of Coaching. Masters had splendid credentials as a player, having represented Australia in the Davis Cup competition in most years from 1972 to 1979. During this period he was a highly ranked player - number four in 1972. He won four ATP tour singles titles including the Australian Indoor championship. In 1974, he partnered Ross Case to win the Australian Open doubles championship before pairing with Case three years later to win the coveted Wimbledon doubles title with victory in the final over John Newcombe and Phil Dent. In the Western Australian Open, Masters also partnered Case for a hat-trick of doubles titles between 1972 and 1974. He had been coaching at the elite and development level for some years in his home State of Queensland and overseas at the Hong Kong Sports Institute (*West Australian*, 5/3/1994, 93). As he had earlier married Western Australian Anne-Marie Crowe, daughter of tennis identity Elsie Crowe, the local link reinforced the view that the appointment offered the WALTA the prospect of extended leadership in all spheres of coaching.

Geoff Masters, Davis Cup player who became Director of Coaching in 1994

One of the responsibilities of the State Coach is membership of the McDonald's State Board. After three years in the chair of the Board, Alan Hicks had relinquished the role to Mel O'Neil, who earlier made his name as a formidable first grade cricketer at Bassendean-Bayswater. And it was soon evident that he was going to apply his sporting acumen to tennis. He was particularly effective in introducing new tournament formats to increase the opportunities for juniors. Not surprisingly, O'Neil's home club of Sorrento won the Australia-wide 1987-1988 McDonald's Tennis Club of the Year Award. This was the outcome of a tennis calendar at Sorrento that was both innovative and interesting. When Robert Bentley, the President, received a $5,000 cheque for the Sorrento club from John Newcombe (the Chairman of the MJTA National Board) he indicated the money would go towards constructing a double sided hit-up wall. Newcombe helped to make the occasion (13 November, 1988) a memorable day by conducting a coaching clinic for juniors in front of Pam Beggs, the local Member of Parliament and a minister in the Labor government, and Wayne Bradshaw, Mayor of the City of Wanneroo. In a reminder that he had not lost his prowess Newcombe then joined Ashley Cooper, the former Wimbledon champion, John Fairchild and leading Sorrento women players Yvonne Ball and Tanya Herd in exhibition games.

Mel O'Neil (Centre), a shrewd cricketer who made his mark in tennis administration O'Neil is with Barry Sanders (left) and John Fairchild (right)

The presence in Perth of Newcombe and Cooper resulted from the organisation of the World Youth Cup at Royal King's Park which had been attended by members of the McDonald's National Board. As well, four ITF staff travelled from London to help run the event. The operations director of the 'classic' was Helen Smith representing McDonald's Junior Tennis Australia and Tennis Australia. Smith, a keen player who had been a schoolteacher before moving into tennis administration, had attended the 1987 World Youth Cup sponsored by NEC at Freiburg, West Germany. Given this experience and the assistance of the WALTA staff, Smith ensured the smooth conduct of the tournament, which was played on the basis of two singles and one doubles between teams aged 16 years and under.

This, the fourth NEC World Cup, was contested by 32 teams from 24 countries in early November 1988. The Australian boys (Joshua Eagle, Greg Doyle, and Lee Holyoach) lost their first round tie against New Zealand although they later defeated number one seed Sweden. The girls proved victorious, defending the title they had won in West Germany a year earlier. The Australian team was made up of Brisbane cousins Lorrae Guse and Kerry-Anne Guse, supported by Sydney's Kerrily Sharpe. The Guse girls fought exceptionally hard in the final against Argentina, which was attended by a large crowd in hot conditions, tempered late in the day by the 'Fremantle Doctor' sea breeze (*Westennis*, December 1988, 20-24).

There were reasons, if a little premature, to believe that the McDonald's program was beginning to pay dividends in lifting the standard of junior tennis across the nation. In Western Australia, the McDonald's Board was continuing to consider new initiatives, including the introduction of a more formalised talent-spotting procedure. Coaches were asked to submit the names of their most promising juniors to participate in training sessions with the State Coach and overseen by the State selectors. The latter were given scope to choose more players to compete in the eastern states with full or half airfares provided. New underage tournaments were added to the calendar during weekends in May and June, helping to provide a better preparation to the July Junior Hardcourt Winter Championships. This event had been added to the McDonald's schedule when, from 1986 the school year was changed to four, rather than the traditional three, terms. The venue for this tournament in its inaugural year was the Sorrento club, where Mel O'Neil continued as manager. For many seasons at Sorrento, O'Neil was supported in the conduct of many tournaments by a small band of volunteers. One member of this group was Gaye Hawthorne, who also offered her services as an umpire. She was the epitome of the valued volunteer upon which the club scene in Western Australia has been so dependent.

Although in 1992 O'Neil relinquished his position as Chair of the McDonald's Board, his successor, Norm Knell, an accountant by profession, was also a Sorrento man. Knell (like O'Neil) had made his name in another major sport; he had a 177-game career as a top league footballer with West Perth club in the glory days of the Western Australian Football League, before the entry of the West Coast Eagles into the Victorian Football League (later Australian Football League) competition in 1987 weakened the local competition. Tennis, for ex-footballers like Knell, had a special appeal because of the relief from physical contact. Perhaps Knell's conversion to tennis was also assisted by his wife Lyn, a keen player, and junior coordinator at Sorrento. His understanding of the needs of juniors was also to be gained through the participation of the Knell children, Karen and Alan, in junior tennis.

While the McDonald's Board benefited from the input of those who had made their names in other sporting codes, many of the initiatives necessarily came from the experienced professionals. In May 1992, Lesley Hunt was appointed to the Board. Many of her achievements as a player have already been documented. After her circuit days, she spent nearly a decade as a travelling coach for several top international competitors; then back in Perth, she became active in the coaching scene before being inducted into the Hall of Champions in 1993. Hunt's appointment to the McDonald's Board had been preceded by Rob Casey's. It was evidence of the priority that Tennis West was giving to junior development. Others who served on the Board, apart from the foundation members, included former Country Week stalwart Henry Ladyman, leading player Robyn Lamb and Brian Beers, following his appointment as Executive Director of Tennis West on 1 August 1988. Throughout, the McDonald's representatives, Norm Sinclair and Greg Weston, were keen contributors who also gave the Board a lay perspective.

One of the foundation members of the Board, Maureen Smith, also served on the national McDonald's Board. Based at the Blue Gum Tennis Club, her influence on the junior and senior scenes in Western Australia was profound. Any assessment of her contribution should be made with the realisation that her husband, Gordon, has also been an important contributor to tennis in both the metropolitan area and in the country zones. From the mid-1970s, Maureen Smith had coached and team-managed nearly all the top-ranked Western Australian women (and some men) players. Eventually, her expertise was recognised at the national level when she was appointed to manage Australian junior teams to Europe and the United States in 1985, 1987, 1988 and 1991. Deservedly, she was appointed as a national selector, a role she also fulfilled with exemplary application for Tennis West. On several occasions Smith was awarded the Coach of the Year Award having earlier being accredited as a Level 3 coach. In local tennis, she proved to be one of the most formidable and enduring competitors, accumulating nearly 30 years of experience in top grade pennants. Given her commitment to juniors, it is ironic that as Maureen Symonds she narrowly missed state selection, particularly because her senior career was notable for numerous doubles titles - a formidable aspect of her game.

One initiative of the McDonald's Board which can possibly be attributed to Smith, and ex-team sportsman Knell, was the decision in 1992 to play a doubles tournament in the second week of the July school vacation at the Sorrento club. Doubles, thought Knell, was a means of developing team spirit as well as providing an avenue for more junior development. This line of reasoning was later strongly supported by Geoff Masters, as the Director of Coaching with a splendid international doubles record. Moreover, Knell (*Westennis*, October 1992, 20) could then claim, 'by arranging the Pepsi doubles we now offer the opportunity to our youngsters to play the same amount of tennis as the eastern states provide for their players during the school holidays'.

Maureen Smith, champion doubles player, who became a leading coach, State and national selector

Reference to Pepsi indicated the entry of another major international corporation into tennis sponsorship. Apart from assistance for the Junior Doubles Classic, Pepsi also supported Tennis West in a launch of the Pepsi League. The object of this competition was to encourage children, many of whom were beginners (in the nine and 10 age groups) to play regular, competitive tennis on a regional basis on Saturday mornings. As both Tennis West and the McDonald's Board fully appreciate, if structured competition is not organised on a suburban and district base, tennis fails to gain its share of youth and talent. It means that the quest to create champions is rarely successful as the best potential can move to other sports.

In 1992, McDonald's signed with Tennis Australia to continue its national sponsorship for another three years. As there had been suggestions that McDonald's was considering terminating their assistance, it did raise concerns about the funding of the junior program if McDonald's do eventually withdraw and another major sponsor is not found. It would almost certainly lead to a curtailment of the metropolitan squads and the availability of assistance for interstate, and possibly international, competition. At any one time, the number of Western Australian juniors receiving assistance was considerable, leaving the State Selectors vulnerable to criticism for selections made without any recognised criteria. For instance, in the October 1992 issue of *Westennis*, State Coach Jeff Schneider reported on Sydney's premier national event the Shell Age Tournament conducted in April as well as the September Glen Iris Tournament in Victoria. Twelve Western Australian juniors had travelled to Sydney assisted by McDonald's sponsorship to pit themselves against Australia's finest, six players being funded to Glen Iris.

Results suggested that the past phobias about the 'kids in the east' were being put to rest, as all 12 reached the round of 16 in the NSW Shell Age. With Sydney as the venue Siobhan Drake-Brockman defeated Monika Sekulov in an all-Western Australian 14 and under final. James Sekulov easily won the boys' 16 and under, with Jaymon Crabb, Mark Andrijcich and Shaun Harrop making quarter-final appearances. In the lead-in tournament to the Shell Age, Drake-Brockman had also won her final, while Craig Civich, Harrop and Jaymon Crabb reached semi-final positions. Andrijcich and Jed Gould made the quarter finals, with the latter coming close to upsetting the number one seed, Dejon Petrovic, from South Australia.

At Glen Iris, the slow surface troubled some of the Western Australians, although Harrop reached the semis and Crabb the quarters. In the feed-in section, Adriana Szymonik made the semi-final. The other three players, Christina Ladyman, Jeremy Bogue and Mark Williams lost in the early rounds in both the lead-in and the major tournament but gained valuable experience, including an opportunity to train with the Victorian state squad at the National Tennis Centre before the tournament.

Paul McNamee and Siobhan Drake-Brockman, Tennis and Sun Protection

Drake-Brockman did not travel to the Glen Iris tournament. This situation arose because for the seventh year in a row, the MJTA had sent national junior teams to compete in Europe and Asia and in August 1992, in company with Annabel Ellwood (ACT) and Reneé Reid (NSW), she was a member of the Australian girls under-14 team in the World Championship played in Tokyo. Under manager Janine Thompson the team finished runner-up to the strong United States side. A few months earlier, Drake-Brockman had also toured Europe in an Australian team. This success, led the Women's Sports Foundation of Western Australia to use an action photograph of her to publicise a major objective of the Council; to increase women's participation in sport.

In November 1993, there was further demonstration of her promise with her performances in the World Youth Cup. Under a headline 'World Honours Drake-Brockman' (*West Australian*, 20/11/1993, 96) the report stated:

> *Teenage tennis star Siobhan Drake-Brockman has confirmed her status as one of the world's leading juniors helping Australia to victory in the under-16 NEC World Cup in New Zealand.*

Drake-Brockman and Annabel Ellwood (ACT) had won their singles rubbers to gain an unbeatable 2-0 lead against the United States in the final at Wellington. Once again Drake-Brockman had called upon her reserves to defeat leading American Stephanie Nickitis in the first match. She won the first set 6/2 but dropped the second 5/7 before regaining control in the decider to win 6/2.

Earlier, in 1990, Drake-Brockman had demonstrated her potential by winning the Australian Twelve and under singles title played at the Corinthian Park club. Although it could be contended that she was advantaged by playing at home on grass, her performance showed she had an excellent temperament. Despite her youth she had nevertheless been exposed to many of the pressures of tennis. Her mother, Jan, was a ranked player in the 1960s and her older sisters Tracey and Marnie had already been in several state junior teams and members of an 'A' grade pennant team at Nedlands and later at Hensman Park. Both were also to win the South West Championship at Bunbury, which was much nearer to their Donnybrook farm. Determination was an attribute that she and her sisters had acquired. It was significant that in winning her first women's senior title in Western Australia, the 1992 Spring Championship at Sorrento, she came back from being a set down in the final to defeat circuit player Joanne Faull from South Australia. She also won in three sets in the semi-final against State senior team member Stephanie Martin. Further proof of Siobhan's development came in the spring of 1994 when, as a 'wildcard' entrant, she defeated the former national number one Rachel McQuillan in the final of the Port Pirie Women's Classic. In January 1995, Siobhan joined Lesley Hunt (twice) and Jenny Byrne as Western Australians to have won the Australian Junior Girls Championship. At the same Flinders Park venue she reached the second round of the Grand Slam singles at the Australian Open.

Another young player who made her initial mark in the national under-12s was Angie Marik. When she reached the 14 and under age group in 1989, after a series of very good performances that included a McDonald's national lead-in tournament victory, she became one of the few Western Australians to gain number one ranking for her age group. She was a regular recipient of McDonald's assistance for interstate experience and was selected for national junior overseas tours, including the Australian World Youth Cup team. By the time Marik won her first senior title in Western Australia, with victory in the annual spring Metropolitan Hardcourt in 1991, she was a seasoned traveller on the junior scene. Thus, during the McDonald's sponsorship period it became more difficult to claim that one of the reasons why champion players had not been produced in Western Australia was due to lack of competition at the national level.

Nevertheless, an unexpected source of assistance, heightening the prospect of producing a champion from the West was the arrival in Perth of Wimbledon doubles champion Paul McNamee. Although his primary objective, commencing in the Christmas period of 1988, was the organisation of the Hopman Cup mixed doubles tournament, he was to conduct regular elite squads. He regularly consulted with the State Coach and Tennis West officials to ensure that his contribution was integrated with the conduct of the McDonald's squads.

By 1994, there had been further rationalisation of the McDonald's program. Throughout the State there were some 80 'development' squads. Five State 'talent' squads were operational in addition to a 'State' squad. Under the guidance of Geoff Masters, the Director of Coaching, and professional John Thorpe, Megan Roper (15), Catherine Rinaldi (14), Tate Roberts (14), Lachlan Menzies (14), Matthew Kirk (15), Jeremy Bogue (14) and Mark Williams (15) had been the promising players selected for more intensive training and interstate opportunities.

The McDonald's assistance remained significant. By 1993/1994 the *WALTA Annual Report* showed direct funding of almost $80,000 dollars. Of course some of the money that flowed to the benefit of Western Australian tennis was being drawn from the national fund. And from 1985-1986 it became obvious that many of the functions previously the responsibility of the Junior Development Committee were being carried out by the McDonald's Board. It was therefore decided that the term 'Junior' should be replaced in the title by 'Schools'. But it should not be assumed that the junior scene can be totally described under the McDonald's banner. The renamed 'Schools Committee' continued many of the programs which had historically been set in place and introduced new measures. As well, the schedule of interstate teams competitions was continued.

Schools development, coaching and junior interstate teams

The two main responsibilities of the Schools Committee, long chaired by Eric McManis, were the conduct of the annual Schoolchildren's State Championships and the School Teams competition. The major sponsor of the Schoolchildren's Championship was McDonald's, with regular further backing from Masters Dairy and the ANZ Bank. The Schools competition was given much support from the Rural and Industries Bank (later BankWest). And the John Horman Agencies (Dunlop/Slazenger) provided assistance for many years.

The Schoolchildren's Tournament continued to be played in the vacation period in August or September. Catering for the championship remained the province of the Women's Auxiliary. For several seasons the championships were centred at the Manning Club which regularly used the nearby courts at the Trinity and Aquinas Colleges and Curtin University. Two-way radio was utilised and the draws and times for play programmed on computer. In 1993, however, the venue was the Sorrento club. Chris Warren, another valued volunteer who had chaired the organising committee for many junior tournaments at the Belmont club, was again in the chair assisted by Mary Hicks. The latter, as wife of the Tennis West President, Alan Hicks, continued her goodwill role as a tennis volunteer.

The Association's links with the rest of the world, arising from the incumbent State Coach's West German connections, bore fruit when 15 juniors from Germany played in the 1989 McDonald's Schoolchildren's Championship. As in the past, there was close monitoring of the entrants and total entries, concern being regularly expressed at the low number of girls participating in nearly all age groups. In 1990, in order to increase the number of matches, it was decided to introduce round-robin qualifying matches in selected events. In some cases, seeded players also played round robins to decide final seeding positions. To maintain and even increase the number of entrants, it was necessary to provide the maximum number of opportunities for the competitors. Tournament play meant a commitment in time for the children as well as their parents or guardians. This time had to be used productively, as the study demands of school environments were becoming increasingly competitive.

The Schools Teams competitions remained under the jurisdiction of the WALTA. After many years of attempting to organise these competitions before Easter and regularly conflicting with club tournament requirements, it was decided in 1992 to transfer the dates to October and November. At the same time it was decided to play the contests under the title of the Rural and Industries [BankWest] Schools Classic. To increase interest, a presentation ceremony was conducted, members of the participating teams in each final receiving gold and silver medallions engraved with references to the sponsors (including a reminder to 'Be Sun-Wise').

The premier event of the Schools Classic continued to be the Slazenger Cup. In the girls section Penrhos College, under the tutelage of champion senior Lyn Cooper had a run of four victories. At this time (1983-1987) three regular state junior players Julia Ledder, Angela Jacka and Michelle Phillips, combined into a strong team assisted at times by capable performers Dale Stronach (Pizzey Cup), Debbie Casey, Jenny Parmley, Melissa Feeney and Cathy Bray. Between 1989 and 1993 Mercedes College also had a sequence of wins with Mrs Beryl Byrne as coach. It had very even teams with players such as Jo-Anne Quinn, Kadina Szymonik and Adriana Szymonik, Natasha Vahala, Angela Chmielewski and Kirsten Butcher. In fact, Mercedes narrowly missed six straight victories, as in 1988 it was defeated by St Hilda's by one game after Karen Vahala and Natasha Vahala had won the first two singles encounters. Although St Hilda's had two Pizzey Cup representatives in Marnie Drake-Brockman and Fiona Lonsdale it was supporting members Sarah Booth and Danuta Butler who made a significant contribution to victory.

Some of the boys' Slazenger Cup finals brought together an array of promising players. In 1986 Hale School, represented by Mark Leuba, Damien Kestell, Michael Simkovic and Grant Chadwick, had a tight victory over Christ Church Grammar School's David Culley, Darren Patten, Paul Kilderry (who was only 12) and Paul Sawyer. A year earlier the result had come down to sets when Hale School narrowly defeated Guildford Grammar. On this occasion, Hale had Mark Hepburn (whose talents were soon to be lost to AFL football) as its top player but he was beaten in straight sets by Guildford's formidable Carl Turich. At that stage, Turich was a nationally-ranked junior, with outstanding prospects for the future. As Hale had won in 1984 with Hepburn, Justin Johns, Damien Kestell, Eugene Simkovic and Justin King, it meant that the school celebrated three consecutive wins.

Some schools invariably performed well in most of the teams events without necessarily winning the historic Slazenger Cup. For instance, in 1989 Aquinas College won the Mursell Shield Division 1 and 2 as well as both divisions of the primary schools Academy Plate. In 1989, Northam High School reached the final of the second division of the Herbert Edwards Cup. The willingness of Northam to enter teams in the schools competition was pleasing from a WALTA perspective but the statistics indicate that only a minority of government schools participated. In the girls' section of the Slazenger Cup, the trophy had not been won by a government school since 1976 and 1977 when Melville Senior High School was successful. In the boys' section, there had been a long break from 1964 and 1965, when John Curtin Senior High School was the shield winner, to 1992 when Duncraig Senior High School dramatically won by two games from Aquinas. The Duncraig team of Shaun Harrop (a Colgate Cup semi-finalist), Scott Perry, Scott Utley and Matt Osborne appeared destined for a narrow loss to the Aquinas combination of Tim Hammond, Vincent Sutisna, Jed Gould and Sam Sewell until there was a dramatic 'turnaround' in the third set of final doubles rubber.

Hale School's performance was later exceeded by Trinity College, which won the Slazenger Cup from 1988 to 1991. Trinity College's inaugural Cup victory had been in 1983 when leading juniors Damian Messer and Phil Hinton were in the team. The later sequence of victories was due to players who were prominent in the junior scene such as Graeme Cox, Marcus Edwardes, Bernard Carney, Tim Fanowrios, Mark Andrijcich and Robbie Firns. These players were also prominent in the Corr Cup which was conducted on Saturday mornings between the major boys metropolitan private schools.

Although the trend in schools throughout the nation was to withdraw from interschool fixtures in favour of weekend club competitions, it should be noted Western Australian Government Schools Sports Association

Pizzey Cup Winners 1990
Back row; Anthony Lewis, Michael Rogers, Jason Scott, Narelle Cox, Angela Green
Middle row, Alan Gooch (Manager), Adam Howard, Bernard Carney, Donna Blackwell, Narelle Kimpton, Erica Martin, Glynis Barber (Manager)
Front row, Shane Orton, Marcus Edwardes, Paul Fairchild (Captain), Stephanie Martin (Captain), Angie Marik Elissa Burton,

(WAGSSA), supported by the Education Department, continued to maintain a tennis sub-committee to organise interschool matches. In 1990, some 50 schools provided tennis opportunities for their students. The Ministry of Education also endorsed a program 'Advantage Lynwood'. At Lynwood Senior High School, in Perth's south-eastern corridor, selected students were given the opportunity to pursue excellence in tennis in conjunction with their normal subjects. Erica Heron and Stephen Doyle, of the school's physical education department had developed the concept in consultation with specialists from Tennis West and the Corinthian Park club.

A particularly significant role played by WAGSSA, in cooperation with WALTA, was the continued conduct of the school interstate teams Pizzey Cup and the individual Colgate Cup. In 1990, this fixture returned to Perth, the main venue being the grass courts at the Mount Lawley Club. With the advantage of home courts and highly-competent and experienced managers Alan Gooch and Glynis Barber, the home State won its first Pizzey Cup teams event title. Four girls Donna Blackwell, Elissa Burton, Narelle Kimpton, and Stephanie Martin gained selection in the All Australian Honour Team. As the remaining members of the girls' section (Angie Marik, Angela Green, Narelle Cox and Erica Martin) were strong performers it is clear why they dominated the points. In the boys' division Paul Fairchild, Shane Orton and Anthony Lewis gained All-Australian honours. They were supported by solid performances from Adam Howard, Michael Rogers, Jason Scott, Bernard Carney and Marcus Edwardes.

Some notable performances were also recorded in the Colgate Cup. Stephanie Martin, the girls team captain, won the final in three sets from her team-mate Donna Blackwell. A Colgate Cup victory had eluded Western Australians since Jenny Byrne had been successful nearly a decade earlier. In 1987, Michelle Phillips reached the final at Penrith (NSW), but lost to future Youth Cup representative Kerrily Sharpe (NSW) in straight sets. Despite this she was selected in the All Australian honour team. In 1994 Sarah Stanley, who in the same season was able to win the women's singles title at the Western Suburbs tournament in Sydney and the Spring Championship at the local Sorrento Club, reached the Colgate Cup final and was selected in the All

Australian honour team. Colgate finals have eluded Western Australian boys but several have gained All Australian honour team selection.

The Pizzey and Colgate Cups were for upper secondary school students, but many of the initiatives in schools tennis from the mid-1980s focused on primary students. In 1986, an Aussie Sports program was inaugurated as part of a national strategy to increase and diversify sports preparation in the last three years of primary school, as an introduction to organised sport. Funded by the Australian Sports Commission (a statutory authority since 1985), the concept involved modifying adult-sized games such as tennis. There was cooperation between the Western Australian Aussie Sports director John Dimmer and Bruce Durston and Eric McManis of the WALTA, where similar ideas had been tried six years before. Sets of rules were published with figures from the Department for Sport and Recreation indicating that some 50,000 primary school children in the eight to 10 age group were said to have participated in mini tennis-Aussie Sports by 1992 (*Westennis*, February 1992, 1). The program was even incorporated into an Expo at Carnarvon for School of the Air students.

"Fun tennis' Pat Roach (Sorrento) at a young age

In late 1991, another scheme 'Ace Tennis', previously known as 'Mini-tennis', was launched in Western Australia as part of a national strategy to provide children with a lead-in to organised tennis. This was a fun-based, skills-oriented program aimed at those six or seven. The fun aspect was based on research that indicated that enhancing children's participation in sport partly depended on the enjoyment factor. Easy-to-follow resource materials, including structured lessons for various age groups, made it easy for teachers and parents with no tennis background to administer the program.

Another opportunity program which had the blessing of Tennis West was known as 'Oz Tennis'. This unique tennis charity created by Paul McNamee had its beginnings in Melbourne as early as 1983, expanded to New South Wales in 1987 and was launched in Western Australia in 1990. The aim was to take tennis to groups which might otherwise not had the opportunity to play the game. The program provided coaching, included the provision of racquets and balls, free to schools designated as disadvantaged by the Ministry of Education and the Catholic Education Office. These schools included three in Broome (including the La Grange Mission), one in Bunbury, one in Collie and the remainder in the Perth metropolitan area. In September 1991 the program was expanded to include a wheelchair group run by professional coach Alan Hartley on courts at Curtin University. By 1994 the program was active in 57 schools, including 17 in country regions from Broome through to Esperance.

TENNIS

GIVING DISADVANTAGED KIDS A BETTER SHOT

The funding for Oz Tennis came from a variety of sources, including Shell and Tennis Australia at the national level. In Western Australia, Paul McNamee, in his role as President of the Oz Tennis Foundation (with support from Chris Johnstone) allocated proceeds from the Hopman Cup Ball to assist. Tennis West also contributed by assisting clubs to conduct an Oz Tennis Awareness Day, with the monies raised going to the project. Moreover, at the Oz Tennis Charity Ball held at the Burswood Resort in October 1990, the administrator, Julie Fernandez, announced the establishment of the Michael Thorpe Memorial Scholarship. As mentioned Michael Thorpe, who had represented Western Australia in the Linton, Reid and Pizzey Cup, lost his life in a road accident in 1990. The purpose of the annual scholarship was to provide private coaching for the most improved student in each group participating in the year's Oz program.

In October 1992, Oz Tennis President Paul McNamee launched a coaching scheme with students from Clontarf Aboriginal College. *Westennis* (April 1989, 30) had previously described how officers from the Ministry for Sport and Recreation's Aboriginal Sports Unit had taken part in a special tennis coaching program conducted by John Whitton from Tennis West and Gavin Plows, the coach at Mosman Park. The Higgins Park club had initiated a scheme to encourage Aboriginals to play tennis. Club member, Ron Hall, with the help of a Sport's Instant Lottery grant and strong backing from Victoria Park MLA Dr Geoff Gallop, was a prime mover for this project (*West Australian*, 2/9/1992, 111).

Of special significance to expanding the base of tennis in Western Australian primary schools was the 'Tennis in Schools Programme', which began in late 1991. Funding emanated from the Health Promotion Foundation of Western Australia. Known as 'Healthway' this organisation had been established by Parliament of Western Australia under the controversial 1990 Tobacco Control Act to administer funds for the arts and sports which had been derived from a tax on tobacco sales. Although there was some controversy about the likely benefits to sport the $209,300 three-year grant to Tennis West for the program helped allay fears that tennis would not benefit from the legislation.

Additional funding for the scheme was provided by the Cancer Foundation of Western Australia, which introduced an accompanying health message, 'Protect Yourself From the Sun'. Michelle Phillips was appointed as the inaugural Coordinator. She was a State Grade player and graduate of the Human Movement Department at the University of Western Australia. Many 11-year-old (year 6) students, particularly those living in less affluent suburbs, were not being exposed to tennis. The 'Tennis in Schools' grant aimed to alleviate this problem. Arrangements were made for the initial clinics to be held indoors at the Claremont Showgrounds. The children were to be trained by professionally accredited coaches, at no cost, except for transport, which the participating schools were to meet. Racquets and balls were supplied as part of the program. It was recognised that the cost of a racquet represented a financial outlay of considerable proportion for children with unemployed parents or those on the average salary or wage (Stoddart, 1986, 39). A follow-up lesson was then conducted by a professional coach at the school's courts, or those nearby. Teachers were encouraged to participate in Level 'O' coaching courses. To help them develop further, a resource booklet, with 20 step-by-step lessons, was published. This included references to the need to encourage students to join local tennis club to begin playing tennis either competitively or socially.

An evaluation of the Tennis in Schools Program was a condition of the Healthway funding: by the end of the first year, over 3,800 students from 95 schools had participated in the coaching sessions and the Cancer Foundation of Western Australia's 'Be Sun-Wise' educative promotion. Survey statistics indicated that some 60 per cent of students who attended the sessions had not received any previous formal tennis coaching. Some 84 per cent of the respondents regarded tennis as a fun game, although surprisingly 44 per cent indicated they did not enjoy watching tennis on television (Phillips, 1994, 34-35). The assessment of the program indicated considerable satisfaction with its presentation (Phillips, 1994) eventually resulting in Healthway granting a further $202,700 for 1995 and 1996. It was apparent, however, that Tennis West still faced challenges in attracting young children to tennis, which Australian Sports Commission studies indicated was highly rated by youth, particularly girls (*Sport for Young Australians*, 1991, 17).

The extent to which special prizes provide an incentive to junior participation is often difficult to gauge. In August 1994 the entrants for the mixed doubles Hyundai Junior Challenge competed for 12 days intensive training at the Hopman Camp in Florida. Reports indicated that the new dimension resulted in quality tennis. The fortunate winners were promising state juniors Kelly Gray and Ashley Dyer. To maximise the benefit of this experience for the players they were accompanied by former champion Lesley Hunt, nominated by Tennis West for the 1994 Quit Coach of the Year Award.

The incentive of an overseas trip also arose with Western Australia 'representing' Australia in the Colgate-Palmolive International Junior Tennis championship conducted in Singapore. The opportunity to convert the proximity to south-east Asia to an advantage, regularly espoused by governments, was being realised by Tennis West. For instance, in November 1994 a team to Singapore comprised of Cameron Fenner, Tim Morgan, Susan Brayshaw and Stephanie Edwardes was managed by State League Player John Campbell. Fenner won the under 11 section while Morgan was the victor in the under 12 division. Morgan, with keen tennis playing parents (Helen and Peter) from the Nedlands Club, had earlier gained top Australian ranking after meritoriously winning a national singles title.

The 1987 Margaret Court Cup winners
Back, Margaret Court, Erica Martin and Andrea Mitchell
Front, Angie Marik and Kerrie Thomas

Some programs developed at the club level also helped to broaden the tennis base. Mention has already been made of the reasons why the Sorrento club had won the McDonald's 'Club of the Year' Award. *Westennis* (February 1992) described how the Higgins Park tennis development coordinator Ron Hall had been awarded the inaugural Vaughan Glare Community Services Award for his formulation of the Victoria Park and districts primary schools team tennis competition. A careful plan was devised to encourage children to visit the club and receive quality coaching under the direction of Tom Luttrell leading to match play. Ultimately it was hoped that the children would became club members and participate in Tennis West pennants and tournaments.

The attempts to plan broader participation in tennis by primary-school students did not lead to Western Australia joining the interstate east coast Bruce Cup competition which had a similar format to the Pizzey Cup but was restricted to primary-school pupils. Clearly the costs of such a venture, even with the advent of cut-price air fares, was too formidable. Tennis West continued to participate in the interstate junior teams events although back in 1982 it had baulked and voted at the national level against the introduction of the 12 years and under competitions known as the Margaret Court and Rod Laver Cups. Many questions had been raised about the possibility of undesirable outcomes of intense competition at this age. In 1990, it was controversially decided not to field teams as the quality of the prospective players did not appear to warrant the cost.

The 1990 Margaret Court Cup winners
Debbie Thomas (Manager), Bonnie Scott, Siobhan Drake-Brockman, and Monika Sekulov

Ironically, however, it was in the 12 and under age group that success twice came to Western Australia in the Margaret Court Cup. In 1987, Andrea Mitchell, who was soon to become prominent in Tennis West administration, managed a winning team at the Adelaide carnival. The team members were Angie Marik and Erica Martin (who combined to be runners-up in the 12 and under national doubles), and Kerrie Thomas. Easily forgotten, at the same venue, with the boys only able to finish sixth, was Blake Brinklow's performance as runner-up in the Australian 12s singles championship.

Wilson Cup winners (1993 competition) From left, Kerrie Thomas, Angie Marik, Jeff Schneider (State Coach), Lesley Hunt (Manager) and Siobhan Drake-Brockman

Three years later, with the rare advantage of the Western Australian representatives playing on home soil at Corinthian Park, the Margaret Court Cup was returned to the West when Siobhan Drake-Brockman (winner of the national singles title), Monika Sekulov and Bonnie Scott were victorious. On this occasion the manager was Debbie Thomas, a prominent coach and 'A' grade player for Corinthian Park, who often conducted squads for the McDonald's program. For the previous under-12 carnival in Melbourne, Debbie Thomas, had managed the Margaret Court Cup team in company with husband Geof who was in charge of the Rod Laver Cup team for boys. Both Debbie and Geof were to win awards for their professional coaching endeavours.

The next victory in the Cup competitions came in December 1992 in Adelaide, when Western Australia won the Wilson Cup for only the second time. Siobhan Drake-Brockman was a member of that team, as were Angie Marik and Kerrie Thomas. The competition was extremely close, with two other States in the running to win the Cup on the final day of competition. At this stage the experience of manager Lesley Hunt helped steer the Western Australian girls to victory.

Although there were no further Cup victories in the junior age groups between 1985 and 1993, there were some very good results; one of the most notable was second place in the 1987 Linton Cup carnival in Sydney. With State Coach John Fairchild as manager, the team included Carl Turich, Johan Anderson and Neil Prickett. Anderson had begun his tennis training in the Swedish junior tennis program before emigrating with his parents to Australia. Turich and Neil Prickett were products of the intense drive in Western Australia to produce players with national standing and were colleagues at the Australian Institute of Sport. They won the 1986/1987 Australian Closed Doubles title and were chosen as members of Australian Overseas touring teams. Anderson, too, had been a member of the victorious Australian Youth Cup team in September 1987. The strongly built Turich became a member of the BP Achievers squad, which was aimed at assisting promising juniors in their transition to circuit play. Ultimately, though, Turich decided against pursuing a professional tennis career and even ceased tournament play in Western Australia. Anderson, who later moved to Sydney remained on the circuit for much longer. Meanwhile, Prickett, after competing on the local tournament scene was soon to be lost to the domestic tennis scene when he began playing and coaching in Germany.

Before moving east, Anderson was eligible to play for Western Australia in the 1988 Linton Cup. Playing in Sydney, and again managed by State Coach John Fairchild, Anderson teamed with Darren Patten and Mark Leuba, to take second place. Patten and Leuba later elected to stay in tennis in the West and become top ranked senior players for many seasons. Patten, with a fine physique, had some very good circuit wins while Leuba, with 'great touch', began to establish his name as a prominent local coach.

In the 1991 Linton Cup, played in Adelaide in late 1990, Western Australia was once again runner-up. Managed by new State Coach Jeff Schneider, the team was strengthened by the inclusion of the much-travelled Paul Kilderry. As he had been living in Canberra, as well as in the United States, there was some uncertainty about his eligibility to represent Western Australia. With Kilderry were Marcus Edwardes and Anthony Lewis, both of whom had been able to obtain some sound results in their junior age groups; in 1990 Edwardes had achieved a national ranking of seven in the boys 16s age category.

Tabulating Kilderry's credentials in junior ranks would be a formidable exercise. He invariably had a high national (and often ITF world ranking) throughout this period. Some highlights included winning a national 14s junior championship, reaching the semi-finals in singles and doubles in the 1991 Junior Wimbledon and the finals of the national 18s and Australian Open Junior doubles. As far back as 1985, Kilderry was a member of the Australian team that played in the International Tennis Federation Sport Goofy Trophy (world 12 and under title) at Disneyworld in Florida. Partnered by Jamie Holmes (NSW), Kilderry was runner-up in the doubles event, losing 9/8 in a rain-shortened match. Even at that early stage Kilderry had a very pleasant disposition, which was recognised with a special sportsmanship award at the event.

Paul Kilderry, National Junior Champion before graduating to the ATP circuit

In Perth for the January 1986 Australian 14 and Under Championships, Kilderry was the runner-up to Holmes in the singles but both shared the doubles title. The newspapers, and even *Westennis*, made much of the so-called 'Kalgoorlie connection'. This focus had arisen for two reasons. Firstly Rob Kilderry, the father of Paul, had been a prominent junior in Kalgoorlie before moving to Perth to be in three consecutive Linton Cup teams (1958, 1959, 1960) and then pursuing a coaching career. Secondly, the winner of the girls Australian 14s title was Emma Peetz, whose mother Kim Blackburne, was also from Kalgoorlie and had national success as a junior. Moreover, an aunt, Jan Blackburne, who learned her early tennis at Kalgoorlie was a member of the Wilson Cup team in 1958 and 1959, when Rob Kilderry was representing the State. A further link, not documented in the articles, was the earlier presence in tennis of Rick Kilderry, who was Rob's brother. Rick had a junior ranking in the late 1950s.

In 1987, Paul Kilderry had the distinction of winning the Australian 14s singles and doubles and this was followed with selection in the Australian 14s European tour. In early 1988, he attended Nick Bolletieri's Tennis Academy in Florida before travelling with the Australian 16s team to Europe and then being offered a scholarship to the Australian Institute of Sport. He then graduated to the ATP circuit and began to improve his ranking. In mid 1994, as proof of his senior credentials, he celebrated a victory over Patrick Rafter in the Tokyo Indoor Tournament. The latter had quickly risen to be one of Australia's top players with several victories over the world's top professionals.

The record of the performances of each interstate team is incorporated in the detailed reports prepared by the respective managers. In 1991, following the sad death of Karen Bucens only a few weeks after her twenty-first birthday, the Tennis West Executive resolved to remember her dedication and determination with an annual award to the best team member in a female state team. As President Alan Hicks said 'the criteria to be taken into account are those most exemplified by the late Karen Bucens - sportsmanship, demeanour, co-operation, team involvement and giving all for the best performance for WA' (*Westennis*, December 1991, 23). The inaugural award went to Adriana Szymonik, playing in the number two position in the 1992 Reid Cup carnival in Burnie, Tasmania. Ironically this team was managed by Kerryl Chute who had also managed the 1986 Reid Cup team in Adelaide when Karen Bucens (along with Christine Foy and Michelle Phillips) had played courageously and with considerable success. Kerryl Chute, who was also Karen Bucens' State Grade captain for several seasons at Hensman Park, likened Adriana to Karen 'as a determined player who gave everything when playing for WA'. A similar judgement could be cast on Siobhan Drake-

The 1986 Reid Cup Team in Adelaide, the scene of some of Karen Bucens' best efforts Back (left toright): Kerryl Chute (Manageress), Michelle Phillips, Christine Foy, Karen Bucens, and Arthur Marshall (Manager) Front (left to right): Pablo Campillos, Darren Patten and Mark Leuba

Brockman and Stephanie Edwardes who were respectively the recipients of the Karen Bucens' award in 1992 and 1993.

Other avenues for interstate team tennis were sometimes available in the universities and the Catholic Tennis Association. Although outside the jurisdiction of the WALTA, they were often afforded the Association's blessing. The Catholic Tennis Association held regular interstate carnivals and university students had the opportunity to play in the annual Intervarsity Summer Games. In 1992 the University of Western Australia won the women's team event for the first time since 1945 with a team captained by Yvonne Ball, an 'A' grade player and interstate representative. Other members, several of whom were regular shield players, were Karlene McIntosh, Adrienne Mansell, Ingrid Mansell, Jenny Grove, Jasmin Sallen, Siobhan Longshaw and Sue Melville. At the end of the carnival Ball and McIntosh were selected in the All-Australian Universities team.

Representing Western Australia could also take another form, although not in a designated team. The Tennis Professionals Association continued to organise the Milo Little Masters Tournament which, until 1991, was used to determine which group of junior players was to represent Western Australia in the national Milo Little Masters. The aforementioned Karen Bucens was twice a member of the Western Australian contingent, which was managed by a local professional coach. Many other promising juniors benefited from participation in these tournaments, but national titles were rarely achieved. In 1989, the pattern of unexceptional performances was broken, with Stephanie Martin defeating Donna Blackwell in the 16s final and Angie Marik winning the 14s title. Two years later, Siobhan Drake-Brockman also succeeded in winning the 14s tournament.

In 1984, the national Little Masters tournament provided a prominent junior, Jodie Bottrill, with the opportunity to tour New Zealand. The Little Masters, attracting some 500 entries, was perhaps the major public focus for the tennis professionals. In the 1987/1988 season, this group revamped its constitution, became an incorporated body and changed its name from the Tennis Professionals Association to the Tennis Coaches Association of Western Australia (TCAWA). This avoided confusion with the touring professional group (the Association of Tennis Professionals) and also better reflected the educational role of the Association. One of its major objectives was promotion of the National Coaching Accreditation Scheme and encouragement of clubs to employ TCAWA members when making their appointments. A number of annual awards to recognise leading coaches and outstanding contributors from an educational, scientific, entrepreneurial or marketing perspective, to the development of tennis was another TCAWA initiative. Unless a coach produces an international champion, his or her expertise is rarely acclaimed, so it was fitting that, from 1984, acting on a suggestion attributed to Arthur Marshall, the following Annual Awards were made:

Yvonne Ball (right), pictured here with leading Cottesloe team-mate Vanya Kelleher(Courtesy The West Australian)

Coach of the Year **Most Improved Coach** **Major Contribution**

Rookie Coach-Level O Award

	Coach of the Year	Most Improved Coach	Major Contribution
1985	Maureen Smith	Rob Murton	Dr Bruce Elliott
1986	Maureen Smith	Ian Walker	Jeff King
1987	Arthur Marshall	Keith Hince	Helen Muir
1988	Maureen Smith	Robert Prouse	Gaye Wearne
1989	Geof Thomas	Pauline Boothey	Lillian Lake
1990	Peter Collier	Stuart Clarke	Arthur Marshall
1991	Rob Casey	Gabrielle Ahern-Malloy	Debbie Thomas
1992	Ian Walker	Peter Holmes	Dr Bruce Elliott
1993	John Campbell	Marnie Drake-Brockman	Keith Hince

A stimulus was given to the coaching scene through a five-week visit to Western Australia by the highly qualified former Western Australian anatomy and biomechanics lecturer, Gundars Tilmanis, from Oregon. This took place in early 1988, as part of the Bicentennial Alcoa Coach-in-Residence Scheme. While the program was aimed at achieving long rather than short-term benefits, through sessions with accredited professional coaches, a wide range of tennis groups in both the city and country was fitted into a busy agenda Tilmanis, widely known as 'Til', created a strong impression with his knowledge and innovative techniques, and was reported (*Westennis*, October 1988, 270) as being convinced that 'WA tennis can go places, the weather is so nice all year and the opportunity for tennis development is here' (*Westennis*, August 1988, 14).

Annual Awards Evening for the Tennis Coaches Association of Western Australia (1991)
Left to right: Sponsor Dennis McInerney (McInerney Ford), with Debbie Thomas, Rob Casey and Ian Walker

Keith Hince, recognised for his major contribution to the Tennis Coaches Association

Resident professional coaches in Western Australia knew very well that the weather, particularly the wind, was not always conducive to the development of better tennis. The TCAWA, with its limited resources, had done its best, in its relatively short history, to be a positive influence on the improvement of tennis in the State. Through the medium of *Westennis*, articles written by TCAWA members have educated readers on many aspects of tennis, including training, tactics, psychology, line-calls and diet. TCAWA members are now welcome as Directors of Tennis West and have become eligible for election to the State Selection Panel. Only the role of Chairperson of Selectors is denied to full-time professional coaches. It is a far cry from the great divide before open tennis.

Overseas opportunities for some juniors also arose from TCAWA member Paul McNamee's desire to ensure that the Hopman Cup made a meaningful contribution to local tennis. Donna Blackwell and Stephanie Martin were nominated in mid-September 1989 to attend the Harry Hopman International Camp, by courtesy of Mrs Lucy Hopman, at Tampa, Florida. They were provided with intensive training and competed in an international junior tournament before returning to Melbourne to play in the McDonald's national championships.

In the following September, Angie Marik and James Sekulov received scholarships to spend a fortnight at the Hopman Camp. Both had successful seasons that had won them places in Tennis Australia junior team tours to Europe. Sekulov had been a member of the 1992 Australian World Cup team which competed in Barcelona. In 1993, he made headlines when he moved into the top 10 on the world junior tour after winning the Indonesian International Junior Open. As Sekulov set out for an official Australian two-month tour of Europe, tennis writer Gary Stocks (*West Australian*, 27/4/1993, 91) commented that this, 'rising young tennis hopeful James Sekulov is fast emerging as the best male player produced in this state'. Later, in recognition of his performances, Sekulov was to win the 1993 Junior Sportstar of the Year.

By 1992, it had been decided to extend the mixed doubles concept to a 16 and under youth tournament. Each State and Territory selected a pairing, with the preliminary rounds being played at Hensman Park and the finals at the Burswood Superdome. Siobhan Drake-Brockman and James Sekulov, who were chosen for Western Australia, added more honours to their records when they combined to win a gripping final against the Australian Capital Territory, represented by Annabel and Ben Ellwood. Drake-Brockman had an impressive singles win but Sekulov lost in three tight sets. However, the West Australians took the tourney after the mixed doubles win against the brother and sister Ellwood combination.

News of the Western Australian victory was accompanied by an announcement that the Junior Hopman would go international, with an initial invitation to Asian teams (*West Australian*, 31/12/1992, 59). It was another example of how Tennis West was benefiting from the entrepreneurial drive of Paul McNamee. A few weeks earlier, there had also been a press release indicating that the Western Australian Institute of Sport (WAIS) and Tennis West would jointly fund the conversion of two courts behind the Perth Superdrome on University of Western Australia land from grass to clay. McNamee had long lamented the lack of clay courts in Perth. Under the joint funding arrangement it was expected that he would conduct a WAIS squad of talented juniors on these courts (*West Australian*, 18/12/1992, 88).

The international flavour of the junior Hopman Cup was duly achieved. Teams from Indonesia and Thailand competed in 1993 but the winners were Cindy Watson and Michael Logaro representing Victoria. In 1994, New Zealand and South Africa also competed when Western Australia surprised some critics by winning the final against New South Wales. Western Australia's two team members, as had been the case in 1993, were Siobhan Drake-Brockman and Jaymon Crabb. During 1994 Drake-Brockman's status as one of the world's leading juniors had been confirmed but Crabb had steadily improved to rise to number two in national age group ranking after winning the Australian Lead-In Clay Court Championship in early October. Both competitors were described as role models for aspiring juniors but there were doubts the pair could win a crucial mixed doubles rubber despite the fact that Crabb had previously won a national junior doubles title with Dalkeith's Craig Gibson. Yet as Burswood Dome singles matches unfolded Drake-Brockman was convincing against Renee Reid with a 6/1, 6/4 scoreline and Crabb lost to Wojtek Stasiak, who had been impressive in the preliminary matches at the Sorrento Club. This meant the trophy was decided by a 6/3, 6/3 victory to the Western Australians in the mixed doubles.

Angie Marik and James Sekulov, both received a scholarship to attend the Harry Hopman Camp in Florida

The Hopman Cup

As early as 1984, the potential of a 'World Mixed Team Championship', combining aspects of the Davis Cup and the Federation Cup, had been discussed between Australian tennis circuit friends Charlie Fancutt, Paul McNamee, and Pat Cash. Upon McNamee's retirement from the circuit, it was decided in consultation with Fancutt to mount the event, which was to be conducted on the Gold Coast or in Perth. McNamee was to be the Tournament Chairman and Fancutt the Tournament Director. At the end of the 1988 Australian Open, Cash (the 1987 Wimbledon champion) agreed to spearhead an Australian team and Mrs Lucy Hopman wholeheartedly endorsed the proposal to dedicate the event to her late husband, the legendary Davis Cup captain.

To help secure Perth's selection as the venue, EventsCorp, an arm of the Western Australian Development Corporation, agreed in April 1988 to underwrite the event, which was to be managed by Paul McNamee Enterprises (PME). Within a month arrangements had been made with Burswood Resort Casino to spend over $3 million to transform the Burswood Superdome into an indoor tennis venue. A contract was also signed with television company TVW Channel 7, which predicted the Hopman Cup would be 'the glamour event of Seven's Summer of Tennis'.

At the Tennis West Council, however, there were concerns that the Hopman Cup would be a 'one day wonder'. Would Tennis West receive a reasonable tournament fee? As the Christmas holiday period had, for many years, been reserved for the City of Perth Tournament (sometimes also designated as the State Open), would this event have to be downgraded in status? Would Tennis West be forced to alter the dates for the City of Perth? And above all, was Tennis West losing control of its own destiny?

As it transpired, the Hopman Cup proved a formidable success. Apart from stimulating tourism, it created widespread public interest in tennis and made an immediate and positive impact on the tennis community in Western Australia. An important factor was the quality eight-team field that McNamee and Fancutt secured. On the first day of competition Cash and Hana Mandlikova represented Australia against Jeremy Bates and Sarah Loosemore from Great Britain in front of 5,000 spectators. Almost 7,000 people attended the match between Australia and West Germany, with Steffi Graf, the current world number one, making her debut in Perth. For the final between Australia and Czechoslovakia, a crowd of 7,500 watched the inaugural Hopman Cup being won by Olympic gold medallist Miloslav Mecir, and Helena Sukova.

At the launch of the second Hopman Cup, McNamee announced that 12 teams would compete, prize money being increased by 40 per cent from $250,000 to $350,000. Following this news came the announcement of a further two-year commitment from the major sponsor, the Swan Brewery (Swan Gold) and host sponsor the Burswood Resort Casino. Ticket sales escalated with the news that John McEnroe and Pam Shriver would lead the United States challenge. However, in the final played on New Year's Day, 1992, Spain became the second nation to win the Hopman Cup when brother and sister combination Emilio and Arantxa Sanchez Vicario respectively won both singles against McEnroe and Shriver. The latter were left to display their great prowess in doubles.

As the tournament grew in stature, Tennis Australia, in March 1990, officially sanctioned the event. In the third Hopman Cup, Western Australians had the opportunity of watching the locally reared champion Elizabeth Smylie (Sayers) play for her country. The total attendance for the week was some 63,000, with a sell-out crowd of 8,500 watching star Monica Seles and the tenacious Goran Prpic win the final for Yugoslavia against David Wheaton and Zina Garrison from the United States. Seles had won 6/1, 6/1 but Prpic took three hard sets 4/6, 6/3, 7/5 for his victory.

In March 1992, McNamee announced that the Hopman Cup was to remain in Perth for the next five years. The first of these Cup fixtures was given a boost when it was announced that Boris Becker and Steffi Graf would represent Germany. Surprisingly, despite being reared in neighbouring towns, they had not played mixed doubles together. Unfortunately, Graf became ill during the tournament and had to default to Czech opponent Helena Sukova in the semi-final. Boris Becker was able to defeat Karel Novacek in the men's singles which had become the second match in the Hopman Cup format. With Graf unable to recover the 'untried German' combination lost to Sukova and Novacek in the mixed doubles. Graf's illness was sufficiently serious for her to return home and miss the Australian Open.

Meanwhile there were more semi-final shocks when Manuela Maleeva-Frangiere and Jakob Hlasek, representing Switzerland, were victors over the Spaniards Emilio and Arantxa Sanchez Vicario. In the final, the Swiss pair, although only seeded at four, were able to clinch the Cup with convincing straight set singles wins over Sukova and Novacek from Czechoslovakia.

The next Hopman Cup, conducted between 2 and 8 January, 1993 drew over 70,000 spectators, with a capacity house of 8,500 people on each occasion that the drawcard, Germany, was in action. Seeded number one, Germany was represented by reigning Wimbledon champion Steffi Graf and former Wimbledon singles winner Michael Stich, and proved too strong in the final against Spain's entertaining Emilio and Arantxa Sanchez Vicario. Earlier, Stich was beaten in the quarter-final by the promising Andrie Medvedev from the Ukraine and then narrowly defeated Guy Forget of France in a third set tie-break to seal victory in the semi-final. An early surprise was Australia's win over South Africa. Wally Masur and Nicole Provis, playing in their first

Hopman Cup for Australia, both produced fine performances to defeat their more highly-ranked opponents Wayne Ferreira and Amanda Coetzer.

The sixth Hopman Cup conducted between 31 December, 1993 and 7 January 1994 at what had been renamed the Burswood Dome, promised record crowds as John McEnroe and Olympic Games gold medallist Jennifer Capriatti, were engaged to represent the United States. Injuries, however, forced both players to withdraw from the team. This provided Ivan Lendl with the opportunity to play his first representative match for his adopted country. But he, and partner Mary Jo Fernandez, were easily defeated in the first round by the German team of Bernd Karbacher and Anke Huber. Germany reached the final but lost to the number one seeded combination, Petr Korda and Jana Novotna from the Czech Republic. The winners shared a cheque of $200,000. Korda had just won $2.5 million for his epic Grand Slam Cup victory and Novotna had also received the runner-up prize to Steffi Graf in the dramatic Wimbledon singles final.

One historic development associated with the Hopman Cup was the trial of an electronic line call system designed and made by Tennis Electronic Lines (TEL). The TEL system is, in effect, a ball tracking system. When the specially made metal-loaded tennis ball is close to the line, data is processed by computers to provide an IN or OUT decision. An audible beep sounds if the ball is no more than 30-40 centimetres out and all information is immediately relayed to the chair umpire's hand computer which also doubles as score book and stopwatch. Frenchman Cedric Pioline's racquet contained a substance that inadvertently triggered the beeper while the central umpire occasionally missed calls that were beyond the antennas buried beneath the court's surface. Most critics, however, judged the initial Hopman Cup trial to be most successful experiment, with the likelihood that 'TEL' will be used in future Grand Slam events (*Sunday Times*, 9/1/1993, 88). Significantly, the 'TEL' system was again employed for the next Hopman Cup. Nevertheless, despite speculation, it was not immediately adopted for Grand Slam fixtures.

Another feature of the sixth Hopman Cup was the need to upgrade security for the 12 competing teams. The injury incurred by Monica Seles, stabbed in April, 1993 by a spectator during a tournament in Germany, shocked the tennis world. Although the crowds at the Hopman Cup series rose to a record 75,000, partly due to Wally Masur and Nicole Provis reaching the semi-final for Australia, there were fortunately no incidents that caused concern. Nevertheless, the total attendance figures did not receive a significant impetus from the National Club Doubles, a joint venture between Pepsi Hopman Cup, Tennis West and the Perth City Council played between 28 and 30 December, 1993. Despite the incentive of a Hopman Cup ticket for nomination, in addition to an opportunity to play on natural grass at one of Perth's historic tennis locations, the response was disappointing. Perhaps the local tennis community had already become accustomed to preserving Hopman Cup time to watching world class tennis rather than competing at the social or tournament level. This view is supported by the observation that the City of Perth Championship, regularly conducted in late December, was not held because no club considered it would be viable.

In late 1994 when the National Cup Doubles was conducted at the Nedlands Tennis Club, the entries were even marginally lower than the inaugural occasion. Although the round-robin tournament was excellently conducted, and highlighted by outstanding performances from competition regular Isla Green and Leederville veteran Hedley O'Neil, the forthcoming Hopman Cup captured the media attention. Nevertheless, the marketing of the seventh Hopman Cup held between 31 December 1994 and 7 January 1995 provided Director Paul McNamee with some real difficulites. Powerful serving Goran Ivanisevic, who was one of the drawcards to represent Croatia, was suspended in November for eight weeks after a flare-up in an ATP Championship event in Frankfurt. To allay some of the disappointment at being precluded from the Hopman Cup, Ivanisevic undertook to play an exhibition charity match in Perth during the Cup. Fortunately, too, at the eleventh hour the 1994 Wimbledon champion Conchita Martinez agreed to anchor the Spanish team. With Boris Becker and Anke Huber representing Germany, Petr Korda and Jana Novotna defending their title for the Czech Republic and Pat Cash making his 'fourth' comeback, the field did ultimately have spectator appeal.

In the first round, Pat Cash played well to defeat South African Christo van Rensburg and then combined expertly with Kristine Radford (Australia's number one woman player at the time) to win the mixed doubles to advance Australia to the quarter finals. As expected, Australia was then defeated by the Czech Republic although this rubber was highlighted by competitive play by Cash in a narrow loss to Korda. The Czech Republic then suffered a semi-final loss to the brother and sister combination of Andrie and Natalia Medvedev representing the Ukraine. Eventually, though, the top seeded combination of Boris Becker and Anke Huber, before a 9,000 capacity crowd, proved too strong with exciting three set singles victories in the final. It confirmed McNamee's assessment that the seventh Hopman Cup would be highlighted by many close encounters.

A major advantage of the Hopman Cup is its predictable date. This facilitates ticket sales and supporting activities. The Hopman Cup New Year Ball at the Burswood Convention Showroom has gained a place on the social calendar and most of the stars appear with more than 500 members of the tennis community regularly taking part. The occasion is used to conduct an auction in aid of the Variety Club of Australia and the Oz Tennis Foundation. The Women's Sport Foundation also conduct a Hopman Cup Breakfast, the State Players Development Trust, a Hopman Cup afternoon tea and Tennis West have a range of associated functions. Whenever, too, a Davis Cup fixture is held in Perth it usually generates a range of activities connected with tennis. However, it is difficult to predict when Perth is to host a Davis Cup tie, even though, like the Hopman Cup it draws spectators far in excess of any Tennis West tournament, including the State Open.

The Davis Cup

A Davis Cup final in Australia invariably captures the interest of the sporting public and, on exciting occasions, even the general public is likely to be aroused. The 1986 final between Australia and Sweden, as in 1983, gave a temporary stimulus to Australian tennis. In 1983, Australia had won without a player ranked in the top 30. Three years later, the team that defeated Sweden had its highest-ranked player, Paul McNamee, at 42 on the ATP list. This was against an opposition that had Stefan Edberg, Mats Wilander, Mikael Pernfors and Anders Jarryd hovering around the top ten in the world.

When Perth was allocated the Davis Cup tie between France and Australia in February 1990 Australia again faced a situation in which its players were lower on the computer rankings than its opponents. And on this occasion Pat Cash was under an injury cloud whereas in 1986 he had been on the rise, with an epic five-set victory over Pernfors, a portent of his 1987 Wimbledon triumph. Nevertheless, even without Cash, Tennis West moved quickly to increase the seating capacity at the picturesque Royal King's Park grasscourt venue, for it was known that the French team would include the highly-ranked and entertaining Yannick Noah and Henri Leconte.

Tennis Australia had warned local officials to cater for about 40 to 50 media personnel, but the huge wave of interest in the tie saw the list of accredited media representatives nearly double. Capacity crowds watched three days of gripping tennis, with Wally Masur emerging as the Aussie hero. After Darren Cahill had lost the opening rubber to Leconte in straight sets, Masur displayed determination to defeat Noah in a three-hour battle that went to five sets. Grand Slam doubles expert John Fitzgerald then combined with Cash to win the crucial doubles encounter against Forget and Noah. On the final day, it frequently seemed that Leconte had Masur's measure, but the Australian eventually prevailed in the midst of controversy when some very close line calls went against the emotional Frenchman.

In the so called 'dead rubber' between Darren Cahill and Yannick Noah, the crowd was entertained in an unusual manner when two ball boys, Jed Gould and Julian Beaumont, were given the opportunity to indulge in a doubles match with the Davis Cup stars. One spontaneous rally, which featured 37 shots, brought the packed stands alive. This reference to the ball boys and girls is a reminder of the voluntary support personnel, both young and old, who are necessary to successfully mount a Davis Cup tie. Professional coach Jeff King and leading player Robyn Lamb were given credit for once again coordinating a proficient group of youngsters for these duties.

The band of line umpires was organised by Steven Stanley, who was becoming a regular in this important facet of the presentation of major events. Another key figure whose help for all important fixtures at Royal King's Park had been greatly appreciated came from head groundsman Bernie Pugh. As the curator at King's Park, like his well known predecessor Bill Cross, it was Pugh's style to perform other duties apart from the expert preparation of the courts. Behind the scenes for this (and other ties), were people such as Dot Connolly, Peg McFarlane and Lucy Nussbaum in the ticketing and gate sub-committee; Estelle Ironmonger in charge of transport, Nancy Cornish the ushering and Anthea McGrath the catering.

Within 12 months (in February 1991) the same volunteers, and numerous others, were again called into service when Tennis West was allocated the first round tie between Australia and Belgium after South Australia had declined an option for the event. This provided a challenge to promote an entertaining event with lower-profile opponents from Belgium. Australia, represented by Wally Masur and Richard Fromberg in singles and supported by Darren Cahill and Todd Woodbridge in doubles, had a convincing five rubbers to nil 'whitewash'. The organising committee reported a 'great result in financial and promotional terms with great support from the media and the public' (*WALTA Annual Report*, 1990/1991).

It was not expected that the Belgium team of Eduardo Musso, Filip Dewulf and Libor Pimek would win the tie. Belgium's top player, Musso, an expatriate Argentinian, was ranked 127 in singles and 137 in doubles on the ATP computer. While Musso did not win a Davis Cup rubber, he did leave a distinctive mark on Western Australian tennis when he won the 1991 City of Fremantle Singles Championship during the Australia Day long weekend. A

Royal King's Park groundsman Bernie Pugh (right) who performed duties in addition to the expert preparation of the courts. Pictured here speaking to Davis Cup captain Neale Fraser. On left is Ian Barclay, at the time, the coach of Pat Cash.

year earlier, the City of Fremantle title had been temporarily designated as the State Open title after six months of unsuccessful searching for a sponsor 'and some trauma with the television industry' (a problem not experienced with Davis Cup ties) (*WALTA Annual Report*, 1989/1990). From the mid 1980s, the State Open caused frequent and vigorious debate for the Association as it tried desperately to give the event premier (or at least significant) status in the Western Australian and Australian tournament calendars.

State Opens

Given the widespread concern about the Open, it was decided to make some radical changes by mounting a men's only non-ATP points tournament at a separate location and time from the women's event. In fact, the 1985 men's open was played prior to Christmas 1984 at Royal King's Park while the women's open was conducted after Christmas in conjunction with the City of Perth Championship at the Cottesloe club.

The decision to play the men's and women's event at different venues, giving the former more funding and focus, was questioned particularly since the State Labor government of the day had recently introduced equal opportunity legislation. The revamped Commonwealth Bank $30,000 32-player men's draw did not generate the losses that had been anticipated, partly because of a growth in sponsorship assistance. Yet, despite attracting one of the best fields in the history of the Open, with many preparing for the Australian Open the following week, the poor attendance was disappointing.

The eventual 1985 winner and first Swede to win the Western Australian Open, was Stefan Edberg with an easy 6/2, 6/4 scoreline over Californian Scott Davis. For Edberg, at 20 years, it was only his second senior tennis title. At the time he was marketed 'as the only player to have won the Grand Slam of junior singles'. Within a fortnight, though, he won the Australian Open and thereafter remained one of the superstars of men's tennis.

Edberg was prominently featured in the publicity for the next two Western Australian Opens. Perhaps less newsworthy was his solid victory in the 1987 Open final, when he easily defeated American Dan Goldie in straight sets.

However, in the 1986 Open (played in November 1985) Edberg sensationally lost in the first round to Roger Grant, at that stage the number one ranked player in Western Australia. The drama that was to unfold was not apparent when Edberg won the first set 6/2 with comparative ease. Grant then changed his tactics from attempting to match Edberg with power to making better use of his ability to vary the pace of the game in the windy conditions. As the 24-year old Grant was quoted as saying '... I tried to mix it up and did not want to allow him to slot into a groove' (*West Australian*, 21/11/1985, 128). This enabled Grant sensationally to take the next two sets to win the match. Both were tie-breaks, which meant that Grant won the match without breaking Edberg's powerful kicking serve.

The post mortem, reported by leading tennis writer Gary Stocks under the heading 'Grant Storms Back to Upset Edberg', revealed that Edberg had arrived in Perth at 5 a.m. on the day of the match and was suffering from influenza. As Grant conceded:

> *It was pretty difficult for Edberg ... he travelled half the world to play here and I thought he would have problems adjusting to the heat after playing most of his recent tennis indoors.*

Regardless of the circumstances it was a big win for Grant, a left-hander, often called 'Chipper' because of the way he often chipped the ball before storming the net. He had experienced the trials and tribulations of the circuit (which he left in October 1985) after having had to play against leading players at a disadvantage in terms of accommodation and practice conditions. Controversially posted to an outside court for the next round, Grant could not continue as a 'giant killer' in the tournament, which was won by another and was Swede, Jonas Svensson, who defeated Tasmanian Simon Youl in an epic 6/7, 6/3, 7/6 struggle. Thus Grant was to remain a member of the notable group of number one-ranked Western Australian men including Rob Casey and Gary Penberthy, who were not able to win their home State's Open. But Grant did twice (1987 and 1988) win the State Closed Championship. Gary Penberthy on one occasion, as well as Chris Johnstone and Brad Properjohn, were also able to wrest this title from Rob Casey who had almost a mortgage in the late 1970s and early 1980s on the State Closed Andy Fanowrios Memorial Trophy.

Another memorable performance in the Western Australian Open was given by Grant in the doubles final of the 1991 event, which was played at King's

Roger Grant, state number one who defeated Stefan Edberg in November 1985. (Courtesy The West Australian)

Mark Leuba, gifted volleyer

Mark Hlawaty, colourful personality

Park in November 1990. Although the singles final was won by American John Simpson from Sandon Stolle in three sets, the doubles was a 'cliffhanger' with Grant and Paul Kilderry defeating David Culley and Mark Leuba in a gripping contest, coming back from the brink of defeat in the tie-break (0/5) in the third set to take the title.

The Western Australian Opens for 1988, 1989 and 1990 titles, even in the men's division, were relatively low profile events. Other tournaments in the calendar were also necessarily designated the Western Australian Open to maintain the historical significance of the event, giving some local players the opportunity to win the Association's premier title. The 'champions' in this category were Brad Properjohn, Darren Patten and David Culley.

In winning the City of Perth at Hensman Park, the tall, powerful Brad Properjohn took the 1988 State Open with his victory over Rob Casey (6/3, 6/1), the former number one in the West. In the doubles, Properjohn partnered Kurt Robinson in an exciting win in three tie-break sets over Roger Grant and Barry Tognolini 6/7, 7/6, 7/6. A year later, when the City of Perth was conducted by the Leederville club the Open was claimed by Darren Patten with a straight-set victory against Robinson. Then, in late January 1990, the speedy Culley defeated the evergreen Casey 6/4, 6/4 in the Fremantle Championship and was also presented with the State Open George Linwood Memorial Championship trophy.

The three 'dual' titles were important in the Western Australian context, but they were a far cry from the 'dual' Western Australian and Australasian Opens of 1909, 1913 and 1921. There was a view in some quarters that it would have been fitting for Casey, as one of the best performing men in the history of State tennis (demonstrated by eight State Closed titles) to win the Open. However, at Fremantle in 1990, Culley was too good on the day and was a worthy Open winner. This tournament was interrupted by poor weather, forcing the organisers to play some of the 'Open' events on a 'first to nine games basis'.

The Executive at Tennis West strove to reinstate the Open, giving it a position on the Australian circuit. Some success was achieved with the 1992 and 1993 Opens, which were played in early December of the preceding years. Supported by the Commonwealth Bank as major sponsor, Alexander Park, with a host of new amenities, took the responsibility of conducting its first fully-accredited Western Australian Open. Under the leadership of Ian White, the club had developed a dynamism which made it a suitable venue for the State's most historic tournament.

The men's draw for the 1992 tournament comprised mainly local players although the number one seed was Andrew McLean from Victoria. However, McLean was beaten in the semi-final by gifted volleyer Mark Leuba. The latter was consistently in the finals of local tournaments with the Champion of Champions, State Hardcourt, Spring Championship and City of Perth titles to his credit. Yet the lack of some old fashioned luck may have denied Mark Leuba the chance of an Open singles title. After winning the first set 6/3 and leading early in the second, an unlucky call on a point to give him a service break appeared to shift the momentum of the match with Darren Patten then securing the final two sets at 6/4 and 6/3. Leuba was to gain some consolation when he teamed with friend Darren Patten to defeat Mark Hlawaty and Scott Marshall in the doubles 7/6, 7/6. The colourful Hlawaty, rapidly making a mark on tennis in the West, must have also wondered if luck had deserted him for in the singles quarter-final against Darren Patten as the latter won

7/6, 1/6, 7/6. It seems, though, that losing tie-breaks is evidence of 'bad luck', but winning them is depicted as 'courageous good play'.

During 1990 Darren Patten was added to the Tennis Australia BP Achievers Squad by the Tennis Australia selectors to join Shane Barr, Neil Borwick and Jamie Morgan. His good performances also warranted his being given a 'wild card' into the 1990 Australian Open. For the 1993 Western Australian Open at Alexander Park, Darren Patten was also given a wildcard for a championship that drew a comparatively strong international field. On this occasion Darren Patten played splendidly, losing in the quarter-finals, to the eventual winner, American Kent Kinnear, in three sets. In an earlier round, Darren Patten had shown his class by defeating Mark Petchey, the number seven seed and English Davis Cup player.

Darren Patten, selected in the National BP Achievers squad

For the 1994 Men's Open, played at Alexander Park (in December 1993), the promising James Sekulov was given a wildcard entry. However, Sekulov along with other Western Australians were not able to make an impression in the draw which included drawcard Jamie Morgan. Yet, the final, sponsored by the Commonwealth Bank, was played between South Australian David Adams and German Peter Moraing. Adams, who had been the runner-up a year earlier, was to win 6/3, 7/5. As this was Adams' first Challenger title it posed a dilemma for him as to whether he should concentrate on singles and possibly place in jeopardy his number seven world doubles ranking with Russian Andrie Olhovsky (*West Australian*, 6/12/1993, 75).

In December 1994, the Open returned to the historic Royal King's Park venue. A feature was the extensive publicity given to the men's Challenger singles event. The first shock was the defeat of the number one seed Jamie Morgan. Local favourite Paul Kilderry played well to hold his seed to reach the semi-final before losing to the eventual winner Jan Kroslak. The athletic Kroslak played 'an irresistible brand of tennis' to score a convincing 6/1, 6/2 victory in the final against the 1992 champion Kent Kinnear (*West Australian* 12/12,1994, 82). Meanwhile, promising juniors Mark Philippoussis and Ben Ellwood went a step further than the previous year when they won the doubles title against Wayne Arthurs and Neil Borwick.

Earlier, in 1987, Alexander Park had conducted its first Western Australian Open title event when its City of Perth Championship for women was given the dual status. This was part of a sequence of State Opens for women which were also known as the City of Perth Championships. In order, these championships were played at Cottesloe (1985), Scarborough (1986), Alexander Park (1987), Hensman Park (1988), Leederville (1989) and Fremantle (1990). Of course, it did provide an opportunity for Western Australians to win what is known as the Perpetual Trophy. The list of victors provides a tabulation of the best women players in the west during those years: Jenny Byrne (1985), Christine Dorey (1986 and 1988), Robyn Lamb (1987 and 1989) and Paula Parentich (1990).

When Byrne won the 1985 Magic Toyota State Open (and City of Perth) as a seventeen year old, tennis scribe Gary Stocks described her as an 'exciting young prospect' (*West Australian*, 31/12/1984, 43). In a tournament marred by rain, Byrne proved too strong and consistent in the final for a gallant Lamb with a 6/1, 7/5 scoreline. The first set took only 23 minutes, but the second set went with serve until the eleventh game when Byrne achieved the vital breakthrough. Lamb had been back in Perth on vacation after a year on scholarship at the University of Oklahoma.

Jenny Byrne, state number one and Federation Cup representative

While Robyn Lamb continued in the college system in the United States, Byrne gradually made her name on the professional circuit. In 1985, before leaving junior ranks she was runner-up in the 1985 Junior Wimbledon, then won the Australian Open junior singles and doubles in December of the same year. She had also reached the third round at Wimbledon and won selection in the Australian Federation Cup team. Some of this success may not have come Byrne's way (as she appeared to have temporarily fallen out of favour with the national selectors) but for support from the Western Australian Institute of Sport (WAIS) which enabled her to participate at Junior Wimbledon. In 1987, after she won the Karen Krantzcke Memorial Award (who had tragically died of a heart attack in 1977 at 30), the national selectors included her in the BP Achievers squad, which had been broadened to cater for talented young women, after having operated for some years for promising young men (*West Australian*, 15/8/1987, 201).

In July 1987, Byrne teamed with Nicole Provis to form the winning Australian team in the Annie Soisbault under-20 years competition. Later, she was selected to play Federation Cup and, in 1992 was in the Australian women's team for the Barcelona Olympic Games. Byrne was not the first Western Australian woman to gain this honour as Elizabeth Smylie (Sayers) won a bronze medal (with Wendy Turnbull) for women's doubles at the 1988 Seoul Olympics. As Byrne matured in senior ranks, it was in doubles (like Smylie) that she collected most of her titles.

In terms of the Western Australian Open, Jenny Byrne also won the trophy for 1992 when she easily defeated Kate McDonald (Victoria) 6/2, 6/4. The tournament was also designated as an ITF tour event. This had ensured a strong draw as was the case with the 1991 Women's Open held at Royal King's Park when Rennae Stubbs (NSW) surprised with an easy 6/1, 6/1 final win over Kristin Godridge from Victoria. Byrne was not an entrant in 1991 or on other occasions (particularly in 1984 and 1989), when either injury or tour commitments prevented her participation.

When the 1986 CSA Credit Union WA Open was played in conjunction with the City of Perth at Scarborough, Byrne reached the final and was expected, as the number one seed, to cruise to victory. However, Christine Dorey (Matison), at 34 caused an upset, to defeat her 6/4, 6/4 with sound, determined play. It was a triumphant win for the veteran, who was hampered by an injured left ankle. Despite her domination of the State Closed Clarrie Mallett trophy with 12 titles, it was Dorey's first WA Open singles title.

Remarkably, though, it was not to be Dorey's last Open for she secured victory in 1988 when she employed her guile in the final to easily defeat Natalie Crutchley 6/2, 6/3 after maintaining her mastery of Lyn Cooper in the semi-final. Even in the 1992 and 1993 Opens, Dorey was still a dangerous player, taking both Stephanie Martin and Donna Blackwell to three sets. By this time Dorey achieved another elusive goal, being selected in an Australian team for the veterans 1992 Young Cup teams event in Dublin.

Another player who figured prominently in several Opens was Robyn Lamb. An athletic player with a fine service, she won the 1987 final in three sets against Karen Bucens, was narrowly beaten by Natalie Crutchley in the semi-final the following year and had another victory in 1989 at the Leederville club against the emerging Donna Blackwell. Competing against an excellent field in 1992, she reached the semi-finals before losing to Jenny Byrne, the eventual winner. A year later she lost the semi-final in a third set tie-break to Stephanie Martin, the number one seed.

During these years Robyn Lamb was invariably formidable in doubles. In 1987, in combination with Kerryl Chute, she narrowly lost a tight three-set match against doubles specialists Lyn Cooper and Judy Lange from the Nedlands club. In 1989, Lamb was the titleholder in combination with Natalie Crutchley, who was also a very strong doubles player. Significantly in the *WALTA Annual Report*, which includes tabulations of the winners of the tournaments, the name of Robyn Lamb during this era appears frequently in the women's doubles and mixed doubles listings. During her time at Oklahoma State University, Lamb was able to achieve a high doubles ranking (*Westennis*, February 1985, 29).

Christine Dorey (Matison), one of the State's great players with an imposing record

Less prominent in doubles contests, but a fine performer in singles was the 1990 Open winner Paula Parentich. Although not a powerful player, Parentich had an excellent command of tactics. In addition, she was extremely fast around the court and had great determination. In her only win in the Open, she demonstrated her application on a surface favoured by her opponent, Robyn Lamb, with a 7/6, 6/4 score when fittingly the tournament was played at Fremantle. Paula's father, Dr Tony Parentich, a keen observer of Paula's play, had been a prominent South Fremantle footballer in his youth. Paula, too, had learnt her tennis in the Fremantle district, where she lived and attended Santa Maria College.

Before attending Law School at Murdoch University, Paula Parentich played club tennis in West Germany. She was a splendid tournament performer, recording many victories in each of the championships on the calendar, beginning with the State Hardcourt title at Esperance in October 1984, when she narrowly defeated Lyn Cooper. On four occasions she won the Champion of Champions and was twice the State Closed winner. Her record as a shield match player for Blue Gum Park and then Alexander Park was also formidable. In the 1992 Shield match final, she was outstanding against Jenny Byrne, the seasoned circuit player.

Parentich's period of local dominance in the second half of the 1980s was challenged by the trio of fine players namely Stephanie Martin, Donna Blackwell and Narelle Kimpton, who had benefited from the McDonald's program and had travelled to West Germany under State Coach John Fairchild. In 1989, with Parentich in Germany Blackwell had reached the final of the Open but lost 6/3, 6/0 to Lamb. While Kimpton, Martin and Blackwell each won a State Closed title, the first of the trio to win the Open (in November 1993 at Alexander Park) was Kimpton when she defeated Martin 6/2, 3/6, 6/3. In the semi-final, Kimpton employed her powerful forehand for a 'fighting' three-set victory against the athletic Blackwell. In fact Kimpton had shown courage in the first round to secure a three set victory as she was down 1/4 in the second set after losing the first to promising schoolgirl Siobhan Drake-Brockman. A year later, Kimpton again showed pluck when she won another Open title with a hard earned victory over Martin in the semi-final and a tight win (7/5, 3/6, 6/4) over Fiona Lonsdale in the 'Be Sun Wise' final. The play of left-hander Lonsdale, in the biggest match of her career, impressed observers (*West Australian*, 6/12/1993, 75). Of course spectators also recalled how Fiona's parents, past champion Keith Lonsdale and Judy Lonsdale, had been prominent in Western Australian tennis circles.

Robyn Lamb, aggressive player with a powerful serve. Top flight doubles player with two State Open singles victories to her credit

The following season, Fiona Lonsdale could not repeat her feat when the 1995 Open was played at her home club of Royal King's Park (in December 1994). Instead another bright prospect emerged when Sarah Stanley, at 17, became one of the youngest players to win the final against her Wilson Cup

Paula Parentich, speedy, determined player who had an excellent command of tactics

teammate Darja Voltnerova. And tennis writer Gary Stocks was to observe (*West Australian*, 12/12/1994, 82) how Fremantle's Stanley, 'has the game to go places and the Commonwealth Bank Open was the ideal place to start'. Although Stanley's promise was salutary, officials were concerned about the small draw of less than one dozen women competitors. For the second year in succession no championship doubles could be played because of the low number of entries.

One of the outstanding doubles combinations was Lyn Cooper and Judy Lange (Kozak). They were renowned for their rapport on court, which helped them to utilise effective tactics. They went close to creating a record in the Open after winning three consecutive titles. However, they were thwarted in the fourth final when they were defeated in 1988 by their keen rivals Christine Dorey and Denise Shevlin (Cole). In the 1930s Myrtle Herbert and Mary O'Mahoney paired for four Open titles, although these were not consecutive victories. In total Myrtle Herbert won seven Open doubles championship trophies while Mary O'Mahoney (Prindiville), despite the intervention of the war years, still won six Open doubles titles. The combination of Miss Ruse and Mrs Constance Blackmore won five titles before the 1914-1918 World War.

In terms of doubles achievements, the pinnacle for a Western Australian was reached by Elizabeth 'Liz' Smylie (Sayers). She married her current coach Peter Smylie in 1984 and moved to Sydney. In July 1985, 'Liz' teamed with Kathy Jordan to win the 1985 Wimbledon crown with a surprising victory over the legendary Martina Navratilova and Pam Shriver. Until that juncture, the latter pair had established a streak of over 100 winning matches. On two further occasions (with Betsy Nagelson in 1987 and with Kathy Jordan in 1990), Smylie proved her great skill in doubles reaching the Wimbledon final. In fact, with Jordan 'Liz' won some dozen titles, including the prestigious Virginia Slims event (*Westennis*, February 1991, 28-29)

In the year of her Wimbledon triumph, Smylie and John Fitzgerald were also runners-up in mixed doubles, losing to Paul McNamee and Martina Navratilova in a memorable encounter. In 1991, she won at Wimbledon in the mixed doubles, partnering John Fitzgerald, with whom she had won the 1983 mixed doubles at the United States Open. The latter title was also won by Smylie in 1990 in combination with Todd Woodbridge. Her fine serve and volley and powerful forehand equipped her for such achievements.

After Smylie had spent several years accumulating major titles, representing Australia in the Federation Cup and Olympic Games and becoming the first Western Australian to win three Sportsman of the Year (1984, 1985 and 1990) awards, she was invited to play for Australia in the Hopman Cup. Tennis West arranged a function to acknowledge her achievements and to present her with a montage of photographs depicting some of her greatest successes through junior to senior ranks. Earlier, Smylie had returned to Perth with Nicole Provis, John Alexander and Mark Edmondson to play an entertaining doubles match to mark the official opening of the Mount Claremont Superdrome, on 22 November, 1987 by the then Premier Brian Burke. Her participation in a number of McDonald's squads was widely appreciated. Apart from her achievements in doubles, she managed to reach the top 20 computer ranking in singles, recording wins over many of the great players in women's tennis. In Australia she had been ranked as high as number two while in Western Australia she reached number one.

Elizabeth Smylie (right), a great circuit doubles player. Won the 1985 Wimbledon doubles crown with Kathy Jordan

Given her international commitments, Smylie rarely played in her home city, or represented the State in the Challenge Cup. She was a member of the Challenge Cup team in 1982 (when WA won) but, despite her absence, Western Australia performed creditably in that competition. It provided the top resident senior players with interstate experience and, it was also contended, helped to keep them in tennis. There were also a number of other competitions sponsored by various companies that gave seniors, in a range of categories, the opportunity for more 'trips'.

The Challenge Cup and other 'trips'

The Challenge Cup continued to be conducted in Tasmania, with Launceston as the main venue. In 1989, the national airline strike led to the cancellation of the event, and when it was resumed in 1990, Robyn Lamb, Paula Parentich, Donna Blackwell, David Culley, Mark Leuba and Darren Patten captured the Challenge Cup. On this occasion each State except Queensland fielded teams.

In the following year, Western Australia retained the trophy with a series of fine performances. Leuba, Patten and Kurt Robinson were undefeated in singles and dropped only one doubles rubber, to South Australia, in the final. The women's trio of the youthful Stephanie Martin, Donna Blackwell, and Narelle Kimpton was equally impressive, with Martin losing the only singles rubber to the highly-rated Louise Stacey of South Australia.

These back-to-back victories were achieved without prize money being offered. However, for the competition played in December 1992, sponsorship funds were offered to the best performing teams. An earlier proposal to incorporate a mixed doubles component in the competition was shelved, as the offer of prize money apparently provided sufficient incentive for each State to enter the round robin and so increased the number of rubbers to be played.

While victory was not always achieved, the competition provided further opportunities for many WA players who could achieve a ranking but could not go the extra step and win major titles. Vanya Kelleher, for instance, was in the 1988 team. As a junior she had competed in a strong age group and

Left to right: Stephanie Martin, Donna Blackwell and Narelle Kimpton an impressive trio

narrowly missed selection in the Pizzey Cup competition. She recorded several good wins in tournaments and State grade tennis. As shown below she finished fourth in the 1988-1989 Westpac Channel 9 Player of the Year Award. This competition continued for most seasons with prize money, but with a lower profile than when it was introduced. The situation changed again in the 1992/1993 season, when the Hyundai automobile company decided to sponsor a senior and junior Player of the Year Award. A Westpac 'player of the week', was also established in 1987/1988 and was continued until the 1992/1993 season.

1988-1989 Westpac Player of the Year Award.

Women

1.	Lisa Askey	(Higgins Park)	204
2.	Robyn Lamb	(Reabold)	156
3.	Jodie Bottrill	(Corinthian Park)	149
4.	Vanya Kelleher	(Higgins Park)	136
5.	Paula Parentich	(Blue Gum Park)	124
6.	Stephanie Martin	(Blue Gum Park)	115
7.	Donna Blackwell	(Reabold)	114
8.	Yvonne Ball	(Higgins Park)	105
9.	Karlene McIntosh	(Nedlands)	87
10.	Michelle Phillips	(Reabold)	84

Men

1.	David Culley	(Dalkeith)	229
2.	Roger Grant	(Dalkeith)	181

3.	Dean Danzi	(Higgins Park)	156
4.	Mark Leuba	(Royal King's Park)	156
5.	Darren Patten	(Hensman Park)	149
6.	Pablo Campillos	(Sorrento)	113
7.	Keith Begley	(Hensman Park)	95
8.	Robert Prouse	(Scarborough)	95
9.	Kurt Robinson	(Scarborough)	93
10.	Eugene Simkovic	(Royal King's Park)	87

The women's winner Lisa Askey, was also in the 1988 Challenge Cup team. She was always a threat in tournaments, winning in the same year both the State Hardcourt title and the Champion of Champions against keen rival Jodie Bottrill. The left-handed Bottrill was chosen in the 1987 Challenge Cup team. For many seasons Jodie played number one in State grade for Corinthian Park and was regularly seeded in tournaments. On the administrative side, she was to later chair a committee reviewing the perennial problem of poor entries in women's tournaments events and the general lack of participation of girls in sport. It is said this situation means that it is easier for a woman to make the Challenge Cup team. Perhaps players such as Erica Andersson (Smith), Glynis Barber (Mitchell), Sue Mack (Taylor), Geraldine Watson (Sayers), Denise Shevlin (Cole), Vanya Kelleher and Michelle Phillips, who were selected in various years, would not agree, as it is often argued that tennis draws most of the best women athletes.

In the men's section (arguably more competitive, if the number of competitors is the main criterion), Robert Prouse was also in the 1987 Challenge Cup side although between 1982 and 1988 he did not receive a state ranking. As a professional coach, he was a regular competitor in tournaments but had broken through in 1987 to win the Champion of Champions Trophy. While the speedy Prouse took his chance to win a major, another player Dean Danzi, prominent in the above award (and ranked above Prouse), could not achieve 'a win in a major'. Danzi, from Pickering Brook, was to be the beaten finalist (against John Campbell) in the 1986 Champion of Champions, the 1992 City of Perth Championship and the 1993 State Closed. Although Danzi was a top performer in State grade and frequently a semi-finalist in the men's championships, Challenge Cup selection proved elusive, because he was either not chosen or was away playing the circuit.

Other 'south of the river' players in the men's divisions of the Challenge Cup who had solid records in local competition were Keith Begley, Tony Luttrell, Neil Prickett and the 'quiet achiever' Lawrence Fiorentino (*Westennis*, February, 1988, 17). The last chose not to try his luck on the circuit but many local players who were Challenge Cup standard pursued their tennis either by playing various satellite tournaments or more commonly, securing coaching appointments and playing club tennis in Germany.

Tony Luttrell was one player who pursued opportunities overseas. He played college tennis in the United States and then moved to Europe. In 1983, while coaching and playing in West Germany, he won the Darmstadt Open. As a junior he had showed considerable promise and was chosen in the 1973 Linton Cup team. Between 1968 and 1976, with his twin brother Reg, he won every junior doubles title from under-10 to under-18 age groups. Later in senior ranks Tony and Reg were both successful in the State Closed Doubles Championship. Both were considered very tough competitors with Tony winning two City of Fremantle Singles Championships.

When the August 1989 issue of *Westennis* listed eleven players furthering their tennis in Germany Tony Luttrell's name was included, together with Lisa Askey, Neil Prickett, Glenn Woodward, Rob Murton, Kurt Robinson, Phil Hevron, Phil Holten, Steve Fletcher, Brad Properjohn and David Culley. Special mention was made of Robinson and Culley who had gained ATP doubles points. Prickett, who had performed well for the Neustadt club, had also achieved doubles success with Culley. Meanwhile, Glen Woodward and Lisa Askey had made particularly favourable impressions.

Back in Perth, Lisa Askey won a trip for mixed doubles competition (sponsored by the *Sunday Times* and Puma) in various regions, leading to a State final and culminating in a national final during the Australian Open at Flinders Park. Noelene Abe (Corrigin) and Mark Douthie (Hyden), from the Kondinin region, were runners-up but they were no match for Lisa Askey and Roger Grant. At the national round-robin Askey and Grant finished fourth. As Grant said 'mixed doubles is a funny game, we played some top tennis, but [we] also played some average tennis' (*Westennis*, April, 1989, 33).

The quest by Lisa Askey and Roger Grant to win the national competition in January 1988 was the second of its kind. One year earlier, Julia Ledder and Mark Tory also gained fourth place at the Flinders Park National Tennis Centre after having won the State regional play-off. At Flinders Ledder and Tory defeated the eventual winners. Both were extremely fine doubles players. Ledder, a ranked player, had a powerful forehand and, at her best, was capable of defeating any woman player in the State in a singles encounter. Tory, runner-up in the 1987 Champion of Champions tournament, was a left-hander whose swinging serve made him particularly effective in doubles.

The apparent increase in the ability of mixed doubles to attract sponsorship was evident when the Nabisco company supported such a competition as part of Tennis Australia's National Tennis Week, a 'Sport 88' event conducted to celebrate the Australian bicentennial. The mixed doubles was conducted on a club basis with the State winners playing at the National Tennis Centre in Melbourne in mid-March. Reabold combination Damien Hampson and Michelle Phillips won the State final and tickets to Melbourne, beating the Royal King's Park pair of Stuart Robinson and Jan McIntyre. In addition, Mark Leuba and Yvonne Ball, nearing the end of their careers as juniors, were chosen to participate in invitational events for singles and doubles. There were also a wheelchair tournament and a teams competition. A particular highlight was a 'legends' Davis Cup contest between Australia and the United States.

Some of the legends of Australian tennis also reappeared in the national father and son/mother and daughter competition, which ran for three years sponsored by the American entrepreneur, Victor Kiam and his company, Remington Products Inc. Throughout Australia, tournaments were played in over 30 centres. The winners then competed in State finals, leading to the national final and, eventually an international play-off. Perhaps unexpectedly, the Western Australian father and son pairing of Don and Darren Patten of Geraldton gained a trip to the La Manga resort in southern Spain at the end of February 1989 for the international final. Originally John Newcombe and his son Clint had won the Australian round, but they were unable to make the trip. So the Patten's won the right to make the trip to Marbella, Spain after they won a semi-final repechage against Victoria's Derek and Wayne Arthurs (*Sunday Times*, 21/2/1988, 124).

The Pattens won the Western Australian section a second time before John Fairchild and his son Paul defeated them. However, as Paul Fairchild had accepted a scholarship to an American University and Darren Patten had committed himself to playing satellites, it was Ken and Cameron Venables from Wembley Downs who became the Western Australian father and son team. They were, in effect, the 'lucky losers' and travelled to White City for the national play-offs. Top-flight player Donna Blackwell and her mother Kaye, also a very capable player (and contibutor to tennis), won the Western Australian division on two occasions. However, the inaugural victory for the mother and daughter competition in 1988 was secured by highly ranked Stephanie Martin and her mother Julie, also a very sound performer. For Julie Martin; as a librarian she helped to preserve the history of tennis in Western Australia.

A feature of the Remington Family Championships, the Bicentennial Nabisco Mixed Doubles and the Puma-Sunday Times Mixed Doubles was an insistence by organisers, in consultation with Tennis West officials, that country regions be given the opportunity to participate. Sponsors were anxious to avoid the claim that they overlooked the needs of rural areas. Likewise, at Tennis West, there was always an awareness of the need to avoid criticism that it was neglecting its country role. Meanwhile, Country Week, one of the biggest operations in Australian tennis, continued to be conducted during January of each year.

Country Week and country affairs

Throughout most of the period since 1985, Rex Richter had been Chairman of the Country Affairs Committee. A fine player in his own right, reaching the final of his Northam club singles championships on a remarkable 27 occasions he knew the country scene intimately. He joined the Northam Tennis Club in 1935 and, between 1942 and 1977, held every position on the club's committee, including President for a total of 13 years. In a review of his contribution after he stepped down in 1992 it was suggested that Richter 'had run a tight ship and would be difficult to replace' (*Westennis*, February 1992, 11). In appreciation of his service to country tennis and, in particular, to Country Week, Trevor Cornford, an Executive Officer with Wesfarmers Insurance Ltd, presented him with a gift on behalf of this sponsor. Wesfarmers clearly recognised the excellent administrative role played by Richter. Likewise, in December 1994, Richter's role was formally recognised by Tennis West when he was presented with a 'Gold Award' for his outstanding services to tennis (*WALTA Minutes*, 15/12/1994).

Sponsorship so necessary to maintain the scale of the operation was taken over by Wesfarmers Rural in 1987 from Elders Pastoral. However, entries for 1987, with the headquarters the Bayswater club, were down, possibly due to the America's Cup, which had filled accommodation in the metropolitan area. For its part, Wesfarmers Rural fulfilled its three-year sponsorship contract and, in 1989 agreed to continue for another three years. The team entries remained 250, whereas in 1985 and 1986 the figures were closer to 350. Difficult economic times in the rural areas were thought to explain this trend.

Katanning veteran Ros Giles kept adding to her illustrious record. She won the over 40s singles against Kay Sandilands and then combined with Joy Ducat (Fleay) in both 1985 and 1986 to win the 'A' grade teams trophy. In 1985, the final was particularly exciting, as Katanning and Kendenup were tied at three sets 24 games all before the decision was made to play an extra set. This resulted in a 6/4 win to Giles and Ducat over Jacqui Phillips and Sandilands. The consolation for Phillips was a decisive win in the singles final against Ducat.

A feature of several Country Week carnivals was the number of team and individual titles taken by tennis families. In the men's section the Pattens of Geraldton were formidable, while the Drake-Brockmans (Bunbury) were very successful in the women's section. Darren Patten won the men's singles in 1987 and Brett Patten, who gradually emerged as a leading player in the State, was champion in the 1989 carnival. In both of those years, Geraldton won the teams title, with father Don Patten a member. Jan Drake-Brockman, formerly ranked player Jan Longson, combined with her daughter Marnie to win the 1988 women's team trophy. Marnie Drake-Brockman won the women's singles in 1986, 1988 and 1994 while in 1987 her older sister Tracey took the same perpetual trophy. If mother Jan had beaten Bronwyn Fewster in the 1982 final, it would have been an even more outstanding family record. Time remains for the youngest daughter Siobhan to win at Country Week, but other challenges may prevent this happening.

Other players from Geraldton in the men's section and Bunbury in the women's also enjoyed success. Ken McCreery, Danny Bowen and Luke Ertzen (Geraldton/Spalding Park) won the team's event in 1990 and 1991, but narrowly lost to Marcus Keizer and Peter Holmes (Albany) in the 1992 final. McCreery, partnered by Peter Harris (Geraldton) lost the 1993 team final to the Albany-Broomehill team of Jeremy Muir, Peter Holmes and Max Loveridge. Unfortunately Geraldton had been weakened by an injury to Danny Bowen on the eve of the final. However, in 1994 Geraldton-Binni was again to take the title. On this occasion Danny Bowen was in the winning team as he had been in the 1989 side. Bowen had won the singles title in 1992 when he defeated Brad Rundle from Katanning. He repeated this performance in 1994 with a straight set win over Glen Hogendoorn. McCreery showed his talents when he reached the 1993 singles final, but he lost a close three-set match to Bunbury's Tim Reynolds.

Diana Thomson, also from Bunbury, whose father Andrew was a tireless worker for tennis, became the women's singles winner in 1989 and 1991. In combination with Faye Parkin in 1987, she caused an upset to win the women's team trophy. In a similar way to the Drake-Brockmans, the experience she gained in the city 'A' grade shield competition and tournaments stood Diana Thomson in good stead for Country Week. She was a member of the Higgins Park shield team beaten in the 1989 women's final by Blue Gum Park. In the Country Week singles, she had three successive epic struggles in the final with Robyn O'Brien from Wickepin. In 1989 Thomson won in three sets. A year later, in another three-set encounter, the result was reversed. As an indication of the priority sometimes given to Country Week competition Thomson had played the 1990 final only two weeks after giving birth to her first child. Moreover, Robyn O'Brien, who as Robyn Hughes originally hailed from the Reabold club in Perth, where her mother Ruth and State ranked brother Don were prominent, also had to care for very young children. Not to be denied, Thomson and O'Brien were back to contest the 1991 final, with another three-set match going to the former.

The Thomson Tennis Family. Left to right: Carolyn, Margaret, Andrew and Country Week champion Diana

The 1992 women's champion Luanne Preston, came from Frankston, Victoria, where she had played some state grade level tennis. On New Year's Eve she married a Western Australian pilot based in Carnarvon and was said to be on an extended honeymoon during Country Week. The runner-up, Joanne Smyth from York was a true Western Australian. Her father Peter Smyth was a champion player in the York district and her mother Robyn was equally well known in the Midlands as a supporter of tennis. Other children David and Melissa regularly competed at Country Week. In 1994, Melissa was the runner-up in the under-18 junior girls section.

The tenacious Luanne Preston also reached the 1993 singles final but Joy Fleay (Ducat) of Kojonup came back from the brink of defeat to win 2/6, 7/5, 6/4. The highlight of the women's division was the formidable record that top Mandurah combination Gail Podsiadlo and Ann Atkinson had accumulated. In 1995 they were to win their seventh consecutive team trophy. This easily exceeded the feat by Katanning's Ros Giles, Val Pain and Cath Ogden who from 1974 to 1977 had won four successive titles. In 1994 Podsiadlo had reached the ladies' singles final, but she was defeated by Marnie Drake-Brockman in three sets. However, part of the secret of Podsiadlo's and Atkinson's success was their splendid doubles play. This was an important factor in Mandurah's 1995 team win when Marnie Drake-Brockman won another singles title from Corrine Ford.

While Mandurah achieved a fine record in the women's 'A' grade section, the record of the traditionally strong Eastern Goldfields Tennis Association (EGTA) in the men's team section, is worthy of mention. Tony Hall and Mal Hodsdon were members of the winning EGTA team in 1985 and 1986. Phil Hevron was also in the 1986 side when it was the victor in the final. Then Hevron, in partnership with Ashley Johns, won the trophy in 1988 after having been runners-up to the Pattens of Geraldton in 1987.

The Country Week program was under continuous review. In 1991, with the impetus to mixed doubles provided by the Hopman Cup, a similar event was introduced. It proved popular for those who had been eliminated in the early rounds of the individual events. In the same year, a special city junior versus country junior match was funded by the McDonald's program. Each team consisted of four boys and four girls in the 12 to 15 age groups.

Gail Podsiadlo (above) and Ann Atkinson, formidable Mandurah pair who gained the team trophy record at Country Week

The Shell Junior Coaching Schemes, introduced in the 1961/1962 season, continued. The January Country Week squad for juniors, under the direction of leading coaches was included. Shell funding was also used to enable coaches to visit country centres for junior clinics. In addition, annual Shell live-in camps for country juniors at nominated metropolitan boarding schools were part of the program. Funds from the State Government were also used for junior development and, between 1982 and 1987, RAC Insurance had sponsored a number of programs in support of the development of junior tennis in rural areas.

For seniors, the annual City versus Country fixture was contested for the Perpetual Cup. In 1985, the size of the combined men's and women's team was doubled from six to 12 men and women. Rounds of men's doubles, women's doubles and mixed doubles were played, with the outcome being determined on a sets and games basis. Generally conducted on the Sunday preceding the beginning of Country Week, the Cup invariably attracted some lesser-ranked competitors in the over-35-years category (a group who gave fine service to tennis), in addition to the main contingent of leading players, many of whom had played metropolitan 'A' (State) Grade or other shield divisions.

Shield tennis/State league (and the 35 years and above seniors)

The conduct of the Shield competition continued to be an integral facet of the Association's activities. Its structure and operation was monitored and regularly modified. At the helm as Chairman of the Shield Match Committee throughout the 1985 to 1993 period was Peter Barrett. He had the capacity to conduct the Herculean task with 'an air of ease'. By the summer season of 1991-1992, over 550 teams (amounting to over 2,300 players) were competing each weekend. There had been a pleasing increase in the junior sections, which since 1986-1987 had operated with 18 and 14 and under age groupings after the intermediate 16 and under category was discontinued. There had been a noticeable growth in the veterans sections, although they were largely wedded to summer grass court tennis. The number of winter teams has varied between 130 and 140 a year. To ease the grading nightmare, Barrett advocated an American rating system, under which all players within a club could be given a grade, ranging from 1.0 (a complete beginner) to 7.0 (a player competing with some success on the international circuit). The details were published in *Westennis*, December 1987, 39, and *Westennis*, March 1988, 26-27. However, the classification was not universally adopted by the affiliated clubs.

In 1990, an Executive sub-committee chaired by Brian Bracewell, assisted by Barrett, Wayne Firns, Sue Heath and Harry Phillips, was established to report on, and make recommendations for, the conduct of the various shield series. This followed the debates in Council during 1989 about the restructuring of the summer calendar. Submissions were sought from club secretaries and pennant supervisors, the Women's Auxiliary, the Tennis Professionals Association, the Veterans, the Umpires Association and individuals, before a series of regional meetings was conducted to discuss the propositions. Finally, a report was tabled on 13 December, 1990 which included a series of recommendations under 10 major headings. Issues referred to included the zoning of the shield competition (with the exception of the State league), the timing of the shield series, publicity, the junior series, additional competitions, rules and penalties, club concerns, the role of clubs in the shield match competition, the improvement of the winter series and the general upgrading of the State grade. In relation to the latter issue, King's Park player John Campbell and Joanne Smith (Bassendean) focused on the players' perspective as part of their research at Edith Cowan University.

Changes to the shield competition then began to be implemented. State Grade (known as 'A' grade until 1985/1986) became known as the State League for the 1991/1992 season. To lift the profile of the State League, a higher nomination fee was introduced, mainly to fund the payment of a referee at each fixture in the men's division. A Board of Management, consisting of the Presidents of the State League clubs, advised on the operation of the League, which was organised on a promotion and relegation basis with victory in the second division leading to promotion to the State League at the expense of the team at the bottom of the State League ladder at the conclusion of each season. To avoid disputes about the completion time for shield matches it was decided that the astronomical sunset time, published in the newspaper, would mark the conclusion of a fixture. Steps were taken to attract more publicity for the competition, which since 1987/1988 had been sponsored by the Westpac Bank. In one respect the Association was particularly fortunate; Gary Stocks, tennis writer in the state-wide morning newspaper the *West Australian*, filed regular well-informed articles about the League as well as major tournaments. A feature article was frequently published on the Westpac Player of the Week, chosen by the Chair of the State Selection Panel on the basis of an outstanding League match performance. Stocks was a regular visitor to the match of the day, as well as often broadcasting the highlights on local radio.

A major change to the format of 'State Grade' which preceded the Select Committee Report was a decision for the 1988/1989 season to increase the size of each team at this level from four to six members. A fixture would then consist of six singles and three doubles matches. The main rationale, applicable to the men's scene, was to expand the opportunities for promising juniors to participate in highly-competitive tennis. Several club delegates were concerned that the expanded teams required the allocation of three instead of two courts on each Saturday afternoon at a time when social matches were the major focus for most club members.

In the women's division, reservations were also expressed, in this case about whether there was sufficient depth to ensure that a high standard was maintained if teams had six rather than four members. Given the popularity and success of the mid-week ladies doubles competition, it was then decided to introduce the notion of a 'designated doubles' pair. A six member team would then contest four singles and four doubles matches. The 'designated doubles' players only participated in two doubles matches. Although it was thought this rule would encourage more senior women back to the top level of shield play criticism of the concept came on equal opportunity grounds, as each member of the women's team did not play a singles match as in the men's competition. So, rather than extend the experiment, women's state grade rules for the 1989/1990 season were amended to ensure that each team member (as in the mens) played one singles and one doubles match. But, when the number of teams in the revamped State League competition for 1990/1991 was increased from six to eight, the lack of depth in women's tennis was recognised, as each team was to consist of the traditional four members. It should be noted that the concept of 'equal opportunity' was then conveniently cast aside, as the men's division retained six member teams.

An alteration to playing conditions that satisfied the quest for equal opportunity was the decision to alternate the men's and women's grand final at Royal King's Park on the concluding Saturday and Sunday of each shield season. No longer was the women's grand final to be played on the back courts on the same afternoon as the men's grand final. It was also decided to play the semi-finals on the home courts of the teams which finished ahead on the premiership table.

Before the increase in the size of the teams, the Nedlands Club achieved a hat-trick of premierships in the women's final in 1986, 1987 and 1988. The 1986 final, in which it scored a convincing win was particularly significant as it marked the decline of the strong Fremantle team. In a fine performance, Lyn Cooper, the Nedlands champion, upset Christine Dorey, the Fremantle 'hero', in the opening rubber 6/3, 5/7, 6/4 to give Nedlands the early ascendancy, a position it maintained on their way to a 5-1 win (*West Australian*, 18/2/1986, 90).

In 1987, Nedlands again caused an upset when it defeated the top-of-the table Reabold, whose players appeared nervous in their club's first grand final appearance. On this occasion, Cooper lost the opening rubber to Robyn Lamb, but the other Nedlands members Judy Lange, Tracey Drake-Brockman and Ann Layman, won their respective singles against Sue Mack, Michelle Phillips and Pam Hatt to set up the victory. A year later, Nedlands, fielding a similar team with Marnie Drake-Brockman taking Judy Lange's place, justified its 'favourite' status with an easy win over Hensman Park. During these years Hensman, which received fine service from Kerryl Chute, Erica Andersson (Smith), Glynis Barber (Mitchell) and Karen Bucens performed reliably, but found it difficult to win finals.

Another strong team during the mid-1980s was Blue Gum. However, this combination's only premiership was in 1989 against Higgins Park The basis of Blue Gum's strength were top-ranked players Paula Parentich, Stephanie Martin, and the powerful Julia Ledder, supported by former Wilson Cup representatives Marie Hill (Bowler), and Sue Clark (Johnson). Leading coach Maureen Smith, who invariably performed well when called upon to play, had an influential hand in the management and tactical direction of the team. Not even a freak accident, which severed a tendon in her left foot just before Christmas 1985, could prevent her coming back 'stronger than ever' (*Daily News*, 16/1/1986, 38).

Reabold also had a strong combination. Its team won successive grand finals in 1990 and 1991 against Blue Gum. Robyn Lamb, Donna Blackwell, Michelle Phillips and Sue Mack were in both Reabold teams, which achieved an almost unblemished record in doubles. A highlight of the closely-fought 1990 final (the last women's six member team) was the epic match in which Karen Vahala for Reabold swung the contest by daring drop-shot tactics to win the third set tie-break against Sue Clark. The latter showed great courage to remain competitive after being struck by cramp in the humid conditions. The weather was even more oppressive a year later, when Reabold was in 'hot' form on the day (23/2/1991) Perth had a temperature of 46.2 degrees Celsius, an all-time record.

The 1990s began with the Reabold team, as the premiership combination, being sponsored by the real estate firm Zadnik Young. This sponsorship provided discounts in membership fees plus the provision of a uniform. Within two years, the scale of sponsorship and the introduction of match payments soon had an impact on the new State League. Royal King's Park were the pacesetters off the court and this led to immediate success on the court. The club, strengthened by Jenny Byrne and strongly supported by Donna Blackwell, Lesley Hunt and Fiona Lonsdale easily defeated Blue Gum in the 1992 final. This dominance was maintained in 1993 after champion Robyn Lamb was lured to Royal King's Park.

For the 1993/1994 season, Cottesloe, with former champion Helen Muir playing a key management role, was successful in obtaining sufficient sponsorship to gain the services of circuit player and former State Open winner Jo-Anne Faull. With strong supporting players Yvonne Ball, Vanya Kelleher, Lisa Askey, Darja Voltnerova and Karlene McIntosh the club was able to win its first premiership in over thirty years. Cottesloe's oppponent in the final was Fremantle represented by the promising Sarah Stanley and veterans Christine Dorey, Denise Shevlin and Judy Kozak. The contest was close with play having to be reconvened the following day to decide the victor. A short extention beyond the official sunset, which Tennis West had employed at the beginning of the season to determine official finishing time for league matches, had not been sufficient to conclude the final doubles rubber on grand final day (*West Australian*, 28/3/1994, 67).

The resources being mobilised to support State League teams were widely debated. It was a break with the past and a pointer to the future. Match payments had begun to creep into the men's division a few years earlier. These were mainly restricted to the higher ranked players in each team, particularly after the change from four to six member teams took place. In this new era of sponsors and match payments, it was more than coincidental that the dominant club in the men's section was Dalkeith, located in a suburb with a particularly high socio-economic status ranking.

Dalkeith won its inaugural premiership in 1987 against Corinthian Park. Both teams were playing in their maiden grand final. The number one for Dalkeith was Roger Grant, who had just taken over the mantle as the State's leading player. Emerging champions David Culley and Darren Patten, supported by Ross Arancini, completed a strong team. Nevertheless, Dalkeith had to play hard for a victory over Corinthian, which had Keith Begley, Brad Hamburg, Neil Prickett and Steve Fletcher.

It was not surprising that Dalkeith, with a similar team, dominated the competition in 1988 when Royal King's Park were its opponents in the grand final. Damien Kestell took the number four spot at Dalkeith to support Grant, Culley and Darren Patten. The threat from Royal King's Park was, however, growing and its team won the Blacklock Shield in the following season. Rob Casey, Mark Leuba, and Damian Hampson, who were runners up with Royal King's Park in 1988, were in winning form in 1989, after the six player format had been launched. Justin Johns, Graeme Cox and Eugene Simkovic had given it the necessary depth.

Nevertheless, Dalkeith, which had one of the largest metropolitan memberships (behind that of Royal King's Park), came back to take the top spot with grand final victories in 1990, 1991, 1993 and 1994. To support Culley in 1994 were Alex Floyd, Scott Marshall, Damian Kestell, John Thorpe and Tim Hammond. Culley, renowned for his court speed, had by this time become the top-ranked men's player, with a succession of fine wins in shield matches and tournament titles, including the Metropolitan Hardcourt, State Hardcourt, Spring, City of Perth and State Closed. Thus Culley and Grant still

David Culley, state number one who was renowned for his court speed

constituted the 'backbone' of the team. However, when Culley missed most of the 1991-1992 season playing college tennis in the United States and Grant moved to Alexander Park, Dalkeith briefly dropped out of the top four.

Roger Grant's move to Alexander Park helped that club to reach the 1992 grand final. However, Hensman Park, led by the colourful Mark Hlawaty (who had had an unbeaten season in the State League) won the Shield in front of a reasonably large crowd. For his part, Grant had a rare bad day, losing to an inspired Ashley Burton, who had previously played for North Beach.

It was Hensman Park's first grand final win since 1986. The earlier title was had been a particularly significant victory, enabling the club to break a 28-year drought. It was a welcome change of luck after being runner-up four times in five years. Hensman set up victory over Higgins Park when Barry Tognolini, Colin Napier and Phil Searle combined to establish a 3 rubbers to 1 lead after the singles. Only the competitive Tony Luttrell won for Higgins, against Rob Murton. The title was then clinched when doubles expert Tognolini, partnered by Colin Napier, had a straight set win over Higgins friends Lawrence Fiorentino and Dean Danzi.

In 1992, Barry Tognolini and Colin Napier were survivors in the Hensman team but their age was probably beginning to tell and they lost their respective singles matches to Greg Quinn and Shane Smedley from Alexander Park. But in 1994 when Hensman met Dalkeith in the grand final it was Tognolini who was able to use his guile and deft volleying to defeat professional coach John Thorpe in a three set encounter. Tognolini, in 1992, had become Chair of the State Selection Panel and was soon joined by the experienced and dedicated shield player Shane Smedley. As mentioned, Tognolini had ironically narrowly missed state selection on at least two occasions. As a senior he represented Western Australia in the 1976 and 1983 Challenge Cup series, establishing a reputation as one the best doubles players produced in the State. By the time Tognolini had played in his second Hensman premiership team, he had begun to compete in some over-35 tournament events and was undoubtedly beginning to pursue opportunities which the rapidly growing veterans' organisation had to offer.

The LTAA, which had noted the growth in popularity of an over-35 group in international men's tennis, requested state associations to provide more opportunities for this category, to 'keep them in tennis'. In response, the WALTA Executive sought to include an over-35 singles event in the 1985 Metropolitan Hardcourt and Spring Championships. Subsequently this became a regular feature of the tournament scene and was even accompanied by a Player of the Year points system. It often figured prominently in *Westennis*, with publicity given to top competitors such as Don Patten, Rod Burton (North Beach), professional coaches Geof Thomas and Keith Hince, former Champion of Champions winners Gary Penberthy and Alan D'Orsogna, John Fairchild and Alan Gooch.

The introduction of the 35 years and over competition was timely, as Penberthy, Fairchild and Gooch were soon to win honour by being selected in the Australian Italia Cup team. Penberthy and Fairchild performed well at Grado, Italy in 1987 (*Westennis*, August 1987, 3) but were not available the following year, when Alan Gooch was chosen to play for Australia in Bol, in what was then Yugoslavia.

For Alan Gooch selection in the Italia Cup was 'a dream come true' (*Westennis*, October 1988, 5). Soon to become a member of the State Executive and Chair of the State Selection Panel, Gooch had achieved several distinctions as a player. He was chosen in the Linton Cup team for 1965 and 1966 and was then a ranked senior for eight years, during which he was a leading 'A' grade player. As a schoolteacher, with a Bachelor of Education (Physical Education major) he did country service and twice won the Country Week singles title. At his home club (Mount Lawley) he had won the singles championship more than a dozen times. Known for his wonderful rapport with people, he was the boys' manager for the winning 1990 Secondary Schools Pizzey Cup team. Poor health in his family intervened to curtail his administrative roles and competitive performance. However, in tennis there is always a future. A return to the real veterans-the 40 and overs, provides scope for this tall right-hander to achieve more of his goals in tennis.

Alan Gooch, leading player with excellent rapport as a manager and coach of junior teams

The Veterans

In the twentieth annual report of the Veterans' Tennis Club of Western Australia (A Division of the Veteran's Tennis Association of Australia and an Associate Body of Tennis West) presented in August 1992, it was reported that the membership had jumped from 754 to 872, the second biggest State membership in Australia. The review of activities was so comprehensive as to suggest that veterans' tennis deserves its own history. Some progress has already been made, with the previously mentioned *The First Decade*, with plans in hand to describe the second decade. It is necessary to recognise more fully the contributions of veterans to the development of tennis in Western Australia. Perhaps the reasons could be evaluated for the decision in 1988 to make Nedlands club the club headquarters after 17 seasons at Royal King's Park. Of course, one important consideration was the availability of grasscourts at Nedlands, thereby answering Veterans' President Doug Brown's plea published in *Westennis* (October, 1990, 21) under the heading 'Let's Keep the Grass'.

After two decades, the organisation has its own uniform, awards and magazine, known as *Vetscene*. Described in each yearly report are the annual tournaments (sponsored by the Commonwealth Bank), the annual Australasian Championships, school matches, women's midweek winter pennants, the winter doubles competition, mixed doubles pennants and the summer night competition. Social matches and functions in both metropolitan and country centres are also given prominence.

The annual report also contained a useful membership list which by 30 June, 1993 had grown to 915. Given that the Veterans had commenced as a men's organisation it was significant that several of the office bearers for the 1992/1993 season were women including President Margaret Thompson, Secretary Bobbie Edwards and Assistant Secretary Geraldine O'Loughlin. Additional women on the committee were Jenny McLure and Lyn Staples. The men holding office were Doug Brown and Rob Ockerby as Vice-Presidents, Fred Gatti as Treasurer, with John Evans and Henry Michael as the remaining members. Clive Wilderspin was the Patron and Dan Carney was the auditor.

Members of the tennis community are reminded that 'life begins at 40' when 'a whole new vista opens up for the talented and the not so talented'. In *Westennis* (October 1992, 31) it was 'advertised' ;

> *One of the options open to the talented after the age of 40 is a series of international events overseas. This year [1992], for example, Christine Dorey was chosen to represent Australia in the Young Cup in Dublin, Ireland;*

Henry Michael, one of the driving forces of veterans' tennis

Rob Ockerby, capable player and Veterans' leader

Margaret Robinson goes later in the year as part of the Connolly Cup team to Texas; Pat Stanley has been to Hungary as part of the Alice Marble team; Gary Penberthy competed with success at the Veteran's International Championships at Palermo (winning the 45 years doubles) and then went to Austria as part of the Dubler Cup team; Jim Black went to Austria as a member of the Bitsy Grant team for over 75 men and Helen Muir went to France in the Bueno Cup.

It was regarded as odd that veteran tennis players sometimes look forward to becoming a year or two older so they can become eligible to compete in the next age group. The veterans segregate themselves by five-year groups, from forty onwards, with national and international rankings determined for each category. While Tennis West administrators have often tried in vain to produce national champions (and circuit players) in the senior and junior ranks, there have been several instances in recent seasons of Western Australian veterans achieving national and even international success.

The first West Australian veteran to represent Australia overseas in competition was Pam Hatt. After reaching the semi-final of the national 40 and over championships, she was chosen to compete in the 1986 Young Cup in the Austrian city of Brand (ironically, Pam's maiden name which she later readopted). John P. Young is credited with being the founder and patron of veterans tennis in Australia. A year later, Pam Hatt was selected as captain of the Young Cup team in Venice. In January 1987, she also had the rare distinction of becoming the national champion in the over-40 singles, doubles and mixed doubles. The latter title was shared with prominent Western Australian veteran Henry Michael, known as one of the driving forces in veterans' tennis. In the men's singles the tall left-handed Michael achieved acclaim when he won the singles title for the over-40 division.

When the Australasian Veterans' Championships were conducted in Perth in January 1988, Western Australians 'scooped the pool' in team and individual events. Former Western Australian Open champion Harry Jacoby (81) teamed with Jim Black, Harold Broadbent, Lloyd Morgan and Sir Ross Hutchinson to win the 70 years Australian title. Geoff Strang, Dawson Hamilton, John Bahen, Keith Holten and Hedley O'Neil excelled to win for the West the 60s title. In the same age group the women's team of Marie Tracy, Pat Jenzen, Joan Davies, Elsie Crowe and Gwyn White secured the title. In the 40s division Western Australia won both the men's and women's titles. The strong men's team consisted of Gary Penberthy, Peter Dyson, Don Patten and Henry Michael and the women's of Kerryl Chute, Helen Muir, Rhonda Perrot and Wendy Weir. Mainly as a consequence of these performances the WA veterans won the Commonwealth Bank trophy for the first time, after achieving the best State aggregate score.

The blue ribbon over-40s singles events produced a WA double. Kerryl Chute employed her speed to upset the seedings and Gary Penberthy won the men's division. Penberthy showed promise of a splendid career in the veterans. As mentioned previously he had already been prominent in the 35 years and over Italia Cup. In Perth he was to win the 40s doubles with friend Peter Dyson as partner. In the women's doubles, Royal King's Park pair Helen Young and Jan McIntyre were successful. The combined 100 years doubles was won by Noel Pearse and Arthur Marshall while Alan Hicks and Clive Wilderspin won the 55 years doubles.

The published criteria for selection to represent Australia in ITF Veterans Cups stated that 'the primary, but not overriding requirement, is for a player to participate with some success in the Australian/Australasian Championships ...,'Not surprisingly therefore Kerryl Chute was chosen in the 1989 Young Cup team to play in Austria. This selection gave the team a fully Western Australian flavour, as Hatt was captain and Jan de Tastes (Blackburne), who had learnt her tennis in the West and soon to return to live, was also in the side. Injury forced de Tastes to withdraw, but Margaret Robinson, who had been competing for Australia in the Bueno Cup in England, was close at hand and able to join the (Western) Australian Young Cup team.

A year later, Pam Hatt nearly gained the tag as the 'oldie of the Young Cup' when she was selected to play in the competition in Kescthely, Hungary. In the same month (June 1990), Clive Wilderspin was selected to play in the Austria Cup in Poertchach, Austria. The name of Wilderspin appears frequently on the lists of past winners of the Veterans' State Championships. Whilst his prowess as a player is widely known his contribution off the court has also been considerable, as he has invariably played a significant role in the organisation of almost all the hallmark veterans events held in Perth. However, before brief reference is made to each of these events, it is necessary to clarify the competitions conducted for the veterans. By 1993 the picture, in addition to the World Veterans Championships, was as follows;

Men		**Women**	
Italia Cup	(35 years)	Young Cup	(40 years)
Dubler Cup	(45 years)	Margaret Court Cup	(45 years)
Austria Cup	(55 years)	Maria Esther Bueno Cup	(50 years)
Von Cramm Cup	(60 years)	Alice Marble Cup	(60 years)
Britannia Cup	(65 years)		
Crawford Cup	(70 years)		
Bitsy Grant Cup	(75 years)		

In recognition of Wilderspin's services as director of the organising committee for the ITF World Veterans' Championships and the Alice Marble and Bueno Cups, conducted in Perth in April 1991, he was named Veteran of the Year. Back in March 1985, Wilderspin had been Chair of the match committee when Western Australia hosted the Dubler and Austria Cups. On this occasion he had worked under Don Clayton, the Chair of the organising committee. Clayton was noted for his attention to detail and desire for perfection. He shared with Wilderspin membership at the Reabold club, terms as president and the honour of life membership of both Reabold and the Veterans' club (*Westennis*, December 1987, 10).

Life membership of the Veterans in the club's first two decades had also been accorded to Sir Ross Hutchinson, Geoff Strang and Arthur Marshall. Strang was the Tournament Director for the 1988 Australian championships. The success of this event led to him being named Australasian Veteran of the Year. Strang was known as 'a glutton for punishment'; he had served for many years as a selector where some of his vast knowledge gained as a long term successful player could be utilised. As a player, he was ranked in the top eight for 15 seasons, during which he teamed with Mervyn Rose to win the 1951 State Open Doubles and repeated the feat the following year with Rex Hartwig (*Daily News* 13/10/1983, 40). After his experience as a selector, he probably regarded his two years as President of the Veterans' Club as 'plain sailing'.

Publicity for most of the major veterans' events was generally the responsibility of Arthur Marshall (*Westennis*, April 1984, 36). Sponsorship, too, was often handled by Marshall, who raised considerable sums for the veterans as well as new tennis courts at Wesley College, his old school with which he maintained a long connection. As mentioned, he had been awarded the Professional Coaches' Association 'Coach of the Year' award and he was particularly adept at raising funds for charitable causes by promoting pro-am days. Until 1992, when the demands of campaigning for State Parliament induced Marshall to forego his weekly newspaper column, the 'power of the pen' was in his hands. He had two years as President of the Veterans and had his share of success in tournament play particularly when he teamed with Bruce Robinson in doubles. In 1989, he was chosen (with Wilderspin) to take part in the International Potter Cup for those who had played in the United States, French or Wimbledon championships. Given his newspaper connections, Arthur was able to give the 'vetscene' regular coverage. As one of the best known identities in Western Australian tennis, it also provided scope for him to air his views about tennis policy. These opinions were not always what officials at Tennis West wanted to hear. However, one concept which Marshall had promoted (*WALTA Minutes*, 2/8/1979) was the creation of a State Players' Development Trust. Now with Tennis West backing the Trust was to provide yet another means of assisting junior development.

State Players Development Trust (and WALTA finances)

Fittingly, Arthur Marshall was elected as the founding Chair of the State Players Development Trust, with Alan Hicks and Andrea Mitchell nominated as trustees. When Gary Penberthy later became the Chair, there was a deliberate attempt to broaden the Committee representation of the various generations involved in tennis so it soon included Dean Williams, Colin Napier, Pat Stanley, Fiona Lonsdale, Michelle Phillips and Sue Mack.

The principal objective of the Trust, which was launched with a dinner at the Perth International Hotel in August 1990, was to raise up to $50,000 to assist talented Western Australian juniors. The main source of funds was to be life membership donations and interest on capital. The membership was to be limited to players chosen to represent Western Australia in senior or junior competition. Research had indicated that 331 people had been State representatives between 1906 and 1988. A special provision permitted the managers of the various State teams to apply for membership.

Strictly speaking, the Trust's management and financial affairs were to operate outside the control of Tennis West, but cooperation between the bodies was clearly expected. An inaugural sporting breakfast, which Trust Secretary Andrea Mitchell said raised over $3,000, was an indicator of strong support for the cause and the goodwill created by the new organisation. In accordance with the Trust requirements, one-third of the net income was to be retained as capital, one-third transferred to Tennis West's Interstate and Overseas Visits Fund, and one-third used to assist young players (under 19 years) to further their tennis careers.

The establishment of the Trust was timely, as the Fund Raising Committee of the Association was forced to grapple with the question of whether or not to conduct an annual Miss Tennis contest. It was a case of 'on again, off again' before social pressures, rejecting the sexism inherent in such events, led to it being discontinued. Nevertheless this left the respective Chairs of the Fund Raising Committee, Gwyn Thomas and Pam Henderson, lamenting that a

Arthur Marshall(left), pictured here with actor Warren Mitchell (Alf Garnett).

very productive means of generating financial support for the Interstate Visits Fund had been lost.

In the scale of Tennis West finances, the contribution of the Trust, while most welcome, was modest. This can be demonstrated by reference to the WALTA (Tennis West) accounts tabled by Treasurer Dene Rundle, for the 12 months to 30 June, 1988. The $340,000 was raised and expended in the following proportions:

Income:	Per cent
Affiliation fees	30
Sponsorship	28
Interest	10
Fees	9
Subsidy (Government-LTAA)	7
Sanction Fees and Levies	6
Tournaments (Proceeds)	5
Competitions	5
Expenditure:	Per cent
Junior development	26
Office overheads	22
Office salaries	19
State coach	11
Development officer	9
Interstate teams	9
Overseas teams	4

Prudence in financial management, which had been one of the characteristics of the Association, was maintained. While some State Associations were in financial crisis, the influence of accountants Harry Spilsbury (1982 to 1990) and Alan Hicks (from October 1990) as the successive Presidents was apparent. Treasurers Dene Rundle (1983-1990), Ian Kuba (1991) and Mike Lee (1992-) were all totally meticulous and responsible in this demanding voluntary role. At the bimonthly Council meetings the accounts were invariably closely scrutinised with delegates such as Hedley O'Neil (Leederville) and Dr Graham Hartill (Royal King's Park) prepared to seek clarification of any matter of concern. Price Waterhouse continued to audit the accounts, as a consequence of a benefactor's will.

Affiliation fees still constituted a major source of revenue, although sponsorship and various government grants were gaining importance. There were some changes in how the extremely sensitive affiliation fees for clubs, were calculated. A constitutional amendment in 1991 provided greater flexibility in the setting of affiliation fees and each minor alteration no longer required a formal constitutional change. Commencing in the 1990/1991 season, the submission of these membership figures was to coincide with the financial year. Over the period since 1985, there was very little change in the number of affiliated clubs, although total membership had steadily increased. The country membership remained virtually static although there were changes in the composition of the zones. From July 1, 1988, Zone 4 was divided with the eastern half to be known as Zone 9 and in 1990 another boundary division was negotiated giving a total of 11 zones. With assistance from the Ministry of Sport and Recreation, particularly the regional development officers, there were subsequent attempts to establish Zone Development Plans.

The extent of club activity and tennis participation outside the jurisdiction of the Association has long been a topic for debate. A national survey conducted during 1992 indicated that 31 per cent of the total population play tennis each year (Sweeney, 1993, 3 and *The Australian*, 4/3/1993, 2), yet only 25,614 players were registered with the Association in 1992 (*WALTA Annual Report*, 1991/1992). With the total population in Western Australia in 1992 standing at 1,662,777 persons (Western Australian Year Book, 1993, 105) it is clear that substantial numbers of tennis players do not join clubs and some clubs do not join the Association. Tennis Australia President, Geoff Pollard, who judiciously adopted the strategy of regularly visiting each State and Territory in the tennis federation, had also indicated that there had been a national decline in tennis numbers. These observations contributed to a decision in 1994 to follow the Victorian example and conduct a Tennis West participation seminar at the Blue Gum Park Tennis Club.

Key speaker, Karen Clydesdale, the highly regarded Tennis Australia National Development Officer, later indicated to the WALTA Marketing Director, Bill Artingstall, that the occasion was one of the best held by any State Association. Council Director Dene Rundle, his committee, together with Paul McNamee and Karen Clydesdale, were specifically praised for the seminar (*WALTA Minutes*, 11/8/1994). A more immediate guide to the health of tennis than waiting for the statistics to be published is a visit to a leading sporting proprietor who retails tennis gear. For instance Reg Hall, known to a generation of Perth tennis players for the professional restringing of racquets and the sale of tennis equipment at his Osborne Park business, can usually provide a sketch of contemporary tennis in the West.

Whether the eventual construction of a tennis centre in the State would increase the incentive to affiliate, particularly for metropolitan-based clubs (and associations) is a moot point. Of course many members of the public, and even some government officials, have laboured under the misapprehension that Royal King's Park is the tennis centre for the Association. As the offices of the Association had been located under the McGibbon Stand at Royal King's Park (since the mid 1960s), which was also the venue for many hallmark events, it is understandable how this view prevailed. However, in August 1992 Tennis West moved its office premises to Leigh Street, Victoria Park. The McGibbon Stand offices had become grossly inadequate. The Leigh Street premises, obtained at a satisfactory rental, had the advantage of being close to the anticipated location of a tennis complex at Burswood on the same tract of land as the Burswood Casino, only a few kilometres from the Perth GPO. At the same time office manager, Verna Pringle, who had given the Association dedicated service, relinquished her position to Julie Philp. The latter, a valuable employee since 1986, greatly assisted in the arduous task of establishing the new offices.

The Tennis Centre

During the 1980s, the prospect of the Association having its own offices and tennis complex always appeared to be just around the corner When Harry Spilsbury assumed the Presidency in 1982, he regarded the building of a hardcourt centre as a priority. His predecessor Barry Sanders also nurtured the idea. When Sanders retired as President he continued as chair of a subcommittee which had already been in existence for four years examining metropolitan area alternatives. In an interview with Gary Stocks in December 1982 (*Westennis*, December, 1982, 10) Sanders even confessed 'that he had hoped to have the facility available by now'.

With the election of the Hawke Labor government in March 1983, funding for national sporting venues was a budget item. But although Hawke learned his tennis in his schooldays in Western Australia he did not sanction federal funds for a tennis centre in the West during his term as Prime Minister. It is noteworthy that the National Tennis Centre at Flinders Park in Melbourne, received $86 million, but the main source was the Victorian and not the federal government. The Australian Open in January 1988 saw the realisation of the 'dream come true' complex (*Westennis*, February 1988, 19). However, the controversy surrounding the playing surface contributed to further delay in Western Australia, because there was a need to evaluate the efficiency of the new Rebound Ace surface (a type of plexi-cushion). In early 1986 Ashley Cooper, the former Wimbledon champion, had been in Perth to discuss the surface proposals with WALTA officials. In the Perth metropolitan area, a survey in July 1988 indicated the affiliated clubs had a total of 768 courts, of which 511 were grass and 257 synthetic. The synthetic surfaces included Plexiplave (180); Chevron (55); Synthetic grass (13); Walktop (10); Bitumen/asphalt (9); HotMix (4); SynPave (3) and concrete (2). Some 149 courts of all types were recorded as having lights.

Given the immediacy of tennis facility considerations the WALTA, in 1989, created a State Tennis Centre Committee, with members Harry Spilsbury, Barry Sanders, Alan Hicks, Mel O'Neil and Brian Beers. Initially they concentrated their investigations on a site near the new Superdrome in Mount Claremont. The incumbent Western Australian Minister for Sport, Gordon Hill, was keen for the centre to be at this location. However, in November 1990 the Committee decided, for several reasons, to discontinue their Mount Claremont quest. Firstly, the Committee had encountered a range of difficulties and frustrations in their negotiations with officials from the Perth City

Council and the University of Western Australia. Secondly, the demands of the University Tennis Club had proven difficult to accommodate. Thirdly, some problems emerged satisfying the requirements of the Disabled Riding School which operated in the area. Finally, too, some environmental concerns became apparent as the project would have necessitated the felling of trees and other damage to the native bushland.

Early in 1990 a consultant with the Burswood resort, John Brennan, had suggested that the Committee consider a tennis centre site at Burswood. Meanwhile, the Committee's membership was reduced to 'a leaner machine' comprised of Harry Spilsbury (Chair), Alan Hicks and Brian Beers leading to a decision to pursue the Burswood option. Bruce Keane, an adviser to the Minister for Sport (with Graham Edwards again in the portfolio) was credited with providing valuable assistance. Then, in April 1991, the Committee on Tennis West's behalf lodged the Burswood application with the State Government, and commenced negotiations with the Federal government for a grant of up to $1 million (interview with Alan Hicks, 15/7/1994).

Recognising that a crucial stage had been reached in the deliberations the committee decided 'to do something every day' to pursue the Association's elusive tennis centre goal. To the delight of the tennis fraternity an official announcement was made on the 26 June, 1992 that the State Government had made a 'founding' $500,000 grant and designated land in the Burswood area for the establishment of a State Tennis Centre. State Government Minister for Sport, Graham Edwards, and the local member for Victoria Park, Dr Geoff Gallop, were present for the occasion. Earlier Premier Carmen Lawrence had written a letter to President Alan Hicks indicating strong support for the plan. As Bryan Rourke, the Western Australian Sport Federation Director remarked (*Westennis*, August 1991, 15); 'the ideal location will undoubtedly provide an ideal focus for tennis players in WA to lift our national ranking's and international profile'. The Sports Federation and the Sports Council had earlier given strong support to the Tennis West submission. State Government Department executives including Jack Busch (Sport and Recreation) and tennis player David Hatt (Planning and Urban Development) had also provided valuable direction.

Much, however, remained to be done to bring the project to fruition. Long serving Executive member, Peter Barrett, accepted a further responsibility and was added to the Committee in October 1992. Moreover, George Bray, City Manager of the City of Stirling and an active playing member of the Royal King's Park Tennis club, agreed to be a consultant. One month later the Federal Government announced a $250,000 grant after Tennis West president Alan Hicks had travelled to Canberra to make comprehensive submissions to Ros Kelly, who was then the Federal Minister for Sport. Kim Beazley, the Minister for Employment, Education and Training and local federal member for Swan, was a key figure in obtaining this grant with strong support also coming from Ministers John Dawkins, Peter Cook and sporting enthusiast Ron Edwards (the federal member for Perth). Discussions, including representation to shadow ministers, continued with all tiers of government. Dene Moore, from the Confederation of Australian Sport, was also involved. As a consequence of the February 1993 State election Richard Court became the new Premier as leader of the Liberal/National Party coalition. Court had strong links with tennis; his sister-in-law, Margaret Court, was a tennis icon and his son, Kris, was a ranked junior and 'A' grade league player. The election also witnessed the seat of Murray being won by tennis personality

Announcement in June 1992 of the Burswood Site for the State Tennis Centre. From left Dr Geoff Gallop, President Alan Hicks, and Minister Graham Edwards

Arthur Marshall. Another newly elected Liberal Party member, Michael Board, had been president of the East Fremantle Tennis Club where Marshall had centred his tennis coaching for many years. Perhaps indicative of the demands upon modern backbench members of parliament neither found regular time to play tennis on the Parliament's grass court. Certainly the days when premiers, such as Bert Hawke (1953 to 1959), could regularly play tennis at lunch time had long gone.

Negotiations at the State level necessarily shifted to the relevant new ministers, their advisers and departments. Richard Lewis, the Planning Minister, a tennis player at the Applecross club, Finance Minister Max Evans, Sport and Recreation Minister Norman Moore (and his predecessor Doug Shave) and even Deputy Premier Hendy Cowan became more central players in the exercise. By December 1993, discussions with the Sport and Recreation Minister's adviser, Hallam Pereira, had reached a crucial stage as to whether the Government would include funding for the Tennis Centre in the 1994/1995 State budget. Subsequently, although the decision to table an early State budget, on 9 June 1994, was criticised by some commentators for its lack of detail it included an item of immense significance for tennis in Western Australia. In the capital works program the Premier and Treasurer, Richard Court, announced a $3.1 million funding allocation for a State Tennis Centre.

As it had been estimated that $5.6 million was needed for the Centre, assistance from State and Federal governments was a pre-condition for the commencement of the project. It was proposed that the centre have 30 hard-courts and an administration building. The project was to be completed in two stages - the first being 18 courts (and offices) with a further 12 courts planned for the second stage (*Westennis*, October, 1992, 6). In April 1993 architectural firm, Hanlin Architects Pty. Ltd., had been appointed Project Managers. This firm's principal, Rob Hankin, proved to be a driving force and his efforts contributed considerably to the progress of the venture. Some of the early advice had been rendered by Graham Mackie and David Bobridge from G.D.H. Pty. Ltd. The architects, in consultation with Tennis West officials, were clearly to face many conundrums before the project was to be

Alan Hicks (President), Minister Norman Moore and Siobhan Drake-Brockman, at 'the breaking the ground ceremony'

completed. Nevertheless, the likelihood of the 'dream' of a long sought tennis centre being realised was a cause for celebration. This occasion moved closer to fruition when Minister for Sport and Recreation, Norman Moore, a former President of the Tom Price and Laverton Tennis clubs, officially launched the new State Tennis Centre on 20 September, 1994 on the Burswood site.

Administrative changes

Before the announcement of the site for the centre, Tennis West had undertaken a review of its Constitution and a series administrative changes to help modernise its operations. The Constitutional Task Force comprised of senior administrators Dene Rundle, Harry Spilsbury and Barry Sanders began meeting in December 1988 and most of its suggested amendments were ratified at a special Council meeting in August 1991. At the annual general meeting in October 1991, an eight-person Board of Directors replaced the 14-person State Executive. Alan Hicks as President was the Chairperson of Directors, the remainder of the Board being Andrea Mitchell (Vice President and Tennis Development), Michael Lee (Finance), Harry Spilsbury (Administration), John Schwarzenburg (Marketing), Peter Barrett (Tennis Activites, including Shield Tennis), Rob Casey (Country Tennis) and Rob Wallman (Club Promotions). With the exception of Wallman, a relatively youthful life member from the Reabold club, all the new directors had sat on the previous Executive. Several members of the Executive who had made a substantial 'voluntary' contribution to tennis at either the Association and/or club level retired, including Dot Connolly (Leederville), Mel O'Neil (Sorrento), Wayne Firns (Mount Lawley), Ian Kuba (Royal King's Park), Rex Richter (Country Clubs) and Barry Sanders (Reabold).

Some of the outstanding features of Barry Sanders' work have already been mentioned. At the meeting of Council in December 1992, Alan Hicks as President of Tennis West (from October 1990) presented Sanders with a polished jarrah box in recognition of his tireless work on the Executive (*Westennis*, February 1992, 4). Not long afterwards, it was also revealed that John Schwarzenberg, the Marketing Director, would be stepping down from the new Board, to return home to the United States. Although Schwarzenberg was to be replaced by Bill Artingstall, a servant of tennis from Hensman Park, the loss of John and his wife Gail to Western Australian tennis was regretted. Both had given many years of service to the East Fremantle Tennis Club Committee. When life membership was granted to John, he indicated that it could not have been achieved without the contribution Gail had also made. On arrival in Western Australia in 1972, he had been immediately employed by leading company Howard Porter Pty Ltd, where he had risen to be a manager. During his term on the Tennis West Executive and Directorate, John brought the benefit of his business acumen to the deliberations - a necessary input to modern sporting administration (*Westennis*, February 1988, 29). He was keen to investigate new marketing strategies, exemplified by the pamphlet 'Meet WALTA Your New Tennis Partner', as well as maintaining some of the established practices such as the annual October newspaper tennis segment (*West Australian*, 6/10/1989, 51-56).

Prior to the revamping of the administration, an important development had been the appointment in August 1988 of Brian Beers as the Executive Director, with John Whitton, the former General Manager, assuming the role of development officer. Beers was selected from some 50 applicants from overseas and interstate. Before turning to tennis he had been a member of the 1958 Collingwood VFL premiership team. In a practical sense he knew something of the Western Australian scene; with Tennis Camps of Australia in the mid-Seventies he had undertaken a key role in organising three Western Australian Open Championships. As an accomplished player and level 3 coach, with experience with Tennis Australia in managing the Open 'Grand Slam' and liaising with players and the media, he had excellent credentials.

Brian Beers, first WALTA Chief Executive, was appointed in August 1988

In December 1992, Brian Beers won the Western Australian Sports Federation Award for the Career Administrator of the Year. The criteria for such awards are invariably contentious, as a balance is required between business profit and loss considerations and managerial efficiency, with the realisation that much of the administration of sports such as tennis is undertaken by volunteers. Reference was made to Beers's role in facilitating the negotiations for the long-term lease (with Harry Spilsbury and Alan Hicks) for the new State Tennis Centre, his role in restoring the profile of the Western Australian Open and assisting the formulation of the submission to obtain the 'Tennis in Schools' grant through Healthway. The latter had been made easier by Tennis West declaring itself a 'smoke-free organisation' from June 1991 and publishing anti-smoking material in *Westennis* (October 1990, 37). He had also been appointed to the influential Tennis Australia Player Adviser National Development Committee. Beers's appointment was made with Harry Spilsbury in the President's chair, but when the award was granted, Alan Hicks had taken over.

When Spilsbury stepped down in October 1990, he was fittingly granted life membership in recognition of his long and distinguished service (*WALTA Minutes*, 13/12/1990). In 1947, Spilsbury had arrived in the west from Queensland to take up a position with a firm of accountants. He was soon posted to Narrogin, where he was an important member of the team which won the 'A' grade Country Week championship. Upon returning to Perth, he became a member at Royal King's Park, teaming in 1953 with Alick Bridge, Alan Hicks, Lloyd Chrystal and John Bahen to win the 'A' grade premiership.

Gradually, however, Spilsbury's administrative role took precedence over his competitive tennis. After experience as a committeeman, he had one term as the President of Royal King's Park, in 1956-1957. Thereafter, he commenced a 14 year-term as WALTA Treasurer. In a 1989 issue of *Westennis* (August, 8) readers were reminded of Spilsbury's long years of service on the Council in addition to his role in veterans tennis. A tabulation of the seasons, when interestingly combined with another dedicated Council contributor John Miller (a life member from the Hensman Club), totalled 75 years. In 1983, Spilsbury was elected as Vice-President of Tennis Australia, a position he continued to hold after relinquishing the position of President at Tennis West to Hicks, another stalwart (*Westennis*, December 1992, 1).

The epitome of 'been there done that' in Western Australian tennis is Alan Hicks. Moreover, his multiple roles have been conducted in a positive tone and supportive attitude. One of the most competent players to hold the Presidency of the Association he first came under notice when he was selected in the 1950 and 1951 Linton Cup teams. He was prominent in 'A' grade pennants and in 1955 won the City of Perth Championship. However, like many of his contemporaries, he regularly encountered Clive Wilderspin, who dominated the tournament scene in that era.

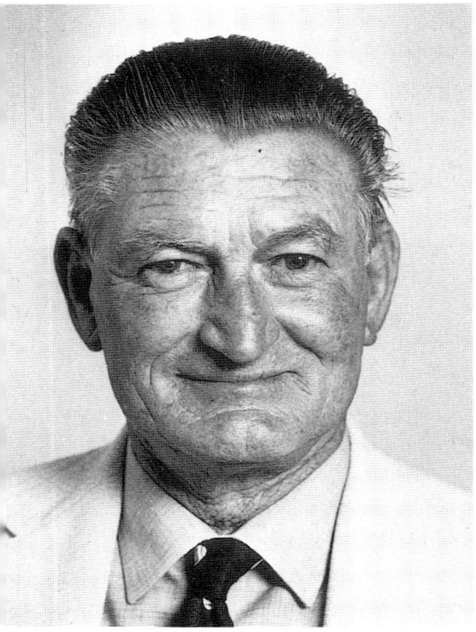

Harry Spilsbury, WALTA President from 1982 after 14 years as Treasurer. Honoured with life membership when he stepped down from the Presidency in 1990

As a chartered accountant with C.P. Bird and Associates, Hicks worked at Bruce Rock and, later, Kalgoorlie. He continued his playing and leading administrative role at the club and zone level. When he returned to Perth, he quickly became a member of the Executive, serving in numerous roles including the post of Chairman of Selectors and Chairman of the Finance Committee. On many occasions, he managed junior touring teams to the eastern States. This responsibility was sometimes shared with wife Mary, who was a Wilson Cup player for Western Australia. She was also regarded as an excellent manager partly because of her supportive disposition. Certainly any reference to Hicks's contribution to tennis must include consideration of the substantial contribution that has also been made by Mary Hicks. As Cec Gardiner, a leading Hensman player and administrator who lived in the eastern wheatbelt in these years, has reminded (interview with Cec Gardiner, 20/12/1993):

> *In both towns [Bruce Rock and Kalgoorlie] Alan and Mary Hicks established junior development programmes that were the envy of all other rural areas.*

In 1975, Hicks became a Vice-President while at the same time he chaired the organising committee which formed the Corinthian Tennis Club. At Corinthian in 1981 he was honoured with life membership. The North Kalgoorlie Club had earlier recognised his services in this manner (*Westennis*, April 1984, 37). At Tennis West, a tradition has evolved of not bestowing life membership until persons 'retire' from an important position. Earlier in the history of the Association, some life memberships appear to be have granted without the recipients satisfying service criteria. However, life membership is not to be confused with honorary membership which was bestowed in 1928 on the three famous visiting French players Jean Borotra, Christien Bousas and J. ('Toto') Brugnon (*WALTA Minutes*, 3/8/1928).

One who satisfied the long service criterion was David Punch who was made a life member in 1989 (*WALTA Minutes*, 14/12/1989). In the same year, after 35 years of dedication to tennis, he had decided to retire from the Executive and relinquish his post as the Senior Vice-President of the Association. Punch had already been made a life member of the South Perth Tennis Club, which he had represented on the WALTA Council since 1954 - after joining the club three years earlier. During his 25 years on the Executive, he chaired or was a member of several committees, including tennis development, junior development, fund raising, joint standing (with Royal King's Park), shield match, LTAA affairs and country sponsored coaching. In addition, he served for many years as a Trustee and steward of the Association and represented WALTA at the Western Australian Sports Federation (*Westennis*, April 1990, 17).

Another Tennis West stalwart was Eric McManis. After suffering ill-health he retired as Vice-President in October 1991 and his life membership was ratified at the Council meeting held during that month. He had begun his involvement in tennis administration in 1954, when he served as secretary of the Kalgoorlie Lawn Tennis Club. After moving to Perth, he began a long association with the Alexander Park Tennis club where as a committeeman for 21 years he was captain, secretary and president. In 1971, he commenced over 20 years of participation on the Executive, being at the forefront of the management of several hallmark events (particularly the Davis Cup ties) and always displaying a keen interest in junior tennis. As a particularly fair minded person, he was well equipped to act as a steward for the Association.

David Punch (second right), is congratulated on his life membership by President Harry Spilsbury, while Vice-President Alan Hicks (left) and Eric McManis look on (Westennis cover page April, 1990).

In Tennis West circles a realisation emerged that the criteria to satisfy life membership had become so exacting that another honour system needed to be devised. In August 1994 at the Council (*WALTA Minutes*, 11/8/1994) a resolution was passed to retrospectively make awards to volunteers 'in appreciation of dedicated services in the development of tennis in WA'. A selection panel comprising the President, General Manager and two Council Delegates was to be appointed annually to recommend Silver, Gold and Grand Slam Awards according to the following general guidelines:

Silver Award

10 years as a Tennis West Delegate or 5 years as an active member of a Tennis West Committee; 'In Appreciation of services to Tennis in WA'.

Gold Award

8 years as a Tennis West Director or 10 years as a Tennis West Chairperson or 15 years as a Tennis West Delegate or Committee Member; 'In appreciation of outstanding services to Tennis in WA'.

Grand Slam Award

Where a minimum of 20 years service has been devoted to tennis in Western Australia, with at least 10 years as a Director of Tennis West; 'In appreciation of dedicated services in the development of Tennis in WA'.

The formidable task of determining the inaugural round of winners was immediately undertaken. Within three months President Alan Hicks made a well received announcement at the December 1994 Council meeting (conducted at the Hensman Park Tennis Club rather than the usual King's Park venue). Hedley O'Neil (Leederville) was the recipient of a Silver Award, Gwyn Thomas (Hensman) and Rex Richter received Gold Awards, with Dot Connolly (Leederville) and Peter Barrett (Nedlands and Cottesloe) being chosen to each receive a 'Gland Slam' plaque. As the President chronicled the contributions of the award winners the delegates were again reminded of the immense scale of service to tennis which these persons had rendered. For instance, Peter Barrett had been a Council delegate since 1968, firstly for Nedlands where he had gained life membership and then Country Zone 4 after he had joined the Cottesloe club. During a period of more than a decade on the Executive he had held the post of Treasurer, followed by Chairman of

Peter Barrett, who with Dot Connolly, received a Grand Slam Award for his dedicated services to tennis

the Shield Match Committee as well as serving terms on the roster, publicity and promotions and State Tennis Centre committees.

Umpires and Etiquette

Umpiring is one of the tennis domains where volunteers make some of the biggest sacrifices. Ramon Connolly, who, until 1989 had five consecutive years as President of the Western Australian Lawn Tennis Umpires Association, was known as a very reflective and perceptive tennis commentator. In the 1985-1986 annual report, he made the following observation in commenting on the State Men's Open final in November 1985 between Jonas Svensson and Simon Youl:

> *The final ... could only be described as an outstanding example of tennis, played in the best traditions of sportsmanship. Perhaps it was their example, or the effects of the Association's Etiquette card, or the points penalty system, or even the absence of some notorious performers from the international scene, but it does seem that court behaviour is improving. Although umpiring will always be a demanding service, it may once again become an enjoyable challenge, instead of a nerve-racking ordeal, if this improvement continues.*

To what extent the 'improvement continues' is a moot point. At the international level, the fading of John McEnroe and the emergence of players such as Stefan Edberg then Pete Sampras, and Steffi Graf, had helped to set the better examples of sportsmanship at the top. Yet in early 1993, under the headline 'Racket Loses its Old Gloss', television critic Pam Casellas suggested (*West Australian* (26/1/1993, 41):

> *The most important reason for us not watching tennis is that tennis players are, by and large, not very nice people. Here they are, feeding in a vast trough of money laid out for them around the world by various tournament organisers and they have the temerity to winge. They scowl at linespeople, they argue with umpires, they ignore hopeful junior tennis players seeking autographs, they sulk at press conferences and whine about the scheduling of events ...*

Rather than relying upon unwritten conventions there was an attempt to establish rules of conduct which complied with the ITF Junior Code and other international codes. Although perhaps working on the assumption that tennis players 'are by and large very nice people', it was necessary to demonstrate that something was being done to eradicate the 'McEnroe Syndrome'. The ITF rules of tennis, the WALTA's own Constitution, the Tennis Australia *Code of Conduct*, the Tennis West *Behaviour Code*, the *Etiquette of Tennis* and a publication entitled 'Footfauting is Cheating' were all given publicity by Tennis West (see *Westennis*, October 1988). The demerit points system was said to provide 'a positive means' of discouraging bad sportsmanship, misconduct, bad behaviour and other detrimental activity and was widely distributed to Association clubs:

	Offence or Misdemeanour	Demerit Points Range
1.	Prejudicial conduct not specifically covered hereunder	Refer to Stewards
2.	Unsportsmanlike behaviour	1-3
3.	Abuse of ball	1-3

4.	Abuse of equipment	1-3
5.	Abuse of racquet	1-3
6.	Audible obscenity, bad language	2-4
7.	Visible obscenity	2-4
8.	Refusal to accept direction of authorised official	2-6
9.	Verbal and/or physical abuse of any official, opponent, spectator, or other person	3-9(6*)
10.	Refusal to umpire	1
11.	Incorrect dress	2
12.	Disqualification from any match (overrides any points imposed previously in that match)	9(6*)

* Amended when the threshold was lowered to six points.

Poster
Footfaulting is Cheating

Demerit points were rarely imposed for incorrect dress. The All England Club (Wimbledon) required players to abide by the 'predominantly white' rule. But in Western Australia, and elsewhere, coloured attire was very popular. Yet standards of dress did cause concern and specifying guidelines became an exercise in semantics. In January 1992, Harry Spilsbury, as Administrative Director, sent a copy of a proposed tennis attire code to affiliated clubs, zones and Council delegates. The memorandum included guidelines on correct attire with a note that company and sponsor identification logos (which had to be limited in number) were not to exceed 13 sq. cm. (2 sq. in.). Acceptable attire was not to include 'football, running or jogging, cycling, board, bermuda, boxer or walk shorts'. Swimwear, leotards, aerobic gear, stretch clothing, leg warmers or body shorts worn under tennis shorts were also deemed unacceptable. The matter proved to be contentious as 'policing' such rules is invariably difficult. In early 1993 it was resolved 'that Tennis West adopt the dress code relating to 'cycle pants' as per Tennis Australia regulations' (*WALTA Minutes*, 15/2/1993). At the Tennis Australia meeting in October 1992 new dress regulations had been adopted. In relation to the wearing of 'cycle pants', it was specified that they may be worn under tennis attire providing they were white, skin coloured, or same colour as the player's shorts (*WALTA Minutes*, 10/12/1992).

Those authorised to impose demerit points in tournaments were referees (and deputy referees), umpires, tournament chairpersons and members of the State Executive or Selection Committee. For shield matches, the president of the home club or its captain or duty captain, and the shield match committee could also impose demerit points. Initially the rules provided that after a player had received 12 points in any 12-month period, he or she would appear before the stewards. However, later in 1990, the threshold was lowered to six points. This not only significantly increased the activities of the stewards but strengthened the relevance of the behaviour code.

In practice, it was the referees and umpires who imposed the demerit points. As noted previously umpiring is a demanding task with very little recompense except the knowledge that top tennis requires top umpiring. To recognise excellence, the Western Australian Lawn Tennis Umpires Association (WALTUA) continued with its Norm Cunningham Umpire of the Year Award and Alf Chave Novice Umpire of the Year. The former, once monopolised by Charlie Brown, was then apparently captured by Dawn Hay. In January 1987,

Dawn and Sandy Hay (above), with Cathy Smith (below), umpiring is now a women's and men's business

Hay had the distinction of being elected President of the Lawn Tennis Umpires' Association of Australia, becoming the fifth Western Australian to be so honoured. Herbert Edwards, who had been instrumental in the establishment of the Australian Association, was the inaugural President. Norm Cunningham was President on three occasions, while Ken Bosworth and Charlie Brown also held the post.

Until 1989, Dawn Hay had been WALTUA honorary secretary for seven years. This role was then assumed by Maxine Connolly, who had quickly risen through the ranks after winning the Alf Shave Trophy. At this juncture, Steven Stanley became the new President of WALTUA. One of Steven's first duties was to present Sandy Hay (Dawn's husband) with an Australian Lawn Tennis Umpires' Association Honour medal for 10 years distinguished service, both on the court and as an official at his local association.

Dawn and Sandy Hay had umpired at the Australian Open. After the completion of the National Tennis Centre at Flinders Park, several members of WALTUA sought to increase their experience by officiating at the annual 'grand slam' Australian Opens. As well, members sometimes attended training courses in the eastern States. For instance in 1991 Cathy Smith obtained a 'White Badge' which is accreditation from the ITF (*WALTA Minutes*, 15/8/1991) rarely obtained by local umpires.

The program for the umpires was never easily administered and the quest for more recruits was always on the agenda. The World Youth Cup posed particular difficulties as several ties were played simultaneously. The rejuvenated State Open, played on week-days, was not easy to cover. Another event which stretched the Association's resources to the limit was the World Veteran's events. The Hopman Cup, like the Davis Cup, was only played on one court but the latter was played over several days and evenings. Often inexperienced umpires had to cope with play that was immeasurably faster than was the norm in local competition.

When calls have been made for volunteers to supplement the WALTUA members, the response has come predominantly from women. For instance, with the Youth Cup over 80 people (mostly women) were recruited and trained as line umpires and eight qualified as Chair Umpires. According to the Tennis Australia Gender Equity Working Party document published in September 1992, the WALTUA had 68 members, of whom 31 were women. One theme of the WALTUA reports to Tennis West has been the genuine drive to attract more women to umpiring. As their membership is above the national average, some success has been achieved in this regard. Of course the question of gender equity has necessarily been considered by both Tennis Australia and Tennis West with umpiring being only one of the areas under review.

Gender equity

In March 1992 the Australian Sports Commission published a document entitled *Towards Gender Equity in Sport*. It was a practical guide for sporting organisations developing gender equity action plans. Tennis was identified as one of the eight sports to be examined so Tennis Australia established its Gender Equity Working Party. Given that the incumbent Tennis Australia President Geoff Pollard had expertise in demography, it is not surprising that this initiative was pursued. Various data on gender equity were obtained and an attitudinal questionnaire prepared. The questionnaire was prefaced with the statement that Tennis Australia and its affiliated State/Territory associations guaranteed, 'Australian men and women, boys and girls equity, whenever possible, in all aspects of the game including participation, training, competition. prizemoney, coaching, officiating and administration'. In essence this represented compliance with the *Commonwealth Sex Discrimination Act* (1984) and the *Western Australian Equal Opportunity Act* (1984).

Tennis is widely regarded as a sport in which women can participate at both the competitive and social levels without facing any obvious barriers. Likewise, there is no apparent reason why women can not exercise a significant administrative role. Historically, though, the number of registered women tennis players has been less than that for men. Tournament entries invariably reveal a much higher number of men and boys. At the Executive level, the percentage of women members has always been significantly below that of men.

Andrea Mitchell, Vice President of Tennis West

Reference has already been made to the number of women umpires in Western Australia. However, some comment is necessary on the data revealed in the broad survey. Tennis Australia's Executive Board (Council) did not have in 1993 one women member. At Tennis West the new nine-person directorate included one woman, Andrea Mitchell, the Vice-President. Later she had the honour of being the first woman to attend a Tennis Australia Board meeting in a representative capacity. By this time, she had filled a host of roles at Tennis West including several team management roles, numerous committees concerned with tennis development and a term as Chair of the State Selection Committee. For the historic Fed (previously Federation) Cup tie between Australia and the Slovak Republic conducted on April 22 and 23, 1995 Andrea Mitchell chaired the organising committee.

Importantly, though, women were gaining greater representation in other forums. The 125 member Council of registered club delegates comprised 96 men and 29 women. At the committee level, there were 50 women from a total membership of 122. In 1990, Tennis West passed a resolution that the important State Selection Panel must have at least two women (or men) on the six-member committee. What, then, did the registered players profile reveal?

Registered Players

	Men	Women	Total
Seniors	8,939	9,421	18,360
Juniors	4,626	2,673	7,299
Veterans	430	390	820
	13,995	12,484	26,479

At the senior and veterans level, the numbers of women appeared to be satisfactory. Nevertheless there were some grounds for concern regarding the significantly lower registration of junior girls. Given that only 71 of the 215 registered coaches were women it made the problem seemingly more difficult to effectively address. The response from Tennis West was to establish a committee on women's tennis within the Tennis Development Directorate. The chairperson was Jodie Bottrill (later Jones), a leading state league player at Corinthian Park. Other members of the committee were coach Debbie Thomas and experienced leading players Jenny Price, Mike Christmas, Scott Marshall and Michelle Phillips. However, the Committee was soon reconstituted with

Michelle Phillips, Tennis in Schools Coordinator (Courtesy The West Australian)

Player Development Director, Andrea Mitchell, as the Chairperson. To face the complicated challenge two men, Darryl Power and Harry Spilsbury, were joined by Lesley Hateley, Stephanie Martin, Helen Muir and Michelle Phillips. As the latter had been appointed Coordinator of Primary Schools Tennis in December 1991 (for a program funded by Healthway), it was evidence of the preparedness of Tennis West to promote women into its administrative structure. A further demonstration of this outlook was the appointment in April 1993 of Jacki Mitchell to the newly created position of Marketing Manager.

A considerable source of strength at Tennis West had been the Women's Auxiliary. On 4 May 1988, a dinner was conducted to celebrate 25 years of mid-week shield competition. Foundation and long-serving president Helen Waters introduced the original committee, provided a brief insight into the more difficult days when their Auxiliary was spurned and proposed a toast to the Association. An Honour Board, which was on display for the first time, showed that the turnover of office-bearers had increased since the early seasons (*Westennis*, October 1988, 37). For instance, in the 1985 to 1994 period, there were four Presidents: Dot Connolly, Marj Hetherington, Peg McFarlane and Lucy Nussbaum.

To lead the Women's Auxiliary meant hard work, its service and fund-raising activities had never been easy to organise. The scale of the mid-week ladies pennant competition required clockwork organisation. By the 1990/1991 season, there were 163 teams in the summer and 79 in the winter competition. So it was not surprising that, at the end of the same season, the Chairwoman of the Shield Match Committee, Jan Graham, decided to stand down. Significantly, though, Graham had moved to another challenge - the Presidency of the Sorrento club.

One woman who was President for several years of the prominent Belmont tennis club was Pam Henderson. She was granted life membership after also serving as treasurer and secretary in addition to being director for many major tournaments conducted at the club. Another role included membership of the Umpires Association. At Tennis West, Henderson was a club delegate for a decade, a member of the Shield Match Committee, and, for a time, the Chair of the Fund Raising committee. Amusingly, husband Tom reported that he had once gone looking for a local tennis club to give her a break from mundane housework. With four children and Pam's commitment to tennis, there is no doubt that Tom Henderson was subsequently required to make an indirect contribution to tennis, a role in the past more often filled by women (*Westennis*, December 1987, 23).

Peg McFarlane, valuable service to tennis

Indicative of changing times was an earlier headline 'Women Play a Big Role on WA scene', preceding one of Arthur Marshall's 'Cross Court' newspaper articles (*Daily News*, 30/1/1981, 29). After noting that the All England Lawn Tennis and Croquet Club continued to exclude women from committee work, Marshall referred to women Presidents in WALTA clubs. Apart from Pam Henderson he mentioned Lesley Portelli at Cockburn and Pat Barblett at Nedlands. Just across the highway, Mary Edwards had two years as President in the early 1980s of the historic Cottesloe club. Mary Edwards ranked as high as number two in the State in 1946 and had been a fine player and major contributor to tennis. Husband Eddie Edwards, who shared with Mary the distinction of club life membership, had been President of Cottesloe two decades earlier (Adamson, 1992). Yet, by the 1991/1992 season, the number of women who held the office of President at the 58 WALTA metropolitan clubs could nearly be 'counted on one hand'. The list read: Kay Seeber

Women's auxiliary 25 years celebration foundation committee Left to right: Mary Ward, Mavis Cooke, Helen Waters, Doris Rapley and Gwyn White

(Bullcreek), Phyliss Rothery (East Fremantle), Miriam Garbutt (Kwinana), Leoni Clymo (Manning), Phyllis Lawrence (Safety Bay) and Jan Graham (Sorrento).

Although it was comparatively rare for women to hold the post of club president, the 1991/1992 *WALTA Annual Report* revealed that 39 of the 58 affiliated clubs had women secretaries. Moreover, six of the 11 country zone secretaries were women. With the barriers being broken down and Dr Carmen Lawrence having a term as Premier of Western Australia and providing a role model, there was an expectation that women would be more prominent in the future administration of both clubs and Tennis West. This was a theme embodied into the Tennis West Corporate Plan which was formulated during 1992.

The Australian Sports Commission has attempted to persuade national sporting organisations to develop corporate plans. Commission statistics indicate that tennis competes with cricket as the major participant sport in Australia so it was appropriate that Tennis Australia should prepare its plan for the future. In Western Australia, the Department for Sport and Recreation had also encouraged the various sporting codes to develop corporate plans. During 1992, Tennis West, with the Tennis Australia document at hand, undertook this exercise. It was the first occasion in the history of the Association that this had been done on a methodical basis. This was soon followed by a review of management practices at Tennis West with a firm of consultants (Compass International) engaged for the task. A comprehensive review of the WALTA Constitution undertaken by dedicated directors Dene Rundel, Michael Lee and Harry Spilsbury, was endorsed at the December 1994 Council meeting.

McDonald's Tennis Australia

The publication of the *Tennis Australia Corporate Plan* 1992-1996 which included an addendum on the benefits of affiliation to both Tennis Australia and the various State (and Territory) Associations (*Tennis Australia Handbook*, 1993, 18-22) was soon followed by a restructuring of the Tennis Australia Council. Voting rights were granted to the Australian Capital Territory and the Northern Territory on the basis of one vote for each Territory.

Queensland, South Australia, Tasmania and Western Australia were each granted two votes, while New South Wales and Victoria, were each allocated three votes. Western Australia, always circumspect about changes to federal compacts regardless of whether they are sporting or political structures, endorsed the changes.

In 1993 federal frictions surfaced when Tennis Australia proposed a revenue raising ball-approval fee levy. Western Australia, represented by Alan Hicks and Harry Spilsbury, expressed concerns about the viability of the scheme. Nevertheless, Tennis Australia decided to go ahead and levy a one dollar per dozen fee to be incurred at the point of import or manufacture as from 1 July, 1994, regardless of whether Western Australia approved (*WALTA Minutes*, 21/10/1993). This action was a reminder that membership in a federation requires concessions and compromises that are not always easy to accept.

Back in 1904, Western Australia was a founding member of the LTAA. Despite the costs incurred 'by the tyranny of distance', for which the Association is not adequately compensated, secession has not been on the agenda at the WALTA. And in December, 1993 Tennis West was partner to a simultaneous announcement in 11 major cities and provincial centres, that McDonald's would continue its sponsorship of Australian tennis for at least three more years.

The agreement, estimated to be worth about S3 million, meant that McDonald's would sponsor the Australian teams in the Davis and Federation Cups, international men's and women's touring squads and maintain the comprehensive junior program. Although some of traditionalists pondered the direction of modern tennis, the President of Tennis Australia, Geoff Pollard, was quoted as saying 'the multi-million dollar alliance, one of Australia's most significant sponsorship agreements [was] a coup for Australian tennis'. Alan Hicks, President of Tennis West, then reminded journalists that 'all existing Western Australian programs will continue thanks to the sponsorship' (*McDonald's Tennis Australia Media Release*, 16/12/1993).

McDonald's money was playing a role in ensuring cooperation between Tennis Australia and its constituent bodies. Some critics, mostly outside of the tennis community, held some reservations about whether tennis had achieved a maximum return for the sponsorship. However, the partnership with McDonald's was clearly having a significant impact on the sport as both Tennis West and Tennis Australia moved towards their respective centenaries.

Chapter Twenty

TENNIS WEST

As already noted, the origins of tennis can be traced back to the Middle Ages, the modern rules of the game, with only minor modifications, were cast by the cricket establishment at the MCC to govern the first 1877 Wimbledon tournament. The popularity of tennis, which could be played by most age groups and both males and females soon spread throughout the world. In Australia it had its beginnings in family homesteads and the first records of tournament play in the West, on a handicap basis, has been traced to Government House in the 1880s.

With the goldrushes in the 1890s quickly swelling the population of the western third of the continent, the family homestead basis of tennis was inadequate to cater for the increasing demand for tournament competition, inter-suburban and inter-town matches and even inter-colonial contests. The response in Western Australia, as in the other colonies, was to establish a tennis association.

In Western Australia, however, the attempt to create a tennis association was originally thwarted partly because of the keen rivalry between Perth and Fremantle. Tennis, too, had to emerge from its status as a winter game for cricketers. As well, many preferred tennis to remain with the homestead structure because this was an effective means of limiting membership of the 'club'.

After three recorded attempts by essentially the same group of 'well to do' people, the Lawn Tennis Association of Western Australia came into permanent existence in April 1903. 'Lawn' tennis, as it was to be known, was to be advanced by the conduct of a State Open and other tournaments, an inter-club pennant competition and inter-State contests. The Association's primary objective was to control competitive tennis, all members of affiliated clubs being 'amateurs'.

In the winter of 1903, Saturday pennants for men were organised and in the same season mid-week pennants for women were commenced. The Association established jurisdiction over the annual State Opens, which were to be completed before the beginning of the cricket season. In 1906, prior to the Open, an interstate match was conducted against New South Wales. For the State Open Championships before the Great War (1914-1918), a small 'company' of gentlemen regularly played the State 'circuit'. This meant that several leading national players often participated in the Open, with the occasional opportunity to play an interstate fixture.

In 1909, the Australasian Lawn Tennis Association (later the LTAA), which had been founded in 1904, allocated Western Australia the Australasian Open at the Zoo grounds in South Perth. This reflected confidence in the capacity of the Western Australian Association to conduct a major event. However, attempts by WALTA officials to gain a Davis Cup fixture, which had already captured the imagination of the sporting public, were not successful, although in 1913 a British Isles team visited Perth.

The 1913 Australasian Open was again played in Perth at Mueller Park in Subiaco. On this occasion Ernie Parker, the champion of the decade (and also a State cricketer) defeated his namesake Harry Parker (NSW) to win the title. In 1909, Ernie Parker had lost in the Open final to Tony Wilding, the great Davis Cup player and Wimbledon champion. Both Parker and Wilding lost their lives in the war-time trenches of Europe.

The Great War had a devastating impact on the Western Australian sporting community, although even by 1913 there had been disconcerting signs that the conduct of feature tournaments had not necessarily benefited the Tennis Association. Resolutions were tabled to terminate the operations of the Western Australian Lawn Tennis Association. With several clubs unable to afford affiliation fees, the Association fell into limbo, although a small Executive conducted medal tournaments for the Patriotic Fund and the schools competition. One significant development in this difficult period was the inauguration of a separate schools competition for boys and girls, known as the Slazenger Cup.

The recovery after the Great War was initially very slow. However, once the dynamic secretary George Linwood took office, there was a rapid increase in the scale of activities. In 1921, another Australasian Open was held in Perth at the Association headquarters, which had become known as Kitchener Park. Notably, none of the 'company' of top players travelled to the West for the tournament. The men's singles was won by Rice Gemmell, a leading local player who unfortunately could not make an impression on the national scene. Mrs Violet Mather, the victor in the State Women's Open, which was conducted at the same time, became a legend in the West and was described as a 'class above the rest'.

When Linwood left the State, to be tragically killed in Calcutta, he had been modestly successful in broadening the base of tennis. A Country Week carnival had commenced. It had been on the agenda for at least a decade as tennis was strong in many country areas. A school children's championship was first conducted by the Association in 1923, with Western Australia joining the annual national junior boys Linton Cup competition a year later. Earlier, in 1921, Western Australia had sent its first senior team to Adelaide to compete in interstate matches.

From the mid-Twenties, tennis grew in popularity as its appeal was broadened to attract a wider spectrum of the population. The newspapers competed to record the activities of the Association, giving rise to the label of the 'golden age of tennis'. Interest lay in Association tournaments and club championships rather than inter-club pennants. Local champions such as Ron Ford and Mollie McGrath (King) were celebrated players. It was not until changes were made in the affiliation fee structure that more emerging clubs were prepared to join the Association. In 1928 the Association made a decision to discontinue its lease of the Kitchener Park (Mueller Park) courts in Subiaco. The cost of maintaining the courts had become a millstone around the neck of the Association. Unfortunately, attempts to establish a tennis centre at another location were not successful.

From the late Twenties, King's Park became the 'Mecca' of tennis' in the West. More style and glamour began to be linked with tennis. It was the venue for several international test matches in which Australia competed against most of the the best players from France, Japan, England and Germany. When coupled with the forceful leadership style of the Association President Sinclair McGibbon, who had strong King's Park connections, there were complaints that King's Park was too central to Association affairs.

McGibbon's successor, Vernon Mursell, had a moderate and conciliatory style. He was also keen to establish a tennis centre separate from King's Park. However, much of Mursell's term (1938 to 1948) had to be devoted to maintaining the Association through the difficult war years and supervising recovery. By the time he retired, the Association, if judged in terms of membership statistics, had only just recovered the position it had achieved when he assumed office. Particularly in women's tennis from McGibbon's and Mursell's terms (and beyond), when Sacred Heart dominated the Slazenger Cup, the Catholic Tennis Association was very strong. Its influence, together with the community basis of tennis in rural towns, helped challenge the thesis that tennis was mainly a 'Protestant pursuit' for the well-to-do.

The Second World War spurred development of fine young players, as the Slazenger Cup and the Schoolchildren's Tournaments continued. Whether the circumstances made these young people more self reliant and disciplined is difficult to establish. Indicative of the increased junior strength was the capacity of Western Australia to win the 1949 Linton Cup with Clive Wilderspin, John Blacklock, Brian Tobin and Noel Pearse. At the same carnival, Wilderspin won the Australian junior boys singles championship and Wilderspin and Blacklock won the doubles title.

In the postwar era Clive Wilderspin became a household name in Western Australia. Wilderspin epitomised the best attributes of the sport such as athleticism, sportsmanship and determination. He represented Australia and defeated many leading players, such as Lew Hoad, but did not gain inclusion in the Davis Cup team. The Davis Cup contests excited great public interest in this era, as Australia was able to regularly produce champions capable of winning many Wimbledon and other Grand Slam titles. Some Davis Cup zone matches were played in Perth. Although this beautiful, but windy and sometimes hot city, was not the venue for a Challenge Round, the WALTA indirectly benefitted financially from these contests.

Western Australians bathed in the Davis Cup glory and had the opportunity to watch many of the Grand Slam champions at King's Park but they did not share in the production of champions. The health of tennis at the social level was generally sound, perhaps sometimes militating against a focus on potential champions. Nevertheless, affiliated club membership numbers briefly dropped in the Sixties. Association officials had to devote attention to bridging the great amateur/professional divide. Although the first open Wimbledon was conducted in 1968, it took several years for signs of the division to disappear. Many of the difficulties arose from disagreements between the LTAA and the WALTA about the best course of action. From 1976, direct WALTA representation on the LTAA Board, which President Barry Sanders regarded as essential to serve the best interests of Western Australia, assisted in the creation of a very productive relationship with the national body.

Once the restrictions on amateurism were fully removed, sponsorship became an important element of the revenue base of the Association and necessary for the mounting of tournaments. As a result conducting tournaments was often viewed with reservations by club committees. Sponsorship assistance was also negotiated for junior tournaments, junior coaching and annual events such as Country Week. Government grants, administered through the Department of Sport and Recreation, also became increasingly significant for the extension of Association operations, such as the creation in 1976 of a development officer position. In 1986, the appointment of a State Coach (John Fairchild), which had been enthusiastically endorsed by President Harry Spilsbury, was also notable.

A large proportion of the sponsorship revenue was directed at junior tennis, with some important agreements being negotiated at the national level. From 1985, McDonald's Company supported a national junior tennis development plan and the number of squads was greatly increased. Opportunities for young Western Australian players to compete in the eastern states were also increased. Moreover, the number of interstate junior teams was expanded and leading juniors such as Carl Turich, Paul Kilderry, Angie Marik, Siobhan Drake-Brockman and James Sekulov, were selected to tour overseas with national teams. The noted junior coach Maureen Smith became a national selector and was chosen to manage national teams to Europe.

The Association lobbied hard for the introduction in 1976 of the Reid Cup interstate competition for 16 and under competitors. It supported the 14 and under Sproule/Stevens for boys and Mary Hawton for girls, which was commenced in 1983, but was initially lukewarm about the decision to extend interstate competition to the Rod Laver and Margaret Court Cups for the 12 and under age groups. Problems with junior tennis, such as poor etiquette, the 'ugly parent' syndrome, and 'burn-out' were of particular concern. On the other hand, as part of a policy to prevent players leaving competitive tennis, several years of advocacy by the WALTA were needed to have the interstate Challenge Cup for senior players introduced.

In senior tennis, an increasing number of players tried their luck on the circuit, but very few won major professional tournaments. When Margaret Court moved to Western Australia, she continued to build on her wonderful record. Lesley Hunt was a local product who reached the top 10 in the world. Another local Elizabeth Smylie (Sayers) developed a reputation as one of the world's leading doubles players, with a win in the 1985 Wimbledon Doubles Championship as the highlight. Jenny Byrne was another, who, at times was able to make an impression on the circuit. Christine Dorey (Matison) and Mary Collins (Sawyer) had the distinction of reaching the semi-finals of an Australian Open. In the Seventies and Eighties, Dorey's record in State competition was formidable.

Elizabeth Smylie (then Sayers) and Lesley Hunt were respectively associated with Western Australia's only two Wilson Cup victories. Elizabeth Sayers led the victorious team in 1981, supported by Robyn Lamb and Sue Johnson. In 1993, Lesley Hunt was the manager when Siobhan Drake-Brockman, Angie Marik and Kerrie Thomas were successful. After participating in the inaugural Wilson Cup in 1931, and controversially sending a women's only team to the Australian Championships in 1933, no women's state teams were selected to tour until 1947. It appears, however, that in recent years the introduction of more underage State teams, together with leading juniors often playing satellite tournaments, has diminished the prestige associated with the Wilson (and Linton) Cup.

In men's tennis, Tim Clayton, Gary Penberthy, Rob Casey and Chris Johnstone emulated Clive Wilderspin by being chosen to represent Australia. Like Wilderspin, though, they did not gain Davis Cup selection. In 1972 Casey had followed in Wilderspin's footsteps to share with Phil Sofoulis, Ross

Olivieri and Phil Chamberlain a rare Linton Cup victory. Nevertheless, Casey and Penberthy remained particularly strong forces in Western Australian tennis and for several years dominated both the local tournament scene and shield tennis. Later both were influential in the coaching and administration of tennis in the West.

The Association undertook several revisions of its expanding shield match competition. In the last decade, as part of a strategy to increase its profile the 'A' grade section was renamed State Grade and eventually State League. Sponsorship by Westpac assisted the Association to strengthen the competition, although player payments at the club level became a source of controversy. There were also several revisions of the junior age categories for inter-club competition. Veterans were provided with opportunities for shield competition.

The scale of interest in veterans' tennis grew to such an extent that a separate organisation was formed. The initially separate men's and women's sections amalgamated and gained associate status with the WALTA. Apart from a program of social tennis, the veterans conduct State and national championships and have also organised international competitions in Perth. The grass courts of Perth may militate against producing ATP champions but they provide an excellent environment for veterans' tennis. Paradoxically, success in the veterans' category has come to many Western Australians. One feature of the growth of the Veterans' organisation has been the cordial and productive relationship that has been maintained with the WALTA.

Two other associate bodies which, at times, have had uneasy dealings with the WALTA have been the Umpires Association and the Tennis Coaches Association. The friction between the WALTA officials and the Umpires' body mainly stemmed from disagreements about umpiring professional matches in Perth. Prominent amongst the Umpires was Norm Cunningham, who was a forceful advocate of open tennis. Obtaining umpires to satisfactorily service hallmark events in Perth has never been easy, as umpiring is often regarded as a 'thankless task'.

The membership of the Tennis Coaches Association has necessarily been confined. It took almost two decades for its members to have various WALTA restrictions (such as those on playing shield tennis and assuming managerial and administrative roles, including membership of the State selection panel) lifted. The Tennis Coaches provide an annual series of awards to foster better coaching and recognise major contributions to the advancement of tennis. Tennis, especially from the professionals' viewpoint, is now a 'sport' rather than a game which requires specialist training from an early age to produce champions on the national and international circuit.

While the professionals focus on the standard version of tennis, the WALTA, with long-serving official John Whitton in the vanguard has had to innovate with mini-versions of the game, under the label of 'ace tennis', partly to counter the popularity of other sports gaining a share of the market for modified rules. The growth of T-ball as a preparation for baseball (and softball) was the most obvious instance. The success of 'ace' tennis cannot perhaps be measured entirely in terms of participants but by its capacity to foster interest for future club membership.

The realisation that many children, particularly in lower socio-economic areas, were not being introduced to tennis was the rationale for the 1992 launch of the 'Tennis in Schools Programme'. Human movement graduate

Michelle Phillips was chosen as the inaugural director, an appointment recognising the Association's need for more expertise in the physical education field. Attempts to place tennis in the school curriculum have been on the agenda for most of the Association's history. Some professional coaches, notably Clarry Treloar, Herbert Edwards and Max Bonner left an imprint on school tennis during the era when professionals were forbidden to play tournament tennis. One of the key objectives of the short-lived Tennis Foundation in the early 1970s had been to extend tennis opportunities in schools. But funding this aspect of Association activities has always been difficult to obtain. The 'Tennis in Schools Programme' was funded by Healthway, which had been established by State government statute in 1990 to administer funds derived from a tax on tobacco. Two years earlier, the creation of a State Players Development Trust, a concept long advocated by player and coach, publicist and innovator Arthur Marshall, provided a further avenue for funds for elite junior development.

Another scheme, known as 'Oz' Tennis, aimed to take tennis to groups which might not otherwise have the opportunity to play the game. This meant the provision of coaching and equipment to participating schools designated as disadvantaged by the Ministry of Education and the Catholic Education Office. Although the scheme had its beginnings at an earlier date in the eastern states, it was not launched in Western Australia until 1990. A key figure in the promotion of the program was Paul McNamee, the former Wimbledon doubles champion, who moved to Western Australia in 1988 to present the Hopman Cup. Although the scope of Oz Tennis was limited, the Hopman Cup soon grew into a hallmark event of international significance.

Association officials initially had some reservations about the introduction of the Hopman Cup, with its men's and women's singles and mixed doubles format. As it was to be conducted in the Christmas-New Year break, it posed a threat to the success of the annual City of Perth Tournament. However, McNamee's capacity to attract top-ranking international players to the event, saw the annual crowds grow from some 40,000 to over 70,000 in the first seven years of the Cup. Further evidence of the acceptance of the concept was the introduction in late 1992 of a junior series. James Sekulov and Siobhan Drake-Brockman, two of the State's most promising juniors who had achieved national recognition, won the inaugural Hopman Junior Cup. Drake-Brockman was again successful in 1994 when she teamed with Jaymon Crabb to win the third Junior Hopman Cup. An international element, which had been introduced to the tournament, enhanced the quality of the field.

Whilst the Hopman Cup required modern marketing and business planning, the same demands were being faced by the Association as it moved towards its centennial. New logos were adopted, and, in keeping with an earlier move by the LTAA to use a trading name (Tennis Australia), the acronym WALTA was cast aside for Tennis West. An Executive Director, Brian Beers, was appointed and the Constitution was revamped. A restructuring resulted in the election of a Board of Directors, followed by a review of office procedures. Reflecting the direction of the operations of Tennis West, a marketing position was created with Jackie Mitchell soon named as the successful applicant. Formerly from Victoria, the home of Tennis Australia, her appointment recalled the impact since the goldrushes that Victorians have had on the history of tennis in Western Australia.

As the administration of sports associations became more professional, the

Tennis West Board of Directors 1994-1995. Back: Michael Lee, Brian Bracewell, Robert Wallman, Bill Artingstall, Dene Rundle, Leonie Bell (Secretary). Front: Andrea Mitchell, Alan Hicks, Brian Beers (General Manager). Harry Spilsbury was absent on international tennis business.

State Ministry for Sport and Recreation advocated the preparation of corporate plans. Tennis Australia adopted the same stance and prepared its own five-year plan, which provided a useful model for Tennis West. Under President Alan Hicks the opportunity for input into the plan was provided to a wide range of people in the tennis community. The presidency, too, required review as it was not afforded any remuneration. When Dr Saw first held the post in 1903 it tended to have nominal status. In the 1950s Justice Walker and Ken Miller were successive Presidents who held the office in conjunction with administrative roles in other sporting codes. By the 1980s, the youthful Barry Sanders found occupying the presidency and a senior position in the Water Authority of Western Australia to be exacting. Thereafter, Harry Spilbury and Alan Hicks as retired accountants, gave the office virtual, full-time commitment.

Tennis Australia had also established a gender equity working party, which produced a document revealing the absence of women from top administrative positions. In Western Australia a committee was set-up to examine the role of women in tennis. A significant development was the appointment, in 1990, of Andrea Mitchell as Association Vice-President. Two newly-created positions, that of Coordinator of the 'Tennis in Schools Programme' and Marketing Officer were gained by women. The number of registered senior women players exceeded that of men but in junior ranks the situation was reversed. The creation of the Women's Auxiliary in 1961 had given a great boost to the participation of women in midweek pennant play, but the low number of women competing in tournaments remained a concern. Given that women from 1934 to 1965 were constitutionally excluded from membership of Council (and the Executive), the administrative role of women only began to significantly alter as the 1990s unfolded.

The Corporate Plan, in concert with Tennis Australia's five-year plan, was futuristic, revealing how Tennis West was moving toward a more professional management of tennis. From uncertain beginnings, the Association has grown from a few small clubs conducting winter pennant tennis to administering one of the state's major sports. Surprisingly, there have been very few rule changes. However, the speed of the game, the equipment and dress of the players has altered remarkably since the turn of the century. Administrators, monitoring international and national developments, have

Alan Hicks, one of the most democratic Presidents.

been forced to take steps to arrest the decline in sportsmanship. A player behaviour code, with the deduction of points for various misdemeanours, has been introduced.

Throughout all these changes the Association's finances have been prudently managed. So pervasive has been this approach that it has led to some assertions that unnecessary caution has prevailed. The Association had no debts but delays over the building of a tennis centre had led to criticism that the Association had too often failed to seize opportunities. Although tennis is a major participation sport in Western Australia, it had not received government assistance for a major facility as had Australian rules football and cricket. Perhaps the best chance for such aid lay during the Forrest government's term in the 1890s when cricket took advantage of having established its association ahead of that of tennis and gained the WACA ground at peppercorn rental. For tennis this situation was soon to be alleviated with the announcement in June 1994 of a State government lease and funds for a tennis centre at Burswood, near the central business district.

So far the Association cannot claim to have produced a wealth of champions. The 'tyranny of distance', which contributes to anti-centralist sentiments can be employed as a motivator in team sports to defeat the best from the East. However, in tennis the isolation factor, particularly before the McDonald's program, limited the opportunities for competition. Producing champions was not a specific objective when the Association was created to establish a more competitive tennis environment. There is no doubt that a Grand Slam singles winner would provide a stimulus to tennis in Western Australia. The Hopman Cup demonstrated some of the latent interest in tennis in the West although this is not being accompanied by significant increases in participation levels. The challenge remains for the Association to fulfil its present functions as well as to harness and develop the positive views in the community of one of the world's great democratic sports. In early 1994 the appointment of Geoff Masters, as Director of Coaching, has offered the prospect of more initiatives for the future. With Alan Hicks, one of the most 'democratic' of Association Presidents at the helm, a basis for optimism prevails.

BIBLIOGRAPHY

Articles and Books

Adamson, P. (1992). *Our Club: The History of the Cottesloe Tennis Club.* The Cottesloe Tennis Club Bi-centennial Committee and Members, Perth: Hawthorn Press.

Alderman, R.B. (1974). The Socio-psychological value of games, sport, and physical activity. In *Psychological Behaviour in Sport.* Toronto: W.B. Saunders Company.

Allen, J. (1979). *Learn to Play Tennis.* Chicago: Rand McNally.

Arnot, R.B. & Gaines, C.L. (1984). *Sportselection.* London: Pelham Books.

Atkin, Ronald (Ed.) (1985). *For the Love of Tennis.* Sydney: Stanley Paul.

Baker, William J. (1982). *Sports in the Western World.* Totowa: Rowman and Littlefield.

Bartlett, Michael & Gillen, Bob (1981). *The Tennis Book.* New York: Arbor House.

Battye, O.K. (1979). 'Sir Winthrop Hackett: The Editor'. In Lyall Hunt (Ed.) *Westralian Portraits.* Nedlands: The University of Western Australia Press.

Bell, Colin J. (1976). *Tennis Coaching in Western Australia.* Thesis: Teachers' Higher Certificate.

Bennett, G. (1985). 'Sport'. In *On This Side: Themes and Issues in Western Australian History.* Perth: Bookland.

Bolton, G.C. (1983). 'Kingsmill, Sir Walter 1864-1935'. In *Australian Dictionary of Biography. Volume* 9, 1891-1939. Melbourne: Melbourne University Press.

Bignell, Merle (1971). *First the Spring: A History of the Shire of Kojonup.* Nedlands: University of Western Australia Press.

Blacker, M. (Ed.) (1993). *The Bulletin Australian Almanac and Book of Facts 1994.* Sydney: ACP Publisher.

Bloomfield, J. (1978). *The Development of Sport in Western Australia.* Perth: Community Recreation Council of Western Australia.

Boyle, J.A.H. (1972). 'Some sporting activities'. In Helen Weller (Ed.) *Recollections from a Shoreline.* Perth: Artlook.

Brabenec, Josef (1980). *Tennis: The Decision Making Sport.* London: Hancock House Publishers.

Brady, Maurice (1959). *The Centre Court Story.* London: Sportsmen's Book Club.

Brasch, R. (1986). *How Did Sports Begin? A Look at the Origin of Man at Play.* Melbourne: Longman.

Broomhall, F.H. (1983). *Mount Marshall: A History of the District and its People from Earliest Times to 1942.* Bencubbin: Shire of Mt Marshall.

Burton, A. (n.d.). *Hale School Perth: The Story of its Foundation and Early Years 1858-1900.* Perth: Co-operative Printing Works.

Campbell, J. (1991). 'An Investigation into the Function and Structure of the Men's Tennis League in Western Australia'. Unpublished research thesis, Edith Cowan University.

Cashman, Richard (1986). 'Sport, big business and the spectator: The anguish of the sports fan'. *Current Affairs Bulletin.* Vol.63, No.1, 12-18.

Clerici, Gianni (1975). *The Ultimate Tennis Book.* (Richard J. Wiezell, trans.) Chicago: Follett Publishing Company.

Colebatch, Sir Hal. (Ed.) (1929). *A Story of a Hundred Years:* Western Australia 1829-1929. Perth: Government Printer.

Coombe, D.C. (1949). *A History of the Davis Cup. Sydney:* Australasian Publishing Company.

Crowley, F.K. (1960). *Australia's Western Third.* London: Macmillan.

Cumes, J. (1979). *Their Chastity was not too Rigid: Leisure Times in Early Australia.* Melbourne: Longman Cheshire.

Crisp, L. (1983). *Australian National Government.* (Fifth edition). Melbourne: Longman Cheshire.

Crowley, F.K. (1971). *Forrest 1847-1918. Volume 1, 1847-91. Apprenticeship to Premiership.* St Lucia, Queensland: University of Queensland Press.

Cunningham, N. (1978). *Southern Suburbs Tennis Association: Golden Jubilee 1982: The First Fifty Years.*

Daly, John A. (1972). 'Sport and Society: The Role of Sport and Games in the Social Development of Early Australia'. *The Australian Journal of Physical Education.* Vol.55, pp†31-37.

Davison-Lungley, R. (1979). *Let's Play Tennis.* London: Octopus Books.

de Garis, Brian (1979). 'Sir George Shenton: The Merchant'. In Lyall Hunt (Ed.) *Westralian Portraits.* Nedlands: University of Western Australia Press.

de Garis, Brian (1981a). 'Political Tutelage 1829-1870'. In C.T. Stannage (Ed.) *A New History of Western Australia.* Nedlands: University of Western Australia Press.

de Garis, Brian (1981b). 'Self Government and the Evolution of Political Parties, 1871-1911'. In C.T. Stannage (Ed.). *A New History of Western Australia.* Nedlands: University of Western Australia Press.

Dowe, H. (Ed.) (1966). *Trollope's Australia.* Melbourne: Thomas Nelson.

Duncan, Tim. (1982). 'The Politics in VFL's Boom'. *The Bulletin.* August 3, 1982, 32-36.

Dunning, Eric (Ed.) (1970). *The Sociology of Sport.* London: Frank Cass.

Dunstan, Keith (1973). *Sports 1973.* North Melbourne: Cassell Australia.

Dunstan, K. (1984). *Tennis, A Dictionary.* Melbourne: Sun Books.

East, A. (Ed.) (1984). *The First Decade: The History of the Veterans Tennis Club of Western Australia (Inc)* 1972-1982.

Easton, Leonard, A. (1971). *Stirling City.* Nedlands: University of Western Australia Press.

Edwards, Herbert A. (1945). *Lawn Tennis: Foundation Strokes.* Perth: Service Printing.

Egan, Jack (1984), in consultation with Adrian Quist. *Tennis, the Greats 1920-1960.* Sydney: ABC/Collins.

Evans, R. (1988). *Tennis: The First Twenty Years.* London: Bloomsbury Publishing.

Evans, Richard (1982). *McEnroe: A Rage for Perfection.* London: Sidgivich and Jackson.

Ewers, J.K. (1959). *Bruce Rock: The Story of a District.* Bruce Rock District Road Board.

Facey, A.B. (1981). *A Fortunate Life.* Ringwood: Penguin Books.

Fewster, Kevin (1984). 'Advantage Australia: Davis Cup Tennis 1950-1959'. *Meanjin.* 43(2). 273-285.

Fraser, N. (1974). *Successful Tennis.* South Melbourne: Thomas Nelson.

Garnett, M. (1983). *A History of Royal Tennis in Australia.* Mt Waverley: Historical Publications.

Gervas, S. (1992). *Kulin (1919) to Tuscany (1989): Journey of a Lifetime.* Perth: Promascio Conventions.

Glanville, Brian (1981). *The Puffin Book of Tennis.* Harmondsworth: Penguin.

Goolagong Cawley, E. & Jarratt, P. (1993). *The Evonne Goolagong Story.* East Roseville: Simon and Schuster.

Greble, William E. (1979). *A Bold Yeomanry: Social Change in a Wheat Belt District, Kulin 1848-1970.* Perth: Kulin Shire Council.

Hagan, J. (1987). 'A Study of the Latent Demand for Night Tennis in the Floreat Area'. Unpublished research thesis Edith Cowan University.

Haley, B. (1978). *The Healthy Body and Victorian Culture.* Massachusetts: Harvard University Press.

Hasluck, Alexandra (1977). *Victorian and Edwardian Perth from Old Photographs*. Sydney: John Ferguson.

Hemery, David (1986). *Pursuit of Sporting Excellence*. London: Willow Books.

Heads, I. & Lester, G. (1988). *200 Years of Australian Sport: A Glorious Obsession*. North Ryde: Angus & Robertson.

Hopman, H. (1972). *Better Tennis*. London: Kaye and Ward.

Horne, D. (1966). *The Lucky Country*. (rev.ed.). Sydney: Angus & Robertson.

Hoch, Paul (1972). *Rip Off The Big Game: The Explanation of Sports by the Power Elite*. Doubleday Anchor.

Hovis, F. (Ed.) (1973). *Tennis for Women*. London: Angus & Robertson.

Howell, R.A. & M.L. (1984). *Foundations of Physical Education*. Queensland: William Brooks.

Hunt, Lyall (1979). 'Sir Walter James: The Social Reformer'. In Lyall Hunt (Ed.) *Westralian Portraits*. Nedlands: University of Western Australia Press.

Hunt, L. (1983). 'Sir John Winthrop Hackett'. *Australian Dictionary of Biography*. Vol.9, 1891-1939. Melbourne: Melbourne University Press.

Humphries, R. (1978). 'Tennis'. In *The Best Years in Australian Sport*. Kurralta Park: Frost Holdings.

Inglis, Gordon (1912). *Sport and Pastime in Australia*. London: Methuen.

Jacques, T.D. & Pavia, G.R. (1976). *Sport in Australia: Selected Readings in Physical Education*. Sydney: McGraw-Hill Book Company Australia Pty Ltd.

Jaggard, Ed. (1993). *Garth: The Story of Graham McKenzie*. South Fremantle: Fremantle Arts Centre Press.

Jaggard, E. (1984). *The Premier Club*: Cottesloe Surf Life Saving Club's First Seventy Five Years. Cottesloe: Cottesloe Surf Life Saving Club.

Jaggard, Edwin (1979). *A Challenge Answered: A History of Surf Lifesaving in Western Australia*. Perth: Vanguard Service Print.

James, Henry C. (1972). Written and compiled. *Western Australia: A Pictorial Parade of 150 Years*. (Second edition). Perth: Rigby.

James, Ruth Marchant (1977). *Heritage of Pines: A History of the Town of Cottesloe*. Perth, Western Australia: Vanguard Service Print.

Jenkinson, M. (1985). 'Overview'. In *Australian Sport: A Profile*. Canberra: Australian Government Publishing Service.

Johnson, J. (1985). *Grand Slam Australia: The Story of the Australian Open Tennis Championships*. Newport: Courtney Books.

Johnson, Joseph (1989). *Amazing Grace: The Story of the Grace Park Lawn Tennis Club 1989-1989*. Hawthorn: Grace Park Lawn Tennis Club.

Joukovsky-Vaisvila, O. (1978). *Around the Rock: A History of the Shire of Nungarin*. Western Australia: Nungarin Shire Council.

Kinross-Smith, G. (1982). *The Sweet Spot: One Hundred Years of Life and Tennis in Geelong*. Melbourne: Hyland House.

Kinross-Smith, G. (1985). 'Chase Better Than a Yard and Worse Than Gallery: Royal Tennis in the Antipodes'. *Sporting Traditions*, 1, 2, 91-95.

Kinross-Smith, G. (1987). 'Privilege in Tennis and Lawn Tennis: The Geelong and Royal South Yarra Examples but not Forgetting the Story of the Farmer's Wrist'. *Sporting Traditions*. 3(2), 189-216.

Kinross-Smith, G. (1994a). 'Lawn Tennis'. In Wray Vamplew and Brian Stoddart (Eds.) *Sport in Australia: A Social History*. Cambridge: Cambridge University Press.

Kinross-Smith, G. (1994b). 'Lawn Tennis'. In Wray Vamplew (Ed.) *The Oxford Companion to Australian*

Sport. Second Edition. Melbourne: Oxford University Press, 248-254.

Lester, Gary (1984). *Australians at the Olympics: A Definitive History.* Melbourne: Kingfisher Books.

Laver, Rod (with Bud Collins). (1971). *The Education of a Tennis Player*. New York: Simon and Schuster.

Lawson, Ronald (1973). *Brisbane in the 1890's: A Study of an Australian Urban Society*. St Lucia: University of Queensland Press.

Matthews, B. (1985). *Game, Set and Glory: A History of the Australian Tennis Championships.* Hawthorn: The Five Mile Press.

Matthews, B. (1987). *Pat Cash: My Story*. Ringwood: Penguin Books.

Mandle, W.C. (1973). 'Cricket and Nationalism in the Nineteenth Century'. In T.D. Jacques & G.R. Pavia (Eds.) (1976). *Sport in Australia*. Sydney: McGraw-Hill.

Mandlikova, H. (1989). *Hana*. London: George Weidenfeld.

McClemans, Sheila (1979). 'Sir Archibald Burt: The Chief Justice'. In Lyall Hunt (Ed.) *Westralian Portraits*. Nedlands: University of Western Australia Press.

McFarlane, D. (Ed.) (1990). *The Guinnes Book of Records*. Barcelona: Guinnes Publishing.

McGregor, Craig (1980). *The Australian People*. Sydney: Hodder and Stoughton.

McKernan, Michael (1993). (Selected and Edited), *The Makers of Australia's Sporting Traditions.* Melbourne: Melbourne University Press.

McLean, Ron (1983). *Country Cracks: The Story of NSW Country Tennis*. Gunnedah, Australia: The Namra Valley Independent.

Medlycott, J. (1977). *100 Years of the Wimbledon Tennis Championships*. London: Hamlyn Publishing Group.

Metzler, P. (1979). *Great Players in Australian Tennis*. Sydney: Harper and Row.

Moore, Ann (n.d.). *History of the Helena Valley Tennis Club.*

Morrison, Bruce (n.d.). 'The History of Tennis in WA". (Unpublished paper).

Naughtin, Richard (1984). 'Margaret Court Looks Back'. *Tennis Australia*. June 1984, 21-23.

O'Farrell, Virginia (1985). 'The Unasked Questions in Australian Tennis'. *Sporting Traditions*. 1(2), 67-86.

Oldfield, Barbara (1993). *A Winning Faith: The Margaret Court Story.* London: Sovereign World.

Pascoe, Robert (1983). *Western Australia's Capital Suburb*. Melbourne: Oxford University Press.

Popham, Daphne (n.d.). *First Stage South: A History of Armidale-Kelmscott District*. Armidale: Town of Armidale, Western Australia.

Potter, E. (1969). *The Davis Cup*. New York: A.S. Barnes and Company.

Phillips, H. (1989). 'The Australian Tennis Championships of 1909'. In L. Layman & T. Stannage (Eds.) *Celebrations in Western Australian History: Studies in Western Australian History*. X, 127-133.

Phillips, H. (1985). 'Sport: A Winner for the Commonwealth'. *Social Sciences Forum*. 11(1), 1-7.

Phillips, M. (1994). 'An Evaluation of the Tennis in Schools Programme, Australia'. Unpublished Master of Education Dissertation, University of Western Australia.

Reynolds, T. (1988). 'An Evaluation of the Level One Tennis Coaching Course in Western Australia'. Unpublished research thesis, Edith Cowan University.

Robbins, C. (1988). 'An Evaluation of the Mini-Tennis Programme.' Unpublished research thesis, Edith Cowan University.

Shannon, Bill (Ed.) (1979). *United States Tennis Association Official Encyclopedia of Tennis*. (Revised and updated). New York: Harper and Row.

Slee, J. (1979). *Calamunnda, a Home in the Forrest: A History of Kalamunda.* Kalamunda: Shire of Kalamunda.

Smith, J. (1991). 'A Study of the Players Attitudes to the Structure of the Women's State Grade League in Western Australia in 1991'. Unpublished research thesis, Edith Cowan University.

Spillman, K. (1985). *Identity Prized: A History of Subiaco.* Nedlands: University of Western Australia Press.

Stannage, C.T. (1979). *The People of Perth.* Perth: Carroll's.

Stewart, B. (1985). 'Financial Support'. *In Australian Sport: A Profile.* Canberra: Australian Government Publishing Service.

Stewart, Bob (1980). 'Sport as a Big Business'. *The Australian Quarterly.* 52(2), 163-177.

Stewart, B. (1989). 'The Nature of Sport Under Capitalism'. *Sporting Traditions.* 6(1), 43-61.

Stewart, B. (1992). 'Athleticism Revisited: Sport, Character Building and Protestant School Education in Nineteenth Century Melbourne'. *Sporting Traditions.* 9(1), 35-51.

Stoddart, Brian (1986). *Saturday Afternoon Fever: Sport in the Australian Culture.* North Ryde: Angus and Robertson.

Stoddard, B. (1981). 'Sport and Society 1890-1940: A Foray'. In C.T. Stannage (Ed.). *A New History of Western Australia.* Perth: University of Western Australia Press.

Sweeney, B. (1993). *Australians and Sport: A Prospectus.* South Melbourne: Brian Sweeney and Associates.

Synder, J. (1993). *Great Moments and Dubious Achievements in Tennis History.* San Francisco: Chronicle Books.

Tatz, Colin (1982). 'The Corruption of Sport'. *Current Affairs Bulletin.* 59(4), 4-16.

Tauman, M. (1978). *The Chief: C.Y. O'Connor. Perth:* University of Western Australian Press.

Terrell, John (1993). *Goldfields Sport: A Centenary of Heroes, Heroines and Happenings.* Bateman: John Terrell.

Tilden, William T. (1922). *The Art of Lawn Tennis.* (Fourth edition). London: Methuen.

Tregonning, K.G. (1993). *Young Hearts Run Free: Hale School 1858-1988.* Wembley Downs: Hale School.

Trengove, Alan (1985). *The Story of the Davis Cup.* London: Stanley Paul.

Trollope, A. (1953). *An Autobiography by Anthony Trollope [1883].* London: Oxford University Press.

Udell, H. (1979). *A History of Gingin 1830-1960.* Gingin: Gingin Shire Council.

Vamplew, W. et al (1992). *The Oxford Companion to Australian Sport.* Melbourne: Oxford University Press.

Whimpress, B. (1992). 'The Value of Facts in Sports History'. *Sporting Traditions.* 9(1), 2-15.

Whitington, R.S. (1975). *An Illustrated History of Australian Tennis.* South Melbourne: Macmillan Co.

Williams, H.W. (1979). *One Day In Collie.* Collie: Shire of Collie.

Williams, H.E. (1984). *Nedlands: From Campsite to City.* Nedlands: City of Nedlands.

Worth, S. (1991). *Rules of the Game: The Diagram Group.* London: Harper Collins.

Yallop, R. (1984). *Royal South Yarra Lawn Tennis Club: 100 Years in Australian Tennis.* South Yarra: Currey O'Neil.

Yallop, R. (1992). *A Serve to Authority: Kooyong: 100 Years of Heroes and Headlines.* Melbourne: Mapp Corp.

Zeigler, Earle, F. (1979). *History of Physical Education and Sport.* New Jersey: Prentice Hall.

<u>Newspapers</u>

The Age (The Tennis Centre, 11 January 1988).

The Australian

The Daily News

The Floreat Post

The Geraldton Guardian

The Perth Gazette

The Inquirer

The Morning Herald

The Phillips River Times

The Sunday Times

The Weekend Mail

The West Australian

The West Australian Times

The Western Mail

The Kalgoorlie Miner

Interviews/Correspondence

Correspondence with Steve Errington 16 June 1986

Interview with Keith Barker 18 April 1986

Interview with Max Bonner 12 November 1991

Interview with Patsy Cough 4 December 1991

Interview with Norm Cunningham 4 February 1987

Interview with Bill Edgar 7 June 1990 and 14 December 1993

Interview with Ron Ford 26 April 1989

Interview with Geoff Hammond 12 June 1989

Interview (telephone) with Olga Hedeman 3 February 1989

Interview with Alan Hicks 13 January 1993 and 15 July 1994

Correspondence with Alan Gooch 3 December 1993

Correspondence with Mrs Ann Hoar 31 May 1989

Interview with Harry Jacoby 30 August 1990

Interview with John Whilton 4 October 1989

Interview with Mrs Molly King (nee McGrath) 29 April 1989

Interview with Mrs Hilda Merry 4 August 1988

Interview with Don Menzies 7 April 1989

Interview (telephone) with Alan Morse 7 September 1989

Correspondence with Alan Morse 20 October 1989

Interview (telephone) with Rod Noble 23 March 1992

Interview with Mary Prindiville (nee O'Mahoney) 14 August 1989

Interview with Dene Rundle 23 March 1986

Interview with Margaret Robinson (nee Heron) 27 September 1989

Correspondence with Len Walker 16 December 1993

Interview with Clive Wilderspin 20 December 1993

Tennis Magazines, Articles, Handbooks

Tennis Australia, Annual Reports

Tennis Australia Handbook 1993 Edition

The romantic story of David Blacklock. *The Retailer.* January 1954, pp.49, 56, 72, 73.

Ernie Parker joins elite. Sportsview. 8(1) October 1992.

Tennis (Australia), *Lawn Tennis in Australia*

Australian Tennis

Reports/Souvenirs/Hansard

Involvement in Sport: Australia. March 1993. Australian Bureau of Statistics (Canberra).

Sport for Young Australians. (1991). Australian Sports Commission, Canberra.

Junior Sports Report. Focus on Children. The Western Australian Sports Council (Dr B. Douge, Chairman, May 1987).

Women, Sport and the Media: A Report to the Federal Government from the Working Group on Women in Sport. Canberra: Australian Government Publishing Service. (1985).

Tennis Australia: Factual Gender Equity Questionnaires. Gender Equity Working Party, September 1992.

Leisure, Recreation and the Role of Government in the 1980's and Beyond. A discussion paper prepared for the Hon. Keith Wilson, MLA, Minister for Sport and Recreation, Government of Western Australia, December 1983.

The Confederation of Australian Sport (1977). *The Financial Plight of Australian Sport.* South Yarra: Confederation of Australian Sport.

Select Committee on Youth Affairs, Legislative Assembly, Western Australia, Discussion Paper No.4, 'Recreation and Leisure', 13 May 1992.

Kings Park Tennis Club (1925) Souvenir. *Report and History* 1895-1924. Perth: Dix Print.

Corinthian Park Tennis Club: *A Short History, the First Ten Years.* (1974) n.p.

Report of the Sport and Recreation Activities in Western Australia, Select Committee. Legislative Council of Western Australia. T. McNeil (Chairman), November 1984.

Hansard, Legislative Assembly of Western Australia.

Involvement in Sport Australia, March 1993. Australian Bureau of Statistics, Canberra.

Western Australian Year Book. 1993. Australian Bureau of Statistics, Perth: Advance Press.

Private Collections

Norm Cunningham Scrapbook file.

Dorey (nee Matison) Christine. Scrapbook files.

Drake-Brockman (nee Longson) Jan. Scrapbook collection.

Tony Hammond - Scrapbook collection

Molly King (nee McGrath). Scrapbook collection.

Arthur Marshall. Collection of newspaper articles.

Sayers Family. Scrapbook collection.

Clive Wilderspin. Scrapbook collection.

Ron Ford - Scrapbook collection

Western Australian Lawn Tennis Association (WALTA)

Minutes of Executive and Council, Annual Reports

Programs (Western Australian Open, Davis Cup ties, Hallmark Events),

Westennis issues.

WALTA Facts and Figures (February 1989).

Tennis West's Corporate Plan 1992-1996, October 1992.

Tennis West: Report of an Organisation Review of Tennis West. Compass International, July 1993.

Review of the Shield Match Competition: Report by the Select Committee (Brian Bracewell, Chairman) December 1990.

Tennis West, Western Australian Women in Tennis Forum 'Let's Get the Ball Rolling', Workshop Proceedings. Tennis Australia. Australian Sports Commission, 13 July 1993.

Veterans Tennis Association of Western Australia (Annual Reports, Vetscene issues).

Tennis Australia Annual Reports.

Western Australian Lawn Tennis Association (Inc.)

Constitution (1928).

Constitution (1934).

Constitution (1984).

Constitution (1989).

Constitution (1995).

APPENDICES

1. **WALTA: Major Office Bearers**
2. **WALTA: Life Members**
3. **Western Australian Open Championship Winners**
4. **The Slazenger Cup - Schools' Tennis Competition**
5. **Country Week Singles Championship Winners**
6. **Country Week Team Winners**
7. **Champion of Champions Trophy Winner**
8. **State Closed Singles Championship Winners**
9. **WALTA 'A' Grade Pennant/Shield Winners**
10. **WALTA Player Rankings**
11. **WALTA Club Affiliation and Membership Statistics**
12. **Affiliated WALTA Clubs**

APPENDIX 1
WALTA : MAJOR OFFICE BEARERS

PRESIDENTS	TERM
A.J.H. Saw	1903-1910
W.H. Kingsmill	1911-1912
A.G. Rains	1913 W.H.
Kingsmill	1914-1922
E.C. Riddle	1923 A.G.
Rains	1924 S.J.
McGibbon	1925-1938
V.B. Mursell	1938-1948
J.L. Walker	1948-1953
K.W. Miller	1953-1962
N.W. Wasley	1962-1971
M.D. Beard	1971-1975
B.S. Sanders	1975-1982
H.M. Spilsbury	1982-1990
A.R. Hicks	1990-

SECRETARIES\ EXECUTIVE DIRECTOR/ MANAGER	YEAR ASSUMED OFFICE
J. Carter	1903
H. Hill	1903
R.H. Kelsey	1904
S.V. Eaton	1909
W. Fry	1911
H.G. Jefferson	1912
G.L. Linwood	1919
E.J.T. Warren	1923
E.H. Hart	1925
S.M. Mortimer	1932
G.H. Carlisle	1935
R.V. O'Shannassy	1953
L. Angel	1966
H.P. Cahill	1976
R.J. Whitton	1978*
B.E. Beers	1988**
G. Allen	1995

* General Manager
** Executive Director 1988-1993
General Manager 1994 -

TREASURERS	YEAR ASSUMED OFFICE
J. Carter	1903
R.H. Kelsey	1904
E.A. Glyde	1907
H.C. Sewell	1908
J.W. Marris	1909
J.S. Triggs	1912
G.V. Eaton	1913
A.M.P. Montgomery	1914
L. Mullen	1914
J. Shadwick	1915
E.J.T. Warren	1916
R. Long	1916
W.R. Corr	1919
E.H. Hart	1935
F.A. Ryan	1943
H.B. Angus	1946
F. Grove	1950
H. Spilsbury	1956
L.C. Richardson	1971
R.A. Casey	1972
F.B.J. Dreyer	1976
P. Barrett	1982
D.P. Rundle	1983
I. Kuba	1989
M. Lee	1991

APPENDIX 2
WALTA LIFE MEMBERS
LIFE MEMBERS
(Documentation Cited)

R.H. Kelsey 1908
(WALTA Minutes 24/4/1908)

W.H. Kingsmill 1923
(WALTA Minutes 8/6/1923)

A.H. Hedeman 1924
(WALTA Minutes 20/6/1924)

E.J.T. Warren 1925
(WALTA Minutes 20/11/1925)

S.J. McGibbon 1926
(WALTA Minutes 21/5/1926)

S.S. Glyde 1928
(WALTA Minutes 6/7/1928)

W.R.J. Corr 1935
(WALTA Minutes 16/8/1935)

E.S. Hart 1943
(WALTA Annual Report 1942/1943)

V.B. Mursell 1949
(WALTA Minutes 27/5/1949)

Q.K. Stow 1953
(WALTA Minutes 10/10/1953)

J.L. Walker 1955
(WALTA Minutes 29/9/1955)

T.E. Robinson 1955
(WALTA Minutes 29/9/1955

F.F. Grove 1961
(WALTA Minutes 28/9/1961)

K.W. Miller 1963
(WALTA Minutes 8/8/1963)

B.D. Morrell 1967
(WALTA Minutes 9/11/1967)

N.W. Wasley 1971
(WALTA Minutes 14/10/1971)

M.D. Beard 1975
(WALTA Minutes 9/10/1975)

E.A. Eastman 1975
(WALTA Minutes 9/10/1975)

B.S. Sanders 1982
(WALTA Minutes 11/12/1982)

H.M. Waters 1983
(WALTA Minutes 13/10/1983)

D. Punch 1989
(WALTA Minutes 14/12/1989)

H.M. Spilsbury 1990
(WALTA Minutes 13/12/1990)

E. McManis 1992
(WALTA Minutes 12/12/1991)

Note:
A.G. Rains and S.A. Mortimer have been listed in some tabulations of those who have been honoured with life membership of the WALTA. Although both gave dedicated service to the WALTA there does not appear to be any official or even circumstantial evidence to support the listing of either Rains or Mortimer. A.G. Rains explicitly denied he had been granted life membership (see WALTA Minutes, 10 June 1936).

APPENDIX 3
WESTERN AUSTRALIAN OPEN CHAMPIONSHIP WINNERS

MEN'S SINGLES
George Linwood Perpetual Challenge Cup

1896	E.R. Boddington
1897	A.W. Hoskins
1898	A.H. Green
1899	J.D. Cramond
1900	J.C. Johnston
1901	J.D. Cramond
1902	L.G. Saxon
1903	E.F. Parker
1904	E.F. Parker
1905	S.N. Doust
1906	H.A. Parker
1907	E.F. Parker
1908	E.F. Parker
1909	A.F. Wilding
1910	S.N. Doust
1911	E.F. Parker
1912	E.F. Parker
1913	E.F. Parker
1914	A.R. Leschen
1915-1918	No contest
1919	A.H. Hedeman
1920	R.T.H. Gemmell
1921	R.T.H. Gemmell
1922	A.W. Phillips
1923	R.T.H. Gemmell
1924	R.T.H. Gemmell
1925	R.T.H. Gemmell
1926	R.T.H. Gemmell
1927	R. Ford
1928	No contest
1929	R.E. Schlesinger
1930	R. Ford
1931	H. Hopman
1932	A. Quist
1933	R. Ewen
1934	M. Carpenter
1935	W.F. Stephen
1936	H.D. Jacoby
1937	W.F. Stephen
1938	G.B. Davis
1939	N.W. Wasley
1940	C. Long
1941-1945	No contest
1946	D. Pails
1947	N. Brodie
1948	F. Sedgman
1949	W. Sidwell
1950	F. Sedgman
1951	K. McGregor
1952	R. Hartwig
1953	K. Rosewall
1954	C. Wilderspin
1955	R. Hartwig
1956	C. Wilderspin
1957	A. Cooper
1958	M. Anderson

MEN'S DOUBLES
S.S. Glyde Memorial Perpetual Trophy

1896	R.K. Kelsey and A. Curie
1897	C.L. Oldham and V. Oldham
1898	K. Bolton and L. Bowen
1899	J.D. Cramond and A.H. Greene
1900	J.G. Greayer and J.C. Johnston
1901	K. Bolton and J.C. Keane
1902	L.G. Saxon and T. Kitchen
1903	K. Bolton and J.G. Greayer
1904	E.F. Parker and J.D. Cramond
1905	E.F. Parker and J.D. Cramond
1906	S.N. Doust and S. Jones
1907	E.F. Parker and J.D. Cramond
1908	E.G Barnard and C.N. Barnard
1909	E.F. Parker and J.C. Keane
1910	E.F. Parker and J.C. Keane
1911	E.F. Parker and J.B. Howitt
1912	H. Rice and A.B. Jones
1913	E.F. Parker and A.H. Hedeman
1914	E.F. Parker and A.H. Hedeman
1915-1918	No contest
1919	I.R. Gibbs and T.C. Hantke
1920	C. Kruger and W. Kruger
1921	R.T.H. Gemmell and S.V. Eaton
1922	E.M. Barker and K. Barker
1923	R.T Gemmell and V.B. Mursell
1924	R.T Gemmell and K. McDougall
1925	R.T Gemmell and K. McDougall
1926	N.J Brearley and V. Trounce
1927	C.L. Evans and F.C. Edmondson
1928	No contest
1929	R.E. Schlesinger and C.L. Evans
1930	M. Carpenter and M. Noble
1931	H. Hopman and K.A. Barker
1932	A. Quist and W.F. Stephen
1933	R. Ewen and T. Fitchett
1934	M. Carpenter and W. Kennedy
1935	W.F. Stephen and R.D. Ford
1936	K. Hough and E. Taylor
1937	M. Bonner and A. Huxley
1938	M. Bonner and G. Davis
1939	M. Bonner and M. McDermott
1940	M. Bonner and M. McDermott
1941-1945	No contest
1946	D. Pails and N. Wasley
1947	L. Brodie and N. Wasley
1948	G. Brown and J. Dart
1949	W. Sidwell and J. Blacklock
1950	H.T. Warhurst and C. Wilderspin
1951	M. Rose and G. Strang
1952	R. Hartwig and G. Strang
1953	D. Candy and D. Hamilton
1954	C. Wilderspin and J. Blacklock
1955	R. Hartwig and J. Blacklock
1956	C. Wilderspin and J. Blacklock
1957	A. Cooper and B. Phillips-Moore
1958	M. Anderson and N. Fraser

Men's singles cont

1959	A. Gimeno
1960	N. Fraser
1961	M. Sangster
1962	R Emerson
1963	R. Hewitt
1964	F. Stolle
1965	R. Emerson
1966	A. Ashe
1967	A. Roche
1968	W. Bowrey
1969	M. Riessen
1970	A. Stone
1971	A. Metreveli
1972	A. Metreveli
1973	P. Proisy
1974	C. Dibley
1975	R. Case
1976	R. Ruffels
1977	R. Ruffels
1978	J. Marks
1979	M. Edmonston
1980	C. Dibley
1981	J. Fitzgerald
1982	E. Edwards
1983	W. Masur
1984	B. Levine
1985	S. Edberg
1986	J. Svensson
1987	S. Edberg
1988	B. Properjohn
1989	D. Patten
1990	D. Culley
1991	J. Stimpson
1992	D. Patten
1993	K. Kinnear
1994	D. Adams
1995	J. Kroslak

Men's doubles cont

1959	U. Schmidt and J. Lindquist
1960	R. Howe and C. Wilderspin
1961	F. Stolle and R. Howe
1962	R. Emerson and N. Fraser
1963	R. Hewitt and B. Bowman
1964	R. Emerson and N. Fraser
1965	R. Emerson and T. Clayton
1966	M. Riessen and T. Okker
1967	W. Bowrey and O. Davidson
1968	G. Stillwell and P. Curtis
1969	K. Rosewall and M. Riessen
1970	G. Battrick and R. Russell
1971	S. Ball and R. Giltinan
1972	R. Case and G. Masters
1973	R. Case and G. Masters
1974	R. Case and G. Masters
1975	C. Dibley and M. Anderson
1976	R. Case and S. Ball
1977	R. Case and R. Ruffels
1978	J. Marks and C. Kachel
1979	J. Marks and M. Edmondson
1980	C. Letcher and S. Ball
1981	D. Letcher and S. Ball
1982	S. Ball and J. Fitzgerald
1983	S. Benson and C. Johnstone
1984	B. Dyke and J. Van Nostrand
1985	C. Warder and D. Graham
1986	S. Youl and D. Cahill
1987	S. Edberg and Y. Noah
1988	B. Properjohn and K. Robinson
1989	R. Grant and B. Hamburg
1990	D. Culley and M. Leuba
1991	R. Grant and P. Kilderry
1992	D. Patten and M. Leuba
1993	L. Bale and D. Nainkin
1994	B. Larkham and P. Kilderry
1995	W. Arthurs and N. Borwick

WOMEN'S SINGLES
Challenge Cup

1897	Miss E. Calder
1898	No entry
1899	No entry
1900	Miss B. Penny
1901	Mrs M. Walsh
1902	Miss E. Black
1903	Mrs Walsh
1904	Miss Hone
1905	Mrs M. Walsh
1906	Miss Payten
1907	Mrs M. Walsh
1908	Mrs M. Walsh
1909	Mrs E. Barker
1910	Miss Low
1911	Mrs E. Barker
1912	Miss Ruse
1913	Mrs V. Mather
1914	Mrs V. Mather
1915-1918	No contest
1919	Mrs V. Mather

WOMEN'S DOUBLES
Challenge Cup

1897	
1898	
1899	
1900	Mesdames Barker and Walsh
1901	Mesdames Barker and Walsh
1902	Mrs Kitchen and Miss Henriques
1903	Misses Henriques and Penny
1904	Misses Hone and Penny
1905	Mesdames Barker and Walsh
1906	Misses Payten and Jones
1907	Mrs Blackmore and Miss Ruse
1908	Mrs Blackmore and Miss Ruse
1909	Mrs Blackmore and Miss Ruse
1910	Mrs Kent and Miss Low
1911	Mrs Blackmore and Miss Ruse
1912	Mrs Blackmore and Miss Ruse
1913	Mesdames Mather and Brook
1914	No contest
1915-1918	No contest
1919	Mrs Lynch and Miss Mountain

	Women's singles cont		*Women's doubles cont*
1920	Mrs V. Mather	1920	Mesdames Mather and Brook
1921	Mrs V. Mather	1921	Mrs Roe and Miss K. Le Mesurier
1922	Mrs V. Mather	1922	Mrs Mather and Miss D. Mountain
1923	Mrs V. Mather	1923	Mrs Wood and Miss M. McDougall
1924	Miss L. Wedin	1924	Mrs Wood and Miss M. McDougall
1925	Mrs R.A. MacBeth (Wedin)	1925	Mrs Wood and Miss M. McDougall
1926	Mrs R.A. MacBeth	1926	Misses M. Officer and E. Whitfield
1927	Miss M. Barker	1927	Misses Officer and Murray
1928	No contest	1928	No contest
1929	Miss P. Smith	1929	Misses P. Smith and M. McGrath
1930	Miss M. McGrath	1930	Miss C. Simpson and Miss M. Herbert
1931	Miss M. McGrath	1931	Miss C. Simpson and Miss M. Herbert
1932	Miss M. McGrath	1932	Mrs L. Eichhorn and Miss M. Herbert
1933	Miss M. McGrath	1933	Misses M. McGrath and P. Smith
1934	Miss M. Herbert	1934	Misses M. Herbert and M. O'Mahoney
1935	Miss J. Glover	1935	Misses M. Herbert and M. O'Mahoney
1936	Miss M. O'Mahoney	1936	Misses M. Herbert and M. O'Mahoney
1937	Mrs A.F. King (McGrath)	1937	Mrs A.F. King and Miss A. Carcary
1938	Miss M. O'Mahoney (Prindiville)	1938	Misses M. Herbert and M. O'Mahoney
1939	Miss F. Trewhella	1939	Misses J. McNamara and A. Peacock
1940	Miss J. Wood	1940	Misses J. Wood and V. Watts
1941-1945	No contest	1941-1945	No contest
1946	Mrs M. McDermott (Wood)	1946	Mrs B. Prindiville and Mrs E. Cooke
1947	Mrs M. McDermott	1947	Mrs M. McDermott and Mrs M. Prindiville
1948	Miss M. Toomey	1948	Mrs H. Hopman and Mrs M. McDermott
1949	Miss M. Grace	1949	Mrs V. White and Miss M. Nicholas
1950	Mrs H. Collins	1950	Mrs V. Bandy and Miss R. Ryan
1951	Miss J. Ryan	1951	Mrs M. Arcus and Miss J. Ryan
1952	Miss J. Ryan	1952	Mrs M. Arcus and Miss J. Ryan
1953	Mrs V.J. White	1953	Mrs V. White and Mrs L. Bandy
1954	Mrs V.J. White	1954	Miss J. Ryan and Miss J. McLeod
1955	Mrs G. Thiele	1955	Mrs C.M. Rogers and Mrs. A.R. Thiele
1956	Miss J. Langley (Bignell)	1956	Mrs N. Collins and Mrs N. Kurts
1957	Mrs H. Collins	1957	Mrs C. Rogers and Mrs A. Thiele
1958	Miss A. Mortimer	1958	Mrs H. Waters and Miss A. Mortimer
1959	Miss R. Schuurman	1959	Miss S. Reynolds and Miss R. Schuurman
1960	Miss M. Bueno	1960	Miss M Bueno and Miss C. Truman
1961	Miss D. Whitely	1961	Miss E. Duldig and Miss H. Plaisted
1962	Miss M. Smith	1962	Misses M. Smith and R. Ebbern
1963	Miss C. Truman	1963	Misses E. Starkey and R. Bentley
1964	Miss L. Turner (Bowrey)	1964	Misses L. Turner and J. Tegart
1965	Miss M. Smith	1965	Misses M. Smith and H. Plaisted
1966	Miss M. Smith	1966	Misses M. Smith and J. Tegart
1967	Miss F. Durr	1967	Misses G. Sherriff and F. Durr
1968	Mrs B.J. King	1968	Mrs B.J. King and Miss R. Casals
1969	Mrs M. Court (Smith)	1969	Mrs M. Court and Miss J. Tegart
1970	Mrs M. Court	1970	Misses K. Melville and K. Krantzcke
1971	Mrs M. Court	1971	Mrs M. Court and Miss E. Goolagong
1972	Miss E. Goolagong (Cawley)	1972	Misses E. Goolagong and B. Hawcroft
1973	Mrs M. Court	1973	Mrs M. Court and Miss K. Sawamatsu
1974	Miss E. Goolagong	1974	Misses E. Goolagong and P. Michel
1975	Mrs M. Court	1975	Ms O. Morozova and Ms M. Navratilova
1976	Mrs H. Mastoff	1976	Mrs L. Bowrey and Miss C. Matison
1977	Ms W. Turnbull	1977	Ms K. Reid and Ms W. Turnbull
1978	Miss A. Tobin	1978	Ms J. Dalton and Ms K. Hallam
1979	Miss J. Davis	1979	Miss D. Evers and Miss M. Sawyer
1980	Miss S. Leo	1980	Ms K. Ruddell and Ms E. Little
1981	Miss A. Tobin	1981	Ms K. Gulley and Miss A. Minter
1982	Miss E. Sayers (Smylie)	1982	Miss A. Tobin and Miss E. Sayers
1983	Miss A. Tobin	1983	Miss C. O'Neil and Miss P. Whytcross
1984	Mrs A. Dingwall (Tobin)	1984	Miss B. Randall and Miss H. Davis

	Women's singles *cont*		Women's doubles *cont*
1984	Mrs A. Dingwall (Tobin)	1984	Miss B. Randall and Miss H. Davis
1985	Miss J. Byrne	1985	Miss J. Lange and Miss L. Cooper
1986	Mrs C. Dorey (Matison)	1986	Miss J. Lange and Miss L. Cooper
1987	Miss R. Lamb	1987	Miss J. Lange and Miss L. Cooper
1988	Mrs C. Dorey	1988	Mrs C. Dorey and Miss D. Shevin
1989	Miss R. Lamb	1989	Misses R. Lamb and N. Crutchley
1990	Miss P. Parentich	1990	Mrs C. Dorey and Miss R. Lamb
1991	Miss R. Stubbs	1991	Misses R. Stubbs and J. Faull
1992	Miss J. Byrne	1992	Misses K. Sharpe and K. McDonald
1993	Miss N. Kimpton	1993	Misses R. Lamb and D. Blackwell
1994	Miss N. Kimpton	1994	No contest
1995	Miss S. Stanley	1995	No contest

MIXED DOUBLES

1903	E.F. Parker and Miss Black	1941-1945	No contest
1904	E.F. Parker and Mrs Walsh	1946	M. McDermott and Mrs M. McDermott
1905	E.F. Parker and Mrs Walsh	1947	L. Brodie and Miss R. Ryan
1906	S.N. Doust and Miss Payten	1948	F. Sedgman and Mrs H. Hopman
1907	E.F. Parker and Mrs Walsh	1949	W. Sidwell and Miss M. Grace
1908	E.T. Barnard and Mrs Walsh	1950	H.T. Warhurst and Mrs M. McDermott
1909	A.F. Wilding and Miss D. Moore	1951	K. McGregor and Mrs V. White
1910	S.N. Doust and Miss K. Bailey	1952	R. Hartwig and Miss J. Ryan
1911	E.F. Parker and Miss Clement	1953	C. Wilderspin and Miss J. Ryan
1912	E.F. Parker and Mrs Barker	1954	C. Wilderspin and Miss J. Ryan
1913	H.A. Parker and Miss Clement	1955	C. Wilderspin and Mrs L. Bandy
1914-1918	No contest	1956	R. Emerson and Mrs L. Bandy
1919	I.R. Gibbs and Mrs Mather	1957	N. Pietrangeli and Miss J. Langley
1920	A.H. Hedeman and Mrs Brook	1958	C. Wilderspin and Miss J. Langley
1921	I.R. Gibbs and Mrs Mather	1959	R. Laver and Miss R. Schuurman
1922	I.R. Gibbs and Mrs Mather	1960	N. Fraser and Miss M. Bueno
1923	W. Kruger and Mrs La Nauze	1961	C. Wilderspin and Miss D. Whitely
1924	C.T.P. Ewing and Miss M. McDougall	1962	N. Fraser and Miss M. Smith
1925	F.C. Edmondson and Mrs Edmondson	1963	O. Davidson and Miss L. Turner
1926	F.C. Edmondson and Mrs Edmondson	1964	K. Fletcher and Miss L. Turner
1927	C.H. Lamb and Miss M.I. Harrison	1965	P. Darmon and Mrs P. Darmon
1928	No contest	1966	A. Roche and Miss J. Tegart
1929	H. Jacoby and Miss M. McGrath	1967	A. Roche and Miss G. Sherriff
1930	M. Carpenter and Miss P. Smith	1968	B. Bowman and Mrs M. Court
1931	H. Hopman and Miss B. Wood	1969	K. Rosewall and Miss F. Durr
1932	A. Quist and Miss M. McGrath	1970	K. Stuart and Miss K. Krantzcke
1933	R. Ewin and Miss M. McGrath	1971	A. Metreveli and Miss O. Morozova
1934	M. Carpenter and Miss M. Herbert	1972	A. Metreveli and Miss O. Morozova
1935	W.F. Stephen and Miss M. Herbert	1973	R. Case and Miss L. Blatchford
1936	D. Harris and Miss M. O'Mahoney	1974	No Event
1937	A. Huxley and Mrs A.F. King	1975	No Event
1938	W.F. Stephen and Miss M. O'Mahoney	1976	C. Letcher and Miss D. Evers
1939	G. Davis and Miss V. Watts	1977	M. Edmondson and R. Fox
1940	C. Long and Mrs M. Prindiville		

	JUNIOR BOYS **Wanda Cup**		JUNIOR GIRLS
1919	R. Forsaith		
1920	W.M. Cleland		
1921	W.M. Cleland	1921	M. Officer
1922	W.M. Cleland	1922	M. Taylor
1923	E.M. Ladyman	1923	M. Officer
1924	E.M. Ladyman	1924	M. Officer
1925	R. Ford	1925	M. Officer
1926	R. Ford	1926	E. Morse
1927	J. Pilgrim	1927	M. McGrath
1928	No competition	1928	No competition
1929	M. Noble	1929	M. McGrath
1930	M. Noble	1930	M. McGrath
1931	M. Carpenter	1931	M. McGrath
1932	W. Stephen	1932	M. McGrath
1933	W. Stephen	1933	M. McGrath
1934	W. Stephen	1934	J. Glover
1935	M. Bonner	1935	J. Glover
1936	M. Bonner	1936	J. Glover
1937	N. Wasley	1937	N. Trewhella
1938	R. Stephen	1938	J. Hunter
1939	M. McDermott	1939	J. Hunter
1940	P. Purdom	1940	V. Watts
1941-1945	No competition	1941-1945	No competition
1946	C. Wilderspin	1946	V. Calnon
1947	G. Worthington	1947	V. Calnon
1948	J. Blacklock	1948	M. Earle
1949	J. Blacklock	1949	P. Cunningham
1950	A.R. Hicks	1950	P. Cunningham
1951	B. Ford	1951	M. Blacklock
1952	L. Hoad	1952	J. McLeod
1953	A. Marshall	1953	J. Langley
1954	D. Napier	1954	J. Langley
1955	R. Emerson	1955	J. Langley
1956	D. Napier	1956	B. Hall
1957	W. Jacques	1957	J. Shearer
1958	R. Kilderry	1958	D. Blackburn
1959	E. Bucholz	1959	D. Whitely
1960	R. Kilderry	1960	D. Whitely
1961	T. Clayton	1961	D. Whitely
1962	T. Clayton	1962	K. Denning
1963	S. Matthews	1963	K. Denning
1964	A. Roche	1964	S. Stephen
1965	E. Russo	1965	J. Longson
1966	A. Hammond	1966	L. Hunt
1967	A. Hammond	1967	L. Hunt
1968	A. Hammond	1968	L. Hunt
1969	A. Hammond	1969	L. Hunt
1970	R. Casey	1970	A. Coleman
1971	R. Casey	1971	P. Reese
1972	P. Kronk	1972	P. Coleman
1973	P. McNamara	1973	S. Taylor
1974	J. Joyce	1974	H. Anliot
1975	C. Casa	1975	L. Mottram
1976	B. Drewett	1976	M. Pekovich
1977	P. Elter	1977	M. Pekovich
1978	R. Kelly	1978	A. Tobin
1979	P. Robinson	1979	C. White
1980	W. Masur	1980	E. Sayers
1981	B. Sharp	1981	M. Yates
1982	S. Marshall	1982	N. Leipus

	Junior boys cont		*Junior girls cont*
1983	A. Lane	1983	E. Minter
1984	M. Kratzmann	1984	J. Thompson
1985	B. Hamburg	1985	N. Crutchley
1986	C. Turich	1986	N. Crutchley
1987	C. Turich	1987	T. Drake-Brockman
1988	D. Patten	1988	K. Bucens
1989	G. Cox	1989	N. Kimpton
1990	A. Lewis	1990	S. Martin
1991	M. Edwardes	1991	S. Martin
1992	P. Petrovsky	1992	S. Drake-Brockman
1993	T. Hammond	1993	A. Szymonik
1994	J. Crabb	1994	S. Stanley

APPENDIX 4
THE SLAZENGER CUP - SCHOOLS TENNIS COMPETITION

	BOYS		GIRLS
Year	**School**	**Year**	**School**
1914	Claremont TC	1914	Perth Modern School
1915	University TC	1915	Presbyterian Ladies College
1916	Claremont TC	1916	Girls High School
1917	Perth Modern School	1917	Perth Modern School
1918	Perth Modern School	1918	Perth Modern School
1919	Perth Modern School	1919	Wanda Tennis Club
1920	Perth Modern School	1920	Presbyterian Ladies College
1921	Perth Modern School	1921	Presbyterian Ladies College
1922	Perth High School (Hale School)	1922	Presbyterian Ladies College
1923	Scotch College	1923	Presbyterian Ladies College
1924	Subiaco TC	1924	Presbyterian Ladies College
1925	Perth High School (Hale School)	1925	Wanda Tennis Club
1926	Subiaco TC	1926	Perth College
1927	King's Park TC	1927	Perth College
1928	South Perth TC	1928	Sacred Heart High
1929	University TC	1929	Sacred Heart High
1930	University TC	1930	Sacred Heart High
1931	Perth Modern School	1931	Sacred Heart High
1932	University TC	1932	Sacred Heart High
1933	Perth Modern School	1933	Sacred Heart High
1934	Perth Modern School	1934	Sacred Heart High
1935	CBC Fremantle	1935	Sacred Heart High
1936	Fremantle Boy's School	1936	Sacred Heart High
1937	CBC Fremantle	1937	Sacred Heart High
1938	Hale School	1938	Sacred Heart High
1939	Hale School	1939	Sacred Heart High
1940	Hale School	1940	Sacred Heart High
1941	Wesley College	1941	Perth Modern School
1942	Wesley College	1942	Methodist Ladies College
1943	Wesley College	1943	Sacred Heart High
1944	Wesley College	1944	Sacred Heart High
1945	Wesley College	1945	Sacred Heart High
1946	Wesley College	1946	Sacred Heart High
1947	Wesley College	1947	St Hilda's CE School
1948	Perth Modern School	1948	Sacred Heart High
1949	Perth Modern School	1949	Presbyterian Ladies College
1950	Wesley College	1950	Presbyterian Ladies College
1951	Perth Modern School	1951	Presbyterian Ladies College
1952	Aquinas College	1952	Presbyterian Ladies College
1953	Perth Modern School	1953	St Hilda's
1954	Not conducted - polio-myelitis epidemic	1954	Not conducted - polio-myelitis epidemic

	Boys cont		*Girls cont*
1955	Perth Modern School	1955	Perth Modern School
1956	Wesley College	1956	Loreta Convent Osborne
1957	Perth Modern School	1957	Methodist Ladies College
1958	Wesley College	1958	Loreto Convent Nedlands
1959	Wesley College	1959	Perth College
1960	Wesley College	1960	St Hilda's
1961	Scotch College	1961	St Hilda's
1962	Wesley College	1962	Sacred Heart High
1963	Wesley College	1963	Sacred Heart High
1964	John Curtin High School	1964	Sacred Heart High
1965	John Curtin High School	1965	Our Lady's College (Mercedes)
1966	Scotch College	1966	Our Lady's College (Mercedes)
1967	Wesley College	1967	Methodist Ladies College
1968	Hale School	1968	Methodist Ladies College
1969	CBC Fremantle	1969	Methodist Ladies College
1970	St Louis	1970	Methodist Ladies College
1971	Hale School	1971	Loreto Convent Claremont
1972	Hale School	1972	St Joachim's
1973	Hale School	1973	Mercedes College
1974	Wesley College	1974	Presbyterian Ladies College
1975	Wesley College	1975	Presbyterian Ladies College
1976	Hale School	1976	Melville SHS
1977	Hale School	1977	Melville SHS
1978	Aquinas College	1978	Iona College
1979	Aquinas College	1979	Iona College
1980	Wesley College	1980	Newman Senior College
1981	Aquinas College	1981	Newman Senior College
1982	Wesley College	1982	Iona Presentation College
1983	Trinity College	1983	Santa Maria
1984	Hale School	1984	Penrhos College
1985	Hale School	1985	Penrhos College
1986	Hale School	1986	Penrhos College
1987	Christ Church	1987	Penrhos College
1988	Wesley College	1988	St Hilda's
1989	Trinity College	1989	Mercedes College
1990	Trinity College	1990	Mercedes College
1991	Trinity College	1991	Mercedes College
1992	Duncraig	1992	Mercedes College
1993	Christ Church	1993	Methodist Ladies College
1994	Christ Church	1994	Presbyterian Ladies College

APPENDIX 5
COUNTRY WEEK SINGLES CHAMPIONSHIP WINNERS

MEN'S		WOMEN'S	
Challenge Cup		Perpetual Trophy	
Presented by Mr Martin Scott			
1923	E.O. Strang		
1924	H.M. Fisher		
1925	E.M. Ladyman		
1926	E.M. Ladyman		
1927	H.D. Kochne	1927	E. Morse
1928	H.V. Halbert	1928	P. Richardson
1929	H.D. Kochne	1929	P. Richardson
1930	R.J. Houch	1930	B. Kings
1931	W. Partridge	1931	C. Simpson
1932	E. Conway	1932	I. Goode
1933	E. Conway	1933	P. Richardson
1934	E. Conway	1934	P. Richardson
1935	E. Conway	1935	P. Richardson

MEN'S *cont*

1936	K. Suraski
1937	P. Graebner
1938	H. Blacker
1939	A.V. Hall
1940	A.V. Hall
1941	J. Smith
1942-1946	No competition
1947	A.V. Hall
1948	A.V. Hall
1949	A.V. Hall
1950	L.E. Quan
1951	L.E. Quan
1952	L.E. Quan
1953	L. Grafton
1954	E. Hamilton
1955	L.E. Quan
1956	L.E. Quan
1957	C.G. Fitzpatrick
1958	A.R. Hicks
1959	A.R. Hicks
1960	M.E. Baddeley
1961	J. Evans
1962	C. Bell
1963	F. Harris
1964	H. Ladyman
1965	K. Harris
1966	H. Ladyman
1967	K. Harris
1968	K. Harris
1969	K. Harris
1970	R. O'Farrell
1971	T. Clayton
1972	R. O'Farrell
1973	C. Bell
1974	C. Bell
1975	C. Bell
1976	C. Bell
1977	P. Rigg
1978	P. Rigg
1979	B. Thompson
1980	C. Bell
1981	C. Bell
1982	A. Gooch
1983	C. Bell
1984	C. Bell
1985	A. Gooch
1986	A. Hall
1987	Darren Patten
1988	J. Johns
1989	Brett Patten
1990	S. Mason
1991	S. Mason
1992	D. Bowen
1993	T. Reynolds
1994	D. Bowen
1995	G. Searle

WOMEN'S *cont*

1936	P. Richardson
1937	R. Collins
1938	S. Counsel
1939	L.E. Gould
1940	S. Lings
1941	P. Graham
1942-1946	No competition
1947	D. Cook
1948	B. Fairclough
1949	B. Fairclough
1950	B. Fairclough
1951	J. Bennett
1952	L. Kurts
1953	E. Stokes
1954	L. Kurts
1955	P. Carry
1956	M. Enderby
1957	M. Enderby
1958	J. Blackburne
1959	J. Blackburne
1960	J. Blackburne
1961	P. Brand
1962	J. Keenan
1963	R. Hall
1964	J. Jones
1965	P. Jenzen
1966	P. Jenzen
1967	P. Jenzen
1968	H. Walker
1969	L. Millard
1970	R. Giles
1971	R. Giles
1972	R. Giles
1973	R. Giles
1974	V. Pain
1975	R. Giles
1976	R. Giles
1977	H. Muir
1978	R. Giles
1979	R. Giles
1980	A. Watts
1981	N. Abe
1982	B. Fewster
1983	J. Lange
1984	J. Lange
1985	J. Phillips
1986	M. Drake-Brockman
1987	T. Drake-Brockman
1988	M. Drake-Brockman
1989	D. Thomson
1990	R. O'Brien
1991	D. Thomson
1992	L. Preston
1993	J. Fleay
1994	M. Drake-Brockman
1995	M. Drake-Brockman

APPENDIX 6
COUNTRY WEEK TEAM WINNERS

	F.W. Goldsmith Trophy		Championship Cup Women's
Year	**Town/Club**	**Year**	**Town/Club**
1923	Katanning	1923	
1924	Katanning	1924	
1925	Katanning	1925	
1926	Katanning	1926	
1927	Cunderdin	1927	Katanning
1928	Bunbury	1928	York
1929	Katanning	1929	Katanning
1930	Katanning	1930	Katanning
1931	Bunbury	1931	Ballingup - Bridgetown
1932	Wyalkatchem	1932	Katanning
1933	Wyalkatchem	1933	Northam
1934	Wyalkatchem	1934	Albany
1935	Wyalkatchem	1935	Northam No.1
1936	Collie RSL	1936	Albany
1937	Geeralying (1)	1937	Eastern Goldfields
1938	Geeralying - Corrigin	1938	Eastern Goldfields
1939	Eastern Goldfields	1939	Victoria Districts Association
1940	Corrigin Williams	1940	Eastern Goldfields
1941	Shackleton	1941	Arrino
1942-1946	No competition	1942-1946	No competition
1947	Dalwallinu-Ballidu	1947	Katanning
1948	Eastern Goldfields	1948	Northam
1949	Pingelly-Narrogin	1949	Moora
1950	Eastern Goldfields	1950	Moora
1951	Eastern Goldfields	1951	Geraldton
1952	Eastern Goldfields	1952	Narrogin
1953	Eastern Goldfields	1953	Geraldton
1954	Eastern Goldfields	1954	Bridgetown
1955	Eastern Goldfields	1955	Mt Barker/Kendenup
1956	Geraldton	1956	Eastern Goldfields
1957	Bruce Rock	1957	Eastern Goldfields
1958	Dalwallinu-Ballidu	1958	Safety Bay/Rockingham
1959	Eastern Goldfields	1959	Safety Bay/Rockingham
1960	Geraldton No.1	1960	Eastern Goldfields
1961	Binnu-Bella	1961	Merridin
1962	Katanning-Broomehill	1962	Katanning-Broomehill
1963	Katanning	1963	Narrogin No.2
1964	Toolibin No.1	1964	Carnarvon
1965	Eastern Goldfields	1965	Tambellup/Cunderdin
1966	Katanning	1966	Corrigin/Cunderdin
1967	Binnu-Carnarvon	1967	Cunderdin/Northam
1968	Binnu-Carnarvon	1968	Narrogin
1969	Binnu-Carnarvon	1969	Northam
1970	Binnu-Carnarvon	1970	Carnarvon
1971	Binnu-Carnarvon	1971	Katanning
1972	Binnu-Carnarvon	1972	Flat Rocks
1973	Albany-Kendenup	1973	Flat Rocks
1974	Albany-Kendenup	1974	Katanning
1975	Albany	1975	Katanning
1976	Albany-Kendenup	1976	Katanning
1977	Katanning	1977	Katanning
1978	Katanning	1978	Wongan/Goomalling
1979	Katanning	1979	Katanning
1980	Geraldton	1980	Beverley/Meckering
1981	Geraldton	1981	Kendenup
1982	Geraldton No.2	1982	Calingiri/Wongan Hills

	Men cont		*Women cont*
1983	Geraldton No.1	1983	Meckering
1984	Geraldton	1984	Meckering
1985	Eastern Goldfields T.A.	1985	Katanning
1986	Eastern Goldfields T.A.	1986	Katanning
1987	Geraldton	1987	Bunbury
1988	Eastern Goldfields T.A.	1988	Bunbury No.2
1989	Geraldton	1989	Mandurah
1990	Spalding Park/Geraldton	1990	Mandurah
1991	Spalding Park/Geraldton	1991	Mandurah
1992	Albany	1992	Mandurah
1993	Albany/Broomehill	1993	Mandurah
1994	Binnu/Geraldton	1994	Mandurah
1995	Albany	1995	Mandurah

APPENDIX 7
CHAMPION OF CHAMPIONS TROPHY WINNERS

	MEN		WOMEN
1964	B. Bowman	1964	D. Whitely (Lee)
1965	B. Bowman	1965	L. Hunt
1966	R. Coulthard	1966	P. Brand (Hattt)
1967	A. Hammond	1967	L. Hunt
1968	J. Evans	1968	D. Whitely
1969	A. D'Orsogna	1969	A. Watts (McKenzie)
1970	A. Fanowrios	1970	C. Matison
1971	G. Penberthy	1971	C. Matison
1972	G. Penberthy	1972	C. Matison
1973	G. Penberthy	1973	L. Cooper
1974	G. Penberthy	1974	S. Taylor (Mack)
1975	G. Penberthy	1975	S. Taylor
1976	R. Casey	1976	C. Matison
1977	R. Casey	1977	M. Sawyer (Collins)
1978	R. Casey	1978	C. Matison
1979	R. Casey	1979	C. Matison
1980	R. Casey	1980	C. Dorey (Matison)
1981	R. Grant	1981	C. Dorey
1982	R. Casey	1982	C. Dorey
1983	R. Casey	1983	C. Dorey
1984	R. Grant	1984	C. Dorey
1985	R. Casey	1985	C. Dorey
1986	J. Campbell	1986	P. Parentich
1987	R. Prouse	1987	C. Dorey
1988	R. Grant	1988	L. Askey
1989	M. Leuba	1989	P. Parentich
1990	P. Askey	1990	P. Parentich
1991	D. Patten	1991	P. Parentich
1992	M. Hlawaty	1992	S. Martin
1993	M. Hlawaty	1993	D. Blackwell
1994	M. Leuba	1994	S. Drake-Brockman
1995	K. Robinson	1995	N. Kimpton

APPENDIX 8
STATE CLOSED SINGLES CHAMPIONSHIP

	MEN		WOMEN
Andy Fanowrios Memorial Trophy		The Clarrie Mallett Trophy	
1975	R. Casey	1975	C. Matison
1976	R. Casey	1976	M. Pekovich
1977	R. Casey	1977	C. Matison
1978	R. Casey	1978	M. Pekovich

	Men cont		*Women cont*
1979	G. Penberthy	1979	C. Matison
1980	R. Casey	1980	C. Dorey (Matison)
1981	C. Johnstone	1981	C. Dorey
1982	R. Casey	1982	C. Dorey
1983	R. Casey	1983	C. Dorey
1984	R. Casey	1984	C. Dorey
1985	R. Casey	1985	C. Dorey
1986	B. Properjohn	1986	C. Dorey
1987	R. Grant	1987	C. Dorey
1988	R. Grant	1988	C. Dorey
1989	D. Culley	1989	P. Parentich
1990	M. Leuba	1990	P. Parentich
1991	D. Culley	1991	N. Kimpton
1992	M. Hlawaty	1992	S. Martin
1993	D. Culley	1993	D. Blackwell
1994	B. Patten	1994	D. Blackwell
1995	D. Patten	1995	S. Drake-Brockman

APPPENDIX 9
WALTA A GRADE PENNANT/SHIELD WINNERS

	MEN		WOMEN
1899	WACA (A)	1899	
1900	Fremantle (A)	1900	
1901		1901	
1902		1902	
1903	Fremantle	1903	WANDA
1904	East Perth	1904	South Perth
1905	East Perth	1905	
1906	East Perth	1906	WANDA
1907	Kings Park	1907	WANDA
1908	WACA	1908	WANDA
1909		1909	
1910	WACA (A)	1910	WANDA
1911		1911	
1912	South Perth	1912	Claremont
1913		1913	
1914	South Perth	1914	South Perth
1915-1919	No competition	1915-1919	No competition
1920	Kings Park	1920	South Perth
1921	Kings Park	1921	South Perth
1922	South Perth	1922	WANDA
1923	WANDA	1923	WANDA
1924	WANDA	1924	WANDA
1925	Kings Park	1925	WANDA
1926	Claremong	1926	WANDA
1927	Kings Park	1927	WANDA
1928	WANDA	1928	Kings Park
1929	Subiaco	1929	WANDA
1930	WANDA	1930	Kings Park
1931	WANDA	1931	Loton Park
1932	WANDA	1932	Loton Park
1933	WANDA	1933	Claremont
1934	Subiaco	1934	Kings Park
1935	Kings Park	1935	Loton Park
1936	Kings Park	1936	Kings Park
1937	Subiaco	1937	Loton Park
1938	Kings Park	1938	Loton Park

	Men cont
1939	Mt Lawley
1940	Kings Park
1941	Subiaco
1942	Subiaco
1943	No competition
1944	No competition
1945	No competition
1946	Nedlands
1947	Subiaco
1948	Nedlands
1949	Claremont
1959	Nedlands
1951	Royal Kings Park
1952	Hensman
1953	Royal Kings Park
1954	Royal Kings Park (1)
1955	Royal Kings Park (1)
1956	Hensman
1957	Hensman
1958	Hensman
1959	Hensman
1960	Hensman
1961	Hensman
1962	Hensman
1963	Royal Kings Park
1964	Royal Kings Park
1965	Claremont
1966	Royal Kings Park
1967	Royal Kings Park
1968	Claremont
1969	Claremont
1970	Claremont
1971	University
1972	University
1973	Royal Kings Park
1974	Bayswater
1975	Claremont
1976	Bayswater
1977	Fremantle
1978	Fremantle
1979	Bayswater
1980	Higgins
1981	Maylands
1982	Scarborough
1983	Maylands
1984	Scarborough
1985	Scarborough
1986	Hensman
1987	Dalkeith
1988	Dalkeith
1989	Royal Kings Park
1990	Dalkeith
1991	Dalkeith
1992	Hensman
1993	Dalkeith
1994	Dalkeith
1995	Wembley Downs

	Women cont
1939	Loton Park
1940	Loton Park
1941	Fremantle Association
1942	Subiaco
1943	No competition
1944	No competition
1945	No competition
1946	Loton Park
1947	Loton Park
1948	Royal Kings Park
1949	Royal Kings Park
1950	Subiaco
1951	Subiaco
1952	Subiaco
1953	Subiaco
1954	Royal Kings Park
1955	Royal Kings Park
1956	Royal Kings Park
1957	Alexander Park
1958	Alexander Park
1959	Royal Kings Park
1960	Cottesloe
1961	Claremont
1962	Claremont
1963	Alexander Park
1964	Alexander Park
1965	Alexander Park
1966	Alexander Park
1967	Loton park
1968	Alexander Park
1969	Royal Kings Park
1970	Claremont
1971	Royal Kings Park
1972	Royal Kings Park
1973	Fremantle
1974	Fremantle
1975	Fremantle
1976	Fremantle
1977	Nedlands
1978	Fremantle
1979	Fremantle
1980	Fremantle
1981	Higgins
1982	Fremantle
1983	Fremantle
1984	Fremantle
1985	Fremantle
1986	Nedlands
1987	Nedlands
1988	Nedlands
1989	Blue Gum
1990	Reabold
1991	Reabold
1992	Royal Kings Park
1993	Royal Kings Park
1994	Cottesloe
1995	Blue Gum

APPENDIX 10
WALTA PLAYER RANKINGS

(As officially listed)

1933

	MEN		WOMEN
1.	Ford, R.D.	1.	McGrath, Miss M.
2.=	Carpenter, M.	2.	Glover, Miss J.
2.=	Jacoby, H.	3.	Herbert, Miss M.
4.	Stephen, W.	4.	McBeth, Mrs.
5.	Kennedy, W.	5.	Wood, Miss B.
6.	Davis, G.B.	6.	Fyfe, Mrs
7.	Hough, K.	7.	Smith, Miss P.
8.	Reitze, R.	8.	Kiesey, Mrs.
9.	Harris, D.	9.	Eichborn, Mrs
10.	Gawler, D.	10.	Carcary, Miss A.

	JUNIOR BOYS		JUNIOR GIRLS
1.	Stephen, W.	1.	Glover, Miss J.
2.	Davis, G.B.	2.	Carcary, Miss A.
3.	Trigg, R.*	3.	O'Mahoney, Miss
4.	Graham *	4.	Donovan, Miss
5.	Dennis *	5.	Cullen, Miss K.
6.	Hyem, J.*	6.	Scadden, Miss
7.	Wilson, A.Y.	7.	Powell, Miss
8.	Wilson, G.	8.	Wansbrough, Miss
9.	Smith, D.	9.	McNamara, Miss
10.	Bonner, Max	10.	Pearson, Miss

* Initial not specified

1934

	MEN		WOMEN
1.=	Carpenter, M	1.	Herbert, Miss M.
1.=	Stephen, W.	2.	Glover, Miss J.
1.=	Ford, R.D.	3.	Carcary, Miss A.
4.	Harris, D.	4.	Smith, Miss P.
5.	Hough, K.	5.	McGrath, Miss M.
6.	Halliday, W.	6.	Veryard, Mrs.
7.	Kennedy, W.	7.	Fyfe, Mrs
8.	Davis, G.B.	8.	McBeth, Mrs.
9.	Reitze, R.	9.	Kiesey, Mrs
10.	Conway, E.	10.	Richardson, Miss P.

NOTE: -Insufficient performances Jacoby, W.

	JUNIOR BOYS		JUNIOR GIRLS
1.	Bonner, M.	1.	Glover, Miss J.
2.	Andrews, W.N.	2.	Carcary, Miss A.
3.	Smith, D.	3.	Jamieson, Miss B.
4.	Halliday, G.	4.	Trewhella, Miss N.
5.	Pittelkow, L.	5.	McNamara, Miss J.
6.	Maley, H.W.	6.	McDermott, Miss J.
7.	Howe, A.M.	7.	Wansbrough, Miss
8.	Angel, L.	8.	Basset, Miss J.
9.	Newman, G.H.	9.	Hunter, Miss J.
10.	McDermott, M.	10.	Augustine, Miss D.

1935

	MEN		WOMEN
1.	Davis, G.H.	1.	Glover, Miss J.
2.	Stephen, W.	2.	McGrath, Miss M.
3.	Halliday, W.	3.	O'Mahoney, Miss M.
4.	Kennedy, W.	4.	Herbert, Miss M.
5.	Ford, R.D.	5.	Kiesey, Mrs J.
6.	Hough, K.	6.	Carcary, Miss A.
7.	Bonner, M.	7.	Jamieson, Miss P.
8.	Reitze, R.	8.	Smith, Miss P.
9.	Thornander, D.	9.	McBeth, Mrs R.
10.	Conway, E.	10.	Peacock, Miss A.

	JUNIOR BOYS		JUNIOR GIRLS
1.	Bonner, M.	1.	Glover, Miss J.
2.	Smith, D.	2.	Jamieson, Miss P.
3.	Wasley, N.	3.	Trewhella, Miss N.
4.	Andrews, W.N.	4.	McNamara, Miss J.
5.	Bennit, W.	5.	McDermott, Miss J.
6.	Halliday, G.	6.	Bassett, Miss J.
7.	McDermott, M.	7.	Hunter, Miss J.
8.	Vincent, J.	8.	Augustine, Miss D.
9.	Stephen, R.		
10.	Bott, C.		

1936

	MEN		WOMEN
1.	Stephen, W.F.	1.	O'Mahoney, Miss M.
2.	Davis, G.H.	2.	McGrath, Miss M.
3.	Ford, R.D.	3.	Herbert, Miss M.
4.	Jacoby, H.	4.	Trewhella, Miss N.
5.	Bonner, M.	5.	Glover, Miss J.
6.	Halliday, W.	6.	Peacock, Miss A.
7.	Wasley, N.	7.	Carcary, Miss A.
8.	Andrews, W.	8.	McNamara, Miss J.
9.	Kinnane, J.B.	9.	Jamieson, Miss B.
10.	Thornander, D.	10.	Williams, Miss M.

	JUNIOR BOYS		JUNIOR GIRLS
1.	Wasley, N.	1.	Trewhella, Miss N.
2.	Stephen, R.H.	2.	McNamara, Miss J.
3.	Vincent, J.B.	3.	Jamieson, Miss B.
4.	Chapman, I.	4.	McDermott, Miss J.
5.	Cairns-Hill, W.	5.	Knox, Miss J.
6.	Collins, N.W.	6.	Hunter, Miss J.
7.	Elliot, I.T.	7.	Paterson, Miss N.
8.	Davey, A.	8.	Fitzhardinge, Miss J.
9.	Main, W.	9.	Nicolson, Miss G.
10.	McAllan, W.	10.	Augustine, Miss B.

NOTE: Insufficient performances McDermott, M.

1937

MEN		WOMEN	
1.	Stephen, W.F.	1.	King, Mrs. A.F.
2.	Bonner, M.	2.	O'Mahoney, Miss M.
3.	Wasley, N.	3.	Trewhella, Miss N.
4.	Kinnane, J.B.	4.	Herbert, Miss M.
5.	Davis, G.B.	5.	Peacock, Miss A.
6.	Ford, R.D.	6.	Carcary, Miss A.
7.	McDermott, M.	7.	Williams, Miss M.
8.	Jacoby, H.	8.	McNamara, Miss J.
9.	Thornander, D.	10.	Halliday, W.

JUNIOR BOYS		JUNIOR GIRLS	
1.	Wasley, N.	1.	Augustine, Miss D.
2.	McDermott, M.	2.	Styants, Miss S.
3.	Stephen, R.	3.	Hunter, Miss J.
4.	Vincent, J.	4.	Knox, Miss J.
5.	Cairns-Hill, W.	5.	Paull, Miss D.
6.	Davey, A.	6.	Nicholson, Miss G.
7.	Mincham, I.A.	7.	Bone, Miss J.
8.	Main, W.	8.	Stein, Miss B.

1938

MEN		WOMEN	
1.	Davis, G.B.	1.	O'Mahoney, Miss M.
2.	Stephen, W.F.	2.	Herbert, Miss M.
3.	Wasley, N.	3.	Trewhella, Miss N.
4.	Stephen, R.H.	4.	Cooke, Mrs M.
5.	Bonner, M.	5.	Peacock, Miss A.
6.	Kinnane, J.B.	6.	Carcary, Miss A.
7.	McDermott, M.	7.	Cullen, Miss K.
8.	Ford, R.D.	8.	McNamara, Miss J.
9.	Andrews, W.N.	10.	Thornander, D.

JUNIOR BOYS		JUNIOR GIRLS	
1.	Stephen, R.H.	1.	Hunter, Miss J.
2.	McDermott, M.	2.	Bone, Miss J.
3.	Davey, A.	3.	Fitzhardinge, Miss J.
4.	Cairns-Hill, W.	4.	Ryan, Miss J.
5.	Hodsdon, W.	5.	Pascoe, Miss C.
6.	Lawrence, E.R.	6.	Knox, Miss J.
7.	Mursell, V.B.	7.	Watts, Miss V.
8.	Graham, R.	8.	Stevenson, Miss M.
9.	Main, W.	9.	Clairs, Miss P.
10.	Mincham, L.	10.	Du Feu, Miss V.

1939

MEN		WOMEN	
1.=	Wasley, N.	1.=	Trewhella, Miss N.
1=	Bonner, M.	1.=	King, Mrs A.F.
3.	Stephen, W.F.	3.	Herbert, Miss M.
4.	McDermott, M.	4.	Cooke, Mrs M.
5.	Davis, G.B.	5.	Peacock, Miss A.
6.	Blacker, H.	6.	Easton, Miss V.
7.	Kinnane, J.B.	7.	McNamara, Miss J.
8.	Stephen, R.H.	8.	McCaul, Miss I.
9.	Cairns-Hill, W.	10.	Thornander, D.

JUNIOR BOYS		JUNIOR GIRLS	
1.	Mursell, V.B.	1.	McCaul, Miss I.
2.	Main, W.	2.	Fitzhardinge, Miss J.
3.	Hammond, G.	3.	Watts, Miss V.
4.	Holten, K.	4.	Pascoe, Miss C.
5.	Davey, R.A.	5.	Ryan, Miss J.
6.	Hodsdon, W.	6.	Lester, Miss D.
7.	Holiday, G.	7.	Pascoe, Miss G.
8.	Stevenson, A.	8.	Clairs, Miss P.
9.	Howman, D.	10.	Conway, D.

1940

MEN		WOMEN	
1.	Bonner, M.	1.	Prindiville, Mrs M.
2.	McDermott, M.	2.	Cooke, Mrs M.
3.	Jacoby, H.	3.	Paterson, Miss M.
4.	Davis, G.B.	4.	Veryard, Mrs E.
5.	Stephen, R.H.	5.	Trewhella, Miss N.
6.	Ford, R.D.	6.	McNamara, Miss J.
7.	Cairns-Hill, W.	7.	Watts, Miss V.
8.	Andrews, W.N.	8.	Ryan, Miss A.

JUNIOR BOYS		JUNIOR GIRLS	
1.	Purdon, P.	1.	Watts, Miss V.
2.	Main, W.	2.	Ryan, Miss J.
3.	Hammond, G.	3.	Fitzhardinge, Miss J.
4.	Holliday, G.	4.	Ryan, Miss R.
5.	Strang, G.	5.	Pascoe, Miss D.
6.	Cullen, G.	6.	Lester, Miss D.
7.	Cox, R.	7.	Wood, Miss E.
8.	Daley, E.	8.	Thornander, Miss A.

1946

MEN		WOMEN	
1.	Wasley, N.W.	1.	McDermott, Mrs J.
2.	Jacoby, H.D.	2.	Edwards, Mrs M.
3.	Stephen, R.H.	3.	Prindiville, Mrs M.
4.	Holten, K.E.	4.	Graham, Miss P.
5.	Kinnane, J.B.	5.	Grace, Miss M.
6.	Davis, G.B.	6.	Bahen, Miss B.
7.	Wilderspin, C.E.	7.	Ryan, Miss R.
8.	Hammond, G.G.	8.	Collins, Mrs H.
9.	Davey, A.L.	9.	Calnon, Miss V.
10.	Harris, R.	10.	Earle, Miss V.

JUNIOR BOYS		JUNIOR GIRLS	
1.	Wilderspin, C.E.	1.	Calnon, V.
2.	Hamilton, D.C.	2.	Nicholas, M.
3.	Genge, T.M.	3.	Earle, M.
4.	McKenzie, D.F.	4.	Higgins, E.
5.	Fletcher, J.F.	5.	Dillon, H.
6.	Lynn, J.S.	6.	Ryan, L.M.

7. Blacklock, J.	7. Prater, U.
8. Bowen, B.K.	8. Lynn, J.
9. Powell, K.H.	9. Treloar, J.
10. Barblett, A.	10. Gilchrist, R.

1947

MEN	WOMEN
1. Wilderspin, C.E.	1. McDermott, Mrs J.
2. Stephen, W.F.	2. Ryan, Miss R.
3. Holten, K.E.	3. Prindiville, Mrs M.
4. Wasley, N.W.	4. Grace, Miss M.
5. Stephen, R.H.	5. Calnon, Miss V.
6. Munro, R.	6. Bahen, Miss B.
7. Hammond, G.G.	7. Earle, Miss V.
8. McDermott, M.	8. Nicholas, Miss M.
9. Harris, R.	10. Davis, G.B.

JUNIOR BOYS	JUNIOR GIRLS
1. Wilderspin, C.E.	1. Calnon, Miss V.
2. Fletcher, J.F.	2. Earle, Miss M.
3. Genge, T.M.	3. Ryan, Miss M.
4. Blacklock, J.	4. Dillon, Miss H.
5. Barblett, A.	5. Prater, Miss U.
6. Anderson, B.H.	6. Lynn, Miss J.
7. Bowen, B.K.	7. Hanlin, Miss J.
8. O'Shannessy, R.	8. Edwards, Miss Q.
9. Loukes, L.	10. Perryman, N.B.

1948

MEN	WOMEN
1. Wilderspin, C.	1. McDermott, Mrs M.
2. Holten, K.	2. Ryan, Miss R.
3. Graham, R.	3. Grace, Miss M.
4. Harris, R.	4. Bahen, Miss B.
5. Hodsdon, W.S.	5. Harrison, Miss J.
6. Strang, G.	6.= Earle, Miss V.
7.= McDermott, M.	6.= Nicholas, Miss M.
7.= McKenzie, D.F.	8. Earle, Miss M.
7.= Blacklock, J.	
10.= Hamilton, D.	
10.= White, V.J.	
10.= Hunt, R.	

JUNIOR BOYS	JUNIOR GIRLS
1. Wilderspin, C.	1. Earle, Miss M.
2. Blacklock, J.	2. Hanlin, Miss J.
3. Fletcher, J.	3. Hanlin, Miss B.
4. Barblett, A.	4. Prater, Miss U.
5. Tobin, B.	5.= Lynn, Miss J.
6. Genge, T.	5.= Blacklock, Miss M.
7. Perryman, N.	7. Cunningham, Miss P.
8. O'Shannessy, R.	8.= Edwards, Miss Q.
	8.= Gilchrist, Miss R.

1949

MEN	WOMEN
1. Wilderspin, C.	1. Grace, Miss M.
2. Holten, K.	2. White, Mrs V.J.
3. Graham, R.	3. Ryan, Miss R.
4. Harris, R.	4. Nicholas, Miss M.
5.= Hodsdon, S.	5. Collins, Mrs N.
5.= Hamilton, D.	6. Calnon, Miss V.
6.= Strang, G.	7. Cunningham, Miss P.
6.= White, V.J.	8. Prater, Miss U.
9. Blacklock, J.E.	10. Hunt, R.

JUNIOR BOYS	JUNIOR GIRLS
1. Blacklock, J.E.	1. Cunningham, P.
2. Tobin, B.	2. Prater, U.
3. Hamilton, E.R.	3. Lynn, J.
4. Hicks, A.R.	4.= Blacklock, M.
5. Randell, C.	4.= Corry, P.
6. Pearse, N.	4.= Heron, M.
7. Shelton, E.	7.= Earle, J.
8.= Hansen, H.	7.= Avery, R.
8.= Mortlock, R.	9.= Einihovici, L.
8.= Robinson, B.	9.= Stirling, J.
8.= Urquhart, A.	

1950

MEN	WOMEN
1. Wilderspin, C.E.	1. Collins, Mrs. H.
2. Holten, K.	2. Ryan, Miss R.
3. Hamilton, D.C.	3. White, Mrs V.J.
4. Strang, G.	4. Bandy, Mrs L.
5. Blacklock, J.E.	5. Grace, Miss M.
6. Quan, L.E.	6. Nicholas, Miss M.
7. White, V.J.	7. Ryan, Miss J.
8. Genge, T.M.	8. Cunningham, Miss P.
9. Hodsdon, W.S.	10. Harris, R.

JUNIOR BOYS	JUNIOR GIRLS
1. Hicks, A.R.	1. Cunningham, Miss P.
2. Pearse, N.	2. Prater, Miss U.
3. Ford, B.D.	3. Blacklock, Miss M.
4. Urquhart, A.	4. Corry, Miss P.
5. Mortlock, R.	5. Einihovici, Miss L.
6. Grafton, L.	6. Earl, Miss J.
7. Robinson, B.	7. Heron, Miss M.
8. Marshall, A.D.	8. Watson, Miss P.

1951

MEN	WOMEN
1. Wilderspin, C.E.	1. McDermott, Mrs Mr.
2.= Hamilton, D.C.	2. Ryan, Miss Joan
2.= Blacklock, J.E.	3. Bandy, Mrs L.
4. Strang, G.	4. White, Mrs V.
5. Quan, L.E.	5. Hesford, Mrs R.

6. White, V.J.
7. Hunt, R.L.
8. Ford, B.D.

6. Cunningham, Miss P.
7. Blacklock, Miss M.
8. Edwards, Mrs M.

JUNIOR BOYS
1. Ford, B.D.
2. Hicks, A.
3. Robinson, B.G.
4. Mortlock, R.
5. Marshall, A.D.
6. Urquhart, A.
7. Grafton, L.
8. Watts, D.

JUNIOR GIRLS
1. Blacklock, Miss M.
2. Corry, Miss P.
3. Heron, Miss M.
4. Einihovici, Miss L.
5. Earle, Miss J.
6. Stewart, Miss M.
7. Johnson, Miss B.
8.= Langley, Miss J.
8.= Irving, Miss J.

1952

MEN
1. Wilderspin, C.E.
2.= Hamilton, D.C.
2.= Blacklock, J.E.
4. Quan, L.E.
5. Hicks, A.R.
6. Strang, G.
7. Marshall, A.D.
8. Robinson, G.B.

WOMEN
1. Ryan, Miss J.
2. Cunningham, Miss P.
3. Bandy, Mrs V.
4. Blacklock, Miss M.
5. Hesford, Mrs R.
6. Arcus, Mrs M.
7. Prater, Miss U.
8. Heron, Miss M.

JUNIOR BOYS
1. Marshall, A.D.
2. Robinson, G.B.
3. Watts, D.
4. Grafton, L.
5. Chrystal, L.
6. Bancroft, G.
7. Purdy, R.J.
8.= Ellis, G.
8.= Francis, B.

JUNIOR GIRLS
1. Blacklock, M.
2. McLeod, J.
3. Langley, J.
4. Einihovici, J.
5. Stewart, M.
6. Earle, J.
7. Blackburn, L.
8. Sayers, M.

1953

MEN
1. Wilderspin, C.
2. Bridge, A.
3. Hamilton, D.
4. Blacklock, J.
5. Marshall, A.
6. Hicks, A.
7. Robinson, B.
8. Quan, L.

WOMEN
1. White, Mrs V.
2. Ryan, Miss J.
3. Collins, Mrs H.
4. Holmes, Mrs P.
5. Arcus, Mrs M.
6. Langley, Miss J.
7. McLeod, Miss J.
8. Stewart, Miss M.

JUNIOR BOYS
1. Marshall, A.
2. Robinson, B.
3. Francis, B.
4. Watson, K.
5. Ellis, G.
6. Purdy, G.
7. Bancroft, G.
8.= Harris, K.
8.= Napier, D.

JUNIOR GIRLS
1. Langley, J.
2. McLeod, J.
3. Stewart, M.
4. Einihovici, I.
5. Irving, J.
6. Earle, J.
7. Sayers, M.
8. Watson, M.

1954

MEN
1. Wilderspin, C.E.
2. Blacklock, J.
3. Bridge, A.
4. Hamilton, D.
5. Marshall, A.
6. Hicks, A.
7. Strang, G.
8. White, V.

WOMEN
1. White, Mrs M.
2. Langley, Miss J.
3. Holmes, Mrs P.
4. Stewart, Miss M.
5. McLeod, Miss J.
6. Ryan, Miss J.
7. Collins, Mrs H.
8. Bandy, Mrs V.

JUNIOR BOYS
1. Napier, D.
2. Watson, K.
3. Chrystal, L.
4. Bancroft, G.
5. D'Orsogna, R.J.
6. Hams, K.
7. Lane, P.
8. Purdy, R.

JUNIOR GIRLS
1. Langley, J.
2. Stewart, M.
3. McLeod, J.
4. Sayers, M.
5. Irving, J.
6. Bloomfield, J.
7. Blackburn, D.
8. Carr, L.

1955

MEN
1. Wilderspin, C.
2. Hamilton, D.C.
3. Bridge, A.
4. Robinson, G.B.
5. Hicks, A.
6. Blacklock, J.
7. Strang, G.
8. White, V.

WOMEN
1. Langley, Miss J.
2. White, Mrs M.
3. Stewart, Miss M.
4. McLeod, Miss J.
5. Bandy, Mrs L.
6. Hesford, Mrs R.
7. Arcus, Mrs M.
8. Earle, Miss J.

JUNIOR BOYS
1. D'Orsogna, R.
2. Napier, D.
3. Harris, K.
4. Greaves, P.
5. Leslie, G.
6. Stanley, R.
7. Evans, J.D.
8. Harris, D.C.

JUNIOR GIRLS
1. Langley, Miss J.
2. Blackburn, Miss D.
3. Sayers, Miss M.
4. Cartledge, Miss L.
5. Blackburn, Miss L.
6. Enderby, Miss M.
7. Bloomfield, Miss J.
8. Flanagan, Miss J.

1956

MEN
1. Wilderspin, C.
2. Hamilton, D.C.
3. Bridge, A.
4. Hicks, A.
5. Blacklock, J.
6. Grafton, L.
7. Robinson, B.

WOMEN
1. Langley, Miss J.
2. McLeod, Miss J.
3. Stewart, Miss M.
4. Collins, Mrs H.
5. Bandy, Mrs V.
6. Sayers, Miss M.
7. Edwards, Mrs M.

8. Napier, D.
9. Harris, K.

8. Holmes, Mrs P.
10. Watson, K.

JUNIOR BOYS
1. Napier, D.
2. Leslie, G.
3. Greaves, P.
4. Evans, J.
5. Harris, D.
6. Brown, C.
7. Metcalfe, G.
8. Diggins, G.

JUNIOR GIRLS
1. Blackburn, Miss D.
2. Hall, Miss B.
3. Enderby, Miss M.
4. Flanagan, Miss J.
5. Lalor, Miss M.
6. Sayers, Miss B.
7. Richardson, Miss E.
8. Selfe, Miss I.

1957

MEN
1. Wilderspin, C.
2. Bridge, A.
3. Napier, D.
4. Harris, K.
5. Robinson, G.B.
6. Ford, B.
7. Strang, G.
8. Blacklock, J.
9. Grafton, L.
10. Evans, J.D.

WOMEN
1. Collins, Mrs H.
2. Langley, Miss J.
3. McLeod, Miss J.
4. Heron, Miss M.
5. Edwards, Mrs M.
6. Waters, Mrs G.S.
7. Sayers, Miss M.
8. Bandy, Mrs L.
9. Holmes, Mrs H.
10. Emslie, Miss A.

JUNIOR BOYS
1. Leslie, G.
2. Paterson, M.G.
3. Taaffe, F.
4. Greaves, P.
5. Harris, D.
6. Lennon, B.
7. Metcalfe, G.
8. Diggins, G.
9. Morrell, H.
10. Brown, C.V.

JUNIOR GIRLS
1. Blackburne, J.
2. Enderby, M.
3. Hall, B.
4. Holbrook, A.
5. Edgar, A.
6. O'Donahoe, E.
7. Sayers, B.
8. Millard, L.
9. Lalor, M.
10. Vance, J.

1958

MEN
1. Wilderspin, C.
2. Bridge, A.
3. Robinson, G.B.
4. Harris, K.
5. Napier, D.
6. Grafton, L.
7. Strang, G.
8. Blacklock, J.
9. Ford, B.

WOMEN
1. Langley, J.
2. Blackburn, D.
3. Robinson, Mrs M.
4. Waters, Mrs H.
5. Edwards, Mrs M.
6. Hall, B.
7. Ward, Mrs J.
8. Sayers, M.
10. Francis, B.

JUNIOR BOYS
1. Patterson, M.
2. Kilderry, Rob
3. Diggins, G.
4. Millen, W.
5. Varney, Kingsley
6. Pearce, E.
7. Morrell, H.
8. Spittel, F.
9. Kilderry, Rick
10. Barrett, B.

JUNIOR GIRLS
1. Blackburn, D.
2. Blackburne, J.
3. Millard, L.
4. Don, L.
5. Laylor, M.
6. Whitely, D.
7. Vance, J.
8. Hall, J.
9. White, J.
10. O'Donohoe, E.

1959

MEN
1. Bridge, A.
2. Strang, G.
3. Watson, K.
4. Robinson, B.G.
5. Napier, D.
6. Grafton, L.
7. Blacklock, J.
8. Francis, B.
9. Ford, B.

WOMEN
1. Langley, Miss J.
2. Holmes, Mrs H.
3. Sayers, Miss M.
4. Wattleworth, Mrs B.
5. Blackburn, Miss D.
6. Davies, Mrs J.
7. Waters, Mrs G.S.
8. Ward, Mrs J.
10. Kilderry, Rob.

NOTE: Insufficient performances Wilderspin, C.

JUNIOR BOYS
1. Kilderry, R.
2. Millen, W.
3. Varney, Kingsley
4. Harris, F.
5. Bell, C.
6. Spittel, F.
7. Watson, D.
8. Morrell, H.

JUNIOR GIRLS
1. Whitely, D.
2. Blackburne, J.
3. Plaisted, H.
4. Millard, L.
5. Paterson, H.
6. Don, L.
7. Edgar, A.
8. Hale, R.

1960

MEN
1. Napier, D.
2. Wilderspin, C.
3. Kilderry, R.
4. Menzies, D.
5. Millen, W.
6. Grafton, L.
7. Strang, G
8. Varney, Kingsley

WOMEN
1. Langley, Miss J.
2. Whiteley, Miss D.
3. Waters, Mrs G.S.
4. Plaisted, Miss H.
5. Holmes, Mrs H.
6. Payne, Mrs (nee Blackburn, D)
7. Ward, Mrs M..
8. Davies, Mrs J.

JUNIOR BOYS
1. Kilderry, R.
2. Millen, W.
3. Varney, Kingsley
4. Watson, D.
5. Clayton, T.
6. McMurtry, D.
7. Harris, F.
8. Cadwallader, R.

JUNIOR GIRLS
1. Whiteley, Miss D.
2. Plaisted, Miss H.
3. Symonds, Miss M.
4. Don, Miss L.
5. Don, Miss G.
6. Gugeri, Miss D.
7. Paterson, Miss H.
8.= Wilson, Miss R.
8.= Rapley, Miss J.

1961

	MEN		WOMEN
1.	Wilderspin, C.	1.	Whitely, Miss D.
2.	Bowman, B.	2.	Plaisted, Miss H.
3.	Napier, D.	3.	Gugeri, Miss D.
4.	Kilderry, Rob	4.	Holmes, Mrs H.
5.	Bell, C.	5.	Don, Miss G.
6.	Grafton, L.	6.	Paterson, Miss H.
7.	Millen, W.	7.	Wilson, Miss R.
8.	Clayton, T.	8.	Waters, Mrs G.
9.	Watson, D.	10.	McMurtry, D.

	JUNIOR BOYS		JUNIOR GIRLS
1.	Clayton, T.	1.	Whitely, Miss D.
2.	Watson, D.	2.	Plaisted, Miss H.
3.	Harris, F.	3.	Gugeri, Miss D.
4.	Rigg, W.	4.	Don, Miss G.
5.	Cadwallader, R.	5.	Paterson, Miss H.
6.	Dyer, J.	6.	Wilson, Miss R.
7.	Varney, Kerry	7.	Ward, Miss J.
8.	Koniuchiwskyj, E.	8.	Treasure, Miss K.

1962

	MEN		WOMEN
1.	Wilderspin, C.	1.	Plaisted, Miss H.
2.	Bowman, B.	2.	Whitely, Miss D.
3.	Napier, D.	3.	Don, Miss G.
4.	Kilderry, Rob	4.	Bignell, Mrs B. (nee Langley, J.)
5.	Clayton, T.	5.	Gugeri, Miss D.
6.	Bell, C.	6.	Brand, Miss P.
7.	Millen, W.	7.	Paterson, Miss H.
8.	McMurtry, D.	8.	Wilson, Miss R.

	JUNIOR BOYS		JUNIOR GIRLS
1.	Clayton, T.	1.	Don, Miss G.
2.	Harris, F.	2.	Gugeri, Miss D.
3.	Street, F.	3.	Brand, Miss P.
4.	Varney, Kerry	4.	Paterson, Miss H.
5.	Dyer, J.	5.	Wilson, Miss R.
6.	Rigg, W.	6.	Ward, Miss J.
7.	Koniuchiwskyj, E.	7.	Benzie, Miss G.
8.	Wall, A.	8.=	Treasure, Miss K.
		8.=	Blackwell, Miss D.

1963

	MEN		WOMEN
1.	Wilderspin, C.	1.	Plaisted, Miss H.
2.	Bowman, B.	2.	Don, Miss G.
3.	Napier, D.	3.	Whitely, Miss D.
4.	Clayton, T.	4.	Gugeri, Miss D.
5.	Menzies, D.	5.	Paterson, Miss H.
6.	Bell, C.	6.	Ward, Miss J.
7.	McMurtry, D.	7.	Treasure, Miss K.
8.	Koniuchiwskyj, E.	8.	Brand, Miss P.

	JUNIOR BOYS		JUNIOR GIRLS
1.	Koniuchiwskyj, E.	1.	Don, Miss D.
2.	Dyer, J.	2.	Paterson, Miss H.
3.	Street, F.	3.	Ward, Miss J.
4.	Penberthy, G.	4.	Treasure, Miss K.
5.	Ladyman, H.	5.	Brand, Miss P.
6.	Fanowrios, A.	6.	Longson, Miss J.
7.	Wall, A.	7.	Jowett, Miss L.
8.	Coulthard, R.	8.	Benzie, Miss G.

1964

	MEN		WOMEN
1.	Bowman, B.	1.	Don, Miss G.
2.	Clayton, T.	2.	Whitely, Miss D.
3.	Penberthy, G.	3.	Plaisted, Miss H.
4.	Koniuchiwskyj, E.	4.	Stephen, Miss S.
5.	Millen, W.	5.	Hunt, Miss L.
6.	Napier, D.	6.	Brand, Miss P.
7.	Wall, A.	7.	Benzie, Miss G.
8.	Menzies, D.	8.	Longson, Miss J.

	JUNIOR BOYS		JUNIOR GIRLS
1.	Penberthy, G.	1.	Stephen, Miss S.
2.	Wall, A.	2.	Hunt, Miss L.
3.	Coulthard, R.	3.	Longson, Miss J.
4.	Fanowrios, A.	4.	McKenzie, Miss A.
5.	Thomson, H.	5.	Tatham, Miss D.
6.	Ladyman, H.	6.	Ward, Miss J.
7.	Gooch, A.	7.	Wall, Miss B.
8.	Hammond, A.	8.	Marshall, Miss J.

1965

	MEN		WOMEN
1.	Bowman, B.	1.	Hunt, Miss L.
2.	Penberthy, G.	2.	Whitely, Miss D.
3.	Millen, W.	3.	Don, Miss G.
4.	Cadwallader, R.	4.	Longson, Miss J.
5.	Harris, F.	5.	Plaisted, Miss H.
6.	Coulthard, R.	6.	Jowett, Miss L.
7.	Strang, G.	7.	McKenzie, Miss A.
8.	Wall, A.	8.	Brand, Miss P.

	JUNIOR BOYS		JUNIOR GIRLS
1.	Penberthy, G.	1.	Hunt, Miss L.
2.	Coulthard, R.	2.	Longson, Miss Jan
3.	Wall, A.	3.	Jowett, Miss L.
4.	Ladyman, H.	4.	McKenzie, Miss A.
5.	Fanowrios, A.	5.	Wall, Miss B.
6.	Gooch, A.	6.	Pilgrim, Miss M.
7.	Hammond, A.	7.	Griffiths, Miss L.
8.	D'Orsogna, A.	8.	Marshall, Miss J.

1966

	MEN		WOMEN
1.	Bowman, B.	1.	Hunt, Miss L.
2.	Clayton, T.	2.	Don, Miss G.
3.	Coulthard, R.	3.	Brand, Miss P.
4.	Cadwallader, R.	4.	Mackenzie, Miss A.

5.	Menzies, D.	5.	Jowett, Miss L.
6.	Wall, A.	6.	Stephen, Miss S.
7.	Millen, W.	7.	Wall, Miss B.
8.	Hammond, A.	8.	Griffiths, Miss L.

	JUNIOR BOYS		JUNIOR GIRLS
1.	Hammond, A.	1.	Hunt, Miss L.
2.	Hunt, H.	2.	Wall, Miss B.
3.	Gooch, A.	3.	Griffiths, Miss L.
4.	Rigg, P.	4.	Lancaster, Miss V.
5.	Hodsdon, G.	5.	Coleman, Miss A.
6.	Ward, D.	6.	Pilgrim, Miss M.
7.	Patterson, M.	7.	Dugan, Miss K.
8.	Morrison, D.	8.=	Bovell, Miss M.
		8.=	Eastcott, Miss M.

1967

	MEN		WOMEN
1.	Bowman, B.	1.	Hunt, L.
2.	Hammond, A.	2.	Brand, P.
3.	Coulthard, R.	3.	Jowett, L.
4.	Millen, W.	4.	Stephen, S.
5.	Ladyman, H.	5.	Wall, B.
6.	Fanowrios, A.	6.	Lancaster, V.
7.	Bell, C.	7.	Treasure, K.
8.	Menzies, D.	8.	Mackenzie, A.

	JUNIOR BOYS		JUNIOR GIRLS
1.	Hammond, A.	1.	Hunt, L.
2.	Hunt, H.	2.	Wall, B.
3.	Rigg, P.	3.	Lancaster, V.
4.=	Hodsdon, G.	4.	Coleman, A.
4.=	McCarthy, T.	5.	Griffiths, L.
6.	Ward, D.	6.	Matison, C.
7.	Morrison, D.	7.	Collins, L.
8.	Holten, P.	8.	Shipley, E.

1968

	MEN		WOMEN
1.	Hammond, A.	1.	Court, M.
2.	Coulthard, R.	2.	Hunt, L.
3.	Penberthy, G.	3.	Whitely, D.
4.	Ladyman, H.	4.	Stephen, S.
5.	Wall, A.	5.	Treasure, K.
6.	Hunt, H.	6.	Jowett, L.
7.	Rigg, P.	7.	Coleman, A.
8.	Hince, K.	8.	Lancaster, V.

	JUNIOR BOYS		JUNIOR GIRLS
1.	Hammond, A.	1.	Hunt, L.
2.	Hodsdon, G.	2.	Coleman, A.
3.	Holten, P.	3.	Lancaster, V.
4.	Pugh, J.	4.	Collins, L.
5.	Worley, O.	5.	Matison, C.
6.	Tognolini, J.	6.=	Shipley, E.
7.	Morrison, D.	6.=	Edmiston, J.
8.	Baker, T.	8.	Eastcott, M.

1968/1969

	MEN		WOMEN
1.	Hammond, A.	1.	Court, M.
2.	Penberthy, G.	2.	Hunt, L.
3.	Hunt, H.	3.	Coleman, A.
4.	Wall, A.	4.	Treasure, K.
5.	Rigg, P.	5.	Lancaster, V.
6.	Kilderry, R.	6.	Hatt, P.
7.	D'Orsogna, A.	7.	Jowett, L.
8.	Millen, W.	8.	Larritt, J.
9.	Holten, P.	9.	Collins, L.
10.	Baker, T.	10.	Watts, A.

	JUNIOR BOYS		JUNIOR GIRLS
1.	Hammond, A.	1.	Hunt, L.
2.	Baker, T.	2.	Coleman, A.
3.	Same, G.	3.	Lancaster, V.
4.	Bougher, J.	4.	Collins, L.
5.	McCarthy, B.	5.	Matison, C.
6.	Hodsdon, M.	6.	Cooper, L.
7.	Casey, R.	7.	Edmiston, J.
8.	Shipley, G.	8.	Worner, E.
9.	Cunningham, S.	9.=	Shipley, E.
10.	Grizich, C.	9.=	Cowan, J.
		9.=	Whitely, M.

1969/1970

	MEN		WOMEN
1.	Hammond, A.	1.	Court, M.
2.	Penberthy, G.	2.	Hunt, L.
3.	Fanowrios, A.	3.	Coleman, A.
4.	Rigg, P.	4.	Matison, C.
5.	D'Orsogna, A.	5.	Jowett, L.
6.	Wall, A.	6.	Collins, L.
7.	Millen, W.	7.	Treasure, K.
8.	Evans, J.	8.	Cooper, L.

	JUNIOR BOYS		JUNIOR GIRLS
1.	Casey, R.	1.	Coleman, A.
2.	Same, G.	2.	Matison, C.
3.	Sofoulis, P.	3.	Collins, L.
4.	Hodsdon, M.	4.	Cooper, L.
5.	Shipley, G.	5.	Worner, E.
6.	Bougher, J.	6.	Edmiston, J.
7.	Olivieri, R.	7.	Shipley, E.8.
8.	Chamberlain, P.	8.	Whitely, M.

1970/1971

	MEN		WOMEN
1.	Penberthy, G.	1.	Matison, C.
2.	Fanowrios, A.	2.	Coleman, A.
3.	Seymour, R.	3.	Chute, K.
4.	Reynolds, J.	4.	Taylor, S.
5.	Kilderry, R.	5.	Cooper, L.
6.	Evans, J.	6.	Young, H.
7.	Gooch, A.	7.	Smith, M.
8.	Casey, R.	8.	Whitely, M.

NOTE: Insufficient performances
Court, M. Hunt, L.

JUNIOR BOYS	JUNIOR GIRLS
1. Casey, R.	1. Coleman, A.
2. Shipley, G.	2. Cooper, L.
3. Sofoulis, P.	3. Worner, E.
4. Olivieri, R.	4. Taylor, S.
5. Chamberlain, P.	5. Whitely, M.
6. Same, G.	6. Sawyer, G.
7. Tognolini, B.	7. Heavey, B.
8. O'Dea, P.	8. Saunders, P.

NOTE: Insufficient performances
Shipley, G. Same, G.

1971/1972

MEN	WOMEN
1. Penberthy, G.	1. Matison, C.
2. Fanowrios, A.	2. Coleman, A.
3. Kilderry, R.	3. Chute, K.
4. Casey, R.	4. Taylor, S.
5. Rigg, P.	5. Cooper, L.
6. Tilmanis, G.	6. Young, H.
7. Gooch, A.	7. Smith, M.
8. Sofoulis, P.	8. Whitely, M.

NOTE: Insufficient performances
Court, M. Hunt, L.

JUNIOR BOYS	JUNIOR GIRLS
1. Casey, R.	1. Worner, E.
2. Sofoulis, P.	2. Taylor, S.
3. Olivieri, R.	3. Whitely, M.
4. Chamberlain, P.	4. Heavey, B.
5. Tognolini, B.	5. Saunders, P.
6. O'Dea, P.	6. Wilkes, H.
7. Hunt, J.	7. Howard, P.
8. King, J.	8. Hall, A.

NOTE: Insufficient performances
Shipley, G. Same, G.

1972/1973

MEN	WOMEN
1. Penberthy, G.	1. Court, M.
2. Fanowrios, A.	2. Matison, C.
3. Hammond, A.	3. Cooper, L.
4. Casey, R.	4. Young, H.
5. Kilderry, R.	5. Chute, K.
6. Tilmanis, G.	6. Taylor, S.
7. Olivieri, R.	7. Smith, M.
8. Holten, P.	8. Whitely, M.
NOTE: Insufficient performances Harris, F.	NOTE: Insufficient performances Hunt, L.

JUNIOR BOYS	JUNIOR GIRLS
1. Casey, R.	1. Taylor, S.
2. Olivieri, R.	2. Sawyer, M.
3. Sofoulis, P.	3. Saunders, P.
4. Tognolini, B.	4. Layman, A.
5. Hunt, J.	5. Wilkes, H.
6. Williams, D.	6. Heavey, B.
7. Ladyman, J.	7. Hall, A.
8. O'Dea, P.	8. Pekovich, M.

1973/1974

MEN	WOMEN
1. Casey, R.	1. Court, M.
2. Penberthy, G.	2. Hunt, L.
3. Wall, A.	3.= Lancaster, V.
4. Olivieri, R.	3.= Matison, C.
5. Hammond, A.	5. Cooper, L.
6. Seymour, R.	6. Chute, K.
7. Dyson, P.	7. Taylor, S.
8.= Sofoulis, P.	8. Young, H.
8.= Ward, D.	

NOTE: Insufficient performances
Fanowrios, A.

JUNIOR BOYS	JUNIOR GIRLS
1. Hunt, J.	1. Sawyer, M.
2. Pushyk, M.	2. Saunders, P.
3. Williams, D.	3. Ladyman, A.
4. Ladyman, J.	4. Hall, J.
5. Seymour, G.	5. Pekovich, M.
6. Williams, R.	6. Hall, A.
7. Walker, I.	7. Wilkes, H.
8. Luttrell, A.	8. Miguel, K.

1974/1975

MEN	WOMEN
1. Casey, R.	1. Court, M.
2. Penberthy, G.	2. Hunt, L.
3. Olivieri, R.	3. Matison, C.
4. Napier, D.	4. Lancaster, V.
5. Dyson, P.	5. Taylor, S.
6. Hince, K.	6. Sawyer, M.
7. Sofoulis, P.	7. Smith, M.
8. Hunt, J.	8. Pekovich, M.

JUNIOR BOYS	JUNIOR GIRLS
1. Hunt, J.	1. Sawyer, M.
2. Hall, L.	2. Pekovich, M.
3. Luttrell, A.	3. Hall, J.
4. Pushyk, M.	4. Layman, A.
5. Luttrell, R.	5. Sayers, G.
6. Williams, R.	6. Lange, J.
7. Bersan, I.	7. Hall, A.
8. Williams, D.	8. Keenan, J.

1975/1976

MEN	WOMEN
1. Casey, R.	1. Court, M.
2. Penberthy, G.	2. Hunt, L.
3. Pushyk, M.	3. Matison, C.
4. Olivieri, R.	4. Cooper, L.
5. Napier, D.	5. Pekovich, M.
6. Hince, K.	6. Taylor, S.
7. Hall, L.	7. Hall, J.
8. Hunt, J.	8. Chute, K.

	BOYS UNDER 19		GIRLS UNDER 19
1.	Pushyk, M.	1.	Pekovich, M.
2.	Hall, L.	2.	Hall, J.
3.	Hunt, J.	3.	Layman, A.
4.	Johnstone, C.	4.	Lange, J.
5.	Williams, R.	5.	Sayers, G.
6.	Bersan, I.	6.	Bovell, K.
7.	Begley, K.	7.	Keenan, J.
8.	Grant, R.	8.	Wheatley, J.

	BOYS UNDER 16		GIRLS UNDER 16
1.	Johnstone, C.	1.	Smith, E.
2.	Begley, K.	2.	Polley, L.
3.	Grant, R.	3.	Sayers, E.
4.	Robinson, P.	4.	Cole, D.
5.	Paskos, A.	5.	Wood, R.
6.	Vinci, T.	6.	Smith, J.
7.	Thorpe, J.	7.	Mitchell, G.
8.	Properjohn, B.	8.	Hullett, M.

1976/1977

	MEN		WOMEN
1.	Casey, R.	1.	Sawyer, M.
2.	Penberthy, G.	2.	Matison, C.
3.	Hall, L.	3.	Cooper, L.
4.	Pushyk, M.	4.	Pekovich, M.
5.	Cadwallader, R.	5.	Mack, S.
6.	Thomson, H.	6.	Chute, K.
7.	Oliveri, R.	7.	Fisher, R.
8.	Bersan, I.	8.	Heavey, B.

	BOYS UNDER 19		GIRLS UNDER 19
1.	Hall, L.	1.	Pekovich, M.
2.	Bersan, I.	2.	Sayers, G.
3.	Johnstone, C.	3.	Lange, J.
4.	Begley, K.	4.	Ainscough, C.
5.	Grant, R.	5.	Bovell, K.
6.	Di Fransesco, A.	6.	Smith, E.
7.	Nicholas, S.	7.	Keenan, J.
8.	Bundell, R.	8.	Cole, D.

	BOYS UNDER 16		GIRLS UNDER 16
1.	Vinci, T.	1.	Sayers, E.
2.	Robinson, P.	2.	Hullett, M.
3.	McEwen, G.	3.	Wood, R.
4.	Properjohn, B.	4.	Mitchell, G.
5.	Thorpe, J.	5.	Tolcon, J.
6.	Feeney, G.	6.	Keenan, A.
7.	Edwards, M.	7.	Johnson, S.
8.	Turner, D.	8.	Casserley, M.

1977/1978

	MEN		WOMEN
1.	Casey, R.	1.	Sawyer, M.
2.	Penberthy, G.	2.	Matison, C.
3.	Hall, L.	3.	Cooper, L.
4.	Olivieri, R.	4.	Pekovich, M.
5.	Bersan, I.	5.	Mack, S.
6.	Johnstone, C.	6.	Maddison, J.
7.	Seymour, G.	7.	Sayers, G.
8.	Sofoulis, P.	8.	Smith, E.
9.	Begley, K.	9.	Smith, M.
10.	Grant, R.	10.	Lee, D.
11.	Di Francesco, A.	11.	Heavey, B.
12.	Tognolini, B.	12.	Lange, J.

NOTE:
Insufficient performances
Hunt, L.

	BOYS UNDER 19		GIRLS UNDER 19
1.	Hall, L.	1.	Sayers, G.
2.	Johnstone, C.	2.	Smith, E.
3.	Begley, K.	3.	Lange, J.
4.	Grant, R.	4.	Ainscough, C.
5.	Di Francesco, A.	5.	Cole, D.
6.	Vinci, T.	6.	Sayers, E.
7.	Thorpe, J.	7.	Bovell, K.
8.	Robinson, P.	8.	Wood, R.
9.	Properjohn, B.	9.	Smith, J.
10.	Turner, D.	10.	Tolcon, J.

	BOYS UNDER 16		GIRLS UNDER 16
1.	Thorpe, J.	1.	Sayers, E.
2.	Properjohn, B.	2.	Tolcon, J.
3.	Turner, D.	3.	Johnson, S.
4.	Watts, A.	4.	Bond, C.
5.	Mason, S.	5.	Sayers, C.
6.	Hall, A.	6.	Keenan, A.
7.	Johnstone, S.	7.	Lamb, R.
8.	Clarke, P.	8.	Marshall, D.
9.	Duncan, J.	9.	Wheatley, P.
10.	Nixon, G.	10.	Worthington, L.

1978/1979

	MEN		WOMEN
1.	Casey, R.	1.	Matison, C.
2.	Penberthy, G.	2.	Sawyer, M.
3.	Bersan, I.	3.	Cooper, L.
4.	Di Francesco, A.	4.	Mack, S.
5.	Tognolini, B.	5.	Smith, E.
6.	Shaw, A.	6.	Maddison, J.
7.	Hunt, H.	7.	Sayers, G.
8.	Murton, R.	8.	Ainscough, C.
9.	Dyson, P.	9.	Sayers, E.
10.	Hughes, D.	10.	Lange, J.

NOTE:
Insufficient performances
Hall, L.
Olivieri, R.
Johnstone, C.
Begley, K.
Grant, R.
Pushyk, M.
Sofoulis, P.

NOTE:
Insufficient performances
Pekovich, M.

	BOYS UNDER 19		GIRLS UNDER 19
1.	Johnstone, C.	1.	Smith, E.
2.	Grant, R.	2.	Sayers, E.
3.	Begley, K.	3.	Lange, J.
4.	Vinci, T.	4.	Cole, D.
5.	Thorpe, J.	5.	Smith, J.
6.	Turner, D.	6.	Wood, R.
7.	Robinson, P.	7.	Lamb, R.
8.	Properjohn, B.	8.	Johnson, S.
9.=	Hall, A.	9.	White, C.
9.=	Watts, A.	10.	Sayers, C.

	BOYS UNDER 16		GIRLS UNDER 16
1.	Turner, D.	1.	Sayers, E.
2.	Hall, A.	2.	Lamb, R.
3.	Mason, S.	3.	Marshall, D.
4.	Johnstone, S.	4.	Wheatley, P.
5.	Cooper, M.	5.	Greig, J.
6.	Thorpe, M.	6.	Worthington, L.
7.	Marshall, S.	7.	Truscott, J.
8.	Power, M.	8.	Clarke, J.
9.	Watts, T.	9.	Lavtas, L.
10.	Slater, C.	10.	Warren, L.

	BOYS UNDER 14		GIRLS UNDER 14
1.	Williams, B.	1.	Greig, J.
2.	Hevron, J.	2.	Warren, L.
3.	Lebedevs, P.	3.	Johnson, J.
4.	Robinson, K.	4.	Hurst, K.
5.	Berry, I.	5.	Watson, D.
6.	Turner, W.	6.	Rushforth, A.
7.	Frick, P.	7.	Worthington, K.
8.	Rundle, G.	8.	Lance, C.
9.	Arnold, E.	9.	Worthington, D.
10.	McLellan, D.	10.	Bowler, H.

1979/1980

	MEN		WOMEN
1.	Casey, R.	1.	Dorey, C.
2.	Hall, L.	2.	Sawyer, M.
3.	Olivieri, R.	3.	Sayers, E.
4.	Penberthy, G.	4.	Cooper, L.
5.	DiFrancesco, A.	5.	Mack, S.
6.	Murton, R.	6.	Ainscough, C.
7.	Luttrell, A.	7.	Smith, E.
8.	Hughes, D.	8.	Sayers, G.
9.	Shaw, A.	9.	Lamb, R.
10.	Tognolini, B.	10.	Chute, K.

NOTE: Insufficient performances:
Johnstone, C.
Bersan, I.

	JUNIOR BOYS UNDER 19		JUNIOR GIRLS UNDER 19
1.	Thorpe, J.	1.	Sayers, E.
2.	Turner, D.	2.	Lamb, R.
3.	Properjohn, B.	3.	Wood, R.
4.	Hall, A.	4.	Greig, J.
5.	Watts, A.	5.	Marshall, D.
6.	Mason, S.	6.	Johnson, S.
7.	Cooper, M.	7.	Wheatley, P.
8.	Vinci, T.	8.	Bond, C.
9.	Duncan, J.	9.	White, C.
10.	Thorpe, M.	10.	Tolcon, J.

	JUNIOR BOYS UNDER 16		JUNIOR GIRLS UNDER 16
1.	Thorpe, M.	1.	Greig, J.
2.	Marshall, S.	2.	Clarke, J.
3.	Power, M.	3.	Bowler, M.
4.	Slater, C.	4.	Lavtas, L.
5.	Watts, T.	5.	Ayres, N.
6.	Edgley, M.	6.	Colquhoun, P.
7.	Lebedevs, P.	7.	Warren, L.
8.	Marsh, A.	8.	Johnson, J.
9.	Campbell, G.	9.	Hurst, K.
10.	Berry, I.	10.	Casserley, E.

	JUNIOR BOYS UNDER 14		JUNIOR GIRLS UNDER 14
1.	Robinson, K.	1.	Johnson, J.
2.	Williams, B.	2.	Hurst, K.
3.	Hevron, J.	3.	Byrne, J.
4.	Hanlin, J.	4.	Jefferson, J.
5.	Napier, C.	5.	McMahon, A.
6.	Turner, W.	6.	Harbron, J.
7.	Arnold, E.	7.	Slater, P.
8.	Messer, D.	8.	Edinger, H.
9.	Frick, G.	9.	Worthington, K.
10.	Jones, R.	10.	Lance, C.

1980/1981

	MEN		WOMEN
1.	Johnstone, C.	1.	Dorey, C.
2.	Hall, L.	2.	Sayers, E.
3.	Grant, R.	3.	Collins, M.
4.	Casey, R.	4.	Cooper, L.
5.	Penberthy, G.	5.	Smith, E.
6.	Tognolini, B.	6.	Ainscough, C.
7.	Olivieri, R.	7.	Lamb, R.
8.	Murton, R.	8.	Greig, J.
9.	Di Francesco, A.	9.	Chute, K.
10.	Shaw, A.	10.	Mitchell, G.

	BOYS 18 YEARS & UNDER		GIRLS 18 YEARS & UNDER
1.	Thorpe, J.	1.	Sayers, E.
2.	Marshall, S.	2.	Lamb, R.
3.	Clarke, P.	3.	Greig, J.
4.	Mason, S.	4.	Johnson, S.
5.	Thorpe, M.	5.	Marshall, D.
6.	Cooper, M.	6.	Wheatley, P.
7.	Lebedevs, P.	7.	Clarke, J.
8.	Slater, C.	8.	Bowler, M.
9.	Armstrong, R.	9.	Howlett, J.
10.	Power, M.	10.	Truscott, J.

NOTE: Insufficient performances:
Turner, D. Hall, A.

BOYS 16 YEARS & UNDER
1. Marshall, S.
2. Thorpe, M.
3. Lebedevs, P.
4. Robinson, K.
5. Slater, C.
6. Power, M.
7. Berry, I.
8. Marsh, A.
9. Watts, T.
10. Campbell, G.

GIRLS 16 YEARS & UNDER
1. Lamb, R.
2. Greig, J.
3. Clarke, J.
4. Byrne, J.
5. Bowler, M.
6. Howlett, J.
7. Phillips, J.
8. Casserley, E.
9. Fraser, H.
10. Hurst, K.

BOYS 14 YEARS & UNDER
1. Robinson, K.
2. Williams, B.
3. Hevron, J.
4. Napier, C.
5. Frick, G.
6. Hanlin, J.
7. Arnold, E.
8. Messer, D.
9. Foote, G.
10. Hamburg, B.

GIRLS 14 YEARS & UNDER
1. Byrne, J.
2. Hurst, K.
3. Johnson, J.
4. Lance, C.
5. McMahon, A.
6. Jefferson, J.
7. Harbron, J.
8. Slater, P.
9. Worthington, K.
10. Ledder, J.

BOYS 12 YEARS & UNDER
1. Robinson, J.
2. Turich, C.
3. Burrows, T.
4. Whitton, M.
5. Venerys, J.
6. Caudle, G.
7. Jones, B.
8. Lewis, R.

GIRLS 12 YEARS & UNDER
1. Ledder, J.
2. Varney, R.
3. Mead, M.
4. Hamburg, V.
5. Gray, L.
6. Crutchley, N.
7. Bignell, J.
8. Finucane, L.

1981/1982

MEN
1. Johnstone, C.
2. Casey, R.
3. Grant, R.
4. Penberthy, G.
5. Luttrell, R.
6. Williams, R.
7. Tognolini, B.
8. Murton, R.
9. Thorpe, J.
10. Shaw, A.

WOMEN
1. Sayers, E.
2. Dorey, C.
3. Cooper, L.
4. Smith, E.
5. Lamb, R.
6. Ainscough, C.
7. Chute, K.
8. Sayers, G.
9. Mitchell, G.
10. Layman, A.

BOYS 18 YEARS & UNDER
1. Marshall, S.
2. Lebedevs, P.
3. Thorpe, M.
4. Robinson, K.
5. Williams, B.
6. Power, M.
7. Marsh, A.
8. Slater, C.
9. Hevron, J.
10. Berry, I.

NOTE: Insufficient performances: Cooper, M.

GIRLS 18 YEARS & UNDER
1. Lamb, R.
2. Byrne, J.
3. Bowler, M.
4. Clarke, J.
5. Howlett, J.
6. Casserly, E.
7. Fraser, H.
8. Hurst, K.
9. Thomson, D.
10. Owens, J.

NOTE: Insufficient performances Greig, J.

BOYS 16 YEARS & UNDER
1. Robinson, K.
2. Williams, B.
3. Hevron, J.
4. Napier, C.
5. Turich, G.
6. Hanlin, J.
7. Arnold, E.
8. Mullany, N.
9. Foote, G.
10. Messer, D.

GIRLS 16 YEARS & UNDER
1. Byrne, J.
2. Hurst, K.
3. Johnson, J.
4. Jefferson, J.
5. Lance, C.
6. Mann, S.
7. McMahon, A.
8. Harbron, J.
9. Madden, M.
10. Edinger, H.

BOYS 14 YEARS & UNDER
1. Robinson, J.
2. Turich, C.
3. Whitton, M.
4. Venerys, J.
5. Caudle, G.
6. Tory, M.
7. Burrows, T.
8. Hepburn, M.
9. Richardson, J.
10. Lewis, R.

GIRLS 14 YEARS & UNDER
1. Mann, S.
2. Ledder, J.
3. Varney, R.
4. Hamburg, V.
5. Gray, L.
6. Mead, M.
7. Crutchley, N.
8. Parentich, P.
9. Bignell, J.
10. Bottrill, J.

BOYS 12 YEARS & UNDER
1. Lindeman, J.
2. Wardell-Johnson, L.
3. Johns, A.
4. Court, K.
5. Campillos, P.
6. Zumpft, M.
7. Adams, B.
8. Watson, G.

GIRLS 12 YEARS & UNDER
1. Jacka, A.
2. Vahala, K.
3. Massey, S.
4. Foy, C.
5. Kelly, S.
6. Bucens, K.
7. Fic, M.
8.= McMahon, S.
8.= Phillips, M.

1982/1983

MEN
1. Johnstone, C.
2. Casey, R.
3. Grant, R.
4. Rigg, P.
5. Properjohn, B.
6. Luttrell, A.
7. Tognolini, B.
8. Murton, R.
9. Prouse, R.
10. Lebedevs, P.

WOMEN
1. Sayers, E.
2. Dorey, C.
3. Lamb, R.
4. Cooper, L.
5. Greig, J.
6. Smith, E.
7. Ainscough, C.
8. Chute, K.
9. Sayers, G.
10. Smith, M.

NOTE: Insufficient performances: Hall, L. Penberthy, G. Thorpe, J.

BOYS 18 YEARS & UNDER	GIRLS 18 YEARS & UNDER
1. Lebedevs, P.	1. Greig, J.
2. Williams, B.	2. Byrne, J.
3. Robinson, K.	3. Johnson, J.
4. Hevron, J.	4. Bowler, H.
5. Napier, C.	5. Hurst, K.
6. Boag, R.	6. Thomson, D.
7. Askey, P.	7. Madden, M.
8. Turich, G.	8. Lance, C.
9. Caplin, N.	9. Ledder, J.
10. Mullany, N.	10. Mead, M.

BOYS 16 YEARS & UNDER	GIRLS 16 YEARS & UNDER
1. Hamburg, B.	1. Byrne, J.
2. Messer, D.	2. Ledder, J.
3. Robinson, J.	3. Mead, M.
4. Turich, C.	4. Crutchley, N.
5. Bransby, S.	5. McMahon, A.
6. Hinton, P.	6. Parentich, P.
7. Sharp, R.	7. Gray, L.
8. Hepburn, M.	8. Varney, R.
9. Tandy, D.	9. Bottrill, J.
10. Whitton, M.	10. Hamburg, V.

BOYS 14 YEARS & UNDER	GIRLS 14 YEARS & UNDER
1. Turich, C.	1. Ledder, J.
2. Danzi, D.	2. Parentich, P.
3. Prickett, N.	3. Drake-Brockman, T.
4. Cunningham, A.	4. Askey, L.
5. Culley, D.	5. Lynch, E.
6. Arbuckle, B.	6. Samson, R.
7. Scott, T.	7. Massey, S.
8. Kestell, D.	8. Jacka, A.
9. Maguire, J.	9. Vahala, K.
10. Hampson, D.	10. Phillips, M

BOYS 12 YEARS & UNDER	GIRLS 12 YEARS & UNDER
1. Martin, C.	1. Vahala, K.
2. Hall, A.	2. Drake-Brockman, M.
3. Evans, J.	3. Quinn, J.E.
4. Woodward, G.	4. Feeney, M.
5. Dalton, S.	5. Pihu, S.
6. Gerrans, P.	6. Churack, E.
7. Patten, B.	7. Ball, Y.
8. Crookes, M.	8. Martin, S.

1983

MEN	WOMEN
1. Johnstone, C.	1. Sayers, E.
2. Casey, R.	2. Dorey, C.
3. Grant, R.	3. Lamb, R.
4. Begley, K.	4. Cooper, L.
5. Properjohn, B.	5. Smith, E.
6.= Robinson, K.	6. Greig, J.
6.= Williams, B.	7. Chute, K.
8. Tognolini, B.	8. Jowett, L.
9. Rigg, P.	
10. Penberthy, G.	

NOTE: Insufficient performances: Byrne, J.

BOYS 18 YEARS & UNDER	GIRLS 18 YEARS & UNDER
1.= Robinson, K.	1. Byrne, J.
1.= Williams, B.	2. Crutchley, N.
3. Lebedevs, P.	3. Johnson, J.
4. Hevron, J.	4. Ledder, J.
5. Napier, C.	5. Parentich, P.
6. Askey, P.	6. McMahon, A.
7. Hamburg, B.	7. Askey, L.
8. Messer, D.	8. Bottrill, J.
9. Robinson, J.	9. Harbron, J.
10. Fiorentino, L.	10. Lance, C.

BOYS 16 YEARS & UNDER	GIRLS 16 YEARS & UNDER
1. Hamburg, B.	1. Byrne, J.
2. Messer, D.	2. Crutchley, N.
3. Robinson, J.	3. Ledder, J.
4. Tandy, D.	4. Parentich, P.
5. Turich, C.	5. McMahon, A.
6. Sharp, R.	6. Askey, L.
7. Bransby, S.	7. Bottrill, J.
8. Hepburn, M.	8. Harbron, J.
9. Danzi, D.	9. Gray, L.
10. Atkin, A.	10. Drake-Brockman, T.

BOYS 14 YEARS & UNDER	GIRLS 14 YEARS & UNDER
1. Turich, C.	1. Ledder, J.
2. Danzi, D.	2. Parentich, P.
3. Prickett, N.	3. Askey, L.
4. Culley, D.	4. Drake-Brockman, T.
5. Kestell, D.	5. Lynch, E.
6. Hampson, D.	6. Foy, C.
7. Cunningham, A.	7. Jacka, A.
8. Scott, T.	8. Vahala, K.
9. Maguire, J.	9. Samson, R.
10.= Campillos, P.	10. Buzens, K.
10.= Leuba, M.	

BOYS 12 YEARS & UNDER	GIRLS 12 YEARS & UNDER
1. Martin, C.	1. Vahala, K.
2. Evans, J.	2. Drake-Brockman, M.
3. Gerrans, P.	3. Ball, Y.
4. Dalton, S.	4. Quinn, J.E.
5. Patten, B.	5. Feeney, M.
6. Hall, A.	6. Pihu, S.
7. Woodward, G.	7. Martin, S.
8. Gibson, M.	8. Vahala, N.
9. Lynch, B.	9. Quinn, J.D.
10. Crookes, M.	10. Kelly, L.

1984

MEN	WOMEN
1. Johnstone, C.	1. Smylie, E.
2. Casey, R.	2. Byrne, J.
3. Luttrell, A.	3. Parentich, P.
4. Properjohn, B.	4. Cooper, L.
5. Grant, R.	5. Smith, E.
6. Robinson, K.	6. Chute, K.
7. Begley, K.	7. Mitchell, G.
8. Tognolini, B.	8. Crutchley, N.

9. Williams, B.
10. Napier, C.

9. Bottrill, J.
10. Askey, L.
NOTE: Insufficient performances: Dorey, C.

BOYS 18 YEARS & UNDER	GIRLS 18 YEARS & UNDER
1. Robinson, K.	1. Byrne, J.
2. Williams, B.	2. Parentich, P.
3. Napier, C.	3. Johnson, J.
4. Turich, C.	4. Crutchley, N.
5. Robinson, J.	5. Bottrill, J.
6. Askey, P.	6. Askey, L.
7. Hamburg, B.	7. Ledder, J.
8. Fiorentino, L.	8. Hamburg, V.
9. Messer, D.	9. Drake-Brockman, T.
10. Heather, M.	10. Fiorentino, C.

BOYS 16 YEARS & UNDER	GIRLS 16 YEARS & UNDER
1. Turich, C.	1. Parentich, P.
2. Robinson, J.	2. Crutchley, N.
3. Heather, M.	3. Bottrill, J.
4. Danzi, D.	4. Askey, L.
5. Tory, M.	5. Ledder, J.
6. Hepburn, M.	6. Hamburg, V.
7. Whitton, M.	7. Drake-Brockman, T.
8. Prickett, N.	8. Fiorentino, C.
9. Culley, D.	9. Lynch, E.
10.= Burrows, T.	10. Butler, J.
10.= Venerys, J.	

BOYS 14 YEARS & UNDER	GIRLS 14 YEARS & UNDER
1. Campillos, P.	1. Phillips, M.
2. Hampson, D.	2. Jacka, A.
3. Patten, D.	3. Bucens, K.
4. Watson, G.	4. Foy, C.
5. Leuba, M.	5. Massey, S.
6. Faulkner, P.	6. Vahala, K.
7. Wardell-Johnson, L.	7. McIntosh, K.
8. Wharton, P.	8. McMahon, S.
9. Court, K.	9. Kelly, S.
10. Woodward, G.	10. Drake-Brockman, M.

BOYS 12 YEARS & UNDER	GIRLS 12 YEARS & UNDER
1. Evans, J.	1. Martin, S.
2. Cox, G.	2. Vahala, N.
3. Cannell, L.	3. Gradisen, D.
4. Floyd, A.	4. Stansfield, M.
5. Morphett, K.	5. Kelly, L.
6. Prendiville, M.	6. Quinn, J.E.
7. Heather, C.	7. Frodsham, A.
8. McIntosh, A.	8. Blackwell, D.
9. Scott, K.	9. Butler, D.
10. Gomez, M.	10. Beale, T.

1985

MEN	WOMEN
1. Grant, R.	1. Dorey, C.
2. Casey, R.	2. Byrne, J.
3. Luttrell, A.	3. Parentich, P.
4. Properjohn, B.	4.= Cooper, L.
5. Penberthy, G.	4.= Crutchley, N.
6. Begley, K.	6. Ledder, J.
7. Tognolini, B.	7. Askey, L.
8. Murton, R.	8. Mitchell, G.
9. Hamburg, B.	9. Chute, K.
10. Robinson, K.	10. Shevlin, D.

NOTE: Insufficient performances: Smylie, E.

BOYS 18 YEARS & UNDER	GIRLS 18 YEARS & UNDER
1. Hamburg, B.	1. Byrne, J.
2. Turich, C.	2. Parentich, P.
3. Prickett, N.	3. Crutchley, N.
4. Danzi, D.	4. Ledder, J.
5. Culley, D.	5. Askey, L.
6. Heather, M.	6. Drake-Brockman, T.
7. Robinson, J.	7. Bottrill, J.
8. McCreery, K.	8. Hamburg, V.
9. Sharp, R.	9. Monger, K.
10. Simkovic, E.	10. Lynch, E.

BOYS 16 YEARS & UNDER	GIRLS 16 YEARS & UNDER
1. Turich, C.	1. Parentich, P.
2. Prickett, N.	2. Ledder, J.
3. Danzi, D.	3. Askey, L.
4. Culley, D.	4. Drake-Brockman, T.
5. Campillos, P.	5. Phillips, M.
6. Leuba, M.	6. Foy, C.
7. Patten, D.	7. Bucens, K.
8. Kestell, D.	8. Jacka, A.
9. Hampson, D.	9. Lynch, E.
10. Cunningham, A.	10. Vahala, K.
11. Keizer, M.	

BOYS 14 YEARS & UNDER	GIRLS 14 YEARS & UNDER
1. Kilderry, P.	1. Vahala, K.
2. Woodward, G.	2. Drake-Brockman, M.
3. Cox, G.	3. Ball, Y.
4. Hall, A.	4. Mori, R.
5. Zsilinszky, K.	5. Feeney, M.
6. Gerrans, P.	6. McMahon, K.
7. Gibson, M.	7. Lindsay, J.
8. Patten, B.	8. Martin, S.
9. Martin, C.	9. Donatti, E.
10. Floyd, A.	10. Scorer, T-A.

1986

MEN	WOMEN
1. Grant, R.	1. Byrne, J.
2. Properjohn, B.	2. Smylie, E.
3. Casey, R.	3. Parentich, P.
4. Robinson, K.	4. Dorey, C.
5. Prickett, N.	5. Crutchley, N.
6. Luttrell, R.	6. Cooper, L.

7.	Hamburg, B.	7.	Ledder, J.
8.	Danzi, D.	8.	Drake-Brockman, T.
9.	Culley, D.	9.	Askey, L.
10.	Tognolini, B.	10.	Bucens, K.

	BOYS 18 & UNDER		GIRLS 18 & UNDER
1.	Turich, C.	1.	Parentich, P.
2.	Prickett, N.	2.	Crutchley, N.
3.	Danzi, D.	3.	Ledder, J.
4.	Culley, D.	4.	Drake-Brockman, T.
5.	Simkovic, E.	5.	Askey, L.
6.	Campillos, P.	6.	Bucens, K.
7.	Leuba, M.	7.	Phillips, M.
8.	Patten, D.	8.	Bottrill, J.
9.	Hampson, D.	9.	Kelleher, V.
10.	Tory, M.	10.	Monger, K.

	BOYS 16 & UNDER		GIRLS 16 & UNDER
1.	Anderson, J.	1.	Bucens, K.
2.	Campillos, P.	2.	Phillips, M.
3.	Leuba, M.	3.	Jacka, A.
4.	Patten, D.	4.	Foy, C.
5.	Hampson, D.	5.	Vahala, K.
6.	Wharton, P.	6.	Cook, R.
7.	Kilderry, P.	7.	Drake-Brockman, M.
8.	Woodward, G.	8.	Ball, Y.
9.	Watson, G.	9.	Martin, S.
10.	Burton, A.	10.	Feeney, M.

	BOYS 14 & UNDER		GIRLS 14 & UNDER
1.	Kilderry, P.	1.	Martin, S.
2.	Cox, G.	2.	Blackwell, D.
3.	Floyd, A.	3.=	Donatti, E.
4.	Cannell, L.	3.=	Kimpton, N.
5.	Morphett, K.	5.	Vahala, N.
6.	Hulbert, J.	6.	Martin, E.
7.	Edwardes, M.	7.	Frodsham, A.
8.	Rogers, M.	8.	Gradisen, D.
9.	Gomez, M.	9.	Nicolay, D.
10.	Kahl, M.	10.	Butler, D.

1987

	MEN		WOMEN
1.	Anderson, J.	1.	Smylie, E.
2.	Turich, C.	2.	Byrne, J.
3.	Grant, R.	3.	Dorey, C.
4.	Properjohn, B.	4.	Parentich, P.
5.	Robinson, K.	5.	Lamb, R.
6.	Casey, R.	6.	Askey, L.
7.	Prickett, N.	7.	Ledder, J.
8.	Culley, D.	8.	Cooper, L.
9.	Danzi, D.	9.	Bucens, K.
10.	Leuba, M.	10.	Kelleher, V.

	BOYS 18 & UNDER		GIRLS 18 & UNDER
1.	Anderson, J.	1.	Parentich, P.
2.	Turich, C.	2.	Askey, L.
3.	Prickett, N.	3.	Ledder, J.
4.	Culley, D.	4.	Bucens, K.
5.	Danzi, D.	5.	Kelleher, V.
6.	Leuba, M.	6.	Phillips, M.
7.	Patten, D.	7.	Vahala, K.
8.	Campillos, P.	8.	Ball, Y.
9.	Hampson, D.	9.	Drake-Brockman, M.
10.	Kilderry, P.	10.	Drake-Brockman, T.

	BOYS 16 & UNDER		GIRLS 16 & UNDER
1.	Anderson, J.	1.	Vahala, K.
2.	Kilderry, P.	2.	Ball, Y.
3.	Woodward, G.	3.	Drake-Brockman, M.
4.	Cox, G.	4.	Martin, S.
5.	Floyd, A.	5.	Kimpton, N.
6.	Gerrans, P.	6.	Blackwell, D.
7.	Zsilinszky	7.	Donatti, E.
8.	Gibson, M.	8.	Cox, S.
9.	Cannell, L.	9.	McMahon, K.
10.	Willen, K.	10.	Marik, A.

	BOYS 14 & UNDER		GIRLS 14 & UNDER
1.	Kilderry, P.	1.	Martin, S.
2.	Willen, K.	2.	Kimpton, N.
3.	Edwardes, M.	3.	Blackwell, D.
4.	Rogers, M.	4.	Marik, A.
5.	Lewis, A.	5.	Green, A.
6.	Scott, J.	6.	Martin, E.
7.	Brinklow, B.	7.	Szymonik, K.
8.	Lemmon, J.	8.	Beale, T.
9.	Carney, B.	9.	Vahala, N.
10.	Orton, S.	10.	Thomas, K.

1988

	MEN		WOMEN
1.	Grant, R.	1.	Byrne, J.
2.	Turich, C.	2.	Dorey, C.
3.	Culley, D.	3.	Parentich, P.
4.	Patten, D.	4.	Lamb, R.
5.	Robinson, K.	5.	Askey, L.
6.	Properjohn, B.	6.	Martin, S.
7.	Leuba, M.	7.	Phillips, M.
8.	Prickett, N.	8.	Blackwell, D.
9.	Danzi, D.	9.	Bottrill, J.
10.	Prouse, R.	10.	Kimpton, N.

	BOYS 18 & UNDER		GIRLS 18 & UNDER
1.	Patten, D.	1.	Martin, S.
2.	Leuba, M.	2.	Phillips, M.
3.	Campillos, P.	3.	Blackwell, D.
4.	Cox, G.	4.	Kimpton, N.
5.	Floyd, A.	5.	Ball, Y.
6.	Woodward, G.	6.	Drake-Brockman, M.
7.	Gerrans, P.	7.	Bucens, K.
8.	Cannell, L.	8.	Marik, A.
9.	Fairchild, P.	9.	Donatti, E.
10.	Gibson, M.	10.	McIntosh, K.

	BOYS 16 & UNDER		GIRLS 16 & UNDER
1.	Cox, G.	1.	Martin, S.
2.	Floyd, A.	2.	Blackwell, D.
3.=	Cannell, L.	3.	Kimpton, N.
3.=	Fairchild, P.	4.	Marik, A.
5.	Lewis, A.	5.	Donatti, E.
6.	Edwardes, M.	6.	Green, A.
7.	Rogers, M.	7.	Martin, E.
8.	Howard, A.	8.	Szymonik, K.
9.	Connell, M.	9.	Perry, R.
10.	Hulbert, M.	10.	Lonsdale, F.

	BOYS 14 & UNDER		GIRLS 14 & UNDER
1.	Lewis, A.	1.	Marik, A.
2.	Edwardes, M.	2.	Green, A.
3.	Rogers, M.	3.	Martin, E.
4.	Brinklow, B.	4.	Szymonik, K.
5.	Orton, S.	5.	Perry, R.
6.	Sekulov, J.	6.	Cox, N.
7.	Lemmon, J.	7.	Thomas, K.
8.	Scott, J.	8.	Brophy, T.
9.	Hammond, T.	9.	Chmielewski, A.
10.	Prentice, B.	10.	Ford, J.

1989

	MEN		WOMEN
1.	Culley, D.	1.	Byrne, J.
2.	Patten, D.	2.	Parentich, P.
3.	Leuba, M.	3.	Martin, S.
4.	Danzi, D.	4.	Lamb, R.
5.	Turich, C.	5.	Blackwell, D.
6.	Properjohn, B.	6.	Kimpton, N.
7.	Robinson, K.	7.	Askey, L.
8.	Grant, R.	8.	Kelleher, V.
9.	Prouse, R.	9.	Phillips, M.
10.	Thorpe, M.	10.	Ball, Y.

	BOYS 18 & UNDER		GIRLS 18 & UNDER
1.	Kilderry, P.	1.	Martin, S.
2.	Cox, G.	2.	Blackwell, D.
3.	Floyd, A.	3.	Kimpton, N.
4.	Cannell, L.	4.	Donati, E.
5.	Fairchild, P.	5.	Burton, E.
6.	Edwardes, M.	6.	Lonsdale, F.
7.	Lewis, A.	7.	Beale, T.
8.	Rogers, M.	8.	Cox, S.
9.	Howard, A.	10.	Carney, B.

	BOYS 16 & UNDER		GIRLS 16 & UNDER
1.	Kilderry, P.	1.	Martin, S.
2.	Edwardes, M.	2.	Blackwell, D.
3.	Lewis, A.	3.	Kimpton, N.
4.	Rogers, M.	4.	Marik, A.
5.	Howard, A.	5.	Green, A.
6.	Carney, B.	6.	Martin, E.
7.	Scott, J.	7.	Perry, R.
8.	Brinklow, B.	8.	Szymonik, K.
9.	Orton, S.	9.	Cox, N.
10.	Wasley, J.	10.	Thomas, K.

	BOYS 14 & UNDER		GIRLS 14 & UNDER
1.	Brinklow, B.	1.	Marik, A.
2.	Sekulov, J.	2.	Martin, E.
3.	Hammond, T.	3.	Thomas, K.
4.	Andrijcich, M.	4.	Palethorpe, M.
5.	Prentice, B.	5.	Chmielewski, A.
6.	Civich, C.	6.	Szymonik, A.
7.	Hargreaves, T.	7.	Gledich, D.
8.	Cotter, J.	8.	Coniglio, I.
9.	Roberts, J.	9.	Stanley, S.
10.	Osborne, M.	10.	Beitmanis, S.

1990

	MEN		WOMEN
1.	Culley, D.	1.	Smylie, E.
2.	Patten, D.	2.	Parentich, P.
3.	Leuba, M.	3.	Martin, S.
4.	Grant, R.	4.	Lamb, R.
5.	Robinson, K.	5.	Blackwell, D.
6.	Danzi, D.	6.	Kimpton, N.
7.	Properjohn, B.	7.	Marik, A.
8.	Turich, C.	8.	Burton, E.
9.	Marshall, S.	9.	Phillips, M.
10.	Schneider, J.	10.	Drake-Brockman, M.

NOTE: Insufficient performances: Kilderry, P.

NOTE: Insufficient performances: Byrne, J.

	BOYS 18 & UNDER		GIRLS 18 & UNDER
1.	Kilderry, P.	1.	Martin, S.
2.	Edwardes, M.	2.	Blackwell, D.
3.	Lewis, A.	3.	Kimpton, N.
4.	Scott, J.	4.	Marik, A.
5.	Rogers, M.	5.	Burton, E.
6.	Orton, S.	6.	Green, A.
7.	Fanowrios, T.	7.	Martin, E.
8.	Brinklow, B.	8.	Cox, N.
9.	Sekulov, J.		
10.	Andrijcich, M.		

NOTE: Insufficient performances:
Carney, B.
Fairchild, P.
Howard, A.

	BOYS 16 & UNDER		GIRLS 16 & UNDER
1.	Edwardes, M.	1.	Marik, A.
2.	Lewis, A.	2.	Green, A.
3.	Scott, J.	3.	Martin, E.
4.	Rogers, M.	4.	Cox, N.
5.	Orton, S.	5.	Thomas, K.
6.	Fanowrios, T.	6.	Palethorpe, M.
7.	Brinklow, B.	7.	Drake-Brockman, S.
8.	Sekulov, J.	8.	Chmielewski, A.
9.	Andrijcich, M.	9.	Szymonik, A.
10.	Harrop, S.	10.	Sekulov, M.

	BOYS 14 & UNDER		GIRLS 14 & UNDER
1.	Sekulov, J.	1.	Drake-Brockman, S.
2.	Andrijcich, M.	2.	Chmielewski, A.
3.	Hammond, T.	3.	Szymonik, A.
4.	Harrop, S.	4.	Sekulov, M.
5.	Civich, C.	5.	Gledich, D.
6.	Collins, N.	6.	Stanley, S.
7.	Perry, S.	7.	Beitmanis, S.
8.	Osborn, M.	8.	Coniglio, L.
9.	Utley, S.	9.	Butcher, K.
10.	King, S.	10.	Berkhout, J.

1991

	MEN		WOMEN
1.	Patten, D.	1.	Byrne, J.
2.	Culley, D.	2.	Martin, S.
3.	Leuba, M.	3.	Marik, A.
4.	Hlawaty, M.	4.	Parentich, P.
5.	Robinson, K.	5.	Blackwell, D.
6.	Danzi, D.	6.	Lamb, R.
7.	Grant, R.	7.	Kimpton, N.
8.	Patten, B.	8.	Kelleher, V.
9.	Marshall, S.	9.	Burton, E.
10.	Heather, M.	10.	Green, A.

	BOYS 18 & UNDER		GIRLS 18 & UNDER
1.	Brinklow, B.	1.	Martin, S.

2.	Edwardes, M.	2.	Marik, A.
3.	Scott, J.	3.	Blackwell, D.
4.	Sekulov, J.	4.	Kimpton, N.
5.	Lemmon, J.	5.	Burton, E.
6.	Fanowrios, T.	6.	Green, A.
7.	Howard, A.	7.	Martin, E.
8.	Harrop, S.	8.	Cox, N.
9.	Civich, C.	9.	Thomas, K.
10.	Roberts, J.	10.	Palethorpe, M.

	BOYS 16 & UNDER		GIRLS 16 & UNDER
1.	Brinklow, B.	1.	Marik, A.
2.	Sekulov, J.	2.	Drake-Brockman, S.
3.	Harrop, S.	3.	Martin, E.
4.	Civich, C.	4.	Thomas, K.
5.	Andrijcich, M.	5.	Palethorpe, M.
6.	Roberts, J.	6.	Stanley, S.
7.	Hargreaves, T.	7.	Szymonik, A.
8.	Perry, S.	8.	Sekulov, M.
9.	Hammond, T.	9.	Gledich, D.
10.	Cotter, J.	10.	Butcher, K.

	BOYS 14 & UNDER		GIRLS 14 & UNDER
1.	Smith, N.	1.	Drake-Brockman, S.
2.	Brinklow, K.	2.	Stanley, S.
3.	Gibson, C.	3.	Szymonik, A.
4.	Sewell, S.	4.	Sekulov, M.
5.	Popovsky, G.	5.	Gledich, D.
6.	Crabb, J.	6.	Beitmanis, S.
7.	Gould, J.	7.	Coniglio, L.
8.	Fullin, A.	8.	Badia, C.
9.	Blanchard, C.	9.	Scott, B.
10.	Fenner, J.	10.	Palethorpe, T.

1992

	MEN		WOMEN
1.	Patten, D.	1.	Byrne, J.
2.	Culley, D.	2.	Marik, A.
3.	Hlawaty, M.	3.	Kimpton, N.
4.	Patten, B.	4.	Martin, S.
5.	Leuba, M.	5.	Blackwell, D.
6.	Robinson, K.	6.	Lamb, R.
7.	Cox, G.	7.	Drake-Brockman, S.
8.	Floyd, A.	8.	Parentich, P.
9.	Danzi, D.	9.	Stanley, S.
10.	Fiorentino, L.	10.	Collins, M.

	BOYS 18 & UNDER		GIRLS 18 & UNDER
1.	Sekulov, J.	1.	Marik, A.
2.	Edwards, M.	2.	Drake-Brockman, S.
3.	Petrovsky, P.	3.	Stanley, S.
4.	Harrop, S.	4.	Szymonik, A.
5.	Brinklow, B.	5.	Sekulov, M.
6.	Hargreaves, T.	6.	Thomas, K.
7.	Roberts, J.	7.	Gledich, D.
8.	Cotter, J.	8.	Butcher, K.
9.	Perry, S.	9.	Palethorpe, M.
10.	Hammond, T.	10.	Coleman, V.

	BOYS 16 & UNDER		GIRLS 16 & UNDER
1.	Sekulov, J.	1.	Drake-Brockman, S.
2.	Harrop, S.	2.	Stanley, S.
3.	Andricich, M.	3.	Szymonik, A.
4.	Cotter, J.	4.	Sekulov, M.
5.	Perry, S.	5.	Gledich, D.
6.	Hammond, T.	6.	Butcher, K.
7.	Utley, S.	7.	Beitmanis, S.
8.	Gallan, C.	8.	Berkhout, J.
9.	Sampson, R.	9.	Badia, C.
10.	Popovsky, G.	10.	Marsiglio, M.

	BOYS 14 & UNDER		GIRLS 14 & UNDER
1.	Crabb, J.	1.	Drake-Brockman, S.
2.	Smieja, E.	2.	Sekulov, M.
3.	Gould, J.	3.	Badia, C.
4.	Fenner, J.	4.	Palethorpe, T.
5.	Roszko, K.	5.	Scott, B.
6.	Davidson, J.	6.	Nunn, C.
7.	Wellington, M.	7.	Roper, M.
8.	Venables, T.	8.	Ford, C.
9.	Bogue, J.	9.	Ladyman, C.
10.	Dickie, A.	10.	Bracknell, C.

1993

	MEN		WOMEN
1.	Culley, D.	1.	Byrne, J.
2.	Patten, D.	2.	Marik, A.
3.	Leuba, M.	3.	Kimpton, N.
4.	Hlawaty, M.	4.	Blackwell, D.
5.	Fiorentino, L.	5.	Martin, S.
6.	Patten, B.	6.	Drake-Brockman, S.
7.	Hargreaves, T.	7.	Lamb, R.
8.	Robinson, K.	8.	Stanley, S.
9.	Harrop, S.	9.	Szymonik, A.
10.	Floyd, A.	10.	Lonsdale, F.

	BOYS 18 & UNDER		GIRLS 18 & UNDER
1.	Sekulov, J.	1.	Marik, A.
2.	Harrop, S.	2.	Drake-Brockman, S.
3.	Perry, S.	3.	Stanley, S.
4.	Hammond, T.	4.	Szymonik, A.
5.	Cotter, J.	5.	Sekulov, M.
6.	Gallan, C.	6.	Beitmanis, S.
7.	Sampson, R.	7.	Badia, C.
8.	Venables, C.	8.	Marsiglio, M.
9.	Crabb, J.	9.	Ladyman, C.
10.	Smieja, E.	10.	Berkhout, J.

	BOYS 16 & UNDER		GIRLS 16 & UNDER
1.	Crabb, J.	1.	Drake-Brockman, S.
2.	Gibson, C.	2.	Stanley, S.
3.	Popovsky, G.	3.	Sekulov, M.
4.	Blanchard, C.	4.	Beitmanis, S.
5.	Smieja, E.	5.	Badia, C.
6.	Sutisna, V.	6.	Roper, M.
7.	Sewell, D.	7.	Ladyman, C.
8.	Gibson, H.	8.	Rinaldi, C.
9.	Fenner, J.	9.	Palethorpe, T.
10.	Fullin, A.	10.	Szefcezyk, S.

	BOYS 14 & UNDER		GIRLS 14 & UNDER
1.	Gould, J.	1.	Roper, M.
2.	Williams, M.	2.	Rinaldi, C.
3.	Menzies, L.	3.	Flindell, J.
4.	Bogue, J.	4.	Sewell, N.
5.	D'Orsogna, L.	5.	Bracknell, C.
6.	Roberts, T.	6.	Gray, K.
7.	Dyer, A.	7.	Ericksson, N.
8.	Devine, P.	8.	Kasendra, P.
9.	Kirk, M.	9.	Towler, E.
10.	Crabb, J.	10.	Koenig, B.

1994

	MEN		WOMEN
1.	Hlawaty, M.	1.	Byrne, J.
2.	Patten, D.	2.	Drake-Brockman, S.
3.	Culley, D.	3.	Faull, J.
4.	Leuba, M.	4.	Marik, A.
5.	Patten, B.	5.	Stanley, S.
6.	Floyd, A.	6.	Martin, S.
7.	Properjohn, B.	7.	Blackwell, D.
8.	Robinson, K.	8.	Kimpton, N.
9.	Hargreaves, T.	9.	Lamb, R.
10.	Roberts, J.	10.	Voltnerova, D.

	BOYS 18 & UNDER		GIRLS 18 & UNDER
1.	Sekulov, J.	1.	Drake-Brockman, S.
2.	Crabb, J.	2.	Stanley, S.
3.	Gould, J.	3.	Voltnerova, D.
4.	Hammond, T.	4.	Sekulov, M.
5.	Perry, S.	5.	Roper, M.
6.	Gibson, H.	6.	Hemachandra, S.
7.	Popovsky, G.	7.	Ford, C.
8.	Sutisna, V.	8.	Prindiville, P.
9.	Blanchard, C.	9.	Nickolich, S.
10.	Sewell, D.	10.	Nunn, C.

	BOYS 16 & UNDER		GIRLS 16 & UNDER
1.	Crabb, J.	1.	Roper. M.
2.	Gould, J.	2.	Ladyman, C.
3.	Williams, M.	3.	Rinaldi, C.
4.	Venables, T.	4.	Ford, C.
5.	Wellington, M.	5.	Prindiville, P.
6.	Fenner, J.	6.	Kasendra, P.
7.	Dickie, A.	7.	Nunn, C.
8.	Dyer, A.	8.	White, B.
9.	D'Orsogna, L.	9.	Flindell, J.
10.	Roberts, T.	10.	Bracknell, C.

	BOYS 14 & UNDER		GIRLS 14 & UNDER
1.	Roberts, T.	1.	Rinaldi, C.
2.	Dyer, A.	2.	Sewell, N.
3.	Menzies, L.	3.	Ericksson, N.
4.	Sewell, M.	4.	Koenig, B.
5.	Gleeson, W.	5.	Gray, K.
6.	Nawrocki, S.	6.	Bryntesson, A.
7.	Cumming, C.	7.	Jungpakdee, J.
8.	Perry, J.	8.	Weiffering, C.
9.	Flindell, G.	9.	Flindell, J.
10.	Offer, R.	10.	Towler, E.

APPENDIX 11
WALTA MEMBERSHIP GUIDE
(Based on WALTA Annual Report)

SEASON	Affiliated Association (Metro)	Affiliated Association (Country)	Affiliated Clubs (Metro)	Affiliated Clubs (Country) * Zones	Aggregate Membership	Aggregate Membership (Country)
1934-35	3	10	25	37	6934	3430
1935-36	3	10	25	39	7810	3686
1936-37	3	10	24	40	7712	3955
1937-38	3	10	25	44	8089	4422
1938-39	3	9	26	40	8416	4579
1939-40	3	8	31	50	8495	4424
1940-41	N.A.	N.A.	N.A.	N.A.	N.A.	N.A.
1941-42	2	4	32	46	6807	3367
1942-43	2	4	23	40	3500	2620
1943-44	Statistics	not	collected -	estimate	[5000]	
1944-45	2	4	19	30	5400	2562
1945-46	2	3	22	34	5211	2234
1946-47	2	3	21	41	7112	3284
1947-48	2	4	26	48	8332	3947
1948-49	3	5	24	53	9436	4668
1949-50	3	5	23	55	9591	4831
1950-51	3	4	26	57	9589	4881
1951-52	3	4	26	60	9453	4853
1952-53	3	4	24	68	9953	5606
1953-54	3	4	25	72	10396	5797
1954-55	3	4	25	76	11179	6323
1955-56	3	4	26	81	11688	6339
1956-57	3	4	28	85	11853	6705
1957-58	3	4	29	85	1230	6975
1958-59	3	8	29	88	12696	6481
1959-60	3	9	29	88	13048	6664
1960-61	3	8	30	67	13404	7172
1961-62	3	3	33	N.A.	13693	7333
1962-63	3		34	8	13226	7218
1963-64	3		36	8	11297	5115
1964-65	2		34	8	11628	5115
1965-66	2		34	8	8875	3547
1966-67	2		37	8	9901	4293
1967-68	2		38	8	10943	4805
1968-69	2		37	8	9866	4150
1969-70	2		38	8	10626	5021
1970-71	2		38	8	10416	4819
1971-72	2		38	8	10597	4685
1972-73	2		38	8	10991	4818
1973-74	1		38	8	10286	4370
1974-75	1		37	8	11732*	5299*
1975-76	1		39	8	12703	5861
1976-77	1		42	8	13667	6297
1977-78	2		45	8	14350	5897
1978-79	2		50	8	16616	6648
1979-80	2		52	8	17289	6909
1980-81	2		52	8	17861	6894
1981-82	2		52	8	18021	6874
1982-83	2		54	8	19613	6858
1983-84	2		54	8	20044	7028
1984-85	2		55	8	20552	7090
1985-86	2		56	8	20841	7266
1986-87	2		56	8	20753	6960
1987-88	2		58	8	21819	7098
1988-89	1		58	9	22776	7224
1989-90	-		57	9	24938	7461
1990-91	-		57	11	24149	8244
1991-92	-		58	11	25614	8959
1992-93	-		61	11	26036	9065
1993-94	-		60	11	24755	8649

*Aggregate membership and aggregate membership (country) includes associate members from 1974-1975. See appendix 12 for the listing of associate bodies in 1992/1993.

APPENDIX 12
AFFILIATED WALTA CLUBS

1903 Founding Clubs
Claremont
Cottesloe
East Perth
Fremantle
Mount
Stock Exchange
WANDA

1933

Metropolitan Clubs
Applecross
Bayswater
Claremont
Crawley
Daglish
East Perth
Hensmen Park
Halvoto
Leederville
Loton Park
King's Park
Midland Junction
Mt Lawley
Nedlands
North Perth
Riverview
Sacred Heart High School
South Perth
Subiaco
Sunning Hill
University
Wanda
West Subiaco
Wembledon
Mt. Ingle

Country Clubs
Albany
Armadale
Beverley
Bridgetown
Boyanup
Bunbury
Bruce Rock
Baker's Hill
Balingup
Carnarvon
Collie
Corrigin
Cunderdin
Denmark
Donnybrook
Geeralying
Greenough
Katanning
Kellerberrin
Merredin, South
Mt. Barker
Mt. Magnet
Moulyinning
Mundaring Weir
Moora
Narrogin
Pingelly
Spring Dallah
Wagin
Woodanilling
Wickepin
Yarding
York
Branch Associations
Catholic
City Houses, Night Tennis
Dalwallinu-Ballidu and District
Eastern Goldfields
Fremantle
Northern Districts
Northam and District
Wyalcatchem
Central Midlands
Bunbury
Harvey District
Wubin

1963

Metropolitan Clubs
Alexander Park
Applecross
Bassendean
Bayswater
Belmont Park
Claremont
City
College Park
Cottesloe
Daglish
Dalkeith
East Fremantle
East Perth
Floreat Park
Fremantle Lawn Tennis Club
Hensmen Park
Royal King's Park
Kitchener Park
Leederville
Loton Park
Maccabean
Midland Junction
Mt Lawley
Nedlands
Nollamara
North Perth
Onslow Park
Peppermint Grove
Reabold
St Luke's
South Perth
University
Branch Associations
Catholic
Fremantle Districts
Southern Districts
Country Zones
Northern Districts' Zone
Moore District Association
Central Districts' Lawn Tennis Zone
Great Southern Zone
Eastern Districts' Zone
South West Districts' Zone
South Coastal District Zone
Eastern Goldfields' Zone

1993

Metropolitan Clubs
Alexander Park
Allen Park
Applecross
Armadale
Bassendean
Bayswater
Belmont Park
Blue Gum Park
Bullcreek
Canning
City Beach
Claremont
Corinthian Park
Cottesloe
Dalkeith
East Fremantle
Floreat Park
Fremantle
Glen Forrest
Greenwood
Hensmen Park
Higgins Park
Kalamunda
Kelmscott
Kensington
Kenwick
Kingsley
Kwinana
Leederville
Lesmurdie
Loton Park
Maccabi
Maida Vale
Manning
Maylands
Melville/Palmyra
Memorial Park
Midland
Mosman Park
Mt Lawley
Nedlands
Nollamara
Noranda
North Beach
North Perth
Ocean Ridge
Onslow Park
Peppermint Grove
Reabold
Rockingham
Royal King's Park
Safety Bay
Scarborough
Sorrento
South Perth
Thornlie
University
Wanneroo
Wembley Downs

Country Zones (See Zone Map)

Zone 1	Zone 2
Zone 3	Zone 4
Zone 5	Zone 6
Zone 7	Zone 8
Zone 9	Zone 10
Zone 11	

Associate Bodies
Gascoyne, Carnarvon TC, Exmouth TC

Pilbara
Dampier TC, Karratha TC, Paraburdoo TC, Port Hedland TC, Tambrey TC, Tom Price

Kimberley
Broome TC, Derby TC, Kununurra TC

TENNIS WEST COUNTRY ZONE MAP

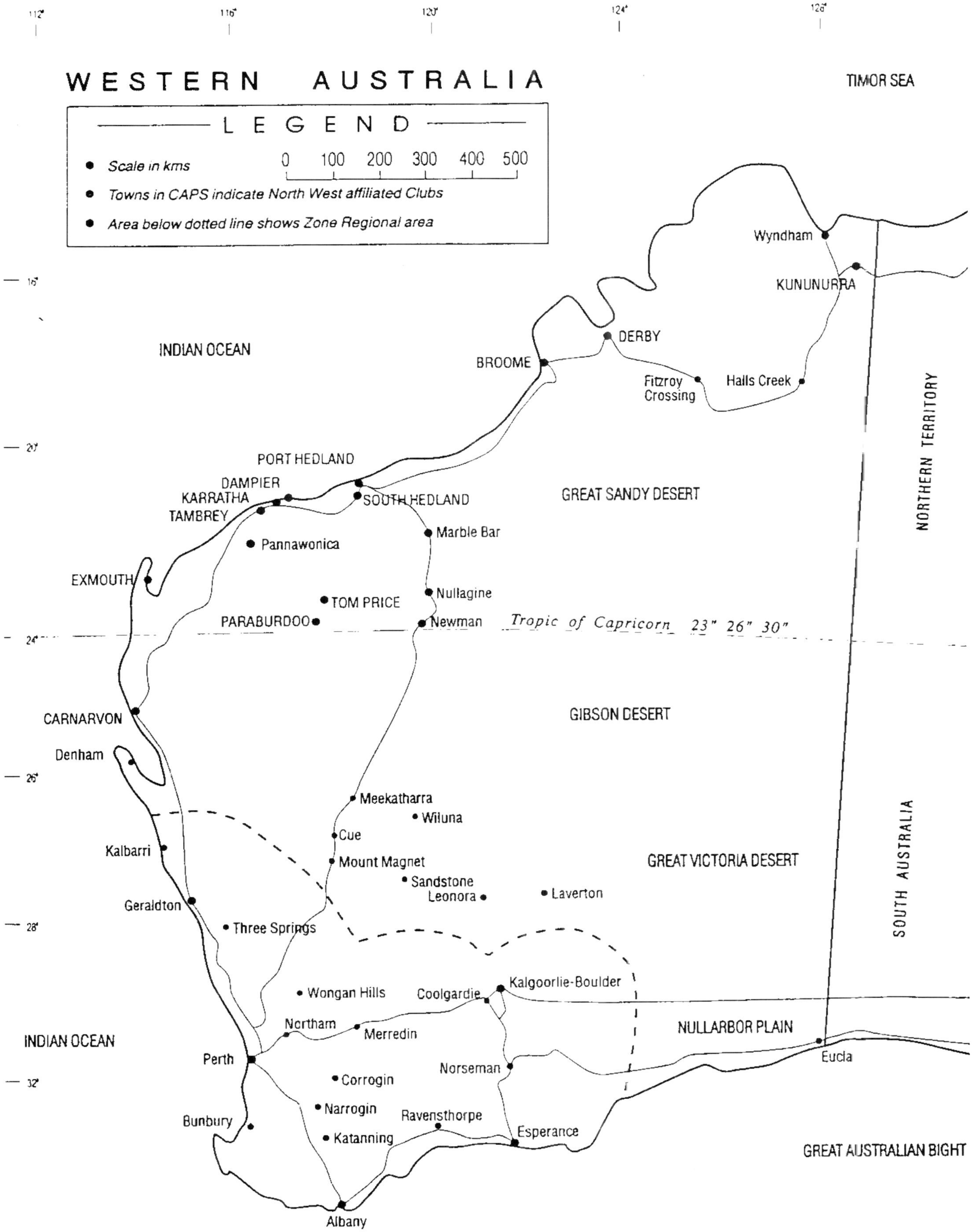

112°
116°
120°
124°
128°
WESTERN AUSTRALIA
TIMOR SEA
LEGEND
Scale in kms
0 100 200 300 400 500
Towns in CAPS indicate North West affiliated Clubs
Area below dotted line shows Zone Regional area
16°
20°
24°
26°
28°
32°
INDIAN OCEAN
Wyndham
KUNUNURRA
DERBY
BROOME
Fitzroy Crossing
Halls Creek
NORTHERN TERRITORY
PORT HEDLAND
DAMPIER
KARRATHA
TAMBREY
SOUTH HEDLAND
GREAT SANDY DESERT
Marble Bar
Pannawonica
EXMOUTH
Nullagine
TOM PRICE
PARABURDOO
Newman
Tropic of Capricorn 23" 26" 30"
CARNARVON
GIBSON DESERT
Denham
Meekatharra
Wiluna
Cue
Kalbarri
Mount Magnet
GREAT VICTORIA DESERT
SOUTH AUSTRALIA
Sandstone
Leonora
Laverton
Geraldton
Three Springs
Wongan Hills
Coolgardie
Kalgoorlie-Boulder
Northam
Merredin
NULLARBOR PLAIN
INDIAN OCEAN
Perth
Eucla
Norseman
Corrogin
Narrogin
Bunbury
Ravensthorpe
Esperance
Katanning
GREAT AUSTRALIAN BIGHT
Albany

also pages 73-74